Spain and Portugal in the New World

1492–1700

# Europe and the World
# in the Age of Expansion

edited by Boyd C. Shafer

Volume I. *Foundations of the Portuguese Empire, 1415–1580*
*by Bailey Diffie and George Winius*

Volume II. *Rival Empires of Trade in the Orient, 1600–1800*
*by Holden Furber*

Volume III. *Spain and Portugal in the*
*New World, 1492–1700*
*by Lyle N. McAlister*

Volume IV. *The North Atlantic World*
*in the Seventeenth Century*
*by K. G. Davies*

Volume V. *Empires to Nations: Expansion*
*in America, 1713–1824*
*by Max Savelle*

Volume VI. *The False Dawn: European Imperialism*
*in the Nineteenth Century*
*by Raymond Betts*

Volume VII. *Islands and Empires: Western Impact*
*on the Pacific and East Asia*
*by Ernest S. Dodge*

Volume VIII. *The Imperial Experience in*
*Sub-Saharan Africa since 1870*
*by Henry S. Wilson*

Volume IX. *The Commonwealth of Nations:*
*Origins and Impact, 1869–1971*
*by W. David McIntyre*

Volume X. *Uncertain Dimensions: Western Overseas*
*Empires in the Twentieth Century*
*by Raymond Betts*

# SPAIN AND PORTUGAL
in the
# NEW WORLD
## 1492-1700

by
LYLE N. McALISTER

UNIVERSITY OF MINNESOTA PRESS□MINNEAPOLIS

Second printing, 1987

**Library of Congress Cataloging in Publication Data**

McAlister, Lyle N.
Spain and Portugal in the New World, 1492–1700.
Bibliography: p.
Includes index.
1. America—Discovery and exploration—Spanish.
2. America—Discovery and exploration—Portuguese.
3. Latin America—History—To 1830.
4. Spain—Colonies—America—History.
5. Portugal—Colonies—America—History. I. Title.
E123.M38 1984     980′.01     83-21745
ISBN 0-8166-1216-1
ISBN 0-8166-1218-8 (pbk.)

*fco*

# Europe and the World
# in the Age of Expansion

## SPONSORS

Department of History of the
University of Minnesota

James Ford Bell Library of the
University of Minnesota Library

## SUPPORTING FOUNDATIONS

Northwest Area Foundation
(formerly Louis W. and Maud Hill
Family Foundation), St. Paul

James Ford Bell Foundation,
Minneapolis

## ADVISORY COUNCIL

Robert I. Crane
*Lawrence H. Gipson
Lewis Hanke

J. H. Parry
Francis M. Rogers
A. P. Thornton

## EDITORS

Boyd C. Shafer
*Herbert Heaton, founding editor
Burton Stein, founding associate editor

*deceased

To My Dear Wife
Geraldine Donaldson McAlister

*whose patience with the
formation of empires was virtually unbounded*

# Editor's Foreword

The expansion of Europe since the thirteenth century has had profound influences on peoples throughout the world. Encircling the globe, the expansion changed men's lives and goals and became one of the decisive movements in the history of mankind.

This series of ten volumes explores the nature and impact of the expansion. It attempts not so much to go over once more the familiar themes of "Gold, Glory, and the Gospel," as to describe, on the basis of new questions and interpretations, what appears to have happened insofar as modern historical scholarship can determine.

No work or works on so large a topic can include everything that happened or be definitive. This series, as it proceeds, emphasizes the discoveries, the explorations, and the territorial expansion of Europeans, the relationships between the colonized and the colonizers, the effects of the expansion on Asians, Africans, Americans, Indians, and the various "islanders," the emergence into nationhood and world history of many peoples that Europeans had known little or nothing about, and, to a lesser extent, the effects of the expansion on Europe.

The use of the word *discoveries*, of course, reveals European (and American) provincialism. The "new" lands were undiscovered only in the sense that they were unknown to Europeans. Peoples with developed cultures and civilizations already had long inhabited most of the huge areas to which Europeans sailed and over which they came to exercise their power and influence. Nevertheless, the political, economic, and social expansion that came with and after the discoveries affected the daily lives, the modes of producing and sharing, the ways of governing, the customs, and the values of peoples everywhere. Whatever their state of development, the expansion also brought, as is well known, tensions, conflicts, and much injustice. Perhaps most important in our own times, it led throughout the developing world to the rise of nationalism, to reform and revolt, and to demands (now largely realized) for national self-determination.

The early volumes in the series, naturally, stress the discoveries and explorations. The later emphasize the growing commercial and political involvements, the founding of new or different societies in the "new" worlds, the emergence of different varieties of nations and states in the often old and established societies of Asia, Africa, and the Americas, and the changes in the governmental structures and responsibilities of the European imperial nations.

The practices, ideas, and values the Europeans introduced continue, in differing ways and differing environments, not only to exist but to have consequences. But in the territorial sense the age of European expansion is over. Therefore the sponsors of this undertaking believe this is a propitious time to prepare and publish this multivolumed study. The era now appears in new perspective and new and more objective statements can be made about it. At the same time, its realities are still with us and we may now be able to understand intangibles that in the future could be overlooked.

The volumes in this series even though they number ten, cover only what the authors (and editors) consider to be important aspects of the expansion. Each of the authors had to confront vast masses of material and make choices in what he should include. Inevitably, subjects and details are omitted that some readers will think should have been covered. Inevitably, too, readers will note some duplication. This arises in large part because each author has been free, within the general themes of the series, to write his own book on the geographical area and chronological period allotted to him. Each author, as might be expected, has believed it necessary to give attention to the background of his topic and has also looked a bit ahead; hence he has touched upon the time periods of the immediately preceding and following volumes. This means that each of the studies can be read independently, without constant reference to the others. The books are being published as they are completed and will not appear in their originally planned order.

The authors have generally followed a pattern for spelling, capitalization, and other details of style set by the University of Minnesota Press in the interests of consistency and clarity. In accordance with the wishes of the Press and current usage, and after prolonged discussion, we have used the word *black* instead of *Negro* (except in quotations). For the most part American usages in spelling have been observed. The last is sometimes difficult for historians who must be concerned with the different spellings, especially of place names and proper nouns, at different times and in different languages. To help readers the authors have, in consequence, at times added the original (or the present) spelling of a name when identification might otherwise be difficult.

The discussions that led to this series began in 1964 during meetings of the Advisory Committee of the James Ford Bell Library at the University of Minnesota, a library particularly interested in exploration and discovery. Members of the university's Department of History and the University of Minnesota Press, and others, including the present editor, joined in the discussions. Then, after the promise of generous subsidies from the Bell Foundation of Minneapolis and the Northwest Area Foundation (formerly the Hill Family Foundation) of St. Paul, the project began to take form under the editorship of the distinguished historian Herbert Heaton. An Advisory Council of six scholars was appointed as the work began. Professor Heaton, who had agreed to serve as editor for three years, did most of the early planning and selected three authors. Professor Boyd C. Shafer succeeded him in 1967.

Boyd C. Shafer

# Preface

This book is about the interaction of Spaniards and Portuguese and numerous Indian and African peoples in a "New World" over a span of two centuries. It may help readers to find their way over the varied terrain ahead if I identify some of the conceptual and organizational problems I encountered while planning and writing and explain how I resolved them.

First, a word about the identities of the Europeans. Until the eve of American expansion Spain was only a geographical and cultural concept. It consisted of a peninsula bound by the Pyrenees, the Atlantic Ocean, and the Mediterranean Sea, and of the folk who dwelt within these confines. Its names—Spain in English, *España* in Castilian, *Espanha* in Portuguese—all derived from Roman Hispania. In the Middle Ages the "Hispanic peoples" included Castilians, Leonese, Basques, Galicians, Navarrese, Aragonese, Catalans, and Portuguese, organized politically into separate kingdoms and counties. Portugal retained its identity as a state and a nation into modern times. The other polities gradually conjoined through a series of dynastic unions culminating in the marriage of Ferdinand of Aragon to Isabella of Castile. The state so formed became known as Spain. It was not yet a nation, however, for its constituent kingdoms and counties retained their cultural and constitutional identities.

Spanish discovery, conquest, and colonization were mainly the enterprises of the Crown of Castile and its subjects. However, I have followed convention and described them as the work of Spain and Spaniards, except when the context requires attribution to Castile or to Castilians. When referring collectively to Spanish and Portuguese actions in America and their results, I use the adjective "Hispanic" rather than "Iberian" or "Latin American," for the common

xiii

homeland of Portuguese as well as Spaniards was then Hispania. Long before
the American discovery, the ancient Iberians had been Hispanicized, so to
speak, and Iberia was re-created in modern times, principally as a geographical
concept. Latin America likewise is a modern invention.

As a basis for ordering the book, I experimented with fitting events into
long-term demographic and economic structures or into general system
models such as dependency structures or the rise of capitalism in the West, but
found that I had too many good pieces left over. I therefore fell back on developing several key themes that struck me as providing unity, continuity, and
meaning to Hispanic expansion in America.

The themes chosen were: (1) the effects of vast distances and extraordinary
extremes of terrain and climate on the direction and forms of Hispanic action
in the New World; (2) the enormous efforts made by Spain and, within its
means, Portugal, to create and to *colonize* territorial empires in those regions;
(3) the elaborate structures that both monarchies developed to give justice and
good government to their American subjects as well as to exploit them; (4) the
formation of American societies with their own reasons for being; (5) the contradictions and tensions among these several processes; (6) the archaic qualities
of American societies and imperial systems; and (7) the great durability of
these societies and systems.

The book is periodized in a more or less traditional way. Part I deals with
the experiences of the Hispanic peoples at home and abroad from roughly the
ninth century A.D. to the first American discoveries. This is a lot of ground
to cover and the number of pages consumed may appear excessive. But Hispanic expansion in America was not a sudden or random phenomenon. It was
a temporal and spatial extension of centuries of experiences gained in peninsular wars against the Moors; dynastic and commercial enterprises in the
Mediterranean; and discoveries, conquests, and colonizations in Africa and
the Atlantic islands. I have therefore tried to do more than sketch out a
"background," a concept that skews the balance and violates the unity of history: I have endeavored to identify and explain persistent continuities in the
behavior of Spaniards and Portuguese in the Old World and the New.

The second period, part II of the book, extends from the discovery of the
New World into the 1560s. It is interpreted as an epoch of dynamic activity,
including the rapid uncovering of the coastlines and the exploration of the
interiors of two continents, the acquisition and organization of vast territories
and innumerable subject peoples, the formation of the main components of
an American population, the establishment of basic patterns of economic

production and exchange, the emergence of incipient social forms, and the creation of prototypical devices of imperial control and exploitation. It was a period of considerable flexibility involving many deliberate experiments but even more ad hoc responses to new situations as they appeared.

The third period, the subject of part III, begins in the 1560s, a decade of transition. After those years territorial expansion continued, but it was accomplished by different methods and different types of men. New elements and new trends appeared in American economies and their imperial extensions. Distinctively American societies and identities emerged and became consolidated. Systems of imperial exploitation and control expanded and became more elaborate and systematic, although not necessarily more effective.

The period and the book end around 1700, because the turn of the seventeenth century marked the beginnings of important changes in the Hispanic New World. In Spanish America signs of quickening economic activity and demographic growth began to appear and, in the early 1700s, the Spanish Bourbons began to reform the antiquated Habsburg imperial systems. In the eighteenth century too, the Indies became more fully incorporated into the North Atlantic World because of the growth of their clandestine commerce with northern Europe and their emergence as major theaters of operations in European imperial wars. In Brazil, the discovery of gold in the backlands just before 1700 generated a new and dynamic economic cycle and sparked the definitive settlement of large parts of the interior. These developments turned Portuguese America from a plantation into a full-fledged colony with an increasingly elaborate and centralized governmental apparatus.

It may be, as some historians contend, that a more appropriate breaking point would be around 1760, since colonial reforms, economic growth, and population increase did not really gain momentum until after that date. Yet around 1700 is a sensible division if not because of what came after, then because of what had happened before. By the end of the seventeenth century, the basic forms of Hispanic American societies, economies, and political behavior had become so firmly fixed that metropolitan reformers and, indeed, political independence did little to alter them.

The history of Spain and Portugal in America contains many informational gaps, especially when it comes to determining how many and how much of people and things. Many disagreements exist, moreover, about how to explain or interpret what is known or believed. Rather than ignoring or avoiding these lacunae and scholarly disputations, I have tried to identify and elucidate them. They are, after all, part of the historiography of the field.

Perhaps the most vexing problem I encountered was how to treat both Spanish and Portuguese expansion in a way that would give cohesion to the book and at the same time recognize the distinctive features of each enterprise. Spain and Portugal today are patently two different states and the Spanish and the Portuguese different peoples. But when Columbus set forth from Palos to discover unknown lands, the political boundaries between them were less firmly fixed and their cultural differences less apparent. They possessed cognate Catholic values, institutions and social forms born of more than a millennium of shared experiences. The Spanish and Portuguese nobility traveled freely between the courts of their respective kings, intermarried, and held fiefs in each others' lands. Portuguese and Spanish seamen sailed on the same ships. Educated Portuguese read Castilian poetry, and Spanish law instructed Portuguese magistrates. Luís de Camões (1524–78), Portugal's greatest poet, regarded himself as a Spaniard, not in a political or national sense but in the sense that he dwelt in the peninsular *concomunidad* (common civilization) of Hispania.

The Portuguese and the Spanish went about their affairs in the New World at a different pace and on different scales, but I think the contrast owed not so much to elusive variations in their "national characters" or "national temperaments," as to differences in the circumstances of their arrival, in the kinds of indigenous peoples and things they came upon, and in their demographic and economic resources. Their American enterprises will be compared in these terms.

The nature of this book determined the forms of scholarly apparatus adopted. It is not a product of original research but rather a synthesis of the published work of many scholars, organized and interpreted as I judged best. Much of the substantive content is known to serious students of colonial Hispanic American history. I have therefore abstained from citing the source of every statement made. Instead I have included a compendious bibliographical essay listing works that I regard as the best, the most useful, or, at least, representative in the several subject categories. It is organized by chapter and, within chapters, following the themes developed in the text. I have used notes mainly for the following purposes: (1) direct attribution to a person or work; (2) substantiation of data that are critical, controversial, or not commonly known; (3) illumination of historiographical contentions; (4) acknowledgment of works to which I am particularly indebted; and (5) citation of items that are too specialized or peripheral to be accommodated in the bibliographical essay.

I have numerous acknowledgments to make: to the many scholars whose works I drew on for information, guidance, and inspiration; to Professors Murdo J. MacLeod, William Woodruff, and Neill Macaulay, who read and criticized several chapters in draft; and to Amy Bushnell-Lisca who typed and edited much of the manuscript scrupulously. Mistakes that may have survived are not her fault. I am especially indebted to several generations of graduate students at the University of Florida. Their seminar papers and more informal observations and comments not only helped fill gaps in my information but suggested new approaches to old subjects and gave me fresh insights into vexing problems.

L. N. Mc.

# Contents

**Part I. Old World Antecedents**

Chapter 1. The Matrix of Hispanic Societies: *Reconquista* and
   *Repoblación*     3
     The Nature of the Christian Reconquest    3
     Forms of Reconquest Warfare    4
     The Resettlement of Reconquered Lands    5
     The Rhythm of the Reconquest    5
     The Reconquest Heritage    9
     Hispania and Europe    10
     The Wellsprings of Hispanic Expansion    11
Chapter 2. Reconquest Hispania     13
     Territorial Organization: Kingdoms and Countries    13
     The Quest for Hispanic Unity    16
     The Reconquest Municipality    17
     Territorial Organization of the Church    18
     Reconquest Economies    19
     The Ordering of Society: The Republic, Justice and
        the Law    24
     The Orders of the Republic    26
     Moors and Jews    32
     Social Mobility    32
     The Monarchy    33
     Social Cleavage and Social Cohesion    38

xix

Chapter 3. Hispanic Expansion in the Old World   41

   The Beginnings of European Expansion: Crusades and
      Trade in the Eastern Mediterranean   41

   Early Hispanic Enterprises: Africa, Italy, and
      the Atlantic   42

   Fourteenth-Century Interruptions: The Four Horsemen
      of the Apocalypse   43

   A Century of Disorder in Castile (1369–1479)   45

   The Brief Portuguese Crisis and the Accession of the
      House of Avis (1383–85)   46

   The Resumption of European Expansion   47

   Juridical Problems of Expansion: Just Title and
      Just War   51

   The Problem of "Race"   52

   Lagging Castilian Overseas Enterprises   55

   The Recovery of Spain: The Reign of Ferdinand and
      Isabella   56

   The Conquest and Colonization of the Canaries   63

   Portugal on the Eve of the Columbian Voyages   66

   Prospects for Hispanic Expansion in 1492   68

   Christopher Columbus and the Patent of Santa Fe   69

**Part II. The Establishment of Hispanic Dominion in America,
1492 to About 1570**

Chapter 4. The Conditions of Conquest and Colonization:
Geography and Peoples   73

   The Columbian Discovery   73

   The Papal Donation and the Line of Demarcation   74

   The Portuguese Discovery of Brazil   75

   Geographical Influences on Spanish Discovery and
      Colonization   76

   Spanish Claims and Aims   77

   The American Indian   83

   Africans in the Enterprise of the Indies   88

Chapter 5: *Mundus Novus*: Discovery and Conquest   89

   The Meaning of "Discovery" and "Conquest"   89

   Rationalization: The *Requerimiento*   90

   Authorization: The Royal Patent   91

The Identification of a New World    92
The Caribbean Cycle of Exploration and
    Conquest    93
The Great Mainland Conquests: Organizational
    Forms    96
The Course of Conquest    100
The End of the Conquest    103
The Spanish Achievement: Explanations    103
Patterns of Conquest: Regional Variations    106
Chapter 6: Colonization: The Populators of the Indies                108
The Meaning and Aims of Colonization    108
The European Component    109
The Indian Population    118
The African Population    121
Mixed Bloods    124
The Population of the Indies around 1570: Summary
    Estimates    130
Chapter 7. Instruments of Colonization: The Castilian *Municipio*    133
The Purposes of Municipalities    133
The Siting and Layout of Towns    133
The Founding of Towns: The "Act of
    Foundation"    134
The Establishment of Municipal Governments    135
The Founding of Parishes    135
Territorial Jurisdiction of Municipalities    136
Municipal Grants of Lots, Lands, and Indians    136
The Construction of Towns    137
The Course of Town Founding    138
Classification of Towns by Function, Size, and
    Status    143
Urban Planning    149
Principal Characteristics of Urbanization during the
    Conquest    150
Chapter 8. Colonization: Efforts to Incorporate the Indians    153
The Rationality of the Indian: Spanish
    Perceptions    153
Early Spanish Indian Policy    154
The Birth of the American *Encomienda*    157

The Evolution of the *Encomienda*    157

Controversial Features of the *Encomienda*    163

The "Spiritual Conquest": The Apostolic Model and the
Mendicant Orders    166

The Evangelization of Mexico    168

The Spread of Evangelization    173

Seventy Years of Spanish Indian Policy: An
Assessment    174

The Conquest Social Order    177

Chapter 9. The Royal *Señorío* in the Indies                                      182

The Legal and Moral Bases of Spanish Dominion    182

Colonial Challenges to the Royal *Señorío*: Captains of
Conquest, Municipalities, and
*Encomenderos*    184

The Instruments of the King's *Señorío*    186

Colonial Capitulations and Rebellions    191

King and Church: The Royal Patronage in the
Indies    194

The Governance of the Indians    197

The Defense of the Indies    197

Royal Government in the Indies: Powers and
Limitations    203

Chapter 10. The Fruits of the Land                                                208

The Factors of Production    208

The Agricultural Sector    214

Forest Products    223

Industry    223

Chapter 11. The Commerce of the Indies                                            231

Local Commerce    231

Regional and Interregional Trade    232

Systems of Trans-Atlantic Commerce    233

Transportation    237

Money and Credit    240

Weights and Measures    242

Governmental Regulation and Taxation    242

Commercial Monopolies    245

Prices and Wages    246

Conquest Economies: An Overview    247

Chapter 12. The Conquest of Brazil                                        250
    The Portuguese Approach to Brazil       250
    The Portuguese Old World Empire       251
    The Course of Conquest in Brazil       257
    Portuguese and Spanish New World Conquests:
       Comparative Features       266
Chapter 13. The Colonization of Brazil to About 1570                      270
    The Brazilian *Município*       270
    The Role of the Indians       272
    The Economics of Colonization       275
    The Commerce of Brazil       279
    Brazilian Populations       280
    The Governance of Brazil       283
    Social Organization       286
    Brazil and the Empire       287

**Part III. Hispanic American Empires from About 1570 to
About 1700**

Chapter 14. The Imperial Context: The Hispanic World in the
  Age of the Habsburg Kings                                      291
    The Reign of Philip II (1556–98)       291
    King Sebastian of Portugal, El Ksar-el-Kebir, and the
       Union of the Hispanic Crowns       292
    The Decline of Spain       293
    The Vicissitudes of Portugal       300
    Spanish America in the Age of Philip II       302
    Years of Transition in Brazil       303
Chapter 15. Territorial Changes in the Hispanic New World:
  Contractions, Expansions, Adjustments                          305
    Territorial Contraction       305
    The Conditions of Territorial
      Expansion       308
    Spanish Expansion: Legal Principles       309
    Territorial Expansion in the Viceroyalty of
      New Spain       310
    Territorial Expansion in the Viceroyalty of
      Peru       317
    Territorial Expansion in Brazil       321

Territorial Changes: A Summary Assessment    329
American Roots of Hispanic Imperial Expansion    331
Chapter 16. Post-Conquest Populations: Components, Numbers,
Movements, Distribution    332
Spanish America    332
The Population of Brazil    340
The Population of Hispanic America at Mid-Seventeenth
Century    343
The Territorial Organization of Spanish American
Populations    345
Urbanization and Ruralization in Brazil    351
Population and Territory: An Overview    353
Chapter 17. Post-Conquest Economies    355
Spanish America: General Trends    355
The Factors of Production    355
Government Regulation and Taxation    362
Economic Sectors    364
The "Seventeenth-Century Depression": Theses and
Countertheses    375
Structural Changes    381
The Post-Conquest Brazilian Economy    381
Structures of Dependency    387
Chapter 18. American Societies and American Identities    391
The Republic of Spaniards and Its Ordering    391
The Republic of Indians: Status and Ordering    395
The "Third Order" of Society: Mixed Bloods and
Free Blacks    396
The Status of Slaves    397
Social Boundaries and Social Mobility    398
Spanish American Identities    401
Social Cleavage and Social Cohesion in the
Spanish Indies    408
Regional Diversities    410
Colonial Brazilian Society: The Sugar Regions    411
Backland Society    415
Brazilian Identities    415
Social Cohesion in Brazil    417
Race, Color, and Class    418

Chapter 19. Imperial Systems                                      423
    New Territorial Jurisdictions in Spanish America:
        Civil and Ecclesiastical    423
    Expanding Functions and Powers of Royal Government
        in the Spanish Indies    425
    Ecclesiastical Government: The Royal Patronage and the
        Royal Vicariate    426
    The Holy Office of the Inquisition    427
    The Defense of the Indies    428
    The Size and the Costs of Government    434
    The Legal and Theoretical Foundations of the State in
        the Indies    435
    The Spanish State in the Indies toward the End of the
        Habsburg Era    438
    Royal Government in Post-Conquest Brazil    439
    Territorial Organization of the Church in Brazil    442
    The Growth of the Powers of the State in Brazil    442
    Metropolitan Agencies of Colonial Government    444
    The Governance of Brazil toward the End of the
        Seventeenth Century    445
    Hispanic American Empires: Imperial Control and
        Imperial Survival    446
Chapter 20. Epilogue: European Reactions to Hispanic Expansion in
    America                                                       452
    Information about the New World: Accumulation,
        Dissemination, and Assimilation    453
    The Intellectual Influence of the New World    455
    European Perceptions of Race: Noble and
        Ignoble Savages    459
    The Economic Impact of the Hispanic New World on
        Europe    462
    Malevolent Transfers: The Case of Syphilis    470
    Hispanic America and European Political Systems    471
    Hispanic American Colonies and Their Mother
        Countries    473
Notes                                                             481
Bibliographical Essay                                             511
Index                                                             565

*Maps 1-6 follow p. 264*

1. The Hispanic Reconquest and Early Atlantic Expansion
2. The Spanish Conquest: North America and the Caribbean
3. Spanish and Portuguese conquests in South America
4. Territorial changes in North America and the Caribbean, c. 1565-c. 1700
5. Territorial changes in South America, c. 1565-c. 1700
6. The Governmental Organization of Hispanic American Empires around 1700

*Tables*

1. Estimated Population of the Spanish Indies in About 1570                131
2. Urbanization in the Spanish Indies in About 1570                      144
3. The Twenty-Five Largest Municipalities in the Spanish Indies
   in About 1570                                                         147
4. Ranking of Municipalities in the Spanish Indies by Population
   in About 1580                                                         148
5. The Portuguese Population of Brazil in About 1570                     280
6. Estimated Population of Hispanic America in About 1650 (as
   Compared with 1570)                                                   344
7. Estimated Minimum Spanish American Bullion Production,
   1571-1700                                                             369
8. Brazilian Sugar Production, 1576-1644                                 383
9. The Governmental Organization of Spanish America in About 1700       425
10. The Governmental Organization of Portuguese America
    in About 1700                                                        441

Part I

Old World Antecedents

# CHAPTER 1

# The Matrix of Hispanic Societies:
## *Reconquista* and *Repoblación*

### *The Nature of the Christian Reconquest*

In the year 718 A.D. or thereabouts, a band of Christians led by the knight
Pelayo strove against a detachment of Muslims near the caves of Covadonga in
the Cantabrian mountains that rim northwestern Hispania. The Muslims were
probably a raiding or tribute-gathering party detached from armies that seven
years earlier had crossed from Africa, occupied most of the Iberian peninsula
in a swift campaign, and then thrust into France until they were finally thrown
back by the Franks at the Battle of Tours in 732. The Christians were fugitives
from the Spanish Visigothic kingdom established in the fifth century and destroyed by the Muslim onslaught.

After several days of intermittent combat, the Muslims withdrew, leaving
the field to the Christians. The fighting, even by the measure of the times, was
rather small scale. Unlike Tours, Sir Edward Creasy did not see fit to include
Covadonga among his *Ten Decisive Battles of the World*. The Muslims apparently were not particularly discomfited by the outcome, nor were the Christians aware that their victory marked a turning point in Hispanic history. But
symbolically, at least, that is what it became when later generations of chroniclers and historians identified it as the beginning of the *Reconquista*, that
prolonged epic in which the Christians regained Hispania and drove thence the
Moors, as they called their Muslim adversaries.

In the most fundamental sense, the Reconquest was a war between Christians and Muslims for dominion over the Iberian peninsula. It was not, however,
an unremitting and relentless crusade waged by great hosts. For most of its

3

duration, a desire for new pasturages and agricultural lands motivated the Christians more strongly than did religious zeal. Territorial and dynastic wars among Christian princes often diverted them from campaigns against the Moors, and frequent truces interrupted hostilities. Christian and Muslim rulers sometimes arranged interdynastic marriages, accepted vassalage and rendered tribute to each other, and negotiated treaties committing the parties to war against their coreligionists. Nor were Christian and Moorish knights very particular about the faith of the lord they served. And, in war as well as in peace, trade moved more or less freely between Christian and Muslim Hispania.

## Forms of Reconquest Warfare

The nature of the frontiers separating the antagonists gave Hispanic warfare a distinctive form. During most of the Reconquest, Christian and Moor did not face each other along a continuous and well-defined front. Instead each manned an irregular and widely spaced line of strong points. Between their lines stretched marches depopulated by war or deliberately emptied of people by Christian kings who wished to place a *despoblado* (wasteland) between their territories and the Muslims. Neither Christians nor Muslims possessed the military and political capabilities to mount sustained offensives across the distances that separated them. Full dress battles and sustained sieges were not the rule, and most campaigns had immediate, limited, and nonstrategic objectives such as the punishment of contumacious vassals and recalcitrant tributaries or the destruction of the enemy's crops and orchards. The most common military operation was the raid for booty. Although on occasion the two antagonists behaved in a most chivalric manner toward each other, they did not feel bound to observe the conventions that ameliorated warfare between Christian and Christian and Muslim and Muslim. They could seize or destroy each other's property without worrying about rules of compensation or restitution, and neither Christian nor Muslim law prohibited the enslavement of infidels and heretics. Both parties accepted ransom as an alternative to enslavement, but only those who had substantial resources could take advantage of this recourse. Hence, human chattel became an important form of booty.

The Muslims called frontier raids *algaras*; the Christians, *cabalgadas*. *Cabalgadas* might be mounted by towns, by temporarily assembled bands of knights, and by lay and ecclesiastical lords. The spoils were divided up (*se repartieron*) among commanders, captains, and soldiers in proportion to rank after the king's fifth (the *quinto*) had been set aside. Even the annual campaigns of kings, emirs, and caliphs had the seizure of booty as a primary or collateral aim. The informal, individualistic, and savage style of such hostilities, some say, forged those qualities of initiative, boldness, and ruthlessness that Spaniards and Portuguese later employed so effectively in Italy and Flanders and against Asiatics and American Indians. Some see in the Reconquest experience the roots of a form of military operations to which the Spanish gave a name — guerrilla warfare.

## The Resettlement of Reconquered Lands

In addition to thrusting back the Moors, the Christians had another problem. They had to occupy and secure territory won. The Spaniards used the term *repoblación* to describe the resettlement of their Reconquest frontier. It derives from the Spanish verb *poblar*, which means to populate or people a region. Thus, the Christians were repopulating or repeopling in the wake of reconquest. But *repoblación* meant more than the unordered movement of settlers into vacant or conquered lands, and it had a value attached. It involved forming civilized communities, providing for their good governance, and seeing to their spiritual and material welfare. These were good and desirable ends, for they extended Christendom and enhanced the *honra del reino*, that is, the honor, prestige, and virtue of the kingdom.

Repopulation had a juridical base resting in Hispano-Roman law and in the declarations of contemporary jurists and theologians. Christian kings possessed a just title to territory that was unoccupied or had been seized from infidels and could grant usufruct of lands within it to subjects who undertook its resettlement or otherwise served the crown well. Title could be asserted formally by the king in person or by others in his name, through a simple act of taking possession that involved raising the royal standard and reciting a set legal formula.

Resettlement was a much more difficult and tedious process than forays against the Muslims. It had to be accomplished initially by depleting the population of previously settled regions. The Christians then had to await the restoration of their demographic resources before they could resume their advance. As the distinguished Catalan historian Jaime Vicens Vives observed, "The borders between Christianity and Islam . . . marked human limits — population limits — and not strategic positions."[1]

## The Rhythm of the Reconquest

The requirements of repopulation, along with the shifting motivations and capabilities of Christians and Muslims, imposed an irregular tempo on the

Reconquest. During its earliest phase, extending roughly from the mid-eighth to the mid-tenth century, the weight of numbers and resources favored the Moors, but they did not exploit their advantage. Finding themselves overextended, and detesting the mists and frosts of northern Hispania, they withdrew their outposts from those regions and consolidated their dominion in the well-watered, fertile, and more temperate southern and eastern parts of the peninsula. Here they created an opulent civilization whose heart lay in the basin of the Guadalquivir River, a land they called al-Andalus, and whose capital became the great metropolis of Córdova. In the north, King Alfonso I of Asturias (739–757), the son-in-law of Pelayo, withdrew the population of the lands along the Duero River (the Douro in Portugal) in order to place a *despoblado* between his kingdom and the Muslims.

The Reconquest really began with the repopulation of these wastelands. Encouraged by a period of political disarray among the forces of Islam, Visigoths, Galicians, and Asturian and Basque tribes drifted down from the humid Cantabrians onto the steppelike *meseta* (plateau) that dominates central Hispania. By the late tenth century they had established a new frontier south of the Duero whose waters and alluvial valley favored human habitation in an otherwise inhospitable environment. Here the advance halted for a century, in part because of a resurgence of Muslim strength but mainly because the Christians lacked the demographic resources to carry them further.

Repopulation of the valley of the Duero was accomplished by various agencies and took several forms. Kings sometimes took possession in person and created rural estates in the lands they claimed. Being still weak and lacking resources, however, they commonly and generously turned the task over to other parties. Acting in their name, nobles also acquired rural manors. The Cistercian order of monks established monasteries and undertook the agricultural and pastoral colonization of surrounding lands. Groups of commoners founded villages holding fields and pastures in common.

By the early eleventh century the repopulation of the valley of the Duero and northern Portugal had provided the Christians with a demographic base to support a new advance, while a breakup of the Caliphate of Córdova into small warring emirates opened the way. The offensive began with a series of powerful raids through the passes of the rugged mountain ranges that traverse central Hispania and thence down into al-Andalus and southern Portugal. By 1085 these campaigns had pushed the military frontier in the center of the peninsula to the ancient Visigothic capital of Toledo on the upper reaches of the Tagus River and, in Portugal, to Coimbra on the Mondega.

Military and demographic factors stalled the Reconquest on this front for most of the twelfth century. The approach of the Christians to the portals of al-Andalus brought a violent Muslim reaction in the form of two waves of reinforcements from North Africa, the first being the armies of the Almoravid sect, which came over in 1086, and the second, those of the Almohads, which arrived in 1146–47. It was during this period that the Reconquest took on the exaltation and ferocity of a holy war for both antagonists. The new African invaders were fanatical believers who waged war cruelly against infidels. On the Christian side, the papacy preached its first crusade as early as 1064, not against the Turks but against the Moors of Hispania. For defense and counteroffense, Christian kings depended heavily upon the medieval military orders: the Knights Templar and the Knights Hospitaler, who entered the peninsula early in the twelfth century, and the indigenous Hispanic orders of Calatrava, Alcántara, and Santiago, formed in 1158, about 1165, and about 1170 respectively. These warrior-monks fought just as ruthlessly as their antagonists. The Christians barely managed to maintain the initiative, and in the mountains south of Toledo, whose passes controlled access to al-Andalus, determined Muslim resistance virtually stalled their advance. To the west, however, they fought their way south to the line of the Tagus (Tejo in Portugal), taking Lisbon in 1147, and in the east they drove the Moors from the valley of the Ebro.

Meanwhile the Christians repopulated the lands they had conquered, but in different circumstances and in different ways than those used in earlier centuries. As they approached the central part of the peninsula, they began to encounter sedentary Muslim populations, and, as they closed in on al-Andalus, they confronted Moorish armies more directly. Repopulation, therefore, required the creation of Christian settlements capable of keeping the subjugated population in check as well as defending a military frontier. Also, as their dominions grew, kings became more powerful, increasingly jealous of their prerogatives, and insistent on maintaining closer control over resettlement. Instead of relying on the loose and informal methods employed in the north, they delegated specific undertakings to private parties and corporations, giving their agents jurisdictional and property rights by particular acts of royal grace.

In central Hispania, between the Duero and the Tagus, kings and, in their name, lay and ecclesiastical magnates, employed towns as the main instrument of repopulation. They did this by granting charters called *cartas pueblas* or *fueros* (*forais* in Portugal) to groups of freemen, authorizing them to found municipalities and giving them privileges and immunities as incentives. The provisions of charters varied from time to time and place to place, but they commonly allowed the establishment of town governments (*consejos* in Castile and Leon, *concelhos* in Portugal) composed of all registered citizens (*vecinos*

in Castile and Leon, *vizinhos* in Portugal). These corporations exercised jurisdiction over an extensive rural hinterland called the *término* or *alfoz* (*termo*
in Portugal). They received a large measure of autonomy in municipal fiscal
and administrative matters; they could dispense common civil and criminal
justice; and they could grant town lots and rural property to *vecinos*. Land
grants to foot soldiers were commonly called *peonías* and were supposed to
be sufficient to support the *vecino* and his family. Mounted warriors received
*caballerías*, which were considerably larger. In Portugal, municipal councils
distributed land to populators in *sesmos*, the *sesmo* being a unit roughly comparable to the Castilian-Leonese *peonía*.

On the military frontier south of the Tagus, towns continued to be instruments of resettlement, but the brunt of the task passed to the military orders
that did most of the fighting. Christian princes gave them vast territorial grants,
which they turned into latifundia worked by the subjugated Muslim population and defended by formidable monastery-castles.

The climax of the Reconquest came swiftly. By the opening of the thirteenth century, the weight of wealth and numbers had shifted definitively to
the Christian kingdoms, and, in 1212, their combined hosts defeated the main
Muslim army at Las Navas de Tolosa, a pass leading down from the central
*meseta* into the valley of the Guadalquivir. They exploited the victory with
powerful offensives that won most of Andalusia, while in the west Portuguese
armies drove south into the Algarve. By the last quarter of the thirteenth century all that remained of Hispanic Islam was the Emirate of Granada, concentrated in the Sierra Nevada mountains of the extreme south, and African garrisons holding the coastal fortresses of Gibraltar, Algeçiras, and Tarifa. What
can be called the "High Reconquest" was over.

One may ask why the Christians did not use the apparent momentum they
had gained to finish the job. Several answers may be adduced. On the one hand,
formidable natural ramparts and virtually impregnable fortresses guarded Granada, and the most intransigent Muslim survivors of the Christian onslaught had
found refuge there. Initial probes indicated that its reduction would be a bloody,
expensive, and prolonged affair. On the other hand, Granada lacked sustained
offensive capabilities and posed no serious threat to Hispanic Christendom unless again reinforced from across the Strait of Gibraltar. Christian princes and
lords, therefore, restricted their military operations to border raids and efforts
to take the coastal fortresses that provided the main points of debarkation for
invasions from Africa. Meanwhile, they had to divide up the enormous spoils
won in the conquest of al-Andalus, and they found it convenient to collect

tribute in gold from the kings of Granada, who acknowledged vassalage to the Christian conquerors.

The lands won from the Moors in the south also had to be settled and secured before a final offensive could be mounted, and the pace of the last stages of the Reconquest had outrun demographic resources. Consequently, re-population at first amounted to military occupation. Castilian and Portuguese kings simply turned over to their nobles and the military orders the rural estates of Moorish lords, making the beneficiaries responsible for defending the marches along the border with Granada. Propertied Muslims were driven or fled from the cities and towns, and their urban holdings together with adjacent rural properties were given to knights and hidalgos from the north. When, in the 1260s, serious revolts erupted among Muslims in the countryside, the Christians expelled most of the rebels. Refugees of all classes found haven in Granada and North Africa, where they fanned hatred against the Christians. Christian lords repopulated the lands left vacant with livestock.

One aspect of the repopulation of the south invites special mention. Some-times encouraged by naval-minded monarchs, sometimes following their own inclinations, Biscayan, Galician, and northern Portuguese seamen settled along the Atlantic coast of Andalusia and in the Algarve. Although separated by po-litical boundaries, they intermingled freely with each other and with Italian sailors to create an international maritime community. Their ports lay at the confluence of Atlantic and Mediterranean seaways. From them fair summer winds blew south along the shores of Africa to the Canary and Madeira islands where northeast trades turned west into an unknown sea.

## The Reconquest Heritage

The Reconquest has many meanings. To the romantically inclined, it was an epic of magnificent proportions with a rich cast of characters who performed memorable deeds ranging from heroic to villanous. Its epic qualities should not be depreciated, for they generated myths, and it is good to remember that in history what people believe happened is often more important than what really occurred.

To the soberminded student of societies and institutions, the Reconquest was a historical period, almost coterminous with the European High Middle Ages, during which the inhabitants of the Iberian peninsula created distinc-tively Hispanic civilizations.[2] The process involved more than simply Chris-tians and Moors. The Christians themselves were by no means a homogeneous people. During the first stage of reconquest and repopulation, they included

Romanized Galicians, partially Romanized Asturian, Basque, and Pyrenean tribespeople, and many thousand Germanic Visigoths and Suevi. The Muslim invaders, numbering, perhaps, 35,000 warriors, also had diverse origins. Among them were desert Arabs, Syrians, Egyptians, and recently converted Berbers from North Africa. Later, in the twelfth century, new waves of African invaders crossed the strait to support Hispanic Moors.

Christian and Muslim warriors together added up to only a small fraction of the population. Several million Hispano-Romans formed the basic human stock of the peninsula. These peoples adjusted to the requirements of Muslim and Christian lords as conscience and circumstance dictated and, in doing so, created new cultural elements. In Moorish Hispania, most converted to Islam and adopted Muslim ways, becoming known as *muladíes* (renegades), and these constituted the laboring and artisan classes. Rather fewer retained their Christian faith but adopted the Arabic language and Arabic names and developed heterodox religious rituals; these were called *mozarabes*. As the Reconquest proceeded, some *mozarabes* emigrated north to escape religious persecution, and Christian raiding parties carried back others. These migrants became the main transmitters of Islamic culture to emerging Hispanic Christian societies.

The peninsula's population also included communities of Jews dwelling in old Hispano-Roman cities. Although numerically inconsequential, they made significant contributions to the commercial, financial, and intellectual life of both Christian and Muslim civilizations. Somewhat later, during the eleventh century, French monks from Cluny, French merchants, and reinforcements of Christian knights from all the countries of northern Europe entered Christian Hispania. During the twelfth century, Italian businessmen made their appearance in the cities of the north. In short, it was the intercourse among this Babel of peoples in war and truce, in courts and humble villages, in urban commerce and rural husbandry, in the marriage bed and the concubine's quarters, that created Reconquest Hispanic cultures.

## Hispania and Europe

The medieval Hispanic experience certainly differed from that of other European peoples, but it was not entirely unique. The northern nations and Italy also had diverse populations including a basic Roman or Romanized stock, Germanic invaders, and influential Jewish communities. Neither was the interaction of Christian and Moor solely a Hispanic phenomenon. It left its mark all around the Mediterranean. Italian cities and the Franks fought and traded with Muslims for centuries, and Henri Pirenne concluded that the impact of

Islam had destroyed the unity of the Mediterranean, ended the world of Rome, and led to the emergence of new civilizations in the Carolingian era. "Without Islam," he asserted, "the Frankish Empire would probably never have existed and Charlemagne, without Mahomet, would be inconceivable."[3] Later, the same flaming of religious zeal that launched the climactic Hispanic offensive against the Moors generated the crusades against Seljuk Turks in the Holy Land.

Throughout the Middle Ages, Hispania experienced the same secular demographic and economic trends that affected the rest of western Europe. The northern peoples, also, had empty frontiers to resettle. In the ninth century, most of their territories consisted of wilderness inhabited by sparse, static, or only slowly growing populations, and they were ravaged by constant warfare among kings and barons. The creation of dynamic new societies and economies required the clearance of forests, the drainage of fens, and the settlement of reclaimed lands in a political environment offering some measure of security.

Hispania, furthermore, was part of a western Christian ekumene. It felt much the same religious and intellectual currents as did its neighbors, and its political and social institutions evolved in the same directions. European influences entered the peninsula in diverse ways. The Muslim conquest did not halt commerce between Barcelona and French and Italian ports. Thousands of devout Europeans made the pilgrimage to Santiago de Compostela, where, it was reputed, the remains of Santiago (Saint James the Greater) had been discovered miraculously in the early ninth century. In the course of the Reconquest, merchants, clergy, and warriors from all parts of Europe entered the peninsula, and many of them remained there. The American anthropologist George Foster contends that "the ethnologist who today digs trait by trait into Spanish culture . . . finds that the majority of the questions he asks lead to Europe, and only a minority to the south and east. The content of religion is that of France and Italy: the same Romanesque and Gothic churches, the same religious services, the same annual festivals." For these reasons, he advises, "Recognize Spain's unique position in Europe and the Near Eastern, African, and Moorish influences which have helped shape her culture, but do not lose sight of the fact that Spain is Europe and Spaniards are Europeans."[4]

## The Wellsprings of Hispanic Expansion

To the student of Hispanic expansion, the Reconquest has a special meaning. It provided the momentum that carried Spaniards and Portuguese across seas and oceans to Sicily, Naples, and Greece; to Africa and the Atlantic islands; and ultimately to America and Asia. At the same time, it gave them prolonged experience in the conquest and colonization of alien lands and it created values and institutions that they carried with them wherever they adventured.[5] And as they went, images of great battles against the Saracens, of Moorish princesses and Moorish gold, of glorious deeds of Christian champions, and of providential divine interventions stirred in their minds. At least, so contemporaries thought. In the mid-sixteenth century, the Spanish historian Francisco López de Gómara wrote, "The Conquest of the Indies began when that of the Moors was over for the Spanish have always fought against infidels."[6] The following two chapters will develop themes that impart continuity to the Hispanic experience in the Old World and the New with particular attention to what happened in Castile and Portugal. Although these kingdoms did not constitute the totality of the Hispanic community, it was under their sponsorship that America was discovered and occupied; their subjects provided the bulk of the conquerors, settlers, and governors of the new lands, and they bore the burden of empire.

# CHAPTER 2

# Reconquest Hispania

## *Territorial Organization: Kingdoms and Counties*

Hand in hand with reconquest and repopulation went the creation of the territorial units that provided the main source of identity for their inhabitants, as well as the spatial framework for civil and ecclesiastical government, economic production, and the formation of societies. The kingdoms and autonomous counties that appeared in the early medieval centuries constituted the superior territorial entities. These included the Kingdom of Asturias, which was created by Pelayo and his descendants in the Cantabrians and which, as the Reconquest moved out onto the tablelands of the Duero, metamorphosed into the Kingdom of Leon; ancient Galicia, a county dependent on Leon that aspired to the status of kingdom and occasionally achieved it; the Kingdom of Navarre, created in the tenth century by Romanized Basques in the western Pyrenees; and the kingdoms of Castile and Aragon, both formed in the first half of the eleventh century, Castile from the eastern marches of Leon, Aragon from a county of Navarre in the central Pyrenees.

Two other polities warrant particular mention. The first was the County of Barcelona, which faced the Mediterranean between the eastern Pyrenees and the lower Ebro River and was more or less coterminous with the geographical region later known as Catalonia. It had its origins in the Hispanic March of the Franks. Toward the end of the tenth century it broke away from Frankish domination but its rulers, although sovereign, continued to hold the title of count. The county retained close ties with France and maintained its ancient Mediterranean associations; it was in Hispania but not entirely of it.

13

The second unit was the Kingdom of Portugal. Its nucleus consisted of Galicians who during the ninth and tenth centuries pushed south to occupy the lands between the Minho and Douro rivers (the Miño and Duero in Spanish). In the late ninth century it became a county dependent first on Leon, later on Castile, and by the early tenth century it was known as Portucale (Portugal in the vernacular) after Porto, one of its principal towns. In 1096 or possibly 1097, Alfonso VI of Leon (1065–1109) and Castile (1072–1109) gave it as a fief to Henry of Burgundy, a French knight who married Alfonso's illegitimate daughter, Teresa. Henry and Teresa had a son, Afonso Henriques, who rebelled against both his mother and his suzerain, now Alfonso VII of Leon and Castile (1126–57), and who in 1139 proclaimed himself king of Portugal. Castile resisted his pretension by invasion and negotiation but when neither prevailed, in 1143 accepted the de facto arrangement. Portuguese independence became official when it was recognized by the papacy in 1179.

These events themselves were not particularly portentous or even noteworthy. They represented one of those dynastic squabbles, very common at the time, that created or dismembered kingdoms. The problem, and a major one in Hispanic historiography, is how Portugal managed to sustain its sovereignty against an increasingly powerful and imperialistic neighbor. Spanish historians attribute the phenomenon to Leonese and Castilian preoccupation with grander affairs, an oversight that could have been corrected with proper attention and enterprise. Portuguese historians regard it, if not as providential, at least as predetermined by geography, which gave their nation a territorial framework and an "Atlantic convergence," and by historical experiences that endowed it with a cultural identity proof against Castilian invasions and conspiracies.[1] The Spanish interpretation, however, appears to be too casual and the case for the uniqueness of Portuguese culture is difficult to sustain. Other Hispanic kingdoms and counties were at one time or another politically independent and possessed individualities just as sharply defined. Yet all of them save Portugal eventually became incorporated into a Greater Spain. The American geographer Dan Stanislawski offers a better-balanced explanation, which may be summarized as follows.[2]

Geographically, Portugal was cut off from the rest of Hispania by tumbled terrain and the absence of east-west roads, the same conditions that frustrated Napoleon's marshals centuries later. During the early stages of the Reconquest, moreover, the depopulation of the valley of the Duero created a demographic gap between the incipient nation and its eastern neighbors. Thus, an isolated people could nurse their individuality unmolested. When Afonso Henriques and his barons won the nation's independence, the *meseta* kingdoms were involved in savage dynastic struggles and soon thereafter in great wars against the Moors, so that Portugal was spared the full attention of Castile-Leon. It could "turn [its] back upon Iberian turmoil, just as Holland was able to ignore Germany."[3] Later, Spanish kings tried on several occasions to "fill out the peninsula" and certainly possessed the military capabilities to do so. Yet their urge was personal and dynastic and lacked sustained force. Spain did not really need Portugal. It possessed the best lands along the border between the two kingdoms, it had Atlantic ports in Andalusia, and it considered its main foreign interests to lie in Africa and Italy. The only genuine reason for acquiring Portugal was strategic, and it is worth noting that when, finally, King Philip II of Spain did so in 1580, his main concern was securing one of the flanks of his Atlantic empire. And when Portugal reasserted its independence in 1640, the power of Spain was fully committed to repressing a rebellion in Catalonia and in wars in Germany and the Low Countries so that it could not respond effectively.

Yet, after reviewing all rational explanations, one suspects that providence or chance had a hand in maintaining Portuguese independence. Up until the time Spain declined into impotence, a timely shift in Hispanic power relations, a modest redirection of Spanish policy, a random dynastic marriage might have undone it all, permanently. The survival of an independent Portugal is the kind of problem that cannot be solved empirically. Yet it must be defined. The existence of two separate Atlantic kingdoms in the peninsula meant that westward expansion would take two independent courses.

As the Reconquest advanced, the early Christian kingdoms grew within generally north-south boundaries, generally agreed upon in advance in bilateral treaties. On the eastern flank, Aragon gained the Muslim Kingdom of Valencia; in the west, Portugal took territories that came to be called Estremadura, Beira, the Alentejo, and the Algarve, while on its left the Leonese occupied most of Spanish Extremadura. Castile, advancing on a much broader front, conquered the region south of the Guadarrama and Gredos mountains, which came to be called New Castile, and al-Andalus, Castilianized as Andalusia. It also obtained the Kingdom of Murcia by gracious donation from James I of Aragon, "the Conqueror" (1213–76), who had seized it from the Moors. By virtue of these conquests, Castile not only became the greatest territorial gainer of the Reconquest but established itself in firm control of the heartland of Hispania. Its kings, moreover, incorporated new acquisitions as integral parts of their dominions, thus creating a single polity. The expansion of Castile and Aragon pinched out the Pyrenean Kingdom of Navarre, which had played such an important part in the early Reconquest.

## The Quest for Hispanic Unity

From the outset of the Reconquest, urges toward the unification of all Hispania stirred. No region in Europe had more clearly defined natural boundaries, and the existence of a common Hispanic faith and church implied territorial and political unity, particularly when all of Christian Hispania was contending against a common sectarian enemy. The Hispanic church and the papacy made this implication explicit in their efforts to mobilize pan-peninsular crusades. In addition, the vision of one Hispania as it had existed under Roman and Visigothic rule flickered intermittently throughout the Reconquest. Asturian-Leonese kings as heirs of the Visigothic monarchy claimed legitimate dominion over all the peninsula, and the idea of a neo-Visigothic empire still lived in the twelfth century.

But there were powerful countervailing forces. The first kingdoms and counties were culturally diverse. Furthermore, they were strung out along a thin linear axis extending through the northern mountains from the Mediterranean to the Atlantic, and the boundaries between them ran through difficult terrain. Thus, cultural diversities were preserved and, as the Reconquest crept south, merged into territorial and political identities. Reconquest Hispania had no locus to which all roads led, no geopolitical center such as Paris or London from which authority could be extended outward or to which subordination could be drawn inward. By the twelfth century, when Toledo emerged as the hub of Hispanic Christendom, it was too late; the individualities of the several kingdoms and counties had become too firmly established to allow a true national union. The several peoples of the peninsula regarded each other as foreigners.

The interests of princes had mixed effects on unification. Asturian-Leonese pretensions to peninsular hegemony did not find favor with neighboring monarchs who themselves dreamt of ruling all of Hispania. Some kings managed a step in this direction by conquest and interdynastic marriages, only to undo their work by subdividing the patrimonies thus joined among their several sons. Yet, in the end, family ambitions expressed through intermarriage provided the main force working for one Hispania, albeit with many setbacks.

The first major step toward peninsular unity did not come until 1162, when, through a fruitful marital alliance, the Crown of Aragon and the County of Barcelona (Catalonia) became joined under a single monarch, Alfonso II of

Aragon (1162–96). Although supported by geographical propinquity, the union had an unnatural character. Aragon was a mountain kingdom, poor in resources and parochial in outlook. Catalonia was a much richer and cosmopolitan state enjoying ancient cultural and political links with France and profitable commercial ties with the Mediterranean world. The constitutional arrangement governing unification permitted each polity to retain its identity, laws, and privileges. Aside from its importance as a step toward one Hispania, the union had other long-range implications. The weight of Catalonian interests in France and the Mediterranean tended to draw the attention of the Crown of Aragon in these directions and away from preoccupation with peninsular and, ultimately, Atlantic affairs.

The second step occurred in 1217, when Ferdinand, the son of Queen Berenguela of Castile (1217) and Alfonso IX of Leon (1188–1230), succeeded to the throne of Castile and, upon the death of Alfonso, to that of Leon. It was he, as Ferdinand III of Castile and Leon, who led the great Christian advances into Andalusia and who, because of his deep piety and exploits against Islam, was canonized as Saint Ferdinand. The prestige and wealth he acquired enabled him to resist Leonese pretensions toward autonomy; the union held, and Leonese institutions gradually merged with those of Castile. Although the banner of the united kingdom continued to carry the Leonese lion rampant, by the end of the thirteenth century Leon had virtually disappeared as a separate territory and polity. These circumstances, along with the territorial acquisitions of Ferdinand III and a geographical position dominating the peninsula, made Castile the largest, most populous, and most powerful kingdom in Hispania. The creation of one *Monarchia Hispania*, however, had to await another time and other rulers.

## The Reconquest Municipality

Below the level of kingdoms and counties the main unit of territorial organization was the municipality. It was constituted not only by an inhabited nucleus but also by a rural hinterland over which its council exercised jurisdiction and in which the council and individual *vecinos* held property. Types of municipalities included the communal villages of Leon, Old Castile, and Portugal; Reconquest towns of the peninsular heartland created ex nihilo to secure frontiers; and burgs situated around the periphery in Catalonia, along the Bay of Biscay, and in maritime Portugal. Some burgs had ancient origins and had been refounded during the Reconquest; others had grown "naturally" in response to economic stimuli. The Spaniard or Portuguese regarded the village or town or city as the true country, the primary source of civic identity, and the locus of territorial loyalties.

## Territorial Organization of the Church

The territorial organization of the church proceeded simultaneously with the formation of kingdoms and counties. In our predominantly secular age, ecclesiastical boundaries are not a general concern, but the medieval Hispanic people were profoundly Catholic and identified strongly with the territorial expressions of their faith. In the course of repopulation, they founded parishes concurrently with villages and towns; parish and community were usually geographically coterminous, and parishioner and *vecino* constituted an indivisible identity. Episcopal units of territory also attracted strong popular allegiances. After the breakdown of Roman civil government, many of the ancient sees managed to preserve their integrity, even in regions later conquered by Islam. To Hispanic Christians they represented continuity and stability in violent and disrupted times, and bishops more than kings and secular lords gave protection to the common folk.

The episcopal reconstruction of Hispania also had strong political connotations. Bishops aspired to elevate the status, extend the jurisdictions, and augment the rents of their dioceses. New sees created in the north competed for preeminence with ancient ones liberated or reestablished as the Reconquest moved south. The main contest developed among Toledo, the capital of the Hispanic church before the Muslim conquest; Santiago de Compostela, which claimed leadership because of Saint James's patronage; and Braga, in Portugal, which strove to maintain its independence from both. On occasion, the competing claims of prelates erupted into violence, as in 1102 when Diego Gelmírez, the contentious archbishop of Santiago, descended on Braga and carried off the holy relics of Saint Fructuoso and Saint Victor.

Monarchs took a lively interest in these matters. Bishops and archbishops were powerful personages, and, by making ecclesiastical and civil jurisdictions coterminous, kings could impose some check on the power of prelates as well as prevent foreign intrusions into their dominions via the episcopacy. Conversely, identification with a powerful see strengthened royal authority. Thus, in the County of Portugal, popular allegiance to Braga unquestionably furthered Afonso Henriques's aspirations to independence from Castile-Leon. The outcome of ecclesiastical wars, diplomacy, and conspiracies was the restoration of Toledo to Hispanic primacy in the twelfth century, an event that contributed further to Castilian dominance in the configuration of peninsular polities. After

Portugal obtained recognition of its independence from the papacy, however, Braga gained jurisdiction over the Lusitanian bishoprics, an ecclesiastical victory that helped to confirm and sustain political separation from Castile-Leon.

## Reconquest Economies

### Agriculture and Grazing

The formation of Hispanic economies conformed in a general way to secular trends affecting the rest of western Europe. Until the last part of the tenth century, populations were static, mainly rural, and subsisted on primitive agrarian pursuits. Manufacturing was limited to household and artisan production of articles essential for war and peace, and trade to local markets and transactions of itinerant merchants. Exchange depended heavily on barter. Within this pattern, however, some distinctive Hispanic traits appeared. In the central part of the peninsula, sheep grazing early became the predominant activity on both manorial and free village lands because of certain advantages it offered. It required fewer hands than agriculture and was therefore more suitable for the sparse populations of early Christian Hispania. Herders could move flocks quickly from the paths of Muslim raids, while immobile crops lay vulnerable; moreover, sheep demanded less constant attention than fields, leaving more time free for fighting. As the Christians moved south onto the central *meseta*, much of the land they occupied was rough in contour, semiarid, and subject to extremes of temperature. This region was more immediately suitable for sheep than for crops. At the same time, the advance facilitated transhumancy, that is, the rotation of flocks between winter and summer pasturage. By about 1000, sheep runs, which came to be called *cañadas*, led from winter enclosures in the northern mountains to summer pasturages on the Duero frontier. This arrangement encouraged an enormous growth in the sheep population.

Grazing also gained organizational and political advantages. As flocks multiplied, owners formed local committees called *mestas* that patrolled pasturages, recovered strays, adjudicated disputes among members, and, in general, defended the interests of sheepmen. As the range of grazing extended, these organizations coalesced to form regional *mestas*. Meanwhile, control of grazing tended to fall into the hands of powerful lay and ecclesiastical lords who could afford to acquire large flocks, who owned or controlled pasturages and sheep runs, and who came to dominate the *mestas*. Finally, Leonese and Castilian kings favored sheep raising over other activities. Not only did they themselves pasture large flocks on crown lands, but the lords of ranges had easier access to the ears of princes than did unorganized agriculturists. Royal favoritism also made fiscal sense, at least in the short run. It was much easier to negotiate with corporations such as the *mesta* for single contributions to the treasury than to collect taxes from dispersed individual grazers.

## Trade and Commerce

About 1000 A.D. a demographic and economic upswing began in Europe, the first phase of a series of Malthusian cycles that have affected the Western world in medieval and modern times.[4] North of the Pyrenees, populations began to increase; lords and peasants undertook the reclamation of large areas of forest, fen, and tidal lands; old towns started to grow and new ones appeared; trade commenced to move more vigorously along rivers, roads, and sea lanes. In Hispania, Leonese, Castilians, and Portuguese exploited the pastoral and agricultural resources of the lands along the Duero and its tributaries that they had repopulated. The slackening of Muslim raids aided their efforts by creating greater security in the countryside, and closer proximity to al-Andalus encouraged enterprising agriculturists to adopt advanced techniques employed by Muslim farmers. Increased food production yielded surpluses that encouraged demographic growth and supported the Reconquest municipalities that the Christians founded in the eleventh century. At the same time, the southward expansion of Hispanic kingdoms incorporated already prosperous towns such as Toledo and Lisbon into Christian economies.

As in northern Europe, the development of commerce followed agrarian and demographic expansion. On land, Hispanic trade followed ancient Roman roads from Muslim territory to towns in Old Castile, Leon, northern Portugal, and Galicia, disregarding the wars between Christians and Moors. At various points in the north, these routes linked to the pilgrimage road leading from France to Santiago de Compostela, and French merchants settled in towns where pilgrims broke their journey as well as in the cities of Leon and Old Castile. By sea, Biscayan ships sailed to Flanders; Portuguese cities traded with Moroccan ports and in the early twelfth century opened commerce with northern Europe; Catalan galleys plied between Barcelona and French, Italian, North African, and Levantine ports, competing vigorously with Italian cities. To service burgeoning mercantile requirements, Hispanic kings and lords licensed — and taxed — annual fairs where Portuguese, Castilian, Aragonese, Jewish, Italian, and northern European merchants gathered to buy and sell with exchange and credit provided by Italian and Jewish bankers.

In the thirteenth century, both internal and external circumstances imparted new vigor to Hispanic commerce. Between the late twelfth century and the early fifteenth century, the population of Castile doubled, from roughly 3,000,000 to 6,000,000 souls, and that of Aragon increased in the same proportion, from 500,000 to 1,000,000. This meant, on the one hand, more mouths to feed and more backs to clothe; on the other, by providing more hands to labor, it kept wages down so that merchants' and landowners' profits rose. The reduction of Hispanic Islam to the Kingdom of Granada in the mid-thirteenth century, moreover, freed Christian Hispania to participate more vigorously in the European commercial renaissance that was then approaching full flood, while the occupation of al-Andalus and southern Portugal provided rich sources of new wealth.

Hispanic commerce received more direct stimulation from two sources. One was the phenomenal expansion of the wool industry resulting from a conjunction of circumstances climaxing around 1300 that collectively have been termed the "Wool Revolution."[5] By the late thirteenth century population growth throughout Europe had created an enormous demand for woolen cloth. Previously, most of the raw wool for the looms of Europe had come from English flocks, but this source became constricted by the disruptions of the Hundred Years' War and the requirements of the domestic textile industry in England. At about this time also, the merino sheep, which produced a high-grade long staple, was introduced into Castile from North Africa, and in 1273 King Alfonso X chartered the *Honrado Consejo de la Mesta de los Pastores de Castilla* (The Honorable Council of the *mesta* of the Shepherds of Castile), thus consolidating the several regional *mestas*. A literal translation of *pastores* may be misleading. The members of the council were not simple shepherds. They were the rich and poweful lords of the *cañadas*, and the *Mesta* became an almost irresistible lobbying and protective organization.

The consequences of the Wool Revolution came quickly and spectacularly. By the middle of the fourteenth century, Castilian staple had largely replaced English in the markets of Flanders and Italy. The incomes of the lords of the *Mesta* soared. Castile created a fleet to carry wool from Seville and the Bay of Cadiz to Italy and from ports on the Bay of Biscay to northern Europe. From this trade the merchants of Castile prospered immensely, and royal revenues from duties and from taxes on production and exchange increased.

Italians provided the other major stimulus to Hispanic commerce. Immediately after the conquest of the south, Genoese and Florentine merchants appeared in the cities of Andalusia and the Algarve to exploit new markets, and, in the 1270s when the Italian cities opened trade with England and Flanders, their merchants settled in Castilian and Portuguese ports that became way stations on the North Atlantic route. It was at this time that Seville and Lisbon began their development as major European maritime centers. Bankers followed merchants and together with them formed Italian colonies whose financial skills were so useful that kings granted them jurisdictional and fiscal immunities. Their enterprise, however, drove many Castilian and Portuguese merchants from business and provided vigorous competition to Hispanic Jews.

Toward the end of the thirteenth century, Hispanic economies showed many signs of vigor, but measured against developments north of the Pyrenees they also had serious deformities. Their most robust growth occurred around the periphery of the peninsula: in Catalonia, along the pilgrimage road to Santiago, and in Cantabrian, Portuguese, and Andalusian ports. The politically and demographically dominant Castilian heartland remained agrarian in structure and mentality. In the agrarian sector itself, grazing increased its predominance over planting. In addition to the great sheep pasturages and *cañadas*, cattle ranches on a fairly large scale began to develop in Leon and Old Castile in the late eleventh century and, as the Reconquest advanced, spread south into Extremadura, New Castile, and Andalusia. Although cattlemen never acquired the formidable organization and influence enjoyed by the *Mesta*, cattle outnumbered sheep in many parts of southern Hispania, and in these regions, one authority proposes, the prototypes of the great cattle haciendas of the New World were born.[6]

The lords of flocks and herds together appropriated vast areas of productive or potentially productive farmlands, particularly in Andalusia. Under Muslim rule this region had been one of the most bountiful in all Hispania, but the conquering Christians expelled the rural population that had made it bloom and turned much of the land into pasture. In all parts of Castile, moreover, grazers won the right to drive their livestock through agricultural properties, thereby doing great damage to crops. It is interesting to note that the expansion of pastoral activities at the expense of agriculture contrasted with the more intensive use of land historically associated with expanding populations and economies.

Overemphasis on grazing also affected other sectors of the economy adversely. The commercial prosperity of Castile depended heavily on the exchange of a single export commodity, wool, for luxury products consumed by the lords of the *Mesta* and other wealthy folk, while the profits of the trade went mainly to foreign merchants and bankers who shipped them from the country. The only industry that developed on any significant scale was wool manufacturing, but its technology was backward. It could not produce the high-grade cloth that was the richest source of profit at home and abroad, and to prosper it needed protection and staple at low prices. These requirements conflicted with those of wool growers, who wanted to sell dear and could get the best prices from foreign manufacturers who also wanted to participate in the domestic market. The contest was quite unequal because the crown, which was heavily dependent on revenues from the *Mesta* and avowedly antiprotectionist, rather consistently favored grazing interests. Inadequate organizational forms also disadvantaged artisan and industrial production. Guilds existed, but they were little more than *cofradías*, confraternities of men practicing the same trade, living on the same street, and attending the same church. Their main functions were helping their parish, providing social security benefits for members, and organizing religious festivals. Kings and municipalities, jealous of their regulatory authority and hostile to restraints on trade, felt reluctant to concede to private corporations the control over production, quality, and prices that gave strength to the guilds of northern Europe.

The Portuguese economy displayed a somewhat better balance. Sheepherding and cattle ranching were important activities in the central and the southern part of the kingdom, and north-south sheep runs traversed Estremadura and the Alentejo. Pastoral interests, however, did not completely dominate the agrarian sector, and various monarchs attempted to balance agriculture and grazing. King Dinis (1279-1325) tried to break up the holdings of the nobility and the church and redistribute them among small proprietors, an effort that failed but won him the sobriquet of "the Farmer." Yet Portuguese economic growth lagged despite intermittent royal favor. Agriculture remained primitive and, although commerce did not depend so exclusively on the exportation of wool as in Castile, it was largely dominated by foreigners. Industrial production was limited mainly to cheap cloth, household and farming implements, and some shipbuilding. As in Castile, the build system atrophied.

It is relatively easy to describe weaknesses in Hispanic economies but much more difficult to explain them. Traditional historiography lays the blame on the Reconquest: the social and political disorders it created and the social attitudes and habits it fostered. But underlying geographic and demographic influences also played a part. In much of the heartland of Hispania, rough terrain, insufficient rainfall, and extremes of temperature in winter and summer discouraged intensive land use. In the broad and rich valley of Andalusia, the circumstances of reconquest severely damaged agricultural productivity. Natural obstacles, unstable political boundaries, the absence of navigable rivers penetrating the interior, and sheer distance hindered the creation of communication and transportation systems. These conditions discouraged thick and well-distributed habitation. The failure of demographic growth to keep up with territorial expansion contributed further to underpopulation.

In short, Hispania's size was out of proportion to its natural and human resources. Its heartland lacked a population density sufficient to support close-knit economic relations between town and countryside, between town and town, between province and province. These conditions contrasted with those prevailing in *l'Europe médiane*, the center of Europe, which lay along an axis running from northern Italy through France, the Low Countries, and western Germany into England. By about 1300, population density in this area had reached forty to fifty persons per square kilometer, a level that the French historian Pierre Chaunu regards as the "takeoff point" for sustained economic growth. Hispania did not reach this verge until about 1500.[7]

## The Ordering of Society:
## The Republic, Justice, and the Law

The Hispanic peoples ordered their societies in much the same way as did other western Europeans. They made no categorical distinction between what was social and what was political. Rather, they subsumed both under the concept of the "republic" (*res publica*, the public entity), whose constitution Saint Augustine had defined in his *City of God*. Augustinian theory entered Hispanic thought through the writings of the learned doctor Saint Isidore of Seville (d. 633).

The republic consisted of an association of persons and "interests" suffering together the exigencies of life on this earth. To prevent contentions among them, their relations had to be ordered in a way that allotted "things equal and unequal, each to its own place." But order had to be more than an accommodation of material interests, for earthly existence was merely an ephemeral sojourn in preparation for the perfect life thereafter. The republic had to serve God's purpose, which was the peace achieved by the harmonious union of souls and which was embodied in the concept of justice. Through justice the citizen was assured true concord. Justice was the sole end of human society, and government was simply applied justice.

The instrument that gave and assured justice was the law. In the first instance, law was divine law, which could never be superseded, but it had to be supplemented and implemented by positive law that derived from usage in a way explained by Saint Isidore: *Mos* was custom sanctified by antiquity. *Lex* was the written law coming from *mos*. Later Hispanic Christian jurists redefined the sequence in Castilian terms. Use came from time; use produced custom, which was unwritten law or *derecho*; *fuero* was written law enacted by the people to sanction custom. Elements of the civil law of the Romans, mainly in the private sphere, also entered Hispanic legal systems through the Theodosian Code and the commentaries of jurists such as Ulpian and Gaius.

Thus, the written law of Hispania came into existence in the form of *fueros*. At first, *fueros* applied to particular classes of people and territorial entities, but from time to time it became necessary to resolve contradictions and establish legal order through compilation and codification. The first major effort in this direction was completed in 694 and was called the *Lex Visigothorum* (Law of the Visigoths) or the *Forum Iudiciorum* (The Bringing Together of the Law), later Castilianized as the *Fuero Juzgo*. The Visigoths intended it to apply to all Hispania, thereby superseding the Roman practice of leaving conquered peoples to abide by their own laws. The early Christian kingdoms adhered to the basic principles of the code, but inevitably different customs and *fueros* appeared in conjunction with emerging national identities and required new and separate compilations.

In Castile, Reconquest codes climaxed in the monumental *Siete Partidas* (Law of Seven Parts), compiled during the reign of Alfonso X, "the Learned" (1252-84).[8] Alfonso intended it only to bring early codifications up to date, but it was prepared by jurists trained in the *Corpus juris civilis*, which had entered Spanish universities, particularly Salamanca and Alcalá, via scholars returning from Paris and Bologna. The effort to reconcile the civil law with Castilian *fueros* produced considerable confusion, but in balance the texts and glosses of the *Partidas* infused a strong measure of Roman law, both public and private, into the Castilian legal system. Innovations included an emphasis on *aequitas* (equity), that is, abstract and universal justice emerging from natural law.

The *Partidas* did not have a direct or immediate impact on Castile's legal system. Castilians of all classes objected to them on the grounds that they replaced revered *fueros* and beautiful and praiseworthy customs with alien principles, an attitude that they tended to display toward all things foreign. Alfonso X never summoned up the resolution to promulgate the code, nor did his successors until Alfonso XI (1312-50) took the step in 1348. Jurists, nevertheless, regularly consulted it as a quasi-official source of law, and magistrates gradually introduced its provisions into the courts. Through translation, the *Partidas* had an important influence on law and political theory in Portugal.

Medieval Hispanic legal thought held what appear to be deep paradoxes. It defined justice, peace, and order as norms in a society organized for war, but war was held to be the ultimate means of establishing peace, and, perhaps, it was universal discord that created such a yearning for concord. In any event, the quest for absolute and perfect Christian justice, along with universal and abstract equity, made the law into a set of moral and ethical precepts intended to guide and instruct conduct rather than a corpus of pragmatic rules governing behavior. The ideal did not take into account original sin, the propensity of mortals to behave evilly and immorally in pursuit or defense of their worldly interests. Only a saint could meet the standards set, and even in most Christian Spain saints constituted only an infinitesimal proportion of the population. Disparities between the ideal and the real, between expectations and performance, created fundamental personal and institutional tensions, reflected in widespread evasions of the law, and even allowed the development of formulae permitting legal circumventions. Thus, although the convention obtained that a king could not knowingly do wrong, his decisions might be ill-advised, in which case his subordinates could suspend execution while his judgment was being illuminated. Such contradictions were not, of course, uniquely Spanish or Portuguese, but in Hispania they appear to have been wider, more deeply rooted, and more enduring than elsewhere in western Europe.

## The Orders of the Republic

### The Clergy

The main interests making up the republic were the functional classes that had developed during the Reconquest and that by the thirteenth century were conceptualized as "orders" of the realm.[9] Each possessed an ascribed status based on the general society's perception of the value or utility of the function it performed. Each, also, had a juridical status expressed in a set of legal privileges and immunities presumed to facilitate the performance of its social task.

The clergy constituted the first order. It had two main components, the seculars and the regulars. The secular branch consisted of the ecclesiastical hierarchy from archbishop to parish priest that had direct charge of the care of souls through administration of the sacraments and in the confessional. The regulars were the religious orders. They included the monastic Cistercians and Benedictines, who entered the peninsula early in the Reconquest, and the mendicant Dominicans and Franciscans, who appeared in the thirteenth century and who devoted themselves to preaching and teaching among the poor.

Although functionally subdivided, the clergy had a single purpose, to guide souls to salvation. Because salvation was the primary end of earthly existence, clerics, secular and regular, enjoyed a preeminent ascribed status supported by ample legal immunities defined in an ecclesiastical *fuero*. The most valued provisions of this code were exemption from personal taxes (*pechos*) and from the jurisdiction of the ordinary courts in many classes of civil and criminal cases in which clergymen might become entangled. The status of the ecclesiastical estate rested on solid material foundations. Prelates, cathedral chapters, monasteries, and other religious foundations held rural estates, urban property, and endowments whose incomes relieved them from complete dependence on the favor and charity of other interests.

## The Nobility

The nobility comprised the second order of the republic. Its nucleus consisted of the old Visigothic ruling class, but during the Reconquest its numbers were augmented and its vitality sustained by co-optation. Persons of common birth who served the king with distinction as mounted warriors could become knights (*caballeros* in Castile, *cavaleiros* in Portugal). Knighthood, however, did not automatically convey *nobleza* (nobility). The aspirant first had to be recognized as an *hijo de algo* (later contracted to hidalgo in Castile, to *fidalgo* in Portugal). That is, he had to be descended from someone of widely known and undisputed honor, courage, virtue, charity, and generosity through a lineage that upheld these qualities. Some sort of formal acceptance or investiture by peers was regarded as highly desirable, if not essential, to confirm and secure *hidalguía* (the quality of being a hidalgo) gained by ascription. The king could also raise commoners to hidalgos directly and immediately by an act of royal mercy (*merced*), but nobility so acquired had a doubtful social legitimacy until it built a lineage.

The nobility was primarily a warrior class, and in an age of almost continuous strife between Christian and Moor and Christian and Christian the survival of the republic depended on its martial skill and valor. It therefore enjoyed an elevated ascribed status. Its importance was recognized formally in an accumulation of immunities that, by the middle of the twelfth century, had been formally defined as the *fuero de los hidalgos*. By virtue of their *fuero*, nobles enjoyed exemption from personal taxes; they could be tried for many classes of criminal offenses only by their peers and under privileged procedural law; and they could not be imprisoned, nor could their property be seized for debt.

Law and custom provided economic and social supports for the nobility's ascribed and juridical status. All its members were supposed to possess landed property providing revenues sufficient to maintain their mounts and military accoutrements and to allow them to live in a style befitting their station. Nobles also enjoyed preference in the allocation of municipal and royal offices. In practice many hidalgos became impoverished and fell into debt because their resources were truly inadequate, especially in periods of inflation, or because they insisted on living beyond their means. Also, the crown did not always respect their precedence in filling public offices, particularly those requiring administrative and fiscal skills. But these deprivations in no way tarnished the luster of their lineage.

Although the noble estate had a common set of qualitites, differences in lineage, wealth, and influence divided it into two ranks. Hidalgos of modest means and office constituted the lower and by far the more numerous. The upper consisted of persons who held large landed estates and high public office and who, in some instances, claimed descent from the old Visigothic ruling class. Nobles of the highest rank held titles recognizing their eminence. During the early years of the Reconquest they were called *optimates* or *magnates*. In the twelfth century, the titles of duke and count came into use, although at first these designated the governor of a large territory and did not become hereditary ranks until much later. Marquises did not appear until the fourteenth century.

## Señorialism and Feudalism

Most of the upper nobility also possessed some measure of *señorío*, a faculty that is difficult to define because its form varied greatly from time to time and from place to place. In a general sense it meant lordship, and one who enjoyed it was a *señor* (lord). More particularly, it conveyed governmental rights: to give laws and to exercise jurisdiction; to coin money; to collect taxes, dues, and services; and to raise military levies. It was commonly associated with the landed estate but it did not necessarily involve ownership of the territory in which it was exercised. Its essential feature was dominion over people. *Señorío* had a high value attached, for it gave the lord political and military bases of power as well as great social honor and prestige.

Originally and ultimately, *señorío* reposed in kings. But they could and did delegate their *señorial* rights to deserving subjects to provide motives or rewards for the conquest and resettlement of territory or because they simply lacked the resources to rule frontier regions personally. Delegation, however, did not amount to an alienation of sovereignty that was imprescriptible. It was also limited in scope and in time. Monarchs reserved for themselves the lawmaking power; jurisdiction in high crimes such as treason, highway robbery, and rape; and the right to coin money. They did not commonly grant *señoríos* in heredity and perpetuity but only for the lifetime of the recipient or, simply, "at the King's will."

In some respects, delegations of *señorío* resembled a feudal arrangement. In effect, the recipient received a benefice for services rendered or anticipated and in return swore fealty and acknowledged vassalage to his sovereign. But *señorial* relationships lacked the essential qualities of feudalism. In contrast with the complex and binding set of benefits and obligations embodied in a feudal contract, the links between Hispanic kings and vassal *señores* were loose and ephemeral. Except in a few instances, also, even the most powerful magnates received only limited jurisdictional rights in their territories. Finally, the *señorial* system had no such elaborate hierarchal ordering of dependency relations as that created by subinfeudation north of the Pyrenees. The king was in fact the only liege lord in his realm.[10]

The failure of a true feudal system to develop in Hispania except, perhaps, in Aragon (which felt strong French influences) is commonly attributed to the Reconquest environment. Empty lands, border raiding, and pastoralism generated among Castilians —and Portuguese —a nomadic life-style characterized by a distates for discipline, a deep feeling of personal identity, an exaggerated self-esteem, and a sense of *pundonor*, which means extreme sensitivity to points of personal honor and dignity. These qualities conjoined in an intense Hispanic individualism and personalism. Carried over into social attitudes, they meant that while the individual accepted the inscrutable fate that raised other men above him in rank, his personal worth remained undiminished by subordination. Concurrently, advancing frontiers made land relatively abundant and favored geographical and social mobility, thereby permitting individuals to indulge their homocentric egos and avoid formal and permanent dependency relations.[11]

After the reconquest of southern Hispania in the mid-thirteenth century, the power of the upper nobility increased greatly. Through the division of the vast territories won, lords of both ancient lineage and new creation acquired *señorial* domains of unprecedented size and became known as *ricos hombres*. The term literally meant men of great wealth, but it also implied elevated social status and great influence in the political affairs of the kingdom. Through royal concessions or by unchallenged assumption, they managed to make their lordships hereditary. To insure the integrity of their family holdings and enhance their prestige, they obtained from the crown the right to create *mayorazgos* (entailed estates) to which a hereditary title of nobility generally attached.

### The Common Order

Commoners constituted the third order of the realm. Their function was to provide the material goods and services required by members of the republic. During the early centuries of the Reconquest, they consisted overwhelmingly of rural laborers of various statuses. Some were free peasants who held allodiums or were residents of landholding villages. Others subsisted in some sort of personal or property dependence on lay and ecclesiastical lords. Still others were adscript serfs. In medieval Hispania, however, serfdom was an unstable institution, because the existence of fluid frontier conditions and empty land encouraged escape from servile conditions. Beginning in the eleventh century, urbanization and economic growth created a new and more influential class of commoners, the *vecinos* of towns, including merchants, guildmasters, and other persons of substance, fixed residence, and decent reputation.

Because of the base nature ascribed to its function, the common order had the lowest ascribed status in the republic and did not have a common privileged *fuero*. Its members were subject to the jurisdiction of royal, baronial, or municipal courts and had to pay capitation taxes. As in the other orders, gradations of status existed among commoners. Townsmen had the highest social reputation and enjoyed liberties set forth in their municipal charters. At first, the provisions of these instruments displayed considerable diversity. In the later stages of the Reconquest, kings attempted to bring them into conformity through codifications of the general laws of the realm and by giving newly founded towns "model *fueros*," that is, particularly praiseworthy charters enjoyed by established municipalities. Avila and Salamanca in Castile, and Santarém in Portugal, furnished widely used models. Portuguese monarchs sometimes drew on Castilian experience. Wishing to refound and repopulate "Elbora [Evora] which we have taken from the Saracens," the king and queen of Portugal gave it the *forum et costume de Avila*.

### The "Underdevelopment" of Hispanic Bourgeoisies

Although townsmen possessed common qualities, their function and status had a curious regional dualism. The *vecinos* of free burgs around the maritime periphery of Hispania included influential mercantile elements. In contrast, civic life in the Reconquest towns of the heartland was dominated by a class called *caballeros villanos* (*cavaleiros vilãos* in Portugal), which translates as knights-commoners, that is, knights who had not won *hidalguía*. Although they might engage in trade and commerce, they maintained a horse, military accoutrements, and, the wealthier among them, bands of retainers. They stood ready to serve in the king's cavalry and in return gained exemption from personal taxes and a virtual monopoly of municipal offices. Neither nobles nor burghers, they constituted an urban patriciate of military origin and function and of knightly mentality. By the thirteenth century, they had become the most powerful element of the common estate in Castile and in central and southern Portugal, a social phenomenon that contrasted sharply with the preeminence of mercantile aristocracies in the towns of Europe from Lombardy to Flanders. Indeed, Hispanic societies had little room for a bourgeoisie. Contemporary texts refer to townsmen as *omos buenos* (*homens bons* in Portugal), *cibdadanos*, or *vecinos*, all of which meant simply men of property and decent social quality, but rarely were they called *burgueses*. The definition of the estates of the realm found in the *Siete Partidas*, moreover, did not accommodate burghers.[12]

Like so many other qualities of Hispanic civilizations, the underdevelopment of Hispanic bourgeoisies is generally attributed to the Reconquest, which created a society organized for war and a set of normative values hostile to economic enterprise. The proper occupation for gentlemen was fighting; the most honorable source of income was rent, booty, and tribute; the firmest source of status was dominion over lands and people. Commerce, manufacturing, and money lending could conveniently be left to Jews and foreigners. For these reasons, even prosperous burghers invested profits from commerce in rent-yielding properties and sought knightly status.

These explanations are widely accepted and plausible, but they should be taken with reservations. After all, the Cid Campeador, that epitome of Castilian *hidalguía*, operated a flour mill for gain; Sancho VII "the Strong" of Navarre (1194–1234) used his loot from the Battle of Las Navas de Tolosa to launch large banking ventures; and the *Mesta* was a great commercial enterprise. In Portugal, the nobility and the crown became deeply involved in gainful undertakings, especially the Flanders trade.[13] All this was not the same as shopkeeping, but it indicates that Hispanic lords and knights were not always mere rentiers and that they had no prejudices against turning a profit. Neither was the defection of the bourgeoisie to the nobility a peculiarly Hispanic phenomenon. The merchants of Flanders, France, and England also aspired to nobility and often achieved it by putting their wealth in the service of princes. Although Hispanic attitudes toward the social value of work and the honorability of commerce may have deviated from European norms, they were by no means unique.[14] Furthermore, the underdevelopment of Hispanic bourgeoisies cannot be explained by cultural attitudes alone. It reflected the underlying structural weaknesses of peninsular economies that were examined earlier in this chapter: inhospitable geographical environments, poor transportation systems, and underpopulation. In any event, Hispanic values and institutions had not crystallized by the end of the thirteenth century, nor were the Hispanic peoples incapable of surmounting demographic and geographic obstacles. The events and circumstances that discouraged and ultimately doomed the development of a vigorous commercial-industrial sector stretched out over several centuries, and the problem will be revisited later.

## Moors and Jews

The Hispanic kingdoms contained inhabitants who were neither clergy nor nobles nor commoners nor, indeed, properly members of the republic, which was an exclusively Christian order. As the Reconquest moved into central and southern Hispania, it overran large sedentary Muslim populations and long-established communities of Jews. By the terms of negotiated surrenders (*pactos protectores*) the victors permitted the vanquished Moors to retain their faith and their property rights as long as they accepted the dominion of Christian princes and paid tribute to them. Although most of the Muslim leaders and the more devout among their followers fled or elected to withdraw into the shrinking territories of Islam, large numbers of the common people accepted these terms and as a class became known as *mudéjares*. The Jews were subject to the same conditions, and most of them elected to remain in their ancient homes. Both elements performed important economic functions. The *mudéjares* served as artisans and rural laborers, and Jews possessed valuable commercial skills and accumulations of capital that could be taxed or borrowed by impecunious princes and nobles. Kings also employed them in the royal household, and they served as clerks and fiscal agents on the estates of lay and ecclesiastical lords. Neither *mudéjares* nor Jews possessed *fueros*. They were governed by the personal law of the monarch.

## Social Mobility

Despite great and generally recognized differences in rank and status, Reconquest societies did not have a rigid or symmetrical ordering. Each order had an internal hierarchy through which its members could ascend by virtue of achievement or favor. Neither were the lines between the orders firmly fixed. Many clergymen came from noble families, and prelates often held great estates either through their office or as individuals. Thereby they became ecclesiastical lords. The commanders and knights of the military orders were considered to be noble, although their status was not hereditary. At the same time they were members of a religious community. In a society organized for war, daring and enterprise could raise commoners to knights and knights to hidalgos, while the church offered avenues of social ascension to devout, astute, and diligent persons of base birth. Jews could enter Christian society by conversion and in time penetrate into its upper ranks, although the stain of their birth could not be cleansed completely.

## The Monarchy

### The King and Lord

To God's ends and by God's grace, the head of the body social and politic was the king. In the early years of the Reconquest, kings held their high office through election by their peers, that is, by the nobility. But very soon it became customary to elect them from the same family, thus establishing the principle of hereditary dynastic succession. Since reigning monarchs normally designated their heirs, elevation to kingship amounted to acclamation. No definite law of inheritance existed, however, until the *Siete Partidas* provided for the succession of all descendants in a direct line, male and female, before collaterals.

Claims for the divine origin of the right to rule reinforced the hereditary principle. They were advanced mainly by the church, which felt that a strong monarchy was essential to provide the internal stability it needed for its mission and to prosecute the wars against the Moors. But divine origin did not mean divine right. The elective principle remained fixed in custom, and contemporary political theory held that kings received their sovereignty not directly from God but rather through a compact with the people to whom God had delegated it in the first instance.

The king held his office in a dual constitutional capacity. He was a public person presumed to stand above interest. His primary function was the adjudication of conflicts among persons and interests through declaring the law that he held in his custody. Reconquest and repopulation, however, created situations not anticipated by ancient *fueros*, so that he also had to create new legal norms. In contemporary phraseology, the monarch became responsible for giving not only justice but good government (*justicia y buen gobierno*), which had as their end the general welfare (*bien común*) of the republic. Thus, he became both chief magistrate and chief legislator in his realm. He also had the responsibility to defend his kingdom against its enemies, a charge that made him the supreme military commander. To perform his several functions, he had to accumulate and husband a royal exchequer, and thus he became the high treasurer of his domain.

The monarch was also a private person, a supreme *señor natural* (natural lord), by virtue of a "natural" order that, in the context of the times, meant through dynastic succession.[15] He not only gave justice and good government to his subjects but also was the sovereign and ruler of his kingdom, which was his family patrimony (the *patrimonio real*). In his sovereign capacity, he possessed various *regalías* (inalienable rights inherent in the crown), which included ultimate title to the lands, waters, and minerals of his realm and the right to grant their usufruct to others, the power to create and fill public offices, and the authority to delegate his *señorío*.

### King and Church

The *regalía* most cherished by Hispanic kings allowed them to intervene directly in ecclesiastical government except in matters of faith and dogma. Following Visigothic precedents, they were regarded as lords protector of the church. As such, they claimed the right to establish sees and monasteries, present prelates (the *patronato*, or right of patronage), convoke church councils, adjudicate episcopal disputes, and censor papal bulls. The papacy disputed these pretensions, but from a rather weak position. The breakdown of church organization on the peninsula after the Muslim invasion had left it without effective channels through which to exert its authority, and it had to acknowledge the special merits of Reconquest kings as crusaders against Islam. For the most part, also, peninsular hierarchies supported the regalist position and, in return, received royal protection and favor. In the eleventh century, the Hispanic kingdoms reestablished formal relations with the Holy See and allowed its legates some voice in domestic ecclesiastical affairs. The church remained, however, essentially a Hispanic institution, and kings managed to retain most of their prerogatives, including an ample royal patronage. Portugal must be entered as an exception to this generalization. In return for papal support for national independence, Afonso Henriques and his immediate successors had to acknowledge subordination to Rome in matters of church governance.

## The Instruments of Royal Government

Law and custom enjoined medieval princes to seek wise and prudent counsel in governing their realms and, in practice, the volume of their duties compelled them to rely on the help of others. Hence, various agencies and offices evolved as appendages of the crown. Early Reconquest kings maintained royal households that conducted the day-to-day business of the court. Their principal functionaries included a chancellor, a chamberlain, a steward, a royal chaplain, a supreme justice, and a high treasurer, all of whom were generally drawn from the upper ranks of the nobility and the clergy. On occasion, monarchs convoked councils to advise them. Normally, these bodies consisted of high-ranking members of the royal household and important personages who happened to be at court, but, when matters of great moment had to be decided, lay and ecclesiastical lords might be summoned from afar to attend.

Beyond the court, kings exercised their writ through several classes of functionaries. The highest ranking among them were counts and other magnates who governed large territorial units in the king's name but held their offices in heredity and often with *señorial* faculties. The crown also appointed directly officials to discharge judicial, military, and administrative functions in smaller districts. Chief among them in Castile were *merinos*, whose duties were primarily judicial, and *adelantados*, who served in frontier regions and who were primarily military commanders. Comparable Portuguese officials were *alcaides* and *meirinhos-mores*.

As the acquisition of new territories and peoples multiplied the responsibilities of kingship, the organs of royal government became more complex and institutionalized. By the late fourteenth century, the kings' councils had evolved from ad hoc convocations to permanent bodies with more or less fixed constitutions. By that time, also, the royal household had become a proto-bureaucracy made up of tribunals and chambers attending to particular functions of government. They were headed by the principal officers of the court, many of whom now held their posts in hereditary proprietorship. The rank and file consisted of clerks, notaries, and accountants drawn from the lower ranks of the clergy and, increasingly, from the common estate.

Meanwhile, new governmental institutions emerged. Beginning in Leon in the late twelfth century, Hispanic kings began to summon parliaments (cortes in both Castile-Leon and Portugal) in which representatives of the orders, meeting in separate chambers, advised the king on the affairs of the realm and confirmed royal successions. The issues on which cortes deliberated were mainly economic, and one of the principal functions of the common chamber was to vote money subsidies to the crown, called *servicios* in Castile-Leon and *pedidos* in Portugal.

Important changes also occurred in regional government. In the fourteenth century Hispanic kings began to send out magistrates (*corregidores* in Castile-Leon, *corregedores* and *juizes de fora* in Portugal) to towns for the purpose of asserting royal authority in municipal affairs. Whatever these officials achieved, however, was counterbalanced by the growing *señorial* powers of the *ricos hombres* and by the tendency of the offices of *merino* and *adelantado* to fall into the hereditary proprietorship of powerful local families.

In theory, the defense of their realms and the giving of justice and good government were the paramount duties of kings. Their most immediate and pressing concern, however, was the state of their treasuries, for neither their personal nor public ends could be achieved without money. During most of the Reconquest, royal revenues came from much the same sources as in other European kingdoms: incomes from estates held directly by the crown, *señorial* dues, and the rental of economic *regalías*, such as the licensing of markets and the exploitation of mineral wealth. Later, in the twelfth century, these sources were supplemented by aids voted by cortes and, as trade expanded, by customs duties and taxes on transit and mercantile transactions. The conditions of the Reconquest produced two special revenues: a fifth of booty taken from the Moors and tributes from Moorish vassals.

The kinds and yields of royal revenues increased substantially during the Reconquest but were rarely sufficient to meet needs. The fiscal immunities of the clergy and the nobility severely restricted tax bases. Kings made lavish grants of money and sources of money to favored nobles and members of the royal family, frequent wars called for extraordinary expenditures, and systems of tax collections were inefficient and corrupt. Also, after the end of the great reconquests, kings could no longer count on windfall booties to replenish their exchequers. They therefore turned to debasement of the coinage to make both ends meet.

The Power of Kings: Law, Theory, and Reality

Law and custom gave Hispanic kings virtually plenary powers. Although technically separate, their functions as head of the republic and their rights as sovereign lords conjoined in the person who wore the crown. As God's instruments of justice and good government they were imbued with majesty. As defenders of Christendom against the onslaughts of Islam they enjoyed great prestige, which the sweeping conquests of Saint Ferdinand of Castile and James the Conqueror of Aragon further swelled. The penetration of Roman law into Hispanic jurisprudence and political theory reinforced traditional sources of royal authority. The text and glosses of the *Siete Partidas* implied, if they did not declare, that the king's will rather than ancient *fueros* was the source of justice and good government. Although political considerations delayed the promulgation of the code, its interpretations by jurists began to lay the foundations of absolute monarchy.

Yet law and custom also imposed powerful checks on monarchs. Despite infiltration by Roman principles, the *Siete Partidas* declared that the sovereignty they possessed was sovereignty restrained and informed by the ends for which God established it, that is, the realization of justice. A prince, furthermore, was bound by the positive law he made, and he could not contravene divine law as revealed in the Holy Scriptures, as expounded by the church fathers, and as illuminated by his conscience. In his deliberations, he was bound to consult his subjects, in whom earthly sovereignty ultimately reposed, and at his coronation he had to swear to uphold the *fueros* and liberties of his kingdom. In short, he could not be a tyrant, although the law made no provisions for public recourse against tyranny.

The several interests making up the republic furnished another and, in practice, more effective check on royal absolutism. The great nobles regarded the king as only the first among equals, as a sovereign elected from among their own ranks. Their territorial estates, their *señorial* jurisdiction, and the hereditary offices they held in the royal administration itself made them so powerful that they could challenge the authority of the crown to the point of contumacy. The institutional church generally supported the monarchy, but it was quick to resist any abridgements of its immunities by royal magistrates; it used its moral authority to restrain royal tyranny; and individual ecclesiastical lords sometimes behaved as independently as the lay nobility. Towns regarded the king as their protector against the depredations of the nobility, but they also guarded their liberties jealously against royal infringements. In cortes assembled, their representatives could petition for redress of grievances, using their power to grant subsidies as leverage.

Still another circumstance weakened the powers of the monarch. He was a private party in a very human sense with a personal and family status to defend and advance as well as a private patrimony (the *patrimonio privado del rey*) to husband. He himself was an interest. This attribute tended to weaken his effectiveness as head of the republic and manifested itself especially in royal successions. Although the line of transmission had been defined, family contentions or paternal affection caused kings to alter the order, in some instances favoring a bastard son. The sudden or anticipated death of rulers, therefore, was apt to provoke acute, bloody, and often prolonged crises in which noble factions and towns supported rival claimants to the throne and in which neighboring princes meddled. Medieval royalty, furthermore, had a life expectancy little longer than that of commoners, so that extended minorities occurred frequently. Such discontinuities dissipated the authority accumulated by even the strongest kings.

The pull and tug of forces in the republic, including the interests of the monarchy itself, required kings not only to adjudicate and moderate conflicts but to accommodate and manipulate what amounted to factions. The practice of kingship was really a political art and, then as now, was the art of the possible. It involved the compromise of constitutional principles and conscience with the practical imperatives of ruling. The effectiveness of its exercise depended heavily on the qualities of the head that wore the crown, and the hazards of succession placed dullards, weaklings, and scoundrels on the throne as well as astute, strong, and noble princes. On balance, medieval Hispanic monarchs gradually strengthened the constitutional and moral bases of kingship, but as functioning heads of state their authority was precarious and they managed to maintain only an unstable equilibrium among the contending interests of the republic.

## Social Cleavage and Social Cohesion

### Religion and the Monarchy

Under the influence of Scholastic social theory, contemporary Hispanic savants conceived of the republic in organic terms. It was a corpus of which the king was the head and whose organs and limbs were the several orders and suborders. Each component had a function that it alone could perform properly, and, to do so, each had to rest in proper structural relationship to the others. Hispanic societies possessed all the essential components of the medieval body social and politic. But, carrying the corporate analogy a step further, the head was not always capable of directing the performance of the body, the organ represented by the nobility was enlarged, and that which performed the mercantile function was weak. The total corpus, furthermore, was "Invertebrate," to borrow an expression used by the Spanish philosopher José Ortega y Gassett to describe the society of modern Spain.[16] It lacked the skeletal articulation that might have been provided by a well-developed feudal system. Today feudalism has a pejorative meaning because it is associated with social inequality and exploitation of one class by another. Yet it did provide a well-understood and generally accepted body of rights, obligations, and procedures that created a social order in northern Europe after ancient sources of authority and cohesion had disappeared, before royal absolutism was practicable, and long before democratic contractualism was even conceivable.

What, then, kept the body from falling apart? One answer may be found in Hispanic Catholicism, the spirit that inhabited the corpus. Spaniards and Portuguese may have been no more devout than other Europeans, but the spectacular acceptance of orthodoxy by the Visigothic court, followed by the prolonged struggle against Islam, intensified their faith to the point of fanaticism. They held a profound conviction that they were especially annointed by God, that they were the most Catholic of all peoples. They believed that their societies were based upon and unified by Catholic faith and values, and that to be a Castilian or a Portuguese was to be a Catholic of impeccable orthodoxy. Thus, a militant Catholicism bridged the deep cleavages between the interests constituting the republic.

The monarchy furnished another source of cohesion, not because of its will or power but because of the mystique that surrounded it. Kings fell short of insuring justice and harmony within their realms and contributed their share to disorder. As individuals they might be contemned and their writ disregarded. Powerful lords might rise against them. But the crown as an institution remained sacrosanct, standing above contending interests as the visible, omnipresent symbol of Catholic unity.

## Kinship and Clientage

The fundamental source of social cohesion, however, lay not in faith and symbols but in two institutions whose origins can be traced back to Roman Hispania and, perhaps, to even more ancient Mediterranean civilizations. One was the *parentela*, an extended kinship group or clan. Its nucleus was the Christian family of blood relatives. Concubinage, disapproved by the church but socially acceptable, swelled its strength with illegitimate offspring. *Compadrazgo* (ritual cogodparenthood) strengthened ties among blood relatives and often brought fictive kin into the fold. In more affluent households, the family included servants and even slaves. It had a territorial base in towns, villages, and manors. Over it ruled the senior male member, the paterfamilias, with authority (*patria potestas*) virtually unbounded.

The other institution was the *clientela*, a system of personal dependency in which powerful persons (patrons) gave protection and favor to the less powerful (clients), receiving in return services and subservience. *Parentela* and *clientela* linked together closely, for the heads of influential families commonly patronized a large clientele, and well-established clients came to be regarded as fictive members of the family. Clans and clientage systems, furthermore, interlocked with others of their kind through marriage, mutual interests, and larger-scale dependency relationships.

The Reconquest sustained and strengthened clan and clientage, for they offered members a measure of physical and psychological security in troubled times. They generated fierce loyalties and frequently cut across formal social divisions to encompass nobles, clergy, and commoners. In these groupings individuals found their most intimate identities and to them alone subordinated their egos. It might very well be said that the primary structure of Hispanic society consisted not of the orders defined in theory and law but of interlocking clans and clienteles loosely held together by a common faith and the mystique of the crown.

# CHAPTER 3

# Hispanic Expansion
# in the Old World

## The Beginnings of European Expansion:
## Crusades and Trade in the Eastern Mediterranean

The vigor of Europe during the High Middle Ages not only opened large internal frontiers but generated that dynamic symbiosis of religious zeal, thirst for territorial conquest, and economic enterprise that characterized the early centuries of European overseas expansion. Beginning with the first expedition to the Holy Land in 1096, Christian warriors established crusader kingdoms guarded by massive fortresses in Syria, Lebanon, Palestine, and Cyprus. Italian towns, Genoa, Pisa, and Venice, provided the transportation, supplies, and much of the capital the crusaders needed to get to their destinations and to maintain themselves there.

In addition to the immediate rewards for their services, the Italians won commercial concessions in the Middle East. By the end of the thirteenth century, they maintained factories in Egypt, throughout the Levant, and along the shores of the Black Sea, linking with Oriental commercial networks whose ramifications had been revealed to them by their countrymen John of Pian de Carpine and the Polo brothers. The trans-Mediterranean trade that they opened contributed heavily to the first European cycle of capital formation, investment, profit, and reinvestment for further profit, and it stimulated the transition from a "natural" to a money economy in the West. In the process, the Italians sharpened their commercial acumen and developed forms of business, banking, and credit organization that, for a consideration, they later put at the disposal of European princes who looked outward into the Atlantic.

### Early Hispanic Enterprises:
### Africa, Italy, and the Atlantic

The main directions of overseas expansion for the Hispanic peoples were limned out even before the Reconquest had halted on the frontiers of Granada. Africa offered the most immediate and powerful attraction. Christian kings and knights felt a strong urge to chase the Moors across the Strait of Gibraltar to their homeland, seize their lands and properties, destroy their power at its sources, and, at the same time, extend Christendom. Africa also held economic attractions. Catalan, Andalusian, and Portuguese merchants as well as Italians resident in Hispanic ports wanted commercial entrepôts along the coasts of Tunis, Algeria, and Morocco. Gold, which in the late Middle Ages fell into increasingly short supply in Europe, could also be obtained in those regions. The Christians did not know its original source but understood that it came northward across the Sahara by caravan to North African terminals. Aragon and Castile regarded these several interests as so important—and so competitive—that in 1291 they negotiated a treaty whereby Aragon obtained rights of conquest and exploitation in the regions of Tripoli and Tunis, Castile in those of Algeria and Morocco.

The two Hispanic kingdoms employed different forms of expansion in Africa. The Crown of Aragon acted primarily on behalf of its Catalan subjects who desired to place commercial factories in North African ports and, at the same time, discommode established Italian competitors and expel Muslim pirates who menaced western Mediterranean seaways. It therefore restricted its efforts to establishing protectorates and spheres of influence. Castile inclined more to military adventures and territorial dominion in the Reconquest tradition. Its rulers from Ferdinand the Saint to Charles the Emperor planned and occasionally mounted expeditions across the strait. In the face of determined Muslim resistance, invasions yielded only a handful of precariously held fortresses, and at enormous costs in lives and money. Yet North African conquests continued to lure and entrap Castilians until modern times.

Off the Atlantic coasts of Africa, the direction of ocean currents and summer winds encouraged voyages to the south and west, where, it was hoped, gold, slaves, and spices might be found. The history of these explorations is obscure. Despite the Aragonese-Castilian treaty of demarcation, Catalans appeared on the Atlantic coast of Morocco in the late thirteenth century and in the early fourteenth century and may have sailed as far south as Senegal. In 1271, or perhaps it was 1291, Genoese navigators apparently reached the

Canaries, which they found inhabited by a Neolithic people who came to be called Guanches. By 1350 or thereabouts, Genoese as well as Mallorcans and Andalusians had visited the archipelago to trade or slave. By that time also, European mariners had probably discovered the uninhabited Madeiras.

A second direction of Hispanic overseas expansion led eastward across the Mediterranean following the military, political, and economic interests of the Crown of Aragon. Through an interdynastic marriage with the House of Hohenstaufen, King Peter III (1276–85) acquired claims to Sicily and Naples. Aragon's dominion in the two kingdoms had to be established and defended against rival French pretensions and papal intervention, and its claims eventually passed to a collateral branch of the royal family. Nevertheless it managed to retain a strong position in Italy. Meanwhile, in the 1340s, Peter IV (1336–87) conquered the Balearic islands of Mallorca, Minorca, and Ibiza from the Moors and incorporated them into his crown. Catalan merchants vigorously supported Aragonese dynastic expansion, for it allowed them to extend their commercial network in the western Mediterranean under preferential conditions and at the expense of their Italian competitors.

Finally, in the ports of the Algarve and the Gulf of Cadiz, bold men looked westward into the uncharted reaches of the Ocean Sea (the Atlantic), where medieval legend placed enchanted lands. In the north lay islands full of marvels which, it was told, had been found by Saint Brendan in the sixth century while he was sailing west from Ireland in search of the "Promised Land of the Saints" and that bore his name. Farther south there was Antilla, sometimes called the Island of the Seven Bishops or the Seven Cities because, it was believed, seven Hispanic bishops and a band of followers fleeing the Saracens discovered it and on it founded seven dioceses and seven episcopal cities. Here the descendants of the first settlers lived in utopian bliss under the paternal rule of successive generations of prelates. The memory of Norse discoverers, moreover, remained alive in northern Europe, although reduced to semilegendary form. Farther south, Portuguese fishermen had ventured many leagues from land, and circumstantial evidence suggests that by the mid-1300s, Europeans had visited the Azores, a third of the way across the Ocean Sea.

## Fourteenth-Century Interruptions:
### The Four Horsemen of the Apocalypse

Around the mid-fourteenth century, European Atlantic expansion halted on most fronts. No compelling commercial, religious, or political reasons existed to probe into the further reaches of the Ocean Sea, whose waters held known and unknown perils. European states lacked national organizations and re-sources for mobilizing sustained oceanic enterprises. Also, around the late 1200s, a long-term reversal of the Malthusian cycle weakened expansionist forces. By that time the agricultural frontier had virtually closed.[1] When much of the land that could be used with existing technology had already been put under plow, food production leveled off, and population growth slowed. Nature accelerated the slackening. In the early fourteenth century, Europe's climate took a turn for the worse, bringing unseasonable cold, excessive rainfall, bad harvests, and widespread famine. Then, in 1347, the Black Death made the first of several appearances that together did enormous demographic damage.

Another Apocalyptic horseman rode with famine, pestilence, and death. The fourteenth century brought more frequent, bloodier, and longer wars than any suffered since the tenth. In the international sphere, England and France strove against each other for more than a hundred years (from 1337 to 1453), involving other powers from time to time and generally disrupting European economies. In each European kingdom, interests contended with each other for shares of diminishing resources, thereby generating the bitterest and most destructive class warfare to be seen before the Industrial Revolution.

Hispania shared in Europe's "Age of Adversity" in ways and measures shaped by its particular circumstances. In the thirteenth century, internal expansion halted along the frontiers of Granada for more than 200 years, thereby restricting lands available for colonization, and the conversion of much of Andalusia into cattle and sheep latifundia severely limited its food-producing capacity. In the first half of the fourteenth century, crops failed frequently, the plague did not spare the Hispanic peoples, and in 1355 a severe earthquake did enormous damage in Portugal.

The end of territorial expansion coupled with plague and famine generated severe tensions within Hispanic societies. Interest strove against interest to preserve or extend its status in an environment whose resources had become visibly finite. *Ricos hombres* rose against monarchies that no longer had newly conquered lands to distribute as patronage, and great noble houses warred among themselves. Towns called up militias to resist baronial invasions of their lands and liberties. Christians found in Jews a scapegoat for misfortune and, in Castile, expressed their rancor in pogroms climaxing in Andalusia in 1391. To save themselves, substantial numbers of Jews converted to Christianity, be-coming known as *conversos* or *marranos* (New Christians), and continued to perform their useful economic and administrative functions. As communicants of the Hispanic church they were able to marry into Old Christian families, including some of the noblest houses of the kingdom, where their wealth and acumen made them quite welcome. Most people, however, suspected that they had acted from prudence rather than revelation, and the *conversos* remained a suspect class.

Civil strife was linked to international wars arising from a new phase in the relations among the Hispanic kingdoms. With the reduction of Islam to the kingdom of Granada, the ancient conception of one *Monarchia Hispania* appeared as an imminent prospect. The basic issue in peninsular politics became under what dynasty this grand aim was to be achieved. The kings of Castile, Aragon, and Portugal, therefore, tried to arrange advantageous interdynastic marriages, intrigued in each others' affairs, and, although they had quite enough to do at home and could ill afford it, made war on each other. France and England intervened on one side or the other to gain advantage in their own hundred years' conflict.

## A Century of Disorder in Castile (1369–1479)

Internal dissensions abetted by foreign meddling provoked severe succession crises in both Castile and Portugal. In Castile a bastard pretender, Henry of the Aragonese House of Trastámara, defeated and slew his legitimate half brother, Peter the Cruel, to gain the throne as Henry II (1369–79). During the struggle, Peter had the support of urban and commercial interests and the aid of England and Portugal. Most of the great nobles rallied around Henry, and Aragon and France intervened on his behalf. Thus, Henry's triumph was the triumph of traditional señorial, agrarian Castile over entrepreneurial elements that, although weak, still had potential for growth in a favorable environment.

The resolution of the succession, however, did not relieve social and political tensions; it only exacerbated them. Henry found himself deeply obligated to the nobles who fought for him and repaid them so munificently with honors, revenues, offices, and *señorios* that contemporaries dubbed him the "King of Concessions." Since these largesse had to be subtracted from a limited royal patrimony, its bestowal unbalanced power relationships between the crown and the *rico hombres* in favor of the latter. After this time also, *títulos de Castilla* (titles of nobility) such as duke, count, and marquis, came into more general use and their most prestigious and powerful holders began to be called grandees, a class so opulent, so magnificent, and so arrogant that its members acknowledged no superior, only peers, and obtained dispensation from removing their hats in the presence of the king. The great noble families became so prideful and greedy that they fell to quarreling among themselves, attacked towns, abused peasants, and usurped royal properties that could not be obtained by concession. In a desperate attempt to survive, the crown lent its support first to one faction, then to another, and cruel wars ravaged city and countryside for a century.

Unstable political conditions disturbed all sectors of the Castilian economy. In the fiscal sphere the beleaguered crown resorted more and more to deficit financing through short-term loans from the church and Jewish bankers and through the public sale of long-term, interest-bearing bonds called *juros*. Persons possessing surplus capital found these instruments to be an attractive alternative to risk-bearing investments in trade and industry.

## The Brief Portuguese Crisis and the Accession of the House of Avis (1383–85)

In Portugal, John, the illegitimate brother of the deceased king Ferdinand I (1367–83) and master of the military order of Avis (a nationalized branch of the Castilian order of Calatrava), contended against King John I of Castile, who had a claim to the throne. John of Avis defeated an invading Castilian army at Aljubarrota in 1385 and, crowned John I (1385–1433), established the Portuguese dynasty of Avis. Despite superficial similarities, the circumstances and the outcome of the two succession struggles were quite different. Portugal was a smaller, more homogeneous, and essentially a more governable kingdom than Castile and hence was better able to withstand political crises. Also, Portuguese nobles, who had many ties of blood and interest with Castilian magnates, supported the foreign pretender while the common estate stood by John of Avis. Thus, the nobility lost credit, the new king won enormous popularity as the champion of a national cause, and, in contrast to its fate across the border, the monarchy emerged in a strong position.

John moved quickly to consolidate his advantage. In 1386, Portugal signed a treaty with England providing for mutual trade concessions and military assistance, and, through a collateral agreement, John of Avis married Philippa of Lancaster, who bore him five sons in this order: Duarte, Peter, Henry, John, and Fernando. At home he associated Henry with himself on the throne to avert another succession crisis and placed him in charge of the indigenous Portuguese military order, the Order of Christ. John and Fernando took over, respectively, the Orders of Santiago and Avis. These maneuvers captured from the nobility one of their major sources of wealth and power. Conversely, John favored his middle-class supporters by appointing them to important posts in the royal government and by confirming the charter of the merchants of

Lisbon, which gave them protection from the competition of foreign mercantile interests.

A longer-range view of the Revolution of 1385 reveals it to have been a turning point in Portuguese history. It not only laid the political foundations of a strong, national state but also reconfirmed independence from Castile, bolstered Portuguese self-confidence, and created a more vigorous sense of national identity. It was at this juncture that the divergence between Castile and Portugal began to widen. The English connection also had far-reaching consequences. Although nobody could have predicted it at the time, it turned out to be the longest alliance in history and the economic and dynastic ties it incubated helped draw Portugal away from complete preoccupation with peninsular affairs.[2]

## The Resumption of European Expansion

### Portuguese Conquests, Explorations, and Commerce in Africa and the Atlantic

The resolution of internal crises, the establishment of a strong monarchy, and the increased influence of mercantile interests quickly led to the resumption of overseas expansion, giving Portugal the lead among the nations of Europe. In 1415, John and Duarte undertook the conquest of Morocco, beginning with the capture of Ceuta. They billed the enterprise as a crusade, and that it was, but it also opened a new frontier which, they hoped, would replenish the royal treasury, give merchants opulent profits, and provide the nobility with booty and, in these ways, create a safety valve for remaining social tensions. African Moors, however, proved to be very obstinate. The Portuguese were unable to seize Tangier, a second major Moroccan stronghold, until 1471, and during the next several decades they could do little more than push a chain of isolated fortresses down the Atlantic coast from Tangier to Agadir and launch *cabalgadas* against vulnerable Muslim towns and villages.

Meanwhile, Prince Henry along with other princes of the blood, nobles, merchants, and muncipal *concelhos* sent maritime expeditions down the coast of Africa for various reasons. Some of those dispatched by Henry were simply exploratory. Most Portuguese expeditions were commercial ventures or combined trade and exploration. The House of Avis, however, regarded all of them as adjuncts to the Portuguese Crusade, which acquired increasingly grandiose proportions and chimerical objectives. John and his sons hoped that by sailing south they could outflank Islam and establish contact with the legendary Christian kingdom of Prester John, indeterminately located in East Africa or perhaps somewhere in Asia. Along with exploring, trading, and crusading, officially sponsored expeditions took possession of the lands they discovered in the king's name, symbolizing the act by erecting stone pillars (*padrões*).

Toward the mid-fifteenth century, two circumstances added impetus to Portuguese expansion in Africa and adjacent waters. First, the caravel, a round-bottomed, lateen-rigged vessel, came into general use. Although small — generally running from thirty to forty tons — it was much more maneuverable and seaworthy than the Mediterranean galley, and, since it required smaller crews, it could carry more provender. Thus, it could sail farther from land and stay at sea longer. Second, more venture capital became available, mainly from Italian merchants who had established themselves in Lisbon and the Algarve in the thirteenth and fourteenth centuries. In the early fifteenth they participated as partners in many Portuguese voyages. The Turkish advance in the east strengthened the Italian presence in Hispania. Although the Turks left the Venetian factories in Egypt relatively unmolested, other cities had to abandon their stations in the Levant. To compensate, Florentines, Pisans, and above all Genoese displaced their main commercial interests westward, reinforcing their establishments in Portugal and Andalusia and supporting Portugal's growing Atlantic orientation.

By 1470 or thereabouts, crusading zeal, geographical curiosity, and commercial enterprise had led the Portuguese and their Italian backers around the bulge of the African continent and eastward into the Gulf of Guinea. In the course of these explorations, they also discovered or rediscovered the Madeira and Cape Verde archipelagos and the smaller islands of São Tomé, Principe, and Fernando Po lying off the Guinea coast. What they found and trafficked in is revealed in the geographical appellations later applied to the lands along the Mauritanian and Guinea shores: the Slave Coast, the Gold Coast, the Ivory Coast, etc. In 1441, an expedition returned with the first recorded cargo of blacks. During the next seven years at least 1000 blacks entered Portugal, and by the 1450s imports reached 700 to 800 annually. The Portuguese, reports affirm, brought back the first Guinea gold in 1442 and during the next two decades became the main gold supplier of Europe. Their success in this sphere had great significance for the Western economies because it occurred at a time when the problem of exchange, particularly with the Orient, had become acute. The Italian bankers who managed exchange sought to stabilize it on the basis of a gold standard. From Guinea the Portuguese also obtained malagueta (red) pepper, cotton, ivory, civet, and diverse exotic products such as parrots. In adjacent waters they took fish for salting and whales, whose oil had a high value in Europe.

The organization of Portuguese trade with tropical Africa developed in haphazard fashion. For several decades after the capture of Ceuta it remained open to anyone with venture capital, provided he paid the *quinto* (the royal fifth) to the crown, apparently an overseas adaptation of the Reconquest levy of one-fifth of booty taken. In the case of slaves, raiding parties at first seized them directly, but later entrepreneurs in the traffic found it easier to get them by barter from Arab traders and local African potentates. The Portuguese never acquired or even precisely located the principal gold mines now known to have lain in the western Sudan. They obtained the precious metal as well as other Guinea commodities in the same way as slaves, by barter, giving in return wheat, cloth, and cheap manufactured goods.

As the volume and value of commerce grew, the crown undertook to control and regulate it more directly. In 1443, Prince Henry obtained a monopoly along with the right to collect the royal fifth. Although private voyages continued and probably exceeded in numbers those sent out by Henry himself, they all had to obtain his license. Beginning also in this decade the Portuguese began to set up factories along the African coast on the model, perhaps, of those established by the Italians and Catalans in the Mediterranean. They put the first of these installations on the island of Arguim, just off the coast of Senegambia, in 1445. At the Portuguese end of the trade, Henry established a receiving and collecting agency in Lagos that became known as the *Casa de Guiné*. After Henry died, the crown moved it to Lisbon and renamed it the *Casa de Guiné e Mina*.

## Portuguese Overseas Colonization

Portuguese expansion during the first half of the fifteenth century also led to the first major European colonization in the Atlantic theater. Along the Guinea coasts, resident and itinerant traders and slavers mixed indiscriminately with blacks, producing a constantly swelling mulatto population that became Portuguese in culture and language and, at least nominally, Christian. These new people clustered around factories and helped to create European-type communities which the crown ultimately chartered as *vilas* (towns), granting them *forais* and municipal councils. Portuguese men, including criminals and renegades transported to Africa, as well as acculturated mulattoes, also made their way into the interior. There some were killed and possibly eaten, but the more fortunate and more cunning settled in native villages, took black wives, served as intermediaries in trade, and became advance agents of miscegenation and acculturation.

The Portuguese colonized the African mainland in an unplanned and desultory fashion and with the thinnest results. They made their main effort on the offshore and Atlantic islands. During the 1420s and 1430s they populated Madeira and Porto Santo, the two main islands of the uninhabited Madeira archipelago, and during the remainder of the century settlement spread to the other seven. The colonization of the Azores, also uninhabited, began in the 1440s, and by the end of the 1460s the main islands had European settlers. The Portuguese also attempted to occupy the Canaries but there ran into two problems. First, the islands had a warlike and hostile indigenous population that had to be conquered before settlement could be undertaken. Second, Castile claimed them by virtue of prior discovery, obtained papal confirmation of title in 1436, and undertook their conquest. Portuguese kings did not accept the Supreme Pontiff's award, but they abandoned efforts to seize the group. Farther south, their subjects began to colonize the Cape Verdes in the 1460s, but in contrast to the Madeiras and the Azores these islands had poor soils, inadequate rainfall, and, in general, no intrinsic attractions, so that the undertaking proceeded haltingly and did not produce an effective population until the early sixteenth century.

Although the population of the Atlantic archipelagos occurred at different times and under different circumstances, the several undertakings employed common procedures and organizational forms deriving from Reconquest experience. The Portuguese crown, acting directly or through Henry or other princes, granted the islands to be settled to captains-donatary through *cartas de doação* (charters of donation). In return for agreeing to colonize their grants, the donataries received *senhorial* rights within them in heredity. They could exercise military and political command and give justice in the king's name; appoint subordinate officials; enjoy a monopoly of mills, common ovens, and the sale of salt; grant land to their followers; and retain a portion of royal taxes and church tithes for their own use. Settlement began with the foundation of villages that, like the African factories, eventually became chartered *vilas*. In spiritual matters, the pope granted the patronage in all lands newly discovered or to be discovered to the Portuguese crown in 1456. The king exercised his rights through the Order of Christ, of which Prince Henry was the grand master.

At first, thinly dispersed settlers on the Portuguese Atlantic islands depended on fishing, subsistence agriculture, and the exportation of woods and dyestuffs for a livelihood. Economic and social development in the main groups, however, soon diverged. Although subtropical Madeira produced important amounts of grain for export to Ceuta and African factories, its soils and climate were also suitable for sugar growing, and a strong market for the sweet existed in Europe. Prince Henry encouraged planting and, in 1452, contracted for the construction of an *engenho* (sugar mill) on Madeira. Four years later the installation exported its first sugar. Aided by black slaves brought over from African stations and infusions of Italian and Portuguese Jewish capital, planting soon became the predominant economic activity. By 1456 production amounted to 6000 *arrôbas* annually (approximately 192,000 pounds avoirdupois).

The introduction of sugar produced important demographic and social changes. By the 1460s, the population of the settled islands stood at more than 2000 souls including Portuguese immigrants, numbers of Flemish settlers, resident Italian merchants and planters, and slaves. Some mill owners became wealthy enough to leave the management of their estates to overseers or tenants and to reside in Funchal or Machico, where they carved escutcheons over their doors, acquired noble status, and founded lineages. The Madeiran sugar estates — producing a tropical product for export, worked by black slaves from Africa, financed by outside capital, and often marked by absentee ownership — were the prototypes of the overseas plantation, that complex social and institutional arrangement so fundamental in the expansion of Europe.

In the more northerly and cooler Azores, where sugar did not grow well, an economy developed based on small and medium-sized family farms that did not require large numbers of slaves. The islands' principal exports during the fifteenth century were, in order of importance, wheat and woad, a plant of the mustard family whose leaves produced a blue dye.

## Juridical Problems of Expansion: Just Title and Just War

As the Portuguese moved into the Atlantic and down the coast of Africa, they encountered practical difficulties that they disposed of in practical ways. But their advance also added new dimensions to ancient moral and juridical problems less easily resolved. The questions were these: Under what circumstances was it justifiable to wage war against non-Christian peoples? How could a just title be established to lands taken from them? What was to be their status under Christian dominion? Until the fifteenth century the issue had been confined mainly to relations with Islam. Learned and common men generally agreed that in the interest of defending and extending Christendom a war against Muslims was by its very nature a just war; conquest of their territories conveyed a just title to them, and the conquered could be disposed of as the conquerors wished. In Hispania, Christians regarded provinces held by the Moors as *terra irredenta*, lands that Christian princes had once ruled and that were being restored to their legitimate lords.

Portuguese expansion down the coast of Africa required another kind of justification, because it involved the establishment of dominion over unoccupied islands or lands whose inhabitants were not Muslims but pagans who had never known Christ. The Portuguese crown took the position that it acquired lordship in these territories by the simple act of discovery and occupation, because they were *terra nullius*; that is, they were not under any true lordship, they were empty, or their people were savages who lived without polity.

Fifteenth-century Portuguese claims were reinforced by the writings of earlier theologians on the nature of sovereignty and just wars. Cardinal Henry of Susa (d. 1271), better known as Hostiensis, made perhaps the classic analysis of the problem. When Christ came into the world, Hostiensis declared, temporal as well as spiritual lordship over all its peoples passed immediately to Him. This faculty He transmitted to His legitimate successors, the bishops of Rome, who came to be called popes. Roman pontiffs, in turn, could delegate lordship over non-Christian lands to a Christian prince, thus conveying a just title to such lands, and, if their inhabitants resisted, a just war could be waged against the recalcitrants. This doctrine guided two papal bulls, issued respectively in 1452 and 1454, that donated to the Portuguese crown sovereignty over the regions its subjects had discovered or might discover as they moved south. In return, the crown was to assume responsibility for the conversion of the peoples encountered. If they forcibly resisted Christian dominion or evangelization or commerical intercourse, they could be conquered, their properties seized, and they themselves reduced to servitude. In addition, the pope declared that no other Christian nation could intrude into the lands and waters donated, thereby giving Portugal a monopoly of expansion into the Atlantic south of Morocco.

## The Problem of "Race"

Early Portuguese explorations raised to prominence another problem that came to pervade and degrade European expansion. What were to be the relationships among the races of people thus brought into close association? The use of the word "race" in this temporal context may appear anachronistic, for, although it existed in western languages in the fifteenth century (*razza* in

Italian, *rasa* in Castilian, *raça* in Portuguese, *race* in French), it simply meant a population of plants, animals, or human beings who through inheritance possessed common characteristics. It did not come into common use or acquire a strictly biological meaning with invidious pseudoscientific connotations until the latter half of the nineteenth century.[3] Even today a respectable number of physical anthropologists believe that after millennia of folk wanderings and miscegenation among peoples the concept of race cannot be applied meaningfully to human groups.

Many social scientists, however, use a cultural rather than a biological definition of race. It is a belief held by culturally identifiable populations that they are different from other populations by virtue of their innate and immutable physical characteristics, that these characteristics are intrinsically related to cultural attributes, and that such differences are a legitimate justification for invidious distinctions among peoples.[4] The word "race" will be used here with this meaning.

Although mainstream Christian dogma held that all of humankind was one and of equal value in the eyes of God because of its common Adamic lineage, Renaissance Europeans were quite aware that humans fell into different categories because of their "natural" physical and cultural qualities. For categorization they used proper nouns such as Moors, Jews, French, Castilians, and the like, or terms such as "nations" or "peoples" inhabiting this or that region and possessing such and such characteristics.

The several European nations, moreover, expressed distaste for deviations from their own norms, and their antipathies deepened in proportion to the magnitude of the deviation. Castilian, English, and French peoples depreciated each other, but all made more invidious distinctions between civilized peoples — themselves — who lived in republics under the dominion of legitimate princes and savages or barbarians who subsisted without law and polity. Religion furnished another strong basis for prejudicial distinctions. European Christians contemned pagans — peoples who had never known Christ — and held even stronger dislikes for Jews and Moors — peoples who had rejected Him. Castilians sometimes referred to Jews as a *mala raza*, a bad or defective race.

Europeans were also color conscious if for no other reason than that skin pigmentation was the most immediately noticeable and most unerasable mark of differences among races. And, as was the case with deviations from their cultural norms and religious beliefs, they regarded darker-skinned races as inferior. Among peoples of color they expressed the strongest distaste for blacks. Perhaps this attitude owed to the fact that an ebony hue was the most extreme deviation from their own phenotypical norm. Perhaps, as some authors maintain, it reflected a "primordial" abhorrence for blackness or, at least, color symbolisms deeply embedded in Western Christian culture, which associated white with purity, virtue, beauty, and the Dove of the Holy Spirit and black with corruption, malignance, sin, and death.[5] Thus, Europeans held stronger prejudices against "Blackamoors," African Moors of sub-Saharan origin, than against lighter-skinned Muslims from the Middle East.

Still another condition affected European perceptions of human superiority and inferiority. Some persons were free; others were slaves and serfs, and their servitude made them infamous in law and fact. Furthermore, following Aristotelian precepts, servitude was a natural state because of the "natural" lack of rationality of persons upon whom it was imposed.

The extent to which the race consciousness of Europeans became overtly hostile depended not only on their perceptions of deviations from their own cultural and physical norms but on the strength of their desire to justify the subjugation of other races and of their fears that other races threatened Christian society. Their desires and apprehensions in turn were closely related to the kinds and magnitude of their interracial associations. Except for the peoples facing on the Mediterranean, most fifteenth-century Westerners knew barbarians, pagans, and colored persons only through hearsay and slaves only as individuals isolated in the general society. These types, therefore, did not concern Europeans greatly.

Moors and Jews were quite a different matter. They were civilized, and their physical characteristics did not differ sharply from those of Mediterranean Christians. However, perceptible numbers of Jews dwelt in European cities, and their financial acumen and enterprise were seen as endangering Christian economic interests while their faith threatened to corrupt the Christian religion. The massive presence of Muslims on the land and sea frontiers of Europe menaced the physical security of Christendom.

The Portuguese advance along the west coast of sub-Saharan Africa changed these conditions radically. For the first time it brought Europeans into regular, close, and large-scale contact with peoples who were neither Jews nor Moors, nor, by European standards, civilized. They were perceived as pagans and savages, they appeared to be eminently suitable for enslavement, and they were black.

The Portuguese as well as Spaniards who intruded on their monopoly did, in fact, enslave as many Africans as they could and sold them in Portugal,

Spain, and the Hispanic Atlantic islands for what they would bring. Some of the individual victims of this traffic may have found kind masters but in mass lots they suffered harsh and degrading treatment. Portuguese writers of the times expressed a strong distaste for their phenotypical characteristics. Around 1450, Gomes Eanes de Zurara (or Azurara), a Portuguese court chronicler, described a load of Guinea slaves arriving in Lisbon in the following terms: "For amongst them were some of a reasonable degree of whiteness, handsome and well made; others black as Ethiopians, and so ill-formed, as well in their faces as their bodies, that it seemed to the beholders as if they saw the forms of a lower hemisphere."[6] A half century later, in 1505, Duarte Pacheco, a well-traveled Portuguese gentleman, expressed prejudices toward West Africans in both behavioral and physical terms. They were "dog-faced, dog-toothed people, satyrs, wild men, and cannibals."[7]

Thus, on the eve of the discovery of America, savagery, paganism, servitude, and blackness became identified in the European mind as marks of racial inferiority.

## Lagging Castilian Overseas Enterprises

Continued internal disorders and a weakened monarchy limited Castilian expansion to occasional and not always productive undertakings. In 1393, Henry III (1390–1406) sent a strong expedition to the Canaries that returned with slaves, and nine years later he issued a patent to Jean de Béthancourt, a French knight-adventurer, granting him *señorial* rights to conquer, settle, and govern the archipelago. Béthancourt managed to occupy some of the smaller islands, thus furthering Castile's claim to the group. Despite the delicate constitution that gained him the sobriquet of "the Sufferer," Henry led into Morocco a large raid that harried the coast and captured and sacked Tetuán, a notorious pirate stronghold. The beginning of Portuguese expansion along the coasts of Africa stirred more positive action in Castile. In 1417 the Castilian crown sent a large expedition to the Madeiras, an intrusion that prompted the Portuguese to move ahead with their settlement of these islands, and between 1420 and 1450 it granted the main Canary islands—Grand Canary, Tenerife, Palmas, and Gómera—as *señoríos* to several nobles. These lords, however, failed to confirm their rights by conquest. Meanwhile, obscure and unsung Andalusian *cabalgadas* traded and slaved along the African coasts in defiance of the king of Portugal's monopoly.

## The Recovery of Spain:
## The Reign of Ferdinand and Isabella

In the 1460s and 1470s, events occurred in Hispania heavy in portent, not only
for the peninsular kingdoms themselves but for all of Europe and for as yet
undiscovered lands beyond the Ocean Sea. These events began in 1469 with the
marriage of Isabella, sister of Henry IV of Castile (1454–74), to Ferdinand, the
heir to the Aragonese crown. They continued with a dispute over who would
succeed Henry, whose alleged incapacity to sire an heir led malicious tongues
to dub him "the Impotent." The ensuing crisis, although perhaps somewhat
more sordid and sanguinary than usual, did not appear to be extraordinary.
Isabella, however, emerged as the successful candidate and was crowned queen
of Castile in 1474. The sequence of events climaxed five years later when
Ferdinand succeeded to the throne of Aragon. Thus, the crowns of the two
kingdoms became united in the persons of the royal couple, and one of the
most dynamic reigns in Hispanic history began.

The policies of the two sovereigns and the measures they took are well
known and need only be summarized here. They gave Castilian affairs their
first attention, not only because Isabella's kingdom had the more pressing
problems but because Ferdinand understood that Castile's central position in
Spain and its population and wealth made it the key to the control of the
peninsula and to the success of Aragonese Mediterranean designs. In Castile
they reduced the nobility and towns to political subordination to the crown.
They introduced the Inquisition in 1478 to root out the heterodox, particularly the *conversos*. Between 1481 and 1492, they conquered Granada. In
1492 they began the expulsion of some 150,000 Jews and more than twice
that many *moriscos* (capitulated Muslims) who refused conversion.[8] Through
negotiations with Rome they obtained in 1482 the right to "supplicate" the
pope in favor of their candidates for vacant Castilian sees and in 1486 the full
patronage for all the churches in Granada, once it was conquered.

To accomplish and consolidate their initiatives, Ferdinand and Isabella re-
juvenated and expanded old institutions of government. At the highest level,
they delegated particular functions of the Royal Council (now called the
Council of Castile), such as justice, war, and foreign affairs, to standing committees. These bodies themselves came to be called councils, although the
crown did not give them formal status until later reigns. The effectiveness of
the conciliar system, however, depended ultimately on personal factors: the
forcefulness of council presidents, their access to the crown, and above all

the cordiality of relations between the royal secretary and council secretaries, who together controlled court communications. The king's confessor also interposed in decision making. Ferdinand and Isabella and their successors placed great store on the royal conscience and he who controlled that sensitive mechanism was a powerful person indeed.

The presence of Ferdinand and his compatriots at court informally linked the governments of Castile and Aragon and influenced Castilian administrative organization. In 1494 he created the Council of Aragon to advise him on the affairs of his kingdom while he was in absentia. Two of its members also served on the Council of Castile. He continued the practice of governing the Aragonese Italian dominions through viceroys but appointed Castilians to that lofty office, much to the indignation of his Aragonese subjects.

To provide for the better administration of high justice, Isabella supplemented the ambulatory royal court of medieval times with permanent territorial tribunals called audiencias or *cancillerías* that took original jurisdiction in important civil and criminal cases and heard appeals from subordinate royal magistrates as well as from *señorial* courts. Appeals from audiencias went to the Council of Castile.

The queen strengthened lower levels of royal government by reviving and reinvigorating the office of *corregidor*, first used by Alfonso XI in the early fourteenth century, to intervene in the management of municipal finances and the dispensation of local justice. Isbella sent out *corregidores* to major Castilian towns, and with her forceful support they took on the functions of provincial governors who not only interposed the royal writ in their capitals but administered subordinate towns and rural areas.

To ensure that her appointed officials performed their duties loyally and honestly, the queen fixed their tenure of office, giving them to know that their posts were not proprietary; she forbade them to marry or acquire property in their jurisdictions lest they develop local interests and loyalties; and she revived two Reconquest investigative institutions. One was the *residencia*, a quasi-judicial inquiry into the conduct of governors and magistrates at the end of their term. The other was the *pesquisa*, a special inspection that might be initiated at any time.

Ferdinand and Isabella took their most innovative measures in the military department, although they probably did not intend them as such. During the long war against Granada, they had to maintain large forces in the field during campaigning seasons, and some units stood constantly under arms. Before postvictory demobilization was complete, Ferdinand's Aragonese interests drew

Castile into war with France in Italy. Some seasoned units, mainly infantry, remained in active service or were reactivated to fight abroad. They soon evolved into regimental formations called *tercios* that dominated the battlefields of Europe for more than a century and formed the core of a standing army, that most fearsome and costly instrument of the modern state.[9]

In staffing their governmental apparatus, Ferdinand and Isabella continued to draw on the upper nobility to fill high offices such as council presidencies, viceregencies, admiralties, and captaincies general. For intermediate posts in civil administration, however, they called on lawyers and jurists (*letrados*) trained in civil and canon law in Castilian universities. Except for Jews and *conversos*, *letrados* were the only class possessing the ability and temperament to handle paperwork and keep complex accounts. Also, in contrast to the nobility, they owed their positions to royal favor rather than lineage. The two monarchs filled the officer and noncommissioned corps of the army with hidalgos and *caballeros*, thus providing honorable employment to the knightly class, which had fallen on hard times.

The political and religious measures of Ferdinand and Isabella had far-reaching results. The two monarchs virtually created Spain as a geopolitical concept. In Castile itself they took the penultimate step toward creating in practice what had heretofore existed only in theory and in the aspirations of Isabella's predecessors: an absolute and patrimonial monarchy in which all *señorío*, territory, offices, and benefices pertained privately and personally to the crown to be held, leased, or donated at the sovereigns' will. The war against the Moors of Granada, the harrying of the *conversos*, and the expulsion of Moors and Jews regenerated among Castilian Catholics a crusading zeal, a prideful sense of accomplishment, and an exalted sense of universal mission. As the mover of these momentous events, the monarchy gained a prestige and, indeed, a sacrosanctity that it had not enjoyed since the days of Saint Ferdinand. The best measure of the achievements of Ferdinand and Isabella is that they were able to pass on their patrimonies and the mystique enveloping the crown to an alien dynasty despite deep-rooted Spanish xenophobia.

The two sovereigns also undertook to regulate the Castilian economy more closely than earlier kings. This was Ferdinand's department, and he appears to have been guided by Aragonese precedents and principles. Abandoning Castilian prejudices against corporate restraints on trade, the crown authorized municipal governments to charter craft guilds enjoying substantial control over wages, prices, and production. In 1474, it chartered directly the *Consulado* (Merchants' Guild) of Burgos, an institution modeled on the Catalan Consulate of the Sea. The monarchs also modified traditional Castilian antiprotectionist policies and introduced some proto-mercantilist measures. These included prohibitions against the export of gold and the import of commodities that might compete with national industry and agriculture, the encouragement of export of items that Castile could produce at competitive prices, and restrictions on the use of foreign bottoms in shipping. In one important respect, however, Ferdinand and Isabella remained true to tradition. Despite a limited measure of protection given to the clothing industry, they still viewed the production of raw wool as the mainstay of the Castilian economy as well as an indispensable source of royal revenue, and they consistently favored the interests of grazers over those of manufacturers and agriculture.

Among the various economic measures of the crown, two stand out as most salutary. First, coming from a Mediterranean background, Ferdinand appreciated business acumen and organization as well as the need for new capital, since existing accumulations were committed to the wool industry and other traditional forms of investment. He therefore encouraged the active participation of Italians, especially Genoese, in Castilian finance and commerce.[10] Second, in 1497 he ordered the replacement of a chaotic mélange of circulating media, often deficient in weight and fineness, with three basic monies. One was the gold *excelente de Granada*, which in weight (3.503 grams) and fineness (23¾ karats) exactly equaled the Valencian *excelente*, the Catalan *principat*, and the Venetian ducat, which provided the basic model. Another was a new silver *real* (weighing 3.196 grams, 0.9306 fine), and the third was the *blanca*, intended to provide small change and struck from *vellon* (copper with a small admixture of silver). The three Castilian coins were all tariffed in terms of a money of account called the *maravedí*. Thus, an *excelente*, commonly called a ducat, equaled 375 *maravedís*; a *real*, 35; and a *blanca*, ½. The reformed monetary system lasted with only minor changes for a century.

The reign of Ferdinand and Isabella also moved Castile into the mainstream of European affairs. The conquest of Granada brought great joy to Western Christendom, at the time very much on the defensive against Islam, and enhanced the stature of the people and the monarchs who won the victory. In 1492, Pope Alexander gave the royal couple the title of the "Catholic Kings" in recognition of their preeminent services against the infidels. It has been alleged, however, that what His Holiness really had in mind was to win their assistance against the Italian depredations of Charles VIII of France, who had earlier obtained from Rome the competitive title of "Most Christian King." Soon thereafter, the victories of their infantry in Italy gave an additional boost

to their prestige. The achievements of the Catholic Kings undoubtedly facilitated their union with the House of Habsburg, accomplished by the marriage
of their daughter, Juana, to the Archduke Philip and of their son, Juan to
Margaret of Austria.

The dynamic quality of the reign of the Catholic Kings invites a fundamental question. How could they accomplish what they did? Their objectives were
not new. Other Hispanic kings had sought the same but had fallen short. Nor
were their measures entirely innovative; Henry IV (1454–74) had anticipated
a number of the reforms introduced by them. Neither were their aims uniquely
Spanish. Part of the answer lies in the special circumstances of their reign.
They both enjoyed youth and abundant energy. As it turned out, they were
a remarkably compatible couple, connubially and politically, and, while re-
specting the sovereignties and sensibilities of their respective realms, employed
the resources of both to order each. They were also strong-minded monarchs
with an exalted conception of the rights and duties of kingship as well as astute
politicians who understood the aspirations and frustrations of their subjects.
They reacted to popular demands as much as they led, especially in their religious policies, which struck a deep responsive chord in a devout people and,
more than anything else, bolstered the prestige of the monarchy. They avoided
gratuitous innovations that would have offended a conservative people, using
instead traditional devices and institutions adapted to their requirements.
They could be ruthless in situations they deemed critical, but they preferred
accommodation and tried to avoid outright confrontations with powerful
interests.

But, while helpful, these explanations are not sufficient. Ferdinand and
Isabella came along at the right time. The reorganization of medieval institutions to accommodate new circumstances was in the air, and "New Monarchs"
appeared elsewhere in Europe to exploit the opportunity. The royal couple
also had the wind at their backs, so to speak. Around the mid-fifteenth century,
the fortunes of Europe took a long-term turn for the better. Plague and general warfare subsided, agricultural production increased, population began to
grow, and commerce quickened.[11]

The realms of Castile and Aragon participated in the upswing. Rough estimates place their population around 1450 at about 6,000,000; in 1482,
at well over 8,500,000, of which Castile claimed 7,500,000 and the Crown
of Aragon, 1,000,000. In the last years of the reign of Ferdinand and Isabella
a precapitalist boom began in the united kingdoms. It was generated mainly
by a revival of the textile industry but also accompanied by a brisk trade with

northern Europe in Castilian wool, Basque iron manufacturers, and Andalusian citrus and wine. Expanding commerce encouraged the shipbuilding industry along the Biscayan coast and in Seville and its outports. It also fed exchange at the great fairs of Medina del Campo and Medina del Rio Seco. In the dominions of the Crown of Aragon, a revival of Catalonian Mediterranean trade paralleled and complemented Castilian economic gains. Prosperity and more efficient treasury management swelled royal revenues from some 800,000 *maravedís* in 1478 to 22,000,000 in 1504.

The reigns of the Catholic Kings were unquestionably productive, but their dispositions and those of their subjects led to acts of omission and commission that, in retrospect, had unfortunate consequences for their realms. They did not unify Hispania in a constitutional sense. Despite their diplomatic and military initiatives, Portugal remained beyond their grasp. Castile and the several states of the Crown of Aragon retained their individual sovereignties. Each kingdom jealously guarded its *fueros* and its liberties. In Aragon Isabella was only a queen; in Castile Ferdinand was only a consort with no authority in his own right. The people of the several kingdoms regarded each other as foreigners. The realms of Spain were united only by a common religion, a common gold coinage, and two monarchs who regarded them as separate components of family patrimonies. The royal couple really did not try to alter this arrangement. They could not conceive of a truly national state.

The prosperity that accompanied their reign had a very uneven distribution, and the Castilian economy remained unbalanced. Its vigor depended heavily on the exchange of raw wool for foreign manufacturers, mainly luxury items, and the boom in textiles rested on the production of low-grade cloth at noncompetitive prices in a precariously protected domestic market. Ferdinand, moreover, introduced monopolistic guilds at a time when northern Europe was moving toward a more efficient organization of production and exchange, and the crown's attacks on *conversos* and Jews dealt a damaging blow to entrepreneurial classes. Agriculture lagged badly owing to antiquated techniques and land systems, discriminatory royal policies, and the persecution of the *moriscos*, who, in the south, formed the bulk of farm labor. In the critical area of grain resources, production just managed to hold its own in good years, but in bad ones, such as came along between 1502 and 1508, supply could not meet demand. Despite attempted fixing, commodity prices rose sharply. In the fiscal sphere, the bonanza enjoyed by the royal treasury did not suffice to support a burgeoning bureaucracy or a court whose elegance reflected the new brilliancy of the monarchy. Even less did it suffice to maintain armies in the field in Granada and Italy. When the queen died in 1504, the crown debt stood at 127,000,000 *maravedís*.

Ferdinand and Isabella made no effort to alter the established order of society, whose hierarchical structure, they believed, faithfully reflected God's plan. Their policies, however, led to some social changes of questionable value. Isabella reconfirmed the rights of serfs to leave the lands of their lords, thereby making all Castilian subjects free men. But, since the beneficiaries had no alternative means of subsistence, freedom simply gave them the right to starve, turned some into vagabonds, and drew many to the slums of overcrowded cities. The Castilian boom gave the indigenous entrepreneurial class a new lease on life, but the persecution of the *conversos* sapped its strength, and favoritism toward wool producers hindered its balanced growth. The expansion of the royal bureaucracy increased another sector of the common estate, the university-trained *letrado*, but it is doubtful that this was a healthy development. The prospects of sinecures in public service encouraged a surplus of graduates whose importunities and family connections led to the creation of new and unnecessary jobs.

The crown's religious policies suppressed, if they did not solve, the *converso* problem, but they created a *morisco* problem. Most of the Moors who accepted baptism rather than suffer exile remained openly Moorish in culture and secretly Moorish in faith and maintained politically subversive ties with North African Islam. The religious policies of the crown also nurtured an older measure of social value. Castilians of all classes became excessively preoccupied with demonstrating their *limpieza de sangre* (blood free from Jewish or Moorish contamination) and, concomitantly, their *viejo cristianidad* (unbroken descent from Old Christian families).[12]

On balance, the reign of Ferdinand and Isabella consolidated an antique and inflexible social structure in Castile. At the top of the pyramid reposed lay and ecclesiastical lords, who made up less than 1 percent of the total population but who monopolized lands, flocks, and high offices and who enjoyed exemption from most direct and indirect taxes. Urban and rural workers, some 85 percent of the kingdom's people, constituted the base. They owned virtually nothing, subsisted in poverty, and suffered the exactions of tax farmers. A "middle sector" squeezed in between. It included impecunious hidalgos and *caballeros*; professional people who depended on royal favor for employment; and merchants, manufacturers, and independent artisans whose fortunes lay at the mercy of royal policies dictated by religious and political rather than economic concerns.

The emergence of Spain as a major European power bolstered the self-esteem of its people, enhanced the prestige of its monarchy, and furthered its mercantile expansion. But it drew the united crown into costly foreign military and diplomatic undertakings. Above all, it contributed to the "fateful alliance" with the Habsburgs, which soon took Spanish *tercios* to the Low Countries and Germany and drained Spanish bullion into the coffers of Antwerp and Augsburg bankers.

## The Conquest and Colonization of the Canaries

The same personal and impersonal forces that created modern Spain generated a vigorous resumption of Castilian and Aragonese expansion. In 1477, Queen Isabella determined to complete the conquest and colonization of the Canary archipelago. As did earlier Portuguese expansion, the undertaking raised juridical and moral problems. In the first place, it brought to a head conflicting Castilian and Portuguese claims in the Atlantic, but the two powers managed to negotiate their differences. In 1479, they signed the Treaty of Alcáçovas, whereby Portugal accepted Castile's claims to the Canaries in return for Castilian recognition of preeminent Portuguese rights in the other Atlantic islands and on the African coast south of Cape Bojador. The second issue was the conditions under which conquest could be undertaken and how a just title to the lands conquered could be obtained. In this instance, the queen and her advisers simply drew on the principle that the extension of the faith justified war against non-Christians and the seizure of their dominions.

The processes of conquest and colonization in the Canaries drew mainly on Reconquest principles and methods but with some more modern devices intermixed. Isabella bought out existing *señorial* rights on Grand Canary, Tenerife, and La Palma, islands that had not yet been conquered, and sent out her own captains to do the job. She granted them the title of *adelantado* and the authority to make *repartimientos* (divisions) of booty and offices and subsequently appointed some of them to the governorship of the islands they pacified. But she reserved the right to control, limit, and revoke at will political functions conceded to *adelantados* and governors. And, as each island was taken, she incorporated it directly into the patrimony of the Crown of Castile. After her experiences with rebellious magnates in metropolitan Castile, she was dead set against the establishment of *señorial* regimes in Castile overseas. She sometimes provided financial subsidies and troops to *adelantados*, but these officials had to rely mainly on their own resources, on occasion obtaining capital from Genoese and Florentine bankers on a partnership basis.

In initiating conquests, *adelantados* generally observed the formal niceties. Upon landing on Grand Canary, Captain Juan de Rejón supplicated that "God, our *Señor*, be pleased to reduce these blind people, and bring them under the yoke of his Sacred Catholic Faith, so that their souls might be saved."[13] He also sent to native chieftains a *requerimiento*, that is a summons, to accept the temporal dominion of Their Catholic Majesties and embrace Christianity, warning them that if they resisted their lands would be taken from them and they would be killed or enslaved. *Adelantados* took possession in the name of the crown in much the same way as their ancestors had done during the Reconquest. They made a formal statement of possession and accompanied it with one or more ceremonial acts deriving from Visigothic custom: cutting a branch or striking the bole of a tree with their sword, raising a cupped handful of soil, or pacing a symbolic portion of land with measured tread.

What happened next depended on circumstances and people. In some instances, the islanders resisted fiercely, and the Spaniards did not complete the conquest of the entire archipelago until about 1497. According to the principles of just warfare, they enslaved the conquered and seized their lands. In other cases the Guanches accepted Christian dominion and the Christian faith preached by Dominicans and Franciscans who arrived with conquerors or closely in their wake. Although the Europeans regarded the Guanches as culturally backward, their customs and their complexions, which ran toward brown, did not seem to have aroused a strong antipathy. Once they had accepted Christianity, the indigenes became technically free Castilian subjects, entitled to full possession of their liberty and property. Isabella and her *adelantados* recognized the natural *señorío* of native chiefs and allowed them to retain this faculty as vassals of the crown. Spaniards of the lower classes married Guanche maidens, particularly the daughters of chieftains, although not much is known about the incidence of such unions. Extramatrimonial miscegenation probably occurred on a larger scale.

In still other instances, Spaniards in the field did not distinguish carefully between military conquest and peaceful occupation. Isabella took the juridical conditions of the Spanish presence seriously. She forbade under severe penalties the enslavement of islanders who became Christians or appeared to be on the way to conversion because, she affirmed, such action "would be a great burden on our Royal Conscience." But captains operating far beyond the limits of royal vigilance reduced the Guanches to bondage illegally, and Portuguese and Spanish slavers from the mainland raided the islands. The Europeans seized the best lands, and the Canarians who avoided slavery subsisted on these properties as tenants. Perhaps Christian principles ameliorated the effect of conquest, but the islanders eventually disappeared as a people under the impact of European exploitation and diseases and through miscegenation.

Colonization and institutional formation followed pacification. Conquerors, immigrants from the metropolis, and acculturated Guanches formed an island population. Each island was organized as a municipality centered on a capital town to which the crown granted *fueros* defining its constitution and privileges. *Adelantados* and *cabildos* made *repartimientos* of land and labor to deserving *vecinos* as well as to religious foundations, influential persons in Spain, and on occasion to Guanche chiefs. The queen took various measures to guard the royal *señorío* and assure justice and good government for her island subjects. She sent out judges to conduct the *residencias* of outgoing governors and, around 1497, established an audiencia on Grand Canary that exercised jurisdiction over all the archipelago. The same bull (1486) that granted her patronage in the kingdom of Granada also applied to the Canaries, and suspicions of pagan heresies among the native inhabitants furnished an excuse for the establishment of the Inquisition in 1504.

The Canaries developed a mixed economy. They produced wheat, cattle, fish, wine, and slaves while they lasted, but sugar quickly became the main cash crop after its introduction, probably on Gómera, about 1480. As in Portugal's Atlantic enterprises, foreigners played an important part in making the land bear fruit. The Genoese not only helped finance the conquest but they invested in sugar planting and refining and played an important role in the carrying trade.[14] By the end of the century, the Welsers, an Augsburg banking family, also had sugar *ingenios* (mills) in the islands.

The conquest of the Canaries extended the faith and added populated lands to the Crown of Castile. The archipelago also lay near the edge of the northeast trades that blew fairly out into the Ocean Sea. The Catholic Kings, however, regarded the islands as peripheral to grander enterprises. In foreign affairs, Ferdinand remained primarily concerned with Aragonese dynastic interests in the Mediterranean and mounting French threats to Naples. Like her predecessors, Queen Isabella had her main interest in Morocco. There she saw an ever-present threat to Hispanic Christendom and, after the fall of Granada, proposed to carry the war across the strait to the enemy's homeland. Although she did not manage to mount an offensive in that direction during her lifetime, in her will she enjoined her successors to crusade against the African Moors.

## Portugal on the Eve of the Columbian Voyages

Developments in late Renaissance Portugal resembled those taking place in neighboring Castile. Around 1450 Portugal's population began to increase and by the last decade of the fifteenth century approached 1,200,000 souls, of whom some 50,000 dwelt in Lisbon. The economic stimulus furnished by demographic growth was strengthened by the planting of large areas of newly reclaimed land and, more important, by continued expansion overseas. Between 1456 and 1470, Madeiran sugar production grew from 6000 *arrôbas* a year (about 192,000 pounds avoirdupois) to 20,000 *arrôbas* (about 640,000 pounds) and, by the early 1490s, reached 80,000 *arrôbas* (about 2,560,000 pounds). In 1482 the Portuguese established the heavily fortified factory of São Jorge da Mina (El Mina) on the northern shore of the Gulf of Guinea and thus were able to tap the gold trade of western Sudan as well as auriferous river sands on the Gold Coast itself. Meanwhile, exploration continued southward, reaching the mouth of the Congo River in 1482–83. Then, in 1487–88, Bartolomeu Dias rounded the tip of Africa, pointing the way to the riches of India and the Spice Islands.

The demands of an expanding economy coupled with availability of Guinea gold induced King Afonso V (1438–81) to coin the *cruzado*, which remained the standard Portuguese gold coin until the eighteenth century. Like the Castilian *excelente* or ducat, it was modeled on the Italian ducat and florin. When first struck in 1457, it contained 3.164 grams of gold, 23¾ karats fine, and was tariffed at 254 *reis* (singular, *real*), the basic Portuguese integer of monetary value and money of account. In 1517 it was retariffed at 400 *reis*, and King Sebastian (1557–78) increased its weight to 3.896 grams and its value to 500 *reis*.

In the latter half of the fifteenth century, also, Portuguese kings joined the "New Monarchs" of Europe. John II (1481–95) moved effectively to strengthen his power vis-à-vis the principal challenges to it, namely, the liberties of the towns and the power of the upper nobility, which, after its discomfiture at Aljubarrota, had regained much of its strength. His efforts were greatly aided by overseas expansion, for as chief merchant of the realm, his profits from trade gave him new sources of revenue and patronage that he could use for political purposes.

John used a combination of measures to chasten the nobility. He confiscated the estates of contumacious lords and resumed the lands of the Portuguese military orders; he asserted the royal writ against *senhorial* jurisdictions and, when his actions provoked schemes against the throne, he executed or exiled the leading conspirators. In addition he and his successor, Manuel I (1495–1521), bought the loyalty of powerful families by granting them pensions, endowments, and, perhaps most important, licenses to engage in overseas trade, a crass activity but one that did not offend their sense of nobility in the least. As for the towns, as early as 1472, the crown began a general revision of their *forais* aimed at standardizing the administration of municipal justice and a hodgepodge of local taxes. This reform included the replacement of *juizes ordinarios* by *juizes de fora* (magistrates appointed and paid by the king). In these actions also, profits from overseas trade gave the monarchy an advantage, for they freed it from dependence on subsidies voted by municipal representatives in cortes.

Reorganization of central administration accompanied the extension of royal authority, with the most important initiatives coming in the spheres of justice and fiscal management. John II created a new court that took care of petitions for pardons, privileges, liberties, and new legislation and thereby centralized the crown's jurisdiction. Reorganizations of the treasury department, systematic budgeting, and more efficient tax collections brought a steady increase in royal revenues during the last two decades of the fifteenth century. To staff the middle and lower ranks of the new bureaucracy, the king drew on university-trained lawyers.

By the end of the 1400s, overseas expansion coupled with the emergence of a New Monarchy gave Portugal a semblance of prosperity and modernity. Yet the kingdom's economy and society had serious structural weaknesses. A population of 1,200,000, most of it abysmally poor, could not begin to absorb the sugar and spices coming from overseas. Most of these commodities, therefore, were reexported, making Portugal merely an intermediary in its own commercial empire. This circumstance in itself might not have been disadvantageous, but the crown lacked a marketing system in western Europe and had to relinquish distribution to Flemish and German merchants who took a good share of the profits. The part that remained at home in the hands of the king and the nobility was used largely for economically unproductive purposes. The practice of planting olives and grapes on reclaimed land further increased Portuguese dependence, for grain had to be imported to feed a growing population.

Despite its increased revenues from sources both old and new, the crown ran into fiscal difficulties; it could not meet the costs of an enlarged bureaucracy, wars in Morocco, weddings in the royal family, and largesse to the nobility.

Beginning in 1500, it began to sell bonds of indebtedness (*padrões de juro*) to cover its deficits.

The survival of an archaic social structure further hampered Portugal's capacity to benefit from its opportunities. Kings John and Manuel did in fact modify the character of the nobility; it became increasingly dependent on the monarchy and, through the trading licenses it obtained, the most commercialized class of magnates in Europe. Nevertheless it continued to dominate Portuguese society through the power of tradition and the ownership and control of most of the land in the realm, despite the inroads on its estates made by John II. Within the common order, the Italian merchant community managed to obtain a share of the profits from a young commercial empire, but the wholesale intrusion of the crown and the nobility into commerce stunted the growth of an indigenous bourgeoisie. Among the mass of commoners, some may have improved their lot by adventuring or emigrating overseas, but most still grubbed a precarious existence from the land.

Portugal also had a religious problem. As in Castile, Jewish communities dwelt segregated in *juderías* in main cities and included families strongly established in commerce, banking, and public office. Portuguese Christians, particularly those who had to compete with them, resented their presence, although not as deeply as did Castilians. Castilian Jews expelled by the Catholic Kings, however, sought refuge across the border, and their presence sharpened Christian animosities. King Manuel I inherited the problem. In addition he had married the daughter of Queen Isabella, who along with her mother pressed for the expulsion of all Jews from the kingdom. Manuel responded to popular and family pressures with edicts in 1496 and 1497 requiring all Jews who would not convert to depart. Many left, but several thousand accepted baptism and became *cristãos novos*, New Christians. As in neighboring Castile, most Old Christians suspected the sincerity of their conversion, and they created an endemic social problem, among other things sharpening Portuguese sensitivity to purity of blood (*limpeza de sangue*).

## Prospects for Hispanic Expansion in 1492

A retrospective view of Hispania toward the end of the fifteenth century reveals that both Spain and Portugal had accumulated a wealth of diverse experiences in overseas undertakings. Both possessed momentum and abundant vitality to carry them further, compounded of a sense of religious mission, commercial enterprise, much of it supplied by the Italian community, and the restless urges of hidalgos, *caballeros*, and commoners denied opportunities for economic and social advancement in their societies. Both, moreover, had dynamic New Monarchies, economic and demographic tides favored them, and they occupied forward bases in the Atlantic. They were somewhat deficient in sustaining economic and social structures, and Portugal in particular still had limited population resources, but the immediate indicators were all favorable. The question was what directions should receive priority. For Portugal, India offered the most glittering opportunity, although, even after rich cargoes of spices began arriving in Lisbon, the crown remained preoccupied with its lagging crusade in Morocco. For Spain, African conquests and dynastic aggrandizements in Italy provided the apparent options.

## Christopher Columbus and the Patent of Santa Fe

At this juncture, or to be more precise in December 1491, one Christopher Columbus, a Genoese navigator, appeared at the court of the Catholic Kings, then established in the encampment of Santa Fe before the walls of besieged Granada. He came to make a final plea for royal support for a voyage he proposed to make into the Ocean Sea to discover new lands and, perhaps, a western route to Cipango and Cathay. After some haggling over terms, in April 1492 Isabella and Ferdinand gave a patent to Columbus known as the *Capitulaciones de Sante Fe*, whose terms appear to have been dictated mainly by the supplicant. In return for his enterprise, the Catholic Kings appointed him viceroy, admiral, and governor in all the lands he might discover and conceded to him the right to one-tenth of the net proceeds of the sale of "pearls, precious stones, gold, silver, spices," and other products he obtained there. They also accorded him the title of Don, thus elevating him to the minor nobility of Castile. The patent provided that all his titles and privileges should pass to his heirs in perpetuity.

One cannot help but wonder at the amplitude of the *señorío* conceded to Columbus by monarchs who had waged a hard struggle against the political independence of the nobility. Perhaps they were in a mellow mood because of the surrender of Granada earlier in the year. Perhaps they attached little importance to the admiral's enterprise, and in any case it cost them little. He himself provided part of the money, which he borrowed from the same Genoese who had helped finance the conquest of the Canaries. The crown made its cash contribution through a loan from the treasury of the *Santa Hermandad*, and Isabella required maritime communities along the Bay of Cadiz to furnish money and ships. Or perhaps the sovereigns simply believed that, if Columbus discovered anything worthwhile, their lawyers could recover what had been given.

Part II

The Establishment

of Hispanic Dominion in America

1492 to About 1570

# CHAPTER 4

# The Conditions of Conquest and Colonization: Geography and Peoples

### The Columbian Discovery

In the darkness of the early morning of October 12, 1492, the lookout on Columbus's ship, the *Pinta*, sighted a white surface glimmering in the moonlight on the horizon and sang out, "Land! Land!" After several hours of excited suspense, first light revealed an expanse of sand and forest rising from the water that, upon reconnaissance, proved to be an island in what later became known as the Bahamas group. Shortly before noon Columbus went ashore in the *Pinta*'s boat and on the strand raised the banner of Castile. He took possession of the island in the name of the Catholic Kings, gave thanks for a safe passage, and christened his discovery San Salvador (Holy Savior). He and his men expressed their delight at the "very green trees and much water and fruit of various kinds" that they saw around them.

San Salvador was inhabited by a neolithic folk, the Lucayans, who were a branch of the Arawak linguistic family. They called their island Guanahaní. Seeing the approach of three monsters from the sea they had fled into the forest, but when outlandishly dressed men appeared on the beach their curiosity overcame their terror and they emerged timidly to meet their visitors. The Europeans offered them gifts of red caps, glass beads, and hawks' bells, and they reciprocated with offerings of parrots, balls of cotton thread, and spears. Columbus and his men marveled at their innocence and generosity and remarked on their splendid physical appearance. The admiral believed that it would be easy to put them to work and, since they had no other religion, to convert them. Observing the small gold pendants that hung from their noses, he asked them where more of the yellow metal could be obtained. Thinking, or wishing others to think, that he had reached the Indies (the Far East), he called them Indians. The name stuck even after his claims had been disproved, and the Spanish and Portuguese soon applied the name Indies to all the lands whose outposts Columbus had discovered.[1]

After spending two days on San Salvador, Columbus explored other islands in the Bahamas group and then continued west, where the Lucayans had informed him gold was to be found. As he proceeded, he came upon two larger islands. One of them he called Cuba, a rough phonetic rendering of its native name; the other, Española (Hispaniola). On both he found Taina Indians who adorned themselves with golden trinkets and who led him to believe that much more of the precious metal lay in the interior of their insular homes. On Christmas Day, the *Santa María* settled on a reef on the northern coast of Española and had to be abandoned. Columbus established a town on the shore, which he called Villa de la Navidad (Town of the Day of Christ's Birth). Leaving thirty-nine men to settle it, he sailed home, reaching Palos, the port from which he had departed the Old World, on March 15, 1493.

## The Papal Donation and the Line of Demarcation

The admiral's return with reports of the rich and populated lands he had discovered supported by a visible assortment of gold trinkets roused great excitement in Andalusian ports and at court. Queen Isabella herself was pleased and directed that his enterprise with "the aid of God be continued and furthered," but before this could be done with confidence the question of who the new lands belonged to had to be settled. The Catholic Kings moved quickly to establish their rights. Upon their request, Pope Alexander VI, conveniently a Spaniard, issued in 1493 a series of bulls that assigned to the Crown of Castile "all islands and mainlands, discovered or yet to be discovered, sighted or not yet sighted, to the west and south of a line set and drawn from the Arctic or North Pole to the Antarctic or South Pole, the line to stand a hundred leagues to the west and south of the so-called Azores and Cape Verde Islands . . . if they were not actually possessed by another king or Christian prince. . . ."[2]

The Portuguese were not satisfied by this division, for reasons that are still controversial. At the time of Columbus's voyage, they knew little about the geography of the South Atlantic and may have felt that the papal award threatened their dominion in Africa south of the Sahara and their route to India. Some historians, however, contend that they already knew of the existence of America and feared that the line as drawn by Alexander would exclude them from discoveries and exploitations there.³ The evidence for this explanation is circumstantial only, but in any case, at Portugal's instigation, the two powers negotiated a bilateral treaty at Tordesillas in 1494 that moved the Line of Demarcation 270 leagues farther to the west.

## The Portuguese Discovery of Brazil

The new line did, in fact, place part of the bulge of Atlantic South America on the Portuguese side, and in 1500 a Portuguese fleet on its way to India touched land in the region. It is not certain what it was doing there. Some historians believe that its commander, Pedro Alvares Cabral, carried secret instructions to establish claim to territory that the Portuguese king believed to be his by virtue of the agreement at Tordesillas.⁴ The alternative and generally preferred explanation is that, sailing first southwest to avoid doldrums along the coast of West Africa, he followed this course too far and came upon Brazil accidentally. In any event, Cabral went ashore, raised a great cross to betoken possession, had a mass of Thanksgiving said, and, thinking that the land was insular, named it Ilha de Vera Cruz (Island of the True Cross). The Portuguese quickly established contact with the friendly and curious people who inhabited the region and bartered with them. After a nine-day sojourn, Cabral dispatched one of his ships to Lisbon to report his discovery, left two *degredados* (exiles) behind to learn the language and customs of the people, and resumed his voyage to India.

The dispatch ship carried a letter to the king written by Pero Vaz de Caminha, an educated royal official, that described the "Island" of Vera Cruz. Caminha remarked on the verdant beauty of the country and the richness of its soil, which, "if it were rightly cultivated . . . would yield everything. . . ." The visitors, however, could not determine whether any gold or silver existed in the region. The letter described the natives as dark brown with well-formed bodies and features. They possessed "the innocence of Adam" and, having no other religion, could easily be converted to Christianity. Indeed, Caminha reported, "the best fruit that could be gathered hence would be . . . the salvation of these people. . . ."⁵

The impressions and actions recorded by Caminha resembled remarkably those of Columbus and his men on San Salvador, but with the departure of the Portuguese fleet the similarity ends. Although Cabral recommended that a settlement be established in the lands he discovered, he was not very excited about the prospect. Neither was his master, King Manuel I. Both were too dazzled by the wealth of India to concern themselves with the conversion of a few natives. Manuel did send out two follow-up voyages, one in 1501 and the other in 1503, which explored the coasts of the continent from just south of the equator to the Rio de la Plata estuary. They discovered great stands of *pau-brasil*, a tree that yielded valuable red and brown dyes and that soon gave its name to the land itself, but found no gold or silver or other precious things. King Manuel turned east to continue the Portuguese crusade in Morocco, to traffic in black Africans, and to follow the lure of spices in the Orient. Meanwhile, Queen Isabella and her successors and their subjects furthered the enterprise of Columbus so that the first half century of Hispanic expansion in the western Indies became mainly a Spanish effort.

## Geographical Influences on
## Spanish Discovery and Colonization

For a brief moment after Columbus came upon islands in the western Ocean Sea Isabella thought only of establishing a factory on Española for trade in gold and whatever other precious things might be found, just as the Portuguese had done in Guinea. But, as new discoveries revealed wonders and riches and countless souls who did not know Christ, the Castilians remembered their past, and the Enterprise of the Indies quickly developed grander dimensions.[6] Discovery merged into conquest and conquest into colonization, and thereby an empire was created.

The Spanish enterprise unfolded along lines shaped by geographical circumstances, among which the immensity of the New World stands out. By European standards Spain was a large country, but it could fit many times into either American continent. The Amazon or Missouri-Mississippi drainage basin could easily accommodate all of Europe west of the Vistula. Only a handful of adventurers to Persia, Cathay, and Abyssinia had ever traversed such interminable stretches of territory. The land overwhelmed and swallowed up discoverers, conquerors, and colonizers and bore hardly a trace of their coming.

The salient physical structures affecting Spanish discovery, conquest, and colonization were two. One was the great central indentation formed by the Caribbean Sea and the Gulf of Mexico, which facilitated and channeled the European approach. In it lay the Greater Antilles, which furnished initial bases for occupation as well as access to the mainland through 270 degrees of the compass. The clockwise flow of Atlantic and Caribbean wind systems, however, detracted from the utility of these bases for return voyages, for it imposed foul sailing from west to east, except in the Gulf of Mexico, where the eastward flow of the Gulf Stream ameliorated its effect.

A second dominating structure was the great mainland cordillera, the backbone of the two American continents. It rose at the Strait of Magellan and then marched northward, dividing and reuniting, rising and subsiding, through the length of South America, Central America, and Mexico, and continued on through the western part of North America. The topography of its several ranges affected Spanish settlement in a number of ways. Between the Tropic of Cancer and the Tropic of Capricorn, altitude tempered latitude. Whereas coastal zones were often unhealthy, hot, and humid, many mountain basins, valleys, and plateaus between 4000 and 10,000 feet above sea level furnished congenial and healthy human habitats. The American indigenes had found them long before the European discovery and had settled them densely, thereby making them doubly attractive to the white intruders who depended on native labor for their existence. In the mountains of the interior, furthermore, the richest deposits of precious metals lay. It was in the cordillera that the main centers of Spanish American civilization developed.

Between the two tropics, also, latitude and altitude often complemented each other. Along much of the Pacific coast of America and the Gulf of Mexico, mountainous regions with cold or temperate climates dropped steeply to narrow tropical and subtropical coastal strips, thereby compressing several ecological zones into relatively short linear distances. The wide range of foods and fibers that the juxtaposed zones could produce encouraged the construction of "vertically" integrated economies by both pre-Columbian peoples and their conquerors.[7]

The cordillera influenced Spanish occupation in still another and adverse way. Its ranges were rugged and passes through them high and infrequent. Also, for much of their length they were badly placed for Spanish interests. In South and Central America they ran much closer to the Pacific than to the Caribbean. This meant that routes from their uplands, where most of their population dwelt, to ports giving direct access to Europe were long and often hazardous. In a very fundamental way, Spanish colonization amounted to the creation of communication and transportation systems under formidable environmental conditions.

## Spanish Claims and Aims

### The Crown

The enterprise of the Indies involved the interaction of peoples of diverse cultures and colors on this vast and overwhelming stage. The Europeans were the prime movers. It was they who crossed the Ocean Sea and imposed their will and their dominion on indigenous populations. Very few Indians came to Europe, and then only as curiosities.[8] But Europeans themselves had different interests and played various roles. The crown authorized, directed, and regulated, following a set of general principles first enunciated by Queen Isabella. These may be summarized as follows.

First, because Columbus had sailed under the auspices of Queen Isabella, the Indies belonged exclusively to the Crown of Castile. Castilian kings, moreover, not only enjoyed full sovereignty over them but had plenary and presumptive rights to all property, real or intangible, in them, including offices and benefices created for their governance. Thus the Indies were not, properly speaking, Spanish possessions or colonies. They were not even regarded as integral components of the Kingdom of Castile but rather as autonomous polities united to the metropolis only by allegiance to a common crown. Thus, contemporary documents refer to *estos reinos* (these kingdoms), which lay in peninsular Spain, and *esos reinos* (those kingdoms), which were on the other side of the Atlantic. These royal rights and prerogatives were essentially the same as those that had governed the establishment of Castilian dominion in lands seized from the Moors. The Catholic Kings, who were trying to recover these rights in Old Spain, simply reaffirmed them vigorously in the Indies, hoping to create in what amounted to a political *tabula rasa*, a more perfect Christian republic, unencumbered by private *señoríos* or pretentious municipal *consejos*.

Second, Castile possessed a just title to the Indies because of its obligation to evangelize the Indians, and, indeed, this was the sole justification for the presence of its subjects in those parts. The bull that defined the Line of Demarcation affirmed this principle. In it Pope Alexander VI disposed:

So that you may with greater liberty and forthrightness assume the duties of these arduous tasks . . . we, by the authority of the omnipotent God granted to us in blessed Peter and the vicarship of Jesus Christ which we hold on earth, by these presents do donate, grant, and assign [these lands], and with them all their towns, camps, territories, villages, and the rights and jurisdictions and all appertaining thereto, to you and your heirs and successors, the kings of Castile and Leon.[9]

Third, the Queen desired lands discovered to be colonized and made to bear fruit. She expected that this be accomplished at minimal expense to the crown and, further, that the Indies produce sufficient revenue to maintain dominion there and, if possible, yield a surplus for transmission to the royal treasury in

Spain. Finally, she declared that once the Indians accepted Christian dominion and the Christian religion, they became her free vassals and were entitled to justice and good government in the same measure as European residents. They could not be deprived of their liberty or property without due process and they could not be made to work against their will or without just compensation. They had, however, to pay an annual tribute to the crown as a mark of their submission.

### Private Interests: Discoverers and Conquerors

The 1500 men who accompanied Columbus on his second voyage, and the thousands more who followed during the next several decades, represented private interests in the establishment of Spanish dominion in the Indies. All were aware that they were subjects of a powerful prince; most never doubted that they were engaged in an imperial undertaking of noble proportions and ends, or that they were militia of Christ. Yet they had compelling personal motives and aspirations. A few, perhaps, sought the intellectual satisfaction that the exploration of new lands might provide. Many dreamt of glory, that elusive combination of self-esteem with public acclaim, honor, and distinction that might be won by heroic deeds performed against great odds.

Yet, despite the adventurous and romantic inclinations of discoverers and conquerors, they were, by and large, practical, hardheaded, and ruthless men. Most came from unprivileged and impoverished families. The scattered data that have been analyzed reveal that their numbers included no titled nobles or prelates and few, if any, masters and *caballeros* of the military orders. These lords fared well at home and had little incentive to adventure in new lands. Instead, the Conquest was accomplished by a few recognized hidalgos, rather more *caballeros* who enjoyed no formal noble status, a few men of urban middle-class origins, a sprinkling of sailors, and a very substantial number of artisans and rural laborers. Juan García de Hermosilla, an old veteran of the conquest of Peru, saw it this way:

This country of Peru was not won, nor was any blood spilled here, by dukes or counts or people titled "don" or relatives of royal judges, because they didn't come in the time of danger, but by Pedro Alonso Carrasco and Juan de Pancorbo and Juan Fernández and Alonso Martín de Don Benito and Pedro Elgarro and other peasants and ordinary hidalgos, and by Juan García de Hermosilla.[10]

In short, most of the first immigrants to the Indies were have-nots, spectators at the feast of life rather than participants. Yet they did not wish to change the society they knew. Instead they left home, as they put it, *ir a valer más en las Indias*. Literally, the expression meant to go to the Indies to become of more worth, but in the context of the times it implied more specific aspirations: to become a lord of vassals, to be addressed as "Don," to found a lineage, to be served by majordomos and menials, to be master of a great house with an escutcheon carved over its door, to dispense patronage to hordes of dependents and to offer lavish hospitality to friends and passers-by. And who knew? If Fortune were gracious enough, perhaps someday they might consort with grandees and wear their hats in the presence of kings.

The surest and quickest route to all that they desired was the acquisition of riches. At first, booty seized from the Indians constituted the most easily obtainable form of wealth. Of all kinds of loot, discoverers and conquerors deemed gold to be the most precious. They made no attempt to hide their avarice, nor did they see anything remarkable about it. Balboa, one of the most levelheaded among them, reported that in Panama tales of gold were so dazzling as "to make us lose our minds,"[11] and Cortés is recorded as saying, "I and my companions suffer from a disease of the heart which can be cured only with gold."[12] The Mexican Indians remarked on this affliction although they could not comprehend it: "The truth is that they [the Spaniards] longed and lusted for gold. Their bodies swelled with greed, and their hunger was ravenous; they hungered like pigs for that gold."[13]

One may wonder at the Spaniards' intense, unremitting, and even manic preoccupation with gold. Today it is useful for fashioning jewelry and for the valuation of baser currency, but it is not necessary to possess it to be rich. Even bankers rarely see it coined or in bullion, while for those who trade in it it is only a commodity. To the Renaissance European, however, gold was a tangible thing. It circulated, and it could be seen, held, exchanged for other valuables, or hoarded. When placed in piles, it glittered like Moorish treasure. It was, moreover, in short supply, and, as the century advanced, Europeans needed it for their commerce. The Spanish, in particular, were incommoded by the rerouting of Sudanese gold through the Portuguese factories on the Gulf of Guinea and, indeed, may have valued the metal more highly than other peoples, although this would be difficult to demonstrate empirically. Gold dazzled just as much the Germans who joined in the conquest of northern South America and the Portuguese when they finally found it in Brazil. In any case, Columbus, who probably spent more time looking for it than he did searching for the Asian continent, summed up its fatal attraction: "Gold is the most precious of all commodities; gold constitutes treasure, and he who possesses it has all he needs in the world, as also the means of rescuing souls from purgatory, and restoring them to the enjoyment of paradise."[14]

Gold and other precious loot soon proved to be an insufficient and ephemeral form of wealth. The Indians possessed only limited hoards, and, when it was divided up among the conquerors, the share of the rank and file fell short of anticipations. What they got, moreover, they dissipated in gambling or expended on horses, arms, and other martial accoutrements at enormously inflated prices. Even captains, who took the lion's share, invested it in chimerical enterprises or spent it on litigation with the crown over the political prerogatives of conquest. Conquerors and first settlers came to regard *repartimientos* (allotments) of Indians as the main reward for their services and sacrifices. *Repartimientos* not only provided wealth in the form of tributes and labor but were also perceived as a form of *señorío*, a status that Spaniards valued above all others except salvation. In conquered areas, however, there were never enough Indians to go around, especially as new arrivals swelled the European population. Thus the search for new clusters of indigenes became a primary motive for new conquests. But the Indies also offered other sources of wealth and social eminence to enterprising conquistadors and to those who did not share in the distribution of the conquered. Canny men could get rich through commerce, and the opening of mines yielded such quantities of treasure as to make the loot of conquest appear trivial.

The Interplay of Royal and Private Interests

Royal and private interests in the Indies had one aim in common, the exploitation of newly discovered lands, but they quickly came into conflict over means and conditions. The crown wished to convert and patronize the indigenous population, establish exclusive sovereignty in its American possessions and, at the same time, gain a profit from the enterprise. Conquerors and settlers wanted to exploit the natives, acquire *señoríos*, and become wealthy. They were not very much concerned about the moral and juridical aspects of dominion or about the treatment of the conquered, and their *señorial* pretensions challenged royal authority.

In pursuing their often conflicting interests both the crown and private parties had advantages and disadvantages. On the one hand, the Spaniards in the Indies felt a deep-seated and chivalrous devotion to the monarchy and the mystique that surrounded it, an attitude expressed by Bernal Díaz del Castillo when he wrote, "As my forefathers, my father and my brother had always been servants of the crown and of the Catholic kings of glorious memory Don Fernando and Doña Ysabel, I wished to be something like them."[15] But their loyalty also held a measure of calculation. They constituted a tiny minority of Europeans existing precariously amidst an imperfectly pacified indigenous population, and they counted on help from home. They also apprehended that swift retribution would follow treasonable action. On the other hand, the conquistadors operated in regions where the king's writ had not been established. They could, in effect, follow their own inclinations, knowing that transgressions would be overlooked in case of resounding successes, diminished by perspective of time and distance, or perhaps be forgiven in recognition of their sacrifices. The king, moreover, felt obliged to reward handsomely subjects who served him well, and he could not prudently push proud captains on distant frontiers too hard.

The condition of the monarchy also affected the interplay of royal and private interests in the Indies. During the interim between Isabella's death in 1504 and the swearing of allegiance to her Habsburg grandson Charles in 1518, regents governed Castile. Some doubts surround the legitimacy of Charles's succession. His mother Juana "la Loca" was first in line for the crown, but he had her declared mad on questionable grounds. Shortly after his reign began, in 1520–21, his Spanish supporters had to put down the Revolt of the *Comuneros*, a rising of Castilian municipalities who feared that a foreign king might abridge their *fueros*. In addition, Charles had imperial problems: the defense of his European dominions against the French, the appearance of the Turks in the western Mediterranean, and the outbreak of religious schism in Germany. These required him to be often abroad, and in his absence regents and councils governed Castile and the Indies. On the whole his agents were men of rectitude and ability, but they could not rule with the majesty of a king present in person. In short, discontinuities in the exercise of kingship meant that the Indies were rather slackly governed during a critical formative period.

Moral and political restraints felt by the crown on the one hand and by conquerors and settlers on the other discouraged open confrontations. Differences between the two parties, rather, created flexible and sometimes unstable conditions in the Indies and over the years resulted in a series of de jure and de facto compromises and accommodations that guided social and institutional formation. They also adumbrated tensions between an imperial system designed to benefit Old World interests and New World societies with their own identities and reasons for being.

## The American Indian

Pre-Conquest Populations

Indigenous peoples played largely a reactive role in the establishment of Spanish dominion in the Indies. Some accepted European mastery willingly or resignedly. Others fought back with determination, but most Indian nations lacked the political, military, and psychological resources for sustained resistance. Once conquered they reacted to the will of their conquerors. Conquest and exploitation along with the introduction of European epidemic diseases did them enormous physical and psychological damage. Their populations diminished, their gods were cast down, and their leaders were destroyed or reduced to Spanish puppets. Their monumental temples were abandoned and often used as quarries by Spanish builders in much the same way as, a millennium earlier, Roman baths, temples, and amphitheaters became the raw materials for Christian basilicas. Inca roads decayed, and the rooting and stamping of European livestock breached Inca terraces, opening the way for erosion and eventual destruction. Zealous Spanish clergymen burned the Mayas' sacred scrolls, and the sophisticated calendrical calculations of the Mayas became arcane lore in the books of Christian scholar-priests. Yet to say that the Indians' role was reactive does not mean that it was inconsequential. On the contrary, their numbers and qualities assured them an indispensable and omnipresent part in the formation of imperial systems and American societies.

No one knows how many Indians inhabited the Western Hemisphere in 1492 and, indeed, the problem has generated one of the liveliest controversies in American ethnohistoriography. The first European visitors to the regions of the Greater Antilles, Mexico, Central America, and Andes spoke of passing through *muy pobladas* and *bien pobladas* provinces, both terms suggesting a population of considerable density. They applied these descriptions even to lands such as western Darién (the eastern part of the Isthmus of Panama) that today are virtual wildernesses. They also made some impressive regional estimates. The island of Española had some 1,000,000 inhabitants, Cuba between 2,000,000 and 3,000,000.[16] Eyewitness accounts of the size of Indian armies and the number of native converts tend to confirm the existence of large populations in many parts of the Indies, and the denunciation of European cruelties by Father Bartolomé de Las Casas, the famous champion and "Protector of the Indians," furnishes additional evidence. According to his "real and true" reckoning, between 1492 and about 1540, more than 12,000,000 Indians succumbed under the Spanish lash.[17]

Four centuries later, in the 1920s, European and North American geographers and ethnographers became interested in the population history of the American Indian before and after the Discovery. Using estimates of the carrying capacity of the land, archaeological evidence, and backward projections of modern censuses, they concluded that the indigenous peoples of the entire New World around 1492 numbered between 40,000,000 and 50,000,000, most of them being concentrated in Middle America and the central Andes.[18] These figures would indicate a fairly dense population in the regions just named.

A second generation of historical demographers arrived at conflicting conclusions. Some assumed that Spaniards of the times consciously or instinctively exaggerated the number of Indians they conquered or converted in order to glorify their achievements and, using various methods of demonstration, revised early estimates sharply downward. The Argentine scholar, Angel Rosenblat, made a painstaking evaluation of regional ethnographic data, applied to them a "verisimilitude" criterion that he never precisely defined, and reckoned an American Indian population of 13,385,000 in 1492.[19] The American anthropologist A. L. Kroeber made evaluations of subsistence potentials of various American regions and, combining the results with a retrospective extrapolation from modern and colonial counts, came up with a pre-Conquest hemispheric total of 8,400,000.[20] Both estimates placed the majority of the natives in Middle America and in the central Andes.

In contrast, the work of the University of California scholars Woodrow Borah, Sherburne Cook, and Lesley B. Simpson tended to confirm and even expand generous earlier estimates. Applying systematic statistical analysis to Aztec and Spanish tribute rolls and to post-Conquest parish records of births and deaths, they concluded that in 1519, about 25,200,000 indigenes dwelt in central Mexico alone.[21] Although the so-called Berkeley School has concerned itself mainly with Mexico and the Caribbean, Borah looked farther afield and in 1962 ventured that perhaps as many as 100,000,000 indigenes inhabited the entire New World on the eve of European discovery.[22] More recently, the American anthropologist Henry Dobyns reckoned a hemispheric figure in the range 90,000,000 to 112,500,000 by determining Indian population nadirs in various parts of America, calculating a standard long-term rate of population decline, and projecting it backward to pre-Conquest times.[23] Thus, observations and estimates made by Spanish contemporaries might not have been, after all, too far off the mark.[24]

When calculations by knowledgeable experts differ so widely, the layperson is apt to be confused and tempted to find a compromise figure by adding the extremes and dividing the sum by 2. This procedure would be methodologically unsound, but the American geographer William Denevan obtained approximately the same result, a hemispheric total of 57,300,000, by a careful reconciliation of various high and low regional totals. Denevan adds that a reasonable degree of error would be 25 percent upward or downward, producing a range of 43,000,000 to 72,000,000.[25] Since all totals, high, low, and moderate, are at best educated guesses, the nonspecialist is free to make a judgmental choice among them. The present author inclines toward Denevan's figures.

In addition to estimating the size of pre-Columbian populations, historical demographers have attempted to determine long-range population trends before the Discovery. Some of their evidence suggests that by 1492 the number of Indians in Mexico and possibly in the Andean region was approaching limits imposed by agricultural systems in use and that a Malthusian crisis loomed not far off. The Berkeley School had some speculations to make on this point. Sherburne Cook suggested that the holocausts of human sacrifice that so appalled the Spaniards in Mexico may simply have reflected the plentifulness and cheapness of human life, and Borah offered a rather striking proposition: "By the close of the fifteenth century the Indian population of central Mexico was doomed even had there been no European conquest."[26]

American Indian Cultures

In 1492 hundreds of different Indian cultures existed in the Americas. For general descriptive purposes these can be grouped into three categories defined by the level of their cultures which, in turn, was determined by the efficiency of food production. The lowest group consisted of primitive hunters, fishers, and food-gatherers whose nomadic life required only the simplest technology and divison of labor. In what later became Hispanic America, these peoples included the Chichemecas of northern Mexico, the Caribs of the Lesser Antilles and northern South America, and the peoples of the South American pampas.

Primitive cultures graded into an intermediate category comprising peoples who depended chiefly on agriculture for subsistence and who, therefore, were sedentary or semisedentary. These conditions required a more advanced technology and more differentiation of social functions. This grouping included the Chibchas of the northern Andes, the Guaraní of Paraguay, the Arawaks of the Greater Antilles, the Araucanians of Chile, the Tupinambá of coastal Brazil, and the Pueblo of New Mexico.

The highest category consisted of peoples who had developed agriculture to the point where it could produce a substantial surplus. This achievement permitted the existence of dense sedentary populations, the emergence of economically nonproductive classes, and the release of mass labor for the construction of monumental cities, temples for the worship of complex pantheons, palaces, fortifications, roads, and terraces. These high cultures or civilizations were the Aztec, Mixtec-Zapotec, Tarasco, and Maya of Middle America and the Inca of the central Andes.

Regardless of level of culture, the primary social and political units of Indian America were the clan composed of interrelated families (the *calpulli* in central Mexico and the *ayllu* in the central Andes), and the tribe formed by associations of clans. Tribes occupied territories with a firmness of dominion and sharpness of delineation increasing in proportion to level of culture. In the high cultures, state structures dominated by warrior and priestly elites were superimposed on clan and tribe. In Middle America the most common superstructure was the city-state. Such states sometimes formed confederations that conquered neighboring peoples and required them to pay tribute, thus creating loosely knit and unstable "empires." The most extensive of these was the Aztec Empire that at its zenith encompassed most of central and southern Mexico. In the central Andes the Incas also created a conquest empire that when the Spaniards arrived stretched from what is now southern Colombia to central Chile. It was much more tightly constructed than that of the Aztecs, because the Incas fully integrated conquered peoples into their state, made elaborate provisions for its government and defense, and organized its economy tightly.

Physical Attributes of the Indian

The physical qualities and conditions of the pre-Columbian indigenes have not yet been well or fully defined. Regional paleopathological research indicates that some groups suffered from malnutrition, especially protein deficiency. A number of endemic diseases were present among them, including several varieties of treponematosis (syphilis, yaws, and *pinta*), tuberculosis, parasite-induced intestinal disorders (among which hookworm has been identified), and, possibly, malaria. Convincing evidence that epidemic diseases afflicted the Indians is lacking, but their long isolation from the Old World left them completely vulnerable to sudden pathogenic invasions.[27] Also, they were not a physically robust people, at least by European standards. Although they had stamina sufficient for their own requirements, they tired quickly under the demands of their Spanish masters. The seventeenth-century Spanish natural historian Father Bernabé Cobo observed that, in Europe, one Spaniard could do more field work in a day than four Indians could in America.[28] But perhaps this disproportion resulted from the Indians' difficulty in adapting to an alien labor system.

## The Indian Ethos

It is relatively easy to catalogue the cultural and phyiscal qualities of the American Indians but much more difficult to comprehend their spirit, for it was and still is quite alien to what people of European origin value. Despite their remarkable achievements in agriculture, in art and architecture, and in astronomy and mathematics, even the Aztecs, the Mayas, and the Incas were primitive peoples by the standards of sixteenth-century conquerors and priests and of twentieth-century anthropologists. They clung to an animistic world view. Not only humans and the gods possessed being but all the things of the universe—stones, stars, winds, and rains—that modern humans classify as inanimate. The dichotomies of humankind and nature, natural and supernatural were inconceivable to the Indian. All things in heaven and earth existed in an integral rather than a categorical relationship. Just as in their intercourse with each other, humans could influence other elements in the universe by cajolery, supplication, remonstrance, and even threat—but only temporarily and for limited objectives. They could not change the eternal order of the universe, and, indeed, the Indians would have regarded any attempt to do so with horror, for it might destroy the rhythms of sowing and reaping, of rain and sun, of death and renewal that determined whether humankind would survive or perish.[29]

The Indian ethos with its values of eternal order and stability bore some superficial resemblance to medieval Christianity, but it was alien to the spirit and values of the Renaissance which, in addition to the physical impact of the Conquest, it had to withstand. Indians' view of the universe made them conservative, nonacquisitive, noninnovative, and fatalistic. These qualities left them highly vulnerable to the dynamic, restless, and ruthless urges of sixteenth-century Europeans but also endowed them with a patience, a resignation and, perhaps, an innate stubbornness that in the long run helped them to survive culturally and biologically.

The quantitative and qualitative attributes of the American Indians shaped the enterprise of the Indies in various ways. They affected the rate at which the Spaniards conquered them, converted them, and put them to work as well as the methods they employed for these purposes. Native labor supported the main sectors of the economy of the Indies, and native women furnished the breeding stock for new ethnic types. The persistence of the indigenes' values and customs influenced social and institutional formation, and their status as slaves, serfs, or servants left an indelible mark on the psychology of European conquerors and their descendants.

## Africans in the Enterprise of the Indies

One other people participated in the establishment of Spanish dominion in the Indies, although its part developed more slowly and less dramatically. Very early, perhaps on Columbus's second voyage, a few Hispanicized blacks appeared as slaves of discoverers and conquerors. Later, traders began to bring in Africans in increasing numbers directly from slaving stations on the coasts of Guinea, the Congo, and Angola, and by the late sixteenth century the number of heads imported amounted to several thousand a year. All together blacks numbered far fewer than indigenous Indians, but their labor helped support the enterprise of the Indies and their fecundity made visible contributions to ethnic formation. And, although torn up by the roots from their native soil and rudely transplanted, they managed to hold on to many ancient beliefs and usages that penetrated Spanish American cultures in innumerable overt and covert ways. The presence of the Indian and the black ensured that societies in the Indies would not be mere replicas of Old World orders.

# CHAPTER 5

# Mundus Novus:
# Discovery and Conquest

### The Meaning of "Discovery" and "Conquest"

If discovery and conquest be followed step by step and league by league over two seas and two continents, they have the appearance of very disorderly affairs. To contemporaries, however, they had definable meanings, rationales, and methods, and, in retrospect at least, their unfolding displays a pattern and a rhythm.

In the language and ambiance of the times, "discovery" meant to reveal or gather knowledge about lands hitherto unknown, but it also had associative aims and values: the revelation of nations hitherto hidden from the light of Christ and the coming upon troves of treasure or, more prosaically, the finding of valuable commodities in which to traffic. It also had a chimerical dimension. Fifteenth-century Europe still credited medieval legends of enchanted kingdoms in far parts of the earth inhabited by Amazons, giants, and even more exotic life forms such as hydras, griffins, and dragons who guarded hoards of precious things. In Renaissance Hispania these fantasies acquired a new vehicle in romances of chivalry whose contents, if not read by all, drifted into popular culture. Such tales had a common theme — the exploits of brave and virtuous hidalgos in fabulous lands — and a stereotypical outcome. The hero returned covered with glory and his fortune gained or restored. The unsophisticated accepted these accounts as factual; after all they were recorded on printed pages just as were royal and holy writ.[1]

To contemporaries, "conquest" (*conquista*) meant the establishment of *señorío* over land and people by force of arms but, within a context established

89

by Reconquest experience and the subjugation of the Canaries, for particular ends: the extension of Christendom and the dominions of Christian kings at the expense of infidels and pagans; and the extraction of tribute and booty from the conquered. It is interesting to note that the Spaniards avoided the word *conquista* in describing their territorial aggrandizements in Christian Italy.[2]

## *Rationalization: The* Requerimiento

Well-established political theories furnished the rationale for discovery and conquest in the Indies. Christian princes could acquire dominion over infidels and pagans to extend Christendom, and a just war could be waged against those who resisted. The Spanish jurist Juan de Palacios Rubios redefined the principle in "Of the Ocean Isles," a learned treatise prepared about 1512 to serve the needs of the Castilian crown. Drawing on the writings of Hostiensis, he declared that popes could annul the jurisdictions of heathens and pagans and confer them on Christian princes, and that was exactly what Pope Alexander VI had done in the Bulls of Donation in 1493. Palacios, moreover, operationalized the doctrine in a formal *requerimiento* to be used in the field. This instrument summarized the genesis of just title as expounded in "Of the Ocean Isles" and called on the Indians to acknowledge the pope as ruler of the world and, in his stead, the king of Castile by virtue of donation. It then informed them that if they accepted the summons they would be received as loyal vassals, but if they did not they would be deprived of their liberty and property and further stated, "We protest that the deaths and losses which shall accrue from this are your fault, and not that of their Highnesses, or ours, nor of these cavaliers who came with us."[3]

Palacios Rubios as well as some other jurists took the *requerimiento* seriously, but in application it was a frivolous document. The conquerors generally employed it in a perfunctory way, and the Indians who heard it could not comprehend its doctrine or even its language since it was read in Spanish or Latin. Father Bartolomé de Las Casas could not decide whether to laugh or cry after he had seen it. The historian Gonzalo Fernández de Oviedo, who served as a notary during the early Conquest, had occasion to proclaim it to the natives and later observed ironically, "My Lords, it appears to me that these Indians will not listen to the theology of this Requirement, and that you have no one who can make them understand it; would Your Honor be pleased to keep it until we have some one of these Indians in a cage, in order that he may learn it at his leisure and my Lord Bishop may explain it to him?"[4] Nevertheless, the document met the juridical requirements of conquest and helped to ease the royal conscience.

## Authorization: The Royal Patent

In the main, the Castilian crown turned over discovery and conquest to private parties at their own expense (*costa y minción*) since it had more pressing uses for its own resources. It retained, however, the right to authorize undertakings and to specify conditions for them. As in the conquest of the Canaries and the agreement with Columbus at Santa Fe, it employed the *capitulación*, or patent, for its purpose. This instrument licensed an impresario to undertake one or more missions in lands described as accurately as contemporary geographical knowledge permitted, generally at his own expense. Types of enterprises specified included not only discovery, conquest, and settlement but trade, a concept expressed in the word *rescatar*, which does not translate well. In some contexts it meant "to ransom," but in the Indies in the early sixteenth century it more commonly meant "to barter". More specifically it referred to trading at an advantage, the most common form of commerical intercourse between Europeans and primitive folk who had no appreciation of the money value of things and who looked on such transactions as exchanges of gifts. Thus, the Spaniards gave cheap cloth and trinkets for gold, slaves, pearls, or whatever they deemed valuable. King Ferdinand, however, tried to keep them from taking undue advantage by decreeing that what they gave must have at least one-third the monetary value of what they received in return. The meaning of *rescatar* also came to include, surreptitiously, the direct taking of Indian slaves.

In return for his investments and services, the impresario received titles and privileges whose amplitude depended on his influence and powers of persuasion, the crown's perception of the importance of his undertaking, or simply on the usages and mood of the moment. At the most modest level, he obtained authorization only to trade and retain a portion of the profits. The most generous patents named the impresario *adelantado*, an adaptation of the Reconquest "Lord of the March"; governor, which conveyed administrative powers; and captain general, which gave military command. These titles and functions subsumed more specific rights for the holder: to lay out territorial subdivisions in the lands he might discover and conquer; to found towns; to give justice and good government in the king's name to his company and to natives in his jurisdiction; to appoint subordinate officials; to grant lands to his followers; to reserve a portion of land and booty for himself; to retain a fraction of taxes due to the crown for his own use; and to draw a salary, although it had to be paid from the revenues of the provinces he governed.

The more generous patents clearly conveyed a measure of *señorío* to *adelantados*, and in granting them the crown speculated with its sovereignty to provide incentives for discovery and conquest. The risk, however, was not excessive; it was *señorío* delegated, not alienated. The beneficiaries exercised their political and judicial functions only as agents of the king, and appeals from their judgments went to royal councils and courts. The rights conceded, moreover, existed in territories as yet unknown, and the manner of their exercise could not be anticipated precisely. Hence, royal tribunals could always interpret them to suit the interests of the sovereign.

## The Identification of a New World

The forms of discovery and conquest in the Indies fell into two stages defined by the relative emphasis given to each process. The first stage, extending roughly from 1493 to 1519, involved mainly maritime reconnaissance and few conquests, for the Spaniards did not find too much to conquer. The second, running from about 1519 into the 1560s, featured the exploration of the interior of the American continents and the establishment of dominion over their richest and most populous regions.

Reconnaissance had aims and dimensions both large and small. The most extended maritime explorations resulted from geographical observations that accumulated rapidly after Columbus's first voyage. To his dying day, the admiral stubbornly maintained that he had discovered the outposts of Asia, but some of his own men as well as other navigators and learned men in Europe could not reconcile what they saw or heard of the configuration of the Indies with what they knew or believed about Asian geography. Voyages consummated by 1500 revealed hundreds of miles of continuous shoreline, snow-capped peaks rising from coastal ranges, and outpourings of fresh water into seas offshore that could only have come from large rivers.

These experiences suggested to European explorers and cosmographers that what had been discovered was a great new landmass rather than a collection of islands. As early as 1494, Peter Martyr, a cultivated Italian gentleman in attendance at the Spanish court, wrote, "For when treating of this country one must speak of a new world, so distant is it and so devoid of civilization and religion. . . ."[5] Columbus himself used the term *otro mundo* (another world) to describe the lands he had discovered, while still clinging to the notion that they were insular or peninsular extensions of Asia.[6]

It was the Florentine navigator Amerigo Vespucci who made an identification that caught on. Between 1499 and 1502, Vespucci made several voyages across the Atlantic — the number is disputed — in the course of which he became quite certain that the lands he saw had no connection with Asia, and, in a letter to his patron, Pier Francesco de Medici, he called the South American continent *Mundus Novus* (New World). The Medici family belonged to a European intellectual community whose members were in close correspondence. The *Mundus Novus* letter circulated quickly and widely through these channels and soon appeared in print in the principal European languages. In 1507, Martin Waldseemüller, a German cartographer, proposed that the New World be called after Vespucci and prepared a map on which he placed the name America on the southern continent just above the Tropic of Capricorn. Gradually, the appellation became accepted in northern Europe, and geographers extended it to all the lands of the Western Hemisphere. Thus, through a better public relations system, the Florentine rather than the Genoese received the largest territorial monument. The Spanish and Portuguese, however, continued to call America the New World of the Indies or simply the Indies until the eighteenth century.

The sudden collapse of Columbian cosmography gave trans-Atlantic exploration a new turn. Princes sent out their captains and admirals to look for a way around or through the obstacle that Vespucci had identified. In the first decades of the sixteenth century, Spanish, Portuguese, English, and French expeditions probed the coasts of both American continents, entering estuaries, bays, and gulfs with excited anticipation, withdrawing in disappointment, but always anticipating that the next coastal indentation would disclose a passage, a confidence bolstered by Balboa's discovery of the Pacific in 1513. As everyone knows, Magellan did discover a strait in 1519, but its waters were so treacherous and the route to the Orient through it so extended that it had little utility.

## The Caribbean Cycle of Exploration and Conquest

The Reconnaissance proceeded in what the Spaniards called the *Islas y Tierra Firme del Mar Océano*. The term *Islas* referred to the Greater and Lesser Antilles. *Tierra Firme* referred to a mainland, a large landmass as distinguished from islands great and small, in this case the northern coast of South America and adjoining Darién. Later the English called these lands and adjacent waters "the Spanish Main." The *Mar Océano* (Ocean Sea), it will be recalled, was the great ocean extending west from Europe.[7]

Early Caribbean exploration had a tentative, probing character, as demonstrated both by the diversity and the lack of specificity in patents granted and by the actions of discoverers. Explorers dreamt of chimerical kingdoms, sought something to conquer, and tried to find a strait. Most voyages, however, had trade as a primary or collateral objective, and some were simply slave raids. Their most common organizational form was the *campaña* or *compañía*, a primitive joint stock company in which participants received a share of the proceeds in proportion to their input in capital or services. These companies generally numbered fewer than a hundred men captained by a *caudillo* and sailing in one or two caravel-type ships, often hastily built in the Indies. They were high-risk operations in which Indian arrows, fevers, reefs, and storms produced heavy casualties in men and ships, and they yielded very uneven profits. Their depredations on the islands and Tierra Firme did great damage to native populations and left those who escaped or lay beyond Spanish reach permanently hostile. Caribbean *compañías* amounted to New World *cabalgadas*.

New World impresarios also produced more positive results. On Santo Domingo, Puerto Rico, and Cuba, they found sufficient dust and nuggets to enable Castile to replace Portugal as the principal supplier of gold to Europe. Despite their often crass motives and villainous behavior, they revealed the location and dimensions of the Greater and Lesser Antilles, the contour of the mainland from Florida to the mouth of the Amazon, and a land route across the Isthmus of Panama to the South Sea (the Pacific). Taken together with European-based oceanic voyages, they defined the latitudinal dimensions of the two American continents and outlined their Atlantic rims from Labrador to the Strait of Magellan.

Whatever their particular interests might be, everywhere the Spaniards went they took possession of the land in the king's name according to ancient usages.[8] Effective occupation, however, lagged behind this act for several reasons. The Arawaks of the Greater Antilles, who at first tolerated the intruders, turned against them when they learned that what the *requerimiento* really did was to make them mine gold, and the fierce Caribs of the lesser islands and Tierra Firme resisted from the outset. The Spaniards, moreover, were few and thinly distributed; they depended for virtually everything they needed for conquests and, indeed, survival on uncertain transport from Europe; and they had to adapt physically and psychologically to alien environments. They began the conquest of Española by about 1496, Puerto Rico by 1508, Jamaica by 1509, and Cuba by 1511, and by about 1519 they controlled the coast and parts of the interiors of these islands. They had, however, to contend with chronic indigenous rebellions. On the mainland, they gained a temporary foothold on Darién in 1509 but did not establish a permanent settlement until 1519, when they founded Panama.

The first twenty-five years of Castilian enterprise in the Indies had many similarities with the Portuguese advance down the coast of Africa. Both Castile and Portugal justified their presence in new lands on the grounds of extending the faith, but their missionary efforts lacked organization and vigor, and their expansion was essentially opportunistic; they looked for whatever might be found that would be profitable. Portuguese African voyages and Spanish *compañías* had much the same organization, forms of financing, and transport. The Spanish seem to have regarded their first settlements on the Antilles and the Main as factories, and in 1503 Queen Isabella established a royal trading house, the *Casa de Contratación*, a Spanish equivalent of the *Casa de Guiné e India*. Whatever their motives might have been, Spanish and Portuguese explorers together greatly extended the limits of the world known to Europeans and claimed the lands they discovered for their sovereigns. Spanish and Portuguese kings both donated rights and privileges to impresarios to further discovery, conquest, and settlement.

These resemblances were more than coincidental. Both Castile and Portugal probed unknown and remote lands inhabited by savages and pagans, and a common cultural heritage governed their reaction to what they found. More direct connections also existed. Each knew what the other was doing. Overt and covert intelligence flowed between the two courts. Spanish traders and slavers intruded into the Portuguese African monopoly, and Spanish seamen sailed on Portuguese voyages. Conversely, Portuguese participated in Spanish oceanic and Caribbean explorations, and on occasion the Castilian crown gave patents to Portuguese captains. Italian merchants, financiers, and navigators serving both Hispanic kingdoms furnished still another informational link.

Despite procedural concurrences, the outcome of early Spanish and Portuguese explorations differed greatly. The Portuguese founded a great commercial empire in Africa and Asia that yielded enormous profits. The king of Castile and his subjects watched enviously, for in the main the New World had been a disappointment. Except for Antillean gold, profits hardly justified investments in men, capital, and materiel, and by 1519 the island mines were beginning to play out. Conditions were generating, however, that changed dramatically the course of the Enterprise of the Indies. Although few had gotten rich in those parts and many had perished, the New World remained a lodestone to the disadvantaged and the ambitious as well as a refuge for scoundrels and political and religious dissidents. Thus, immigration swelled the population of the islands, and European plants and animals arrived, adapted, and reproduced. Old Caribbean hands, *rancheadores* and *baquianos* as they came to be called, acclimated and learned how to adapt European military organization and tactics to Indian fighting.

## The Great Mainland Conquests: Organizational Forms

Meanwhile, rumors and wisps of information began to accumulate about rich and populous kingdoms lying behind the coastal jungles and escarpments of the mainland. The Spaniards desperately wanted to credit this intelligence and had no difficulty doing so, for it seemed to substantiate what medieval legend and contemporary romances of chivalry told and foretold. Suddenly all their dreams came true. In 1519 a reconnaissance of the Mexican coast commanded by Hernán Cortés encountered incontestable evidence of an opulent civilization existing on the interior plateau. Without waiting for formal permission, Cortés undertook to conquer it and two years later stood victorious on the ruins of Tenochtitlán, the Aztec capital, with the loot of an empire at his disposition.

The news of the bonanza spread like flame through the Indies and Spain, bringing new waves of fortune seekers across the Atlantic and depopulating the islands as settlers rushed to share in the spoils. The magnitude of Cortés's success won ex post facto approval of his enterprise from Emperor Charles along with titles and honors. Thereafter, Spaniards continued to trade and slave and look for a strait, but they directed their main efforts to finding and conquering *otros Méxicos* (other Mexicos), which, they firmly believed, were bound to exist somewhere on the two American continents. At this juncture exploration turned inland, discovery merged directly into conquest, and the Caribbean *compañías* quickly evolved into the expedition of conquest, sometimes called the *entrada* (a penetration into the mainland). It now became the Portuguese turn to watch with envy.

As the Enterprise of the Indies turned toward great mainland conquests, its organizational forms adapted to new circumstances. The royal patent continued to be the authorizing and regulating instrument, but its provisions tended to become more specific and standardized. Thus, to a *capitulación* given in 1526 for the conquest of Yucatán, the crown appended a General Provision to be observed by all *adelantados*. Reflecting the discovery of millions of indigenes living in a semblance of polity, it reminded impresarios that the main justification for Spain's presence in the New World was evangelization and required each expedition to include two priests, who were to introduce the Indians to Christ.

Expeditions of conquest varied in size, depending on the magnitude of the lure and the appeal of the leader but probably more than anything else on the availability of manpower. Francisco Pizarro began the conquest of Peru in 1524 with only about 180 men. Years later, when the European population of the Indies had increased substantially, Gonzalo Jiménez de Quesada set forth to find the Golden King in highland Colombia with about 900 men, although only 166 reached their destination. Most of the *entradas* fell between these extremes, but some of the smaller enterprises numbered fewer than 100 conquerors.

Expeditions had a fairly standard organization. The king's appointee held command, sometimes with the titles of *adelantado*, governor, and captain general, but he did not possess absolute authority. Law and custom required him to take counsel with his men when important decisions had to be made, and the possibility of rebellion or deposition restrained authoritarian inclinations. The second level of command consisted of captains, sometimes elected by the company but more often appointed by the commander on the basis of their martial qualities or experience, social status, friendship or kinship with the leader, or material contributions to financing and equipping the undertaking. A detachment of mounted men and rather more foot soldiers comprised the rank and file. Although no formal distinction of military rank existed between cavalry and infantry, horsemen enjoyed a superior status; they were *caballeros*. In addition to its military personnel, the company included a representative of the king's treasury to see that the royal fifth was taken from booty, one or more notaries to record significant occurrences, and one or more priests to minister to the spiritual needs of the Europeans and preach to the Indians. Some conquerors took along black slaves, and most drafted Indians as auxiliaries and bearers.

But the Conquest was by no means an exclusively male affair. Spanish wives and mistresses sometimes accompanied their men in travail and adventure, foraging for food, binding wounds, giving courage and comfort in misfortune and defeat, and, in the long run, imparting an air of permanence to the early Spanish presence in the Indies. Among them was Inés Suárez, who followed her husband to the Indies only to find him dead. She became the mistress of Pedro de Valdivia, the conqueror of Chile, sharing in the hardships of his marches and battles. She sometimes fought at his side and won her share of the booty. Later, she achieved Christian respectability by marrying Rodrigo de Quiroga, who became governor of Chile. In Mexico, Isabel Rodríguez's devotion to the care of the wounded during the siege of Tenochtitlán made her the Florence Nightingale of the Conquest. The most famous woman of them all was Doña Marina, "La Malinche," a daughter of a chief who was tributary to the Aztecs. After being captured in a battle in Tabasco, she became Cortés's chief interpreter and adviser on Indian affairs as well as his mistress. Eventually, she married one of the lesser conquistadors and became a solid *ciudadana* (citizen) of Mexico City.

Neither can the animals of the Conquest be overlooked. Everyone, of course, knows about the role of the aristocratic horse. Horses provided mobility on the march and mass and velocity in the charge and at first had a devastating psychological effect on the Indians, who regarded rider and mount as a single monstrous corpus. There was also the noble dog, probably of the mastiff breed, trained to attack Indians in battle. Among those whose identities have survived are Leoncico, owned by Balboa, and Bercerillo, who belonged to Ponce de León. It was said of Bercerillo that he could distinguish at a distance between hostile and friendly natives, and for his aggressiveness in combat he received one-half of a crossbowman's share of the booty. But the unsung hero of the Conquest was the plebeian swine, a long-legged, tough Castilian breed that adapted easily to almost any climate or terrain. It foraged for its sustenance, reproduced regularly on the march, and provided a self-propelled source of animal protein for the conquerors.

Since the crown's contribution was only occasional and generally niggardly, financing expeditions required private venture capital. Like Caribbean *compañías*, most expeditions were organized as primitive joint stock companies. Each member, in addition to providing his services, was expected to supply his own arms and equipment, although in some instances leaders advanced funds for this purpose. The impresario and his captains raised the money, often by borrowing, to purchase more expensive supplies and transport. Variations from this pattern of capitalization sometimes occurred: Francisco Pizarro, Diego de Almagro, and Father Luque formed a partnership for the conquest of Peru; in the conquest of Chile, Pedro de Valdivia had a Peruvian merchant as a silent partner; and Hernando de Soto used his share of booty taken from the Incas to finance the conquest of Florida. The Castilian Law of Spoils governed returns on investment of capital and services. After the king's fifth and a sum for general expenses had been set aside, the leader was entitled to from one-seventh to one-tenth of the booty. The remainder was to be divided into shares of which simple foot soldiers received one, harquebusiers and crossbowmen one and one-half, and mounted soldiers two or more. Often, however, different schedules of shares were specified in patents or decided in the field. Such irregularities tended to stir bitter dissensions among the company.

Conquistadors employed the standard armament of the time. Mounted warriors carried lances and swords; foot soldiers used pikes, harquebuses, and crossbows; and the expedition dragged along artillery when obtainable. All fighting men started out with partial or complete European-style armor. It was, however, expensive and heavy and, in the tropics, generated almost unbearable heat. Also Indian flint projectiles shattered against it, causing dangerous ricochets. Many soldiers therefore came to prefer the quilted cotton type of armor used by the Indians. For food, conquerors depended on European staples such as dried meat, wheat, olive oil, and wine to the extent that they were available but often had to resort to manioc, beans, and other unappetizing native fare. And, of course, there were the ubiquitous pig and game taken along the way. As for transport, those who could afford it rode horses. For passage by sea leaders bought or constructed ships and for river travel requisitioned Indian canoes.

In structure, the expedition of conquest was multiform and, in function, multipurpose. Although it had military objectives and a quasi-military organization, it could not properly be called an army. Some of its personnel might have served in the campaigns against the Moors of Granada, in the Italian wars, or in the conquest of the Canaries, but many had had no military experience before coming to the Indies. It was organized for a particular undertaking, and, when that was accomplished or frustrated, it disbanded. It had a loose command structure; maintenance of discipline depended more on the leadership qualities of the commander than on formal codes of military justice. Members received no regular pay.

If the expedition was something less than an army, it was something more than a band of warriors. It had political functions and a political structure. Patents and the instructions that accompanied them constituted primitive bodies of law; they were the seeds of the monumental Laws of the Indies, which accumulated during the sixteenth and seventeenth centuries, slowly became codified, and were finally published in 1681. The *adelantado* not only held the military title of captain general; as governor and chief magistrate he exercised civil authority over his own men, and, when after a successful undertaking the expedition of conquest became an expedition of occupation, he assumed the governance of the indigenous population. His captains became his political subordinates, and when the conquerors founded towns they became *vecinos* and *ciudadanos*, that is, political persons.

The company of conquerors possessed a social organization that sometimes paralleled, sometimes intersected the formal command structure. Even in the free and easy camaraderie of the Conquest, European distinctions in rank existed. Hidalgos were still hidalgos and commoners remained commoners. Inherited status, however, might be improved by contributions of capital to the enterprise, by prowess in battle, or by demonstrated qualities of leadership. The expedition might also be permeated by ties of personal dependence based on patronage dispensed by leaders and on kinship. Relatives of the first conquerors flocked to join them, and present with Alonso Pérez in the storming of Tenochtitlán were sixteen of his brothers, uncles, and cousins. Status deriving from these several sources imposed a loose hierarchal order on the expedition that, although conditioned by European social standards, had a distinctive American tone.

Expeditions of conquest also had economic dimensions. Men joined them for gain, and in the larger undertakings a wide range of occupations were represented. Companies might include armorers and gunsmiths, sailors, miners, agriculturists, apothecaries, barbers, leatherworkers, ironworkers, tailors, cobblers, scribes, and even men of letters. Such an assortment of skills enabled the company to survive for extended periods far from European settlements. In sum, the expedition of conquest constituted a self-contained segment of Spanish society capable of survival, expansion, reproduction, and adaptation.

## *The Course of Conquest*

### North America

The Conquest had a discernible although irregular rhythm which is depicted graphically on map 2. It advanced from staging area to staging area, the intervals between advances being determined by the time required to mobilize manpower, collect supplies and transport, reconnoiter and gather intelligence, and acclimate to new natural and cultural environments. Using Santo Domingo as their principal base, the Spaniards spent nearly two decades establishing themselves on the Greater Antilles and Tierra Firme. Then, with the fall of Tenochtitlán in 1521, this city, renamed Mexico by its conquerors, became the base for the establishment of Spanish dominion in North America, and the pace of conquest quickened. From Mexico, a pre-Columbian communications network provided expeditious routes for expansion in almost every direction. Spaniards flocking in from the Antilles and Europe to share in the spoils or discover *otros Méxicos* swelled available manpower, and the wealth of the Aztecs furnished ample supplies.

Aided by this conjuncture of circumstances, within six years after the defeat of the Aztecs, Cortés's lieutenants fanned out from Mexico City and conquered central and southern Mexico, Tehuantepec, Chiapas, Salvador, and highland Guatemala and began the conquest of Yucatán. Very soon thereafter, in 1529, Spaniards departed Mexico City to subjugate New Galicia, a vast "kingdom" extending northwest from central Mexico into what is now the states of Jalisco and Sinaloa and on into the Gran Chichimec (the land of the wild Chichimeca tribes). Owing to repeated native uprisings, however, Yucatán and southern New Galicia were not pacified until the early 1540s, and the Gran Chichimec remained a *tierra de guerra* (land of war) until well into the seventeenth century.

While these great enterprises were afoot, hopes of finding a western and Spanish route to the Spice Islands remained very much alive and generated far-ranging searches for its two essential components, a trans-American strait and a practical route across the Pacific. To these ends Cortés sent out expeditions that in the 1520s and 1530s explored the western coast of Mexico from the tip of lower California to the Isthmus of Tehuantepec, and he also dispatched three ships to the Moluccas. In 1542 expeditions sailed from Mexican Pacific ports east to the Philippines and north as far as Oregon. Pacific explorations, however, yielded no immediate fruit. On the American side of the Ocean, the Spaniards could not find an interoceanic passage, although they continued to believe that somewhere in the north the "Strait of Anian" crossed the continent. In Asia, Portugal claimed that all the islands discovered lay on its side of the Line of Demarcation as extended into the Eastern Hemisphere, and in 1529 Emperor Charles ceded his pretended rights to the Moluccas for a sum of money he needed for his wars with France. Perhaps more important, trans-Pacific voyagers from Mexico could not find the proper combination of winds and currents to carry them back home.

## South America

In South America, Darién proved to be a false approach to the interior, for it had an unhealthy climate and gave access to little more than dense rain forests and misty mountains. In 1519, therefore, the Spaniards moved their mainland base to Panama on the South Sea. From there reconnaissance, and then conquest, proceeded in two directions. The first turned northwest to Costa Rica and Nicaragua and on into Honduras, where it led to a violent confrontation with Spaniards coming down from Mexico. The second followed the Pacific coast of South America to Peru, at first moving slowly. With the discovery of the Incas, however, the pace accelerated. In 1533, the Spaniards occupied the Inca capital of Cuzco, and it became the springboard for new conquests. Just as in Mexico latecomers arrived, too late to share in the spoils but swelling available manpower. Inca wealth and population provided additional support. From Cuzco, a well-developed road system gave access to Quito, the Chibcha principalities in Colombia, and the central valley of Chile, all of which were conquered by the early 1540s, and to Alto Peru (Upper Peru, now Bolivia), which came under Spanish dominion in the 1550s.

These conquests in turn furnished staging areas for new advances. In the 1560s men from Santiago de Chile crossed the Andes and occupied Mendoza in western Argentina, and in the same decade conquerors from Upper Peru moved down into northern Argentina to pacify the province of Cuyo. Meanwhile, the Antilles continued to serve as bases for enterprises on Tierra Firme. In the 1520s and 1530s the Spaniards managed to establish enclaves on the coasts of Venezuela and Colombia, and in the third quarter of the sixteenth century they penetrated into the more temperate and salubrious valleys of the Venezuelan Andes. These acquisitions, however, were poorly regarded, for they held little booty.

In the Rio de la Plata area, conquest followed a rather unique course. In 1536 an expedition coming directly from Europe established the settlement of *Nuestra Señora de Buenos Aires* on the west bank of the estuary. The hostility of the pampas Indians, however, made the site a horror of sudden attacks, siege, and starvation. Five years later the Spaniards moved their base upriver to Asunción and within a decade established dominion over the Guaraní. Here they subsisted, separated from other conquered regions in the Spanish Indies by great reaches of mountains and jungles and from Europe by thousands of miles of river and ocean.

## Penetration of Continental Heartlands

The lure of "other Mexicos," "other Perus," and diverse chimerical kingdoms also generated explorations deep into the heartlands of the New World. In 1541 and 1542 an expedition departing from Mexico under the command of Francisco Vázquez de Coronado wandered over a great part of the American Southwest and into the Great Plains, hoping to find in those parts the fabled Seven Cities of Cíbola, which were said to be even richer than Mexico, and the equally opulent land of Gran Quivira. During almost the same time span, from 1539 to 1542, another company, under the command of Hernando de Soto, explored the southeastern part of North America and penetrated as far west as Oklahoma seeking kingdoms reputed to possess more precious gems and metals than the realms of the Aztecs and the Incas. Taken together these two *entradas* nearly spanned the continent 250 years before Meriwether Lewis and William Clark made their crossing.

In South America, expeditions based on Quito and the Colombian highlands pushed across the high cordillera into the basins of the Orinoco and the Amazon. The most famous among them, commanded by Gonzalo Pizarro, Francisco's brother, set out from Quito in early 1541 to seek the "Province of Cinnamon and the Lake of the Golden King" in the lands beyond the Andes. In late December of the same year, Francisco de Orellana left the expedition and descended the Amazon from the river's upper tributaries to its mouth, which he reached in August of 1542. In neither North nor South America did the great continental *entradas* find anything to conquer, and they returned decimated and disillusioned. They did, nonetheless, add immensely to geographical knowledge.

## The End of the Conquest

When did the Conquest end? The answer depends on definitions. In the early 1540s champions of the Indians at court induced Emperor Charles to back away from the concept of conquest and to require peaceful pacification of newly discovered lands. Furthermore, after 1542 patents no longer required the use of the *requerimiento*, and in the 1550s and the 1560s royal instructions forbade the use of war to bring the indigenes to obedience and Christianity. Men in the field paid little attention to such strictures, and conquest as a process involving a particular set of motives and methods lingered on until the seventeenth century. By the 1560s, however, the Spaniards had subjugated all the major Indian civilizations of the New World and controlled its most desirable territories. What might be called the "High Conquest" was over. Its spatial limits were determined in part by natural obstacles, in part by native resistance, but mainly by the dimming of a vision. It had become increasingly evident that no other Mexicos or other Perus existed.

## The Spanish Achievement: Explanations

One must ask another question about the Conquest. How could a few thousand Europeans bring down in such a short span of time great empires whose populations numbered in the tens of millions? Only two decades elapsed between Cortés's march to Tenochtitlán and the reduction of the Chibchas in the Colombian Andes. Some of the reasons have been touched on, but a recapitulation is in order. Traditional explanations emphasize military factors. Europeans unquestionably possessed superior weaponry and equipment. Firearms at first had a devastating physical and psychological effect on the natives, and horses terrorized them. Spanish discipline and tactics that permitted the immediate application of force at critical points and places on the battlefield gave the conquerors an enormous advantage over unwieldy Indian armies. A rather limited concept of the nature of war further handicapped the natives. The Aztecs took the field to impose their tribute system on other nations and, on occasion, simply to take captives for ceremonial sacrifice. To inflict heavy casualties on the enemy would have contradicted their purposes. The Spanish, however, thought of war in crueler terms. Its purpose was the destruction of opposing forces so that they would be unable to fight again. This objective became an imperative for small bands campaigning far from their bases in the midst of large, hostile populations. Survival required total victory. Yet the indigenous peoples quickly overcame their terror of European arms, adjusted to European tactics, and, as it dawned on them that they were being conquered, regrouped and resisted vigorously. These circumstances suggest that other factors must be taken into account to explain the rapid success of the Conquest.

The diversity and distribution of Indian cultures undoubtedly favored the Europeans. The several nations spoke a babel of tongues, and the major civilizations existed isolated from each other, thus inhibiting the exchange of intelligence and prohibiting military cooperation. Pizarro could repeat the successes of Cortés ten years later because the Incas had not heard of the fate of the Aztecs.

The political and social structures of the major Indian nations also affected their fate. In them, small military and religious elites dominated and exploited passive masses that, although they might fear, revere, or obey their leaders, did not render political loyalty to them. Thus, after indigenous leadership had been destroyed, decimated, or discredited, the rest of the population had neither the capabilities nor the incentive to fight on. Instead, they accepted European masters and in this way the Conquest amounted to a displacement of elites.

The Europeans, furthermore, happened to arrive at a time when internal crises had weakened indigenous political systems. In central Mexico, the vitality of the Aztec confederation had passed its peak, and nations tributary to it hated and feared their exploiters. "The Mexican," lamented the Otomí, "is an inhuman person. He is very wicked. . . . There is none who can surpass the Mexican in evil."[9] In Yucatán, Mayan leagues had fallen apart, and cities warred against each other. In Peru, the death of the ruling Inca, Huayna Capac, precipitated a war for the throne between his sons, Huascar and Atahualpa. The conquerors exploited these tensions adroitly, making alliances with disaffected or contending elements and defeating resistance in detail.

Certain subjective factors also affected the course of conquest. At first, the Indians did not know what to make of the Spaniards. The strangers arrived in sea monsters, dressed in outlandish fashion, carried sticks that belched flame and thunder, bore tidings of a remote and faceless god, demanded gold, and required submission to an unknown king who ruled vast dominions across the waters. Europeans knew that the world was full of strange and wonderful things, but nothing had intruded into the Indians' ordered conception of the universe for millennia. Perhaps the strangers were themselves deities, and the Mexicans suspected that Cortés was the Toltec god and culture hero Quetzalcoatl, who had treacherously been driven from the land in earlier ages and had now returned to claim his dominion. Such doubts, along with ominous signs and portents observed by his soothsayers, made Moctezuma reluctant to resist the approach of the Europeans and induced among the Mexicans a paralysis of will that one author compared to the malaise that overcame France in the face of the German invasion of 1940. In short, the Indians, beset by uncertainties about the motives and, indeed, the identity of the conquerors, at first adopted a neutral or defensive posture. By the time they realized that they were up against ruthless and determined antagonists who knew exactly what they wanted, it was too late.

Still another, and perhaps decisive, factor in the Conquest was the intervention of microscopic allies on the side of the Europeans. In December 1518 or January 1519 an epidemic struck the Antilles. The Spanish called it *viruelas*, a term that they sometimes used to describe eruptive fevers in general but that applied more specifically to smallpox. In this instance it was probably smallpox accompanied and aggravated by measles. The Europeans had a high degree of immunity to it, but the Indians lay at its mercy. Within the next two years imported *viruelas* and respiratory infections of pandemic proportions spread to the mainland, arriving in Mexico one year after Cortés and appearing in Central America and Peru before the conquerors. No one knows how many indigenes perished, but according to contemporary reckonings in some areas casualties ran as high as 50 percent of the population. The onslaught demoralized the uncomprehending and defenseless natives, cut into the fabric of their societies and economies, and killed many warriors. Like the European plague, moreover, it had no respect for rank. It carried off princes and nobles including the old Inca Huayna Capac, thereby precipitating a bitter succession war. The micropathogenic invasion unquestionably diminished the Indians' will and capacity to resist.

## *Patterns of Conquest: Regional Variations*

Although generalizations can be made about forms and methods of conquest, they conceal different patterns that developed in the several parts of the Indies and that, together with diverse pre-Hispanic natural and cultural environments, help to explain the many regional variations in social, economic, and political formation that subsequently appeared. Everywhere conquerors went they began their enterprises in much the same way: taking possession, reading the *requerimiento*, and founding a town as a base of operations and a symbol of their presence. These preliminary acts, however, had different sequels. The Mexican and Peruvian experiences contrasted sharply. Within a decade after the fall of Tenochtitlán, virtually all the Indians of central and southern Mexico accepted the *señorío* of the king of Spain, although not without many silent doubts and reservations. Except for incessant squabblings among Europeans over spoils and prerogatives and for frontier disturbances, the land lay at peace and ready to embark on vigorous economic and social development. In Peru, nominal conquest proceeded just as rapidly, but pacification lagged, and thirty years after the Spanish occupation of Cuzco disorder prevailed in many provinces.

The differing Mexican and Peruvian experiences can be attributed to several circumstances. The Inca state had a relatively firm and legitimate foundation, and after the fall of Cuzco pretenders set up a "Neo-Inca State in Exile" in the remote eastern Andean province of Vilcabamba. It retained the allegiance of many native peoples nominally under Spanish dominion until its physical destruction in 1572, and the mystique of the imperial crown remained alive in indigenous Peru until the nineteenth century. In contrast, the more fragile political structure of the Mexicans collapsed quickly. Hostile subjects and neighboring tribes denied its chieftains a refuge, and in any event the Spaniards had discredited, slain, or executed the most powerful among them.[10] Geography also favored the more rapid pacification of Mexico. Although a rugged land, its long stretches of open country and relatively low passes allowed the conquerors greater mobility in putting down uprisings than did the towering ranges and broad deserts of Peru.

The behavior of the conquerors also differed in the two regions. In Mexico, the Spaniards disputed fiercely over spoils but managed to maintain a united front against the conquered. In Peru, contentions between the adherents of Francisco Pizarro and of Diego de Almagro erupted into open civil wars that not only delayed pacification but set a very bad example for the natives. Nor can the role of leadership be ignored. Cortés employed an extraordinary combination of audacity, diplomacy, and calculated ruthlessness, not only to conquer the Mexicans but to put down rivals and contain dissensions among his followers. More important, he had a vision of empire, of a "New Spain," which he pursued by giving justice and good government, as he saw it, to the conquered and by fomenting the economic development of the lands he won. No one can challenge the martial qualities of Pizarro and Almagro, but these leaders lacked the political skills of Cortés and did not look much beyond the immediate requirements and booty of conquest.

Differing patterns of conquest can be observed in other parts of the Indies. In Quito, which had never been completely incorporated into the Inca system, and in Chibcha lands, divisions among the indigenous population allowed the Spaniards to gain quick victories and discouraged the formation of post-Conquest resistance movements. In contrast, the conquest of Central America was a very disorderly affair owing to the depredations of Spanish slavers and to civil war among the conquerors over jurisdiction, booty, and control of a transisthmian route that ran up the San Juan River and, via the Nicaraguan lakes, to the Pacific. In Chile, the conquerors quickly subdued the indigenes of the central valley, but in the south they encountered the fierce Araucanians who not only held the intruders at bay but on occasion raided deep into pacified territory, making Spanish tenure precarious. In remote Paraguay, after overcoming initial Guaraní resistance, the Europeans consolidated their control by marrying the daughters of chieftains and thus acquiring a certain legitimacy in the eyes of native subjects.

# CHAPTER 6

# Colonization:
# The Populators of the Indies

## The Meaning and Aims of Colonization

Just as the discovery merged into conquest, conquest blended into colonization. Rendered by contemporaries as *población*, colonization retained its medieval significance. It meant the settlement of newly gained territories but for particular purposes and in particular ways. It required the establishment of a Christian republic where men lived in polity and justice according to their rank and station and made the land bear fruit. And it remained a good and desirable thing. It extended Christendom, increased the patrimonies and revenues of princes, and "ennobled" the land. Indeed, it was the logical and desired end of discovery and conquest, despite the notion still persisting in otherwise respectable histories that, whereas the English came to America to settle and till the soil, the Spaniards came only to plunder.[1] The mystique of *población* persisted long after Spanish dominion in the Indies had passed. In 1853, the Argentine statesman Juan Bautista Alberdi expressed it in his famous aphorism, "*gobernar es poblar*" ("to govern is to populate").[2]

In the Indies *población* acquired a new dimension. It involved not only colonization by Europeans but participation by indigenous peoples in a multiple role that Queen Isabella defined in 1503 in instructions to Nicolás de Ovando, the first royal govenor of Española:

Item: Because we desire that the Indians be converted to our Holy Catholic Faith and their souls be saved and because this is the greatest benefit that we can desire for them, for this end it is necessary that they be instructed in the things of our faith, in order that they will come to a knowledge of it and you will take much care to see that this is accomplished. . . . Item: Because for mining gold and performing other work which we have ordered done, it will be necessary to make use of the service of the Indians, compelling them to work in the things of our service, paying to each one a wage which appears just to you . . . .[3]

To these precepts, the queen shortly added another:

We ordain and order that our Governor of the said Indies, undertakes with much diligence to see that *poblaciones* be established in which the Indians can live together, as do the persons who live in these our Kingdoms [in Spain].[4]

Fourteen years later Father Bartolomé de Las Casas restated this aim more explicitly. He recommended that forty Spanish farmers with their wives be settled in Indian communities in the Antilles to provide a model of industry and thrift for the indigenes, and predicted:

Thus will the land be made fruitful and its people multiply, because they will plant all manner of trees and vegetables. Your Majesty's revenues will be increased, and the islands ennobled and be, therefore, the best and richest in the world. And if as time goes on the Indians should prove themselves able to live alone and govern themselves, and serve your Majesty in the same way as your other vassals do, this is provided for in the laws.[5]

In short Indians were not only to be put to work to support Spanish colonization but were to be taught to live in Christian polity, to be acculturated, as modern anthropologists say. And thereby they would become populators in their own right.

## The European Component

### Influences Governing Emigration to the Indies

The Spaniards had some preconceptions about how to go about colonizing the Indies, but the changing numbers and qualities of the populators themselves conditioned the methods and instruments employed. Beginning with the European element, its formation occurred through immigration and natural increase. The gross number of immigrants to the Indies and their qualities depended on both individual initiatives and royal policies. Individuals and families went to the New World for diverse reasons: to win a fortune, to improve their status, to escape royal justice or the attentions of the Holy Office, to serve God as missionaries and the king as royal officials, or to accompany or find husbands. The crown had fairly definite ideas about who should go and who should not. In general, it encouraged the immigration of Catholic Castilians of good character and provided incentives in the form of grants of land, agricultural supplies and implements, and exemption from direct taxes for first settlers and their eldest sons. It particularly encouraged the immigration of women, because it regarded the monogamous Christian family as the basis of social formation in the new lands, and of artisans and laborers, who, it hoped, would not only perform essential productive tasks but would also provide a model of thrift and industry for the indigenous peoples. It also tried to direct emigrants to less favored provinces that had shortages of settlers.

Isabella discouraged the emigration of non-Castilians but never absolutely prohibited it, and upon her death in 1504 Ferdinand formally opened the Indies to Aragonese. Emperor Charles adopted an even more liberal policy by extending the right to the subjects of his non-Hispanic kingdoms. But on one point the Catholic Kings and their successors remained adamant. They absolutely forbade Jews, crypto-Jews, Muslims, *moriscos*, and heretics to go to their American dominions. To enforce its policies, the crown required all emigrants to obtain licenses from the *Casa de Contratación* (Royal House of Trade) in Seville, excepting clerics, soldiers, sailors, and servants. It is likely, however, that individual initiatives and ingenuity had more to do with the quantity and quality of emigration to the Indies than did the wishes of kings.

The Volume of Emigration

The number of emigrants to the Indies during the period of discovery and conquest cannot be determined with any exactitude. The main source of information on the subject is the registers of licenses issued by the *Casa*, some of which have been gathered and published by the Archivo General de Indias as *Catálogo de pasajeros a Indias durante los siglos xvi, xvii y xviii*.[6] This source lists 15,480 persons but has several shortcomings. Despite its ambitious title, it covers only the years 1509–59, and even within this span registers for a number of years are fragmentary or missing. The licensing system, moreover, functioned loosely. Although crown regulations required all vessels sailing for America to register with the *Casa* in Seville, many departed clandestinely from other Spanish ports and even from Portugal carrying unlicensed passengers. Not a few persons avoided controls by passing themselves off as sailors, soldiers, and servants. Licenses could be forged or purchased from legitimate holders or from venal officials. Finally, registers do not reveal how many people actually departed, how many survived the long and hazardous trans-Atlantic passage, how many perished quickly in the unhealthy

American tropics or became casualties of the Conquest, and how many returned to Europe.

Because of deficiencies in passenger lists, it has generally been surmised that the number of persons who actually emigrated exceeded substantially the number of registered passengers, and this is confirmed by the American historical linguist Peter Boyd-Bowman in connection with his research on the origins of New World Spanish dialects. Supplementing passenger lists with information gleaned from a variety of other published and unpublished contemporary sources, Boyd-Bowman identified 45,374 persons of European origin known to have resided in the Indies between 1493 and 1579. He believes that this count represents almost one-fifth of the actual number of such individuals and that, if it is accepted and multiplied by five, then the total volume of emigration must have approached 226,870. This is the best estimate presently available.[7]

National and Regional Origins of Emigrants

Using the same sample, Boyd-Bowman calculated that almost 95.0 percent of emigrants hailed from the dominions of the Crown of Castile, only 2.0 percent from the realms of the Crown of Aragon and from Navarre, and 2.8 percent from outside of Spain. Andalusia provided more than a third of the total, and this province, along with Extremadura and the two Castiles, better than three-quarters. Over the eighty-six-year span, no really significant change occurred in proportions furnished by the several regions of Spain. Thus, the conquest and colonization of the Indies was accomplished mainly by individuals from the south and west of Spain.

This pattern developed from several circumstances. In part it was a function of time and distance. Seville, in the southwestern extreme of the peninsula, was the center of communications with the Indies and the principal port of embarkation for those parts. The circulation of tidings from America, the main inducement to emigration, decreased in proportion to distance from Seville, and, furthermore, it was easier for prospective emigrants to get to that port from Andalusia, New Castile, and Extremadura than from Old Castile and Leon and the remote northern and Mediterranean provinces. But other factors also affected the scant representation of northerners and easterners. Some historians have proposed that, if these enterprising peoples had played a larger role in the colonization of the Indies, they would have created a more vigorous and more modern imperial system, and critics have blamed Castilian exclusivism for their absence. As for Aragonese subjects, it is true that they were technically

foreigners. The Cathloic Kings, moreover, distrusted their constitutionalist pro-
clivities and wished to prevent the spread of political infection to the New
World. But the crown never absolutely denied them access to the Indies, and in
any case if they had really wanted to go there they would have found a way. The
fact of the matter is that the Discovery aroused little interest in the dominions
of the Crown of Aragon or along the Bay of Biscay, where people were preoccupied with other matters: the Catalans, with the restoration of their commercial empire in the Mediterranean; the Aragonese, with French and Italian
affairs; and the Basque ports, with the wool and iron trade to northern Europe.

The predominance of Andalusians also reflected ancient historical trends
combined with particular social circumstances. In Hispania, long-term population movements flowed from north to south, and the resettlement of Andalusia
was the last stage in internal migration. Here the monopolization of land by
*ricos hombres* and grandees turned many settlers and their descendants into
urban proletarians living on a bare subsistence level in overcrowded quarters,
into seasonal laborers in the countryside, and into impoverished hidalgos, all
without any domestic prospects for improving their lot. The relief of overpopulation in the south through emigration to the Indies, therefore, became
the next step in Spanish population movement.

Non-Spaniards, that is, persons who were not subjects of the combined
crowns of Castile and Aragon, comprised only a small percentage (2.8) of the
sample, but their importance was disproportionate to their numbers. They
played significant roles in navigation and in commerce, legitimate and illicit.
Portuguese made up the largest group of foreign immigrants. Despite political
boundaries separating them from the rest of Hispania, they were never really
regarded as foreigners. Castilians and Portuguese possessed a common historical,
cultural, and linguistic heritage; they maintained many family, *señorial*, and
economic ties that crossed political boundaries, and the Algarve and the Atlantic coast of Andalusia held a seagoing population that was truly international.
In addition, the Portuguese possessed navigational skills greatly in demand, and
many enlisted in the crews of Spanish ships engaged in discoveries and trans-
Atlantic trade. As sailors they did not have to obtain licenses to go to the Indies.
The expeditions of conquest included Portuguese *fidalgos*, and Portuguese merchants established themselves in New World ports with or without licenses.
These immigrants rapidly assimilated into the Spanish population. The main
objection to their presence derived from a belief, rather well-founded, that
many of them were *conversos* fleeing the Inquisition. Indeed, in the Indies
the terms "Jew" and "Portuguese" became almost synonymous.

Italians, mainly from Genoa and other points along the Ligurian Coast, constituted the second largest foreign element. As a result of Aragonese expansion, the Italian kingdoms were closely linked to Spain, and, like the Portuguese, the Italians were skilled navigators and assimilated easily. They were well established in Seville at the time of the Discovery and wielded considerable influence in diverse matters including the procurement of licenses for their compatriots. Many of the Italian residents of the Indies, temporary or permanent, came from the Sevillian community.

The third largest group of foreigners consisted of subjects of Emperor Charles's northern principalities, and their presence can be attributed to the emperor's political and financial obligations in those parts. By and large, they engaged in commercial activities. The fourth largest non-Spanish element was French, despite the almost continuous hostilities that prevailed between the Houses of Habsburg and Valois during the first six decades of the sixteenth century. A sprinkling of English, Irish, Scots, Greek, and central European immigrants complemented the foreign population of the Indies.

American Destinations of Emigrants

Europeans went to different parts of the Indies for various personal reasons or because of official assignments, but for the most part the flow of emigration followed the rhythm of conquest and the successive opening of new sources of American wealth. Boyd-Bowman's sample shows that until 1520 the majority of emigrants chose Española, for it was the economic and governmental center of the Indies as well as the point of departure for most American-based expeditions of discovery and conquest. Considerably fewer selected the other islands of the Greater Antilles. During the period 1520-39, newly conquered Mexico attracted nearly a third of the new arrivals (32.4 percent), followed by Española with 11.0 percent and Peru, where the conquest was still incomplete, with 10.8 percent. Between 1540 and 1559, emigrants to Española dropped to 4.4 percent and to Mexico to 23.4 percent, while Peru's share rose to 37.0 percent. This pattern reflected the general shift of Spanish interest from the islands to the mainland and the economic attractions of Peru, especially after the opening of the mines of Potosí after 1545. During the span 1560-79, Mexico regained the lead with 39.8 percent, Peru's share dropped to 21.5 percent, and Española made only a slight gain, to 6.1 percent. The resurgence of Mexico is probably attributable to the pleasant climate of its extensive uplands, its diversified and rapidly expanding economy, and the opening of its northern provinces.

Among other parts of the Indies, New Granada consistently attracted the largest number of immigrants, about 8.7 percent of the total arriving between 1520 and 1579. The remaining regions experienced surges during their conquests, but later their share dropped to 5.0 percent each or less.

Some propositions about the significance of regional origins and destinations suggest themselves. It may be assumed that the peoples who went to the Indies brought with them the attitudes, values, prejudices, and practices of the towns and provinces from which they came and that these attributes guided cultural and social formation in the New World. The American anthropologist George Foster refined this assumption into a particular theory of "Conquest Culture."[8] During the first stages of conquest and settlement, the Europeans had to make quick, spontaneous decisions about how to conduct their enterprises and organize and exploit the conquered peoples. Familiar patterns of thought and behavior guided their choice of action. During this period Andalusia, Extremadura, and the two Castiles provided the majority of immigrants. Therefore the values of traditional, pastoral, *señorial* Hispania, the region where the memory of the Reconquest was most alive, predominated in the formation of incipient Spanish American cultures.

Scattered data suggest that after about 1600 the proportion of immigrants coming from the more "modern" and more "Europeanized" provinces of northern and eastern Spain increased, but by that time cultural forms had crystallized and new arrivals adapted to them. As for linguistic development, Boyd-Bowman concludes that the Castilian-Andalusian spoken by more than half the the women and more than one-third of the men who went to the New World during the Conquest period played the decisive role in the formation of the *primitivo español antillano* (the Spanish spoken in the early Antilles), which, carried to the mainland, constituted the base of other Hispanic American dialects.[9]

In other areas of cultural formation, however, such correlations have not been systematically demonstrated, and the American social historian James Lockhart has some reservations about them. Speaking of Peru in the period 1532–60, he observes that, although regional origins represented real divisions among immigrants, they "were far from clearcut" and the several groups were "not yet very conscious of themselves." Furthermore, although Andalusians predominated, "the real distinction was between the Castilian majority and the minority groups from the semi-alien fringe areas of Spain." The significance of this pattern, he concludes, "is not so clear; we are as far as ever from knowing whether Spanish American civilization can be said to have Andalusian origins."[10]

Social and Ethnic Backgrounds of Immigrants

Data on social backgrounds of passengers to the Indies have been less systematically collected than information on regional origins, but they reveal some rough proportions and trends. Analyses of expeditions of conquest along with Boyd-Bowman's samples and other sources show that during the first three decades of the century immigrants included no titled nobles and only a handful of legitimate hidalgos. Most arrivals were of base birth. Laborers and artisans predominated, followed by men-at-arms of common estate, sailors, and a few clerics and representatives of the urban middle classes. Although the rosters of expeditions generally listed an *oficio* (occupation) for each member, it is likely that many were simply adventurers or became so immediately upon arrival.

As pacification proceeded, the quality of immigrants gradually changed. Between 1540 and 1579, the proportion of hidalgos remained low, slightly over 4.0 percent of Boyd-Bowman's sample, but among commoners new types appeared. Between 1560 and 1579 one of every sixteen was a merchant or business agent. Between 1540 and 1559 almost 10.0 percent were classified as servants, and during the next twenty-year period 13.6 percent were so classified. New immigrants also included sober artisans come to ply their trades, missionaries come to evangelize the indigenes, and officials come to staff expanding agencies of royal government. Lawyers arrived in increasing numbers. Colonial governors protested that their presence only fomented unnecessary litigation, and in response the crown discouraged and, on occasion, forbade their immigration, but they continued to come. One of the most significant trends was the steady increase in the percentage of women. The sample figures are: 1493–1519, 5.6 percent (308 out of 5481); 1520–39, 6.4 percent (845 out of 13,262); 1540–59, 16.4 percent (1480 out of 9044); and 1560–79, 28.5 percent (5013 out of 17,587).

One other element in Hispanic migration to the Indies must be mentioned. Despite rigorous prohibitions, *conversos* and crypto-Jews from Spain and Portugal made their way across the Atlantic to escape the attention of the Inquisition or, like Christian Spaniards, simply to improve their lot in life. As early as 1506, ecclesiastical officials on Española denounced the steady arrival of "Hebrews," and the conquerors counted New Christians among their companies. Indeed, one of Cortés's followers became the first New World martyr of his race when he was burned at the stake for relapse into Judaism. Also, American inquisitorial records provide presumptive evidence of the presence of the People of the Book in the major urban centers, where they engaged mainly in artisanry and small entrepreneurial activities. Their numbers cannot be determined. They lived in secret communities, practiced endogamous marriage, and adjusted to their environment by adopting pseudo-Catholic practices. Unless apprehended by the Holy Office, they were not officially identified and became invisible in population counts.

Natural Increase in the European Population

It is impossible to calculate the rate of natural increase among the European population because of the lack of firm data on natality, mortality, and other variables in the demographic equation. Scattered contemporary evidence points to rapid multiplication. Despite a badly unbalanced sex ratio, the efforts of crown and church to promote domesticity bore fruit. A census of Española taken as early as 1514 revealed that Spanish wives lived with their husbands in every town on the island. The Spanish, moreover, were a fecund people, their households abounded in servants, and they populated the land in true biblical fashion. Royal cosmographer and geographer Juan López de Velasco, who between 1571 and 1574 prepared the first general census of the Indies, reported 300 *vecinos* in Asunción and "more than 2,900 children of Spanish parents."[11] Such discursive observations produce no statistics, but they suggest that by the 1560s natural increase had surpassed immigration as a source of European population growth.

Estimating the Total European Population in About 1570

Although much remains to be learned about the processes that formed the European population, the quantitative results can be estimated using López de Velasco as a point of departure. In his day censuses were not head counts of men, women, and children but enumerations of *vecinos* in a community, that is, residents who owned houses and freeholds and whose names were inscribed in registers maintained by municipal councils. To arrive at a total population, contemporaries customarily multiplied the number of *vecinos* by five, the estimated average size of a household, which included the nuclear family, dependents, and servants. Relying mainly on López de Velasco's census, the Argentine historian Angel Rosenblat estimates that 23,364 *vecinos* dwelt in the Spanish Indies around 1570.[12] Applying a conversion factor of 5 produces a total population of 116,820, or 120,000 rounded out. López de Velasco himself, however, estimated in his summary of the temporal and spiritual state of the Indies that 200 *pueblos de españoles* (Spanish towns) and around 32,000 *vecinos* existed in Spanish America, figures somewhat greater than the sums of his local counts.[13] Perhaps he made a mistake in addition, or perhaps he allowed for towns for which he did not have specific information. In any case, multiplying his general estimate of *vecinos* by 5 yields a total European population of 160,000. The count of *vecinos*, moreover, does not include clerics who dwelt in the Indies or Spaniards living in Indian communities and on rural estates.

Modern investigation tends to support an even higher figure. Some scholars believe that a multiple of 6 rather than 5 should be used to calculate the total European population in the Indies because of "the great number of children of the Spaniards" and the large numbers of relatives and hangers-on who attached themselves to patriarchal households. Applying the larger multiple to Rosenblat's tally of 23,364 *vecinos* produces a total of 140,184 and to López de Velasco's general estimate of 32,000, a total of 192,000. Woodrow Borah, furthermore, found partial downside errors in the chronicler's count in Mexico, and, if these are corrected the number of *vecinos* increases from 6114 to 10,061.[14] Whether comparable errors exist in López de Velasco's data for other regions is not certain. Let us, therefore, go along with the Argentine historian Nicolás Sánchez-Albornoz and guess that somewhere in the neighborhood of 220,000 Europeans dwelt in Spanish America around 1570.[15] At first glance this figure raises an awkward problem when compared with an estimated European immigration of 226,870. Among other things, it leaves little room for natural increase, a patently absurd result. But, assuming that Boyd-Bowman's count actually constituted a 20 percent sample, the apparent discrepancy can be accommodated by supposing that many of the persons he identified had died by 1570, some had returned to Europe, and others were not registered *vecinos*.

Some qualitative changes in the European population accompanied gross quantitative trends. As conquest merged into colonization, conquerors settled down to live on the tribute and services rendered to them by their charges. The diverse occupational types who arrived too late to become conquistadors or who, perhaps, preferred more sedate life-styles, settled in towns and cities to practice their Old World skills. The growing proportion of women immigrants encouraged family formation, and the number of female children they bore accelerated the process. Taken together, these developments created a more complex but less volatile population.

## The Indian Population

Post-Conquest Decline and Its Causes

In contrast to an ascending curve for European populators, all evidence points to a continuing decline of the indigenous population after the blows it suffered during the first stages of the Conquest. Father Las Casas blamed losses mainly on Spanish brutality — massacres, an infinite variety of tortures, and excessive labor demands. Franciscan missionary Toribio Motolinia wrote that "God struck and chastised this land [Mexico] and those who were in it . . . with ten disastrous plagues" among which he enumerated the casualties of the Conquest, the famine that followed it, the heavy tributes and services imposed on the Indians, tortures and cruel imprisonments, work in the mines, and the building of Mexico City. "In this work," Motolinia affirmed, "during the first years, more people were engaged than in the building of the temple of Jerusalem. . . . In this work numerous Indians died. . . ."[16]

But Motolinia listed as the first plague the epidemics that broke out during the Conquest, and modern scholarship confirms that the main killers were infectious diseases in epidemic form. After the first onslaught of 1520–24, which expedited the Spanish victories, pandemics swept through Mexico with almost decennial regularity: 1529–35, 1545–46, 1558.[17] The tragic story repeated itself in Central America, New Granada, Peru, and Chile. Between pandemics, local epidemics wrought further damage to the indigenous population.

The identities of the killers were several. Smallpox, as observed earlier, appeared in the Antilles in 1519. Measles struck the Caribbean in 1529 and spread to Mexico in 1531 and thence to Central America and Panama. The American pandemic of 1545 was caused mainly by a disease that the Aztecs called *matlazáhuatl* and that modern scholars think was either influenza or typhus. It devastated Mexico first and within the year affected New Granada and Peru. The Aztecs spoke of another new affliction, *cocolitzli*, that caused burning fevers. Diptheria came to the Indies, and there is some evidence that humankind's ancient enemy, the Black Death, made its appearance. Two or more diseases often worked in conjunction, and a common pattern seems to have been the onset of respiratory infections after eruptive fevers had weakened body resistance.

Demographic decline stemmed not only from immediate casualties. Epidemics carried off the young and fertile as well as pruning away the aged and infirm, and when they struck so frequently they crippled successive generations before losses could be replaced. Mobilization of Indian labor broke up families, thereby reducing reproductive capacity. Disruptions of native systems of food production and distribution occasioned by European conquest and colonization resulted in malnutrition and starvation. Arduous toil joined with malnutrition to weaken resistance to Old World diseases. Perhaps the shock of conquest also played a part in the disaster. Contemporaries reported that Indians, overcome by despair at their fate, lost their desire to live and, indeed, sickened and died by acts of will.

Europeans and their African slaves contributed to native populaton decline in a more indirect way. They took Indian women as concubines or mistresses on a large scale, frequently forming veritable harems. The subject of miscegenation is examined in detail later in this chapter, but it may be observed here that more or less permanent liaisons of these kinds withdrew Indian women from the indigenous gene pool. Mothers bore mixed-blood rather than Indian sons and daughters. The magnitude of such a drain cannot, of course, be measured.

Indian population decline appears to have come sooner and been sharper and more final in the Antilles and in tropical continental lowlands than in the highlands of the mainland. In the former regions, populations were smaller to begin with and therefore less able to withstand large losses. In them Spaniards and Africans first appeared with their Old World diseases. From them Spaniards took thousands of slaves, many of whom died from harsh treatment. In tropical zones, also, the indigenes died not only from smallpox and influenza but from malaria and, possibly, dengue fever and hookworm. And, as populations dropped sharply, Spaniards and Africans monopolized native women more fully. The highlands, in contrast, were conquered after Indian slavery had been generally proscribed. Tropical diseases did not reach these regions, and, although sickness and exploitation caused heavy losses among their population, its numbers and density provided it with strategic reserves.

The Magnitude of Decline: General and Regional

What was the magnitude of indigenous population losses in the Spanish Indies during the Conquest era? The first step toward answering the question is to review the various hemispheric estimates given in chapter 4 of this book and to adjust them to exclude Indians living in regions not conquered or occupied by Spain in the sixteenth century. The estimates, it may be recalled, were: Angel Rosenblat, 13,385,000; William Denevan, 57,300,000; and Henry Dobyns, 90,000,000 (his minimum figure). In the case of Rosenblat's calculations, a rough approximation of the native population of what became Spanish America can be obtained by subtracting from his total the 2,130,000 Indians listed by him as dwelling in North America north of the Rio Grande and in the Lesser Antilles, the Guianas, and Brazil. The result is 11,255,000. The way in which the other two hemispheric estimates are broken down regionally does not permit the same kind of calculation. Yet, regardless of differences in totals, 16 percent is a reasonable estimate of the number of indigenes in regions unconquered by Spain, and, if this percentage is subtracted from Denevan's and Dobyns's totals, the results are, respectively, 48,132,000 and 75,600,000.

The second step is to estimate the number of indigenes in the Spanish Indies toward the end of the Conquest era. Again, López de Velasco's census made around 1570 provides a point of departure, but the use of his data presents several problems. Following the common usage of the times, López did not count all Indians but rather counted only those who paid tribute. Other sources, however, indicate that his tally was incomplete. In addition, to arrive at a total figure, the number of tributaries has to be multiplied by the average size of a tributary household. Modern scholars disagree on what this factor was in the several parts of the Indies. Finally, López did not count classes of Indians not subject to tribute or groups in incompletely pacified areas who had not been made tributaries.

In calculating his hemispheric total for 1570, Rosenblat attempted to resolve these difficulties in the following way.[18] Drawing on data from other sixteenth-century sources, he adjusted the number of tributaries to 1,873,370. Then, applying a conversion factor (for the size of a tributary household) that varied regionally from 4 to 5 and adding an estimated 1,675,300 Indians living outside the tribute system, he arrived at a sum of 10,827,150. Some historical demographers believe that his conversion factor is too high, resulting in an inflated total.[19] But, since no other comprehensive figure for the period is available, let it be used for a penultimate calculation: subtracting from it 1,920,000 indigenes estimated by him as living in America north of Mexico and in the Lesser Antilles, the Guianas, and Brazil leaves a total of 8,907,150 in the Spanish Indies.

The magnitude of population decline now depends on which pre-Colombian estimate (as adjusted for Spanish America) is accepted as a base for calculations. For the three authorities cited earlier in this exercise, absolute and percentage losses are: Rosenblat, 2,347,850 (21 percent), Denevan, 39,224,850 (81 percent), and Dobyns, 66,692,850 (88 percent). Because of the conjectural nature of the estimates on which they are based, none of these figures has a real statisical value, but the two higher sets suggest that the indigenous peoples of the Spanish Indies were almost decimated in the seventy or so years following the Discovery.

More exacting regional studies confirm a picture of catastrophic losses. Borah and Cook calculated that the some 25,200,000 indigenes they proposed as the population of central Mexico in 1521 fell off to 16,800,000 by 1532, to 6,300,000 by 1548, and to 2,650,000 in 1568.[20] Comparable trends have been proposed for other parts of the Indies. Investigations by Cook and Borah corroborate earlier opinions that the native inhabitants of the Antilles had virtually disappeared by the middle of the sixteenth century and show that the Mayas of Yucatán suffered terrible losses.[21] The Scottish historian Murdo Macleod calculated that in Guatemala the Indian population of the highland pueblo of Santiago Atitlán fell from 48,000 in 1524 to 4020 in 1585, and he believes that decimation occurred throughout Central America during roughly the same period.[22] In the case of New Granada, a recent examination of the tribute and *visita* records of the province of Tunja reveals that between 1537 and 1564, the number of indigenes in that jurisdiction declined from 232,407 to 168,444.[23] As for Lower Peru, it has been generally assumed that the decline there was less precipitous and stretched over a longer period. Nonetheless, it was severe. Noble D. Cook, who has published the most comprehensive and thorough study of colonial demographic trends in that region, calculates a drop from 3,300,574 in 1520 to 1,290,680 in 1570.[24] In summary, the weight of evidence indicates that a demographic disaster of continental proportions occurred in the New World in the sixteenth century.

Qualitative changes in the indigenous population also contrasted with the European experience, which, in the main, involved constructive formation and stablization. The Four Horsemen who rode with the conquistadors destroyed ancient and stable structures. Primary families broke up into widows, widowers, and orphans, and some evidence exists that casualties ran higher among men than among women, thereby unbalancing the sex ratio. Entire communities suffered decimation, and survivors fled to distant places or wandered the countryside. The disintegration of family and community loosened kinship ties. The quantitative and qualitative devastation of the indigenous population far exceeded anything accomplished by the Black Death in Europe.

## The African Population

### Estimating the Volume of the Slave Trade

A third primary population component, the black African, began to appear in the Indies very shortly after the Discovery. Its first representatives were Hispanicized blacks whom the Spaniards brought with them as slaves or servants and whom they called *criollos* (creoles) or *ladinos*. Some left their names in history. One, Nuflo de Olano, saw the Pacific along with Balboa's company. At least one came to Mexico with Pánfilo de Narváez and allegedly introduced smallpox into the land. Perhaps the most famous was Estevanico, who accompanied the Spanish explorer Cabeza de Vaca on a long odyssey through the American Southwest (1528-36) and later served as an interpreter for Fray Marcos de Niza, who explored the New Mexico region in 1539 and saw the Seven Cities glistening on the distant horizon. Also, as early as 1510, a few *ladino* freemen and freewomen began emigrating to the Indies under license from the House of Trade and settled on Española and the other main Antilles. These early arrivals, Christian and Spanish in culture but few in number, were accepted as populators.

After the second decade of the sixteenth century *bozales* ("wild" or savage blacks) brought directly from African slaving stations became the main source of the black population. Conflicting circumstances affected the rate of their arrival. On the one hand, Spanish settlers needed them in places and situations where the supply of indigenous labor fell short or the crown restricted its use. Although a few clerics voiced moral reservations about the enslavement of blacks, Castilian kings did not object in principle. No bulls of donation imposed obligations upon them to protect Africans, and the enslavement of Africans raised no questions about just wars. On the other hand, the crown disliked using Spanish money to make purchases from the Portuguese, who controlled the source of supply. It feared that savage Africans would corrupt the morals of innocent Indians. And, since in the early days of the Atlantic slave trade many of its victims came from areas influenced by Islam, the danger existed that American indigenes would suffer religious contamination. Lastly, Africans showed a disposition to rebel against servitude. The upshot was that the king required special licenses for the introduction of slaves, a policy that in effect limited supply.[25]

The number of blacks who entered the Indies is as conjectural as the number of European immigrants, and for the same reason: data on imports are deficient in quantity and defective in quality.[26] Records of licenses issued are incomplete for most of the sixteenth century, and those surviving show only imports authorized, not numbers who actually arrived. At the African end of the slave trade, dealers and carriers recorded "bodies" loaded, but few manifests have survived or, at least, been collected, and in any case they do not account for attrition on the Atlantic passage, which might have run from 20 percent upward. At American terminals royal officials tallied imports for purposes of taxation but, again, records are incomplete and they do not include clandestine introductions. Slavers, moreover, used their trade to cloak illicit traffic in other merchandise and, to account for hold space, overdeclared the number of blacks carried. Customs officers connived with traders to manipulate import figures. Finally, the unit of account confuses calculations. It was not an individual slave but a *pieza de Indias*, that is, a unit of labor equivalent to a prime young male. Males and females who did not meet the standard counted as fractional parts, but *asientos* (contracts for the introduction of slaves) do not report fractions. Since cargoes always included blacks who were not prime, theoretically the number of heads delivered invariably exceeded the *piezas* contracted for.

Despite these difficulties, the work of the French scholars Huguette and Pierre Chaunu and of the American Philip Curtin permits a rough estimate of slave imports during the Conquest period. The Chaunus identified 263 licensed slaving ships sailing to ports in the Indies between 1551 and 1595 and, using an estimated average cargo of 138 *piezas* per vessel, calculated that 36,294 *piezas* arrived during the forty-five-year span. The annual average of imports was 810, which, when applied to the years 1551–70, yields a total of 16,200.[27] Curtin believes that on the average *piezas* equated with heads. He also conjectures that an average of 500 slaves a year was brought in between 1521 and 1550, "the total of 15,000 being intentionally large in order to account for the trickle that entered the Spanish possessions before 1521, and for some between 1551 and 1595 that might have escaped from the Chaunu net."[28] Adding the figures produced from the Chaunu average (16,200) and Curtin's supplement for the earlier years (15,000) yields a total of 31,200. This figure may be slightly high, since the general trend of the volume of the sixteenth-century Spanish American slave trade was upward, and the numbers brought in annually before 1570 probably fell below the Chaunu average for 1551–95. Nonetheless, let 31,200 be taken as a rough approximation of the number of African slaves introduced into the Indies through 1570.

Old World Origins and New
World Destinations of African Slaves

Available samples, chiefly from Mexico and Peru, indicate that around 80.0 percent of slave imports came from Senegal, Gambia, Guinea, and, after midcentury, the mouth of the Congo.[29] Most were in fact savages as contemporaries defined them, but some from Senegal and other points along the northern coast of the Gulf of Guinea were taken from civilized nations. Labor requirements determined American destinations. Concentrations appeared on the Greater Antilles, on the circum-Caribbean, in enclaves along the Pacific coasts of New Spain and Peru, and in subtropical valleys in the lower reaches of the American cordillera. In highland regions, substantial numbers labored in the gold mines of Central America and New Granada and rather more in the silver centers of northern Mexico and Upper Peru. In rural agricultural areas blacks were scattered thinly among native villages as overseers for Spanish masters, or they worked as *vaqueros* (cowhands) on ranches. Substantial numbers (perhaps a majority), however, labored as household servants, artisans, or unskilled laborers in Spanish towns and cities. Black slavery in colonial Spanish America was essentially an urban phenomenon.

## Estimates of the Total
## African Population around 1570

The slave trade was the chief source of the African population in the Indies, but, in arriving at a total, two others must be taken into account: the number of free blacks who emigrated from Spain and natural growth among both free blacks and slaves. No reliable data are available on either. The number of free blacks was probably small relative to the number of slaves, and the natural growth rate among the slave population was undoubtedly small, perhaps even negative, for several reasons. Unhealthy working environments, malnutrition, and arduous toil produced a high mortality rate among slaves working on plantations or in mines. Birth rates were held down by separation of the sexes in the organization of servile labor and by the overwhelming predominance of males over females. In addition, the degrading condition of slavery itself created psychological barriers to reproduction.

In the absence of any reliable demographic data, can a total figure be proposed? López de Velasco reported 40,000 blacks living in the Indies around 1570.[30] This figure accommodates estimated slave imports, a small number of free immigrants, and a modest natural growth rate. It is as good as any that can presently be found.

## Mixed Bloods

### Origins and Kinds

The Spanish scheme for the colonization of the Indies included only Europeans, Indians, and blacks. Another population element, however, soon appeared. It could not have been long after Columbus landed on Guanahaní that a European mariner lay with an Indian woman, who in the time allowed by nature brought forth the first of countless mestizos. Not long after that portentous accouchement blacks, free and slave, began to arrive in the New World, and the matings of blacks and whites gave birth to mulattoes and of blacks and Indians to *zambos*.

Circumstances in the Indies favored a rapid rate of miscegenation, or, as the Spanish say, *mestizaje*, among Europeans and indigenes, mainly through Spanish fatherhood. Conquerors and first settlers were predominantly males. They were virile and a long way from home. And, like the Portuguese in Africa, their perceptions of somatic and cultural deviancy did not inhibit their concupiscence. Indian women existed in unlimited abundance and were at the disposal of the Spaniards by virtue of their subjugation and not uncommonly by their inclination. Cieza de León described a mutual attraction: around Cuenca, in the kingdom of Quito, the native girls "were beautiful and not a little lascivious, and fond of the Spaniards."[31] Or perhaps the Spaniard's perception of comeliness was affected by his long separation from women of his own kind, and young Indian women may have been a bit calculating. To consort with conquerors gave them status, and the offspring of the union might aspire to join the dominant race.

Miscegenation proceeded in part through holy wedlock. Whatever their original intentions might have been, many Spanish immigrants struck roots in the Indies and wished to establish a legitimate lineage perpetuating their name. In selecting brides they considered women of their own kind to be more culturally compatible, and, although they had no strong prejudices against the color and features of Indian women, they measured desirability by their own somatic norms. Historian Gonzalo Fernández de Oviedo described the daughter of a Panamanian chieftain as "beautiful, because she in truth looked like a woman of Castile in whiteness, and in her mien and gravity."[32] There were, however, too few white brides to go around, and Spaniards who could not obtain them had to settle for what was available, preferring daughters of caciques (Indian chieftains) because of their social status and the dowries of land and labor they brought.

Public policy condoned and to some degree encouraged marriages between conqueror and conquered. Canonical law interposed no objections so long as both parties were Christians. Indeed, this principle had been explicitly declared during the conquest of the Canaries. On the other hand, crown and church inalterably opposed illegitimate cohabitation, for it violated the ideal of the unitary Christian family, which they regarded as the cornerstone of social formation in the Indies. Consequently they repeatedly enjoined *vecinos* living in sin to legitimize the union. Social and political considerations reinforced moral concerns. In 1503 Queen Isabella ordered Governor Ovando to arrange marriages between Spaniards and Indians so that within the intimate bonds of matrimony the indigenes would learn to live like Christians and loyal subjects.

The crown also encouraged racial intermarriage indirectly and perhaps unwittingly through its interest in increasing the Europeanized population and promoting social stability. In 1528 it ordered that married settlers be preferred in filling municipal offices and in 1538 that the same preference be observed in granting new *repartimientos* of Indians. In the following year it made sterner demands. It required all single men holding *repartimientos* to marry within three years under penalty of loss of their Indians. The authors of these measures probably had Spanish brides in mind, but some bachelors affected sought out Indian wives or legitimized unconsecrated unions in order to get the grants they wanted or to keep those they had.

The conditions of family formation produced not a few marriages between Spanish men and Indian women and a generation of legitimate mestizos. The 1514 Santo Domingo census showed that 54 of 146 married *vecinos* had Indian wives,[33] and Las Casas reported that in the town of Vera Paz, Guatemala, most of the 60 *vecinos* were married to natives.[34] Almost all the founders of Santa Fe de Bogotá took Chibcha brides.[35] As the century wore on, however, the number of such unions fell off, at least proportionately, because of several circumstances. The crown discovered that in the Antilles Europeans living in close association with indigenes exercised a bad rather than salutary example, and, as colonization moved to the mainland, it came around to a policy of racial segregation expressed in prohibitions against the residence of Europeans and mestizos in indigenous communities. But a demographic factor also contributed to the decline of interracial marriage. An increasing number of European women came to the Indies, and a growing population of American-born Spanish brides became available.

In the end, the conqueror-conquered relationship, the easy availability of Indian women, and the social acceptability of concubinage in Hispanic culture determined that miscegenation should proceed mainly through illegitimate unions. Virtually every conqueror from captain to peon had Indian mistresses and illegitimate mestizo offspring. Some among them performed prodigiously. One, Alvaro, a soldier in the conquest of Mexico, is said to have fathered thirty bastards within the span of three years. In Paraguay, reported Chaplain Francisco González Paniagua, "some Spaniards had seventy women; unless they were poor none had fewer than five or six; most had from fifteen to twenty and from twenty to forty."[36] It is no wonder that contemporaries came to call Asunción "Mohamet's Paradise."

A different set of circumstances affected the miscegenation of African and European. In the flexible conditions of the early Conquest years, blacks sometimes surmounted their various disabilities. Juan Valiente, a mulatto and originally a slave, participated in the conquest of Chile, won the affection and esteem of his comrades "despite his skin," received a grant of land and a *repartimiento* of Indians, and settled down as a respected *vecino* of Santiago. Such instances of acceptance, however, occurred infrequently. Although Europeans might disdain Indians' rational capacities, they held much stronger prejudices against Africans. They perceived them as savages beyond rationality and quite possibly tainted by Muslim infidelity. They were slaves or descendants of slaves and therefore infamous. Their color and features stood much further removed from the Spanish ideal of comeliness than did the Indians'. The nightmare of slave rebellions sharpened Spanish antipathies toward them.

Spanish prejudices strongly discouraged intermarriages between white and black, and, although the crown did not expressly forbid such unions, it discouraged them on the grounds that the vices of the black partner would corrupt the white and that the issue would be tainted by infamy. But neither social attitudes nor public policy discouraged Spanish men from concubinage with African women, slave and free. Indeed, settlers appeared to have esteemed black and mulatto mistresses above all others. Only a few Spaniards, generally of the lowest classes, took colored brides, and even more than mestizos, mulattoes had illegitimate origins.

The crown adamantly opposed both illegitimate and legitimate unions between black and Indian, fearing that the depraved Africans would corrupt the innocent American indigenes and spread political and religious subversion among them. As in the case of Spaniards and mestizos, it forbade blacks to live in native communities, but biological urges and social circumstances frustrated public policy. By all accounts, the African male in the Indies was sexually vigorous, while black women were in short supply and white women inaccessible, leaving only one outlet for his urges. Free blacks circulated among the indigenous population of urban centers, and in rural areas they served Spaniards as majordomos and tribute collectors. The Indians had no racial prejudice and their women identified the African with the European conqueror. Free blacks and even slaves managed to arrange liaisons with indigenous girls, and, it was reported, some collected veritable harems.

The Demographic and Cultural Destinations
of Mixed Bloods: Assimilation and Rejection

In terms of population structure, *mestizaje* led in three directions. The destiny of the mestizo varied. Those of legitimate birth were accepted socially and legally into European society, and many illegitimates did not fare badly. Hispanic cultures took a tolerant view of bastardy, and some of the great figures of the Reconquest — Alfonso I of Asturias, Ramiro of Aragon, Alvaro de Luna — were born on the wrong side of the blanket. A number of conquistadors were also illegitimate, including Francisco Pizarro, who, nevertheless, became a marquis; Cortés's captain Francisco de Lugo; and Juan de Alvarado, the brother of the conqueror of Guatemala. Many Spaniards in the Indies, moreover, felt a genuine affection and responsibility for their illicit offspring, recognizing them and legitimizing them. The will of Martín de Irala, the first governor of Paraguay, illustrates their paternal attitude.

Item. I say and declare and confess that I have and God has given me in this province certain daughters and sons, who are: Diego Martínez de Yrala and Antonio de Yrala and Doña Ginebra Martínez de Yrala, children of myself and María my servant, daughter of Pedro de Mendoza who was the principal [Guaraní] chief of this land; and Doña Ysabel de Yrala, daughter of Agueda my servant; and Doña Ursula de Yrala, daughter of Leonor my servant; and Martín Pérez de Yrala, son of Scolastica my servant; and Ana de Yrala, daughter of Marina my servant; and María, daughter of Beatriz, servant of Diego de Villalpando, and . . . I own and declare them as my sons and daughters. . . .[37]

Irala further declared that those named were to share in his estate.

The crown, if it could not prevent concubinage, favored legitimization for political as well as moral reasons and, in fact, adopted a policy of what might be called cultural legitimization. In 1533, Emperor Charles ordered that all mestizos in Mexico living with Indian mothers and relatives be brought together and given a Spanish education. This ambitious project never bore fruit, but a step in that direction was taken around midcentury with the establishment of the Colegio de San Juan de Letrán, an academy devoted to educating foundling mestizo boys and girls, and from time to time the crown issued instructions to pick up and educate illegitimate children who had no home.

Thus, illegitimate mestizos who benefited from fatherly solicitude and royal favor were also co-opted into European society, and the marriage of Spaniards with legitimate and legitimized *mestizas* produced offspring called *castizos*, who completely reverted to the European side of their lineage. In general,

Europeanization seems to have been mainly an urban phenomenon, and its main agents were the feminine *mestiza* and *castiza* rather than the male mixed blood, for the simple reason that a much greater demand existed for brides than for grooms among the European population, and Spanish suitors found legitimate *castizas* quite acceptable, particularly when they were wealthy and comely.

The second direction of *mestizaje* ran toward Indianization. Mestizos who could not find a place in Spanish society gravitated into the native sections of Spanish cities or to indigenous communities in the countryside, where they identified with the distaff side of their parentage. They commonly took Indian wives or concubines, and the product of these unions reverted completely to the conquered race. A parallel but smaller-scale process also contributed to reversion. By and large, the conquerors left the native nobility in possession of its rank and function, and, down to the lowest *cacique*, nobles tended to select wives and concubines from among Hispanicized *castizas* as status symbols. The offspring, however, became Indians.

A third direction led into a limbo inhabited by mixed bloods, illegitimate by birth, who did not find a home in primary parental groups. They included an uncounted number of mestizos but were increasingly suffused by African blood for a variety of reasons. Male slaves outnumbered female slaves two to one, forcing the excess men to mate outside their race, which in effect meant with Indians and mixed bloods. White males, moreover, appeared to have preferred black and *mulata* mistresses to Indian. Also, mestizos assimilated more easily into European and Indian societies than did mulattoes and thereby lost their hybrid identity. Mulattoes, in turn, spread their seed among *mestizas* and Indian women, and so it went.

Guessing the Mixed Blood Population

The total number of unassimilated mixed bloods is especially difficult to estimate because contemporary Spaniards saw no point in counting them. They were not *vecinos* and rate payers nor were they tributaries until declared to be so by the crown in the 1570s. In any case, a census of them would have been difficult because most had no fixed residences. López de Velasco simply reported that there were *muchos* (many) in the Indies and that their number was increasing daily.[38] In his population summaries for about 1570, Rosenblat lumps black and mixed bloods together for a total of 232,000, and, if López de Velasco's 40,000 blacks be subtracted, 192,000 mestizos, mulattoes, *zambos*, and various more complex mixtures remain.

Again, these figures are the roughest of estimates, but a partial check against them exists. Using statistical techniques developed in their studies of Indians, Cook and Borah calculated that in 1568–70, the population of Mexico between Tehuantepec and the northern limits of Spanish settlement was 2,733,412, breaking down as follows: Europeans, 62,866 (2.3 percent); mestizos, 2417 (0.1 percent); *pardos*, that is, free blacks and others with African blood, 22,566 (0.8 percent); Indians, 2,645,573 (96.8 percent).[39] These results may be suspect on the grounds that the authors had to rely on incomplete data and that they make unverifiable assumptions about the ethnic identities of many persons counted. Cook and Borah, however, do go a step beyond guessing. And in their calculations mestizos and *pardos* together amount to 24,983, a sum that closely approximates Rosenblat's total for blacks and mixed bloods in Mexico around 1570.

## The Population of the Indies around 1570: Summary Estimates

Table 1 summarizes the population of the Indies around 1570 by racial components and by regions. It is based on López de Velasco's enumerations of *vecinos* and tributaries converted into total inhabitants by Rosenblat's formulae and on Rosenblat's estimates of numbers of blacks and mixed bloods. It has several shortcomings. The figures listed are based on insufficient and defective data, and Rosenblat's methodology can easily be challenged. Other studies cited earlier suggest a larger European element, perhaps as many as 220,000, and a smaller number of Indians. The figures for blacks and mixed bloods are at best educated guesses. Furthermore, one must bear in mind that cultural as well as purely ethnic factors influenced sixteenth-century counts. The "Europeans" undoubtedly included an indeterminable number of co-opted mixed bloods, the "Indians" an uncertain number of mestizos who became Indians, legally and culturally. Yet the figures in the table are the only comprehensive set available for the closing years of the Conquest period. Although totals and subtotals may be wide of the mark, proportions by component and regional distribution fall within the range of probability.

A review of population formation during the Conquest epoch reveals several basic trends. Around 1570 the indigenous peoples still constituted more than 96.0 percent of the inhabitants of the Indies, but their growth rate was sharply negative. The number of Europeans, including assimilated mixed bloods, remained tiny, some 1.3 percent of the total. It was, however, increasing steadily, perhaps at a rate of 2.0 percent annually, primarily from natural increase,

Table 1
Estimated Population of the Spanish Indies in About 1570

| Region | Europeans | Indians | Negroes, Mixed Bloods | Totals |
|--------|-----------|---------|-----------------------|--------|
| Mexico | 30,000 | 3,500,000 | 25,000 | 3,555,000 |
| Central America | 15,000 | 550,000 | 10,000 | 575,000 |
| Española | 5000 | 500 | 30,000 | 35,500 |
| Cuba | 1200 | 1350 | 15,000 | 17,550 |
| Puerto Rico | 1000 | 300 | 10,000 | 11,300 |
| Jamaica | 300 | · · · | 1000 | 1300 |
| Colombia | 10,000 | 800,000 | 15,000 | 825,000 |
| Venezuela | 2000 | 300,000 | 5000 | 307,000 |
| Ecuador | 6500 | 400,000 | 10,000 | 416,500 |
| Peru | 25,000 | 1,500,000 | 60,000 | 1,585,000 |
| Bolivia | 7000 | 700,000 | 30,000 | 737,000 |
| Paraguay | 3000 | 250,000 | 5000 | 258,000 |
| Argentina | 2000 | 300,000 | 4000 | 306,000 |
| Uruguay | · · · | 5000 | · · · | 5000 |
| Chile | 10,000 | 600,000 | 10,000 | 620,000 |
| Totals | 118,000 | 8,907,150 | 230,000 | 9,255,150 |
| Percentage of total | 1.3 | 96.2 | 2.5 | 100.0 |

Source: Adapted from table 4 in Angel Rosenblat, La población indígena y el mestizaje en América, 1492-1950, 2 vols. (Buenos Aires: Editorial Nova, 1954), I, 88.

secondarily from immigration. The black element was also growing but more slowly, mainly through the importation of approximately 800 slaves annually.

Unassimilated mixed bloods constituted a rapidly increasing component for both social and demographic reasons. The Spanish population expanded mainly through the instrument of the monogamous Christian family, whose formation was slowed by the unbalanced sex ratio still prevailing at the end of the Conquest. But this restraint did not affect mestizaje. Despite the shrinkage of the indigenes, an abundant supply of Indian women remained, supplemented by burgeoning numbers of mestizas and mulatas and by black females, slave and free. The absence of social and moral restraints on cohabitation outside the narrow confines of the European community, along with universal male dominance, made this breeding stock easily accessible to sires of all races.

Demographic trends during the Conquest had far-reaching effects on the formation of the Spanish colonial regime. During the early years of their presence in America, the Europeans could rule tens of millions of Indians and exploit their labor and production through native potentates in much the same manner as did the Portuguese and, later, the English and the Dutch in Southeast Asia. Indeed, the Spaniards had no alternative to this method. The disastrous decline of the indigenous population that followed, however, induced them to intervene more directly in the governance of the Indians in order to conserve and allocate a shrinking supply of labor. In addition, large indigenous population losses facilitated the appropriation of land by the Spaniards and encouraged the growth of the great estate. Another important demographic development was the formation of a multiracial or multiethnic population. Its several elements, with statuses assigned by the conquering race, became the constituent groups of the colonial social order.

# CHAPTER 7

# Instruments of Colonization:
# The Castilian *Municipio*

## The Purposes of Municipalities

The Castilian *municipio* constituted the main instrument of European colonization by virtue of tradition, necessity, and policy. The Spaniards could conceive of no other way to live together; a republic was a city. Ample precedent
existed from the Spanish Reconquest; the valley of the Duero and Old and
New Castile had been settled and secured by the founding of towns. In a vast
and hostile New World, moreover, Europeans had to gather in nucleated
settlements not only for physical security but for defense against loneliness.
The crown understood all of these things and also that the municipality provided the only device immediately at hand to organize vast territories, to distribute land and other resources, and to reduce restless bands of conquerors
to civility.

## The Siting and Layout of Towns

As exploration revealed the immensities of the New World, Castilian monarchs
evinced an intense interest in the location and physical layout of towns, recognizing, perhaps, that as in other matters America offered an opportunity to
begin anew, avoiding mistakes of the European past. When Governor Pedrarias
Dávila founded Panama in 1519, he followed royal instructions that he had
brought with him. These read in part:

Let the city lots be regular from the start, so that once they are marked out
the town will appear well ordered as to the place which is left for a plaza, the site
for the church and the sequence of the streets; for in places newly established,

proper order can be given from the start, and thus they remain ordered with no extra labor or cost; otherwise order will never be introduced.[1]

Four years later Emperor Charles set forth more general prescriptions for siting and laying out towns in the Indies. They were to be placed in proximity to water and building materials and should have pastures and firewood nearby. Furthermore, "sites for settlement are not to be selected in very high places, because of discomfort from the winds and difficulties of service and transportation, nor in very low places, near swamps and lagoons, because they are generally unhealthy, but they are to be located in moderate altitudes, and in places where winds from north and south blow freely." Sites subject to fogs were to be avoided, and, if on a river, they should be located so that the rising sun shown first on the town and was not reflected from the water's surface into the eyes of the inhabitants. Slaughterhouses, stockyards, fishmarkets, and "other dirty and ill-smelling businesses" were to be situated outside of the town precincts, preferably across a river or on the seashore.[2]

Although guided in a general way by royal instructions, populators in the field made ad hoc decisions about when and where to found towns on the basis of their immediate requirements. These might include a coastal base for penetrating the interior and advanced posts en route to their objectives. They almost always included a location from which conquered territory could be dominated and that had an immediate supply of Indian labor. The Conquest, however, proceeded at such a headlong pace that founders often made mistakes in town siting. They misjudged the lay of the land, the salubrity of the climate, or the strategic value of a location or discovered that persistent native hostility rendered a site untenable. Or they could not anticipate that future communications routes might pass them by, that declines in the indigenous population would leave them short of labor, and that hurricanes, floods, and earthquakes might damage or destroy communities. In many instances, therefore, towns had to be abandoned or refounded on new sites. Also, settlers moved about restlessly from one town to another, seeking brighter prospects or evading royal justice. These circumstances gave early European colonization in the Indies a very unstable character.

## The Founding of Towns: The "Act of Foundation"

The imperatives that guided settlement created the most typical sixteenth-century Spanish American municipality, which may appropriately be called the "conquest town." It was founded *por via de capitulación*, that is, by the authority granted to adelantados in their patents and instructions. The founding took place "according to the customs and order of founders observed in the lands of Castile" and began with a formal "Act of Foundation," duly recorded, witnessed, and notarized. The ceremony commonly proceeded as follows. The captain or *adelantado* drew up his company in military formation and with arms at present before a tree or implanted stake (*arbol de justicia*) that symbolized royal justice. Then, in full martial accoutrements, he mounted his steed, proclaimed in a loud voice that on behalf of the king he proposed to found a town of Spaniards on that site, and gave it a name commonly compounded of a prefix honoring a saint or the Holy Virgin and a suffix associated with some secular attribute of the location. (More than 200 places in Latin America still commemorate Santiago.) He then commanded that anyone who would gainsay him stand forth to defend his opposition at point of sword or lance. If no one answered the challenge, the founder dismounted, announced that he took possession of the new land in order to found there a city or town in His Majesty's name, and struck the tree of justice five ringing blows with his unsheathed sword. The soldiers responded by discharging their harquebuses and shouting in one voice, "Viva el Rey." The notarized record of the act was then sent to the king.

## The Establishment of Municipal Governments

A number of practical measures followed the ceremonial act. The founder appointed or, in some cases, the company elected the *justicia* of the town consisting of two *alcaldes ordinarios* (municipal magistrates) and its *regimiento* (aldermen), generally four to eight in number. *Justicia* and *regimiento* together constituted the municipal council, called, in the Indies, a *cabildo* or *ayuntamiento*. All the founders inscribed their names in the Book of the Cabildo as *vecinos*, and municipal government was rounded out by the appointment of an *alférez real* (herald and standard bearer), an *alguacil mayor* (chief constable), a *fiel ejecutor* (inspector of weights, measures, and prices), a *receptor de penas* (collector of fines), and a *síndico* or *procurador general* who was the attorney and spokesman for the town.

## The Founding of Parishes

As in Reconquest Hispania, the Spaniards created a parish simultaneously with a civil community. The *vecinos* became parishioners by inscribing their names on the parish register, and the senior chaplain of the company provided the curate. Early in the existence of the community, the settlers formed a *cofradía*, a lay brotherhood that had the functions of raising funds for the construction and support of the church; providing aid to the poor, aged, or infirm and to widows and orphans; and, by no means the least, organizing merry processions and festivities on the numerous saints' days that sprinkled the Hispanic religious calendar. By these several acts, an expedition of conquest became transformed into a civil and religious corporation, and conquistadors into *primeros pobladores* (first or original settlers), a class that enjoyed high status in the early society of the Indies and held preeminent claims on the generosity and mercy of the king.

## Territorial Jurisdictions of Municipalities

The municipality was also the first and primary unit of territorial jurisdiction in the Indies. As in Castile, its authority included not only its urban nucleus called the *fondo legal* but a *término* extending in all directions to the limits of other towns that might exist in the district. In newly conquered or thinly settled regions, towns encompassed vast expanses of territory. In 1519–20, Veracruz theoretically included all of Mexico, known and unknown, and after the founding of Mexico City in 1521 its *cabildo* claimed jurisdiction eastward to the limits of Veracruz and, in other directions, over all of New Spain. In New Granada, the *término* of Popayán ran sixty-six miles to the north and sixty miles to the south. Municipal boundaries, however, were defined only in loose metes and bounds, and, as new settlements filled in interstices, frequent jurisdictional disputes among *cabildos* occurred.

## Municipal Grants of Lots, Lands, and Indians

After the formal acts of foundation, the populators attended to the physical organization of the new municipality. A surveyor laid out the town plan "by line and rule," first defining a rectilinear *plaza mayor* (main or central plaza), which would be the center of community life. He then designated streets running perpendicular to each of its sides and others intersecting them at right angles to form blocks, usually divided into four lots each. The founder retained the most desirable lots and distributed the remainder to the *vecinos* with choice determined by rank among them. Generous space was reserved around the main plaza for a church and public buildings.

Outside the town proper, the founder or, by delegation from him, the *cabildo* set aside an *ejido* (commons), allocated lands to provide income for the municipal government and the parish, and made *repartimientos* of agricultural and grazing properties to *vecinos*. The basic units of private distribution were *peonías* for foot soldiers and *caballerías* for horsemen, both being of Reconquest origin. In 1513 the crown laid down specifications for their size and quality. The *peonía* was to be large enough to maintain a *vecino* and his household and might be a hundred acres or less. The *caballería* was about five times as great and could run to a thousand acres. In practice, size varied according to the quality of the land, and distribution was to be made so that each person received "part of the good and part of the middling and part of the worst." Allocations might be made in multiples of basic units, although, for the most part, individuals were limited to five *peonías* or three *caballerías*.

Conditions of tenure also derived from Reconquest precedents. All newly conquered lands were regarded as *tierras de realengo* (royal lands). To encourage colonization, the crown delegated by *capitulación* the authority to make *repartimientos* to *adelantados* and *cabildos* but reserved the right to confirm such distributions. Recipients were required to build a house on their town lots and to put their rural properties to productive use within a specified period of time, commonly five years. If they did so, they acquired usufruct in heredity and perpetuity, although the crown retained ultimate title. If they did not, the properties reverted to the royal domain. Lands not included in municipal distributions remained crown lands and could be granted by royal *merced* to corporations and to deserving individuals who might or might not be first settlers. *Realengos* lying within a municipality's *término*, however, remained under its political jurisdiction in the first instance.

Very often founders also made *repartimientos* of Indians of the region, reserving a substantial portion for themselves and allocating the remainder among *vecinos* by rank. The crown, however, was very sensitive about the disposition of its native subjects by private persons. It conceded authority to *adelantados* to make distributions reluctantly and provisionally and insisted on the right to confirm or disallow such actions.[3]

All in all, the forms and procedures of early colonization in the Indies suggest a historical continuity with the repopulation of Castile and Leon during the Reconquest. In neither instance did towns grow organically from crossroads markets, religious centers, or fortified strongholds. In both situations they were created ex nihilo to occupy and secure lands empty of Christian inhabitants.

## The Construction of Towns

The Spaniards began to build their towns at once, employing drafted Indian labor supervised by settlers who knew something of construction principles and methods. Their first residences were temporary and made from whatever materials happened to be at hand—wood, wattle, or adobe. They gave rather more care to constructing the church and public buildings, using, when available, quarried stone or rubble from demolished Indian structures. It took a decade or more to raise the monumental edifices and extensive utilities that characterized even the more modest colonial Spanish-American municipalities. It is rather curious that in view of their strategic and military functions very few conquest towns had permanent walls, except for those on the Araucanian frontier. In Mexico, and occasionally elsewhere, the Spaniards met the requirements of defense by fortifying the nucleus rather than the periphery. They placed their churches in great courtyards surrounded by crenelated walls and provided the main edifice with battlements, embrasures, and sometimes moats.[4]

## The Course of Town Founding

### The Caribbean Islands

Different natural and human environments, along with the irregular rhythm of conquest, produced different rates and patterns of urbanization in the several regions of the Indies. In the Antilles, the process at first moved along rapidly. Between 1502 and 1515, the Spaniards founded twenty-seven towns on the four major islands. Between 1520 and 1530, however, the exhaustion of the gold fields, the dwindling of the native population, and the magnet of mainland conquests not only halted the foundation of new towns but led to the abandonment of many existing ones. Intermittent raids by French corsairs during the next two decades discouraged the growth of surviving municipalities and forced the resiting of some coastal settlements in the interior. The most significant step taken was to move Havana in 1519 from the southern to the northern coast of Cuba in order to place it on the Gulf Stream, which carried the outbound traffic of the Indies eastward to the Atlantic. The transfer allowed the city to develop into one of the major ports of the Indies.

The Spaniards gave scant attention to the other Caribbean islands, except as sources for slaves. They discovered and named the Lesser Antilles but made no attempt to settle them. Carib Indians inhabited most of them, and these tribes were much fiercer than the Arawaks of the Greater Antilles, as well as being cannibalistic. No incentive, moreover, existed for conquering the smaller islands. They held no gold; most had dense forest cover that made them unsuitable for grazing, and, while northeast trades made them easily approachable from the Atlantic, contrary winds hampered access from settlements in the Greater

Antilles. For practical purposes, Florida was insular and was regarded as a part of the northern Caribbean. Several expeditions went there in the first half of the sixteenth century but found nothing to induce them to conquer and settle the region. In summary, by the 1560s the insular Caribbean was only sparsely settled. Santo Domingo was its only major city, and it had seen better days. Havana was only beginning to stir as a rendezvous and revictualing station for fleets bound homeward to Spain.

## Mexico

In central Mexico, conditions favored the rapid foundation of European municipalities. The advanced indigenous civilizations already possessed a well-developed network of settlements that suggested to the conquerors the most advantageous sites for conquest towns. The Spaniards subjugated the natives swiftly, and despite the ravages of post-Conquest epidemics enough Indians survived to support a substantial European population. In addition, Cortés promoted colonization vigorously and effectively. By 1531 some fifteen municipalities had been founded in this region. Chief among them was the City of Mexico, raised on the site of the Aztec capital of Tenochtitlán.

From central Mexico colonization followed conquest in three directions. One led into highland Guatemala and El Salvador. Here, also, a substantial sedentary Indian population lived in organized communities that, after offering brisk initial opposition, surrendered to Spanish domination. By 1531 six European municipalities existed in the two provinces. Another line of colonization led into Yucatán, but the lowland Mayas put up a stubborn and prolonged resistance, and the Spaniards did not found their first permanent towns there until the 1540s. Even then, settlement proceeded slowly, and, as late as 1570, the peninsula contained only four towns populated by scarcely 300 *vecinos* in all.

The third line of settlement ran north and west from central Mexico, first into New Galicia. Here, in the early 1530s, several towns were founded, including Guadalajara (1531), which became the capital of the Kingdom of New Galicia although it had to be resited twice. Spanish settlement of these territories, however, was precarious. The subjugated Mixton Indians harbored bitter resentments against the brutal treatment they had suffered during their conquest, and to the north and west savage Chichimeca tribes roamed a vast and barren *despoblado*. In 1540 the two Indian groups formed an alliance, began to attack European communities, and even managed to besiege Guadalajara. The uprising required mobilization of all the resources of New Spain, and only after several months of bloody campaigning did the Spanish manage to put it down. After the Mixton war, the advance of settlement resumed, but by means other than the founding of conquest towns. Beginning with a great silver strike at Zacatecas in 1546 and extending through the 1560s, mining settlements appeared in the desert regions north and west of the Valley of Mexico. The mines had to be supplied and miners fed, and, to meet the need, the Spaniards traced a highway from Mexico City to Zacatecas, with roads leading from it to other mining communities. A little later they opened a track linking Zacatecas and Guadalajara. In the lands along these routes, they established ranches that produced wheat and cattle. They also had to protect the mines and the roads leading to them against the still hostile Chichimecas, and, as one element of defense strategy, they founded towns at key sites along communication routes. In this manner the triangle Mexico City-Zacatecas-Guadalajara was secured and settled. Its heart was a large region of fertile river bottoms and rich grasslands that came to be called the Bajío and which developed into the breadbasket of northern New Spain.

Central America

The colonization of Central America south of Guatemala and El Salvador proceeded slowly. Panama was the first permanent settlement (1519), but its hinterland lacked the agricultural resources and a sufficient supply of Indian labor to support a stable European population. It survived mainly as a trade and communications center linking Peru with the Caribbean and the route to Europe. Nombre de Dios, its counterpart on the other side of the isthmus, was founded first in 1510, was soon abandoned, and was refounded in 1519, but it amounted to little more than a roadstead, populated only when fleets from Spain arrived.

To the north and the west of Panama, the dense Indian population in the basin surrounding Lake Nicaragua provided the first attraction for settlement, and here the lieutenants of Pedrarias founded Granada in 1524 and Leon in 1525. These towns at first served mainly as centers for rounding up and marketing slaves, but, after this resource had been depleted and the slave trade proscribed, they became agricultural communities subsisting on the labor and production of the surviving natives. The Spaniards also found gold in the streams draining west and north from the mountains of Nicaragua and Honduras into the Caribbean, but tumbled terrain and hostile Indians made access to the fields difficult, and they tended to be quickly exhausted. As a consequence of these circumstances, Nicaragua west of the lake remained largely uncolonized. In Honduras the conquerors founded the Caribbean port of Trujillo in 1525 and

Gracias a Dios ten years later, but native intransigence and contentions among the Spaniards delayed effective colonization of the interior until the 1540s. As late as 1570, the province held only 200 to 300 Spaniards scattered among six insignificant towns. It was not until the 1560s that settlers penetrated into the volcanic basin of Costa Rica and founded Cartago (1564).

## South America

The colonization of the northern littoral of South America ran into even more formidable obstacles. Much of the coast was low lying, swampy, and fever ridden, and rain forests covered the hinterland. The Indian population was sparse, warlike by disposition, and highly sensitized against the Spaniards because of slave raids that had been directed against it since the beginning of the century. On what is now the Caribbean coast of Colombia, conquerors founded Santa Marta in 1525 and Cartagena in 1533, but there was not much to conquer around either town. Both struggled along as centers for barter, slaving, and grave-robbing until the settlement of the highlands of New Granada established them as port cities serving the interior. Even then their situation remained precarious because of intermittent French corsair raids along the coasts of Tierra Firme during the middle decades of the century.

On the Venezuelan coast, the Spaniards founded four towns in the early 1500s as slaving or pearling stations, but only two—Cumaná (1520 or 1521) and Coro (1527 or 1528)—survived for long. A third, París, came to nothing, and in 1541 a hurricane struck the fourth, New Cádiz, causing its inhabitants to move to a new location, which they later abandoned. In the third quarter of the century, fourteen new communities including Caracas (1567) were established in the more temperate and salubrious valleys of the interior of the province, but they had to fight desperately to maintain themselves against Indian attacks and lacked a sufficient labor supply. Some were abandoned, and a plague of ants forced one to relocate. In 1570 only eight towns remained in the province, and they were populated by a scant 200 *vecinos*, all of them poor.

As in central Mexico, circumstances in the northern Andes favored rapid European colonization. In the mountain valleys and basins of this region lived a dense population of agricultural Indians who, after brisk but short-lived resistance, were pacified and put to work. By chance, furthermore, their conquerors included a number of men who looked beyond the extraction of loot and booty. In 1534 the energetic colonizer Sebastián Belalcazar founded San Francisco de Quito in the center of a valley running north and south through highland Ecuador and blessed with rich, well-watered soil, an industrious Indian population, and a springlike climate. In 1535 the Spaniards founded Puertoviejo on the Pacific to serve the interior. Fire destroyed it a short time thereafter, but its populators moved to the rival port of Guayaquil, established in the same year.

From Quito, Belalcazar moved north into the valley of the upper Cauca River and there between 1536 and 1540 founded several towns whose prosperity was stimulated by gold strikes in tributary streams. In the higher valleys to the north and east, the conquerors pacified the Chibcha peoples quickly and found in their territories a well-distributed network of native administrative centers. In the late 1530s and through the 1540s, the Spaniards established on or near these sites their own towns, including Santa Fe de Bogotá (1538), which became the Spanish capital of the kingdom of New Granada. Also in the 1540s, the first of a series of gold strikes on the middle reaches of the Cauca and the tributary Nechí initiated the settlement of the mountainous region lying above the river to the east, which later became known as Antioquia. In the 1550s a line of towns appeared, running along the easternmost spur of the Andes to the confines of Venezuela. Highland New Granada's main connection with the outside world, however, led down the Magdalena Valley to Santa Marta and Cartagena on the Caribbean through a *despoblado* of jungles and swamps, and shoals, rapids, shifting channels, and flood runoffs hampered the navigation of the river itself. As a result, vast regions between the uplands and the coast remained virtually unsettled, and Bogotá and its subordinate towns were isolated from other centers of American empire and from metropolitan Spain.

In Peru urbanization lagged for nearly a generation after the foundation of such early conquest towns as Cuzco (1534) and Trujillo and Lima (1535). The vast extent of the kingdom and the rugged terrain of the central Andes made for difficult communications between regions and districts. The much-touted roads of the Incas pointed out directions to conquerors but did not serve well for transport. Having been built mainly for human bearers, they were narrow and ascended precipitous slopes by long stretches of steps that horses and even mules found impossible to mount. Instabilities occasioned by native intransigence and civil wars among the conquerors also slowed European settlement. Not until royal governors established a measure of internal order did colonization move forward significantly, first into Upper Peru (roughly modern Bolivia) after the discovery of a mountain of silver that came to be called Potosí, in 1545 and then slowly south and east from this region into northern Argentina, where *entradas* founded several isolated towns in the 1550s and 1560s. It is a defensible proposition that, although the Potosí mines encouraged the settlement of immediately adjacent territory, they constituted overall a deterrent to colonization because they diverted attention and resoures from town founding in regions that did not promise spectacular bonanzas. In any event, by 1570, when New Spain boasted thirty-five Spanish municipalities, New Granada thirty, and Ecuador thirty, the vast reaches of Lower and Upper Peru together held only twenty-one.[5]

Spanish colonization in the southern part of the continent occurred in rather distinctive circumstances. When, in 1541, Indian hostility forced the Spaniards to abandon Buenos Aires, they moved far up the Paraná River into Paraguay and there founded the town of Asunción. For three decades it was the only Spanish municipality in the basin of the vast Rio de la Plata system and, indeed, in the heartlands of South America.

On the western side of the Andes, conquerors established themselves in the central valley of Chile with the foundation of Santiago in 1541, but because of determined native resistance settlement proceeded slowly and, on occasion, suffered serious reverses. Indians destroyed Santiago eight months after its founding, and the city had to be rebuilt. During the next decade, the Spaniards pushed slowly into Arauco, the land of the Araucanians, where they founded Concepción and Imperial in 1550 and Valdivia two years later. But in 1553 the Araucanians rose in a general revolt under the leadership of their brilliant chieftain Lautaro, forcing settlers to abandon their southern outposts and threatening central Chile itself. A total mobilization of the European population and five years of hard and bloody campaigning were required to regain lost territory and establish a precarious and shifting frontier south of the Bío Bío River. Even afterward, Chile remained a military colony and a military society. Meanwhile, with expansion to the south blocked by continued native resistance and that to the north by the Atacama desert, colonization moved eastward across the Andes. In 1561 settlers from Santiago founded the towns of San Juan and Mendoza in what is now western Argentina.

## Classification of Towns by Function, Size, and Status

Table 2 shows the results of town founding in the Indies during the first eighty years of Spanish dominion. The communities enumerated in the table can be classified in several ways, beginning with function and structure.[6] By virtue of good judgment or good luck in site selection, a few conquest towns evolved into centers of civil and ecclesiastical administration. By 1570 Mexico City and Lima, the "City of the Kings," were the respective metropolises of North and

Table 2
Urbanization in the Spanish Indies in About 1570

| Region | Spanish Towns and Cities |
|---|---|
| Mexico | 35 |
| Central America | 26 |
| Española | 10 |
| Cuba | 8 |
| Puerto Rico | 3 |
| Jamaica | 3 |
| New Granada | 30 |
| Venezuela | 12 |
| Ecuador | 30 |
| Peru | 15 |
| Upper Peru (Bolivia) | 6 |
| Paraguay | 1 |
| Argentina | 2 |
| Chile | 11 |
| Total | 192 |

*Source:* Angel Rosenblat, *La población indígena y el mestizaje en América, 1492-1950*, 2 vols. (Buenos Aires: Editorial Nova, 1954), I, 88. Rosenblat derives his count mainly from Juan López de Velasco, *Geografía y descripción universal de las Indias*, ed. Don Marcos Jiménez de Espada, Biblioteca de Autores Españoles vol. 48 (Madrid: Ediciones Atlas, 1971), *passim*.

South America. Both were the capitals of New World viceroyalties, the seats of metropolitan dioceses, and mercantile and financial centers. They were also the main loci of intellectual and cultural life. They possessed *colegios* (secondary schools). In 1551 the crown decreed the establishment of the Royal and Pontifical University of Mexico, which opened its doors in 1553. The king also authorized, in 1551, the founding of the University of San Marcos in Lima, but the institution was not endowed and organized until twenty-five years later.

The monumental architecture of Mexico City and Lima attested to their magnificence. Each boasted a viceregal palace, a cathedral (in both cases still under construction), and a municipal hall of impressive proportions. Both were centers of regal ceremony with well-developed social hierarchies. Present at high masses held in the cathedral to celebrate important occasions such as the crowning of kings or the birth of princes were His Excellency the Archbishop, who conducted the services; His Excellency the Viceroy; the learned lawyers of the audiencias (high courts) that sat in each city; the deans and canons of the cathedral chapter; the abbots and priors of metropolitan convents; the members of the distinguished *Cabildo*; *caballeros*; and other notable *vecinos*. All were seated according to rank and status, a provision that caused endless contentions over preeminence. Outside the portals the viceroy's halbardier guard stood at attention, ready to present arms when the host was raised. In the courtyard gathered lesser folk—artisans, shopkeepers, vendors of food and drink, transients, and pickpockets. In the homes of even the lowliest Spaniards, Indian servants swept, washed, polished, and prepared repasts in anticipation of their masters' return.

In addition to the two metropolises, administrative centers of secondary rank existed from New Spain to Chile. They were Guadalajara in the Kingdom of New Galicia, Santiago de Guatemala in the Kingdom of Guatemala, Santa Fe de Bogotá in the New Kingdom of Granada, San Francisco de Quito in the Kingdom of Quito, Cuzco in the Kingdom of Peru, and Santiago in the Kingdom of Chile. All except Santiago de Chile were seats of royal audiencias; all were cathedral cities where bishops dwelt. Although less populous and splendid than Mexico City or Lima, they possessed thriving mercantile communities and socially diverse inhabitants.

A second type of European settlement, the most numerous in the Indies, also evolved from conquest towns. This was the agricultural community, which depended for its existence on the fields and pastures in its hinterland. In some, the *vecinos* were mainly *encomenderos*, that is, those who held *repartimientos* of Indians and whose subsistence came from the tributes and services rendered by their charges. Various service sectors catered to their requirements and those of their enormous families, legitimate and illegitimate, while parish clergies ministered to their spiritual needs. Thus, in 1570, Asunción in the province of Paraguay, had "somewhere in the neighborhood of three hundred *vecinos*, almost all *encomenderos*, and more than two thousand, nine hundred children born in the land of Spanish parents, who sustain themselves from the products of the soil and trade in them."[7] Mendoza, in trans-Andean Chile, had twenty-eight to thirty *vecinos*, all of them *encomenderos*. In Cali, in the New Kingdom of Granada, twenty-four of the thirty-six *vecinos* were *encomenderos*; Valladolid, in New Spain, numbered thirty-six *encomenderos* among its fifty *vecinos*.

Other agricultural towns had few if any *encomenderos*, because peculiar circumstances attending their founding had placed them in localities where there were no pacified Indians, because the native population had virtually disappeared, because available *repartimientos* had been granted to monasteries in the vicinity or to absentee lords living in the large administrative centers, or because the crown had retained or resumed control of the Indians of their districts. Their principal *vecinos* hired labor to husband their fields, herds, and flocks or, in some poor regions, toiled themselves. Thus, Cuenca in the Kingdom of Quito had eighty *vecinos*, of whom only three were *encomenderos*, the rest being small farmers and ranchers. Although some 8000 native tributaries existed in the district, they had been commended to other parties. Coro, in Venezuela, was a provincial capital and the seat of a diocese, but it had only thirty *vecinos*, all poor, with no *encomenderos* among them. The 200 tributaries in the province were commended to the church but provided such a scanty income that the bishop and other ecclesiastical officials rarely came to the city, and there was talk of moving the diocesan capital to a more prosperous location. Antequera de Oaxaca, in New Spain, a provincial capital and the seat of a diocese, had 350 *vecinos*, all "poor and needy." Although an abundance of Indians lived in the province, most belonged to the *repartimientos* of the Cortés family.

The mining centers in Mexico and Upper Peru made up a third type of settlement. Most of them were not properly founded. They began simply as camps and only later became municipalities by royal grace. They had a distinctive population mix exemplified by the Imperial Villa of Potosí, whose 400 European inhabitants included no *encomenderos* but rather were almost all miners, merchants, and shopkeepers.

Port cities constituted a fourth urban type. Some, such as Veracruz, Panama, and Cartagena, began as bases for conquests. Later, as commerce developed with Spain, their fortunate locations encouraged their evolution into maritime centers. Others such as Callao, in Peru, were founded specifically as ports. Like mining communities, their primary function gave them a distinctive population. Of Cartagena's 250 *vecinos* in 1570, only 16 were *encomenderos* and the rest merchants and traders. Merchants also predominated among the *vecinos* of Veracruz and of Panama, where, because of the lack of Indians and farms, commerce was the only available form of livelihood.

A fifth type of settlement had primarily defense functions and might be classified as praetorian. It guarded the outposts of the empire against intruders. Its inhabitants consisted mainly of garrison troops and a small service sector. In 1570 the presidios of St. Augustine, Santa Elena, and San Pedro in the province of Florida were the only pure cases of this type. Their total enumerated population consisted of about 150 officers and men whose civic status was not clearly defined. However, some cities and towns in other parts of the Indies had a marked military character. On the southern frontier of Chile, settlements were fortified, and their principal citizens, mainly *encomenderos*, were prepared to stand to arms. Havana, Veracruz, and Cartagena were primarily ports serving commerce, but they, too, were fortified and their inhabitants organized into militia companies to withstand corsair attacks.

Municipalities can also be ranked and classified by the size of their populations, which, in the sixteenth century, meant the number of *vecinos* they boasted. Such a ranking is made in tables 3 and 4. Except for the two cities of first rank, the municipalities tabulated in table 4 would not qualify as urban centers by modern quantitative standards even if total populations were counted instead of *vecinos* only. The smallest among them, however were more than

Table 3
The Twenty-Five Largest Municipalities in the
Spanish Indies in About 1570

| Municipality | Number of Vecinos |
|---|---|
| Mexico City, Mexico | 3000 |
| Lima, Peru | 2000 |
| Cuzco, Peru | 800 |
| Bogotá, New Granada | 600 |
| Guanajuato, Mexico | 600 |
| Guatemala City, Guatemala | 500 |
| Puebla, Mexico | 500 |
| Santo Domingo, Española | 500 |
| Panama, Panama | 400 |
| Potosí, Upper Peru | 400 |
| Arequipa, Peru | 400 |
| Oaxaca, Mexico | 350 |
| Santiago, Chile | 350 |
| Asunción, Paraguay | 300 |
| Guamango, Peru | 300 |
| Huánuco, Peru | 300 |
| Orepeso, Upper Peru | 300 |
| Trujillo, Peru | 300 |
| Zacatecas, Mexico | 300 |
| Cartagena, New Granada | 250 |
| Ciudad Real de Chiapas, Mexico | 200 |
| Veracruz, Mexico | 200 |
| Granada, Nicaragua | 200 |
| Chachapoyas, Peru | 200 |
| San Juan, Puerto Rico | 200 |

*Source:* Juan López de Velasco, *Geografía y descripción universal de las Indias*, ed. Don Marcos Jiménez de Espada, Biblioteca de Autores Españoles, vol. 48 (Madrid: Ediciones Atlas, 1971), *passim*.

Table 4
Ranking of Municipalities in the Spanish Indies by
Population in About 1580

| Attributed Rank | Number of *Vecinos* | Number of Towns | Total Number of *Vecinos* in Rank | Percentage of *Vecinos* in the Indies |
|---|---|---|---|---|
| I | 2000 or more | 2 | 5000 | 22 |
| II | 500 or more | 6 | 3500 | 15 |
| III | 90 or more | 50 | 9730 | 42 |
| IV | 25 to 90 | 85 | 4030 | } 21 |
| V | 10 to 25 | 46 | 756 | |
| Totals | | 189 | 23,016 | 100 |

Source: Adapted from tables 2 and 4 in Jorge E. Hardoy and Carmen Aranovich, "Urban Scales and Functions in Spanish America Toward the Year 1600: First Conclusions," *LARR*, 5 (no. 3): 60, 77 (Fall 1970). As in the case of Rosenblat, Hardoy and Aranovich derive their count from López de Velasco, *Geografía y descripción universal de las Indias*, ed. Don Marcos Jiménez de Espada, Biblioteca de Autores Españoles, vol. 48 (Madrid: Ediciones Atlas, 1971), *passim*, but they show two fewer towns than Lopéz.

mere villages and hamlets. They performed urban functions of an administrative, economic, religious, and social nature and provided the services and amenities that the Spaniards thought essential in a republic.

Sixteenth-century Spaniards ranked municipalities by status, just as they did social classes and people, and *vecinos* were quite sensitive about the position of their community in the urban hierarchy. The most distinguished rank was *ciudad* (city); the second, *villa* (roughly, town); and the lowest, *pueblo* (peasant village). In the Indies few European *pueblos* could be found, since there were no admitted Spanish peasants. The Indians provided the American equivalent, and it was they who lived in *pueblos*. A newly founded *ciudad* or *villa* acquired its rank by royal grant, the criteria being the preeminence or promotional ability of the founder, the crown's perception of the service rendered by its foundation, and its anticipated size and influence. Promotion from *villa* to *ciudad* was possible by royal favor, but rank, once obtained, was rarely lost. Many communities were founded as cities but, when the tides of empire passed them by, retained their status as in the case of Santiago de los Caballeros, on Española. It was founded with high hopes in the early 1500s but had only seventy *vecinos* in 1570. The status of both *villas* and *ciudades* could be enhanced by obtaining from the king coats of arms and special honorary titles.

Thus Potosí became the Imperial Villa of Potosí, and Mexico City, Cartagena, Santa Fe, and other cities won the designation "Very Noble and Very Loyal."[8]

Some rough correlations exist among function, size, and status. Among the eight communities making up ranks I and II in table 4, five—Mexico City, Lima, Bogotá, Guatemala City, and Santo Domingo—were major administrative centers, the seats of audiencias and dioceses, and enjoyed the status of *ciudad*. Of the remaining three, Cuzco ranked as *ciudad* and, although it was not the home of an audiencia, was a cathedral city and an important provincial capital. Puebla had exactly the same attributes. Guanajuato was only a *villa* and owed its ranking to its mining boom. Moving into rank III, correlations disappear, but in ranks IV and V, small, agricultural-based *villas* predominate.

## Urban Planning

The physical plans of cities and towns in the Indies varied in a way that bore some relation to function. Most were initially laid out on a gridiron pattern. The orgins of this arrangement are uncertain. Some architectural historians hold that crown and colonists were directly influenced by Italian Renaissance town planners who, in turn, drew their inspiration from classical Roman architects, particularly Vitruvius. Empirical evidence supports this proposition in cases of town planning in the later decades of the sixteenth century, but meanwhile the Spaniards did not have to go very far afield for either guiding theory or example. The Catalan Francex Eiximenic (1340–1409) published a treatise on proper urban layouts in which he not only laid down the requirments for siting but prescribed a formal gridiron plan centered on a main plaza, a cathedral, and civic buildings. Also, physical models existed in Spain. During the twelfth, thirteenth, and fourteenth centuries, a number of cities were constructed with regular geometric plans, and the *castra* (fortified camps) built by the Catholic Kings during the last campaigns against the Moors provided a more immediate precedent. The camp of Santa Fe, facing the Muslim stronghold of Granada, was a fortified rectangle at whose center two perpendicular avenues intersected and led outwards to four cardinal gates. Governor Ovando seems to have used it for a model when he resited and rebuilt Santo Domingo after the hurricane of 1502, and it is worth noting that some of the conquerors had seen Santa Fe, all of them knew about it, and many of them passed through Santo Domingo on the way to their destinations. In the Indies the regular layout of indigenous cities on whose ruins the Spanish built their own municipalities undoubtedly affected town planning. When in 1522 Alonso García Bravo made his famous *traza* (trace or survey) for Mexico City, he followed the reticulated system of canals that ran between *chinampas* (floating gardens) of Tenochtitlán.

But it may have been that the Spaniards needed no historical guidance. They simply adopted a generic solution for the organization of human habitation. The use of a gridiron or rectilinear plan was the most obvious and sensible way to lay out a town where none had existed before and where space and terrain allowed a choice. In any case, the bold geometrism of so many Spanish towns probably derived from a variety of local pragmatic experiments, and as in so many aspects of colonization in the Indies, the detailed and systematic prescriptions that the crown eventually provided simply confirmed and legitimized a form that had been adopted in practice.[9]

Not all the European municipalities in the Indies had or retained a gridiron layout. In many instances, as towns grew, the need to conform to land contours or to accommodate natural barriers prevented the rectilinear extension of the original streets. Thus, some port cities, although founded on a gridiron pattern, grew concentrically around a bay with new streets radiating obliquely from the original nucleus to form triangular or trapezoidal blocks. In other cases, founders had no plan; the original layout was irregular, and from it growth occurred haphazardly. Mining cities constituted a case in point. They appeared spontaneously on the site of strikes and grew linearly following the valleys whose hilly sides encased veins of silver or in whose streams gold was washed.

### Principal Characteristics of Urbanization during the Conquest

Several general characteristics of Spanish urbanization in the Indies stand out.[10] One was its rather haphazard and unstable character, a characteristic already mentioned. Some further examples will emphasize the point. In 1502 a hurricane destroyed Santo Domingo, first founded in 1496, and it had to be re-sited and rebuilt. Because of poor site selections, Havana had to be moved and refounded twice. Guatemala City was also moved twice, the occasion for the last shift in location being an earthquake that destroyed the second city. San Salvador was founded in 1524, refounded in 1528 and 1545, and later in the century ravished by earthquakes three times. Angol, in Chile, had to be refounded nine times because of earthquakes and Indian depredations. In addition to these misfortunes, the peripatetic propensities of conquest populations often drained towns of their *vecinos* or filled them with rootless and restless inhabitants.

A second characteristic was the dispersal and isolation of centers of population. Several circumstances imposed this pattern. Except where concentrations of precious metals offered irresistible attractions, the Spaniards built their towns in congenial natural environments and where large supplies of native labor were available, conditions that tended to coincide because the sedentary Indians had long before found the best places to live. But the extremes of altitude and climate, along with the vast expanses of jungle, swamp, and desert, that characterized the geography of the New World severely limited such favorable situations and isolated them one from the other. Even in the most attractive regions the Europeans had to spread out their settlements so as to allow equitable *repartimientos* of indigenes. And, when all is said and done, even if all the Indies had been like the valleys of Mexico and central Chile, there were not enough Spaniards in the world to colonize thickly and evenly such boundless territories.

A third and derivative characteristic was the weak articulation of urban networks. The distances and natural barriers that separated centers of settlement discouraged communications among them, and they tended to develop purely local identifications. Many regions, furthermore, produced few commodities or manufactures beyond their immediate needs, so that commercial incentives were insufficient to foment a lively intermunicipal intercourse. Insofar as communities looked outward, it was toward the major administrative centers, the loci of the authority that dispensed privileges, immunities, and exemptions and the locations of the main markets for exportable commodities and whatever imports were needed. These centers, in turn, were in closer touch with Seville than with each other. And, as communications routes developed to serve this pattern, towns whose founders had not anticipated their directions found themselves even more isolated.

Finally, unbalanced growth and the primacy of a handful of cities characterized Spanish settlement in the Indies. The pattern is indicated by the percentages of the population of major territorial units living in capitals around 1570: for the Isthmus of Panama, 69 percent in Panama City; for the Audiencia of Mexico, 48.1 percent in Mexico City; for the Kingdom of Quito, 45.7 percent in the city of Quito; for the Audiencia of Lima, 39.8 percent in the city of Lima; for the Greater Antilles, 29.2 percent in Santo Domingo.

The characteristics of urbanization that appeared in the Indies in the sixteenth century—widely dispersed settlements, underdeveloped urban networks, inordinate population concentrations in a few administrative centers—persisted long after Spain's dominion in this region ended. They can be regarded as demographic deficiencies that adversely affected the social, economic, and political development of Spanish America. Yet Spanish colonization cannot be depreciated. Although a less spectacular process than discovery or conquest, it required a much more sustained and persistent effort, and it was quite remarkable that a few handfuls of Spaniards left a visible and permanent mark on a land so vast as to make the peninsula from whence the came appear a cozy neighborhood.

# CHAPTER 8

# Colonization:
# Efforts to Incorporate the Indians

### The Rationality of the Indian: Spanish Perceptions

Queen Isabella desired to incorporate the American indigenes into the Spanish scheme of colonization by converting them, acculturating them, and putting them to work, but she underestimated the magnitude of the task. Indeed, a sharp difference of opinion arose as to whether it could be accomplished at all. The dispute turned on the essential nature and identity of the American indigene and, in a broader sense, was an extension of the problem first raised by Portuguese expansion along the coast of Africa when Europeans encountered savagery and paganism on a large scale.

The first settlers in the Indies had a low opinion of the Indian's rationality, and Governor Ovando shared it. When he arrived in Española in 1501, he found a situation that was duplicated again and again as the Conquest advanced. The Indians, he reported, worshiped idols and devils and showed little disposition toward Christianity. They lived in savagery, ate bugs and lizards, indulged in bestial sexual practices, and bathed frequently, a practice that the queen was informed did them much harm. Of more immediate concern, they preferred feasting, drinking, dancing, and idleness to honest toil, and to avoid serving the Spaniards they fled to the hills and forests. As a result of native fecklessness, the European settlers starved, the gold mines went unworked, and royal revenues languished. Indeed, the first Spanish colony in the Indies faced a crisis of existence. A little later, historian and public official Gonzalo Fernández de Oviedo described the natives he saw on Española and Tierra Firme as "naturally lazy and vicious, melancholic, cowardly, and in general a lying, shiftless people. . . .

[But] what could one expect from a people whose skulls are so thick and hard that the Spaniards had to take care in fighting not to strike on the head lest their swords be blunted?" Teaching them Christianity, he observed ironically, "is like chewing on a cold piece of iron."[1] Some persons believed the Indians to be not only depraved but subhuman. Although he changed his mind on his deathbed, Dominican Friar Domingo de Betanzos sent a memorial to the Council of the Indies declaring the natives to be beasts, condemned by God for their sins and doomed to perish.[2]

Father Las Casas took a more positive view. "God created these simple people," he affirmed, "without evil and without guile. They are most obedient and faithful to their natural lords and to the Christians whom they serve. . . . Surely [they] would be the most blessed in the world if only they worshiped the True God."[3] He believed further that they could be truly converted and taught the arts of civilization.

The crown and its most influential advisers consistently supported Las Casas's position, at least in theory, and in 1537 Pope Paul settled the question officially by declaring: "We . . . consider . . . that the Indians are truly men and that they are not only capable of understanding the Catholic Faith, but according to our information, they desire exceedingly to receive it."[4] The question of the rationality of the American indigenes, however, remained very much alive and generated intense debate in Spain and the Indies throughout discovery, conquest, and colonization. Generally speaking, esteem for Indians was highest among savants in Europe who had never seen one, lowest among officials and settlers who had to deal directly with their exasperating resistance to European ways. It must be said, however, that most Spaniards in the New World had a vested interest in regarding Indians as inferior beings.

## Early Spanish Indian Policy

Enslavement

But, even if the essential humanity and rationality of the Indians were accepted, at first no one had any clear notion of how to redeem them from sin and sloth. The most obvious way to put them to work was to enslave them. Columbus tried it but received a severe reprimand from his sovereign. The queen had no scruples about the ancient and universally accepted institution of slavery, but she objected to the disposition of her subjects without her express approval. She and her successors, moreover, consistently affirmed that the Indians, once they accepted Castilian sovereignty, became vassals of the crown and as such were free, although conditions in the Indies produced two exceptions to this principle. First, natives could be enslaved if captured in a just war, that is, when they refused to admit Spaniards to their territories or attacked Spanish settlements or openly rebelled against royal authority. Second, if they were already slaves of Indian masters, Europeans could acquire them legitimately by gift, barter, or purchase.

Conquerors, settlers, and traders operating far from the scrutiny of the crown interpreted restrictions on Indian slavery loosely. During the first stages of conquest in the several regions of the Indies, a lively slave trade developed, and tens of thousands of indigenes lost their liberty. But, as pacification progressively reduced the number of natives who could be legally enslaved, and as more royal governors arrived in the Indies, slavers had more difficulty justifying or obscuring their depredations. The trade also involved considerable financial and even physical risk, and Indian slavery turned out to be a very wasteful system. Natives died in large numbers when transported from one climate to another, and the unaccustomed labor demanded of them took a heavy toll. Although traffic in Indian slaves continued both legally and clandestinely until the 1540s, when the crown finally prohibited it in most parts of the Indies, it was an unsuitable device for exploiting the labor of the mass of pacified natives, and another means had to be found.

Early Evangelization

As for evangelization, Spain might have been a crusading nation, but it had little missionary experience and no missionary tradition. During the Reconquest, the kings of Castile and Leon had been content to let Moors and Jews retain their faith as long as they accepted Christian dominion and paid tribute. For sixteenth-century Spaniards, only two direct precedents existed, and they offered few lessons. Hernando de Talavera, who became bishop of Granada after the fall of that city, attempted to convert the defeated Moors by gentle persuasion, but the good work proceeded so slowly that the Catholic Kings turned instead to forced mass conversion. The fruits of their efforts were highly suspect. The Spaniards also tried to convert the Canary Islanders, but the effort was on too small a scale and the results too uncertain to provide a model. Little could be learned from the Portuguese. Their spiritual offensive in Africa had aborted, and their missionary work in the Orient was scarcely under way when the Spanish Conquest began. During the Antillean phase of colonization, individual clergymen preached to the Indians and claimed a few converts, but missionary efforts lacked effective leadership, organization, and method.

Social Experiments

The Spaniards made several experimental attempts to teach the Indians how to live like civilized Christians. During the early sixteenth century, some authorities in Spain believed that this end could be accomplished by *buen ejemplo* (good example), that is, by placing the subjugated people in close association with Europeans. Queen Isabella tested the theory by ordering Governor Ovando to bring the natives out of their mountains and forest retreats, where they lived isolated from the Spaniards, and to congregate them in towns, preferably near the mines, where each would have a house and a plot of land on which to raise crops and graze livestock.

Isabella further required the governor to place in each new community a Spaniard of known virtue to administer justice to the inhabitants and protect them from abuse. Each town was to be provided with a church and a chaplain, who would baptize the Indians and instruct them in matters of faith. Finally, the queen instructed Ovando to arrange that "some Christians [that is, Spaniards] marry some Indian women and that Christian women marry some Indian men so that both races will communicate with each other and the Indians [be] instructed in the things of our Sacred Catholic Faith and, likewise, learn to work in their plots of land and manage their households and the said Indians be made into men and women of reason."[5] The queen did not inform the governor where, among the European adventurers and vagabonds who infested the island, he was to find men of virtue and industry to instruct the natives by example. In any event, nothing came of her orders.

Responding to the representations of Father Las Casas and other friends of the Indians at court, in 1520 the crown again ordered the formation of villages of free natives on Española under Spanish civil and religious tutelage. It authorized a similar undertaking on Cuba that lasted from 1526 to 1535. Owing to the opposition of European settlers and the indifference of island officials, the two experiments aborted. Las Casas himself directed a third, which was designed to create Indian villages on the Pearl Coast (in Venezuela) under the care of two Dominican missions already established there. He also arranged for the crown to send over fifty Spanish farmers to teach the natives the arts of husbandry. But everything went wrong. Storms prevented additional friars assigned to the project from reaching America, and Indians destroyed the missions. The Spanish "farmers" proved to be political dissidents who had been proscribed for their part in the *comunero* rebellion in Spain. In America they promptly deserted and joined Ponce de León's expedition to Florida.

## The Birth of the American Encomienda

Meanwhile, an institution had been evolving that, if it did not fulfill all of Isabella's aims, served to mobilize Indian labor systematically and legally. Its origins lay in an ad hoc response to the early sixteenth-century subsistence crisis on Española. Yielding to Governor Ovando's warnings of imminent disaster, in 1502 the queen issued an order reaffirming the freedom of the Indians and her primary commitment to evangelization. But she also authorized the governor to "compel and force" the Indians to gather and mine gold, to produce food for the Spaniards, and to work on the construction of public buildings. For their labor they were to be paid a wage that Ovando deemed just.[6]

Ovando interpreted the queen's orders in a way shaped by his experience. He was a *comendador mayor* (knight-commander) of the military order of Alcántara, which in Spain held many *encomiendas*. An *encomienda* was a form of *señorío* consisting of towns, villages, castles, monasteries, and other populated places in the royal domain that the crown commended into the charge of deserving persons or corporations for a specified span of time, giving them the right to collect stipulated dues and services from the inhabitants. Commendation, however, did not convey property title.

Guided by this precedent, the governor retained some Indians to work in the royal mines but commended the remainder to Spaniards he thought deserving. Through commendation, the beneficiary obtained the right to collect for his own use most of the tribute owed by his charges to the crown. Tribute due in money or kind could be commuted into personal service, that is, labor. Island settlers preferred personal service because the Indian had little else with which to pay. They also construed it as a *señorial* due owed to themselves, in contrast to tribute in money or goods, which was simply a royal tax. The crown rationalized the abridgment of Indian freedom by requiring those who received commendations to gather their Indians into settled communities and to build churches and provide chaplains for them. Thus, the *encomienda indiana* (the *encomienda* in the Indies) was born.

## The Evolution of the Encomienda

The Antillean Phase

During the next four decades the American *encomienda* developed into the single most important institution for transforming conquest into colonization. Several factors shaped its evolution. The first was the conflicting interests of the crown and American settlers. Queen Isabella accepted Governor Ovando's arrangement for expedient reasons, but she did not like it, nor did her successors. It had a questionable legality since it required the forced labor of Castilian subjects. It involved a partial donation of sovereign rights and threatened to create a class of *encomenderos* (holders of *encomiendas*) with *señorial* pretensions. And as it spread through the Antilles, reports accumulated that the Spaniards were using their charges as slave gangs, thereby doing them great damage. The crown therefore looked forward to its ultimate replacement by free wage labor and meanwhile sought to regulate its more objectionable features and prevent its spread.

For their part, settlers in the Indies quickly became dependent on the *encomienda*. Without it, they contended, they would have no means of support, royal revenues would shrink to nothing, the land would be abandoned, and the great work of conquest undone. The natives themselves would relapse into idleness and idolatry. On a more aggressive note, colonists urged that *encomiendas* be granted in perpetuity so that the Indians would not be treated as borrowed property but as capital assets to be husbanded. They also sought jurisdiction over their charges on the grounds that it would create a lord-vassal relationship that would guarantee social stability as it had done in Castile since time immemorial. Royal officials in the Indies tended to support the *encomenderos*. Some held *encomiendas* themselves, but they were also practical administrators who recognized that behind self-interest and specious arguments lay a fundamental reality. The Spaniards had not come to the New World to toil in mines or on plantations, and in any event there were not enough of them to constitute a sufficient labor force. The indigenes did not wish to work for them even if paid a just wage. Without some device such as the *encomienda*, the Enterprise of the Indies would have faltered badly.

The conflicting interests of crown and settlers became apparent in a series of official actions and colonial reactions. In 1512 representations of Dominican friars prodded King Ferdinand into promulgating the Laws of Burgos, which redefined the arrangements set by Ovando but regulated conditions of work and pay for *encomienda* Indians and established a system of royal supervision and inspection.[7] The code, however, merely legitimized the *encomienda* without ameliorating the lot of the natives, for royal officials ignored its provisions. Five years later, at the instance of Las Casas, the crown sent two commissioners of the Jeronymite Order to the islands to investigate the possibility of freeing the Indians and authorized them to take action toward this end if they saw fit. The good friars met such unanimous and intransigent opposition from colonists that they took little action and made no positive recommendations. Moved in part by Las Casas's charge that the *encomienda* was responsible for the dwindling of the Antillean population, Emperor Charles forbade its introduction into recently conquered Mexico, but Cortés had already made a general distribution of Indians, reserving some for the king and a generous portion for himself. Charles not only accepted the accomplished fact but suffered the institution to be established in other parts of the Indies. Despite its abuses and its threat to the royal *señorío*, in the end the crown could think of no other way to reward deserving conquerors and secure Spanish tenure in the New World.

### The Mainland *Encomienda*

On the mainland a new set of circumstances affected the evolution of the *encomienda*. Here there were many, many more Indians than in the Antilles, and most of them were much more amenable to systematic exploitation than the easygoing and improvident islanders. They were distributed in dense clusters and lived in a semblance of polity, residing in organized communities, obeying their natural *señores*, and rendering service and tribute to them. The Europeans had only to appropriate an already existing system and adapt it to their own requirements.

On the mainland, also, the crown's interest in checking abuses of the *encomienda* and the *señorial* propensities of *encomenderos* was linked to changing official attitudes toward Spanish-Indian relations in general. Intimate association between the two peoples, it became apparent, not only facilitated exploitation of the indigenes but, according to Vasco de Quiroga, the erudite Mexican churchman, caused the Indians to become corrupted by "the bad example we give them of arrogance, lust, avarice, sharp trading, and all manner of profanities, so that they see in us hardly any behavior that could be called Christian."[8] Thus a fear of bad example replaced a naive belief in good example, and the crown moved toward a policy of racial segregation expressed in orders forbidding Spaniards to live among the indigenes and requiring the Indians to remain in their towns and *pueblos*.

New environmental conditions and changing perceptions of the Indian altered the *encomienda* in several important ways. It acquired a distinct territorial dimension. In the Antilles, commendations had consisted of tribal units that possessed a certain mobility, but, on the mainland, the *encomendero* received towns and villages of Indians or caciquedoms, which were well defined administrative-territorial units. The crown ordered that these be left intact and Indians not be taken from them to work elsewhere, except for temporary assignments and then only with the consent and supervision of royal officials. The arrangement, however, did not convey property rights to the *encomendero* in the district of his grant; the natives retained possession of their lands. Spaniards obtained their land by *repartimiento* in newly conquered regions or later by royal grant.

Mainland *encomiendas* had an enormous range in size. The great captains of conquest obtained and retained a disproportionate share of the human booty of the Conquest. The crown gave Cortés twenty-three separate *encomiendas*, which, according to his reckoning, totalled 115,000 natives. Francisco Pizarro took for himself 20,000 tribute-paying Indians. In the most densely populated parts of the New World, grants of 2000 tributaries were not uncommon. At the lower end of the scale, conquerors without rank and influence or out of favor with distributing authorities obtained only a village or less.

On the mainland, the conditions of commendation changed, and tenure became stabilized. The crown consistently held that *encomiendas* were rewards for outstanding service in the Indies and repeatedly ordered that, in granting them, conquerors and first settlers should enjoy preference. Charles, however, continued the practice, begun by Ferdinand, of giving them to other persons and corporations who importuned for a share in the spoils and whom he thought "deserving." Thus, latecomers to the colonies, royal officials, ecclesiastics, and religious foundations in the Indies, as well as court favorites in Spain, became *encomenderos*. In 1536 the crown compromised in the matter of tenure by adopting in principle grants for *dos vidas* (two generations) although it made the continuation of title dependent on the "good behavior" of both generations. It refused, however, to yield jurisdiction.

The mainland *encomienda* acquired important military functions, which were defined in a royal order of 1536:

Within four months computed from the day that *encomenderos* receive their cedulas of *encomienda*, they are obligated to have horse, lance, sword, and other arms, offensive and defensive, which to the governor of the province appear to be necessary according to the qualities of their *repartimientos* and the forms of war, so that they will be prepared for any occasion, under penalty of deprival of the Indians which have been commended to them.[9]

In part because of this provision, the *encomienda* became closely tied to what the Spanish called *vecinidad*, that is, fixed, permanent, and legal residence in a municipality. As the conquest expanded, *encomenderos* showed a propensity for abandoning their homes and Indians to join *entradas* promising new booty. Their departure left entire regions devoid of Europeans and left the land undefended. The crown, therefore, ordered them to establish and maintain residence in one of the towns of the province or district in which their grant lay as a condition of title. To ensure further their domestication, it required them if married but alone to bring their wives from Spain and if single to find a bride in the Indies without delay.

Lastly, the crown tried both direct and indirect means to prevent excessive exploitation of the indigenes and to protect its own political and fiscal interests. It declared that *encomienda* Indians could not be compelled to carry heavy burdens or work in the mines except when "absolutely necessary." Neither could they be forced to perform intensive plantation labor. Instead, more arduous forms of toil were to be left to slaves, Indian or black. Such enactments implied, however, that the commended indigenes could work voluntarily in the several forbidden areas. As observed earlier, they could not be removed from their *pueblos* and towns for extended periods, and they could not be loaned or rented to other *encomenderos* or to non-*encomenderos*. As for their tribute, the crown attempted to fix who should pay, how much, and in what kind on the basis of their obligations to caciques before the Conquest.

*Encomienda* and *Corregimiento*

The crown also created an institution that counterbalanced and undermined the *encomienda*. Since the first distributions in the islands, not all Indians had been commended to private parties. Some remained *en la Corona*, that is, under direct royal control, and in the 1530s this reservation was formalized as the *corregimiento de Indios*, whereby uncommended natives were placed under the jurisdiction of royal officials, who "shall be called *corregidores*, so that even by their titles the Indians shall know that they are not their lords."[10] By this arrangement, the natives continued to render labor or tribute, but to the king rather than to *encomenderos*. In addition to collecting these dues, *corregidores* were ordered to settle the Indians in their charge in towns governed by indigenous *cabildos* and to provide royal justice within their *corregimientos*.

The *corregimiento* had several apparent advantages for the crown. Immediately, it kept the faculty of jurisdiction out of private hands and provided convenient sinecures with which to reward deserving subjects. In the longer run, it created a repository for newly conquered natives and *encomiendas* confiscated by or escheating to the king. Through the cumulative effect of such reversions, it could lead ultimately to the extinction of the private *encomienda*. Perhaps Emperor Charles's advisers had this end in mind. In terms of the welfare of the natives, however, it is questionable whether they fared much better under the *corregimiento* than in *encomiendas*, because *corregidores* received their salaries from the tribute they collected and they controlled the personal service owed by their charges. In connivance with caciques, they often extorted more than was their due.

## The "Tamed" *Encomienda*

The climax in the history of the *encomienda* came in the 1540s. Although by that time it had struck deep roots in the Indies, it still had powerful enemies at court who opposed it on legal and humanitarian grounds. In addition, the crown still distrusted a powerful *encomendero* class in the Indies that continued to press for perpetual tenure and for jurisdiction and that often exercised de facto *señorial* faculties, as revealed in a report from a royal agent in Mexico: "Twenty leagues outside Mexico City there is little or no judicial system . . . and I know that in some regions the villagers consider the lords and *encomenderos* of the villages as their kings, and they know no other sovereign."[11] Other observers reported that *calpixquis* (majordomos and overseers) judged and punished Indians, suspended caciques, and appointed Indian *alcaldes* in *encomienda* villages.

These several considerations moved Emperor Charles to promulgate, in 1542, the famous Laws and Ordinances Newly Made by His Majesty for the Government of the Indies and the Good Treatment and Preservation of the Indians. One section of the "New Laws," as the code is commonly called, dealt with the general organization of colonial government. The remainder, as the title indicates, dealt with the governance and treatment of the Indians. One provision outlawed their enslavement and ordered all those taken illegally to be freed. Other articles dealt a near mortal blow to the *encomienda* by declaring that: (1) no new *encomiendas* could be granted; (2) those to which no legal title could be proven and those held by royal officials, ecclesiastics, and religious orders reverted immediately to the crown; and (3) even those legitimately held escheated upon the death of the present holder.[12]

In effect, the New Laws terminated the *encomienda* upon the death of the longest-lived *encomendero*. The colonists understood this clearly and raised cries of outrage and indignation. Virtually the entire civil and ecclesiastical establishments in the Indies supported them through conviction or because their own *encomiendas* were endangered. In Mexico rebellion threatened; in Peru and Nicaragua it erupted. The crown backed off, suspending the articles of the code that would have terminated the institution, but its retreat was only tactical. In 1549, it made a flank attack by ordering that *encomenderos* could no

longer require personal services from their charges; they could only collect tribute from them. The Indians, furthermore, did not have to pay in money; they
could render what they owed in kind with amounts adjusted to their means.
Over the next two decades, the king also introduced an arrangement whereby
*encomienda* Indians rendered their tribute directly to the royal treasury, which
then paid *encomenderos* amounts due to them.

During roughly the same period, evolving social policy also affected the *encomienda*. As the native population declined, smaller *encomenderos* became
impoverished and took up residence in the villages of their Indians, where they
could subsist directly on goods and services owed them. Also, Indian communities became infested by Spanish and mixed-blood vagabonds who lived a life
of idleness, supported by the native inhabitants. *Encomenderos* and other intruders not only imposed an intolerable burden on the scant resources of the
indigenes but provided a scandalous model of behavior. The crown therefore
issued a series of orders restraining all Europeans, excepting priests, and all
mixed bloods from residing or tarrying in native communities. Although often
evaded, these measures helped to weaken further the *encomendero*'s control
over his Indians.

By 1570 the *encomienda* still survived in the Indies. Contemporary geographer and cosmographer Juan López de Velasco reported that the Indians
who had been pacified and reduced (settled in Christian communities) were
divided into 3600 *repartimientos*, some held by His Majesty (*corregimientos*)
but most by private parties (*encomiendas*).[13] *Encomenderos* continued to extract personal services from their charges or rent them out through subterfuge
and collusion with royal officials, particularly in remote parts of the Indies
such as Paraguay and Venezuela where the king's writ ran faintly. The institution, nevertheless, had lost much of its vitality. As Professor Lesley Byrd
Simpson put it, it had been "tamed."[14] It amounted to little more than a
charge on the royal treasury, and *encomenderos* became little more than pen-
sioners of the king. The fact that the crown came to allow a third *vida* in 1555
and by 1629 a fourth simply meant that it felt the *encomenderos* were under
control. Meanwhile, as holders died off without heirs, more and more Indians
escheated, and a continuing decline in the native population diminished the
size of surviving *encomiendas* and the income from them in proportion.

## *Controversial Features of the* Encomienda

Despite a rather substantial corpus of scholarly literature on the *encomienda
indiana*, its attributes still stir historiographical controversy, and the main issues

deserve review.[15] One is the connection between Old World and New World forms. Historian Robert Chamberlain, a pioneer investigator of the problem, believes that the origins of the institution in the Indies "are to be sought not in any one of the Castilian grants, donations, and institutions, and forms of rights over land and people . . . but in these as a whole."[16] Yet, circumstantially at least, a direct historical connection exists between the *encomienda* in the Indies and in Spain. Governor Ovando was a *comendador* of the Order of Alcántara, which held many *encomiendas* in Castile. He was familiar with their organization and management, and it is plausible that he drew on this experience when he commended Indians to Spanish settlers on Española. Also, the form of the grants on both sides of the Atlantic displayed similarities. In each case they involved commendation under specified curcumstances and for specified periods or at the royal will; they both had territorial bases and military functions. The main difference was that, in law, American *encomenderos* did not enjoy *señorial* rights. They consistently pretended to them, however, referring to their Indians as vassals, and in practice exercised extensive jurisdiction over them. In short, the *encomienda* was one of the many Spanish institutions transplanted to the Indies and there adapted to new circumstances.

The connection between the Spanish and the American *encomienda* relates to another controversial issue. Was the institution in the Indies essentially capitalist or essentially feudal or, better to say, *señorial* in character? The feudalistic-capitalistic dichotomy has little meaning except within a Marxist theoretical framework, and empirically it is specious. In legal terms, the *encomienda* clearly had medieval origins, the rights and obligations of crown and *encomenderos* patently constituted a *señorial* arrangement, and contemporaries thought and spoke of it as such. Many *encomenderos*, however, were active entrepreneurs, renting out their Indians, selling tribute in kind on the open market, and investing their revenues in mining, commerce, and manufacturing. In short, they used a *señorial* instrument for capitalistic purposes. The adaptation should not be surprising. The Spaniards came to the Indies at a time when all over Europe medieval institutions were being adjusted to the requirements of New Monarchies and the first stages of a commercial revolution.

More specific problems of understanding also exist. One is the distinction between *repartimiento* and *encomienda*, since contemporaries used the terms almost interchangeably. The relationship was as follows. Generically, a *repartimiento* was a division or distribution of something. More particularly, during the Reconquest and in the Canaries it commonly meant a divison of spoils. In America, Indians were a form of spoil. The *encomienda* was simply an institutionalized *repartimiento* characterized by legal prescriptions for tenure and use. Thus, sixteenth-century documents speak of *"repartimientos of encomiendas."* The crown preferred the word *encomienda* because it connoted a donation by royal grace. Settlers preferred *repartimiento* because the term implied control of labor and territory won by conquest, although they liked to be called *encomenderos*, a title that smacked of nobility, very much reminiscent of the *comendador* of the Spanish military orders. In both popular and official usage, however, *repartimiento* triumphed and *encomienda* occurred mainly in set legal phrases, such as "to have [or receive] Indians in *encomienda*."

A more venerable and persistent misunderstanding is that the *encomienda* was a grant of land as well as Indians and the nucleus of the Spanish American hacienda. A connection between the two institutions unquestionably existed. Colonists received both *mercedes* of land and *repartimientos* of Indians, sometimes in the same document, and, not infrequently, the two grants coincided territorially. In these circumstances, the use of land and *encomienda* service tended to merge. But juridically the crown kept the titles to the two resources separate, fearing that combination would encourage the *señorial* aspirations of the conquerors and first settlers.

Most of the disagreements and misunderstandings about the *encomienda indiana* derive from its inherently complex nature. The institution is generally treated as an instrument for exploiting indigenous labor. That it was, but it was something more. It was in intent a general-purpose institution, designed to Christianize and Hispanicize American Indians. Also, it was constantly evolving and developed many regional variations. In Paraguay the conquerors married the daughters of Indian caciques, assumed control of the labor of the chief's subjects, and called the arrangement *encomienda*. Somewhat later the regular institution was introduced, so that the two forms coexisted and sometimes overlapped. In Chile the formal *encomienda* was instituted during the Conquest, but later the Spaniards put Araucanians captured in war to work on their estates and regarded them as *encomienda* Indians. In short, any general description of the *encomienda* amounts to the construction of an ideal type.

But, if modern scholars are uncertain about the qualities of the *encomienda*, they may take heart from the bafflement of contemporaries. After the institution had been in existence for nearly fifty years, Antonio de Mendoza, the first viceroy of New Spain, complained, "As far as the Indians are concerned, there have been so many changes that as I have said repeatedly we are going crazy with so many experiments. After sixteen years in this government I could swear that I am more confused about them than at the beginning."[17]

Putting aside definitional and historiographical problems, the *encomienda* unquestionably fulfilled what all contemporaries knew to be its primary function. It ensured European tenure in the Indies by providing a means for conquerors to subsist on the surplus production of the conquered directly (through the collection of tribute from them) and indirectly (through the use of their personal services). It visited incalcuable cruelties and brutalities on the Indians, but, given their cultural indisposition toward free wage labor and their status as a conquered people, they were bound to be exploited, and the mature mainland *encomienda* was the only viable alternative to mass enslavement of the native population.

The *encomienda*, however, failed to do the one thing that, in the minds of legalists and moralists, justified its existence. It produced little Christianity among the Indians. Some wealthy *encomenderos* built churches and provided curates for their charges, but many were too poor to do so. In any event, as a class they were more interested in material returns than in evangelization. The "spiritual conquest" of the Indies, therefore, passed to other hands and to other institutions.

### The "Spiritual Conquest": The Apostolic Model and the Mendicant Orders

Early missionary efforts in the Antilles had been rather desultory, but, when the Spaniards reached Mexico with its large populations and advanced cultures, evangelization acquired a sense of urgency and challenge. "The natives of these parts," Cortés wrote in his third letter to Emperor Charles, "are of much greater intelligence than those of the Islands; they seem to us indeed to possess sufficient intelligence to conduct themselves as average reasonable beings." In his fourth letter he remarked, "In no letter that I have written to your Majesty have I failed to point out the opportunity that exists to convert certain of the natives in these parts to our holy Catholic Faith, and I have begged your Majesty to dispatch religious persons of saintly life and character for that purpose."[18]

Cortés's reports and other intelligence arriving from Mexico led crown and church to seek more effective methods of evangelization. Early church history provided the most obvious model. The sudden revelation of countless souls who had never heard of Christ presented a challenge comparable only to the task of the apostles when they set forth among the pagans of the Roman world to tell of the Savior's death and resurrection. The conversion of the American Indians, therefore, should be entrusted to bands of simple and virtuous missionaries, untainted by mundane ambitions. The apostolic model, moreover, had a particularly exalting prospect. In religious as well as secular matters, America was a *tabula rasa*, and it might be possible to raise there a spiritual order as pure and spotless as the primitive church before it became corrupted by false doctrines and the ways of the world.

Crown and church agreed that the most appropriate source of apostles for the Indies were the two mendicant orders, the Franciscans and the Dominicans, and the older Order of Saint Augustine. As a result of reforms sponsored by Cardinal Jiménez de Cisneros, all three had reaffirmed their commitment to the primitive Christian virtues of poverty and humility; the Franciscans, especially, had extensive experience teaching and preaching among the rural and urban poor of Castile, and all three possessed disciplined organizations that could mobilize their resources expeditiously. The Observant, or Reformed, branch of the Franciscans had a particularly apostolic orientation containing a strong strain of millennialism, that is, the belief, rather widespread in the late Middle Ages, in the imminence of a thousand years of earthly perfection during which the devil would be bound as predicted in the Revelation of Saint John and that would be preceded by the conversion of "false" Muslims, "perfidious" Jews, and "blind" Gentiles who had no knowledge of the Sacred Scriptures. To the millennialists, the Discovery took on a mystical meaning. They transplanted their hopes for a millennial kingdom to the New World, where, they believed, the Gospel must be preached to its multitude of Gentiles before the great day dawned.

Because of the urgency of evangelization and the shortage of secular priests in the Indies, the papacy issued bulls in 1521 and 1522 that dispensed with standing prohibitions against the orders engaging in parish ministry and management and granted them extraordinary powers normally reserved to bishops: the right to administer all the sacraments, to absolve from excommunication, to confer and confirm minor orders, and to consecrate churches and provide them with ministers. No cleric might interfere with their work, under pain of excommunication. It was understood, however, that these concessions were temporary and that the work of the friars constituted only the first step in the incorporation of the American Indian into the church. After they had converted groups of natives, they were expected to return to their traditional teaching and preaching functions or move on to new missionary frontiers, leaving their neophytes in the care of secular clergy.

## The Evangelization of Mexico

Early Problems and Experimental Methods

In 1524 twelve Observant Franciscans arrived in Veracruz to begin the evangelization of the Indies. The commission that they carried from the general of their order reveals the apostolic inspiration of their mission. "I send you with twelve companions," it read, "for this was the number which Christ took in his company for the conversion of the world. . . . You are called of the Father to labor in His vineyard, not as hirelings for wages, but as sons of the great Father, seeking nothing for yourselves but the things of Jesus Christ."[19]

The first Dominicans, also numbering twelve, arrived in New Spain in 1526, and a company of Augustinians came over seven years later. During the next three decades, new contingents of the three orders joined their brethren, with the result that by 1559 central Mexico had 380 Grey Friars residing in eighty convents, 210 Black Friars in forty houses, and 212 Augustinians also in forty houses. Geographically the houses of the missionary orders were fairly evenly distributed in the Valley of Mexico and immediately adjacent regions. Beyond the central region, however, a rough territorial divison of labor existed with the Franciscans dominating in Michoacán and New Galicia, the Augustinians in a zone running north toward Tampico, and the Dominicans to the south in Oaxaca.

The first friars had a general doctrine of evangelization and an exalted sense of mission, and the Franciscans among them had a feeling of urgency imparted by the imminence of the millennium. But they did not have a systematic program for extirpating idolatry, instructing the Indians in the basic mysteries of the faith, baptizing converts, and catechizing neophytes. And they faced formidable obstacles. They were few; the Indians, multitudinous and dispersed. Although a number of indigenous urban centers existed, most of the population lived in huts or small hamlets, and the impact of conquest had caused many to flee to remote and inaccessible places. The Indians, furthermore, understood no Spanish, and the friars knew not one of the myriad native tongues. Finally, many indigenes resisted conversion, obstinately preferring their ancient gods and suspecting the missionaries of being but one more instrument of oppression.

Indian resistance raised another problem. To what degree could the fathers employ force in their ministry? After all, Christ did not dispatch soldiers to establish his *señorío* on earth but sent out humble, saintly men who spread the word by precept and example. On this issue jurists and theologians disagreed. Las Casas and other purists in the Dominican order denounced any resort to coercion, insisting that only apostolic methods could be employed. Humanists such as Juan Ginés de Sepulveda agreed that the primitive apostolic church, that is, the church before Constantine, had not used compulsion but argued that the emperor's official acceptance of Christianity created a unified Christian society, *Christianorum Imperium*, possessing a secular arm that could legitimately compel the conversion of infidel, Jew, and pagan.

Despite the monumental proportions of the challenge, the friars plunged into their work, employing pragmatic and eclectic methods. They went first to existing native administrative and religious centers that they called *cabeceras* and that were surrounded by *pueblos sujetos*, that is, subordinate pueblos. In the *cabeceras* they broke up the native idols, pulled down pagan temples, and built their convents and parish churches, often using the ruins of destroyed pyramids as foundations. At first the magnitude of their mission forced them to resort to perfunctory instruction and mass baptisms, and on occasion they lured the natives with promises of food and protection. Martín de Valencia, the leader of the twelve Franciscan apostles who had arrived in 1524, boasted that in that year alone he and his companions baptized more than a million natives and that later "it is said that they [each] baptized more than one hundred thousand persons and some more than four hundred thousand counted numerically."[20]

As they accumulated experience, the missionaries devised more systematic methods of conversion. Some of the first generation laboriously compiled vocabularies and constructed grammars of the principal Indian languages of their provinces, learned to speak them, and taught them to their brothers. A few became accomplished linguists. One, Franciscan Father Francisco de Toral, preached in two native languages every Sunday and feast day; another could deliver his message in three; and one exceptional case, Father Andrés de Olmos, wrote catechisms and preached Christian doctrine in "more than ten." Some of the friars also became convinced that to extirpate idolatry, they must learn as much as possible about native cultures and religions in which the devil manifested himself. Therefore, they assiduously collected ethnographic data, employing native codices and informants in a methodologically sophisticated way. They were the fathers of American Indian anthropology, and their writings remain a main source for the study of pre-Conquest civilizations.

On the question of the use of force, in 1559 a Dominican, Fray Palatino, published a learned treatise in which he reaffirmed that conversion must be accomplished by persuasion but allowed that, if the Indians refused to listen to the message, they could first be subjugated. This compromise suited King Philip's conscience, and in the following year he ordered it accepted in the Indies. Meanwhile, as in other matters, missionaries in the field adopted pragmatic solutions. They cajoled, bribed, threatened, and occasionally called on the secular arm to get the attention of the Indians and to induce them to listen. And they adopted a posture of stern paternalism toward neophytes who showed signs of relapse or laxity in attending services.

### Indian *Doctrinas* and *Congregaciones*

The friars also developed two organizational forms to facilitate their task. These were the *doctrina* and the *congregación*, the most exclusively American of all the institutions employed by Spain in the Indies. The *doctrina* was a center or school of religious instruction located in the convents of the several orders. Periodically the fathers summoned their neophytes to the cemetery adjoining the convent church and, grouping them around the raised crosses, required them to recite the catechism, listen to a sermon, and hear mass. The sons of caciques and *principales* (chiefs and subchiefs) received special attention. Recognizing them as the future leaders of their people, the friars brought them to the convents as boarders and there catechized them daily and taught them to serve at mass and assist with other religious duties. Youths trained in this manner aided in the instruction of their people. The missionaries also extended their ministry to *pueblos sujetos* in which they induced the Indians to construct churches. The larger villages might be provided with a resident priest, but most were *pueblos de visita*, so called because one of the fathers visited them periodically to catechize, preach, and say mass.

*Congregaciones* were new Indian communities formed for several mutually supporting purposes. The fathers intended them to facilitate conversion by bringing the natives together in convenient locations and, at the same time, to halt the disintegration of native societies occasioned by conquest. Congregation also acquired a rationale that expressed formally Queen Isabella's ideas for converting and acculturating the indigenes and that established priorities among her several objectives. Father Bartolomé Hernández defined the order of purposes in a letter to the Council of the Indies: "As your Graces know, it is first necessary that they [the Indians] be men who live in polity, in order to make them Christians."[21] For Hernández, to live in polity meant to abandon savage and rustic customs and to reside in ordered communities like rational men — clean, barbered, eating on tables with proper utensils, sleeping on beds, and eschewing drunkenness and sodomy.

The reduction of Indians to polity, one of the announced functions of the *congregación*, involved politicizing them in the modern sense of the word. The friars saw to the appointment of indigenous governors from among chiefs and subchiefs and in all organized communities required the Indian *vecinos* to elect *alcaldes* and *regidores* to constitute a *cabildo* that, in turn, appointed *alguaciles*, majordomos, and other municipal officials. Under missionary supervison, the *cabildo* allocated properties for the support of town government and church; marked out commons; distributed agricultural and grazing lands on the basis of need and merit; collected revenues, which were deposited in the corporation's treasury *(caja de comunidad)*; and undertook the construction of public works and utilities.

Congregation also involved providing the Indians with means of subsistence and of paying their tributes to the crown and *encomenderos*. The friars of the several orders introduced European plants and animals, developed improved methods for cultivating native corn, and taught their charges new arts of husbandry. Such instruction also had nonmaterial ends. As one missionary put it, "It was also a kind of catechism and training in good habits."[22] Most of the territory in which the missionaries labored was semiarid or had dry seasons, so that agricultural development depended on irrigation. All the orders brought water to their *congregaciones* by aqueducts and canals and made desert regions bloom.

The missionaries further strove to relieve the physical miseries of the Indians, a task made particularly urgent by the ravages of epidemics. The Franciscans and Augustinians built hospitals in their *congregaciones* with the labor, money, and alms of their charges, who also provided the nursing staff. These establishments had ameliorative as well as medical functions. They were places where the poor and infirm might find care and sustenance, and the troubled-in-spirit refuge and spiritual comfort; they were free provisioning depots where, in time of need, the Indians could obtain food and clothing; and they served as hostelries for visitors and transients, thereby relieving the individual members of the community of what might have been a considerable burden.

Congregation, like conversion, encountered serious obstacles. Many parts of central Mexico had terrain too broken to accommodate conveniently located settlements. Each of the orders demanded and received missionary provinces much too large to be administered efficiently by the friars at hand, many of whom came to prefer a comfortable life in well-established convents to forming new communities in the wilderness. The Indians often balked at deserting ancestral homes, and many of those resettled later fled to remote places where they could follow their ancient customs and un-Christian practices in peace.

Congregation brought with it political problems. The friars rather quickly adopted a highly paternalistic attitude toward their charges. They came to believe or, at least, to contend that American indigenes were too simple to adapt to European ways and, indeed, too innocent to be exposed to them. They even opposed teaching Spanish to them, holding that a knowledge of the language would simply facilitate the transmission of harmful habits and, perhaps, heretical doctrines. As one Augustinian friar observed, "All these Indians are like nestlings whose wings have not yet grown enough to allow them to fly themselves. . . ." The missionaries, he continued, "are their true fathers and mothers, their advocates, and representatives, who take for them all the blows of adversity. . . ."[23] But the missionaries' concern for the care of their neophytes was complemented by a vested interest in the institutuions that they created and that consumed their time, energy, and devotion.

The paternalism of the missionaries inevitably brought them into contention with every important interest in the Indies. The crown fully supported congregation in principle. In 1538 Emperor Charles declared: "I have been informed that for our sacred Catholic Faith to be extended among the native Indians of that land, it will be necessary for them to live in human polity so that there be a road and method to give them a knowledge of the divine, and, for this reason, you should order them to live together in the streets and plazas."[24] Eight years later, Prince Philip redefined the basic objectives of Spanish Indian policy when, in the name of the emperor, he ordered viceroys and governors in the Indies "to execute, using moderation and good judgment, the *reduccion congregacion, poblacion*, and religious instruction of the Indians."[25] Severe epidemics that devastated both old and new Indian communities gave an additional impetus to resettlement. In 1551 and again in 1558, the crown ordered survivors to be congregated in communities of European design situated near monasteries. Yet its policy had internal contradictions. While supporting congregation and segregation, it still wished the Indians to be Hispanicized and insisted that the natives learn Castilian. And, as in the case of the *encomenderos*, it distrusted the pretensions of the missionaries to what amounted to *señorío*.

Since congregated Indians also belonged to royal or private *repartimientos*, the friars incurred the enmity of *corregidores* and *encomenderos*, not only because they tried to protect their charges against exploitation but because the construction of monasteries, public works, and habitations in indigenous communities competed for a shrinking labor supply. In the spiritual sphere, the missionaries outraged the episcopacy. They claimed that their Indians were exempt from tithes and that by virtue of the papal bulls of 1521 and 1522 they enjoyed virtual exemption from the authority of bishops. In addition, they steadfastly resisted secularization of their *congregaciones*. Indeed, some of the fathers advocated the erection of a separate native church under the governance of the orders and insulated from the moral and doctrinal corruptions of the European establishment.

Despite obstacles and setbacks, Indian resettlement went ahead during the middle decades of the sixteenth century, although it is not certain how rapidly. Some missionaries reported that by 1570 the task was virtually completed in central Mexico, and López de Velasco supports their testimony.[26] Others lamented that much remained to be done or redone even in such centrally located provinces as Tlaxcala, where the program had had an early start. But, leaving quantitative evaluations to future scholarship, something more can be said about the qualities of the *congregaciones* known to exist. Like the *encomienda*, they were multifunctional institutions. As religious associations they were theoretically bodies of neophytes undergoing spiritual instruction, but in fact they were also Indian parishes complete with native *cofradías* in which the friars performed the administrative and sacramental functions of priests more or less independent of episcopal authority. They were also civil communities, the native equivalent of the European municipality. The agricultural innovations of the friars contributed significantly to the economic development of the colony, and the religious and civil activities they introduced could not help but contribute in some measure to the Hispanicization of the indigene. In short, the *congregación*, like the *encomienda*, served as a primary institution of colonization.

## The Spread of Evangelization

Central America

The early experiences of the orders in New Spain provided the model for the evangelization of other thickly populated parts of the Indies. Beginning in the 1540s, Mercedarians, Dominicans, and Franciscans, many of them with experience in Mexico, moved into Guatemala where cultures cognate to those of central Mexico provided them with familiar missionary environments. Here they founded their monasteries and baptized on a vast scale. Here too they undertook to congregate the Indians, a particularly urgent task because the Conquest had virtually destroyed the political and social organization of the indigenes and left them scattered and disoriented in caves and *barrancas*. The bishop of Guatemala, Francisco Marroquín, stoutly supported resettlement, and by 1550, it was reported, virtually all the natives of highland Guatemala,

Chiapas, and Honduras were baptized and congregated in Spanish-style towns and pueblos. In Yucatán, where the Conquest sputtered, the Franciscans began large-scale evangelization in the 1550s, but Indian resistance along with indifferent church leadership slowed progress, and by 1570 conversion and congregation were far from complete.[27]

## Peru

Dominicans, Mercedarians, and Franciscans, some with Mexican experience, began arriving in Peru in the early 1530s, and in the 1550s Augustinians followed. The missionaries, who still had the apostolic tradition very much in mind, often came in bands of twelve, and in 1563 the Franciscans organized the "Province of the Twelve Apostles of Peru." The several orders established their monasteries in major cities and undertook the conversion of the natives, but they found less auspicious conditions for their ministry than in Middle America. In Peru the conquest was uncompleted; multitudes of Indians who were supposedly subjugated reserved their loyalty for old rulers and gods and stubbornly resisted the Christian message, and wars among the conquerors disrupted city and countryside. Consequently, the missionaries could not get down to serious work until the 1550s, and even then they lacked numerical strength to proselyte beyond large population centers. Although they claimed hundreds of thousands of converts, in Peru evangelization lagged far behind New Spain. And, although they made some preliminary attempts to congregate the Peruvian indigenes, around 1574 López de Velasco reported that in "these Indies of the South" the natives were not resettled in *poblaciones* as they were in the northern continent.[28]

### Seventy Years of Spanish Indian Policy: An Assessment

An overview of seven decades of colonization in the Indies shows mixed results. The Republic of Spaniards was firmly established in its cities and towns and subsisted at various levels of comfort on the labor or tributes of the indigenous population. The reduction of the Indians to Christian polity proved to be a task of greater magnitude and for the most part lagged badly. In matters spiritual, the Indians unquestionably accepted baptism by the millions in the middle decades of the sixteenth century, and large numbers of those converted were undergoing religious instruction and receiving sacraments. It is difficult to say, however, how many were truly Christian. Contemporary judgments varied. Friars on the missionary front, especially the Franciscans, affirmed the efficacy of their apostolate, for to have done otherwise would have been to repudiate decades of toil and sacrifice. In 1561 Father Jacinto de San Francisco, who worked in the evangelical vineyards of New Spain, "found his soul filled with joy on seeing the Christianity of these people." Dominican Agustín Dávila Padilla defended at length the fervor with which the Mexican Indians confessed and their enthusiasm in matters of religion. Even in Peru, where evangelization lagged, Juan Polo de Ondegardo had no doubt in 1571 that large numbers of Indians ought to be saved, since at the hour of death all sought the sacraments with great faith and in the confessional gave moving evidence of their devotion.[29]

Civil authorities had strong reservations. In 1554 the viceroy of New Spain wrote to Philip II that the Indians of Tehuantepec "had no more feeling for our faith than brute animals," and in Peru Governor Vaca de Castro informed an assembly of provincials of the religious orders in 1565 that, according to his information, "out of more than three hundred thousand men [Indians] who are baptized, no more than forty are truly Christian and as many idolatries exist here as before." The Jesuits, who did not arrive in the Indies until the 1560s, viewed the work of their predecessors skeptically. In 1572 Father Bartolomé Hernández thought that most of the Peruvian indigenes were like the *moriscos* of Granada, without any understanding of the faith that they professed or any devotion to it, Christians but in outward appearance, and this only for fear of punishment. Farther north, fellow Black Robe Father Jerónimo Ruíz de Portillo judged that "millions of Indians remained without conversion in the city and district of Cartagena." On one closely related matter, religious and civil observers generally agreed; the Indians stubbornly resisted Christian morality and the monogamous family.[30]

When the conversion of the Indians is viewed from a modern perspective, it appears that they exercised a measure of selectivity. They found it spiritually satisfying, or at least prudent, to continue surreptitiously many of their ancient devotions. As one modern writer expressed it in the title of a book, long after the missionaries passed from the scene there were "idols behind altars." From the new faith offered to them or imposed upon them,[31] they selected those features of doctrine and ceremony that appealed to their spiritual, emotional, aesthetic, and practical needs. The interaction of the old and new faiths created a syncretic Indian religion whose character and qualities were not exactly what the Spanish crown and church had in mind. Yet depth of the Christianity of the American Indian in the sixteenth century cannot really be evaluated empirically. It is a theological issue akin to problems such as the relative spiritual value of faith and works and the old *ex opere operatio* debate, which questioned whether the due bestowal of the rite confers grace regardless of the subjective state of the minister and the recipient.

In matters secular, the Indians came under diverse European influences. Outside the selective and limited associations envisioned by crown and church through *encomienda, corregimiento,* and *congregación,* segregation broke down on a broad front. Despite legal injunctions and the paternalism of missionaries, *encomenderos* and their agents dwelt in indigenous communities, and European vagabonds tarried in them; Spanish merchants set up shop in major towns, and itinerant traders visited smaller ones. Around European municipalities, the need for labor created native *barrios* (wards) at first populated by *encomienda* Indians but increasingly swollen by migration from countrysides disrupted by new conquests, civil wars, native resettlement, and epidemics.

For these several associations, Indians picked up many things. The tribute system, designed to provide goods for Spanish consumption, pushed them into raising European crops, animals, and fowl. Some of these introductions they adopted for their own use, but they retained a primary dependence on pre-Conquest crops and cultivated them in traditional ways. European labor requirements set them to new tasks and imposed different work rhythms upon them, but they did no more than they had to, and at their own pace.

Under pressure from missionaries, the Indians reluctantly began to wear European-style shirts and pantaloons, but they also wove their traditional mantles, using wool instead of indigenous feathers and fibers. They learned European artisanry, but the madonnas and angels they carved for monasteries and churches sometimes had a distinct Indian cast. In the sphere of nonmaterial culture, they accepted large numbers of loan words, chiefly nouns, to describe newly acquired things and concepts. In many regions they accommodated to European-style town life and developed a remarkable skill in municipal government, although their old chiefs still dominated the system. They also acquired an addiction to litigation and considerable ingenuity in tax evasion and counterfeiting.

All in all, the Indians showed a remarkable endurance and resiliency in responding to the multiple and conflicting demands put upon them, adapting in ways that their European masters never anticipated. They saved what they could from the wreckage of their ancient ways; they selected from among European requirements and offerings those things within their reach that suited them and molded them to their own needs. They rejected what they found unacceptable, and they covered the process of selection with a display of passive acquiescence.

## The Conquest Social Order

The Republic of Spaniards

The social values of the Spaniards applied in an American environment of conquest and colonization created what might be called a "Conquest social order." As in Old Spain, it was formed by ranks and classes of people, each with an ascribed and juridical status determined by its social function.

During the early stages of colonization, the orders consisted simply of a class of conquerors lording it over a mass of subjugated Indians distributed in *encomiendas*, Neo-Scholastic theory furnished a rationalization of the relationship. In 1541 Domingo de Betanzos, a Dominican friar resident in Mexico, expounded:

It is necessary that for a republic to be well ordered and sustained, there be in it valorous and powerful and wealthy persons and *caballeros* and nobles, because these are the bones whose structure sustains the republic; . . . no republic could be more unfortunate and deprived than one in which all are poor, cast down, and needy, because such people cannot . . . aid each other which would be the case if no one had villages in their charge or *señorios*.[32]

The need to accommodate new social groups in the American republic soon produced a more elaborate ordering, which conformed roughly to the European society of orders. Conquerors turned *primeros pobladores* and *encomenderos*, who formed some 2 percent of the Spanish population in 1570, gave promise of evolving into a colonial nobility, retracing the process that created the nobility of Castile. Although a few among them were hidalgos of established lineage, most were commoners who gained honor by virtue of military service rendered or owed to the king. They were the American equivalent of the *caballeros villanos* of Reconquest towns. Through the progressive extension of rights granted to first settlers in Española, they enjoyed exemption from head taxes. Some among them obtained the *fuero* of hidalgos by special royal grace. A few won knighthoods in the Spanish military orders that, although not hereditary, were considered to be marks of nobility. And to a very few the crown gave noble titles. Cortés became the marquis of the Valley of Oaxaca; Pizarro, the marquis of Pizarro.

The possession of Indians gave the conqueror-*encomendero* class an economic and territorial base of power and a measure of de facto *señorio*. Its members dominated the *cabildos* of conquest municipalities. In the style of the

Castilian nobility they built townhouses as large as their means permitted. In them they ruled as paterfamilias over wives and concubines, legitimate and illegitimate progeny, close and distant blood relatives, fictive kin, clients and hangers-on, and household servants and slaves.

The clerical estate took quick and deep root in the Indies. Within two decades after the fall of Tenochtitlán a complete ecclesiastical organization, from archbishop to parish priest, had been created, and the main orders of the regular clergy taught, preached, and meditated, each having its provincials, abbots, brothers, and lay brothers. As a corporation, the church enjoyed essentially the same *fueros* and reputational status as the clergy of metropolitan Spain. Pious bequests and endowments, the favor of royal officials, and entrepreneurial activities provided it with an economic base of power and influence.

An incipient third estate consisted of *vecinos moradores*, that is, townsmen who did not hold *encomiendas* but possessed freehold houses and properties in the cities and *villas* in which they dwelt. Preeminent among them were the wholesale merchants who established themselves in the main urban centers of the Indies. Although they did not possess honor, they enjoyed wealth, which was the next best thing. They constituted, moreover, a de facto urban guild and thereby acquired the substance of corporate status that, in Hispanic culture, gave the whole a social weight greater than the sum of its parts. It also enabled them to exert collective pressures against public officials to advance their business interests. In predominantly commercial centers, such as Veracruz, Cartagena, and Panama, well-to-do merchants obtained seats on *cabildos*.

Professional men constituted a second important element of the *morador* class. *Letrados* were the most prominent group among them. At first they came from Spanish universities, but after the 1550s graduates of the Universities of Mexico and Lima swelled their numbers. They served the king, colonial corporations, and private parties. Their social status derived from their association with the majesty of the law, their university degrees, and their leadership in the intellectual life of the Indies. Although they did not constitute a guild, common backgrounds, functions, and interests gave them a degree of internal cohesion. They could qualify as *vecinos*, but very few became members of *cabildos* except in a service capacity. The professional class also included substantial numbers of notaries, who enjoyed less prestige than degree-holding lawyers. Not enough doctors of medicine practiced in the Indies to form an identifiable social group.

Artisans formed a third major sector of the common element. Because of the mechanical nature of their offices, they held a social rank inferior to that of merchants and professional men, and, except for master craftsmen, most lacked the substance to qualify as *vecinos*. As fast as cities and *villas* were founded, however, they organized themselves into chartered guilds and gained corporate status. Guilds also sponsored *cofradías* that played an important part in municipal social life.

The Spanish population included elements that did not fit into traditional functional categories and had no collective identities. Owners of mines who did not possess *encomiendas* could qualify as *vecinos moradoes* and, in predominantly mining communities, were well represented in *cabildos*. Much more numerous was a transient and unpropertied lower class consisting of unincorporated craftsmen who plied their arts illegally; petty tradesmen; overseers of *encomiendas*, rural estates, and mines; and uncounted vagabonds whose idleness and depravity caused civil and ecclesiastical officials unceasing concern.

### The Uncertain Status of the Indians

The Spaniards had more difficulty accommodating non-Europeans in civil society, for they conceived of it as an organic unity in which all elements from highborn to low shared a common Catholic heritage and culture. In addition, at the time of the Discovery the concept held the implicit assumption that, regardless of rank, all were free subjects of the crown.

The millions of indigenes did not quite meet these conditions. Technically they were free subjects of the crown, but in the eyes of Europeans they were manifestly an inferior race. The Spaniards, armed with superior valor and virtue, had conquered them. They spoke incomprehensible tongues and had vicious customs. Much worse, they secretly worshiped Satan and his minions; they accepted European labor requirements reluctantly and slowly; and in many parts of the Indies they were so imperfectly pacified that they posed a threat to European dominion.

Queen Isabella, Emperor Charles, and many churchmen of good will proposed to remedy the Indians' defects by precept and example, but, pending the realization of these intentions, European hopes, prejudices, and apprehensions assigned them an extraordinary and provisional juridical status defined in both paternalistic and discriminatory terms. On the one hand, the law tried to protect them from their own vices and European exploitation. On the other, it required them to pay tribute as a mark of subjugation. It also forbade them to leave their communities except for labor assignments and then only temporarily, to dress in European finery, to bear arms, to go about on horseback, and to matriculate in universities. The church, moreover, refused to ordain indigenes in the secular or regular clergy, and most guilds excluded them from membership.

The survival of the cacique class complicated the incorporation of the indigenous peoples into the republic. The crown felt obliged to respect its natural *señorío*, needed its assistance to govern the Indian masses, and, perhaps, viewed it as a political counterbalance to the *encomenderos*. For these reasons, Emperor Charles confirmed its preeminence by granting its members the *fuero* of hidalgos, the privilege of being addressed as Don, and the right to hold land for its private use. He also dispensed it from the payment of tribute and the restrictions on movement and behavior imposed on the Indian masses. A few chiefs of royal blood such as the descendants of Moctezuma obtained noble titles (the counts of Moctezuma). Thus, the native nobility ranked juridically in the second estate, but it remained reputationally Indian.

### Free Blacks and Mixed Bloods: Social Anomalies

The accommodation of blacks in the Conquest social order at first presented no serious difficulties. They were familiar, although inferior, peoples to whom law and tradition had already assigned a status. Those who were slaves were not properly a part of the republic. They subsisted as a separate juridical entity. Those who were free technically enjoyed the same legal status as European vassals of the crown, although in fact they bore the taint of infamous origin. In any case, during the earlier years of the Conquest both enslaved and free blacks were few, dispersed, and Hispanicized. But, as the importation of savage *bozales* mounted, the presence of Africans became more visible and menacing, and Spanish prejudices against their perceived physical and cultural defects deepened, extending even to the free colored and beclouding their status in the republic.

By the end of the Conquest, a burgeoning population of unassimilated mixed bloods constituted the most serious obstacle to the formation of a well-ordered republic. The Spaniards had no place for such peoples in their scheme of things, no precedents for guidance. They regarded the products of miscegenation as a social embarrassment and, like blacks, a social menace. Contemporary Peruvian jurist Juan de Matienzo summarized European attitudes: "The free Negroes and mulattoes, and some mestizos . . . are restless, mischievous, and incorrigible, and there are so many of them and they are increasing so rapidly, that the time could come when they will roister about in bands, committing assaults and robberies, or they will concert with the Indians and seduce them into rebellion."[33] Geographer and cosmographer López de Velasco concurred.

For the most part, mestizos are well-disposed, agile, of good strength and industry, and clever enough for anything. But they are poorly inclined toward virtue and for the most part given to vices. They do not enjoy the laws and liberties which the Spaniards have nor can they hold Indians in *repartimientos*, except for those born of legitimate matrimony. . . . There are many mulattoes and sons of Negroes and Indian women who are called *zambaigos*, and these people have come to be the worst and vilest in these parts. Because there are so many of them and also of mestizos, some regions are in danger of disorder and rebellion.[34]

Like the conditions that gave it birth, the Conquest social order was unstable. Its constituent elements did not have clearly defined reputational and juridical qualities. But by the same token it had a high degree of flexibility. European immigrants and established *moradores* who enjoyed royal favor could still obtain *encomiendas* and enter the proto-nobility. Enterprising settlers could become rich in mining and commerce, and, although the possession of wealth in itself did not convey honor, it provided the means to buy honor. Among the lower orders, Indians could flee their rural bondage and, like the medieval European serf, find "freer air" in towns and cities. Legitimate and legitimized mixed bloods could still find a home in European society.

# CHAPTER 9

# The Royal *Señorío* in the Indies

The Crown of Castile gained the Indies by conquest, but it had to confirm, consolidate, and defend dominion so acquired. It was also obliged to provide justice and good government to its trans-Atlantic subjects, European and Indian, for contemporary political theory still held that this was the first duty of princes. Administratively, these multiple tasks involved the enactment of laws suitable for New World kingdoms and the creation of a governmental apparatus to exercise in them what Spanish jurists recognized as the four primary functions of government: *jurisdicción* (judicial), *gobierno* or *policía* (legislative and administrative), *capitanía general* (military command and defense), and *hacienda* (treasury management).

## The Legal and Moral Bases of Spanish Dominion

In a society that set great store on moral and religious bases of action, the Castilian crown had the primary obligation of establishing a just title to the Indies. Two immediate and quite acceptable sources lay at hand in the discovery and occupation of uninhabited lands and, as in the Canary Islands, the conquest of non-Christian lands and people. But to legitimize further her claims, Queen Isabella secured the Alexandrine bulls of donation. As the advance of conquest and colonization uncovered the complex realities of relations between Christians and pagans, savants cast about for alternative or supplementary justifications and found them in the Aristotelian doctrine of the natural servitude of barbarians, in the law of nations that upheld the freedom of civic and commercial intercourse among peoples, and in the replacement of pagan tyrannies

182

by Christian justice and good government. In the Indies royal officials negotiated directly with native princes to obtain formal acknowledgment of Castilian sovereignty.

Differences of opinion among Castilian jurists and theologians on such a vital issue generated prolix and acrimonious disputes and produced propositions verging on lese majesty. The crown listened patiently but rather consistently found the title conveyed by the papal donations sufficient to satisfy its conscience and support its political and diplomatic interests. Meanwhile it got on with the business of incorporating American discoveries and conquests into its patrimony. In 1493 Isabella charged Juan Díaz de Fonseca, archdeacon of Seville and a member of the Council of Castile, with the direct administration of her new dominions. At about the same time, the general accountants (*contadores mayores*) of Castile took charge of royal revenues deriving from those regions, and the Council of Castile assumed jurisdiction in legal cases originating in them or affecting them. By 1511 the increasing volume of overseas affairs led to the formation of a special committee of the Council of Castile to manage them. In 1519 a royal order formalized these several arrangements by annexing Española to the Crown of Castile. In the following year its provisions were extended to the rest of the known Indies, and in 1523, to New Spain. In 1524 the king elevated the special committee of the Council of Castile to the status of an independent body, the Council of the Indies, which assumed general control over administrative, judicial, fiscal, and military matters in the American kingdoms.

Several considerations affected the giving of laws to the Indies. Castilian legal theory, increasingly infiltrated by Roman principles, conceived of justice in ideal, abstract, and universal terms and of law as a set of ethical and moral precepts to instruct conduct rather than as rules to regulate it. The rapid advance of conquest and colonization created innumerable particular situations that had to be dealt with justly. And as a private person confronted with the direct responsibility of ruling the king had to accommodate numerous conflicts of interest; that is, he had to act politically. Finally, to guide him, he had only spotty and faulty intelligence, often furnished by interested parties.

The laws actually promulgated derived from several sources. At first, they consisted of miscellaneous orders and provisions including the papal bulls of donation, royal patents for discovery and conquest, instructions to overseas governors, and particular enactments such as the Laws of Burgos. The accumulating corpus of legislation, however, had many gaps, and Emperor Charles attempted to fill them by ordering that the Laws of Toro, the most recent compilation of Castilian law (1505), should prevail in America. At the same time he directed that Indian usages and customs be respected so long as they did not conflict with this code, the imperatives of evangelization, or royal prerogatives. But he also provided that the application of particular provisions of Castilian law or the elevation of indigenous custom to the status of law required a special royal order.

The conditions of its formation produced a *derecho propiamente indiano* (corpus of law distinctively Spanish American) that had complex and contradictory characteristics. First, in spirit it was eminently casuistic, setting standards of behavior far beyond mortal capacity to meet and imposing an organic inflexibility on the whole. Second, the effort to give justice in each and every particular instance led to an inordinate concern with minutiae. Third, abstract principle and social reality formed a dialectic in which law became the synthesis. Finally, the dialectic along with the rapidity of legal formation led to numerous inconsistencies and contradictions between particular enactments. Taken together, these several qualities provided a constant temptation to law evasion, an invitation to litigation, a paradise for lawyers, and an impregnable refuge for bureaucrats.

## *Colonial Challenges to the Royal* Señorío: *Captains of Conquest, Municipalities, and* Encomenderos

The creation of de jure sovereignty in the Indies was a relatively simple matter. It involved only the reconciliation of opinions of jurists and theologians in a form acceptable to the crown, along with the extension of the king's law to the Indies. The establishment of de facto *señorío* was a task of much greater magnitude because it ran squarely up against the aspirations and pretensions of the most powerful interests in the New World: the captains of conquest, the conquest towns, and the *encomendero* class.

By the terms of their *capitulaciónes*, *adelantados* generally held the titles of governor and captain general and they had authority to dispense justice and collect revenues, distribute lands, and, sometimes, to make provisional *repartimientos* of Indians in territories they discovered and conquered. These faculties they held dear, as their rewards for service and sacrifices and as the foundations of great lordships, and they were reluctant to relinquish them.

In the course of conquest and colonization, the towns of the Indies acquired a set of rights and privileges that together amounted to *fueros*, although in both Spain and the Indies in the sixteenth century this term tended to be replaced in official documentation by *ordenanza* (ordinance), implying the supersedure of granted or contractual privileges by royal law. Unlike the medieval Castilian charters, individual municipal ordinances in the Indies were not single documents; they were rather accretions of provisions deriving from patents for conquest, general and particular royal enactments affecting towns, concessions extracted from the king by founders or granted by him for special services, and municipal legislation that might or might not have royal approval.

Because of their diverse origins, the ordinances of conquest towns were often ill-defined and contradictory and varied from locality to locality, but they contained a more or less common set of rights. They vested municipal government in a corporate *cabildo* whose organization was outlined in chapter 7. During the first stages of colonization, *cabildos* could grant *peonías* and *caballerías*, issue local regulations for trade and business as long as their provisions did not conflict with the laws of Castile or the Indies, vote ordinary and extraordinary taxes, and convene *cabildos abiertos* (deliberative assemblies of invited *vecinos*). They also had the right to send their *procuradores* (town attorneys) to court to present grievances or solicit favors and could hold regional procuratorial assemblies as a means of communication among towns or to formulate collective petitions to the king. At least forty such gatherings took place in Española, Cuba, Chile, Mexico, and Peru in the 1500s, most of them during the first half of the century.

In the decades immediately following conquest, the American municipalities exercised their rights and privileges with a vigor reminiscent of the Reconquest towns of Castile. The crown approved their initiative as long as they directed it toward the organization of conquered territory, but Habsburg kings had a congenital mistrust of municipal liberties that was further sensitized by developments in both its old and new kingdoms. In Castile, the Revolt of the *Comuneros* had threatened Charles's succession to the throne. In the Indies, the ambiguities of municipal ordinances and the insulation provided by distance encouraged towns to interpret their rights broadly and enact legislation conflicting with royal policy and law.

The *encomendero* class acquired control over the labor and tribute of a large part of the conquered population in the Indies. Its members pretended to *señorial* rights over their Indians, regarded them as vassals, and in practice exercised a substantial measure of jurisdiction in rural areas. Like the captains of conquest, they believed that they had preemptive rights to their *encomiendas* because of the services they had rendered to the king and the suffering they had endured during the Conquest. The interests of *adelantados*, municipalities, and *encomenderos* had a substantial congruence. The captains of conquest themselves were the greatest *encomenderos* and the titular leaders of other conqueror-*encomenderos*. *Encomenderos* dominated the *cabildos* of most of the conquest towns.

## *The Instruments of the King's* Señorío

### Treasury Officials, Investigating Officers, and Royal Governors

The imposition of royal sovereignty in the Indies constituted a task not unlike the ordering of Castile by the Catholic Kings, and the crown had the same means at hand that it had used to discipline the *ricos hombres* and the *consejos* of Old Spain: the law, a set of royal judicial and administrative institutions, and a corps of magistrates and accountants to staff them. The ordering of New World dominions, however, presented particular difficulties. They were far away. Contemporary political mores obliged Christian princes to be generous to subjects who served them well, and prudence dictated that proud and powerful captains should not be pushed too far. Furthermore, conquest and colonization proceeded more rapidly than the resources of the crown could be mobilized. Isabella and her successors, therefore, proceeded diplomatically, often deviously, giving with one hand and taking with the other, retreating from confrontations and compromising when expedient.

The great *adelantados* presented the most immediate challenge to the royal *señorío*, and, while their enterprises were still under way, the king began to send out functionaries to recover sovereign faculties donated to them or usurped by them. The process followed a fairly standard sequence in each region as it was conquered and pacified. It is perhaps indicative of royal priorities that the first crown agents to appear were *oficiales reales de hacienda* (treasury officials), often accompanying expeditions of discovery and conquest to see that the king got his honest share of booty and profits. This temporary provision rapidly evolved into permanent treasury offices (*cajas reales*) placed in major towns and cities and headed by a *tesorero* (chief treasurer), a *contador* (accountant), and a *factor* (manager of the crown's business enterprises and transactions).

As pacification and colonization proceeded, income from loot and booty declined and the main sources of crown revenues came to be: (1) the *quinto*, a royalty on bullion produced, which at first came to as much as two-thirds of assayed value but later dropped to the standard one-fifth or less to stimulate production; (2) Indian tribute; (3) an *almojarifazgo* (customs duty) on European imports; (4) profits from business enterprises owned by the crown or in which it invested; (5) the *diezmo* (tithes); and (6) *bulas de la Santa Cruzada*, which were indulgences sold to provide funds for wars against the infidel. The last were first used during the Middle Ages. They had outlived their function but not their fiscal utility. Between 1534 and 1543 the yield of the American treasury averaged 252,000 ducats a year, and by 1557 it had risen to 1,203,235 ducats, about 11 percent of total crown revenues.

The second step toward establishing the royal *señorío* in the Indies was the dispatch of investigating magistrates (*juezes pesquisadores* and *juezes de visita*) to look into charges of misgovernment of *adelantados* acting as governors and magistrates, or the sending out of judges to take their *residencias*. If the king's agents cast their eyes in the right directions, they could easily find cases of misconduct—usurpation of authority, frauds against the treasury, mistreatment of the Indians—that provided legal justification for depriving offenders of their administrative and judicial offices.

A third step was the appointment of royal administrators to govern the "provinces," roughly delineated during conquests and centered on conquest towns. The status and nomenclature of these units varied. The most prestigious were called *gobernaciones* and had a governor at their head. They were generally situated where external defense was an important consideration, that is, in frontier regions molested by unpacified Indians and maritime districts exposed to corsair raids. Thus, the provinces of Zacatecas, Veracruz, and Cartagena were *gobernaciones*. Others were called *alcaldías mayores* and were governed by *alcaldes mayores* (not to be confused with *alcaldes ordinarios*, who were municipal magistrates). They tended to be organized around important Spanish towns that served as their capitals. A third type was the *corregimiento*, administered by a *corregidor*. It was originally introduced for the governance of the Indians, but, as European colonization expanded, the crown began to appoint *corregidores de españoles* to govern provinces dominated by Spanish cities and *villas*. In many instances the king appointed conquistadors to these posts, but they held them at the king's will, not by *señorial* patents.

Despite differences in nomenclature and rank, all provincial administrators exercised much the same functions. Within their territories they proclaimed and enforced the crown's orders and assisted in the collection of its revenues. As magistrates they took cognizance of litigation to which the crown was a party and heard appeals from municipal justices. They had the right to intervene in municipal government when the king's interests were at issue, to confirm the election of *alcaldes ordinarios*, and to sit ex officio in the meetings of the *cabildos* in their provinces. On military frontiers, governors frequently held the title of captain general.

Royal Audiencias and Viceroys

Misgovernment, real or alleged, provided the justification for the penultimate step in the recovery of the king's sovereignty in newly conquered regions, namely, the establishment of royal audiencias. Like the Castilian *cancillerías* on which they were modeled, American audiencias had primarily judicial functions. They decided appeals from subordinate magistrates, although important civil suits could be appealed from audiencias to the Council of the Indies; they possessed original jurisdiction in criminal cases originating in the cities in which they were seated and its immediate environs, as well as in civil suits to which the crown or its officials were parties. But, in addition, the king gave them governmental authority in order to curb the power of the *adelantados* and to end the turbulence of conquest.

The first American audiencia, that of Santo Domingo, was created in 1511 with its seat in the city of the same name. It was given jurisdiction and political command over the Antilles and Tierra Firme at the expense of the heirs of Columbus. The second, the Audiencia of Mexico, was established in 1528 and seated in Mexico City. It exercised jurisdiction and political command in all of New Spain, thereby supplanting Cortés as chief magistrate and governor of the lands he had conquered.

Despite their august presence and ample powers, the first American audiencias failed to bring justice and good government to the new kingdoms of the Indies. Collegiate administration bred dissension and caution, which in turn delayed decisions and impeded energetic action. Moreover, even royal magistrates succumbed to the temptation to enrich themselves at the expense of the king and his Spanish and Indian subjects. In Mexico, the audiencia and its president, the conquistador Nuño de Guzmán, behaved with a rapacity and licentiousness that gained them enduring notoriety and led, in 1530, to their dismissal and the appointment of a second audiencia, whose members were carefully selected for their rectitude.

The disorders in Mexico convinced King Charles that he needed a personal and powerful representative in the Indies. In 1535 he sent out a viceroy to govern the kingdom of New Spain, the ultimate step toward establishing full royal sovereignty in the Indies.[1] The qualities of his appointee, Antonio de Mendoza, testified to the importance he attached to the post. Mendoza was a scion of one of the greatest families of Spain, one whose noble lineage ran far back into the Reconquest and whose members had served the crown faithfully in civil, military, and ecclesiastical offices. Antonio himself had led loyalist troops against the rebellious *comuneros*, had been chamberlain of the queen, and, at the time of his selection, was Charles's special ambassador to Hungary.

Mendoza's titles conveyed almost plenary powers to him. As viceroy he was the king's alter ego in the Indies and therefore entitled to the same reverence and obedience from European and Indian subjects as the king would have enjoyed had he been present in person. In addition, Charles named Mendoza ex officio president of the royal audiencia of Mexico and governor and captain general of New Spain, which, at the time, extended southward into Central America, northward into the *tierra incognita* beyond the frontiers of settlement, and thence eastward to include Florida. For governmental purposes it also incorporated the Antilles. He was also appointed superintendent of the royal treasury within these territories.

During the three decades following Mendoza's installation, the crown extended and consolidated audiencial and viceregal government. A milestone in its efforts was the New Laws of the Indies, promulgated in 1542. The New Laws provided for the establishment of two new audiencias, their immediate purpose being to enforce the anti-*encomienda* legislation of the code. One was the Audiencia of Lima, seated in the city of the same name and exercising jurisdiction and political command over the Isthmus of Panama and all of Spanish South America excepting the settlements on the coast of Venezuela, which remained under the authority of Santo Domingo. The other was established for the governance of Central America. During the first few years of its existence, its seat and limits shifted about, but it finally settled down in Guatemala City and took its name from its capital. Its jurisdiction and command extended from the Isthmus of Tehuantepec to Panama, excepting Yucatán, which remained attached to the Audiencia of Mexico. In addition, the New Laws contained provisions for standardizing the organization and procedures of American audiencias.

The New Laws also had an indirect but far-reaching effect on the structure of royal government in the Indies. The Audiencia of Lima not only failed to enforce their anti-*encomienda* provisions but supported the protests of Peruvian *encomenderos*. This situation, coupled with the general turbulence prevailing in conquered Inca lands, induced the crown to create in 1544 a second American viceroyalty, the Viceroyalty of Peru, whose capital was fixed in Lima and whose territory included Panama and all of Spanish South America excepting Venezuela. Like his counterpart in New Spain, the viceroy of Peru also had the title and functions of president of the audiencia seated in his capital and of governor, captain general, and secretary of the royal treasury within his realm.

As conquest and colonization advanced, new audiencias were created in regions that, because of distance, could not be administered effectively from existing centers of government. These were the Audiencia of New Galicia (1548) in northwestern New Spain, with its seat in Compostela; Santa Fe de Bogotá (1549), with its seat in the city of the same name and jurisdiction over the Kingdom of New Granada; Charcas (1559), with its capital in La Plata (Chuquisaca) and with jurisdiction over upper Peru, including the rich mines of Potosí, and over Paraguay; Panama (1567), exercising jurisdiction over the Isthmus of Panama from its seat in the city of the same name; Quito (1563), whose territory extended from northern Peru into modern Colombia and whose capital was the City of Quito; and Chile (1565), which was seated in the City of Concepción.

The personnel of American audiencias normally consisted of a president who, if not trained in the law, presided ex officio, at least four *oidores* (magistrates), a *fiscal* (crown attorney), an *alguacil mayor* (chief constable), a chaplain, a solicitor for the poor, assistant attorneys, notaries, and scribes.

The status of audiencias in the Indies varied. As judicial bodies all had equal or coordinate jurisdiction; appeals went from each directly to the Council of the Indies. In terms of their relationships with other superior agencies of royal government, however, they fell into three types.[2] Those of Mexico and Lima have been termed "viceregal" by modern scholars because their presidents (ex officio) were, respectively, the viceroys of New Spain and Peru, and they served viceroys as advisory councils of state in administrative, military, and treasury matters. Another type was called, in the terminology of the times, a *presidencia* because it had its own president, resident in its capital. In modern typologies such audiencias have been called "subordinate," because the viceroy in whose realm they lay served as governor, captain general, and secretary of the royal treasury within their jurisdictions. Into this category fell the Audiencia of New Galicia, in the Viceroyalty of New Spain, although formally it did not actually have its own president until 1575 and, in the Viceroyalty of Peru, the audiencias of Panama, Quito, Charcas, and Chile. In practice, dependent audiencias exercised as much administrative authority as they could appropriate and were in frequent contention with viceroys.

A third type of audiencia was located in regions where defense was a major concern of government but that were too distant from Mexico or Lima for viceroys to exercise effective military command. Its president was also the captain general, governor, and superintendent of the royal treasury of its district. Because of its military character contemporaries referred to it as a *capitanía general* (captaincy-general), and modern scholars classify it as "pretorial."

Although captaincies-general were nominally subordinate to viceroys in defense matters, they enjoyed virtual autonomy in all functions of government, reporting directly to the Council of the Indies. This class included Santo Domingo and Guatemala, in the Viceroyalty of New Spain, and New Granada, in the Viceroyalty of Peru.

To keep his American viceroys, magistrates, and governors on the path of rectitude, the king retained the *visita*, *pesquisa*, and *residencia*, first used in the Indies to bring *adelantados* to book. For the highest level of investigations the Council of the Indies selected the judge-commissioners, who took the *residencias* of senior colonial officials and conducted visitations of their administrations. The appointees of American audiencias conducted *residencias* and made visitations at the provincial level. If found guilty of malfeasance or misconduct, the subjects of the several forms of investigation were subject to fines, confiscations, imprisonment, or combinations of these penalties. As another method of control, the crown forbade its colonial officials to marry, hold property, or engage in business within their districts lest they become involved in conflicts of interest or develop local identifications.

## Colonial Capitulations and Rebellions

The extension of royal government to the Indies effectively deprived *adelantados* of their *señorial* prerogatives. For the most part, they accepted their demotions as became loyal and chivalrous vassals of the king. They might go to Spain or send envoys to represent their merits at court, and some entered into prolonged litigation to recover donations made in their patents. They all received gracious thanks but, beyond that, only nonpolitical favors and awards. The crown allowed the heirs of the first of them, Christopher Columbus, to retain the title and privileges of Admiral of the Indies, granted them a perpetual annuity of 10,000 ducats, and created for them the dukedom of Veragua and the marquisate of Jamaica. These fiefs, however, lay in poor and virtually unpopulated regions.

Cortés, the greatest among them, came off the best, perhaps because he added such rich and populous dominions to the royal patrimony, perhaps because he was such a powerful figure in the lands he had conquered that he could not safely be treated ungraciously. In any event, in 1529 Emperor Charles created for him the marquisate of Oaxaca, which encompassed some of the richest lands in central and southern Mexico, granted him *encomiendas* totaling 23,000 tributaries, and gave him civil and criminal jurisdiction in his territories. The marquisate was a true *señorío*, one of the few the king permitted in the

Indies, but Cortés held it not by right of conquest, only by royal grace and mercy.

The expansion of royal government also curtailed the liberties of towns. The appellate jurisdictions of audiencias and provincial administrators limited the judicial authority of *alcaldes ordinarios* to minor cases. Viceroys had the authority to confirm, review, and amend municipal ordinances and the exclusive right to grant land in pacified areas. Provincial administrators could intervene directly in municipal affairs. Emperor Charles also extended the practice of appointing *regidores perpetuos* (councilmen with permanent and hereditary tenure), which not only permitted the placement of non-*encomenderos* in *cabildos* but also provided an important source of royal patronage. As for procuratorial assemblies, the emperor believed them to represent a dangerous tendency toward democratic government in the Indies and as early as 1530 pronounced that "without our express command it is not our intention or will that the cities or towns of the Indies meet in convention."[3] Except on newly won frontiers, by the end of the conquest the municipalities in the Indies had lost much of their earlier vitality and, in effect, were appendages of royal government. This outcome, however, cannot be attributed entirely to royal policy. By that time, towns had completed their main task, the colonization and organization of conquered territory, and not much remained for their governments to do except deliberate over narrow local issues, engage in factional local politics, and spend time and money on the innumerable fiestas and ceremonies that enlivened municipal life.

In most instances, the captains of conquest and the towns accepted the loss of their political privileges docilely, but the crown's offensive against the *encomienda* in the 1540s appeared to settlers as a threat to their very existence and provoked the first violent political crisis in Spanish American history. The epicenter of the disturbance lay in Peru, where the New Laws had a special impact. One of their articles provided that everyone who had participated in the wars between the Pizarrists and the Almagrists should be deprived of their *encomiendas*, and most of the conquerors had been compromised on one side or the other. When Blasco Núñez de la Vela, the first viceroy, arrived in 1544 to exact compliance with the code, he encountered intransigent hostility not only from settlers but from the audiencia and the episcopacy. When negotiations broke down, Gonzalo Pizarro led a revolt, cloaked as a "supplication" to the king for justice, which crown officials and loyalist settlers did not put down until 1548 and then only by concessions to *encomenderos* and promises of amnesty to rebels, which together induced most of them to defect to royalist forces. Summary courts-martial condemned Gonzalo and his principal captains to execution and lesser rebels to banishment, flogging, and penal servitude in Mediterranean galleys. Another uprising occurred in Nicaragua in 1550, encouraged by refugees from Peru who had escaped the king's justice. The rebels gained control of the province and threatened Panama before loyalist forces destroyed them.

In New Spain, Viceroy Mendoza averted rebellion by persuading *Visitador* Gonzalo Tello de Sandoval to suspend the exection of the New Laws that he had been sent to enforce. The resentments and apprehensions of the Mexican *encomenderos*, however, carried over into the second generation. In 1564, the brothers Alonso and Gil González de Avila hatched a plot to overthrow the vice-regal government, proclaim Don Martín Cortés, the great conqueror's son, king of New Spain, and redistribute the spoils of conquest among the sons of the conquerors. The conspiracy gained widespread support among *encomenderos* and among Indian caciques who transferred their reverence for Hernán to his heir. The death of Viceroy Luis de Velasco in 1564 also favored the plot since it left the government of the kingdom in the hands of a rather timid audiencia. The conspirators, however, managed the affair badly, talking so much that everyone knew about it, while Don Martín vacillated, sometimes appearing to lend his support but covering his position by maintaining cozy relations with royal officials. Finally, in 1566, the audiencia plucked up the courage to act. It arrested Don Martín and sent him back to Spain and imprisoned the González brothers in Mexico. These measures panicked the other conspirators, who hastened to denounce each other. King Philip sent over a judge armed with plenary powers, who arrested all those touched by suspicion and, after summary trials, executed many of the scions of conquerors and first settlers. The marquis fared not too badly. His trial in Spain failed to produce sufficient evidence of treason to convict him, a finding that might have been affected by a personal loan of 100,000 pesos which he made to the king. He escaped with a fine of 50,000 pesos but never returned to Mexico.

The conspiracies and rebellions of the *encomenderos* threatened the very foundations of the royal *señorío* in the Indies, but, in the end, the crown triumphed. For the most part, the American settlers were poorly organized, and, although they harbored deep resentments, most drew back from renouncing irrevocably their allegiance to a monarchy that they held in reverence, that was the source of all legitimate favors and titles, and whose retribution they feared. The king and his officials in the Indies exploited American weaknesses with an efficacious combination of amnesties, tactical withdrawals, and calculated ruthlessness. The royal victory, nevertheless, did not allay the discontents of the conquerors and first populators and their sons, who made up the elite of the Spanish Indies.

## King and Church: The Royal Patronage in the Indies

The establishment of full royal sovereignty in the Indies, as the Castilian kings perceived it, involved the subordination of the church to the crown in all spheres except the definition of dogma and the maintenance of religious discipline. This end had to be obtained at the expense of the papal jurisdiction, but in negotiations and contentions with Rome the kings of Castile held many advantages. The Bulls of Donation had given them sole responsibility for the evangelization of the Indies, and they could claim that they required plenary powers to fulfill their mission. The Spanish hierarchy accepted this position, and, to ensure its continued support, the crown honored the church and favored prelates with important posts in colonial administration. Thousands of miles and the entire apparatus of Castilian civil and ecclesiastical government intervened between Italy and the Indies. In addition, Rome could not press its claims too militantly, for it was beholden to Their Catholic Majesties for creating millions of new communicants; it needed their military and diplomatic support in Italian affairs and depended on them increasingly for the defense of the Catholic faith against Lutheran heresy.

The accumulation of regal rights began when the Enterprise of the Indies was scarcely underway. In 1501, the Catholic Kings obtained a bull granting them the tithes in America. These revenues, however, were to be used mainly for the support of the church, and, in fact, this became the practice. A second bull, issued in 1508 and based on precedents established for the Kingdom of Granada and the Canary Islands, gave the king the right of presentation (nomination) for all ecclesiastical benefices in the Indies from archbishoprics to parishes, allowed him to approve or reject the nominations of commissary generals for important offices in the religious orders, and gave him control over the founding and construction of churches and monasteries.

The crown also obtained from the Holy See, first on an ad hoc basis and in 1543 by a general pontifical concession, the right to establish episcopal jurisdictions in America, define their limits, and fix their seats. As in creating civil units of government, it set up bishoprics closely in the wake of conquest. At first, New World dioceses were suffragan to the archbishop of Seville, but beginning in the late 1540s archepiscopal sees were erected independent of peninsular jurisdiction. Thus, between 1511 and 1564 Castilian kings erected a complete ecclesiastical organization in the Indies composed of twenty-two dioceses roughly coterminous with major civil provinces and suffragan to five archdioceses founded in Santo Domingo (1545), Mexico (1546), Lima (1546), Tegucigalpa (1561), and Santa Fe de Bogotá (1564).

Papal donations and concessions formed a most ample *patronato real de Indias* that Castilian kings regarded as the most honorable and prestigious of all its *regalías*, "the richest stone, the most precious pearl, in the royal diadem."[4] Around it they unilaterally erected legal and institutional safeguards. They required clergymen to obtain a royal license to go to and from the Indies and regulated their movements while there. They demanded that, before entering their office, prelates swear an oath of loyalty and fealty to the crown and vow to respect patronal rights. They closed off direct communications between Rome and the church in the New World by providing that no bull, brief, rescript, or other pronouncement of popes could be published or enforced in America without the royal exequatur and by forbidding papal legates and nuncios to go there. They asserted the right to convoke and prorogue church councils and synods and to suspend the publication of their proceedings. They circumscribed the ecclesiastical *fuero*, which had been extended to America, by ordering that disputes over competence be decided by royal courts. As an ultimate resort, they declared that jurisdiction in *causas de patronato* (contentions over patronal rights) be determined by their own councils and audiencias rather than by ecclesiastical tribunals.

The crown held the *patronato* to be indivisible and imprescriptible, but, because of the volume of work entailed and the remoteness of its American dominions, it delegated patronal functions to royal agencies and officials. In Spain, the Council of the Indies recommended to the king the churchmen who were to be presented to the pope for prelacies and to American bishops for offices in cathedral chapters. In the New World, viceroys, audiencias, and governors, acting as vice-patrons, nominated candidates for curacies to bishops, managed the collection and use of tithes, and had direct control over the construction of religious edifices.

The attitudes of the missionary orders, particularly in New Spain, where they were most firmly established, posed a special kind of threat to the royal *señorío* in matters of ecclesiastical government, one which was analogous to the challenge of the *encomenderos* in the temporal sphere. Even after episcopal jurisdictions had been established and secular clergy became available for the ministry of parishes, the friars tenaciously resisted secularization of their *congregaciones* on the grounds that only they possessed sufficient devotion and experience to care for the fragile souls of the indigenes. Indeed, some of the more exalted spirits among them aspired to create a separate Indian church, independent of the authority of bishops. The pretensions of the friars, if sustained, would have divided the *patronato* and complicated its exercise. But, more important, they would have removed permanently the spiritual control of much of the native population from the episcopacy, which, in the main, accepted subordination to the crown, and placed it in the hands of the regular branch of the church, which, historically and because of its command structure, had stronger and more direct ties with Rome.

As with the *encomenderos*, the crown did not move forcefully or directly against the missionary orders. It had a deep commitment to the rapid and universal evangelization of the indigenous population and realized that the religious orders possessed the best qualifications for the task. In addition, the establishment and manipulation of balances of power among contending interests, ecclesiastical as well as civil, constituted a key element in evolving imperial government, and kings may have deemed it politically inexpedient to give a spiritual monopoly to the bishops. In the 1560s a number of circumstances conjoined to erode the pretensions of the friars. The second generation among them lacked the total commitment of the first apostles to the Indies; they divided into factions disputing over doctrine and method; and the several orders contended with each other over territorial jurisdiction so violently that on one occasion the Augustinians challenged the Franciscans to resolve a dispute at point of lance. The orders managed to hold on to their congregations and to govern them in matters spiritual and temporal with considerabl autonomy, but the central issue of secularization remained very much alive.

Despite occasional setbacks and frustrations, by 1560 or thereabouts Spanish sovereigns enjoyed a control over ecclesiastical government in the Indies that was quite unusual when compared with church-state relations in other European monarchies and, indeed, in Spain itself. The crown managed to intrude even in matters of religious dogma and discipline. Its right of presentation enabled it to influence the opinions of bishops, and its authority over church councils allowed it to intervene in their deliberations. It also possessed inquisitorial powers, which were exercised in the Indies by bishops and abbots under the general direction of the Council of the Inquisition in Castile.

As the American political scientist J. Lloyd Mecham wrote, "It can be contended with considerable truth that the king was more than a patron in America; he exercised quasi-pontifical authority."[5] And in the political sphere the church became an arm and a shield of royal authority. In return for the moral and material support it received from Spanish kings, the clergy, high and low, preached obedience and loyalty to the monarchy and contributed generously to the reverence in which it was held by Europeans and Indians alike.

## The Governance of the Indians

The governance of the Indians presented special problems. The conquerors found millions of indigenes subsisting under well-developed political hierarchies and were content to govern through existing systems as long as they provided labor and tribute. At first the crown adopted the same policy and formalized it by appointing native leaders as governors of provinces and, at the municipal level, allowing them to hold key posts in government. In these several capacities, they ruled their subjects according to ancient customs and usages that did not conflict with the Laws of Castile.

The vulnerability of the Indians to exploitation, however, and the fiscal interests of the royal treasury soon led to modifications of government through intermediaries. Many of the laws of the Indies dealt specifically with the treatment of the indigenes, and the crown created special offices to see that they enjoyed justice and good government. At the superior level of administration it appointed senior civil and ecclesiastical officials as "Protectors of the Indians," and at the provincial level *corregidores de indios* provided a direct link between Spanish and Indian government. The functions of inspection and investigation also acquired a special form in the Indian *visita*, which, in addition to collecting tribute data, looked into the conduct of *corregidores, encomenderos*, and chieftains. Many *visita* records survive to provide a major source for modern ethnohistorians. But, despite the intervention of the crown in Indian administration, by the end of the Conquest *encomenderos* retained considerable political influence in the countryside, and in congregations the friars disputed the temporal authority of both *corregidores* and *encomenderos*.

## The Defense of the Indies

### Indian Frontiers

While the kings of Spain were reducing their American subjects to polity and obedience, they also had to develop the function of *capitanía general* to cope with peoples and princes who did not accept their exclusive *señorío* in the Indies. Around the peripheries of Spanish settlement, wild Indians resisted conquest, developed an intransigent hatred for the intruders who wished to enslave them, and menaced European settlements and communications. The main threats came on the extreme southern and northern frontiers of the empire. In Chile, south of the Bío Bío River, dwelt the Araucanians, a robust and bellicose race that quickly developed a sophisticated military organization and body of tactics. They surrounded their settlements with stockades and, in the field, constructed trenches fronted by abatis. They captured and stole Spanish horses and created a formidable light cavalry. They learned quickly that harquebuses and cannons take time to load, and by ambush, swift charges, and maneuver they overcame much of the military advantage that the Spaniards possessed by virtue of their monopoly of firearms. Throughout the sixteenth century they defended their forested redoubts stubbornly and from them raided far north into the central valley, making Chile a land of war.

In northern Mexico lay the Gran Chichimec, inhabited by unsubdued Indian tribes. After their defeat in the rebellion of New Galicia, they simply withdrew into remote mountain regions. They were fierce warriors, who, before battle, stimulated their courage by taking a hallucinogen, probably mescaline. Their main weapon was the bow, which they could fire rapidly and accurately, and their slim arrows had a penetrating power that amazed and confounded the Spaniards. Like the Araucanians, they evolved new organizational and tactical devices to fight the Europeans. They quickly adopted the horse, which provided them with mobility and allowed them to strike suddenly and withdraw just as rapidly into their mountain and desert fastnesses; they sent spies into Spanish towns and engaged in strategic destruction of livestock; they adopted the Spanish practice of surprise attacks at dusk and dawn and specialized in ambuscades. Contemporary European observers marveled at their military skills: "They have so many strategems that I doubt that they are equalled by soldiers long in Italy and, above all, they never fail in anything they try." And, "They defend well their property without having any, and they fight and skirmish as if they were Moors of Granada."[6] During the 1550s and 1560s, Chichimeca peoples mounted increasingly ferocious attacks on the mines and cattle ranches of the north and harassed the roads leading from those regions to Mexico City.

For frontier defense, the crown at first called on *encomenderos* to fulfill their military obligations. This class provided the army that subdued the native rebellion in New Galicia, and in Chile it was the only military force at hand. The feudal host, however, did not provide an effective force for sustained warfare. The geographical dispersion of *encomenderos* made for slow mobilization. The mentality of the conquerors, moreover, changed with remarkable rapidity. As soon as they became populators with fixed residences and properties, they lost their martial spirit, devoted themselves to extracting revenues from their lands and Indians, and argued that if they were summoned for extended campaigns their sources of subsistence and status would go unattended and the work of colonization be undone. The second generation of settlers showed an even stronger distaste for arms. In addition, many *encomiendas* fell into the hands of female heirs, and, after the New Laws, others reverted to the crown, thereby diminishing the number of *encomenderos* available for military service.

Beginning in the 1550s the crown turned to different kinds of forces to defend Indian frontiers. One was companies of soldiers, paid from its treasury and officered by its appointees, whose mission was to search out and destroy bands of hostile Indians. The other was municipal militias whose formation was based on ancient Castilian laws requiring all able-bodied *vecinos* to maintain arms and muster to the defense of their communities in time of danger. On occasion they mobilized to reinforce the king's companies. In addition, colonial governors fortified towns in southern Chile and, in northern Mexico, built presidios at strategically located sites. These measures, however, were not very efficient, because royal troops were raised only for particular campaigns and received little regular training and discipline. The militia had no formal organization, and no permanent provisions existed for military supply and finance.

### Defense against Foreign Interlopers: Diplomatic Countermeasures

Spain's European neighbors presented a threat of a different order to its dominion in the Indies. The papal donation as revised at Tordesillas settled for the time being rival Spanish and Portuguese claims in the West, but Francis I of France, it is reported, expressed a desire to see the clause in Adam's will that excluded him from a share in newly discovered lands, the English held that the pope had no authority to give or take away kingdoms, and the king of Denmark refused to accept the Supreme Pontiff's determination of dominion in the East Indies. The issue at stake in these contentions actually broke down into two parts, linked by a common origin in the bull *Inter Caetera* of 1493. First, Spain advanced what can be distinguished as a "Territorial Claim," that is, the exclusive right to discover, settle, and rule all lands west of the line of Tordesillas. Second, it maintained a "Navigation Law Claim"; that is, Spanish laws regulating commerce with the Indies bound the subjects of all nations.

Spain tried to defend its American interests in two ways, one of which was diplomacy. Its ambassadors at the English and French courts repeatedly sought to secure unconditional acceptance of both its territorial and navigation law claims, but the effectiveness of such representations depended principally on the state of Spanish relations with the two northern European nations. Until well into Elizabeth's reign, England maintained its traditional alliance with the rulers of the Netherlands, and this meant peace with the Spanish Habsburgs. English monarchs therefore restricted their challenge to gaining entry into the commerce of the Indies. At its European end, they negotiated an agreement permitting English Catholics to reside and trade in Spain. In addition, John Hawkins made three voyages to Spanish America (1558–62) with Elizabeth's support, but he did not have overtly hostile intentions. He sought, rather, to offer assistance in policing the Caribbean against corsairs in return for commercial privileges. Philip did not accept the scheme, but Hawkins and other Englishmen began a clandestine traffic in slaves that breached Spain's commercial monopoly but not the peace between the two nations.

The French caused much more trouble. Their kings conceded partial recognition of Spain's territorial and navigation law claims but held that its exclusive dominion in America pertained only in regions actually settled. In any event, the almost continuous Habsburg-Valois wars in the first six decades of the sixteenth century precluded a permanent agreement between the two powers and gave France an excuse for overt intrusions into the Indies and their commerce. As early as 1504, Gallic corsairs began raiding Spanish trans-Atlantic shipping in the triangle of waters bounded by the Azores, the Canaries, and Andalusian ports. In 1523, Jean Fleury, commanding a squadron belonging to Jean d'Ango of Dieppe, seized two vessels of a fleet bringing back the loot of conquered Mexico to Emperor Charles. The yield of spectacular gold ornaments, jewels, and feathered cloaks opened French eyes to what the Spanish were really up to in the New World, excited their cupidity, and induced them to step up their attacks. In some years as many as seventy of their ships prowled the Atlantic approaches to Seville and its satellite ports.

Beginning in the 1530s, French corsairs extended their marauding to the Indies themselves, first in the Antilles and later along the Main, attacking not only Spanish shipping but also coastal settlements. Up to the Treaty of Crespy (1544), which terminated the fourth Habsburg-Valois war, they limited their hostilities to wartime. Thereafter they raided during interludes and truces, thus foreshadowing a principle of European international relations that later came to be expressed by the phrase "no peace beyond the line"; that is, peace between nations in Europe had no force west of the longitude of the outermost of the Azores and south of the Tropic of Cancer. The peak of the corsair offensive came during the mid-1550s, when as many as thirty French ships appeared annually in the Indies virtually dominating the seas around the Antilles and pillaging coastal towns on Española, Puerto Rico, and Cuba at will. Meanwhile, beginning in the 1540s, they supplemented raiding with contraband trade.

The Treaty of Cateau-Cambrésis (1559) ended a half century of warfare between the houses of Habsburg and Valois, but French corsairs in diminished numbers continued to raid Spanish shipping in American waters, especially along the Main, where swelling shipments of silver from Nombre de Dios offered tempting prizes. In addition, French contraband trade with small Spanish settlements on the Antilles and the northern coasts of South America became routine. Ironically, peace in Europe enabled French merchants to establish themselves as "naturalized" persons in Andalusian ports and thereby gain legitimate entry to the Indies trade.

Safeguarding the Sea
Lanes: The *Carrera de Indias*

A second and more direct method of defending the Indies and their commerce was the construction of military and naval defenses. First priority went to securing the *Carrera de Indias*, the maritime lifeline linking Spain and the Indies. The patterns of conquest and colonization, along with the directions of winds and currents, shaped its course. During the Antillean phase of settlement, it followed favorable winds from Seville and its outports on the Gulf of Cadiz to the Canaries, which provided revictualing, and on across the Atlantic to San Juan, Santo Domingo, and Santiago de Cuba. After the conquest of Mexico, it continued on to Veracruz, passing along the southern coast of Cuba and through the Yucatán channel. Following the conquest of Peru, a branch developed running from an American landfall in the Lesser Antilles along the Main to Nombre de Dios on the Isthmus of Panama. After its discovery around 1513, the Gulf Stream took homeward-bound ships from Havana through the Bahama Channel and north along the coast to the latitude of the Carolinas, where fair winds blew east toward Europe.

Like most of Spain's policies in the New World, the defense of the *Carrera* developed in an ad hoc fashion. Immediately after Fleury's coup in 1523, the crown organized a naval squadron called the *Armada de la Guardia de la Carrera de las Indias* to police waters at the European end of the route. Convoy sailings for Atlantic crossings became the general practice very early, because they pooled navigational skills and provided collective security against disorders in the weather. The appearance of French marauders, first in European waters and then in the Caribbean, furnished an additional incentive to send ships in convoy. After the outbreak of the fourth Habsburg-Valois war, in 1542, the Council of the Indies forbade departures of groups of less than ten sail and required all ships to be armed. Meanwhile, security requirements along with the growing volume of trade encouraged the use of larger and larger vessels that could carry not only more cargo but heavier armament. This trend culminated in the 1550s with the appearance of the galleon, a vessel of 500 or more tons burden, square rigged, with heavy broadside batteries and wooden castles perched fore and aft.

Fortifications and Coast Guards in the Caribbean

The first American convoys had no fixed organization or schedule of sailings. Usually they consisted of vessels that gathered at Seville and its outports and then sailed to America when all were ready, which meant irregularly. After crossing the Atlantic and entering the Caribbean together, they divided into two flotillas, one going to Tierra Firme and Panama and the other serving the Greater Antilles, Honduras, and Mexico. In each flotilla the two heaviest armed vessels served as the *capitana* (flagship of the captain in command) and the *almirante* (flagship of the admiral second-in-command). On the return voyage both fleets stopped at Havana for victualing and repairs but did not always return across the Atlantic together.

In the Indies themselves defense meant not only the security of the *Carrera* but the protection of interisland commerce and of settlements exposed to corsair raids. To these ends the Spanish adopted several interrelated strategies. Beginning in the 1530s colonial governors began to fortify important ports and and organize militia companies to defend them. Then, in the 1540s, when trans-Atlantic convoys were in American waters, their commanders detached frigates to partrol the Caribbean, Finally, in the 1550s, light mobile squadrons based on Santo Domingo were organized for this purpose.

The continuation of French corsair depredations into the 1550s demonstrated the inadequacy of these measures. As on Indian frontiers, those who benefited directly were expected to bear the burden of defense, but the population of the Antilles and Tierra Firme was sparse, impoverished, and little disposed to make financial and personal sacrifices even for its own security. Locally based naval patrols sailed irregularly, and fortifications of ports languished. In 1560 only Santo Domingo had a reasonably complete set of permanent works. Elsewhere installations were limited to masonry central keeps and artillery bastions, sometimes linked together by walls of wood and rubble. Permanent garrisons consisted only of an *alcaide* (commander), one to three artillerymen, and a few black slaves, while armament was insufficient in quantity and in poor repair. It was expected that, when attack threatened, garrisons would be reinforced by mobilized militiamen, but the effectiveness of this reserve depended almost entirely on the energy of local leadership. Except in main towns and cities, companies existed only on paper; *vecinos* were reluctant to confront corsairs who generally outnumbered them, and many preferred to work out a modus vivendi with the interlopers based on illicit trade.

## *Royal Government in the Indies: Powers and Limitations*

By the end of the Conquest era, the Crown of Castile had promulgated a body of laws and created an apparatus of government that fully established its *señorío* in the Indies. This achievement represented the overseas extension of a well-established monarchical system but with some of its features strengthened and others weakened. On the one hand, the king not only created positive law for his New World realms but created those realms themselves, by an act of will. He not only ruled them but possessed them as integral parts of his patrimony. No great lords challenged his sovereignty. Leaving aside native princes, who did not count for much, he was the sole natural *señor* in his newly conquered dominions. Nor did his American kingdoms possess liberties and *fueros* that he had to swear to uphold upon his succession to the throne, and there were no American *cortes* that had to agree to new taxes or approve royal enactments. The crown's economic and political *regalías* were virtually unlimited and included an extraordinary measure of power in the governance of the church.

On the other hand, a number of juridical and circumstantial influences tempered the exercise of royal sovereignty. In the Indies as in Castile, the king was morally and legally obliged to give justice and good government to his subjects, and he was bound by divine and natural law. He could not be a tyrant. On these points learned jurists instructed his intelligence and his confessors illuminated his conscience. Although he often compromised principle for political and fiscal reasons, legal and moral considerations unquestionably restrained any arbitrary or tyrannical impulses he may have felt. From a more practical standpoint, the ever-present threat of colonial rebellions induced him to avoid or back off from the full exercise of his authority.

The law also provided a number of peaceful recourses against royal actions that subjects deemed injurious to the commonweal or to their own interests.

Colonial authorities could, on their own initiative or upon petitions from *vecinos*, invoke the formula *Yo obedezco pero no cumplo*. This translates literally as "I obey but do not comply," but in a legal sense it "suspended" or "stayed the execution" of an order pending an appeal to the crown for reconsideration. In addition, individuals had legal means to protest or evade the king's writ. They could "supplicate" him as chief magistrate to reverse or amend an action he had taken as chief lawgiver, or they could use the device of *composición*, that is, dispensation from wrongdoing in return for a payment, generally nominal, to the royal treasury.

The organization of royal government itself further diluted the force of the king's laws and decisions, for at each level its several offices and agencies possessed coordinate and overlapping authority in the exercise of the principal functions of government: justice, legislation and administration, defense, and treasury management. Thus, in Spain, the Council of the Indies was responsible for all of these, but in each it acted through standing committees whose membership overlapped. In the New World, audiencias were encharged with the administration of justice, but in viceregal and pretorial audiencias viceroys and captains-general served as their ex officio presidents and in viceregal and dependent audiencias viceroys could determine whether contentious cases should be resolved administratively or judicially.

With respect to the other functions of government, viceroys and heads of pretorial audiencias, as governors and captains-general, held supreme political and military command within their districts, but treasury officials had to approve extraordinary expenditures they wished to make, and the law required them to seek the advice of the audiencias seated in their capital in making important policy decisions. Furthermore, these audiencias assumed full governmental authority when the office of viceroy or captain-general fell vacant without a successor having been named. Treasury officials were primarily responsible for managing the king's revenues, but viceroys and captains-general superintended their work, and audiencias made preliminary examinations of their accounts before these were sent to the Council of the Indies for final audit. As vice-patrons in the Indies, viceroys interposed themselves in ecclesiastical administration but also found it politic to consult archbishops and bishops about secular matters, and on occasion prelates became interim viceroys.

In lower echelons of administration, provincial governors intervened in municipal affairs and informally shared their several functions with *encomenderos* and missionaries. And in every office and at every level, functionaries could interpret orders from above in ways that they deemed professionally correct or that suited their personal interests.

The overlapping and coordinate competences of governmental agencies created a system in which each checked and balanced the other and that traditional historiography attributes to the king's desire to ensure his exclusive *señorío* by diffusing power among his servants overseas. This may very well have been so, but other influences also contributed to the arrangement.[7] It was inherent in the constitutional personality of the monarch, which made him chief magistrate, chief lawgiver, and chief administrator. The union of these functions in his subordinates was a perfectly normal procedure and, indeed, had ample precedents in metropolitan Spain. It also reflected the immediate imperatives of the Conquest era, when royal officials in the Indies had to be given whatever kinds of authority they needed to establish order and law. Finally, it offered a way to save salary money, a consideration always pressing on the king's mind. In any event, while the system of checks and balances unquestionably helped to prevent concentration of governmental authority in the Indies, it also encouraged bureaucratic "buck-passing" and jurisdictional disputes that delayed and diffused the application of royal orders and laws.

The qualities and conditions of employment of the servants of the king in the Indies also weakened the effectiveness of his rule. Drawing on Max Weber's models, they formed a "patrimonial" rather than a "rational" bureaucracy in that governmental offices were regarded as parts of the royal patrimony and were staffed on that basis.[8] The principal requirement for appointment to them was not professional merit but demonstrated loyalty and previous service to the monarchy, not necessarily in the capacity for which the office called, and an influence with the king or with persons who had his ear. Once they were appointed, the tenure, remuneration, and advancement of officials still depended more on royal favor than on meeting objective standards of performance. While it is true that *residencias* and *visitas* inquired into their conduct, the crown could set aside or suspend the judgments of its investigators at its pleasure.

The judiciary constituted a partial exception to these generalizations. Royal magistrates and attorneys were required to have doctorates or licentiates in civil or canon law, but, the qualifications of candidates being more or less equal, personal or family influence governed their selection. When exercised by strong and conscientious monarchs, patrimonial government could and did produce some outstanding administrators, such as Antonio de Mendoza, the first viceroy of New Spain. However it could and did lead to the appointment of incompetent, indifferent, and venal officials, especially at lower and less visible levels of government, where, in practice, patronage was controlled by the Council of the Indies and American viceroys.

The honesty and effectiveness of the royal bureaucracy was further undermined by the propensity of its members, at all levels and in all departments, to acquire local kinship and business connections, despite repeated prohibitions against this practice. Such associations created conflicts between private interests and public duty that all too often were resolved to the detriment of the latter.

Overextended communications systems provided another kind of check on royal authority overseas. Some 4000 statute miles, measured lineally, stretched between Madrid and San Juan, Puerto Rico, the easternmost port in the Indies, another 2200 miles from San Juan to Mexico City, the capital of the Viceroyalty of New Spain. It was more than 700 miles from Mexico to Culiacán, the northernmost outpost of the viceroyalty, and 1300 to Costa Rica, its southernmost province. From Madrid to Panama, it was 5100 miles and another 1550 from Panama to Lima, the capital of the Viceroyalty of Peru. Within the viceroyalty, 1600 miles separated Lima from Cartagena at its northern extreme, and 1800, from Concepción, Chile, at its southern limit.

But these figures merely define the gross dimensions of communications systems. For people and ships and horses, linear distances were immeasurably lengthened by the interposition of natural and human obstacles and hazards: at sea, the direction of winds and currents, storm patterns, reefs and shoals, and lurking corsairs; on land, precipitous slopes, raging rivers, deserts, thick forests, swampy flood plains, and hostile Indians. Spanish imperial communications, therefore, can best be described in terms of the time required to travel from one point to another.

Reliable statistics are available for elapsed times on the *Carrera de Indias*. Convoys took from 70 to 179 days to get from the mouth of the Guadalquivir to Veracruz. The average time was 91 days. Those sailing to Panama consumed an average of 92 days on the outbound voyage, with the shortest time recorded being 43 days.[9] It took less than two months to sail from Chile to New Spain, but the return voyage might consume a year. Father Reginaldo de Lizarraga told of a Spaniard he knew who was conceived and born on the southward passage and whose mother became reimpregnated before the ship reached Coquimbo, in Chile.[10] Reliable compilations of travel times by land are not available, but following are some random estimates based on contemporary accounts: Veracruz to Mexico, 7-9 days; Mexico to the mines of Zacatecas, 15 days; Lima to Cuzco, 22 days; Cuzco to Bogotá, 23-24 days; Bogotá to Cartagena, 21-28 days.[11]

The enormous extension of imperial communications determined that intelligence move very slowly from outlying provinces of Spanish America to major capitals, thence to ports, and then across the Atlantic to Seville and the Spanish court. In the course of its transmission from place to place it might very well be lost, overlooked, or deliberately distorted or, at best, become outdated. Royal measures based upon it were likely to be unrealistic or inconsistent and therefore were susceptible to evasion or suspension. Laws and policy statements moved equally slowly along reverse routes, and, at each point where action was indicated, they could be reviewed, suspended, or temporarily tabled. Thus it might be said that a rule of distance applied to the governance of the Indies; that is, the force of the king's writ diminished in proportion to the increase in distance between its point of declaration and its point of application.

Ultimately, royal sovereignty in America depended not upon its imposition but on the general acceptance by colonial elites of the king's right to rule. To ensure acceptance he had to act with restraint and moderation. The system of government that evolved step by step and piece by piece to meet these conditions appears inordinately cumbersome and inefficient, but efficiency is a modern value and has never stood at the top of the Spanish scale. The primary aim of Hispanic government was the accommodation of interests within the republic, and it would have been thwarted by excessive zeal and rational organization.

By the end of the Conquest era the sovereignty of the king in the Indies had also been secured against Spain's enemies. Chichimecas and Araucanians still harassed European settlements and communications on the frontiers of the empire, but they reconquered no territory, in part because of Spanish military superiority but more fundamentally because the weight of demographic and material resources inclined heavily to the European side. In the Caribbean and on the Main, shipping and settlements lay vulnerable to privateers, and smuggling was endemic, but the territorial integrity of the Indies remained intact. In truth, however, this apparent success resulted less from the efficiency of Spanish military measures than from geopolitical circumstances. Spain established itself firmly in the New World before its European rivals developed the national will, organization, and logistical capabilities to seize and hold significant lodgments there.

# CHAPTER 10

# The Fruits of the Land

*Población* required that the land be made fruitful so that its people prosper and multiply and royal revenues be augmented. In the broadest sense, fructification included the exploitation of everything the land yielded, animal, vegetable, and mineral, or, to put it in modern terms, the development of the economy of the Indies. A description of this process begins with a look at the primary factors of production — natural resources, labor, and capital.

## The Factors of Production

### Natural Resources

Land furnished the main natural resource of the Indies and, in regions where the Spaniards first settled, it was abundant. Before the European discovery, some Indian cultures may have been facing Malthusian crises, but most of their agricultural systems used only a fraction of the arable and very little of the grazable potential of the soil.

Many parts of the Indies had rich endowments of minerals. Auriferous sands and ores existed in Española, Puerto Rico, and Cuba, in central and southern Mexico, on the Caribbean side of Central America, in the Colombian Andes, and at scattered sites in Ecuador, Peru, and Chile. The main silver deposits lay in northern Mexico and Upper Peru, with smaller concentrations in the uplands of Honduras, northern Peru, and Chile. Other metallic ores included iron, in northern Mexico, Cuba, Venezuela, and the central and southern Andes; copper, in Mexico, Cuba, Peru, and Chile; and tin, in Mexico and Upper Peru. The

Spaniards, however, esteemed base metals much less than gold and silver. Oviedo reported that copper had great value and utility in the Old World but no one, not even the poorest, bothered to extract it in the Indies because of the Europeans' feverish preoccupation with gold.[1] Behind their neglect, however, lay sound economic reasoning. Nonprecious metals had a low weight-value ratio and could not be transported on long hauls as profitably as gold and silver. Other forms of mineral wealth to be found included precious diamonds and emeralds in northern South America and less exotic and more widely distributed things such as salt, lime, and various kinds of building stone.

In addition to cultivatable land and mineral wealth, the Indies had vast plant resources, including wood, which could be employed for construction and fuel; leaves, roots, barks, saps, and flowers useful for food, beverages, drugs, dyes, fabrics, and cordage; and grasses to sustain grazing animals. In many regions flowed streams and rivers that could be tapped for irrigation or diverted to provide power.

In the main, European settlers found the resources of the Indies easy to acquire. By virtue of discovery, papal donation, and conquest, not only did the Crown of Castile hold dominion over the New World kingdoms, but all their lands, waters, minerals, forests, precious gems, salt deposits, and hidden treasures were *regalías*. The crown could give them over to private parties and did so under generous terms. In the case of land, it allocated enough to Indian communities to meet their estimated needs and made grants to European settlers by various devices. *Adelantados* received donations in the regions they discovered and conquered running up to tens of square leagues, and they could make allotments of *peonías* and *caballerías* to their followers. *Cabildos* exercised the same rights. The king or, in his name, viceroys, audiencias, and governors made land grants to persons who agreed to settle in newly founded towns and to others considered to be deserving of royal mercy and grace. The only limitation placed on such concessions was that to receive *el dominio pleno e irrevocable* (full title) the recipient had to place the land under cultivation within a specified period of time, generally four or five years, and to obtain royal confirmation of the grant if it had not been received directly from the crown.

The king found it economical to grant, rent, or sell rights of exploitation of subsoil resources to private parties on liberal terms but reserved ultimate title and required the impresarios to pay a royalty, the *quinto*. He rented, contracted, or simply licensed the right to harvest the fruits of the forest and to grow and process high-value plantation crops such as silks and dyestuffs.

The location of many primary resources tended to offset their abundance and ease of acquisition. Some were remote from population centers and ports, so that their exploitation entailed high labor and transportation costs. Some having a complementary relationship were disadvantageously placed. Two instances of maldistribution stand out. One was the distribution of water with respect to cultivable land. Much of the most fertile grain land was concentrated in areas with only marginally sufficient rainfall. The other was the location of wood vis-à-vis silver deposits. At the time of discovery, forests had been depleted in the main centers of Indian civilization, and the requirements of the Europeans for construction and fuel accelerated deforestation. A particularly acute situation existed in silver-mining districts, which needed large and continuous supplies of timber to shore up shafts and tunnels and to provide fuel. Unfortunately, they happened to be located in terrain virtually devoid of forests. Also, the few and intermittent streams of the Mexican silver districts could not provide enough water to drive machinery.

## Labor: Indian Sources; the Repartimiento-Mita and Free Wage Labor

The conquered status of the indigenes determined that they would be the main source of labor in the Indies. "Without them," the contemporary Peruvian jurist Juan de Matienzo explained, "the republic could not be preserved, since the Spaniards do not work, nor is it fitting that they should."[2] During the first half of the sixteenth century, the labor supply was so abundant that the conquerors and first settlers used it wastefully, through slavery, the repartimiento-encomienda, and the corregimiento. Noninstitutionalized forms of exploitation also existed. Before the arrival of the Europeans, Indian lords possessed servants who had, in one way or another, lost their tribal or community identities and were bound perpetually to their masters. The conquerors simply appropriated them and added to them from the numerous indigenes dislocated by conquest and congregation. In New Spain and the Antilles, such workers were called naborías; in Peru, yanaconas. Under Spanish rule they possessed a shadowy legal status. Because they had no tribal or village affiliations, they paid no tribute; they were not free, for they could not leave their masters; neither were they chattel, for they could not be bought or sold. Some settlers managed to accumulate enough of them to constitute a personal labor force that they employed on their own properties or rented to others.

Around the mid-sixteenth century, a conjuncture of human and divine acts produced a major labor crisis in the Indies. By that time Indian slavery no longer counted as a major source of workers, because most natives were incorporated into *encomiendas* and *repartimientos*, and the New Laws of 1542 put an end to Indian bondage except in very special cases. Seven years later the crown prohibited personal service under the *encomienda* and the institution lost its utility as a direct source of labor. In the 1540s, also, new epidemics diminished the supply of indigenous workers available under any system. But, as the labor supply decreased, the demand grew, owing to the subsistence needs of a growing European and mixed-blood population and to the opening of the great silver mines.

Out of the crisis emerged a new form of the *repartimiento*. It differed from the *encomienda* in that it did not involve direct, long-term grants of native labor or tribute to private parties or institutuions. Instead, it provided drafts of crown and *encomienda* Indians to employers for specified tasks under an arrangement whereby villages sent assigned quotas serving in rotation. The crown closely regulated conditions of service and required beneficiaries to pay a just *jornal* (daily wage), which in practice amounted to a deduction from tribute owed. The arrangement was not entirely novel. In pre-Conquest Mexico, an institution called the *catequil* required the common folk to furnish labor drafts for work on state lands and on "public works" such as temples, palaces, roads, causeways, and ditches. A comparable arrangement called the *mita* functioned in Inca Peru. The Spaniards simply took over well-rooted indigenous practices, adapted them to their uses, and defined them in their terms. The crown justified the new *repartimiento* on several grounds. In legal terms it was defined as a commutation of tribute; it was presumed to combat vagabondage by putting "idle" Indians to work, and it was to be used only in enterprises contributing to the common weal. Colonial officials, however, construed the general welfare to include virtually all productive activities. In practice, the system provided a means to ration a rapidly diminishing human resource.

By 1560 or thereabouts, the new *repartimiento* had become the main supplier of labor in the Indies, especially in mass lots. It was supplemented, however, by other forms. On military frontiers enslavement continued, and in remote regions *encomenderos* still extracted personal services from their charges, openly or under various guises. The use of free wage labor increased owing to several circumstances. Epidemics and abortive congregation broke up traditional residential patterns and turned loose Indians who roamed the land seeking employment. It is likely also that in some instances working for hire simply represented a certain measure of rational adaptation of the indigenes to European labor systems. Those who sought work found it easily in mines, in workshops, and on Spanish agricultural properties. Yet, free wage labor was not always literally free. Indians who acquired skills in great demand commanded good wages and enjoyed mobility, but the unskilled often became bound to their employers by debt. By 1560, also, the free labor force included a growing number of mixed bloods and a smattering of emancipated blacks.

## Black Slave Labor

The Spaniards used black slaves as a supplement, complement, or substitute for Indian labor. Their employment had both advantages and disadvantages. On the one hand, Africans possessed greater physical stamina than Indians. Many came from iron age cultures, possessed artisan and agricultural skills, and, having been rudely uprooted from their native habitats, had no choice but to adapt to European requirements. On the other hand, they were in chronically short supply. The crown limited imports because it feared the effect of large African populations on public order and morality and because it did not like to use Spanish silver to buy from foreign suppliers. Probably no more than 31,200 black slaves entered Spanish American ports before 1570. Shortages along with speculation in import licenses also made slaves expensive. During the latter half of the sixteenth century, their price ranged from ninety to several hundred pesos a head, depending on sex, age, physical stamina, and market conditions.

Supply and cost factors made the use of black slaves economical only under certain circumstances: They could be employed as mass labor in enterprises such as gold mining or sugar planting that promised high returns on capital invested, or as individuals they could serve in occupations where their skills or dependability surpassed that of the indigenes. Consequently, African slaves constituted only a tiny fraction of the total labor force.

## Capital

Of necessity, the first capital in the Indies came from Europe through the media of Castilian, Italian, German, and Flemish investors. It was put to work in gold mining, slaving, pearling, and the sugar industry in Española, at interest rates that colonists and the archbishop of Seville thought excessive. In later years, European capital remained indispensable, especially in the commercial sector, but the Indies began to generate their own supply. The first sources were the gold fields of the Antilles, which yielded more than 8 million pesos, slaving, and the loot of mainland conquests. Cortés collected from Moctezuma a gift or, better to say, a tribute of about 162,000 pesos, and the ransom of

Atahualpa tallied out at 40,850 marks of silver and 971,125 pesos of gold, not counting the king's portion.[3]

As pacification proceeded, the tribute of the Indians rendered in money or in kind became a primary source of income for Europeans, supplemented by profits from agriculture, commerce, manufactures, and mining. Conquerors turned *encomenderos* displayed an entrepreneurial vigor that belies their image as feudal-minded lords of vassals content with revenue and status furnished by rents and dues. Using their loot and tributes, they made diversified investments in basic food production, commercial crops, extractive industries, textile manufacturing, and urban real estate. Some had annual incomes in the tens of thousands of pesos. Merchants settled in the major cities of the Indies also became wealthy, and by the end of the Conquest the church enjoyed substantial incomes from rents, tithes, and pious bequests.

How capital so generated was husbanded is one of the least-known chapters in the economic history of the Indies. Scattered evidence suggests that long-term accumulation faced many handicaps and hazards. A portion was used to pay taxes, especially the *quinto*, but, given the colonists' ingenuity in evading such obligations, the drain was probably small. Considerably more went to pay for European imports. In the Indies themselves investment practices had a highly speculative nature. When enterprises failed to yield bonanza-type profits, impresarios abandoned them for others that glittered more brightly, including chimerical El Dorados. They also spent inordinate amounts of money on lavish hospitality and other forms of conspicuous consumption, dowried their daughters generously, and gave large endowments to the church. Merchants tended to be more cautious, but throughout the private sector no structures existed that encouraged long-term capital accumulation. The most common forms of business organization were the family firm and temporary partnerships whose organization derived from the *commenda* or *societas* developed by the Italian cities for their Mediterranean trade and that the partners formed for a particular enterprise. The managers of capital were individuals, and the continuity of their fortunes depended on the initiative and acumen of their heirs. Among the *encomenderos*, at least, these qualities appeared to have diminished by the second generation. Finally, hazards of transportation, sharp price fluctuations, and changes in royal regulations could destroy fortunes suddenly. In contrast to land and labor, supplies of capital were limited and unstable. Hence, settlers favored land and labor-intensive rather than capital-intensive enterprises. Or, it might be more accurate to say, economic forces supported the Spaniards' culturally derived desire for *señorial* dominion over land and people.

## The Agricultural Sector

Introduction of Old World Plants and Animals

Although mines produced the most spectacular form of wealth, the husbandry of plants and animals constituted the basic economic activity in the Indies. It was the greatest employer of labor and produced most of what today is called the Gross National Product. As Father Las Casas observed, "It is a general rule that those who dug gold always lived in need and even in the jails for debt, while those who dedicated themselves to farming and husbandry became rich according to the standards of the times."[4]

Husbandry in the Spanish Indies began with the continued production of native crops, but the Europeans, although they accepted some of the garden vegetables cultivated by the Indians and ate corn and manioc when they had to, much preferred foods with familiar tastes and textures. They also wanted meats, fibers for clothing, and other products of the soil that were not indigenous to the New World. Hence, they devoted intensive efforts to the introduction of plants and animals from Europe. The crown required ships sailing to the New World to carry seeds, cuttings, roots, and breeding stock; it offered prizes and tax advantages to agricultural innovators; and it instructed colonial governors to devote particular attention to agricultural development. The missionary orders induced their charges to cultivate European crops and herd European animals, and captains of conquest understood that the permanence of their achievements depended on promoting husbandry.

The Spaniards experienced many difficulties in matching up Old World plants and animals with suitable American habitats. Among their staples of food and drink, wheat had a wide range of adaptability, but it ran to stalk instead of head in the tropics, and the seed mildewed and rotted in the humid passage across the Atlantic and the Caribbean. After many trials it finally found suitable conditions in the valleys and basins of the American cordillera lying at altitudes between 5000 and 10,000 feet, along coastal streams in Peru, in the central valley of Chile, and in the Rio de la Plata region. Wheat production in the Indies, however, did not begin to meet local needs until after the mid-sixteenth century.

The grape was more particular about its habitat, but it ultimately found a congenial home in the irrigated valleys of the Peruvian coast. In 1551, the Lima district produced the first American vintage. In the last half of the sixteenth century, cultivation spread to central Chile and across the Andes into the Argentine province of Mendoza. The olive was even more selective. The Spaniards finally found suitable soils and climates in coastal Peru and central Chile, but the delicate stock had to be conveyed from Europe to those remote regions without benefit of intermediate staging areas; the tree grew with excruciating slowness; and the first harvests did not appear until rather late in the century. These limited and hard-won successes did not quite live up to anticipations. Settlers found American vintages too harsh for their tastes and regarded American olive oil as inferior in flavor and consistency. Those who could afford it bought Spanish imports.

Colonists had varying success with other familiar food plants. Garden vegetables and melons did well except at extremely high altitudes and in unirrigated desert regions. Fruits such as peaches and apricots adapted quickly in temperate American climates, but apples, pears, and plums had more difficulty, producing yields inferior in quantity and quality to those of European orchards. Three Old World plants took especially well to the American tropics and subtropics. By the end of the Conquest, citrus fruits brought over from Andalusia and sugar and bananas introduced via the Canaries flourished in warm climates from central Mexico to Asunción, in Paraguay.

Among the animals that the Europeans brought to the New World, the tough Spanish swine adapted most rapidly, universally, and prolifically. It survived all but the most extreme climates, altitudes, and terrain; foraged for its sustenance; and produced copious litters thrice annually. By the mid-1500s practically every part of the settled Indies had an enormous swine population, and Cieza de León reported that Peru was curing bacon as good as that produced in the Sierra Morena of Old Spain.

Spanish cattle also took readily to life in most parts of the Indies. They were fast and mean and intimidated all predators except the largest felines. After Columbus brought the first breeding stock to Española in 1493, they multiplied rapidly there, quickly spread to the other Greater Antilles, followed the conquest to the mainland, and prospered wherever they could find grass and water. When they reached the boundless and bounteous grasslands of northern Mexico and the Rio de la Plata, their population exploded. They also flourished exceedingly on the rich pasturage of central Chile. Cattle adapted to Andean valleys and basins but did not multiply so spectacularly in those regions, because altitude and precipitous slopes restricted ranges.

For human purposes the horse provided the complement to the cow, since cattle could not be herded without highly mobile mounts. Fortunately, horses tended to prosper in the same natural environment that favored large bovine herds, although they were less hardy and reproduced more slowly. In 1531, ten years after the Conquest, Mexico bred only about 100 head a year, but, as set-tlement moved north into the grasslands, the equine population increased rap-idly. In the 1550s contemporaries reported some 10,000 horses grazing in the Mexican Bajío. In South America horses reproduced slowly in highland regions, but in Chile and Paraguay fine herds appeared quickly.

The sheep that Columbus brought over in 1493 did not find the heat and humidity of the Antilles congenial. The species did not begin to flourish in the Indies until the 1530s and 1540s, when Antonio de Mendoza introduced me-rinos into New Spain and gave special attention to their husbandry. The Span-iards brought sheep to South America immediately after the conquest of Peru. The creatures adapted well in the valleys and basins of the Andes and, like other European animals, found central Chile to their taste. From there they crossed the Andes into the province of Mendoza.

Other animals introduced by the Spaniards in the New World included goats, which were hardier than sheep and adapted to a wider range of environmental conditions; oxen, although they were not bred or used extensively; and asses. The mare, bred with the ass, produced the mule that was used throughout the Indies for transportation and animal power in mines and mills. The Europeans also brought with them common barnyard fowl, including chickens, ducks, and guinea hens. Chickens adapted to as wide a range of environmental conditions as swine, and, although they found formidable natural enemies among Amer-ican felines, foxes, and serpents, they scratched in every barnyard from northern Mexico to Arauco and Asunción.

In addition to deliberate transfers, other species found their way surrepti-tiously from the Old to the New World. Insect larvae and adults attached them-selves to roots and cuttings and animal breeding stock. Seeds of "Kentucky" blue grass, dandelions, daisies, and myriad "useless" plants arrived mixed with wheat and barley. Ships sailing to the Indies carried rats, mice and other un-registered animal passengers.

European Introductions and Ecological Changes

Old World flora and fauna introduced deliberately or accidentally into the New World had effects just as revolutionary as the impact of human conquest and the invasion of micropathogens. Transference unquestionably initiated far-reaching changes in landscape and ecology. Throughout the Antilles and the tropical circum-Caribbean, as well as in temperate forest lands, exotic importa-tions replaced indigenous vegetation. In some instances changes resulted from simple competition among species, but the clearing of land for agriculture and the cutting of timber for fuel and construction helped along the process by creating space for European transplants. In upland valleys, European grains and fruits displaced Indian maize, beans, and squash on a large scale and were planted in hitherto uncultivated regions. These transformations proceeded so rapidly and on a scale so vast that a century after Columbus discoverers would have found much of the landscape unfamiliar. Jesuit Father Bernabé Cobo, writing in the second quarter of the 1600s, grasped their magnitude: "The abundance with which all the animals and fruits and vegetables and all kinds of plants which the Spaniards have brought, flourish in the Indies . . . in many parts without the industry and aid of men. . . . [This] has led some, guided only by what they see, to believe that any of these things were not introduced but native to these lands."[5]

European animals contributed to ecological change in various ways. In the Rio de la Plata region and in northern Mexico, cattle and horses populated vast ranges that formerly had been virtually empty of large fauna, and in central Mexico cattle literally replaced the indigenous human inhabitants through a tragic circle of events. The decline of the native population occasioned by epidemics opened land to Spanish herds; the livestock invasion encroached on land still occupied; the hapless natives withdrew to marginally productive areas, thus reducing their food supply and making them more susceptible to disease. Further population losses opened additional land for grazing, and so it went. North of the thickly inhabited regions of Mexico, grazing livestock destroyed ground cover, bringing erosion and desiccation and opening the way for the replacement of indigenous grasses by shrubs and plants that withstood aridity. In the Peruvian Andes, the passage of animals breached retaining terraces, thereby facilitating heavy runoffs, erosion, and floods.

Ecological changes had debatable implications for long-range human habitation, but in the short term they had some positive consequences. Within two or three decades, introductions from the Old World doubled and perhaps tripled the number of plants cultivated in the Indies, relieved the paucity of domesticated animals, and created a quantitative increase in food supplies. The transference of the banana into the American tropics produced spectacular results. A small grove, requiring little attention, could provide basic subsistence for a family throughout the year. Furthermore, a wider selection of edible plants permitted diversification against drought and disease. Despite the many damages they did, the introduction of grazing animals made possible the exploitation of vast territories that before had had no utility except for scattered transhumant Indians.

The appearance of European animals also produced a revolution in the sources of animate energy. The pre-Columbian Indians had relied mainly on human power, and the Spaniards did the same during the early years of the Conquest. But as indigenous labor became scarcer and more closely regulated, the Europeans turned increasingly to the mule, the ass, and the ox for transport and for power to operate mines and mills. The Indians themselves quickly adopted the European ass, which became the ancestor of the burro, so endearing to tourists but so exasperating to those who had to prod it along.

Agricultural Production: Basic Foods and Fibers

Conquerors and conquered put the fruits of the land, indigenous and immigrant, to work according to their needs, capabilities, and values. The immediate requirements of both peoples was subsistence. After the coming of the Europeans, the Indians continued to cultivate maize, manioc, beans, squash, potatoes, and other traditional crops on their village lands. In addition, they selectively adopted a number of Old World cereals, fruits, and vegetables and took quickly to what the Spanish called *ganado menor*, which translates roughly as small livestock. Within a decade after the Conquest, pigs, goats, and chickens were a common sight in their yards and on their commons.

In highland regions, the Indians acquired flocks of sheep, which they used not so much for their meat as for their tallow, skins, and fleece. Except in isolated instances, the indigenes did not keep cattle. The Spaniards preempted pasture lands and also forbade the pacified natives to own horses, which were a symbol of the conquering race and a military threat in the hands of unsubjugated or rebellious peoples. Without this noble animal the Indians lacked the mounted mobility needed for herding.

During the early stages of colonization, the Spaniards obtained the foods they needed in two ways. First, they planted whatever would grow—vegetables, fruits, cereals—on their *peonías* and *caballerías*, and their pigs rooted on the commons. Their cattle grazed beyond cultivated zones, but ranching was unorganized, with an open-range system prevailing, and little attention was paid to land titles, Spanish or Indian. Second, they used native products selectively and required the Indians to plant European crops, appropriating a portion of both as tribute.

Local subsistence agriculture could not supply for long a growing population of Europeans and mixed bloods, especially the inhabitants of burgeoning administrative centers and mining communities. Commercial grain ranching developed, therefore, to meet the need. Enterprising first settlers extended their original *repartimientos* of land, and new arrivals acquired rural properties through royal grants. Both groups further increased their holdings through informal occupation of public lands (*tierras baldías*) and usurpation of Indian commons. On the ranches so created, they planted wheat and other cereals for sale to urban populations. Most holdings, however, did not exceed 100 acres, and only part of the land was planted in wheat each year.

Stock Raising

Stock raising expanded along with grain ranching. It provided a range of marketable commodities: meat, hides, skins, fleece, lard, and tallow. Compared with agriculture, it had economic advantages. Since breeding stock was cheap and ranges virtually free, it required little capital investment, and the management of flocks and herds needed only a minimal labor force. Grazing had an additional attraction for Spanish settlers. They associated the ownership of livestock and extensive grazing rights with the great *señoríos* of Old Spain, and they were well aware of the royal favor shown to the stockmen of Castile.

Spanish husbandry multiplied domestic livestock where favorable environments existed. In Andalusia and Extremadura, cattle herds rarely ran more than 800 or 1000 head, but, in Mexico by the 1550s and in Chile by the 1560s, some numbered in the thousands. At mid-sixteenth century contemporaries noted large flocks of sheep in the Mexican Bajío, and, in 1567, some 150,000 head, of which Indians owned a third, grazed in the vicinity of Santiago, Chile.

As herds of cattle and sheep multiplied, it became necessary to impose some sort of organization on their husbandry, particularly in the matter of grazing rights. Hence stockmen obtained from the crown or its officials in the Indies particular types of grants called *sitios* or *estancias*. In general, these conveyed the right to establish an installation, including housing and corrals, at specified sites on public lands and to graze animals on surrounding territory. In other instances cattlemen or sheepmen simply established *sitios* on unclaimed land without bothering to obtain a formal grant. Often, however, ranch installations were impermanent, and the boundaries of ranges were not defined or, at best, were expressed only in terms of rough metes and bounds, such as "as far as the eye can see in all directions," from the top of a specified natural eminence. *Estancias* and *sitios* appeared wherever the Spanish herded stock in large numbers, but they were most numerous and most extensive in New Spain north and west of the Valley of Mexico and in central Chile.

In contrast to the preeminence of sheepherding in Old Spain, cattle ranching predominated over sheepherding in Spanish America. A *mesta* was organized in

New Spain in 1537, but it was controlled by cattlemen. This reversal of position can be attributed to several circumstances. Wool exported from the Indies to Europe could not compete with the production of a firmly established and protected peninsular industry, whereas a growing European market for American cattle hides existed. Cattle, furthermore, could be raised more easily and economically than sheep, because they required less human care in breeding and herding and were less vulnerable to predators. Another influence may have been that during the first phases of colonization most settlers came from Andalusia and Extremadura, where cattle ranching also predominated over sheep grazing; hence, they simply inclined to the form of pastoral activity with which they were the most familiar.

### Sugar

Spaniards profited by raising basic food crops but, in general, neither quickly nor largely. Grain prices rose steadily in the middle decades of the sixteenth century, but the cost of labor increased even more rapidly, while the price of meat held steady or dropped. Poor transportation facilities limited the market range of these commodities. Because of its perishability, meat could not be sold far from the place of slaughter. In addition, everything had to be carried by Indian bearers or pack animals over rough trails so that the cost of moving bulky animal by-products or grain ate up profits except on short hauls. Enterprising settlers, therefore, began to cast about for products that had two qualities: one, an unsatisfied demand in either the Indies or Europe; the other, a high ratio between value and bulk or weight.

The product that first struck the colonists as meeting these requirements was sugar, which Europeans used mainly for making pastries and preserving fruit. Spaniards were already growing cane in the south of Andalusia and in the Canaries, and they knew that an insatiable sweet tooth existed on both sides of the Atlantic. Sugar processing also yielded molasses, a nourishing food item, and *aguardiente*, a cheap, raw, and potent rum. Columbus brought sugar cane to Española in 1493. Colonists began planting it on Puerto Rico and Jamaica shortly after the conquest of these islands. Cortés introduced it into Mexico in the early 1520s, and Pizarro into Peru in 1533, a year after his arrival. Planting began around Asunción in the 1540s.

### Dyestuffs

Dyestuffs also promised high and quick profits, for a booming European textile industry and an infant industry in the Indies required them in ever-growing quantities. Two sources lay immediately at hand. The forests of the Antilles, Tierra Firme, Honduras, and Campeche held stands of trees that produced blacks, browns, and dull reds. The Spaniards began cutting them shortly after 1500. In central and southern Mexico, the Indians used cochineal to dye their cloth with scarlet, crimson, and purple hues. They made it by reducing into cakes the bodies of tiny insects that infested the nopal cactus. It took some 70,000 of these creatures to yield a pound of dye, a statistic that may seem frivolous except that it attests to the infinite amount of labor that went into processing.[6] The Spaniards discovered that cochineal had ten to twelve times the dyeing power of kermes, a Mediterranean tree-dwelling insect upon which the European industry had relied to produce its crimsons, and also gave superior colors and fastness. Colonists in Mexico exploited it by taking it as part of their tribute. As early as 1526, they sent a shipment to Spain, and by the 1540s Mexican dyers had begun to use it. By the 1560s, annual production reached from 2000 to 3000 *arrobas* (about 76,000 U.S. pounds) and fetched 25 to 30 pesos an *arroba* on European markets.

For a blue dye, the Europeans turned first to woad, a plant cultivated in the districts of Thuringia and Toulouse that furnished the main source for Old World dyers since the superior Oriental indigo leaf was scarce and expensive. In 1537 a German partnership introduced woad planting around Jalapa, Mexico, but the harvest proved to be of such poor quality that in 1554 they abandoned the enterprise. At about the same time, however, the Spaniards discovered a wild species of American indigo growing in southern Mexico, Yucatán, and Guatemala that they compelled the natives first to collect then to cultivate. Sales of the New World product were recorded in Rouen as early as 1565, but profitable planting did not really get under way until the 1570s, mainly in Yucatán and Guatemala.

Cacao

The Europeans exploited a number of other plantation-type crops of both New and Old World origin. When they arrived, they found the Indians growing cacao, with the main centers of cultivation lying along the Pacific coast from Sonsonate, just southeast of the Isthmus of Tehuantepec, to the Gulf of Nicoya, in present-day Costa Rica. Secondary zones of production existed in various tropical and subtropical regions of central and southern Mexico. The bean had two uses among the indigenes. It served as money of exchange and account throughout Mesoamerica, and, when ground and mixed with lukewarm water, it produced a thick liquid or gruel that the indigenous nobility consumed copiously. Europeans found the potion nauseous, and it was not until toward the end of the sixteenth century that experimentation produced recipes acceptable to their tastes. Meanwhile, native demand remained high, and enterprising Spaniards undertook to expand production either on their own plantations or by requiring the Indians to plant more. They obtained their profits through the collection of tribute in cacao or by buying native production cheap and selling it dear. Cacao cultivation experienced a boom that peaked in the 1550s when some *encomenderos* received as much as 4000 pesos a year in tribute, in addition to what they collected illegally. In the 1560s, however, Central American production fell on hard times owing to poor land management, careless cultivation, and a decline of the native work force in plantation regions.

## Silk

Settlers learned that the European silkworm would feed on an American variety of mulberry and introduced sericulture into the Antilles early in the sixteenth century, using breeding stock from Granada. The worm did not take to the West Indian climate but found parts of New Spain to its taste, and, between 1540 and 1555, production boomed in primary centers located in Oaxaca and the Mixteca and in secondary zones scattered through central Mexico, around Guadalajara and Tampico, and in Yucatán. Its successful introduction owed much to the patronage of Viceroy Mendoza, and its diffusion, to the Dominicans who taught their Indian congregations how to nurture the worm. Many of the producing regions, however, proved to be climatically unsuitable for consistent yields. After 1555, entrepreneurs began to abandon marginally profitable plantations for mining and other more promising enterprises, and cultivation stabilized in the primary centers.

## Cotton, Tobacco, and Coca

The Europeans grew American cotton commercially in the Antilles, the semitropical valleys of central Mexico, the Cauca Valley, trans-Andean Ecuador, and the irrigated coastal regions of Peru. In the Antilles they produced American tobacco, although not in large quantities. Smoking had not yet caught on widely among Europeans, and the leaf was used mainly for medicinal purposes. In South America they took over coca planting from the Indians. Before the Potosí silver boom it was the most profitable enterprise in the kingdom, and around 1570 Pedro Pizarro reported that "it is the thing which is worth the most and has the highest price there is among the natives, and I believe there is a yearly traffic in this herb to the amount of more than six hundred thousand pesos, and it has made many men rich."[7] But there were those who saw multiple evils in coca culture. It encouraged idolatry among the natives, since it was the devil who planted the notion in their heads that chewing the leaf relieved hunger and fatigue; it diverted labor from the mines; and the descent of workers from the highlands to the warm climates where the plant grew caused them to die. But Juan de Matienzo had a rebuttal to these arguments. God did nothing without a reason, and since He caused coca to grow in Peru, He must have intended that the Indians use it.[8]

## Forest Products

In addition to developing the agricultural and pastoral potential of the Indies, the Europeans harvested the fruits of its tropical and subtropical forests, including cassia, whose leaves produced senna and whose pods held a mild laxative; balsam, whose sap yielded unguents and cosmetics; and sarsaparilla, whose roots were thought to be efficacious in the treatment of fever, plague, scrofula, and syphilis.

## Industry

### Agro-Industry

The first and most universal form of industry in the Indies was the processing of the yield of farms, ranches, and plantations. Almost every town had a mill that ground grain, produced locally or brought from other places, and a slaughterhouse that provided meat for local consumption. In the production of many commodities, planting and harvesting merged with manufacturing in a single unit of production. Ranchers turned their milk into cheese and butter, growers of grapes and olives pressed their fruit into wine and oil, cochineal collectors and indigo planters boiled down their insects and leaves into cakes of dye, and sericulturists spun thread from the webs of their worms.

Sugar was the most intensively organized agro-industry in the Indies. In addition to fields producing cane it required a large, disciplined labor force, mills driven by water (*ingenios*) or animal power (*trapiches*) to grind the cane, boiling vats and cauldrons to reduce the juice to coarse-grained cakes for market, skilled technicians to supervise the refining process, additional fields to grow food crops for the workers, and woodlands providing timber for construction and fuel for boiling. Because of large capital requirements for machinery and labor, production was not always vertically integrated into single units. Planters who could not afford *ingenios* or *trapiches* brought their cane to the mills of larger plantations, whose owners processed it for a percentage of the yield.

Large capital requirements along with early shortages of technicians created a substantial time lag between first plantings and the production of marketable sugar. Although Columbus introduced cane in Santo Domingo on his second voyage, settlers did not build the first *ingenio* on the island until 1516 and not on Puerto Rico and Jamaica until the 1520s. Santo Domingo did not send its first exports to Europe until 1521; Puerto Rico, not until 1533. Although planters received up to two ducats an *arroba* (25.35 U.S. pounds) for their sugar, it took the intervention of the crown to put the island industry on its feet. In the 1530s, Emperor Charles ordered that technicians be brought over from Europe and that treasury officials advance credit for the construction of mills. With this boost, planting and refining entered a period of growth. Española, the main beneficiary, had 35 *ingenios* and *trapiches* by 1548. The larger plantation complexes included 100 acres or more of cane lands yielding up to 80 *arrobas* of sugar per acre, *ingenios* capable of refining 10,000 *arrobas* a year, and up to 900 black slaves. By that time, also, the industry began to prosper on Puerto Rico and, more modestly, on Jamaica.

On the mainland, the sugar industry also developed slowly. In 1524 Cortés began the construction of a mill at Tuxtla, on the coast of Veracruz, but it did not begin to produce until ten years later, and in 1550 only two large *ingenios* operated, the Tuxtla mill and another belonging to the Cortés estate near Cuernavaca. After midcentury, planting and refining began to develop more rapidly in both these regions and in new zones in Michoacán and Oaxaca. All that is known about the early history of sugar in South America is that settlers began to build small mills in coastal Peru in the late 1530s or early 1540s and that they were refining sugar around Asunción in the 1550s. Mainland planters produced almost exclusively for local consumption, in part because they could not compete in the export market with the Antilles industry, which enjoyed the advantages of immediate access to water transportation, a shorter haul to Europe, and royal favor. More importantly, a growing American population consumed all the sugar they could grow.

Textiles

Outside of food processing, textile manufacturing was the main industry in most parts of the Indies and, except for mining, the most advanced in terms of organization and technology. Several circumstances contributed to its position. A constantly growing demand existed for articles of apparel and household items made of cloth. Prices of imports were high, and, in any case, Spanish producers could not meet home demand, let alone supply overseas markets. Spanish Americans, moreover, could supply most of the factors of production. Profits from agriculture, stock raising, mining, and commerce provided initial capital. Proliferating herds of sheep and locally grown cotton, flax, silk, and agave offered abundant fibers; American dyes were available; Indians working for nominal wages, voluntarily or in *repartimientos*, furnished cheap labor; and in textile-producing regions sufficient water flowed to drive looms.

In the Indies, the textile industry used two basic forms of production. One was domestic, involving no more than six looms, owned and operated by Indian families. The second, and by far the more productive, was the *obraje* (workshop), using six or more looms along with fulling mills, employing perhaps several hundred workers, and generally powered by water. *Obrajes* appeared in New Spain in the 1530s, in Peru by 1545 or thereabouts, in New Granada by 1547, and in remote Tucumán by 1549. By 1571 Spanish North America had some eighty workshops, located mainly in the Valley of Mexico and in Puebla and Oaxaca. South America did not lag far behind, with production centered in Quito, Cajamarca, and Cuzco.

Much remains to be learned about the variety, volume, and organization of production of *obrajes*, but some generalizations can be made about them. They wove wool, cotton, silk, flax, and hemp depending on local and regional demands and the type of fibers available. Most, however, concentrated on the production of wool and cotton, with woolens predominating in the cool highlands and cotton in tropical and subtropical regions. They not only wove and dyed cloth of diverse consistencies, textures, and colors but manufactured a wide variety of items from it. Finished products included hats, jackets, trousers, shawls, priestly vestments, stockings, gloves, underclothing, handkerchiefs, ribbons, lace, carpets, tablecloths, napery, counterpanes, hemp sandals, match cords for ordnance, and saddlebags.

In terms of ownership and management, *obrajes* originally fell into two classes. Some belonged to Europeans, not uncommonly the same ones who also owned herds of sheep and cotton lands. Others were *obrajes de comunidad*, that is, shops owned and operated by native communities belonging to *encomiendas* and *corregimientos* whose workers paid their tribute from wages or profits. In practice, caciques managed to skim off a large part of the earnings, and, when *encomiendas* fell vacant or escheated to the crown, Europeans leased communal shops so that by the end of the sixteenth century they owned or controlled the textile industry in the Indies.

During the early years of colonization, *obrajes* used the pre-Conquest techniques of the Indians for making cloth, but around midcentury owners brought over master-weavers, shearers, dyers, and fullers from Spain to introduce European methods of production. Native workers learned these techniques quickly. The textile industry in the Indies, however, did not reach the level of technical development attained in Castile and much less the efficiency achieved in Italy and northern Europe. For the most part, it manufactured coarse-fibered, loosely woven, and poorly dyed fabrics. European settlers much preferred imports despite their cost, and most American production went to clothe Indians and lower-class mixed bloods.

### Other Manufacturers

Other important manufactured items included leather and leather goods, pottery, glass, furniture, soap, gunpowder, rough ironwork, and gold and silver jewelry and ornaments. Some regions developed specialties according to their human and natural resources. Puebla, in Mexico, became famous for its ceramics; Arequipa, in southern Peru, founded church bells and cannons; northern Peru fashioned lamps for mines; the pans along the Venezuelan coast yielded salt; Guayaquil, in Ecuador, and Realejo, in Nicaragua, had important shipyards. The highland pine forest of Nicaragua and Honduras provided naval stores. The organization of these manufactures varied. Most involved some measure of domestic production, but Mexico City began licensing craft guilds in the 1530s, and by the 1570s they existed in the main economic and administrative centers of the Indies, where they fashioned as wide a variety of consumer items as their peninsular counterparts. And, although the *obraje* is associated primarily with the textile industry, workshops also produced pottery, leather goods, and furniture. As in the case of cloth, however, European settlers generally regarded other American manufactured goods as inferior and bought imports when they could afford them.

### Mining: The Gold Cycle

Although agriculture and food and fiber processing provided the greatest source of wealth for the inhabitants of the Indies and employed most of the labor in those parts, in the eyes of crown and settlers precious metals remained the most attractive fruits of the land. The Spaniards began mining gold on Española in 1494 and on Puerto Rico and Cuba as soon as they occupied those islands. Production involved mainly washing auriferous sands and in some regions pulverized surface ore, using Indian labor gangs. Miners took their raw gold, or at least were supposed to take it, to royal *casas de afinación* (assay houses), where officials cast it into bars, each numbered and stamped with its weight, fineness, and date of assay, set aside the king's share, and returned the remainder to its owner.

Gold mining proved to be a very volatile enterprise, owing chiefly to the rapid exhaustion of deposits that could be worked profitably with existing technology. What might be called the "island cycle" lasted scarcely thirty years. Until 1515, most of the treasure came from Española. From 1516 to 1530, Puerto Rican production almost equaled that of its western neighbor, and Cuban gold amounted to about half as much. Thereafter, island mining declined sharply, but the yield from streams and veins in Panama, in highland Nicaragua and Honduras, and in the mountains of Michoacán and New Galicia replaced it. These sources played out by midcentury, but American production remained alive because of new strikes elsewhere, including those in the Zaruma region of the Province of Quito, at scattered locations in Upper and Lower Peru and in Chile, and in Antioquia. Black slaves furnished a large part of the labor.

In general, the peak years of sixteenth-century gold production in the Indies fell between 1541 and 1560, but no one knows how much gold the Spaniards obtained from their New World mines during these early decades. Existing records are incomplete, and those that can be found deal only with registered imports of precious metals at the *Casa de Contratación* in Seville. They do not take into account dust, nuggets, and bullion that remained in the Indies for local exchange or passed into the hands of smugglers, or bars that clandestinely bypassed the *Casa*. The best estimate available holds that between 1503 and 1560 legal imports at Seville amounted to some 112,581,960 grams (26,684,513 *pesos de oro de minas*) of fine gold, of which 67,577,210 grams (16,017,352 pesos) arrived during the peak years, 1541-60.[9]

Silver Production

European-managed silver mining in the Indies began shortly after the conquest of Mexico with the exploitation of surface deposits already being worked by the Indians around Taxco, Sultepec, and Zumpango, in central Mexico, and Tamazula and Compostela, in New Galicia. Gonzalo Pizarro began to work the Inca mines at Porco in Upper Peru during the late 1540s. Production from these sources was substantial but hardly spectacular, because the natives had already skimmed off the easily accessible surface ore and their smelting methods, which they continued to use under Spanish direction, were primitive and gave a low rate of recovery. In the 1530s a party of German experts introduced the stamp mill and lead smelting in Mexico, but the high cost of fuel and the falling quality of ores rendered their method uneconomical.

A conjuncture of circumstances occurring in the mid-sixteenth century launched the first American silver bonanza. First, the Spaniards made a series of major strikes: the *Cerro Rico* of Potosí in 1545, at Zacatecas in 1546, and at Guanajuato and Pachuca, in Mexico, in the 1550s. Second, in 1554 or 1555 Bartolomé de Medina, a Mexican miner, devised a process for extracting silver from its encasing ore through amalgamation with mercury, a metal obtained from the royal mines at Almaden in Spain and in the Austrian Habsburg's dominions. Although it cost money, it had the advantage of yielding a higher rate of recovery than smelting and used much less wood fuel. Third, in 1563 the Spaniards came upon an enormous deposit of cinnabar at Huancavelica, in Peru, which produced quicksilver for Potosí although it took them ten years to perfect the amalgamation process for use there.

The technology of silver production in the sixteenth-century Indies can be summarized as follows, bearing in mind that the lay and qualities of ores produced numerous regional variations. The initial step was extraction. At first miners dug the weathered and oxidized surface ores, which were easily workable and which, because of their reddish color, were called *colorados*. After these had been exhausted, workers followed the veins underground to the darker sulphides, which they called *negrillos*, driving vertical shafts and linking them to horizontal tunnels to provide drainage as well as access. Miners broke rock and ore with picks, sometimes cracking it with heat first. Gunpowder blasting did not come into use until the first part of the eighteenth century. Broken ore was sacked and, in shaft mines, carried to the surface on the backs of workers clambering up a series of rough wooden ladders. As in the case of blasting, mines did not employ the whim, a poweful animal-driven hoist, until the eighteenth century.

The next step in production depended on the kind and quality of ore obtained. Smelting continued to be used for high grades and some sulphides, but most underwent mercury amalgamation. The details of the process as used in the sixteenth century are uncertain, but generally speaking it involved: (1) pounding and grinding the ore to a powder in *haciendas de minas* (stamp mills) driven by water in Peru and by animal power in Mexico; (2) mixing the pulverized product with quicksilver, salt, and other reagents that amalgamated the silver and the mercury; (3) separating the amalgam from sludge by washing; and (4) distilling the amalgam, a process that vaporized the mercury and left fine silver or, in some ores, silver alloyed with gold. Much of the mercury could be reused. Like gold, the refined silver went, or was supposed to go, to royal assay houses, where the staff recast it into bars of standard size, stamped it with a number, its weight and fineness, and the royal seal, set aside the king's fifth, and returned the rest to its owner.

For labor in the silver industry, miners and refiners employed black slaves mainly for surface tasks, since they were expensive and, if used in damp shafts and tunnels, succumbed to respiratory infections. Indians did most of the underground toil, but in ways that differed regionally. At Potosí and in central Mexico mine owners used the *mita-repartimiento*, but the rich veins of northern Mexico lay too far from the centers of indigenous populations to make this system feasible. Here free or nominally free wage earners made up the bulk of the native labor force.

Silver production was the most complex economic enterprise in the Indies. It involved not only an advanced technology but multiple separate operations and large outlays of capital for machinery, mercury, chemicals, timbering, animal power, and human labor. For these reasons, the industry was rather loosely organized in the sixteenth century. Few individuals had the capital or the organizing ability to finance or to manage all the steps in production, making vertical integration uncommon. Instead, the several facilities tended to be owned and operated independently. Ownership of mines themselves was widely dispersed. In 1585, some 612 mines honeycombed the *Cerro Rico* of Potosí, and registers listed 500 mine owners. Refiners, much fewer in number, bought the ore from the miners. Both classes frequently obtained capital on a loan or share basis from wealthy merchants, and middlemen intervened at various stages of production, buying and selling ore and refined silver.

The volume of silver yielded by American mines in the first six or seven decades of the sixteenth century is as uncertain as that of gold and for much the same reason: the main source of information is the statistical series recording registered precious metals entering Seville whose shortcomings were described in the preceding section.[10] These figures do, however, reveal approximations of production and delineate production trends. In the decennium 1531–40, when the Spaniards first began to exploit the mines of central Mexico, fine silver registered in Seville came to 86,193,876 grams (3,372,217 pesos). In the next decennium, 1541–50, when Potosí and Zacatecas came into production, the amount doubled to 177,573,164 grams (6,944,307 pesos). In 1551–60, the figure jumped to 303,121,174 grams (11,859,201 pesos) and in 1561–70 to 942,858,792 grams (36,888,066 pesos).[11] The spectacular increases are attributable to the introduction of mercury amalgamation and the opening of new mines in Mexico. Although proportions varied from year to year, one-quarter to one-third entered Seville on the royal account and the remaining on private accounts. The boom beginning in the 1560s dramatically changed the relative values of gold and silver production in the New World. In the decennium 1551–60, the proportion in terms of the total value of Sevillian imports, was 2:1 in favor of gold. In the next decade it shifted to 3:1 in favor of silver, and the disproportion continued to mount throughout the century.[12] It was reflected in the widening of the bimetallic ratio (the value of gold in relation to silver) in Spain from 10.11:1 during the years 1497–1536 to 12.12:1 during 1566–1608.[13]

The yield of American silver mines made Moctezuma's tribute to Cortés and the ransom of Atahualpa appear paltry indeed. By bullionist standards, the Enterprise of the Indies had finally paid off, and handsomely. Yet few miners got rich or at least kept their fortunes. The silver industry did not have the high volatility of gold mining, but it had an essentially speculative character and cyclical ups and downs. Veins played out or were lost as shafts penetrated deeper; costs increased in geometric proportion; and flooding often forced the abandonment of mines. Capital was scarce, and the prices of mercury and silver fluctuated. The miner had little control over these variables, so that most of the profits of the industry went to refiners, silver merchants, and the crown.

The importance of the silver industry cannot be measured by its production and its profits alone. It gave a powerful stimulus to virtually every other sector of the economy of the Indies. Mining installations had to be supplied with articles of iron, leather, tallow, wood, and cloth, and miners had to be fed and clothed. In New Spain, stock ranching and agriculture developed rapidly north of the Valley of Mexico to provide sustenance to Zacatecas and Guanajuato, and the fertile regions of Arequipa performed the same service for Potosí. Some of the larger mine owners and refiners themselves acquired cattle and wheat ranches. The needs of miners stimulated the growth of *obrajes* in central Mexico, Quito, and Cuzco, and the demand for animal power in pits and refineries created mule-breeding industries in the Mexican Bajío and in Tucumán and Córdova. The flow of supplies to the mines and the return movement of silver to the viceregal capitals and ports was mainly responsible for the development of permanent transportation routes. Of the utmost importance was the fact that silver furnished bullion and specie for exchange against the large volume of imports that a growing European population demanded.

# CHAPTER 11

# The Commerce of the Indies

The commerce of the Indies involved the exchange of goods at the local level, between adjacent regions, between widely separated American provinces and kingdoms, and between America and Seville, where it linked to long-established European trade routes. Through Portuguese connections it extended to India, to the Spice Islands, and to slave stations on the African coast. Its patterns and forms were shaped by complex and changing market conditions, by the nature of the transportation systems it used, by the kinds and availability of money and credit, by government policy, and by the intrusions of foreign corsairs and smugglers.

## Local Commerce

The most universal form of local commerce was the public market. It was primarily an indigenous institution but one with which Europeans were familiar through their own markets and fairs. They appreciated its utility in the Indies and encouraged its survival. Its organization remained essentially unchanged, but it expanded its functions to serve Spaniards and mixed bloods as well as Indians. In villages and small towns, markets were generally weekly affairs with days and conditions set by municipal authorities. In large urban centers, they were fixed installations functioning seven days a week. Mexico City had two, one in the native quarter and another in the Spanish city. Cortés reported in his Fourth Letter to Emperor Charles:

The same good order is observed [in them] and in their transactions as in former days, [and] in [them] are to be found all such manner of produce as is grown throughout the land, for there is nothing which is not brought there for sale; and the variety of merchandise is not less than in the former days of prosperity. It is true that there are now no ornaments of gold or silver, nor featherwork, nor other treasures as there were wont to be; a few small pieces of gold and silverwork appear, but not in the quantity as before.[1]

But, if precious items disappeared, they were replaced by useful things: cackling hens, squealing pigs, bleating goats, cheap clothing, hardware, and glasswork.

In Spanish towns and cities, European forms of trading supplemented markets. Larger merchants not only dealt in goods wholesale but maintained retail stores, mainly for the sale of imports, despite the social onus attached to merchandising over the counter. Petty merchants opened shops and stalls in the colonnades of town plazas where they haggled with buyers over the prices of apparel, hardware, and household equipment obtained from wholesalers on commission or consignment. On streets running from the plaza, metal smiths, leather workers, shoemakers, apothecaries, pastry cooks, and diverse other artisans made and sold their specialties and sometimes maintained outlets in plaza shops and municipal markets. Peddlers cried their wares from door to door. Special arrangements existed for the distribution of basic foodstuffs. Towns built slaughterhouses, to which contractors supplied livestock on bid, and granaries of two kinds: one distributing cheap maize and wheat to the poor, the other selling at higher but regulated prices to the more affluent.

## Regional and Interregional Trade

The rhythm of conquest and colonization determined the first extended patterns of trade in the Indies. The Antilles furnished horses and foodstuffs for the conquest of Mexico, receiving in return portions of the loot. As New Spain became pacified and its fields and pastures began to produce, it provided supplies for the subjugation of other regions. As early as 1537, Cortés sent two ships to South America carrying food and arms. What he received in return is uncertain, although it is recorded that a Peruvian merchant, Baltasar García, promised to pay him 4005 gold pesos.[2]

The advance of the Conquest also provided a major trade item—Indian slaves. In the early 1500s, Spanish expeditions raided the Bahamas and Tierra Firme for natives to be sold on Española, Puerto Rico, and Cuba for gold. In the 1520s and the 1530s, Mexico exported Indians in large numbers to the Antilles in exchange for foodstuffs and livestock. After the mid-1520s, Nicaragua became the major slave mart of the Indies, exporting its indigenous population wholesale to Peru, the West Indies, and the Central American gold mines. No one knows the total volume of this vicious traffic; but its victims must have numbered in the tens of thousands.

Around mid-century, the interregional trade began to assume more stable forms. Grain-producing regions exchanged their surpluses with tropical and subtropical provinces in return for such products as sugar, *aguardiente*, cotton, and tobacco. Agricultural and pastoral districts provided mining settlements with grain, meat, potatoes, sugar, leather, sheepskins, tallow, and animal transport and power in return for bullion and specie. The *obrajes* of Mexico, Puebla, Quito, and Cuzco supplied cloth and clothing to extended hinterlands. The irrigated coastal valleys of Peru exported foodstuffs to Panama. Arequipa sent wine to Quito.

The diverse demands of a vast empire along with specialized regional production generated a wider exchange linking American kingdoms and continents. Central America sent large quantities of cacao to Mexico and South America in the middle decades of the sixteenth century. By the mid-1540s, Mexico supplied most of the grain needed by the Antilles. The slow development of the economy of Peru, however, and that kingdom's heavy dependence on mining, were the main factors shaping the patterns of long-distance commerce in the Indies. While its irrigated coastal valleys and uplands produced a variety of foods and fibers, Peru depended heavily on imports of basic commodities, for which it could pay in silver. It obtained grain from Chile, mules from Argentina, cloth from Quito, and wood planking, maize, and horses from Nicaragua. Mexico continued to be its main trading partner, sending south at first foodstuffs, seeds and seedlings, and animal breeding stock; later, black slaves, sugar, cochineal, and luxury items, including reexports from Europe.

## Systems of Trans-Atlantic Commerce

### The *Carrera de Indias*

Trans-Atlantic commerce moved through four systems. In terms of volume and value of goods carried, the *Carrera de Indias* was the most important by far. Its structure consisted of two components. One was the fleets that sailed to and from the New World whose routes and organization were outlined in chapter 9. The other was the ports that served the fleets. At the European end of the *Carrera*, the crown very early, in 1503, gave Seville a monopoly on the Indies trade. After 1510, when disillusionment with the economic prospects of America set in, it allowed Cadiz to participate. In 1529, Charles V adopted a much more liberal policy, opening trans-Atlantic commerce to nine Castilian ports: Coruna, Bayonne, Avilés, Laredo, Bilbao, and San Sebastián in the north and Cartagena and Málaga along with Cadiz in the south. Even so, Seville remained the most important entrepôt, and, when, in the early 1570s, the inflow of precious metals in large quantities induced the crown to establish strict control over their circulation, Seville regained a virtual monopoly. At the American end of the *Carrera*, ships at first called at major and minor ports as markets dictated, but the lines of development of the colonial economy, especially the opening of the mainland gold and silver mines, soon established Veracruz, Nombre de Dios, and Cartagena as the main American destinations of the fleets. Havana emerged as a fourth major port by virtue of the victualing and repair services it provided for ships returning to Europe. These changes reduced Santo Domingo to secondary status.

Goods carried by the *Carrera* varied in volume and kind during the Conquest period, depending mainly on market conditions in Europe and America and the level of corsair activity. From 1493 to 1520, exports to the Indies rose steadily to provide for the needs of conquest and colonization, which included arms, powder, horses and other livestock, barrels of flour, jars of oil, and tuns of wine. The New World returned mainly gold from the Antilles. During the next three years volume fell off sharply. In the islands, the diminished production of mines and the decline of the native labor supply lowered the purchasing power of the settlers; in Spain, a bad wheat harvest in 1522 reduced the supply of grain for export; and along the Atlantic approaches to Seville, the outbreak of war with France in 1521 loosed corsairs against Spanish shipping.

In 1524 a recovery began that extended into the 1530s. It was generated by several developments. The influx of settlers into newly conquered New Spain and the conquest of Peru greatly increased the demand for consumer goods in the New World. At the same time, the range and value of exportable items from the Indies grew, thereby producing exchange for purchases from Europe. In addition to gold, which by the 1530s came mainly from Mexico and Central America, exports included the first yields of Mexican silver mines, sugar and hides from the Antilles, pearls from the Venezuelan coasts, dyewoods from Campeche and Honduras, the first shipments of cochineal from Mexico, and from the tropical forests of the West Indies and the Caribbean small quantities of leaves, roots, and bark deemed to possess medicinal qualities. The value of gold exported probably exceeded that of all other items combined.

During the next decade, 1540–50, trans-Atlantic trade boomed, with volume doubling. Again, the surge resulted from the rapid expansion of colonization and exportable production in the Indies. Immigrants from Europe continued to flow into New Spain and began to populate newly conquered regions of South America, while shipments of silver from Potosí and Zacatecas increased the exchange available to Spanish Americans.

In 1550 another sharp decline began which lasted for a decade. During this period Spain, along with the rest of Europe, suffered a sharp recession accompanied by a drop in commodity prices. At the same time, the development of agriculture, food processing, and textile manufacturing in the Indies decreased the demand for European imports. In the 1550s, the Habsburg-Valois wars reached a climax, and French corsairs ranged almost unchecked in American and European waters, virtually blockaded Andalusian ports, and attacked Spanish settlements on the Antilles and the coasts of Tierra Firme. These several circumstances made Sevillian merchants reluctant to invest in what amounted to high-risk enterprises.

The slump ended in 1559, and trans-Atlantic trade grew steadily for the next three decades, owing essentially to two influences. One was the general political and economic stabilization of Spanish America that followed the disorders of the Conquest. The other was favorable demand-supply conditions. In the New World, the growth of the European and mixed-blood population created more consumers; exportable supplies of hides, sugar, and dyestuffs increased; and bonanza levels of Peruvian and Mexican silver production increased American purchasing power. In Europe, expanding economies and populations demanded more and more bullion and specie, raw materials, and sweet stuffs. The upturn was assisted by the Treaty of Catcau-Cambrésis (1559), which relieved corsair pressure on the *Carrera*.

The African Slave Trade

A second trans-Atlantic system handled the African slave trade. Its organization varied according to vacillations in royal policy. For twenty-five years after the Discovery, the crown allowed the introduction of slaves from Europe with virtually no restrictions except for an import fee of three pesos a slave imposed in 1513. This procedure proved hard to police. In 1518, therefore, Emperor Charles began issuing monopolistic licenses to bring in slaves directly from Africa, favoring northern European merchants to whom he was beholden and who already had commercial connections with Portuguese interests controlling the source of supply. Generally speaking, these instruments authorized the importation of a prescribed number of slaves from specified African regions to particular places in the Indies within a designated period of time. Traders continued to pay the three-peso head tax. The new arrangement, however, limited supply, raised prices, and offended the monopolists of Seville. In 1532, the king turned over the trade to the *Casa de Contratación* in Seville, which continued the licensing system, but on a nonmonopolistic basis.

As observed in chapter 6, the number of Africans entering the Indies during the first decades of the slave trade is highly conjectural. Philip Curtin estimates that, from the Discovery to 1550, it amounted to about 15,000 and, for the next twenty years, some 16,200, bringing the total for the Conquest period to approximately 31,200.[3] In the Indies themselves, marketing had no particular organization. Blacks were handled like commodities. At the port of entry, shipmasters acting for themselves, or as agents for other licensees, sold them individually to users of labor or to merchant middlemen for whom the slave was generally only one of the wares in which he dealt.

The Canaries Trade

A third system handled direct commerce between the Canaries and the Caribbean. Emperor Charles authorized the traffic in 1534, and in the 1550s King Philip established mercantile tribunals on the three main Canary islands subject to the ultimate jurisdiction of the *Casa de Contratación* in Seville. The trade consisted mainly of exports of Canarian wheat, oil, and wine to ports in the Antilles and on the Main that were bypassed by regular fleets, in exchange for local products and whatever gold and silver could be extracted from American settlers.

The Contraband Trade

The fourth trans-Atlantic system carried clandestine trade. It met an unsatisfied demand for European goods and African slaves or provided them at lower prices than legitimate merchants. Colonists paid for them with sugar, hides, and illicit precious metals. Its main American loci were neglected and undefended settlements in the Caribbean. Its principal agents were French corsair-smugglers, Canary Islanders, and slave traders who used their legal traffic as a cover. The *Carrera* itself accommodated some illicit traffic through the collusion of ship captains, merchants, and customs officials. Data on contraband trade during the Conquest years are virtually nonexistent, but it probably amounted to no more than a fraction of all trans-Atlantic commerce.

## Transportation

### Land Routes

Although market conditions constituted the most fundamental force shaping the domestic and overseas commerce of the Indies, other influences intervened to affect its flow, in the main adversely. In the 1550s, corsair activity unquestionably disrupted both the *Carrera* and interregional trade in the Caribbean, but in the long run extended and hazardous transportation systems were a much greater hindrance.

Land routes generally corresponded to those defined by pre-Columbian Indian nations for governance, trade, and war. The Spaniards extended and supplemented what they found already in use, mainly to facilitate the exploitation of new mines. In the Viceroyalty of New Spain, they pushed a road from central Mexico first to Zacatecas, then to more northerly mining districts. In Panama they developed a route across the Isthmus to carry Peruvian silver to the Caribbean. Farther south, they connected Cuzco with Lima, and Potosí with Arica, the main loading point for Potosí's silver.

The Spaniards also improved pre-Columbian networks, all of which had been designed for foot traffic only. Even the famed roads of the Incas, although surfaced and graded, were narrow, ascended steep slopes by steps, and crossed rivers by unstable bridges. On major routes, such as that connecting Mexico City and Veracruz, Spanish engineers widened old tracks and detoured hindrances to traffic. At important stream crossings, they built Roman-arched stone bridges. Where heavy use demanded and gradient permitted, they constructed proper roads, among which the best developed ran from Mexico City north to the mines and from Lima to its port of Callao.

The forms of transport used depended on the quality of routes. Despite European improvements, most "roads" were really nothing more than trails, and in wet seasons they were vulnerable to slides, erosion, and flooding. In the immediate post-Conquest years, indigenous bearers called *tamemes* did the carrying, using a simple pack frame and tumpline. After the development of mule and ass breeding, the most common form of land transport became animal pack trains (*recuas*), driven and cursed along by black and mixed-blood *arrieros* (professional muleteers). In the more remote regions of the Indies, however, Indians continued to serve as bearers, and on better roads the Spaniards used the *carretera*, a primitive two-wheeled cart that had traveled the roads of Castile since time immemorial. On the Mexico-Zacatecas route, the growing weight and bulk of traffic led, in the 1560s, to the introduction of the *carro*, a ponderous vehicle borne by two great iron-rimmed wheels six to eight feet in diameter and drawn by eight to twelve mules. Aside from their carrying capacity, *carros* had another use. Like the wagons that later carried Anglo-Saxon settlers to Oregon and California, they could be brought together to form a field fortification against Indian attacks.

## Water Routes

The Spanish Indies suffered a poverty of navigable inland waters, particularly in regions where commerce needed them. On the Pacific side of the two American continents, rivers were only navigable in their lower stretches. They gave no direct access to the upland regions where most of the settlers lived. On the Carribbean and Atlantic seaboards nature was somewhat more accommodating. The San Juan River provided a route into the intermontane basins of Nicaragua, and the Magdalena linked New Granada to the Caribbean. Shoals and rapids, however, hampered the navigation of both rivers, and the central cordillera intervened between Bogotá and its river port. The Amazon and the Orinoco were navigable, but they traversed regions that had little attraction for European colonization. In the southern half of the continent, the Rio de la Plata system gave access to interior settlements. Despite the hazards of its shallows and sandbars, it alone among American rivers regularly navigated by the Spaniards permitted the use of sail for significant distances upstream.

Several transportation systems carried the domestic seaborne commerce of the Indies. In terms of the value and volume of goods transported, the most important connected Huatulco, Mexico, with Lima and served intermediate Pacific ports in Central America and Ecuador. Pacific wind systems favored northbound traffic but slowed southbound traffic interminably. On the New World's Atlantic approaches, one network handled interisland traffic; another linked the Antilles to ports in Mexico, in Central America, and on the Main; a third ran from Veracruz to Venezuela, generally following the coast and touching at intermediate ports in southern Mexico, Yucatán, and Central America. Natural forces and features as well as corsairs hindered sailing in the Caribbean and the Gulf of Mexico. Prevailing winds blew generally west and north, making it difficult to sail east along the Main and from Cuba to Santo Domingo, except that north of Cuba the Gulf Stream aided eastbound vessels. Hurricanes threatened sea traffic from June to October. Also, in contrast to the

Pacific coast of Central America, the Caribbean side was deficient in defensible ports, and shoals, reefs, and shifting currents endangered navigation.

Trans-Atlantic commerce suffered several handicaps. Sheer distance, hazards created by corsairs and Atlantic storms, and obstacles imposed by bureaucracies made the passage slow and difficult. At both ends of the *Carrera*, serious bottlenecks existed. The stretch of the Guadalquivir between Seville and the sea, which substituted for a harbor, was narrow and shallow, so that congestion of vessels assembled at sailing time delayed departures and returning fleets had to wait weeks to discharge cargoes. At the American end of the fleet route, inbound merchandise destined for Peru and outbound silver from Potosí had to be shipped across the Isthmus of Panama by mule train, a passage that consumed from five to seven days, while the fleet had to wait in an exposed roadstead.

The difficulties of the Panama crossing prolonged efforts to find an alternative either through the discovery of a strait or the development of transisthmian routes in Nicaragua and Tehuantepec. Contemporaries also conceived artificial solutions. In 1534, Emperor Charles ordered a feasibility study made for an interoceanic canal across the Isthmus of Panama. Nothing came of the project for reasons put forth by Father Joseph (José) de Acosta: "It is a plan as vain as it is pretentious . . . because no human power would suffice to level the great and impenetrable mountain which God put between the two seas. . . . And even if it were possible for humans, in my opinion it would be right to fear the punishment of heaven for changing the works which the Creator, with complete harmony and accord, ordained in the formation of the universe."[4]

The Spanish employed various types of vessels for water transport, with draft, tonnage, design, and rigging depending on the service required. For several decades after the Discovery, they continued to rely on the caravel for trans-Atlantic maritime carriage. Toward midcentury this versatile craft that had served explorers so well tended to be replaced on long hauls by the *não*, a square-rigged merchant vessel of greater capacity capable of carrying heavier armament. By the 1560s, vessels of this type ranging from 300-600 tons appeared on the *Carrera* and from 200-250 tons on the Mexico-Peru run. In the 1550s, the needs of maritime defense induced naval architects to develop the galleon, a specialized type of *não* of 500 tons or more that had finer lines and heavier armaments than merchant vessels. In addition to providing escort service, it carried particularly valuable cargoes, including the king's silver and gold. Smaller ships served intercoastal and interisland trade, including caravel-built craft and *barcos*. The later were vessels of from 50-60 tons propelled by

both sail and oars. Still smaller craft of local design, construction, and nomenclature plied rivers and threaded their way through coastal waters to serve local needs.

The nature of transportation systems unquestionably had an adverse effect
on the economy of the Indies. Goods flowed along them slowly and with frequent interruptions, thereby restricting supply, increasing haulage costs inordinately, and raising consumer prices so high that they constrained the
growth of markets. Problems of transport also limited the range of profitable
trade in many commodities, thus hindering the development of integrated regional economies.

## Money and Credit

The supply and kinds of money and credit constituted another major influence
affecting commerce. As early as 1497, Queen Isabella considered striking standard Spanish gold coins on Santo Domingo, but nothing came of the notion.
During the first three decades of the sixteenth century, the crown occasionally
shipped Castilian coins to the Antilles. In principle, however, it resisted the export of precious metals in any form, and the amount that arrived was quite insufficient. In the absence of money, colonists at first relied on barter, but, as
placer fields and silver mines opened, they worked out their own monetary
system based on the *peso*, which although sometimes roughly and illegally
coined was primarily a raw weight of gold or silver of varying purity. Colonists
and treasury officials used it both as a medium of exchange and a money of
account. The finest and, therefore, the most standard was the *peso de oro de
ley perfecta*, often called in New Spain the *peso de oro de minas* and in New
Granada the *peso de oro bueno*. It was assigned a weight of 4.219 grams, 22-
22½ carats fine, and a tariff of 450 *maravedís*, thus giving it the same weight
and value as the Spanish *castellano* but a slightly reduced fineness. Settlers also
used gold and silver pesos of lesser quality and local and regional nomenclature.
Because of crude assay methods and surreptitious debasements, the several
pesos did not always meet official standards of weight and quality.

Responding to complaints of money shortages and monetary disorder coming from the Indies, Emperor Charles authorized the establishment of a mint
in Mexico City, which began operation in 1536. It struck three kinds of coins,
one being the silver *real*, which weighed 3.196 grams, 0.9306 fine, and had a
tariff of 34 *maravedís*. It was also issued in denominations of ¼, 2, 3, and 4.
A second was a silver peso with the same fineness but a weight of 25.56 grams
and a tariff of 272 *maravedís*. It was considered to contain eight *reales*, and

therefore contemporaries named it the *peso real de á ocho*. Later in the century it came to be called the *peso duro* (hard peso), *peso fuerte* (strong peso), or, simply, the peso. A third type of coin struck consisted of small copper pieces for petty change, but the Indians distrusted them and threw them into the lakes or melted them down for use in their artisanry. In 1564, therefore, the mint discontinued their coinage.

In 1565 the crown also authorized a mint in Lima to cut silver pesos and *reales*, but it was so far from the mines that it did not receive enough bullion to pay expenses. Although it continued to operate sporadically, in 1572 its main operations were transferred to Potosí, a region so remote that circulation of its coinage in the rest of the viceroyalty was deficient, and the commerce of Lima suffered a chronic shortage of circulating media.

No reliable data on Peruvian coinage in the sixteenth century exist, but the Mexican mint struck 1,500,000 whole and fractional silver pesos in the period 1536–48, 2,300,000 in 1549–58, and 3,000,000 in 1559–1600. Although the two mints together put a good amount of money into circulation, a major share of it drained away to pay for imports, and the Indies continued to suffer for lack of minted coins. Also, the circulation of money was fairly well limited to major commercial centers and trade routes. In the hinterlands, the Europeans met the shortage by cutting small pieces of gold and silver for local exchange. Indians who could not get their hands on silver pesos or *reales* and who, perhaps, had a preference for old ways continued to employ in their petty commerce coca leaves, *maté*, bits of cloth, pieces of copper and tin, shells, beads, stone counters, and, above all, cacao. The bean had a wide circulation and, in Mexico, an exchange rate that fluctuated around 140 beans for a silver *real* during most of the sixteenth century.[5]

Those who needed money but did not possess it had either to borrow it or obtain credit for their transactions. They paid dearly for both. The Genoese of Seville were the main financiers in the trans-Atlantic trade. In addition to participating directly in overseas ventures, they made loans to other parties for purchasing merchandise and arming ships to be sent to the Indies. Because of the high risks involved on the *Carrera* they demanded interest ranging from 50 to 90 percent. This rate may be compared to the annual rate of 5-5½ percent charged by the great Italian Banco di San Giorgio to its prime European borrowers. The Genoese also delivered goods on credit to traders to the Indies, adding interest to the valuation of the merchandise. At the American end of the *Carrera*, overseas branches or correspondents of Genoese firms loaned money or extended credit to merchants and brokers at interest rates ranging from 58 to 65 percent. Loans and credits on both sides of the Atlantic were almost invariably short term, with settlement expected immediately after goods purchased had been resold.[6]

Much less is known about commercial loans and credit in the domestic trade of the Indies, but scattered evidence suggests some tentative observations. Venture capital was much scarcer than in Europe. The crown advanced credit mainly to stimulate mining and the Antillean sugar industry, leaving commerce to its own resources. The church possessed capital to loan but preferred to invest it in real estate mortgages. Hence, the wealthier merchants of Mexico City, Lima, and a few subordinate audiencial capitals were the main sources of credit. In comparison with the Genoese of Seville, they made few direct loans, and, when they did make them, they used deeply discounted notes, taking a very sizable interest from the principal before delivering the balance to borrowers. Also, rather than extend credit to middlemen and retailers, they preferred to distribute their goods on consignment or commission to agents in their headquarter cities or in the provinces.

## Weights and Measures

Although not as serious a problem as money and credit, the different metrological systems used in Spanish America had at least a nuisance effect on trade. Despite intermittent efforts of kings from Alfonso the Wise to Ferdinand and Isabella to establish uniform weights and measures, at the time of the Discovery each province, each district, and, sometimes, each town in Castile had its own standards. Immigrants to the Indies introduced the systems with which they were familiar, thus replicating the disorder prevailing in the metropolis and forcing merchants and carriers engaged in long-distance commerce to make numerous conversions.

## Governmental Regulation and Taxation

Still another factor affecting Spanish American trade was the commercial and fiscal policies of the crown. By law and by custom, the determination of what was to be bought and sold, by whom, at what prices, and under what conditions was a *regalía* to be exercised in the public interest. A just prince was obliged to see that his subjects could obtain adequate quantities of goods and services of standard quality at prices that did not gouge the consumer and provided a fair profit for the seller. Furthermore, he had to protect merchants and manufacturers against unfair competition. Reasons of state also inclined kings toward the regulation of trade and commerce. It facilitated the collection of taxes, and, at the time the Enterprise of the Indies was born, the belief was growing that economies should be managed so as to maintain strong national monarchies.

In the Indies, the crown exercised its regulatory rights in both direct and indirect ways. By the terms of their individual charters and a general declaration of Emperor Charles, municipalities issued licenses to trade, manufacture, grind grain, and slaughter livestock within their jurisdictions. They also fixed local prices for consumer staples and goods sold by artisans and conducted systematic inspections to see to the observance of their regulations.

The crown displayed a rather liberal policy toward interprovincial and interregional trade in the Indies. It permitted all of its subjects, including Indians, to participate as long as they were licensed by royal officials, and it discouraged internal customs duties. It made no serious efforts to control types, volume, and prices of commodities exchanged, except for precious metals and items such as mercury and salt, which were royal monopolies. At seaports the king charged officials with inspecting vessels to see that they were seaworthy, properly rigged, and adequately provisioned and with testing the competence of pilots. Voyages had to be licensed, cargoes registered and inspected upon departure, and manifests checked upon arrival. These regulations, however, appear to have been applied only loosely except on main routes and, particularly, on the New Spain-Peru run.

Spanish kings attempted to regulate trans-Atlantic more closely than interAmerican commerce because it was the most accessible source of taxes and because mercantilist policies required it to be watched carefully. They held in principle that it should be conducted only by properly licensed Castilian merchants and carried in Castilian bottoms, that only Castilian goods should supply the colonies, and that American production, especially of precious metals, should be reserved for the crown and its subjects. On both sides of the Atlantic, it required special licenses to export and import goods believed to have a particular national importance or special taxability.

Three royal taxes bore most directly on commerce. One was a customs duty (almojarifazgo), imposed in stages beginning in the early sixteenth century. By 1566, the customs office in Seville collected 5 percent on imports and 5 percent on exports. In Indies ports the rate was 10 percent on imports and 2½ percent on exports, the assessment on imports being based on American prices, which were many times higher than in Sevillian schedules. A second tax was the avería, levied on all imports and exports at Seville, including bullion, and earmarked for the expenses of the American fleets. Its rate varied from 6 to

30 percent, depending on the prevailing security of the *Carrera* and, especially, on the level of corsair activity. The third was the pernicious *alcabala* (sales tax). In 1543 it had been levied on American imports in Seville at the rate of 10 percent whether the goods were sold or not. The Indies enjoyed exemption from the tax by virtue of a series of royal concessions made when they were first colonized, and, although several attempts were made to introduce it, settlers raised such a cry that the crown retreated.

Excepting the fluctuating *avería*, American merchandise entering Seville paid a total charge of 17½ percent, consisting of the 2½ percent export duty levied in America, the 5 percent tax on imports, and a 10 percent *alcabala*. European merchandise going to the Indies paid a 5 percent export duty in Spain and 10 percent upon arrival, for a total of 15 percent. In intercolonial commerce, American products paid customs duties at the Sevillian schedule. European goods reexported to other ports in the Indies were assessed on accrued increase in value.

The *Carrera* provided the matrix for regulating and taxing trans-Atlantic commerce. Although the fleet system had developed in part through the natural flow of trade, in part for purposes of defense, it also channeled traffic in a way that facilitated supervision. At its European end, the official regulatory and fiscal agency was the *Casa de Contratación* of Seville. Established originally in 1503 as a royal trading house, it continued to receive, register, and remit to treasury agents gold and silver arriving from America on the royal account. It organized the outbound fleets, issued sailing licenses to the privately owned vessels that made up most of their strength, inspected cargoes and provided manifests, and collected export duties. Upon the return of the fleets from the Indies, it registered and taxed what they brought. In addition to its strictly regulatory duties, the *Casa* served as a court of law in civil suits affecting crown revenues from commerce and in criminal cases arising from violations of commercial codes. It also advised the crown upon request or on its own initiative about all matters relative to the Indies trade and, in effect, became a ministry or council of commerce. In 1526, Emperor Charles made it subordinate to the Council of the Indies, but in practice it continued to enjoy a large measure of autonomy in its own sphere. In American ports, royal treasury officials exercised regulatory functions and collected duties.

Royal taxation and regulation did not impose an intolerable burden on the commerce of the Indies. By the standards of the time, excises and duties were not extraordinary, nor did mercantilist controls restrict the flow of trade unduly. In America, goods moved about more or less freely, and, in trans-Atlantic traffic, the number of articles that could be exported exceeded those on the restricted list. The crown applied mercantilist restraints so loosely that they did not limit the supply of goods. When it became apparent that Castilian industry and agriculture could not accommodate a growing American market, the king on occasion gave licenses to Italian, Flemish, German, English, and French merchants to trade with his New World dominions, to import foreign goods for that purpose, and to reexport American products. Foreigners further participated in the Indies traffic by using Castilian merchants as commission agents, and many specially licensed foreign ships sailed in the fleets.

## Commercial Monopolies

Another aspect of government policy had more pernicious effects on commerce, namely, the use of private monopolies for indirect regulation and revenue collection. In 1543 the crown organized the *Universidad de Cargadores a las Indias* (Guild of Merchants Trading with the Indies), better known as the *Consulado* of Seville, and gave it a monopoly of trade with the Indies through all Spanish ports. In return for its privileges, the *consulado* collaborated with the *Casa de Contratación* in organizing and loading outbound fleets and unloading inbound fleets; it acted as an agent for collecting the *avería*, regulated the business practices of its members, and took jurisdiction over commercial suits in which they became involved. Spanish kings did not see fit to charter *consulados* in America until the end of the sixteenth century, but meanwhile a few great mercantile houses in Mexico City and Lima acquired a de facto monopoly of trade with Seville and the distribution of European goods in the Indies. Like their Sevillian counterparts, they helped in the organization of fleets.

Monopolists on both sides of the Atlantic used their privileged position to create an artifical market in the Indies, one in which they tried to control supply so as to insure maximum profits. Fray Tomás Mercado, an astute observer of contemporary Sevillian business practices, believed that gross profits on exports to America ran as high as 100 percent and net as much as 50 percent.

Mercado also remarked on the effect of monopolistic profit margins, credit charges, and, presumably, transportation costs and taxes on prices in America: "A *vara* [about 33 bolt inches] of velvet worth 1,000 *maravedís* in Seville would cost 2,000 *maravedís* in the Indies. When it was bought on credit, its price became 1,900 *maravedís* in Seville, and 2,800 *maravedís* in the New World."[7] The American prices quoted are probably those that wholesalers paid at ports of entry. Retail prices would have been even higher.

## Prices and Wages

Serial data on the prices of domestically produced and imported goods would illuminate subjects discussed in this chapter. Unfortunately, only scattered figures and intermittent sequences exist even for those regions most intensively studied, and, if combined, they have little statistical value. They do, however, permit some speculative inferences. In most parts of the Indies a three-stage price movement developed that closely paralleled the progress of conquest and colonization. At first, in each newly conquered region, everything was scarce and therefore very dear. Then, as the Spaniards devised ways to collect surpluses produced by the indigenes, and as the yield of European-managed farms, ranches, and workshops came on the market, basic commodity prices either fell or, at least, tended to level off. The third stage was a steady and, sometimes, steep rise occasioned by the demands of a growing European and mixed-blood population that could not be supplied adequately by a shrinking native labor force. Thus, between 1530 and about 1570, the price of corn in New Spain increased slightly more than three times; of wheat, two and a half times; of *ropa menuda* (shirts, trousers, and skirts worn mainly by Indians), five times; and of bolt cotton cloth, nine times. An exception was meat. Its abundance caused its price to fall or remain stable.[8]

The prices of imported luxury goods went through much the same stages: first, exorbitant levels, reflecting shortages of everything; then, some relief as more ships arrived from Europe; and, finally, a long-term rise in which European inflation, monopolistic controls, and increasing taxation were the main forces at work.

Within the three-phase movement of prices, sharp short-term fluctuations occurred. For goods produced in the Indies, they owed to the irregular alternation of good and bad crop years and the shifting availability of native labor. Prices of European imports rose and fell in response to scarcities and gluts in the American market. These were occasioned by irregularities in fleet arrivals in the Indies and the lack of reliable commercial intelligence in Seville, which led merchants to underestimate or overestimate American demands. In more general terms, the period 1500–70 was marked by great price instability underlaid by long-term inflation.

Data on wages are, if anything, even scarcer than on prices, especially because a large part of the work force did not receive direct cash payments. Probably the rapid economic development of the Indies, coupled with the sharp drop in the idigenous labor supply, pushed direct and indirect wages up faster than prices. Professors Cook and Borah hypothesize that the demographic disasters suffered by the Indians eventually enabled them to extract better treatment as well as higher pay from their masters, thus helping to reverse the decline in their numbers.[9]

## Conquest Economies: An Overview

By the 1560s human urges, sometimes helped, sometimes hindered by nature, had pretty well set the basic structure of the economy of the Indies, or, better to say, the economies of the Indies, for the organization of production and trade had a dual character. One economy was oriented toward Europe and based on money. Its major exports in order of value (in *pesos de oro* of 450 *maravedís* each) were: precious metals, 14,141,216 (1566-70); hides, 583,438 (1568-70); cochineal, 478,856 (1568-70); and sugar, 268,040 (1568-70).[10] Secondary exports consisted mainly of dyewoods and other products of the forest. Prices obtained depended mainly on European market conditions. including considerable manipulation by monopolists and speculators. In exchange, the Indies received hardware, fine clothing and wines, olive oil, diverse luxury items, slaves, and mercury. The prices of these items were determined in part by American demand-supply conditions, in part by private or government monopoly. The mercantile economy's loci were mines, plantations, and urban commercial centers. Its main axes ran Zacatecas-Mexico City-Veracruz-Havana, and Potosí-Lima-Panama-Havana. Its production relied for the most part on compulsory labor systems, the *repartimiento-mita*, and black slavery, supplemented by a free labor force of Indians and mixed-bloods, especially in the Mexican mines. In brief, it had a proto-capitalistic structure and placed the New World in economic dependency on the Old.

Various circumstances gave the mercantile economy an unstable and cyclical character. Plantation crops could be damaged or destroyed by droughts, floods, winds, insects, and fungi. Production was often hindered by poor land management and capital and labor crises. Transportation was subject to delays or interruptions occasioned by terrain, bureaucratic sluggishness, and corsair attacks. Prices of American products rose and fell in European markets, and delayed or faulty commercial intelligence prevented producers from making rational adjustments to fluctuations. The bestowal of the crown's favor on an industry might cause it to boom, but a shift in royal policy could bring it ruin. Mining had to contend with capital and labor shortages, the exhaustion of veins and the flooding of shafts, the availability and price of mercury, and changes in the rate of the *quinto*. The bonanza mentality of the colonists, generated, perhaps, by the great windfalls of conquest loot, contributed to instability. Entrepreneurs were prone to abandon enterprises, before patiently and fully developing them, for others that appeared to offer quicker profits.

Another economy served the basic needs of the American population. Some of its sectors, such as the textile industry and wholesale merchandising, were urban centered and linked to the mercantile system, but its main loci were the vast rural hinterlands of the Indies, and its organization resembled the "natural economies" of medieval Europe, bearing in mind that such forms never existed in a pure state. It produced grain, meat, and other basic foodstuffs, cheap clothing, leather goods, and household items. For exchange, it supplemented scarce pesos and *reales* with barter, uncoined metal pieces, gold dust, and traditional native monies. Its labor base consisted of Indians working their communal lands in traditional ways and, despite the best efforts of the crown, delivering their surplus labor and production to Spanish masters through dependency relations such as the *encomienda* and debt peonage. In short, it had a neo-*señorial* structure. Although it suffered intermittent agricultural crises, it had a much more stable base than the export economy.

Important regional variations existed in the systems just described. Mexico had the most versatile and best balanced economy. The kingdom possessed rich mines, lands and climates that could produce a wide range of export and subsistence crops, an adequate labor supply, a relatively well organized system of internal transportation, access to European markets, and the advantage of prudent management during its critical formative stage. Highland New Granada, Ecuador, Chile, and Paraguay had productive subsistence economies based on rich agricultural and pastoral resources and sufficient native labor. A lack of precious metals, however, and the prohibitive cost of transportation for less valuable products, denied these regions significant participation in export trade. Because of a limited range of resources and, perhaps because of habits developed during the early stages of settlement, the Antilles and the tropical circum-Caribbean and Pacific leaned heavily on monocultural production for export: Guatemala on cacao; Santo Domingo and Puerto Rico first on gold, then on sugar; Tierra Firme on slaves and gold. Peru constituted a special case. It possessed a wide range of resources and adequate labor supplies, but civil strife, royal and private preoccupation with the Potosí mines, and lack of economical access to European markets for its nonmineral production hindered balanced economic development.

The economic organization of the Spanish American possessions was as cumbersome and inefficient as the political apparatus that governed them. But it provided subsistence for millions, plenty for thousands, and affluence for some, which is about the best that can be said for most economies, then and now. Its construction was just as striking an achievement as the speed with which the Spaniards conquered the Indies and the rate and range of their colonization. It says a great deal about their persistence, enterprise, and ruthlessness, as well as about the endurance of the indigenes who had to do most of the digging and fabricating and carrying.

# CHAPTER 12

# The Conquest of Brazil

## *The Portuguese Approach to Brazil*

In the eighteenth century, a French historian compared Spanish and Portuguese expansion in the New World in the following terms:

The conquests of the Portuguese in the New World are not as pleasing on a broad view as the conquests of Mexico and Peru. In the latter we see a single Conqueror who . . . successfully conquers a mighty State in a short space of time with few men to establish himself solidly on the ruins of a great Empire. As in the epic Poem, it appears as a single action embellished by a few Episodes. With the former, on the contrary, it is a long period of years, a multitude of different lands, an infinite number of actions, many Chiefs who succeed one another with different ideas, an assemblage of disparate things which have neither unity nor sequence, and a kind of chaos from which a single whole emerges only because it is the same nation which acts everywhere and to which all is related.[1]

The differing paces and patterns of conquest described above derived mainly from two circumstances. One was that, through a combination of Columbus's reckonings and the vagaries of Atlantic winds and currents, the Spanish first came upon their Indies through a great continental indentation, the Caribbean, and they placed their first settlements in its midst. From these points, interior seas gave access to the shores of the two continents, which, in turn, provided convenient bases for approaching the centers of indigenous wealth and population as they became known. In contrast, the first Portuguese who sailed to America bumped into the outer rim of a continental landmass. Boundless jungles, bush and swamp, mighty rivers, and towering mountains separated them from the treasures of America, and in any event at the time they had no way of knowing of the existence of those riches.

## The Portuguese Old World Empire

### Territorial Organization

The other condition slowing Portuguese expansion in America was that while Spain was laying the foundations of a territorial empire there, Portugal was creating an imperial system of a different order in other parts of the world (its genesis was examined in chapter 3). It is essential to examine some of its main features because they explain more fully why the Portuguese at first left the lands discovered by Cabral virtually unattended and why they acted as they did when they finally turned their eyes to the New World. Leaving aside the fruitless, costly, and beleaguered fortresses in Morocco, four of which King John III (1521-57) sensibly abandoned, the Portuguese Old World empire in the early 1500s had three territorial components. One consisted of the agricultural colonies on the Atlantic archipelagos—the Azores, the Madeiras, and the Cape Verdes—and on São Tomé and Principe, immediately off the coast of Nigeria. Another was made up of an intermittent line of trading and slaving stations stretching along the Atlantic coast of Africa from Sierra Leone to the Congo and anchored on the fortified settlement of São Jorge da Mina (El Mina).

A third, and by far the richest, component of Portugal's Old World empire was the *Estado da India*, whose formation began with the arrival of Vasco da Gama in Calicut in 1498. It consisted of a string of coastal enclaves and offshore islands running around the Indian Ocean from Sofala, in lower Mozambique, to Cochin, on the Malabar coast of India, and thence around the tip of the Indian subcontinent to the Coromandel coast, to Ceylon and Malacca, to the Moluccas, and to Macao on the China coast. It was anchored by major fortifications at Mozambique on the east coast of Africa, Ormuz at the head of the Persian Gulf, Goa, and Malacca. Most Portuguese settlements were essentially trading stations, acquired by negotiation or force and enjoying extraterritorial rights in the midst of native states. In a few regions such as Ceylon, alliances with local princes allowed the Portuguese to extend their political and economic influence into the interior. The lifeline of the *Estado* was the *Carreira da India*, the long maritime route from Lisbon to Goa and Cochin.

The Economics of Empire

Until da Gama's voyage, income from the Portuguese overseas empire came mainly from African gold, slaves, and malagueta (red) pepper. The crown managed trade in these items through the lease of monopolies to private parties, requiring only that they pay a 5 percent import duty, or by entering into an investment pool with them.

After the opening of the sea route to India, eastern spices—black pepper, ginger, cinnamon, cloves, nutmeg, and mace—took over first place from African products. Profits from the spice trade appeared so promising that, in 1503, the king declared it a full royal monopoly. Only the crown could send ships into the Indian Ocean, and returning cargoes all had to be delivered to the royal *Casa da India* in Lisbon. Beyond this point, however, an exclusive monopoly proved to be impracticable. The main market for spices lay in northern Europe, and the *Casa* did not have any system for selling them directly in those regions. It therefore sent them to the Portuguese factor in Antwerp, who contracted distribution through merchant consortia of Germans, Florentines, and, ironically, Jews recently expelled from Portugal. Thus, Lisbon became only a point in transit. The real center of the spice trade was Antwerp, and foreigners took a substantial part of the profits. Direct costs of the spice trade were also heavy. Between 1522 and 1543, reinforcements for the Indian fleets cost about 800,000 *cruzados*, and, between 1522 and 1551, more than 100,000 *cruzados* a year were lost on ships wrecked on the *Carreira* and between Lisbon and Flanders.[2]

Despite these expenses, the spice trade produced handsome revenues. In 1506 they accounted for 27 percent of royal income. By 1518 the percentage had increased to 39, more than the value of all other overseas commerce and of all the crown's income from metropolitan Portugal.[3]

Imperial Governance

In constitutional terms, the Portuguese Old World empire grew by incorporating each new territorial acquisition as an overseas extension of the metropolis. It several components were subject to Portuguese law as codified in the *Ordenações Afonsinas*, completed during the reign of Afonso V (1438–81), and in the superseding *Ordenações Manuelinas*, a simplified version of the *Siete Partidas*, which appeared in its final form in 1521. As in the Spanish Indies, the provisions of these codes had to be continuously supplemented and adapted to new circumstances by royal orders, decrees, and *regimentos* (standing instructions to governors), but these never evolved into a separate corpus of colonial law. With the exception of the *Casa da India* and its predecessor institutions, which amounted to royal trading and customs houses, the crown did not see fit to create separate home agencies of government such as the Spanish Council of the Indies to handle overseas affairs. Instead, such matters were managed by royal secretaries.

Overseas agencies of royal government reflected the changing circumstances of expansion. The Atlantic Islands and Guinea remained in the hands of captains-donatary who were the descendants of the original grantees or who had acquired charter rights by purchase. In practice, successive Portuguese kings had gradually obtained control of the captaincies by sending out royal treasury officials, magistrates, and *corregedores* to supervise them. From the beginning, the creation of the *Estado da India* was a royal enterprise, and the crown governed it directly through its appointees. The principal official was the governor-general, named for a three-year term, who had his seat in Goa. When circumstances required a more prestigious representative, or when the appointee was of pompous lineage, the king gave him the additional title of viceroy (*vice-rei*), but between 1505 and 1550 only four of the fifteen governors sent out received this distinction. In addition to governing Goa, the governor-general was responsible for coordinating naval defense against the eastern Muslim states into whose domains the Portuguese had forcibly intruded. The other settlements in the *Estado* had royal governors nominally subject to Goa, but in practice the sprawling extent of the empire allowed them a good deal of autonomy. Governors-general and local governors had as their ranking subordinates *ouvidores geral* (auditors-general and chief magistrates) and *provedores môr* (quartermasters-general).

The kings of Portugal consistently held that the main justification for their intrusion into the lands of pagans and infidels was the extension of Christendom, and, to this end, a close alliance was established between crown and church in the *Estado da India*. The soldier-chronicler Diogo do Couto described the connection thus: "The Kings of Portugal always aimed in their conquest of the East at so uniting the two powers, spiritual and temporal, that one should never be exercised without the other."[4] The pope institutionalized the arrangement by granting to Portuguese kings a very ample *padroado real* (royal patronage), first in the Atlantic and Africa, later in the *Estado da India*. Originally it was exercised by the Order of Christ with considerable independence, but in 1495 the crown assumed the order's grand-mastership and gained direct control of the patronage. Its rights included the establishment of ecclesiastical jurisdictions, but in this sphere it acted rather slowly. Not until 1514 did it create the first overseas diocese, which it seated in Funchal in the Azores. Goa did not become a bishopric until 1534. No new sees were created until 1557, when bishops were appointed to Cochin and Malacca, suffragan to Goa, which was elevated to an archbishopric in the same year. Macao did not gain episcopal status until 1575.

## Colonization and Overseas Social Organization

At first glance, it might appear that the Portuguese paid less attention to colonization (*povoamento*) than did the Spanish. By the mid-sixteenth century hardly more than 200 or 300 Europeans lived in the factories (*feitorias*) on the Atlantic coast of Africa, and in 1540 a rough census counted only some 1800 European-descended families in all the *Estado da India*. Many of these were probably assimilated mixed bloods. The Portuguese, nevertheless, did the best they could, considering the opportunities and means available. As observed in chapter 3, they colonized the uninhabited Azores and Madeiras vigorously. The pestilential lands of Africa south of the Sahara held little attraction for them. In the Orient they found brighter prospects, but without extensive territorial conquests the dense native population could not be dispossessed of its lands to make way for Europeans, nor could it be enslaved or commended to support settlers. Perhaps more important, a nation of little more than 1,000,000 souls lacked the resources to colonize two continents.

But within these limitations, the Portuguese colonized Africa and Asia in spirit and fact. From Mina to Macao, they built European towns, laying out streets and building churches, public edifices, and houses in the form and manner prescribed by tradition. The crown granted the settlements *forais*, which among other privileges, allowed them to establish municipal *concelhos* or *câmaras*. Their liberties, however, were somewhat straitened by the fact that the territorial jursidictions of towns generally coincided with those of the resident royal governor, who personally, or through his minions, intervened in local affairs. Parishes were established simultaneously with towns and the communicants formed into religious confraternities (*irmandades*). These voluntary associations contributed to the construction and maintenance of churches, conducted pious observances, celebrated the innumerable saints' days of the religious calendar with merry games and processions, and performed social ameliorative functions such as the support of hospitals and orphanages and the distribution of alms to the poor. They also provided a means of social identification and a source of emotional sustenance for settlers far from home.

Because of their shortage of human resources, the Portuguese, even more than the Spanish, relied on the acculturation of natives to provide a Europeanized population in the *Estado da India*. In general they exhibited a good measure of political tolerance toward the native peoples of their territorial enclaves. Once Muslims and Hindus accepted Portuguese dominion, they were left in possession of their liberty and property, given the protection of Portuguese law, and, if they became Christians, granted the privileges and immunities enjoyed by European settlers.

The crown also tried to use miscegenation to advance Europeanization. To Portuguese who married respectable native women it offered various subsidies. Afonso de Albuquerque, who came to Goa as governor-general in 1506, reported on the first results of this policy:

We took here some good-looking Muslim women, of white colour. Several of our men, well-born and gentlemanlike, asked them in marriage, in order to settle in this land. For that purpose, they asked for money, and I had them married, according to the orders received from Your Highness, and to each of them I have given a horse, land and cattle. . . . All together there will be about 450 souls.[5]

Six years later, another contemporary gave the king a quite different assessment of the governor-general's matchmaking:

Your highness is to be blamed for everything that is happening here, because sometimes we all think that you are ordering him (*Albuquerque*) to do everything he does. . . . Believe me, the married men here are not those that Your Highness would wish to be married. They are men of low birth who have married their slaves in order to get the advantages of the dowries bestowed by Your Highness. . . .[6]

The author was an enemy of Albuquerque, and his views may have been colored by personal animus. Nevertheless, they probably reflected Portuguese attitudes toward interracial marriage better than did the governor-general's report, for this type of union dropped off sharply after the crown ceased to provide dowries for Asian brides.

Meanwhile miscegenation took a more natural and fruitful course; Portuguese men took harems of native concubines. Crown and church fulminated against such arrangements but could not prevail against powerful social influences. The European male in India, far from his native environment and without the companionship of females of his own kind, enjoyed freedom from traditional sexual restraints. He found an abundance of native women who were untroubled by Christian sexual ethics and aware of the advantages to be gained through liaisons with men of a conquering race. Thus, it was through illicit unions rather than marriage that the Portuguese peopled their Asian enclaves with Eurasians.

## Colonization and Evangelization

Efforts to colonize by acculturation merged closely with evangelization. Not only did the kings of Portugal feel bound to extend Christendom, but the Portuguese, as well as the Spaniards, believed that a true civil society must be a Christian society. In the Congo, the crown mounted a quite substantial missionary effort, but the depredations of slavers aborted the undertaking. In the *Estado da India* missionaries, with the Franciscans taking the lead, arrived closely in the wake of the first spice fleets but ran into a different set of problems. The Muslims, although less militant than their breathren in North Africa, were virtually impervious to conversion, and the Hindus possessed an ancient and sophisticated religion that did not yield easily to either Muslim or Christian teaching and preaching. And, since the Portuguese presence in Asia was still precarious, the missionary fathers had to rely on the carrot rather than the stick. Infidels and pagans who did not accept the new religion were not to be ill-treated, but those who became "brethren in Christ" received preferential treatment in matters of taxes and civic privileges.

Around 1540 evangelization became more militant. By that time Portuguese civil and ecclesiastical authority was well established in the East, and the church, acting through the secular arm, began to destroy idols, temples, mosques, and other odious symbols of alien religions in Goa and neighboring territories. Also, in early 1542, Father Francis Xavier, of the Society of Jesus, arrived in Goa, heralding the appearance of a new and vigorous missionary order. Within twenty-five years the Jesuits had stations throughout the *Estado da India* and in remote Japan. In them they developed methods of evangelization that quickly gained them leadership in the field. Eschewing force and bribery, they adjusted their approach to the cultures of the peoples with whom they worked; learned their languages; preached aggressively; engaged in doctrinal disputation with Brahmins, Mullahs, and Buddhist priests; founded schools (*colégios*) for the instruction of neophytes in religion, reading, and writing; and sent out young converts to spread the faith beyond their missions.

No one knows how many Christians the Jesuits and other missionary orders made in the East. In some areas, such as Goa, the Coromandel coast, and Ceylon, conversions during the sixteenth century probably ran to the hundreds of thousands. Evangelization tended to be most successful in areas controlled directly by Portuguese and among the lower classes and castes who stood to gain socially and materially by conversion. Perhaps, also, the disadvantaged found in the new faith some spiritual consolation for their lot. The missionaries in the *Estado da India*, however, did not attempt conversion on a continental scale as did the Spanish in the Western Indies, nor could they have done so. There were too few of them, they had to work with populations much more sophisticated than the American Indians, and they did not possess the power and prestige that large territorial conquests conveyed to missionaries in the Spanish New World.

The formation of societies in the Portuguese Old World empire was guided both by traditional values and by attitudes generated by expansion. Within their limited territorial possessions, the Portuguese (almost exclusively male) constituted the elite since they were the masters and set the values. But they also had to assign statuses to alien peoples in the territories they controlled. Various considerations affected their judgments—level of culture, legitimacy of birth, and personal achievement—but the overt standard of measure was color. It will be remembered that when Albuquerque selected brides for his gentlemen, he tried to make sure that they were not only comely but white. The status of non-European peoples in the Portuguese Old World graded downward from "white" Muslims and Hindus, through various shades of half-castes, to Africans of midnight hue. Some legitimate, pale-faced Eurasians and mulattoes obtained nominal acceptance in European society, but they were not welcomed at respectable dinner tables.

## The Course of Conquest in Brazil

### The "Period of Neglect," 1500–30

Preoccupation with extracting wealth through "Golden Goa" along with the burdens of governing and defending the *Estado da India* quite understandably diverted Lisbon's attention from its American possessions, which, initial reconnaissance had determined, held no precious metals or valuable spices. For some thirty years after Cabral came upon the Ilha da Veracruz, the Portuguese presence in Brazil was limited mainly to the exploitation of the wood that gave the land its name. The means employed followed a well-established pattern. The crown rented monopolies to private companies financed by Portuguese New Christians, Genoese, and Florentines. Very little is known of the details of their enterprises, but available sources show that as in Africa they established factories along the coast and obtained brazilwood through barter with the natives. The Brazilian historian Roberto Simonsen calculated the average annual volume of the trade during the period 1500–30 at 300 *toneladas* (a *tonelada* equaled about 921.6 kilograms), that is, enough to load three to five ships of the time. The value of production for the thirty-year period totaled about 250,000 *cruzados*, of which the crown obtained about one-quarter from the rent of its monopoly.[7] The net profits of concessionaries are not known.

Compared to the India trade, the exploitation of dyewood was a very modest enterprise, but it was sufficient to keep interest in Brazil alive and led to the first step in colonization. Although some factories were seasonal, little more than ports of call, a few such as Pernambuco (1502?), Porto Seguro (1503), São Vicente (1508?), and Bahia de Todos os Santos (1509?) may have developed into small settlements, perhaps protected by simple forts.[8] Because of the difficulties of obtaining food from distant Portugal, their inhabitants planted subsistence crops, principally indigenous manioc and maize.

In addition to exploiters of dyewood, two other classes of Europeans appeared in Brazil during the early 1500s. One comprised missionaries of the Franciscan and Arrábida orders, but little is known about their strength or ministry. *Degredados* (criminals and other undesirables) dumped at various points along the coast constituted the other. These men, if not of heroic stature, were certainly the most romantic figures that the first stages of Portuguese occupation produced. They also made some practical contributions. The Indians undoubtedly killed and perhaps ate some of them but took others to be superior beings. The fortunate survivors adapted quickly and comfortably to a life that provided them with freedom from toil, virtual *senhorio*, and unlimited access to women. They learned indigenous languages and customs, sired numerous illegitimate progeny, and became veritable patriarchs of extended families. Because of their influence among the indigenes and their bilingualism, they were of immense assistance to traders and, later, to Portuguese settlers.

## Preliminary Reconnaissance

In 1530 or thereabouts King John determined to occupy Brazil more definitively for reasons he set forth in a letter to Duarte Coelho, who participated in the undertaking:

Dom João, etc. To whomever may see this letter of mine I make it known that, considering how much it serves God and is to my advantage and to the good of my kingdoms and landholdings as well as that of their natives and subjects, that my coastal area and land of Brazil be more settled than they have been up to now, in order to have the divine worship and services celebrated there, and to exalt our holy Catholic faith by bringing to it and interesting in it the natives of the aforesaid land who are infidels and idol worshippers, as well as because of the great profit which would accrue to my kindgoms and landhold- ings, and thus to the natives and subjects of them, if they settle and take ad- vantage of the aforesaid land. . . .[9]

In other words, much the same concerns motivated the king as those that took the Portuguese to Africa and Asia and impelled the Spanish toward American conquest.

But John had more immediate and specific reasons for his new interest in his American dominions. The first and most pressing was intrusions by the French, who had no more respect for Portugal's titles to the New World than for Spain's and who, for purposes of making war, regarded Portugal as a Span- ish appanage. In the very early 1500s, French corsairs began raiding Portuguese as well as Spanish shipping in the Atlantic triangle formed by Portugal, the Azores, and the Canaries. Also, as early as 1504, French ships appeared along the Brazilian coast, combining logwood trading with raids on Portuguese fac- tories. Beginning in 1516 John sent out occasional "coast guard" fleets to chastise and expel the interlopers, but these expeditions could not police ef- fectively 3000 miles of indented coastline.

In the 1520s, at about the same time they began raiding in the Spanish In- dies, the French stepped up their aggression in Brazil. Their depredations cut into the king's revenues from his brazilwood monopoly and did great mischief to his subjects. Should the French establish themselves permanently in Brazil, moreover, they would be in a position to threaten the flank of the *Carreira da India* whose route extended westward across the Atlantic before swinging south and east to round the tip of Africa.

King John also had precious metals very much in mind—especially silver, which the Portuguese needed for exchange in their oriental spice trade. Al- though early coastal reconnaissance had found none, intelligence received later caused him to believe that mines might exist somewhere in the interior of South America. In 1524-25, Aleixo Garcia, a Portuguese sailor shipwrecked on the southern shores of Brazil, had led a party inland looking for a "White King" reputed by the coastal Indians to rule lands rich in minerals. He probably reached the outposts of the Inca realms, where he learned of their mines and treasures, and, although some of his native followers later slew him, accounts of his exploits reached Europe. Shortly thereafter, John Cabot made a voyage to southern South America (1526-30) and, sailing up a great river in search of a strait, he found a few items of silver among the Guaraní Indians. Although their value was paltry, the trinkets raised excited anticipations in Madrid and Lisbon, and Cabot named the river up which he had voyaged the Rio de la Plata (The River of Silver).

These *entradas* and discoveries merged with a legend of a mountain of silver glittering somewhere in the interior and approachable from the Rio de la Plata region, which became known as the "coast of gold and silver." King John, therefore, was anxious to obtain control of those regions if they lay on his side of the Line of Demarcation. When the tidings of Pizarro's approach from the Pacific side of the continent reached Lisbon, his interest acquired a certain urgency.

John began by sending Martim Afonso de Sousa, a nobleman in his confidence, to find out more about his American dominions. More specifically, he ordered Martim Afonso to explore the coasts from the Rio Maranhão to the Rio de la Plata (with particular attention to determining whether the coast of gold and silver lay on the Portuguese side of the Line), to take formal possession of the land, to expel the French, to set up a system to administer the scattered factories, to establish a permanent agricultural colony, and to settle persons in places from which mines might be discovered. The king provided his captain with a fleet of five ships carrying 400 sailors and colonists and gave him full administrative, military, and judicial authority over his personnel and the lands he settled.

Martim Afonso performed his several missions truly and well. Departing Lisbon in December, 1530, he made landfall two months later on the northeast coast of Brazil. Turning south and east, he rounded the hump and followed the coastline southwest, erecting *padrões* (stone pillars) signifying Portuguese possession and naming prominent landmarks after saints' days as they came up in succession. Near present-day Pernambuco, he captured three French ships loaded with brazilwood. Off the Island of Cananéa (on the coast of present-day Paraná) Martim Afonso's flagship and another of his vessels were shipwrecked, but he led the remaining three to the Rio de la Plata. He then returned to the Bay of Santos and on its shores founded the settlement of São Vicente. Through the good offices of the *degredado* João Ramalho, the settlers established cordial relations with the Indians in the hinterland and were able to found a satellite village, Piratininga, on the plateau that lay back of the bay. Martim Afonso returned to Portugal in 1533 to report that Brazil offered favorable prospects for colonization and to receive gracious thanks and more substantial rewards from his sovereign.

The Donatary Captaincies

Even before Martim Afonso's return, King John had decided on a plan of colonization that had well-established antecedents in the settlement of the

Atlantic islands and that would cost him no money. He determined to divide his American dominions from Pernambuco to the Rio de la Plata into captaincies, each possessing some fifty leagues of coastline and with latitudinal boundaries running inland to the meridian of Tordesillas, wherever that might be determined to lie. The captaincies would be granted to donataries who agreed to settle them at their own expense in return for extensive political and economic rights within their territories.[10]

The king made the grants between 1534 and 1536, although with some departures from the original plan. The exploration of the Sousa brothers, along with data from other sources, indicated that in the south the coast of gold and silver unfortunately fell on the Spaniard's side of the Line. In the northeast, however, the coast between Pernambuco and the Rio Maranhão lay within the Portuguese donation. Thus, the limits of the lands to be granted shifted northward. Also, the changing slope and contour of the coast made it necessary to vary the number of leagues granted. As it worked out, twelve donataries received fifteen captaincies between the Maranhão and a point near the boundary between modern Brazil and Uruguay. The grants had ocean frontages varying from thirty to sixty leagues. Martim Afonso obtained two noncontiguous strips whose coastlines totaled 100 leagues. His brother, Pero Lopes de Sousa, who had accompanied him on his voyage, received three totaling eighty leagues of shoreline. These multiple grants to the Sousas account for the numerical discrepancy between captaincies and donataries.

Like the Spanish captains of conquest, none of the donataries came from the titled nobility of the realm, a class that had no need to undertake risky adventures overseas. They were *fidalgos* and respectable commoners who obtained their captaincies for meritorious service to the crown and on the assumption that they possessed the resources to settle them. Of the twelve, four had served in a military capacity in the Orient and North Africa, four as civil functionaries, and three on various court missions. Little is known about one, Pero do Campo Tourinho. At least eight had some experience as mariners, and four had been to America before they received their grants. At least nine were men of some means, although only one, Jorge Figueiredo Correia, was reputed to be rich.

As in the colonization of the Azores and the Madeiras, the constitutions of the several captaincies consisted of two primary documents, a *carta de doação* (charter of donation) and a *foral*.[11] The charter set forth the donatary's rights and privileges. In the political category, he received his grant in heredity, inalienable and indivisible, and obtained the title of governor and captain with the option to name a lieutenant to act in his stead. He could govern his territory without interference from royal *corregedores* and could found towns, grant charters to them, appoint certain municipal officers, deny suffrage to any *morador* (settler), and set aside municipal elections. The donatary exercised jurisdiction without appeal in civil cases involving claims worth less than thirty ounces of gold. In criminal cases he enjoyed original jurisdiction and the power to impose fines and imprisonment of up to ten years on *fidalgos* and penalties up to and including death on plebeians (*peões*), slaves, and Indians.

Charters also gave generous economic privileges. The donatary could set aside one-fifth of his captaincy, laid out in four or five noncontiguous strips, as his personal property. Although the rest of the land technically belonged to the crown, he could distribute it in *sesmarias* (individual grants) to his followers. He received a monopoly of salt mines and of grain and sugar mills, and he could enslave a limited number of Indians and export them to Portugal free of sales taxes. He enjoyed exemption from personal taxes and was assigned a portion, generally one-tenth, of various revenues he collected for the crown, as well as a percentage of the tithe owed to the Order of Christ.

The *foral* defined the authority retained by the crown and the rights and privileges of settlers. Regal prerogatives included monopolies of trade in brazilwood, drugs, and spices, which in practice were often rented out, and the collection of the royal "fifth" on precious metals and gems mined. The king could also send *môrdomos* (treasury officials) into the captaincies to look after his fiscal interests. The settlers had the right to receive *sesmarias*, to which they could obtain title after five years of cultivation, and to trade with Indians, other captaincies, the metropolis, and those foreign nations with whom Portugal was at peace. They enjoyed exemption from personal taxes, except the tithe, from certain excises such as those levied on soap and salt, and from export and import duties except those on goods carried by foreign ships. Finally, they could not be prosecuted for crimes committed before coming to Brazil. In general, the *foral* applied to foreigners who settled in Brazil as well as to Portuguese.

The settlement of the several captaincies encountered two common problems. First, the indigenous inhabitants were either hostile by disposition or became so when the Portuguese tried to enslave them or when the French incited them. Second, like the Spaniards in the Antilles, the first Portuguese settlers of Brazil constituted a volatile and ungovernable lot. Not only were they set down far from home and freed of traditional social and civil restraints, but they included a high proportion of *degredados*, particularly after a royal decree of May 31, 1535, whereby Brazil replaced the island of São Tomé as the main dumping ground for Portuguese criminals and other undesirables.

Aside from these difficulties, the fate of the captaincies depended on a variety of circumstances, but mainly on the enterprise, leadership, and resources of their donataries. The men who held the charters for Piauí, Rio de Janeiro, and Sant' Ana did not even try to colonize them. The donataries of Pará, Maranhão, and Ceará organized a large expedition of ten ships and 1000 men to exploit their grants and established the small settlement of Nazaré on the island of Maranhão. The enterprise, however, turned out to be, and perhaps was conceived as, a Spanish-style *entrada*. Most of the personnel plunged inland to search for gold and silver mines, and two-thirds of them perished in the jungles. The survivors settled down at Nazaré for a time, but, discouraged and beleaguered by hostile Indians, they soon abandoned the settlement. The Portuguese did not renew efforts to occupy these territories for nearly a century.

The donataries of the remaining captaincies all settled their grants either in person or through lieutenants (*loco tenentes*), but with varying degrees of success. Two captaincies, São Vicente and Pernambuco, prospered. The first had an initial advantage, since it was the only one that was financed directly from the substantial resources of the crown. Also, Martim Afonso de Sousa was a capable leader. Shortly after his return from Brazil, the king appointed him governor-general of India and he never saw the New World again, but he had the good judgment to appoint capable lieutenants to manage his affairs there. By 1548 the captaincy had three settlements: São Vicente and Piratininga, founded by Martim Afonso, and the port of Santos, which was established later. Togther they held some 600 European settlers. The land surrounding them was planted in sugar, citrus, and subsistence crops. From these locations, settlement spread into neighboring Santo Amaro, which became in effect a dependency of São Vicente.

Pernambuco also had initial advantages. Located on the bulge of Brazil, it was relatively close to Portugal, and a factory already existed there when the captaincies were chartered. Equally important, the donatary, Duarte Coelho, invested heavily in his enterprise and directed it vigorously and in person. He founded two towns, Iguaraçú and Olinda, the second of which became his capital. Guided by his military experience in India, he fortified them strongly and defended them against hostile natives. He saw to it that the settlers planted sugar; he financed initial purchases of stock, tools, and equipment; and he administered the king's law firmly. By the mid-1540s, the two towns had more than 500 settlers, and surrounding cane fields produced enough sugar to load forty to fifty ships annually for Europe. Dyewood cutting also remained a profitable activity in the region.

The remaining captaincies settled in the 1530s fared less well. In general they were underfinanced and plagued by Indian uprisings, and the donataries or their lieutenants could not maintain control over the settlers. Bahia and São Tomé prospered initially but had to be abandoned. Ilhéus, Porto Seguro, Espírito Santo, and Itamaracá survived, but only precariously. All told, four donataries lost their fortunes and two their lives attempting to conquer Brazil.

By the late 1540s, about fifteen towns and villages holding perhaps 2000 settlers survived in Brazil, but only two areas had been colonized effectively. Most of the coast from Maranhão to the Line of Demarcation in the south was as barren of European occupation as it had been when Martim Afonso made his reconnaissance. The security of the infant colony was precarious, for the French continued to harass the coast and incite the Indians against the Portuguese. The great distances between settlements made a coordinated defense difficult, and, in any event, no central military command existed; each donatary was individually and directly responsible to the king. In 1548 a refugee from one of the beleaguered settlements who found safety in São Vicente summarized the plight of Brazil in a letter to the king: "If Your Majesty does not succor these captaincies soon, not only will we lose our lives and goods but Your Majesty will lose the land. . . ."[12]

## The Governership-General and
## the Royal Captaincy of Bahia

Plaints such as this as well as more official intelligence convinced King John that the effective occupation of Brazil needed a more centralized administration. In 1548, therefore, he appointed Tomé de Sousa, a cousin of Martim Afonso, who had served the crown well in India and Africa, governor-general of the colony. An accompanying regimento defined his tasks and his authority. His primary mission was the establishment of a royal captaincy from which the governance of the several donatary captaincies could be coordinated. The site selected was the spacious bay of Todos os Santos (Bahia), which occupied a central location between Pernambuco in the north and São Vicente in the south. To recover title to the territory, the crown purchased the charter rights of the original donatary.

The regimento gave the governor-general more specific assignments. It named him military and naval commander of the colony and required him to see that the settlements in the several captaincies were well fortified and that their

# Maps

Map 2. The Spanish Conquest: North America and the Caribbean

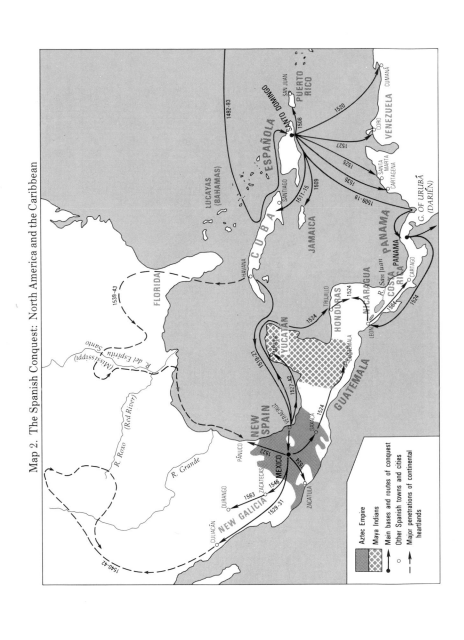

# Map 3. Spanish and Portuguese Conquests in South America

SANTA MARTA  CORO

PANAMA

VENEZUELA

1530-33

NEW  GRANADA

R. Cauca

R. Magdalena

1536-38

1536-39

Orinoco

BOGOTÁ

1536-39

POPAYÁN

ECUADOR

QUITO

LINE OF
TORDESILLAS
(1494)

1560-61

1541-42

R. Marañon  (Amazon)

1560-61

1530-33

1536

PERNAMBUCO

1549

CAJAMARCA

1533

BAHIA

PERU

LIMA

CUZCO  1548

R. São Francisco

B   R   A   Z   I   L

AREQUIPA

1535

LA PAZ

1540

1535

R. Paraguay

1548

UPPER
PERU

POTOSÍ

1540-53

1565-67

1530-33

RIO DE JANEIRO

PARAGUAY

R. Paraná

SÃO VICENTE

ASUNCIÓN

1524-26

C

H

I

L

E

SANTIAGO
DEL ESTERO

1535-41

R. Paraná

1535

1540-59

SAN JUAN

MENDOZA

SANTIAGO DE CHILE

CONCEPCIÓN
1550

VALDIVIA  1552

OSORNO
1558

Inca Empire
Chibcha Indians
Guaraní Indians
Tupinambá Indians
●─▶ Main bases and routes of conquest
● Other Spanish and Portuguese cities and towns
--▶ Major penetrations of continental heartlands

Map 4. Territorial Changes in North America and the Caribbean, c. 1565–c.1700

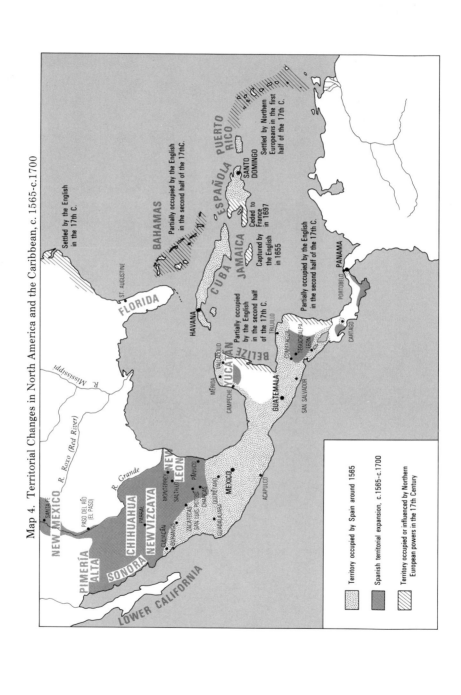

Territory occupied by Spain around 1565

Spanish territorial expansion, c.1565–c.1700

Territory occupied or influenced by Northern European powers in the 17th Century

# Map 5. Territorial Changes in South America, c. 1565-c. 1700

Territory occupied by Spain and Portugal around 1565

Spanish territorial expansion, c. 1565-c. 1700

Portuguese territorial expansion, c 1565-c. 1700

Spanish mission provinces in the 17th C.

Territory occupied by Northern European powers in the 17th C.

Territory seized by the Dutch and regained by the Brazilians, 1630-1654

Directions of penetrations of the interior by the Paulistas

# Map 6. The Governmental Organization of Hispanic American Empires around 1700

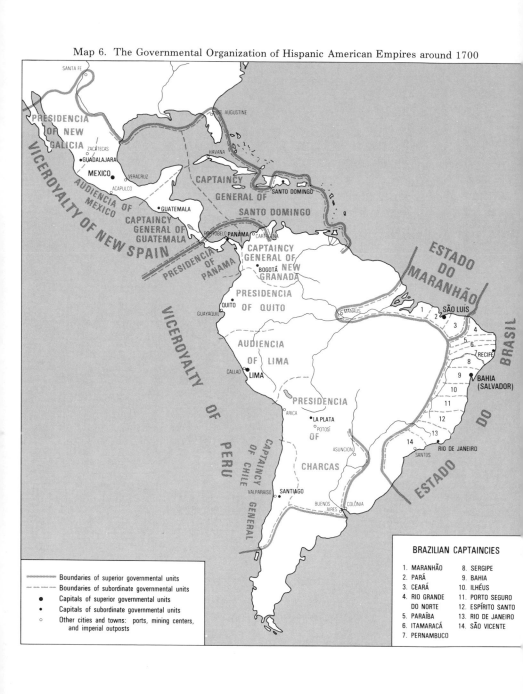

SANTA FE

PRESIDENCIA OF NEW GALICIA

ST. AUGUSTINE

ZACATECAS
GUADALAJARA

HAVANA

MEXICO
VERACRUZ
ACAPULCO

VICEROYALTY OF NEW SPAIN

AUDIENCIA OF MEXICO

CAPTAINCY GENERAL OF GUATEMALA

GUATEMALA

CAPTAINCY GENERAL OF SANTO DOMINGO

SANTO DOMINGO

PORTOBELO PANAMA
CARTAGENA

PRESIDENCIA OF PANAMA

CAPTAINCY GENERAL OF NEW GRANADA

BOGOTÁ

ESTADO DO MARANHÃO

PRESIDENCIA OF QUITO

QUITO
GUAYAQUIL

MANAUS

SÃO LUIS

1
2
3
4
5
6
7 RECIFE
8
9 BAHIA (SALVADOR)
10
11
12
13
14

BRASIL

ESTADO DO

AUDIENCIA OF LIMA

CALLAO LIMA

VICEROYALTY OF PERU

PRESIDENCIA OF CHARCAS

ARICA
LA PLATA
POTOSÍ

ASUNCION

RIO DE JANEIRO
SANTOS

CAPTAINCY GENERAL OF CHILE

VALPARAISO SANTIAGO

BUENOS AIRES
COLÔNIA

---

Boundaries of superior governmental units

Boundaries of subordinate governmental units

● Capitals of superior governmental units

• Capitals of subordinate governmental units

○ Other cities and towns: ports, mining centers, and imperial outposts

santa fe

## BRAZILIAN CAPTAINCIES

| | |
|---|---|
| 1. MARANHÃO | 8. SERGIPE |
| 2. PARÁ | 9. BAHIA |
| 3. CEARÁ | 10. ILHÉUS |
| 4. RIO GRANDE DO NORTE | 11. PORTO SEGURO |
| 5. PARAÍBA | 12. ESPÍRITO SANTO |
| 6. ITAMARACÁ | 13. RIO DE JANEIRO |
| 7. PERNAMBUCO | 14. SÃO VICENTE |

inhabitants possessed serviceable arms. It also directed him to form a navy and with it drive the French from the coasts.

The *regimento* tied Indian policy to defense. It reaffirmed that "the principle reason for motivating my [the king's] decision to settle the land of Brazil was in order that the people of that land be converted to the Holy Catholic Faith. . . ." But the king also asserted that, according to reports he had received, enslavement of the indigenes was the main cause of their hostility. To satisfy the royal conscience, therefore, and to establish internal tranquillity, the document directed the governor-general to put a halt to slaving. It further required him to concert with the donataries to establish friendly relations with the Indians, to hasten their conversion, and to concentrate them in villages near Portuguese towns where, from the good example set by Europeans, they would learn to live in Christian polity.

The *regimento* provided for the economic growth of Brazil by ordering de Sousa to grant liberally lands for commercial agriculture, which, for all practial purposes, meant sugar planting. The size of the allotments, the king declared, should be in proportion to the means of the settlers to exploit them, but excessive concentration of ownership should be avoided. Agriculture remained exempt from all taxes except the tithe.[13]

Tomé de Sousa arrived in the Bay of Bahia to take up his charge on March 29, 1549. He had under his command some 1000 men, thus increasing the European population of Brazil by a third in one stroke. His company included a staff of military, judicial, and treasury officials as well as settlers, among which were counted *fidalgos*, commoners of some substance, artisans, peasants, and some 400 *degredados*. It also had with it six Jesuits under the leadership of Father Manuel da Nóbrega, the vanguard of their order in the New World. They represented the first effort by the crown to implement its announced reason for colonizing Brazil. They had the mission of converting, congregating, and protecting the Indians.

The governor-general went to work at once. He founded and fortified the town of Salvador (Bahia), which became the first capital of Brazil. Combining a show of force with the good offices of the *degredado* Caramurú, he pacified the neighboring Indian population and distributed land as he had been ordered to do, except that some of the grants were larger and more concentrated than the king had intended. The property owners planted cane, put the Indians to work by various legal and illegal means, and, under royal license, brought in black slaves from Africa. In 1550 and in 1551 the crown sent over additional settlers to hasten the growth of the colony.

The Royal Captaincy of Rio de Janeiro

The most urgent task confronting Tomé de Sousa was the expulsion of the French, and he and his successors harried privateers and smugglers with some success. A few years later, however, the Gallic presence assumed a more menacing form and led ultimately to another major Portuguese conquest. In 1555 a company of French Huguenots under the command of Vice Admiral Nicolas Durand de Villegaignon founded a settlement that they called France Antarctique on Guanabara Bay within the unoccupied captaincy of Rio de Janeiro. The undertaking constituted a direct territorial invasion of the dominions of the king, affronted his honor, and provided a base from which a hostile power could menace the western flank of the *Carreira da India*. The Portuguese reacted rather slowly but, in the end, effectively. In 1565, Mem de Sá, the third governor-general of Brazil, built a fort at another place on the bay as a base from which to attack the intruders. After a two-year siege, he forced their surrender, expelled them, and founded the town of Rio de Janeiro on the site of his fort. The crown declared donatarial rights to the region in default and established it as a second royal captaincy under a governor nominally subordinate to Bahia.

## *Portuguese and Spanish New World Conquests: Comparative Features*

The founding of Rio de Janeiro climaxed formal Portuguese efforts to occupy Brazil in the sixteenth century and, chronologically, corresponded roughly to the end of the Conquest in the Spanish Indies. It provides, therefore, a convenient occasion for making further comparisons between early Spanish and Portuguese expansion in the New World.

The Portuguese moved much more slowly and less deliberately than the Spanish in exploiting their territorial claims, for reasons alluded to in the opening pages of this chapter. They found no precious metals to motivate them. Perhaps equally important, they encountered no large concentrations of sedentary Indians. This meant that Spanish-type *encomiendas* could not be used as incentives or rewards for conquest. It also meant that Portuguese kings did not have to assume responsibility for the governance and conversion of millions of natives as did the Spanish crown. Portugal, therefore, devoted most of its scant resources to its more promising Old World empire.

Despite the different conditions they encountered, the two Hispanic peoples went about establishing their dominion in the New World in quite similar ways.

It is sometimes said that the Spaniards conquered their Indies while the Portuguese simply occupied Brazil. The distinction has some juridical validity. Contemporary Portuguese jurists held that the Brazilian natives did not possess properly organized societies; they lived without polity. Technically, therefore, the land was "empty" and belonged to the first Christian occupant—*prima capientis*—as had the Azores and Madeiras.[14] The charters and *forais* issued by King John made no mention of conquest. But in this connection it will be remembered that the term "conquest" did not appear regularly in Spanish patents until after the discovery of the great native "empires."

Nevertheless, the Portuguese were quite familiar with the juridical nature and practical advantages of conquest. Lusitanian *fidalgos* joined Spanish *entradas* and shared in their miseries and rewards. As reported in chapter 3, Portuguese kings undertook to conquer Morocco, and they referred to territory seized from Hindu and Muslim states in the East as their "conquests." In a charter given in 1571, King Sebastian authorized Paulo Dias de Novais to "conquer" Angola, in Africa. The document refers to Angola as a "kingdom," that is, it was a properly ordered state, and Sebastian justified its conquest on the grounds that the enterprise would extend Christendom and the dominions of a Christian king. He also had an economic incentive for conquest; Angola was reputed to have rich silver mines.[15]

As for the occupation of Brazil itself, the Portuguese were quite familiar with what the Spaniards were doing on the other side of the Line of Demarcation and tried to emulate them in deed and word. Captains-donatary did, in fact, subjugate native populations by force of arms. They called their achievements conquests, and contemporary authors did the same. Thus, Duarte Coelho, the captain-donatary of Pernambuco, complained that "we are forced to conquer by inches what Your Majesty granted by leagues."[16] Pedro Magalhães de Gondavo, Brazil's first historian recorded that Pero Lopes de Sousa "first conquered" the captaincy of Itamaracá and that Duarte Coelho "conquered" Pernambuco.[17] The word also crept into official documentation. A royal letter of instructions accompanying Coelho's charter stated that his captaincy would run inland "as far as my conquest extends."[18] The view of the Portuguese toward New World conquests may be summed up simply: they did not have as much to conquer as the Spaniards but wished they had.

The Portuguese and the Spaniards also used cognate institutional forms of conquest. The provisions of Brazilian charters of donation and *forais* closely resembled those of Spanish-American *capitulaciones*, and the Brazilian captain-donatary has his counterpart in the Spanish American *adelantado*. The reasons for the similarity are evident. Both sets of institutions, Spanish and Portuguese, had their immediate origins in closely comparable experiences: the occupation of the Canaries, the Madeiras, and the Azores. But both trace back to the *adelantados* and *meirinhos-mores* and to the *fueros* and *forais* that reconquest Hispanic kings used to occupy frontier regions. Both were *señorial* in spirit and in substance. They involved the delegation of a measure of royal sovereignty to private parties as a means to establish dominion in new lands.[19]

Some differences in emphasis, if not in kind, may be found between Portuguese charters and *regimentos* and Spanish *capitulaciones* and royal instructions governing conquest. The Portuguese authorizations appear to have granted *señorial* faculties more amply and unreservedly than did those given by Spanish kings. Indeed, the powers and privileges conceded to donataries led one of Brazil's distinguished historians to declare: "In this fashion, the [Portuguese] Crown ceded most of its sovereign powers to the benefit of the donataries and reserved but a limited protectorate over the new Brazilian captaincies. . . . We can almost say that Portugal recognized the independence of Brazil before colonizing it."[20] The main reason for King John's generosity, perhaps, lay in the timing. The *señorial* crisis that climaxed in Spain on the eve of the Discovery and that carried over into the Catholic Kings' distrust of their *adelantados* in the Indies had been largely resolved in Portugal a hundred years earlier. In any event, Portuguese kings do not seem to have had any apprehensions about the political ambitions of their captains in Africa, India, or Brazil, nor did they have any occasion to be uneasy. But they might have been less self-confident had their Brazilian donataries been conquering great native empires and discovering rich mines of gold and silver.

Portuguese authorizations and instructions also showed less concern with the legalities of conquest, especially the rights of the Indians, and more with the practicalities, especially in military matters. The reasons for the differences have already been touched upon. Technically, Portuguese jurists contended, Brazil did not have to be conquered, since its indigenous inhabitants did not live in polity under the rule of natural lords. The Portuguese crown acquired a just title to the land simply by discovery and occupation. In fact, however, the establishment of secure dominion required decades of almost continuous warfare in which the main enemy was the French, acting alone or in alliance with the natives. Fundamentally, the conquest of Brazil was a contest between two European powers for American dominion. The pattern foreshadowed the eighteenth-century struggle between France and England for control of eastern North America.

In contrast, the Spaniards recognized the natural lordship of Indian princes and felt compelled to rationalize the seizure of their lands. But the Spanish conquest proceeded rapidly, region by region, and its outcome was never really in doubt. The Indian alone lacked the technological and psycholgical resources to withstand the intruders, and Spain's northern European enemies did not appear in strength until after its dominion was secure. The Spanish monarchy, therefore, could afford to indulge its moral and legal concerns.[21]

# CHAPTER 13

# The Colonization of Brazil to About 1570

## *The Brazilian* Município

Like the Spaniards in their Indies, the Portuguese in Brazil used the municipality as the primary instrument of settlement, and for much the same reasons. They could conceive of no other way to live in polity than in urban centers; in an empty and hostile land they felt the need to cluster together for physical and psychological security; and the king desired that towns be founded to consolidate his dominion in newly acquired territory. The first formal step taken by donataries or their lieutenants and by royal captains upon their arrival in Brazil was the founding of a town (*vila*). The Act of Foundation followed the Hispanic tradition. The founder selected a location that in terms of climate, access to the sea and the hinterland, quality of the land, and defensibility appeared advantageous. At the center of the site he directed that a *pelourinho* (a stone column with an iron shackle attached) be raised as a symbol of the king's justice. He then traced the outlines of the town, gave lots to the *moradores* in order of their rank, and appointed the municipal *senado da câmara* (municipal council) from among the *homens bons* (men of decent quality among the company).

The organization of the municipal council throughout the Portuguese empire closely resembled that of the Spanish *cabildo*. Members with voting rights were called *oficiais da câmara* and consisted of two *juizes ordinarios* (magistrates) and from two to six *vereadores* (councilmen), depending on the size and importance of the town. An *escrivão* (clerk) and a *tesoureiro* (treasurer) sometimes counted among the *oficiais*, although they did not always have voting rights. The numbers and identities of subordinate officials varied from one place to the other, but they generally included an *almotacél* (market inspector); a *juiz dos orfãos*, who cared for the interests of widows and orphans; an *alfares* (standard bearer); a *porteiro* (doorkeeper); and a *carceiro* (jailer). The *oficiais* were perpetuated through annual elections by *vizinhos* under the supervision of a crown judge. In contrast to Spanish monarchs, however, throughout the colonial period the kings of Portugal did not issue a single order dealing specifically with municipal government. Instead a metropolitan *regimento* issued in 1504 and incorporated into the *Ordenações Manuelinas* governed Brazilian towns.[1]

A number of practical and religious acts followed or accompanied the foundation of towns. In surrounding lands, the captain allocated small agricultural properties (*roças*) to settlers of modest means and *sesmarias* to wealthier or more influential *moradores*. A parish was created simultaneously with the civil community, with the chaplains of the expedition serving as rectors, and a church was raised for divine services. As the settlement became established, the parishioners organized *irmandades* (confraternities) for pious, charitable, and social purposes. The jurisdiction of *câmara* and parish were not limited to the immediate confines of the town but, as in Spanish America, included a *termo* extending to vaguely defined limits in the hinterland.

According to Spanish cosmographer López de Velasco, in 1570 Brazil had sixteen towns, the main ones being Olinda, Salvador, Rio de Janeiro, and São Vicente.[2] They had the same initial function as Spanish American municipalities; they served as points of departure for the occupation of territory. But patterns of urbanization developed differently in Spanish and Portuguese America. Whereas the Spaniards immediately plunged inland to plant their most important settlements on high plateaus among dense Indian populations, the Portuguese, as one of their seventeenth-century chroniclers observed, were "content to scrape along the seaside like crabs."[3]

Restriction of early settlements to the coast, however, cannot be attributed to contentment. The lure of the *sertão* (the vast and mysterious interior) was a constant force in the settlement of Brazil. The Spanish had found gold and silver in their Indies and the Portuguese could never believe that God had not placed precious metals on their own side of the Line. They shared with the Spanish an "Edenic Vision," a belief that in some unexplored corner of the globe a terrestrial paradise lay hidden, and they too were haunted by medieval legends of shining mountains of silver or precious gems, lakes and rivers of gold, lost cities, and Amazonian warriors. In order to prevent the dispersion of population, the crown tried to limit settlement to defensible coastal sites, but some of the northern donataries lost their companies and their substance in *entradas*, and it will never be known how many settlers and adventurers perished during the first decades of the Portuguese presence in the New World in forgotten or unrecorded penetrations of the *sertão*. What really held the population on the seashore was the failure of these shadowy enterprises to find anything.[4]

Another difference lay in the organization of urban networks. In Brazil they were even more poorly articulated than in the Spanish Indies. At the end of the sixteenth century no usable land routes connected the widely spaced coastal settlements, and maritime traffic between them was inconsequential. Almost exclusively, Brazilian towns were tied economically, culturally, and politically to the mother country rather than to each other.

The physical layout and architecture of towns in Portuguese and Spanish America also differed. The Portuguese in Brazil did not adopt the grid pattern until the eighteenth century, meanwhile accommodating their towns to the lay of the land and the imperatives of maritime defense. They did not mark out spacious central plazas or, until much later, indulge in the construction of monumental civic and religious buildings. Salvador in 1570 was a small settlement mounting in a haphazard way the steep escarpment lying behind the Bay of All Saints. It represented a typical Portuguese urban ecology, still in evidence in Lisbon and Porto, of an upper city occupied by fortifications, public buildings, and residences and a lower city of quays and warehouses. Although nominally the capital of Brazil, in appearance it was a poor place compared with Mexico, Lima, and even many Spanish American provincial towns. But, of course, the Portuguese did not have at their disposal armies of virtually free native labor.

## The Role of the Indians

### Providers of Labor

The Portuguese never defined the role of the Indian in colonization as explicitly or as elaborately as did the Spanish, nor did they institutionalize it to the same extent, mainly because the indigenous physical and cultural presence did not loom as large in their part of America. In theory and practice, however, the two Hispanic peoples took a common approach to the problem. Portuguese kings, if they be taken at their word, expressed the same official position as did their Castilian cousins. The primary justification for the conquest of Brazil was the opportunity to convert the natives, and their spiritual and physical welfare weighed heavily on the royal conscience. In 1532, about the time of the inception of the donatary system, King John III created the *Mesa de Conciência e Ordens* (Board of Conscience and Religious Orders) to advise him on the moral and ethical aspects of the governance of native peoples.

Portuguese settlers were just as interested in exploiting the Indian as their Spanish neighbors and tried to do so in much the same ways. The first Europeans in Brazil relied on the natives for subsistence and for bringing logwood to collecting points, giving in return cheap European goods, that is, bartering at great advantage. After the arrival of donataries and their settlers, however, the Indians could not or would not feed the new European population from their limited production, nor would they work voluntarily on plantations. The Portuguese therefore enslaved the indigenes to meet their labor requirements. The practice produced in Lisbon the same resistance as it did at the Spanish court and generated the same kind of debates among jurists and theologians, the outcome being a declaration by King Sebastian in 1570 that only natives taken in a just war could be placed in bondage. The restriction seems to have had little influence on Brazilian slavers.

As early as 1559 colonists in Bahia wanted the Indians distributed in *repartimientos*, "as was done in the Antilles and in Peru," and requests to the king to authorize such allocations continued throughout the century.[5] The Portuguese crown never acquiesced, perhaps because it knew of the damage done by the *repartimiento-encomienda* to the natives of the West Indies and, more certainly, because of the opposition of the Jesuits.

Meanwhile, other circumstances diminished the utility of the Indians as a primary source of labor. As elsewhere in the New World, European-introduced diseases did them great harm. In 1562 a smallpox epidemic lasting about three months broke out in Bahia, and one Jesuit estimated that it killed 30,000 blacks and Indians. Later in the year, another began in Ilhéus and, spreading to Bahia in 1563, carried off between one-fourth and three-fifths of the surviving indigenes of that captaincy.[6] The Brazilian Indians, moreover, had an option unavailable to the sedentary populations of Middle and Andean America. They could simply run away into the back country, as the historian Pedro de Magalhães de Gandavo reported in the early 1570s:

There were so many of these Indians on the coast near the Captaincies. The whole coast was inhabited by them when the Portuguese began to settle the country; but, because these Indians revolted against them and practised much treachery upon them, the Governours and Captains of the land overthrew them little by little and killed many of them; the others fled to the sertão [the back country]; thus the coast remained unpopulated by the natives, near the Captaincies; however, some Indian villages, peaceful and friendly toward the Portuguese, were left.[7]

Evangelization

The Portuguese crown appears to have moved more slowly than did Castilian kings in the missionary field.[8] Organized evangelization in Brazil did not begin until 1549, when six Jesuits arrived in Bahia with Tomé de Sousa. But it must be remembered that the spiritual offensive did not really take shape in the Spanish Indies until thirty years after the Discovery. Between 1549 and 1563, ninety-four more Jesuits came to Brazil from Europe, and sixteen Brazilian-born Portuguese were recruited into the society. Members of other orders also answered the call but, as in the *Estado da India*, the enterprise and discipline of the Society of Jesus gave it the lead.

The Jesuits undertook their mission first in Bahia and São Vicente, later in Pôrto Seguro, and then in Ilhéus, Pernambuco, and Rio de Janeiro. They employed methods very similar to those developed earlier by the mendicant orders and the Augustinians in Mexico. Through persuasion and with some help from the secular arm, they congregated dispersed tribes into *aldeias* (villages) and *reduções* (groups of villages, or "reductions").[9] At the center of the *aldeia* lay the church, constructed, of course, by the congregated natives. Here the fathers taught their charges the fundamentals of the faith, baptized and catechized them, and saw to it that they attended mass regularly. To facilitate their task the missionaries learned Tupí-Guaraní, the lingua franca of native Brazil. In the larger communities they established *colégios* to give youths, particularly the sons of chiefs, advanced instruction in religion as well as to teach them to read and write Portuguese. The Jesuits also trained their Indians in agriculture, artisanry, and other arts of civilization. They placed civil administration in the hands of Indian notables, but in practice they exercised authoritarian control in their reductions.

In most regions the missionaries encountered the same kinds of problems as their co-workers in the Spanish Indies. The natives with whom they labored generally accepted reduction and Christianity, but they only dimly comprehended the meaning of their conversion, commonly relapsed into idolatry, and persistently refused to abandon polygamy, a practice that lay deeply embedded in their culture. Unreduced Indians harassed the *aldeias*, and the depredations of Portuguese slavers hindered the reduction of new groups. Settlers regarded the Jesuit congregations as convenient mobilizations of labor. The fathers, supported by the king, vigorously resisted European exploitation accomplished by force or persuasion but eventually made some accommodations. They allowed their charges to grow food for the Portuguese and in some instances loaned them out to planters for particular periods and for specified tasks, an arrangement that resembled the Spanish-American *repartimiento* as it developed after the New Laws and one that had the same vulnerability to abuses.

The year 1562 marked the peak of the first phase of the Jesuits' spiritual offensive. Their largest reductions lay in Bahia, where the immediate presence of the king's governor-general favored their enterprise. Here they counted some 30,000 neophytes grouped into eleven reductions. In São Vicente, the peace that had been established between settlers and indigenes advanced their efforts. One of the substantial results of their presence in that captaincy was the merger of the impoverished European village of Piratininga with one of their reductions to form the town of São Paulo, the main center for expansion into the interior during the late sixteenth and the seventeenth centuries.

The year 1562 also marked a shift in direction of the Jesuits' evangelization. At first they had established their reductions close to European towns where the Indians could be taught religion and good habits by example. But the fathers soon learned that their charges suffered morally and spiritually as well as physically from proximity to the Portuguese, and they gradually began to shift their activities to more inaccessible regions. The population losses suffered by coastal missions also encouraged the Jesuits to seek new fields. Slavers followed them and the contest over the control of the body of the Indian lasted throughout the colonial history of Brazil. By the end of the sixteenth century, however, it had become mainly a frontier problem.

The sixteenth-century Jesuits also played a civilizing role among the European population. They educated the male children of the Portuguese, both white and colored, in their *colégios*, acted as the conscience of the crown in the New World, served as confessors to the rich and powerful, and, through their preaching and teaching, ameliorated in some measure the morals and manners of the Portuguese, who like other Europeans far from home in an exotic environment tended to relax Old World standards of behavior.

## The Economics of Colonization

### The Primary Role of Sugar Production

Dyewood helped to keep Portuguese interests in Brazil alive during the first three decades of the sixteenth century, and, after the establishment of the captaincies, it continued to be an important commercial product. Traders obtained it principally from coastal forests between Pernambuco and Cabo Frio north of Rio de Janeiro. In the last quarter of the 1500s, average annual exports came to about 10,000 hundredweights.[10] Other products of the land included subsistence crops, among which manioc was the staple; tobacco and cotton grown for local consumption; and cattle and oxen. In the 1550s a small whaling industry developed, centered on Bahia and devoted to collecting ambergris. The volume and value of its production is unknown, but around 1570 Magalhães de Gandavo wrote: "From it some of the inhabitants have become rich, and others are getting rich, as is well known."[11] But logwood cutting, subsistence agriculture, and whaling could not sustain colonization. Some other resource had to be found that would attract and hold settlers.

Circumstances dictated that the mainstay of Brazilian colonization would be sugar. By 1530, when the crown determined to occupy its American possessions effectively, the price of that commodity had begun to rise, reversing a long downward trend. In 1506, it stood at a little over two grams of gold an *arrôba* (about 32 pounds avoirdupois); at the end of the sixteenth century, it was six times as much. Thanks to their Old World plantations, the Portuguese already had a well-developed marketing and credit system at their disposal and were familiar with the technology of production.

In Brazil, itself, the Portuguese found stretches of coastal land between Pernambuco and São Vicente whose soils (a type called *massapé*) and climates were suitable for planting. Land, furthermore, could be acquired for nothing and in large amounts. The Portuguese Law of *Sesmarias*, which supposedly guided the distribution of lands in Brazil, provided for relatively modest properties of a size that could support a man and his family with, perhaps, the help of a hired hand or two. And as noted above, the crown warned donataries to avoid the concentration of properties in the hands of a few. Captains and *câmaras* did in fact make small allotments to settlers of modest means and status, but the more affluent and high-ranking colonists as well as influential and wealthy persons in Portugal obtained grants that ran from 10,000 to 13,000 hectares.

Sugar production required intensive labor. The Portuguese who came to Brazil did not wish to cut, haul, and mill sugar personally, and, in any event, there were not enough of them to perform these tasks. Neither could the Indians provide an adequate supply. They did not adapt well to plantation labor, and death and flight reduced their availability. Planters still depended heavily on them but also turned to another source of hands. In 1559, the crown authorized the opening of the slave trade between Africa and Brazil. Little is known about its volume in the sixteenth century. Philip Curtin estimates that it brought 10,000 slaves to Brazil during the years 1551–75.[12] Most of them probably arrived during the latter half of the period, when planting spread rapidly. Data on slave prices are also scarce. About the best that can be said is that the supply of slaves at acceptable prices was sufficient for the needs of an expanding industry.

Sugar planting needed substantial capital outlays for machinery as well as for slaves. In the 1550s, an average-size mill cost upward of 40,000 *cruzados*. Little is known about the sources and amounts of capital available to early Brazilian planters. Most of it appears to have been furnished by Europeans, especially Flemings and Germans. As with labor, the supply was sufficient to support the industry's expansion.

Still another circumstance favored the Brazilian sugar industry. Since no precious metals had been found in the colony, the crown gave planting undivided and full support, including a ten-year exemption from production taxes for new plantations, first granted in 1549 when Tomé de Sousa founded Bahia.

The early history of Brazilian sugar production is not well known, but its general course can be profiled. The Portuguese planted cane around their factory at Pernambuco in the early 1520s, and Lisbon customs records of 1526 show imports from that point. Large-scale planting did not begin until the permanent occupation of Brazil under the captaincy system, a step that happened to coincide with the emergence of a strong European market for sugar. In 1533, Martim Afonso de Sousa had several mills built at São Vicente, and shortly thereafter Duarte Coelho began planting and milling around Pernambuco. The royal captains introduced the sugar industry in Bahia and Rio de Janeiro almost immediately after the founding of those settlements. It developed on a smaller scale in the minor captaincies.

### The Organization of Sugar
### Production: Plantation and *Engenho*

The main unit of production was the large plantation. As in the Spanish Indies, only a portion of its lands were planted in sugar. Part of the remainder was left in forest, which furnished fuel for boiling. Other sections were used to grow food crops and to graze the oxen that were employed in hauling and grinding cane. The mill constituted the central component of the production complex. Planters used two kinds: large *engenhos d'agua* (water-powered) and smaller animal-powered installations called *trapiches* or, sometimes, *almajarras*.

Small planters called *lavradores* also contributed to production. They fell into two classes: independent proprietors and persons who leased or share-cropped parts of larger plantations. Neither class could afford to buy mills and had to use *engenhos* or *trapiches* belonging to plantation owners. In return they gave a portion of the yield of their cane that, for independent *lavradores* amounted to one-half and for lessees and sharecroppers, between three-fifths and two-thirds. Under these arrangements, many mill owners found it more profitable to lease or sharecrop their lands than to plant them. The key to wealth and power was the possession not so much of sugar lands as of mills. Hence, the entire production complex including its lands became known as the *engenho* and the owner as a *senhor de engenho*, literally lord of the mill.

By 1570 some sixty mills ground cane in Brazil. They were distributed as follows: in the southern captaincies, mainly in São Vicente and Rio de Janiero; thirty-one in the central region, of which eighteen were in Bahia; and twenty-four in the north, twenty-three of which lay in Pernambuco.[13] Driven by either water or animal power, on the average they had a much greater capacity than the earlier small, manually driven mills of the Atlantic islands or the *ingenios* and *trapiches* used in the Spanish Indies. Many could produce 3000 *arrôbas* of sugar (about 96,000 pounds avoirdupois), the largest ones as much as 10,000 *arrôbas* (about 320,000 pounds avoirdupois) annually.[14]

No serial statistics are available on early Brazilian sugar production, but some scattered observations and estimates can be found. By the late 1540s yields had surpassed those of all Portuguese Old World plantations together, and by 1570 the industry had entered a boom phase. In that year, according to conservative reckonings, the colony exported about 180,000 *arrôbas* (some 5,760,000 pounds avoirdupois) annually, which sold in Lisbon for eleven grams of gold an *arrôba* and whose total value came to more than 90 percent of all Brazilian exports.[15]

### The *Engenho* as an Instrument of Settlement

Not only was sugar the economic mainstay of Brazilian colonization, but the plantation that produced it was a fixed and well-ordered place of habitation, a form of settlement comparable in importance to the town. Its permanent population consisted of slaves who performed common and semiskilled labor; overseers; *lavradores*; technicians who operated and maintained the mill; and artisans who fashioned equipment used in planting, transport, and processing, as well as household articles and cheap cotton clothing. Quarters for the work force clustered around the mill. Since planting extended beyond easy commuting distance from towns, *senhores de engenho* found it convenient to build permanent residences on their plantations where they lived a good part of the year, surrounded by their extended families and numerous dependents. Large plantations had chapels and a resident priest who gave spiritual care to masters, slaves, and freemen.

A social and political symbiosis quickly developed between town and plantation. *Senhores de engenho*, even if they lived on their plantations, generally maintained town houses; the towns remained the centers of civic life, and even the most remote *engenho* lay no more than a day's journey from the nearest *vila*. Through their wealth and elevated social status, mill owners acquired control of the *câmaras*, held the most important offices in religious confraternities, commanded the local militia, and came to constitute powerful local oligarchies.

It might be said that sugar played much the same part in the colonization of Brazil as did precious metals on the Spanish side of the Line of Demarcation. Both commodities invited and sustained permanent settlement. The comparison, however, can be overdrawn. Parts of the viceroyalties of Mexico and Peru did, indeed, depend almost exclusively on the extraction of gold and silver. Their treasure provided the principal export and the main source of capital for Spanish America as a whole. Yet many provinces developed other sources of wealth and more diversified and self-sufficient economies. Settlers also received *encomiendas*, which not only were an economic resource but conveyed an element of lordship to which a high social value attached. It is a reasonably safe conjecture that the Spaniards would have colonized and held large parts of their Indies, especially the uplands of Middle and Andean America, with their rich agricultural and human resources, even had they not found mines there. In contrast, Brazil had no known source of wealth other than sugar to attract and hold European settlers. Without planting, the donatary system would probably have failed.

## The Commerce of Brazil

The internal commerce of Brazil was mainly local, involving the exchange of agricultural and pastoral products, simple artisanry, and European imports. Trade among the several captaincies was negligible, owing in part to the long distances that separated them and the hazards of land and sea transportation. But, more important, they produced much the same things under much the same conditions and therefore had little to trade with each other.

To a much greater extent than in Spanish America, Brazilian commerce was external. Its basic pattern was the exchange of sugar and dyewood and other forest products for wheat, wine, olive oil, hardware, machinery, luxury items, and slaves from various parts of the Old World. By the late 1560s, its value was substantial and growing, although still less than that of the India trade and amounting to only a tiny fraction of Spain's trans-Atlantic commerce. The Portuguese monarchy, however, did not attempt to control commerce with America as tightly as did Spanish kings. Instead of organizing convoyed fleets, it permitted individual vessels, including those of friendly foreign nations, to sail between Brazilian and metropolitan ports under the loose supervision of the *Casa da India*. The crown intervened most directly and effectively in fiscal matters. It collected an ad valorem tax on sugar and contracted its monopoly of trade in dyewood and slaves to private parties. Its rather relaxed mercantile policy probably owed to its conviction that the Brazil trade did not really require expensive convoys and mercantilist controls, especially since it did not involve the transport of precious metals. On the contrary, the costs of such mechanisms would have diminished the comfortable revenues received under existing arrangements.

## Brazilian Populations

### The European Element

Data for the population history of Brazil are even spottier than for Spanish America. The first comprehensive counts of European *vizinhos* (municipal householders) were made around 1570 by the Portuguese historian Pedro de Magalhães de Gandavo and the Spanish cosmographer Juan López de Velasco. Their figures are summarized and compared in table 5:[16]

Table 5
The Portuguese Population of Brazil in About 1570

| | Vizinhos | |
| --- | --- | --- |
| Captaincy | Magalhães | López |
| Bahia | 1100 | 1000 |
| Pernambuco | 1000 | 1000 |
| São Vicente | 500 | 500 |
| Porto Seguro | 220 | 200 |
| Ilhéus | 200 | 200 |
| Espírito Santo | 180 | 200 |
| Rio de Janeiro | 140 | 400 |
| Itamaracá | 100 | 100 |
| Total | 3440 | 3600 |

Magalhães and López prepared their accounts at about the same time, and the concurrence of their figures in some instances is so close that one is tempted to suspect that one author had a peek at the other's notes or that both drew on the same sources. In any event, multiplying Magalhães' count of 3440 *vizinhos* by 5, which contemporaries considered to be the average family or household size, yields a total European population of 17,200. Using López de Velasco's *vizinho* count, the same operation produces a total of 18,000. The Brazilian Jesuit José de Anchieta, however, calculated that a Portuguese American house-hold had 6 members.[17] Applying this multiple to Magalhães' and to López's *vizinho* counts, the results are respectively 20,640 and 21,600. The upper and lower extremes of the four sets of multiplications are 17,200 and 21,600. The true figure, perhaps, lay somewhere between them.

The spotty information available about the European backgrounds of Por-tuguese Americans suggests the following generalizations.[18] Most were immi-grants. Natural increase in the New World was slow because of a shortage of white mothers. Proportionally fewer women came to Brazil than to Spanish America in the sixteenth century and particularly before 1550. The Portuguese, even more than their peninsular neighbors, kept their womenfolk in haremlike seclusion, and the crown appears to have discouraged their emigration because the demands for women on three continents would have damaged the repro-ductive capacity of a nation with a population of only a little over a million souls.

The best authorities declare that most immigrants were young, single men, but this datum does not reveal how young was young and how many were single in fact or simply in spirit. As for social origins, they included some *fidalgos* and, as Brazil became more settled and prosperous, merchants and lawyers. But most were more humble folk: peasants, artisans, soldiers, sailors, and laborers who hoped to improve their lot in a frontier land, as well as *degredados*, who emigrated involuntarily. Jews and New Christians also found refuge in Brazil, where the hand of the Portuguese Inquisition rested lightly. In short, immi-grants represented a verisimilar, if not exact, cross section of the middle and lower strata of Portuguese society.

New settlers were drawn from all parts of metropolitan Portugal as well as from the Azores and the Madeiras, with the largest percentage coming from the provinces north of the Tagus and, particularly, from Minho, which was the most densely populated part of the kingdom. European immigrants also in-cluded an indeterminate number of foreigners. Duarte Coelho brought Galici-ans from Spain and Canary Islanders to Pernambuco. In the south, Martim Afonso's colonizing expedition of 1530 included a few Germans, Italians, and Flemings, and later families of Italian sugar growers came to São Vicente from the Madeiras. In all probability, Spaniards formed the largest group of aliens for the same reasons that Portuguese predominated among non-Spaniards in the Spanish Indies: cultural compatibility. They were most numerous in the southernmost settlements that lay closest to Spanish Paraguay and the Rio de la Plata.

### The Indian Element

Angel Rosenblat estimated that the indigenous population of Brazil dropped from about 1,000,000 in 1492 to 800,000 in 1570.[19] The figures are highly conjectural and, in addition, are for all of the territory constituting modern Brazil. Whatever the total might have been, only a fraction of it lived along the coasts, and it was there that European diseases struck first and took their greatest toll. In 1562 the Jesuit *aldeias* in Bahia alone still held 34,000 natives, but in 1585 Father José de Anchieta could account for only 18,000 reduction Indians in all the colony. Their numbers were still shrinking because of disease, flight, and genetic dilution occasioned by miscegenation.[20]

### Africans and Mixed Bloods

Rosenblat reckoned that in 1570 some 30,000 "Negroes, mestizos and mulattoes" dwelt in Brazil.[21] He does not break down the total by group, nor can reliable estimates of the size of each be found elsewhere. If Curtin's reckoning of the volume of slave trade during the period 1551-75 —some 10,000 —be accepted, it provides an indirect clue to the size of the African population. Most Africans were imported slaves, and, since their death rate was very high and their birthrate very low, they must have numbered considerably less than total imports. As for their provenance, scattered records show that the great majority came from the Guinea coasts and its hinterlands and from the Congo.

Although the number of mixed bloods in the colony is conjectural, there is little doubt that the most dynamic force in population formation was *mestiçagem*, as race mixture is termed in Portuguese. The same conditions existed there that favored the process in Africa, India, and Spanish America: an acute shortage of European women, the dominant position of the European male, his relaxed moral standards, and the availability of willing or unresisting Indian and black females. The patterns of mixture were much the same as in the Spanish Indies. White mated with Indian produced the *mameluco*; unions of whites and blacks yielded mulattoes; intercourse between black and brown produced *cafusos*. Other descriptive terms also appeared. *Mestiço* was sometimes used to describe the offspring of both white and black and white and Indian; mulattoes were sometimes called *pardos*, and *caboclo* might be used as a synonym for *mameluco* or to speak of any lower-class person of color.

Most mixed bloods were illegitimate. Crown and church accepted mixed marriage between Portuguese and Indians, but they were rare. In 1551, Jesuit Father Nóbrega reported that European settlers regarded matrimony with an Indian woman as a "great infamy."[22] At their instance he repeatedly urged the king to send orphan girls and even women of bad repute from Portugal to provide wives for settlers. This, in fact, was done from time to time. Despite the degraded status of prostitutes in the mother country, lonely Brazilian Portuguese willingly took them as brides. Crown, church, and colonials all opposed marriages with black slaves, and very few, if any, occurred.

In many cases Portuguese fathers recognized and legitimized their *mameluco* offspring and gave them Portuguese names, thus opening the way for their assimilation into European society. In other instances illegitimate *mamelucos* were raised by their Indian mothers and absorbed into indigenous communities. Recognition by a Portuguese father brought mulattoes release from servitude, but the whites did not co-opt them as readily as they did *mamelucos*, and those not recognized remained slaves.

## The Governance of Brazil

The Portuguese crown incorporated Brazil into its patrimony in the same way it had annexed Africa, Asia, and the Atlantic islands. The Brazilian charters of donation declared that donataries would govern according to the laws of Portugal. Brazil was to be simply another overseas extension of the mother country. As in Spanish America, metropolitan codes had to be supplemented from time to time by *regimentos* issued to royal governors and by royal edicts, orders, and decrees. Although these instruments accumulated as colonization progressed, they were not as numerous as those issued by Spanish monarchs, nor were they regarded as a body of law distinctively American.

Within this constitutional framework the crown tried to assert its sovereignty in several ways.[23] One was the creation of royal captaincies, first Bahia, then Rio de Janeiro. Administratively, these actions involved the resumption by purchase or default of titles and powers conceded earlier to donataries. Royal objectives, however, were not so much to displace private government as to stimulate colonization and strengthen defense. Portuguese kings made no further resumptions until new regions were occupied in the seventeenth century.

The crown also intervened in the government of private captaincies. In some instances, the initiative came from Lisbon and took the form of royal orders and regulations and of visitations from Portuguese officials. In others, the governor-general acted as a royal agent. In theory, this dignitary exercised military and political command over all Brazil, and, like his counterparts in India, he had a corps of officials to assist him: a *capitão môr da costa* (commander of the coast guard fleet), an *ouvidor geral* (chief justice), a *tesoureiro das rendas* (treasurer), and a *provedor môr* (quartermaster and business manager), along with lesser functionaries, secretaries, and technicians. Tomé de Sousa, the first governor-general, exerted his authority by sending his chief magistrate and his treasurer to reform judicial and fiscal practices in Pôrto Seguro and Ilhéus and by replacing the donataries' lieutenants in both captaincies with his own appointees. He also made a personal tour of inspection of the several southern captaincies.

Although de Sousa himself acted vigorously, the power of his office was restricted by two circumstances. One was the ambiguous policy of the crown. The *regimento* given him did not revoke any of the charter rights of the donatary captains. But he also received a separate letter of appointment that affirmed his superior authority in the following terms:

I [João III] hereby inform all of the Captains and Governors of the said lands [captaincies] of Brazil . . . that Tomé de Sousa will have the titles of Captain of the city of Salvador and the captaincy of Bahia, and Governor-General of the said captaincy and of the other captaincies . . . and you will obey him, and comply with and do whatever Tomé de Sousa, in my behalf, requires . . . I think it good . . . to repeal the said donations (*cartas de doaçao*) and all that is contained in them which might be contrary to what is contained in this letter, or in the said regimentos and decrees. . . .[24]

Whether by design or oversight, the crown never resolved the contradiction between the two documents. As a result, numerous disputes arose between successive governors-general and donatary governors that Portuguese kings settled individually. Their decisions very often reflected the relative influence of the contending parties at court, but, in a more general way, they tended to uphold donatarial privileges in those private captaincies that were being governed effectively and, especially, in those that produced good revenues for the royal treasury.

Another influence restricting the governor-general's power was the same "law of distance" that loosened the authority of Spanish viceroys. Brazil was simply too large and its settlements too far apart to be governed effectively from any one center. Pernambuco and São Vicente, which lay at the colony's geographical extremes and also flourished under proprietary government, remained virtually independent of Bahia except to some degree in military matters. They had to rely on the royal coast guard for maritime defense, but they still retained command over their own militia.

Royal indecision and geography combined to give the government of Brazil a dual character. One component was the governorship-general of Bahia, whose governor exercised nominal civil and military command over all Brazil; the other consisted of the donatary captaincies, whose proprietors regarded Lisbon as the sole font of royal authority and disregarded Bahia.

The crown attempted to impose its authority on municipal government more directly. During the last half of the sixteenth century, it ordered royal judges to assume the presidency of the most important councils in Brazil, a policy comparable to that of Habsburg kings in the Spanish Indies. But, whereas *cabildos* wilted under pressure from viceroys and audiencias, Brazilian *câmaras* successfully resisted intervention from distant Lisbon and Bahia.[25]

The ecclesiastical organization of Brazil developed along much the same lines as its civil and military administration. In 1551 the crown obtained from Rome the permanent patronage in its New World dominions, and in the same year it removed them from the jurisdiction of the bishop of Funchal, in the Azores, and created the diocese of Brazil, with its seat in Bahia. The bishop of Bahia encountered some of the same problems as the governor-general. He had little success in establishing episcopal authority over the secular clergy in the other captaincies, who, in general, were just as undisciplined as lay colonists.

Although sixteenth-century Portuguese kings had much the same exalted concept of the rights and obligations of their office as did Spanish monarchs, they asserted their authority in America more slowly and less deliberately and fully. The preceding chapter touches on some of the reasons for this difference, but they may be reduced to two. One was simply that Brazil did not require as much government as did the Spanish Indies. Its effectively occupied territory was much smaller and its inhabitants far fewer, it had no large indigenous population that needed special governance, and from a purely fiscal point of view, the limited wealth of Brazil did not require a large administrative investment in the colony. The king could obtain a comfortable revenue from America by collecting ad valorem taxes on its exports at home ports and by leasing his monopolies there.[26] The other reason was that Brazil did not have a powerful conqueror-*encomendero* class whose *señorial* aspirations had to be checked by a powerful royal presence.

The obvious and significant differences between the governments of Brazil and of Spanish America obscure a fundamental characteristic that they shared.

In theory, both were authoritarian. The king ruled; he gave the law; his courts adjudicated the law he gave; subjects had no practical recourse against tyranny. But in both parts of Hispanic America two influences diluted and dissipated royal authority. One was extended and overburdened communications systems. The other was diffusion of power, effected in Spanish America by the overlapping of the functions and authority of royal agencies and offices, in Brazil by the division of authority between royal governors and private donataries.

## Social Organization

The Portuguese who came to America had much the same concept of a properly organized republic as did their Spanish American contemporaries. It should be constituted by classes and orders ranked according to their social virtues. The Portuguese had no doubts about their own status. Because of their Christianity, their civilized ways, and their physical qualities, they believed themselves to be a superior race, and they possessed the will and the means to establish their dominance. Thus, conquest society in Brazil had the same basic form as in Spanish America: a European elite lording it over subjugated and enslaved people.

Nevertheless, owing to different conditions of conquest and colonization, early Brazilian and Spanish American societies differed in important structural details. In Brazil, the traditional orders appeared only in the most rudimentary form. Some first settlers were legitimate *fidalgos*. Among the common majority, some aspired to that status and achieved it reputationally. But conquest in Brazil lacked the heroic qualities that in the Spanish Indies promised to create an American nobility. The Portuguese crown rarely elevated conquerors and first settlers to the *fidalgo* class, nor did it give titles of nobility to even the most successful donataries. Neither did it create *encomiendas*, which in Spanish America were the substance and symbol of exalted social status. The closest Brazilian counterpart of the *encomendero* class was the *senhores de engenho*. As their title suggests, they enjoyed ascriptive lordship, but their status derived fundamentally from bourgeois enterprises—the exploitation of land, labor, and capital for profit—rather than from noble deeds in the Reconquest tradition. And they owned slaves rather than exercising *señorial* faculties over a conquered people.

The other orders also failed to acquire strong identities in Brazil. Compared with their position in the Spanish Indies, the clergy were few in number, widely dispersed, poorly endowed with temporal resources, and lacking in an ecclesiastical hierarchy to give their estate luster and prestige. Among the common order, the merchants of the main Brazilian ports could not compare in wealth and influence with the great mercantile houses of Mexico City and Lima. A sparse and scattered population and a small royal bureaucracy could not support a large professional sector of lawyers and notaries.

The position of non-European peoples in the social order also differed in the two parts of Hispanic America, mainly because of differing population structures. To both the Spaniards and the Portuguese, the Indians were a new race whose essential human qualities had yet to be clearly and precisely defined, but they were unquestionably a naturally inferior people. Here the similarity ends. In most regions of Spanish America, indigenes constituted an overwhelming majority of the population. Their presence as vassals of the king and communicants of the church could not be ignored. They were also an indispensable source of labor. In contrast, by 1570 Indians in Brazil were a visibly shrinking element whose services were not essential to the survival of the colony. For both moral and economic reasons, therefore, Spanish monarchs and jurists felt much more obliged to fix the legal status of the Indian, firmly and in detail, than did their Portuguese counterparts.

By the time the Spanish and Portuguese arrived in America they had already fixed the status of Africans. They perceived them as naturally inferior because of their defective physical and cultural attributes. As slaves or descendants of slaves they bore the stain of infamy, institutionalized in the law. In Brazil, however, Africans formed a more appreciable social element than in Spanish America because their numbers were proportionately larger and growing rapidly. It might be said that in the Spanish Indies the most basic social distinction was between Spaniards and Indians, who, although nominally free, existed in a state of dependence on their conquerors, institutionalized in the *encomienda* and the *repartimiento-mita*. In Brazil, the primary distinction was between free Portuguese and enslaved Africans.

Mixed bloods were a rapidly increasing group in both Brazil and Spanish America, and their presence had to be taken into account. But for the Spanish, they were a new and ominous social phenomenon. In contrast, the Portuguese were already familiar with miscegenation through their behavior in Africa and Asia. Although it would be hazardous to affirm that they were better disposed toward its products than were the Spanish, they were better prepared psychologically to accept their existence.

### Brazil and the Empire

The conquest and colonization of Brazil introduced a new and increasingly dynamic element into Hispanic expansion. In a broad geographical context, it brought about a restructuring of the Portuguese empire into an eastern and western division. The eastern component continued to be the *Estado da India*. The western component included West Africa, the Atlantic islands, and Brazil. Aside from having a common south Atlantic location, its integrating feature was the plantation economies of São Tomé, Principe, the Madeiras, and Brazil, all dependent on slaves from Guinea and the Congo. During the sixteenth century the *Estado da India* yielded the most spectacular profits, but the beginning Brazilian sugar boom portended a westward shift in the economic center of gravity of the empire.

The wealth flowing in from east and west made Lisbon one of the greatest ports in Europe and created the appearance of prosperity and affluence. A contemporary observer, Damião de Gois, reported that he often saw merchants coming into the *Casa da India* with sacks full of gold and silver to pay what they owed, "and this money the officials told them, they should bring back another day, because there was no time to count it."[27] The crown shared heavily in these riches through the rent of monopolies and ad valorem taxes, and the court through royal largesse. But a serpent lurked in the golden Eden. Openhanded and improvident kings could not meet expenses and had to resort to deficit financing. Lisbon, like Seville, was merely a point of transit for goods arriving from overseas. Spices, sugar, and logwood had their main markets in northern Europe. Italian, German, and Flemish merchants arranged their transport to destinations where the merchant-bankers of Antwerp managed their sale. Thus, the wealth of empire was essentially transient. Meanwhile, Portuguese agriculture could not meet the demands of a growing population, and, beginning in the 1540s, the sustenance of the nation depended on the import of wheat from France, North Africa, and the Baltic. Prices of basic commodities rose, while the urban poor starved in the streets of Lisbon and Porto. In the countryside, peasants scratched out a scanty subsistence, and the more enterprising among them went off to the East or emigrated to Brazil.

Part III

Hispanic American Empires

from About 1570 to About 1700

# CHAPTER 14

# The Imperial Context:
# The Hispanic World in the Age
# of the Habsburg Kings

## *The Reign of Philip II (1556-98)*

The reign of Philip II was a transitional period in Hispanic history. The shift began in 1556 when the bequests of the Emperor Charles gave the Habsburg patrimonies in eastern Europe to the Austrian branch of the family, leaving to Philip Spain, the Low Countries, Franche-Compté, the Italian possessions of Aragon, and the Indies. Three years later Philip returned to Spain from the Netherlands, where he had been commanding Spanish forces fighting the French. He was a Spaniard by birth and upbringing and never left his home again. In 1560 he established the royal court permanently in Madrid, in the heart of Castile. He was welcomed home, so to speak, by swelling quantities of treasure arriving from the Indies, which, toward the end of his reign, accounted for about 20 percent of crown revenues. In 1571, the victory of Spanish and Italian naval forces at Lepanto ended the Turkish threat in the Mediterranean. This sequence of events symbolized the emergence of an empire whose character was distinctively Spanish, whose center was Castile, and whose main interests lay in the Atlantic world.

Philip's purposes as king were several. As a Christian prince he felt obliged to give justice and good government, as he saw them, to all his subjects. As a devout Catholic he intended to extirpate heresy and heterodoxy in his realms and to defend the Holy Religion wherever his influence extended. Although a Spaniard, he was also a Habsburg and therefore committed to defending the family patrimonies in other parts of Europe. His aims struck a responsive chord in the hearts and minds of his Spanish subjects, especially his championship of Catholic orthodoxy.

Philip applied a considerable array of abilities to the exercise of kingship. He possessed a powerful mind, and he had been apprenticed in his craft by his father. He was certainly one of the most diligent princes in history, working interminable hours and giving his personal attention to every detail. But he also had an arbitrary turn of mind and a conviction that he ruled directly by God's will. He deliberated at great length before acting on matters large and small, a quality that won him the sobriquet "the Prudent," but that some of his modern critics characterize as indecisiveness and procrastination. During his long reign the constitution and government of Spain acquired the indelible stamp of his personality.

### King Sebastian of Portugal, El Ksar-el-Kebir, and the Union of the Hispanic Crowns

King Sebastian (1557–78) did not have the abilities, the resources, or the opportunities that gained lasting fame for his Spanish contemporary. He possessed, nevertheless, certain eccentricities that indirectly had profound effects on Hispanic imperial affairs. As a youth he was headstrong and much given to morbid religiosity and to violent and martial exercises. Inspired by the Christian victory at Lepanto, he conceived a new Portuguese crusade in Africa. Against all sound advice, including cautions from Philip II, in 1578 he led a great host across the water to Africa and to a confrontation with the forces of Islam on the field of El Ksar-el-Kebir (Alcácer Quibir, or the Battle of the Three Kings). After four hours of striving under the burning Saharan sun, 8000 Christians lay dead and another 15,000 fell captive to the Moors. Sebastian himself disappeared from the ken of Europeans, although it is believed that he perished in battle or in a Moroccan prison.

The disaster at El Ksar led to the realization of an ancient Hispanic dream, one *Monarchia Hispania*. Sebastian had not produced an heir, and his death left the Portuguese succession beclouded. The claimants to the throne included Philip II of Spain, whose mother was a Portuguese princess of the blood. Philip reinforced his dynastic claims with distributions of Mexican "silver bullets" (silver pesos) among influential Portuguese and by invading Portugal with a Spanish army. In 1581 the Portuguese cortes crowned him Philip I. As he himself said of his new realm, "I inherited it, I bought it, and I conquered it."[1] By conjoining under his rule Spain and Portugal and their dominions in Africa, Asia, and America, he created the first empire on which the sun never set. The contemporary Spanish theologian and geographer Antonio Vázquez de Espinosa put it in more timely terms. "In all the countries which His Majesty holds under his empire, continually, at every hour, and without pause, the Holy Sacrifice is being celebrated."[2]

Constitutionally, the union of the Hispanic crowns was simply a dynastic arrangement of the same order as the earlier joining of the realms of Castile and Aragon. Philip swore to uphold the liberties of Portugal and to leave the governance of that kingdom and its overseas possessions in the hands of Portuguese nationals, save that he reserved the right to keep a Spanish viceroy in Lisbon to see to his interests. For the most part he kept his promises.

Although many Portuguese, especially the lower orders of society, resented the rule of a foreign king, others perceived that in practical terms the advantages of union outweighed the disadvantages. Portuguese merchants gained easier access to the Indies trade, especially in slaves, while the terms of the union excluded Spaniards from participation in Portugal's imperial commerce. Spain's enemies became Portugal's, but Philip felt obliged to use Spanish resources to defend Brazil, for in hostile hands it would have threatened Spanish South America, the Caribbean, and the *Carrera de Indias*. The Portuguese had to pay nothing for this protection. The union also made it easier for them to disregard the Line of Tordesillas as they pushed inland from their coastal settlements in Brazil.

## The Decline of Spain

The era of Philip II brought not only a transition in the character of the Spanish monarchy but a shift in the long-term course of Spanish history. At midpoint in Philip's reign Spain stood at the zenith of its power. Its population was still growing, its armies dominated the battlefields of Europe, it could assemble seemingly invincible armadas, and a swelling volume of treasure from America flowed into the royal treasury and into private coffers. Its people looked forward to a Golden Age when there would be "but one shepherd and one flock in the world," and "one monarch, one empire, and one sword."[3]

The hour of splendor and hope passed quickly. During the last half of Philip's reign weaknesses in the Spanish imperial system became obvious. Overspending and excessive borrowing had reduced the royal treasury to insolvency, and the Spanish economy showed signs of weakening. By 1580 Castile could not produce enough grain to feed its people, and by the 1590s the Castilian textile industry was severely depressed. Economic troubles spread during the rules of Philip III (1598–1621) and Philip IV (1621–65). In the early seventeenth century Basque iron production began to drop, and Basque shipbuilding declined in quantity and quality. These reverses made Spain increasingly dependent on foreign imports and foreign shipping. In the early 1600s, also, a decrease in the volume of American trade and in the amount of American silver reaching Seville dealt a severe blow to the commercial sector.

Beginning in the late sixteenth century Spain suffered a series of demographic setbacks. Between 1596 and 1602 a great plague struck Castile, claiming from 600,000 to 700,000 lives. During the remainder of the seventeenth century new epidemics in the several Spanish kingdoms, along with famines, war casualties, and the expulsion of about 275,000 *moriscos* from the realms of Aragon, caused further losses. The net result of these misfortunes is uncertain. The Spanish population probably peaked at between 8,000,000 and 8,500,000 souls at the very end of the sixteenth century. Some authorities contend that it then began to decline, dropping to about 6,500,000 by 1700. Others believe that it remained stagnant throughout the seventeenth century at around its 1600 level. It is generally agreed that significant shifts occurred in population distribution, especially in Castile, where tens of thousands of destitute peasants migrated to towns and cities, turning the countryside into a desert.[4]

Troubles on foreign fronts also appeared during Philip's reign and mounted after his death. The final decree of the Council of Trent, issued in 1563, effected a definitive division of European Christendom into mutually hostile camps. Philip felt obliged to assume the championship of the Catholic cause. The religious issue, along with Spanish dynastic and commercial interests, drew the nation into a long series of wars with its old enemy France, with England, and with the fledgling Dutch Republic, which had emerged from the revolt of the Spanish Netherlands in 1566. Spain's military undertakings in Europe climaxed in 1621 when the count duke of Olivares, Philip IV's favorite secretary, brought the nation into the Thirty Years' War, an involvement that lasted until 1648. Meanwhile, Elizabethan privateers and Dutch West India Company fleets harassed Spanish shipping and settlements in the Indies.

The fortunes of these wars gradually turned against Spain. In 1588 English seamen and Atlantic storms destroyed the Invincible Armada, which Philip had sent against England. The losses were quickly replaced, but in 1639 a Dutch fleet dealt a nearly mortal blow to the Spanish navy in the Battle of the Downs, fought in the English Channel. Four years later the redoubtable Spanish infantry suffered a stunning defeat in the Battle of Rocroi. The disaster marked the end of Spain's military predominance in Europe.

While reverses accumulated abroad, serious political crises developed in the homeland, owing immediately to the efforts of Olivares to create a "Union of Arms," that is, a national military reserve to which each of the Habsburg realms would contribute quotas of men, paid from its own revenues. The measure provoked strong resistance, especially in Catalonia and Portugal, where it was regarded as an infringement of constitutional liberties. The Portuguese, furthermore, had become disenchanted with the union of the crowns, which they had come to call their "Babylonian captivity." After the death of Philip II, Spanish officials began to intervene in their affairs, the government in Madrid attempted to exclude them from the Indies trade, and Spanish protection did not prevent the Dutch from invading northeastern Brazil in 1630. In the spring of 1640 Catalonia rebelled, and in the autumn of the same year the Portuguese followed suit, replacing John, of their noble house of Bragança, on the throne. The Catalan revolt was not suppressed until 1652. The Portuguese successfully defended their independence, which Spain formally recognized in 1668.

When Philip II's great-grandson, Charles II (1665–1700), ascended the throne, Spain still survived, but its armies and navies were broken, its influence in European affairs negligible, its economy in a prolonged depression, and its monarchy completely bankrupt. The optimism of Philip II's reign had changed to *desengaño*, a spirit of disillusionment and hopelessness. Although Spain began a slow recovery in the last years of Charles's reign, it never regained the power and prestige it had enjoyed under its second King Philip.

It is relatively easy to trace the course of decline and to identify particular contributory causes. But how can these be weighed and ordered? An underlying factor was certainly long-existing weaknesses in the underpinnings of the Spanish nation. Spain at the peak of its power was deficient in natural and human resources. Much of its soil was poor and much of its territory was semiarid, deficiencies compounded by centuries of deforestation and erosion. It was traversed by high and rugged mountain ranges, and its main rivers descended swiftly from the interior to the sea. These natural features limited its agricultural potential and hampered the development of internal communications and transport.

The size and density of Spain's population reflected the inhospitality of its physical environment. Toward the end of the sixteenth century, after more than a hundred years of demographic growth, its people numbered no more than 8,500,000. By way of comparison, the realms of France, its neighbor and perennial enemy, had about the same area, but they were much better endowed by nature and had about 18,500,000 inhabitants.

Antiquated political and social structures hampered the full exploitation of Spain's limited resources. In 1600 one monarch ruled the several Spanish kingdoms, but each retained its cultural individuality and its particular constitution and liberties. These features hindered the creation of a truly Spanish identity and the mobilization of genuinely national efforts. In consequence the strength of Spain depended mainly on the Kingdom of Castile, which made up about 80 percent of Spanish peninsular territory, held about 85 percent of the Spanish population, provided most of the crown's revenues, and, among all the realms of Spain, identified most closely with the Habsburg monarchy and its aims.

Castile, however, had its own structural weaknesses. At the zenith of Spanish power, the Castilian nobility and clergy still held a virtual monopoly of wealth and privilege. They continued to enjoy their ancient *fueros*, including immunity from personal taxes. Lay lords and ecclesiastical foundations held the most productive lands of the kingdom under *señorial* jurisdiction and protected by entailment and mortmain. Such conditions of tenure discouraged intensive agricultural production. The mercantile and industrial sectors, which had shown considerable vitality in the first half of the sixteenth century, fell under the domination of monopolistic guilds. The peasantry, about 80 percent of the Castilian population, suffered exploitation by landlords and cruel exactions from tax farmers and were burdened by inflated production costs while forced to sell their grain at prices kept artificially low by the government. It was their helpless lot that induced them to abandon the countryside. The social order was supported by an ethic that exalted the noble qualities of leisure and ostentation and depreciated the bourgeois virtues of enterprise, productive labor, and thrift.

Although little could be done to alter Spain's geography, other infrastructural weaknesses were not beyond alleviation when Philip II came to the throne. During the first half of his reign, at least, he possessed enough authority, prestige, and popular support to effect a closer union among his Spanish realms, to redress some of the more grievous social imbalances in Castile, and to introduce economic and fiscal reforms. But he also had a very traditional turn of mind. He respected the liberties of his several kingdoms and he believed the established social order to be ordained by God. He regarded the nobility and the clergy as the bulwark of the crown. He granted new titles liberally and sold *señoríos* from the royal domain to lords old and new. He made no concerted effort to cultivate and elevate the economically productive sectors of society. The intellectual climate created by his uncompromising defense of religious orthodoxy discouraged the advance of science and technology.

Philip's successors, the third and the fourth of the same name, were much less able than he was and, moreover, no more disposed to change the established order. On the contrary, they continued to create new titles and new *señoríos*.

They further favored the nobility by granting to them endowments, pensions, and annuities at the expense of the royal treasury. Their largesse amounted to what modern economists call transfer payments, that is disbursements by the government for which the nation receives no goods and services in return. Under the three Philips, also, the numbers and wealth of the clergy increased substantially, thereby withdrawing manpower and capital from economically productive enterprises.

Spain's problems did not go unnoticed by contemporaries. A group of seventeenth-century political economists — the so-called *arbitristas* — analyzed the sources of Spanish decadence with considerable perspicacity and proposed *arbitrios* (remedies). Their writings, coupled with the imperative of strengthening the nation after the breakdown of the twelve-year truce with the Netherlands (1609–21) and Spain's entry in the Thirty Years' War, induced Olivares to undertake a number of fundamental reforms. In addition to the Union of Arms, these included sharp reductions in royal favors and pensions, taxation of the privileged orders, inquiries into the sources of mysterious fortunes accumulated by the king's ministers, measures to increase the population, and prohibitions against the importation of foreign manufactures. But by that time inertial forces were so great and the government so weakened that all his efforts came to nothing.

Weaknesses in its underpinnings unquestionably made it difficult for Spain to sustain the preeminence it gained in the sixteenth century. They also made the nation especially vulnerable to the crises that affected Europe in the 1600s. Alone, however, they cannot account for its rapid and almost total collapse. The direct cause of the debacle was the foreign commitments of the Spanish Habsburgs and the methods they employed to finance them.

From the accession of Philip II to the death of Philip IV, Spain was almost constantly at war for causes that its rulers and many of its people regarded as just and righteous. Military and naval undertakings cost immense amounts of money, but royal income was barely sufficient to meet the expenses of the court and the government even in times of peace. The tightness of revenues owed in part to the limited wealth of the nation, in part to an antiquated and inefficient fiscal system, but more directly to a very narrow tax base. Castile bore most of the burden. Not only was it the largest and wealthiest kingdom in Spain, but its cortes was the most amenable to voting revenues to the crown. As observed earlier, however, much of its wealth was exempt from taxation because of the immunities of the nobility and clergy.

The Emperor Charles and Philip II were reluctant to increase the burden on their taxpaying subjects, who, they well knew, were already heavily laden. They resorted instead to deficit financing to meet their imperial needs, employing two fiscal instruments. One was the *asiento*, a short-term contractual loan, generally negotiated with foreign bankers, to be repaid on specified dates and pledged against particular crown revenues. *Asientos* bore interest rates ranging from 10 to 14 percent per annum, with an additional 10 percent imposed on payments in arrears. Outstanding *asientos* constituted an unfunded or floating debt. The other device was the *juro de resguardo*, a fiduciary long-term bond paying annual interest rates of from 5 to 10 percent to holders. *Juros* formed the government's funded debt.

Charles borrowed so heavily that when he abdicated in 1556 royal revenues were pledged years in advance, and the cost of debt servicing alone amounted to more than the crown's annual income. In the following year Philip II declared a *medio general*. This expedient, sometimes rendered as bankruptcy, involved a repudiation of outstanding *asientos* and compensation of holders with *juros* at lower interest rates, that is, a forced conversion of the floating debt into a funded one. Although Philip's income doubled between 1556 and 1573 and redoubled by the end of his reign, imperial expenses increased at a greater rate. Like his father, he turned to the moneylenders, with predictable results. In 1575 and again in 1596, he resorted to *medios generales*.

Deficit financing weakened the Spanish and more especially the Castilian economy in several ways. Along with the influx of American treasure, it contributed to long-term inflation. Based on an index of 100 for 1501, Spanish prices rose fourfold by 1600. Wages increased at a more or less comparable rate. These circumstances contributed heavily to the decline of Spanish industry, for it received little protection from the crown and could not compete with imports from foreign countries where the costs of production rose at a slower rate. Habsburg fiscal policies also harmed the economy in more subtle ways. Entrepreneurial elements, already infected by the hidalgo mentality, discovered that it was safer and just as profitable to invest in rent-yielding real estate and government bonds as in commercial and industrial enterprises.

The seventeenth-century Habsburgs were even more desperate for money than their predecessors, for the scale of foreign wars grew while economic contraction at home and the decline of the Indies trade and of American silver imports decreased their revenues. They continued, therefore, to use deficit financing, resulting in new *medios generales* in 1607, 1627, 1647, and 1653 that further eroded the full faith and credit of the government. They also introduced

new excise taxes, which weighed most heavily on productive classes, and confiscated shipments of private silver entering Seville.

The late Habsburgs compounded their fiscal improvidence by tampering
with the value of the Castilian currency, a recourse that the Emperor Charles
and Philip II had avoided. In 1599, when the supply of American silver started
to level off, they began to mint *vellon*, the common coinage of the realm from
copper alone. A long period of monetary instability followed. When the crown
needed more funds it coined more *vellon* or recalled that in circulation and
stamped it with a higher value. Both procedures returned a handsome profit
to the treasury. But, when their inflationary results could no longer be ignored,
the government reduced the volume of mintings or recalled and devaluated the
*vellon* in circulation, thereby producing sudden deflations. Sharp and abrupt
fluctuations in the supply and value of money brought the economy to the
brink of collapse and completed the ruin of the entrepreneurial classes. In
1680, after a period of especially severe inflation, the government introduced
currency reforms involving strict limits on current mintings of *vellon* and the
rapid retirement of copper. These measures stabilized the currency and marked
the beginning of a modest economic recovery.

The financing of wars had still another pernicious effect. Expedient considerations induced the monarchy to abandon still-underdeveloped centralized
mechanisms for creating, maintaining, and deploying armies and navies. Instead
it turned these functions over to private contractors, commonly foreigners, and
to nobles, towns, and semiautonomous regions of Spain, all of which were compensated with money, favors, and privileges. This system was not only inefficient and wasteful; it helped to perpetuate the power of traditional, *señorial*
elements in society and further weakened the fragile underpinnings of the Spanish national state.

What, then, can be concluded about Spain's decline? Fundamentally, it was
a particular case of adversities that afflicted most of Europe in the seventeenth
century: demographic and economic contraction, social and political disruptions, and international wars. The troubles of Spain were simply more acute
and prolonged than elsewhere because the nation's faulty infrastructures made
it less able to withstand severe crises and because overcommitment in Europe
strained its human and natural resources beyond their limits. As the English
historian Robert Watson so neatly put it in 1783, "Her power corresponded
not with her inclination."[5] And, since the strength of Spain lay in the resources
and spirit of Castile, so the decline of Spain was essentially the failure of Castile.

## The Vicissitudes of Portugal

In 1572, Luís de Camões, Portugal's greatest national poet, published *Os Lusiades*, an epic glorification of the deeds of Lusitanians overseas. The event caused a great stirring of national pride and, symbolically at least, marked the zenith of the kingdom's power and prestige. At that time, Portugal held strong military or commercial bases on the west coast of Africa, around the shores of the Indian Ocean, in the Spice Islands, and at Macao, on the China coast. Great fleets brought the wealth of the East to the *Casa da India* in Lisbon. In Brazil the coast had been secured against the French from São Vicente to Pernambuco, and sugar production had begun to boom.

But setbacks soon occurred. The Portuguese crusade in Morocco, begun a century and a half earlier, ended forever in 1578 at El Ksar-el-Kebir. The disaster stunned the tiny kingdom and shook its faith in its destiny. It lost the flower of its nobility, and the ransom of prisoners drained it of cash, jewels, and precious ornaments. Camões, then mortally ill, declared himself willing to die "in and with" his country.

By that time, also, Portugal's position in the East had begun to weaken. In 1575 Ternate, its bastion in the Spice Islands, fell to an East Indian sultan. Meanwhile Venice had contrived to reopen the Red Sea route and regain a share of the spice trade. As supplies reaching Europe from this source increased, prices fell. In 1580, pepper was down from its mid-sixteenth century peak by 25 percent in London, 12 percent in Castile, and 8 percent in Vienna.[6] But the *Estado da India* still had to be defended at enormous cost to the nation, and the *Carreira da India* devoured ships and men. Not uncommonly on the six-month outbound voyage half of the fleet's complement died of scurvy and many ships went to the bottom in storm and shipwreck.

Portugal's position deteriorated further after the union of the Hispanic crowns in 1580 provided the Dutch with a welcome opportunity to attack its overseas possessions and trade. In 1602 the Hollanders organized the Dutch East India Company to advance their interests in the East, and during the next several decades the company's forces seized most of the Portuguese stations in India, Ceylon, and the Spice Islands. The British East India Company, chartered in 1600, followed closely on the heels of the Dutch. In 1622 a joint English-Persian expedition captured Ormuz on the Persian Gulf, and by about 1650 English factories were scattered around the periphery of the Indian Ocean from Madagascar to the western tip of Java. By the late 1660s the only major bases still held by the Portuguese in the *Estado da India* were Goa, Macao, Mozambique, and Mombasa. The Spice Islands had fallen into the hands of the Dutch and the English, and after 1639, when Japan expelled the Portuguese, the Dutch obtained control of the Island Empire's commerce with Europe. Expatriate Portuguese merchants managed to retain a portion of the carrying trade in the East, but very few of their profits found their way back to the mother country.

Portugal also suffered major losses in the Atlantic theater. In 1638 the Dutch West India Company, organized in 1621, seized El Mina (St. George of the Mines) on the Guinea coast and three years later drove the Portuguese from the coasts of Benguela and Angola. In the 1630s it seized a large part of northeastern Brazil, although it had to withdraw in 1654.

At first glance the histories of Spain and Portugal from the late sixteenth century to the mid-1600s appear to have followed the same course—from imperial greatness to virtual impotence—and for much the same reasons. Portugal's human and natural resources were even more meager than those of its neighbor. Its population toward the end of the sixteenth century probably numbered no more than a million and a half. It had virtually no industry and was dependent on foreign grain. Its social structure was just as archaic as Castile's. Its monarchy constantly teetered on the brink of bankruptcy, owing to the favors it granted to privileged estates and to the costs of defending its empire.

Yet major differences existed between the forms, causes, and courses of the imperial trajectories of the two Hispanic powers. Although smaller and poorer than Spain, Portugal possessed greater internal strength. It was a single nation, unencumbered by the constitutional divisons that sapped Spain's vitality. Modern research suggests that its population, rather than stagnating or declining, increased from about 1,500,000 toward the end of the sixteenth century to about 1,800,000 by 1640 and to some 2,000,000 by the early 1700s.[7] Whereas Spain's European commerce suffered severely because of the nation's wars in Italy and northern Europe, Portugal's remained relatively healthy despite the struggle with the Dutch. The Portuguese India trade fell off badly beginning in the 1570s, but commerce in Brazilian sugar helped make up for the losses sustained. In contrast, Spain's trade with the Indies declined sharply in the 1620s and remained depressed for the rest of the century. Although the Portuguese crown was chronically destitute, it eschewed the misguided monetary policies that undermined the Spanish economy.

External developments saved Portugal from further misfortunes and, indeed, helped it to reconstruct its empire. On the Iberian peninsula, Spain committed most of its resources to subduing the Catalan revolt, thereby aiding Portugal's concurrent rebellion against Spanish rule. Growing commercial rivalries between

England and Holland led to three naval wars between the two powers (1652–54, 1665–67, and 1672–74), which relieved Dutch pressures on Portugal's overseas possessions. Meanwhile, in 1654, Portugal and England negotiated a commercial treaty that was solidified in 1661 by the marriage of the newly crowned Charles II of England to the daughter of Dom John IV and by an Anglo-Portuguese defense pact. These arrangements led to large-scale English intrusion into Portuguese domestic and overseas commerce. But, in return, Portugal gained a formal ally in its continuing struggles against Spain and Holland and obtained the protection of what was soon to become the world's most powerful navy.

Thus, it might be said that, in contrast to Spain, Portugal never rose to great imperial heights only to decline sharply into impotence. In 1700 it was essentially what it had been in the 1570s, a small, poor European nation, heavily dependent on an overseas empire for whatever prosperity it enjoyed. The locus of its empire had simply shifted from the *Estado da India* to the Atlantic.

## Spanish America in the Age of Philip II

In the Indies, as in Spain, the reign of Philip II was a period of transition. By the 1560s the Conquest had lost its momentum, but territorial expansion continued, responding to new motives, employing new methods, and being led by new types of people. At the same time, however, northern Europeans began to nibble away at the peripheries of the king's American dominions.

Significant changes occurred in Spanish American population and social structures during Philip's rule. The number of white inhabitants grew steadily, and, among them, the preponderance of American-born over European-born Spaniards increased rapidly. Between 1551 and 1575 imports of black slaves into the Indies doubled over those of the preceding twenty-five-year period. Like mestizos, mulattoes and *zambos* were no longer individual cases of miscegenation but large classes of people whose existence demanded recognition. In contrast with other population elements, new epidemics and pandemics diminished further the indigenous peoples and hastened the destruction of their traditional social institutions. These trends, coupled with a broader range of contacts with Spaniards and mixed bloods, furthered the acculturation of the indigenes, although the pace remained slow. In short, by the end of Philip's reign, society in the Indies no longer consisted of a handful of European intruders lording it over a seemingly inexhaustible Indian population through native intermediaries and institutions. It had become much more complex and was assuming distinctively Hispanic American qualities.

During the last quarter of the sixteenth century the economy of the Indies continued to expand, trans-Atlantic trade increased steadily, and exports of American silver mounted. In the early seventeenth century the mercantile and mining sectors of the economy entered a depression whose magnitude and duration is still being debated. Domestic manufacturing and agriculture, however, remained relatively healthy and moved Spanish America well along the road to self-sufficiency in basic consumer goods.

In matters of imperial policy, the early years of Philip's rule were a period of stocktaking, a respite after the hectic era of the Conquest. Jurists and administrators in both Spain and the Americas industriously gathered data from archives, *visitas*, and interrogatories, reflected on their findings, and suggested new measures for the good government of the Indies. Philip carefully read and annotated the voluminous reports and recommendations that crossed his desk, evaluated them in terms of his interests and his duty, and defined two principles that guided his colonial policies and those of his Habsburg successors: Spain's American dominions were to be more tightly and uniformly governed, and their resources were to be employed more fully and effectively to further the ends of the monarchy.

Philip's policies produced a surge of *ordenamiento* and *reglamentación* (the issuing of ordinances and regulations): in 1562, the Ordinances of Monzón, regularizing the structure and functions of American audiencias; in 1564–65, regulations for the convoyed fleet system; in 1573, the Ordinances for New Discoveries and Settlement and the definitive establishment of the Sevillian monopoly of trade with America; in 1574, the Ordinance for the Laying Out of New Towns and the *Ordenanza del Patronazgo*, which reaffirmed the amplitude and imprescriptability of the *real patronato de Indias*. Governors in the Indies followed the king's lead. Francisco de Toledo, fifth viceroy of Peru (1569–81), is particularly noted for his regulatory zeal. During his administration he produced a spate of decrees and orders governing, among other things, *corregimientos*, *mitas*, the collection of tribute, new congregations of Indians, muncipalities, and the mining industry.

## Years of Transition in Brazil

The reign of Philip II was also an era of transition in Brazil, although he himself had little to do with the changes. When he succeeded to the Portuguese crown, its American dominions consisted of widely scattered coastal settlements from Pernambuco in the northeast to São Vicente in the south. By the time he died, Brazilians had begun a long period of territorial expansion that took them, along the coasts, to the mouth of the Amazon and the banks of the Rio de la Plata estuary and, in the interior, far beyond the Line of Tordesillas.

In Brazil, as in Spanish America, significant economic, demographic, and social changes followed the era of the Conquest. Between 1570 and 1580 the colony's sugar production doubled, and its demand for black slaves added an important element to the Portuguese Atlantic economy. In Brazilian sugar zones, growing imports of African slaves helped to replace a rapidly diminishing indigenous population, contributed to the formation of a large class of mulattoes, and consolidated a social system whose primary relationship was between white masters and colored slaves. In the interior, a much more homogeneous and loosely stratified society developed through the thorough blending of white, black, and brown people in a frontier environment.

While the Habsburgs ruled Portugal, Spanish example and influence induced the kingdom's ministers to adopt new institutions and stronger measures for the governance and exploitation of Brazil. The Bragança dynasty also attempted to tighten up colonial administration. Compared with Spanish efforts in this direction, the Portuguese moved much more slowly and less deliberately. Nevertheless, the result was more government and more regulation than had existed under the House of Avis.

It is ironic that both Spain and Portugal tried to impose stronger government on American dominions that were growing in wealth and population during an era when the Old World sources of metropolitan strength were diminishing. The tension between Hispanic American societies with their own reason for being and imperial systems is an underlying theme of the following chapters.

# Territorial Changes in the Hispanic New World: Contractions, Expansions, Adjustments

In the last decades of the sixteenth century and throughout the seventeenth, far-reaching territorial changes occurred in the Spanish Indies and in Brazil. The dominions claimed de jure by Spain suffered substantial contractions; the lands occupied de facto by both Spain and Portugal expanded enormously, and Portuguese expansion produced major readjustments of the territorial claims of the two Hispanic powers in South America.

## Territorial Contraction

### The Beginnings of Northern European Colonization

Territorial contraction in Hispanic America resulted not from the withdrawal of Spain and Portugal from lands they had already settled but from northern European colonization in regions they had left unoccupied. During the sixteenth century the French and the English had attempted to plant settlements along the coasts of North and South America, but these undertakings were ill-planned and supported and came to bad ends. By the end of the 1500s circumstances had changed. The northern European nations had grown stronger and more able to support overseas empires. Their expanding economies required more raw materials and larger markets, and mercantile elements had gained a greater voice in their governments. Permanent colonies in America could not only facilitate the penetration of Hispanic American commerce but would provide a direct source of furs, dyes, hides, and plantation products. Thousands of French, English, and Dutch had crossed the North and South Atlantic. They were familair with its winds and currents and with the lay of the land along the east coast of the American hemisphere and in the Caribbean. By the end of the sixteenth century, also, northern European naval power had increased vis-à-vis that of Spain and Portugal, and the rule of "No peace beyond the line" allowed foreign intrusions in America without disrupting international relations in Europe.

Insofar as northern Europeans needed a legal justification for doing what they would have done anyway, they countered the Hispanic claim of *uti possidetis de jure* (right of possession by law), based on the papal donation and prior discovery, with the doctrine of *uti possidetis de facto* (right of possession by effective occupation).

Northern European colonization began modestly and in regions far removed from Spanish and Portuguese attention. Around 1599, the Dutch built two small forts on the lower Amazon and, in the early 1600s, established posts in the regions that became known as the Guianas. These settlements were little more than factories, although some small-scale planting took place around them. In 1611 the Dutch built Fort Orange at the mouth of the Hudson as a fur trading post. The English, most notably Sir Walter Raleigh, also attempted to settle in the Guianas in the 1590s and in the early 1600s but failed. Much farther north, however, they managed to establish their first permanent colony at Jamestown in 1607.

The Naval Offensive of
The Dutch West India Company

In the 1620s northern European colonization in the New World gained momentum and began to intrude into more sensitive parts of lands claimed by Spain and Portugal. The initiative came from the Dutch West India Company, chartered in 1621 on the model of the Dutch East India Company of 1602. Shortly after its founding, the West India Company began to send powerful naval expeditions into American waters. In 1624, one of them took Bahia but was driven out by a combined Spanish and Portuguese fleet. Four years later, the Dutch admiral Piet Heyn fulfilled the dream of generations of privateers by capturing the Mexican treasure fleet in Cuban waters. The booty came to 15,000,000 *florins*, enough to pay the company's debts and declare a 50 percent dividend to stockholders. During the next two years, other Dutch commanders ranged through the Caribbean, ravaging its islands and coasts.

The Dutch Conquest of Brazil

Piet Heyn's success also allowed the company to capitalize large new enterprises and it turned its attention to Brazil, this time to the rich sugar lands of the northeast. In 1630 its forces took Recife and during the next few years extended its occupation along the coast southward to the Rio São Francisco and northward into Ceará. The conquest, however, proved to be short-lived. In the 1640s, Brazilian troops mounted a counteroffensive that gradually pushed the invaders back against their main base at Recife. The Dutch also encountered other problems. Their hold was weakened by policy disputes between their governor, Maurice of Nassau, who wished to develop a true colony, and the directors and stockholders of the company, who were interested only in immediate profits. Then came the outbreak of the first Dutch-English war in 1652, which made so many demands on the United Provinces' naval strength that they could no longer defend the company's Brazilian acquisitions. In 1654, the garrison of Recife, now closely beleaguered, surrendered to a Portuguese fleet.

Northern European
Colonization in the Caribbean

The Dutch West India Company also contributed to more permanent Spanish territorial losses in the Caribbean. Its naval offensives so weakened and dispersed Spanish defenses in that area that the English and the French were able to establish themselves first in the Guianas, then in the islands of the Lesser Antilles that Spain had never occupied. The Dutch themselves settled on St. Martins and St. Eustatius in the island chain and on Curaçao and Bonaire along the coasts of Venezuela.[1]

During the middle decades of the seventeenth century a combination of circumstances placed further strains on Spanish American defenses. At the Battle of the Downs in the English Channel (1639) and the Battle of Itamaracá off the coast of Brazil (1640), the Dutch dealt near-mortal blows to the Spanish navy. In addition, their settlement of the Lesser Antilles provided foreigners with American bases for hostile activities, and, beginning in the 1650s, buccaneers—international bands of American-based marauders—began to attack Spanish American shipping and settlements in the Caribbean in force.

The northern European nations took advantage of Spain's weakness to extend their colonization in the Caribbean. In 1655, after a badly managed and abortive attempt to seize Española, the English took the less well defended and settled island of Jamaica. About this time, also, English logwood cutters established themselves around Belize on the coast of Honduras. In 1665, the king of France sent out a governor to assert control on the island of Tortuga, lying just off the northwestern coast of Española, which had been occupied from time to time by the Spanish, the English, buccaneers, and the French. During the next several decades, French planters gradually established themselves in the northwestern part of Española itself, a region that English and buccaneer raids had caused the Spanish to abandon.

While northern European colonization in the Caribbean expanded, it also, continued in regions farther removed from Spanish sea power. By the end of the seventeenth century, the French and English were well established along the coasts of North America from the Carolinas to Quebec.

Territorial Losses: An Assessment

The Portuguese in America managed to withstand seventeenth-century foreign intrusions, in part because of vigorous defensive actions, in part because of the diversion of Dutch interests to other parts of the world. In contrast, the Spanish suffered rather extensive losses of territories to which they had laid claim. They reacted by lodging diplomatic protests and by devising strategies to expel foreign intruders and to prevent further inroads. The defense of the Indies will be treated in more detail in chapter 19. For the purposes of this chapter, it is sufficient to say that Spain lacked the military and demographic resources to occupy all the territory it claimed.

During the course of the seventeenth century, Spain came to realize the unreality of its territorial claims and the limits of its capabilities. In the Treaty of Münster (1648), it acknowledged Dutch title to Curaçao and St. Eustatius; in the Treaty of Madrid (1670) it confirmed England's possession of its several Caribbean and North American colonies, excepting the logwood stations around Belize; in the Treaty of Ryswyck (1697), it ceded the western half of Española to France, a colony that the French named St. Domingue. In short, it abandoned grudgingly the doctrine of *uti possidetis de jure* and accepted that of *uti possidetis de facto*. But losses and concessions, while damaging to Spain's pride, were really not severe. At the end of the seventeenth century, the main centers of wealth, population, and power in the Spanish Indies remained intact.

## The Conditions of Territorial Expansion

While foreign intruders nibbled at the peripheries of the Hispanic New World, in its heartland the subjects of the kings of Spain and Portugal occupied vast new territories, sometimes in interstices between existing population clusters, sometimes on open frontiers. In some instances the spirit of the Conquest lived on, and Spanish *adelantados*, Portuguese captains, and the missionary orders led the way. Increasingly, however, new motives and methods guided expansion, new human types provided the vanguard, and new institutional forms were employed.

## Spanish Expansion: Legal Principles

King Philip II first set forth the legal principles that were to govern territorial expansion in the Spanish Indies in the Ordinances for New Discoveries and Settlement of 1563. Its provisions were reaffirmed and elaborated in the more famous Ordinances for New Discoveries, Conquests and Pacifications promulgated in 1573.[2] The Ordinances of 1573 reveal a number of continuities with the policies of the Catholic Kings and Emperor Charles. They provided that new acquisitions of lands and people be accomplished at no expense to the royal treasury and under patents issued by the king to private parties. As in earlier years, these instruments granted to the leader of the expedition titles and prerogatives as incentives and rewards for his initiative. They named him *adelantado*, governor, and captain-general of the lands to be occupied and authorized him to appoint royal treasury officials. They gave him the right to found towns and name their officers; to grant land to his followers, reserving a generous portion for himself; and to enjoy a salary derived from the revenues of the territory he won. The ordinances also reiterated the crown's commitment to colonization of new provinces by Indians as well as by Spaniards and required *adelantados* to see that the indigenes be brought together in communities where they could be taught to live in Christian polity.

The provisions of the new ordinances, however, differed from earlier regulations in two important respects. They insisted more strongly that new territorial acquisitions be made with no aggravation to the Indians and, indeed, directed that in the future the word "conquest" be eschewed and "pacification" be used instead. The code of 1573 also reflected compromises made by King Philip with the crown's deep-rooted distrust of *señorialism* in the Indies. It permitted *adelantados* to grant *encomiendas*, a right hitherto reserved to the king, and, if they were operating beyond the limits of established territorial jurisdictions, they were not answerable to any colonial authority, only to the Council of the Indies. The titles and offices they received in their patent were inheritable for at least one generation. Members of an expedition of pacification, in their capacity as first settlers, were to be regarded as *hidalgos de solar conocido* (of well-established reputation), and the *adelantado* himself could establish "one or two" *mayorazgos* (entailed estates) and might, at royal discretion, be granted a title of nobility.

King Philip's apparent generosity owed to several circumstances. The crown lacked the resources to undertake discoveries and pacifications itself, especially in view of its deepening fiscal insolvency, and, as the prospects of finding "other Mexicos" and "other Perus" dimmed, it had to provide other incentives to private initiative. But also, by the 1570s, it had suppressed rebellions in Peru and Nicaragua and the Avila conspiracy in Mexico, and it had created an apparatus of royal government in the Indies to guard its interests. It therefore felt much more self-confident about its authority in those kingdoms.

## Territorial Expansion in the Viceroyalty of New Spain

### Florida

In terms of area occupied, the most important territorial expansion in Spanish America occurred in northern New Spain, from Florida at the eastern extreme to Baja (Lower) California at the western. The occupation of Florida represented the completion of unfinished business. During the first half of the sixteenth century, conquerors and missionaries had penetrated the region but failed to establish any permanent footholds. King Philip, however, regarded Florida as having a special strategic importance, for homebound treasure fleets passed close to its eastern shores.

Philip's concern acquired an immediate urgency when French Huguenots made an unsuccessful attempt to plant a settlement at Port Royal in South Carolina in 1562 and then returned to America in 1564 to build Fort Caroline at the mouth of the St. Johns River. When the news of the French reappearance reached the king, he negotiated a contract with Pedro Menéndez de Avilés, a trader to America and sometimes commander of the Indies fleets, to expel the intruders and make a permanent settlement in Florida. The provisions of the agreement generally conformed to the principles set forth in the Ordinances of 1563. The king required Menéndez to undertake the enterprise at his own expense and to subjugate the Indians of the region by means of reason. Menéndez obtained the title of *adelantado* along with valuable economic privileges and ample governmental powers for himself and his heirs. The French presence at Fort Caroline, however, so alarmed Philip that he later agreed to make direct contributions of men and supplies to the gathering expedition.

Menéndez executed his orders with dispatch. Arriving in Florida in August, 1565, he established a fort at a site he called St. Augustine. Then, marching swiftly overland by night, he fell upon Fort Caroline and put its garrison to the sword, sparing only women and children. Shortly thereafter, he found two bands of shipwrecked French reinforcements, induced them to surrender unconditionally, and then massacred them save for a handful of professed Catholics.

Missionaries played an important part in consolidating and extending Spanish dominion in Florida. Jesuits began to arrive in St. Augustine shortly after its founding and quickly established a line of missions running north along the Georgia and Carolina coasts. The hostility of the Indians and several martyrdoms, however, induced the Black Robes to abandon Florida in 1572 for new fields in Mexico, where they will be encountered later.

In 1573 the Franciscan order assumed responsibility for missionary work in Florida. During the late 1500s and in the course of the next century, it established two strings of missions which, at their maximum extent, ran northward into southern Carolina and westward into the lands of the Apalachicola Indians. In addition to their religious functions the missions formed a strategic buffer against the aggressive English to the north. They were, however, greatly overextended because of the limited strength of the friars at hand and of the military support available. Indian defections, climaxing between 1702 and 1706, forced the missionaries to withdraw from their northern and western provinces to the protection of St. Augustine.

In the early eighteenth century Spanish Florida consisted only of the garrison town of St. Augustine, a small grazing and agricultural hinterland, several outlying forts, and the surviving Franciscan missions. For nearly 150 years, nevertheless, it had served effectively as the northeastern bastion of the Spanish empire in America and continued to do so until it was acquired by the English in 1763, not by conquest but by cession.

The Mexican North:
New Vizcaya and New Leon

In northern Mexico, expansion occurred on a more massive scale and for different reasons than in Florida. The Spaniards advanced along several axes emanating from Zacatecas into what became known as Nueva Vizcaya (New Vizcaya), a region that included most of the great interior basin lying between the eastern and western Sierra Madre ranges. It was inhabited by transhumant Indian tribes of hostile disposition whom the Spaniards called, collectively, Chichimecas. Its main attraction was the deposits of silver ore located along the eastern flank of the western Sierra amidst semiarid grasslands. A secondary axis led south and east from Zacatecas to silver-bearing ores, undiscovered and bypassed during the Conquest.

The principal instruments of expansion were *adelantados* who obtained patents to pacify and settle these hostile regions and who hoped to profit by exploiting their mines. Up to a point they observed the spirit of the Ordinances of 1573, if only for tactical reasons. The preceding decades had demonstrated the futility of *guerra a fuego y a sangre* (war of fire and blood) as a means of subjugating the native population, and the new generation of *adelantados* tried conciliation and negotiation. Franciscan friars aided their endeavors, acting as advance agents to gain the confidence of the Indians and on occasion winning martyrdom. When, however, pacific measures failed, captains did not hesitate to resort to war and the word "conquest" continued to appear in contemporary documents. Despite frequent failures and setbacks, by about 1600 missionaries and soldiers had achieved a sufficient measure of pacification to open the north to colonization.

The pattern of settlement on the northern frontier conformed to that established around Zacatecas and in other older silver districts. Mining camps sprang up around new strikes, and at the richer sites, such as Durango (1563), Charcas (1573), San Luis Potosí (1592), and Parral (1630), developed into permanent municipalities and capitals of provinces. But, as contemporaries observed, "mines neither sowed nor harvested nor bred."[3] To feed hungry miners, farms producing wheat and maize appeared in accessible watered valleys. On drier range lands cattle ranches spread, producing not only meat but hides and tallow for the use of the mining industry. In many instances the ownership of mines, agricultural properties, and grazing lands became conjoined in the hands of the northern *adelantados*. They and their descendants managed to consolidate and extend their holdings into enormous estates, the prototypes of the Latin American hacienda-latifundia.

The growth, organization, and economic and social functions of the hacienda will be described in more detail in chapter 17. The institution is considered here only as an instrument of territorial expansion. The desire to create a landed estate was a powerful motive for the northward movement of the frontier, and, like the Brazilian *engenho*, the hacienda was a populated place that consolidated the occupation of new territory. Although the great *hacendados* (masters of haciendas) maintained residences in provincial capitals, they spent part of the year on their rural estates accompanied by members of their family, clients, and hangers-on. More lowly elements of the hacienda's population included overseers, artisans, *vaqueros* (cowhands), laborers both permanent and seasonal, and household servants. Resident curates ministered to the spiritual needs of all. The physical manifestations of settlement were permanent residences for masters and workers, chapels, storehouses, tanneries, forges, grain mills, and wine presses. For purposes of defense, the central installations were fortified, and able-bodied workers were organized into militias.

Another axis of expansion led into northeastern Mexico, a region that came to be known as Nuevo León (New Leon). The advance began with the settlement of Saltillo in 1577 on the western frontier of New Vizcaya where abundant grasslands attracted stockmen from Zacatecas. Nineteen years later, in 1596, the Franciscans founded a mission at Monterrey that ultimately became the locus of a civil settlement. The colonization of New Leon lagged, however, because of the absence of precious metals and the hostility of the Indians, which the slaving activities of *adelantados* and settlers intensified.

Toward the middle of the seventeenth century the Spanish crown gave stronger support to the settlement of the province owing to its fear that foreign nations, now firmly established in the Caribbean, might intrude on the undefended coasts of Texas and Louisiana. Beginning in the 1650s, the royal governor of New Leon founded several towns and attracted a few settlers with proffers of large land grants and *encomiendas*. Later, in the 1680s and the 1690s, the viceroy of New Spain responded to French attempts to settle Louisiana by establishing several missions and presidios in eastern Texas, but Indian resistance forced their abandoment in 1694.

The Northwest: Chihuahua,
Sonora, and Lower California

In the occupation of New Vizcaya and New Leon, the religious orders played an important supportive role. In the Mexican northwest, they formed the *punta de lanza* (the point of the lance). Beginning in the early 1600s, Franciscans pushed north from Durango along the western edges of the central plateau into a region that became known as Chihuahua, where they established missions among the Conchos Indians. On their left flank, Jesuits followed a parallel route along the eastern slopes of the Sierra Madre, which were inhabited by the Tarahumara Indians. The northwestern advance of both orders was followed by the founding of towns, the construction of presidios, and the formation of cattle ranches. In the mid-1600s, it was interrupted by a series of savage Indian rebellions that destroyed most of the Chihuahuan missions. After the risings had been subdued, however, the missionaries and settlers returned and resumed their advance. By 1700, they were approaching the upper reaches of the Rio Grande.

Across the Sierra Madre, on the west coast of Mexico, the first stage of the northward movement was exclusively a Jesuit enterprise. Beginning in Sinaloa in 1593, the Black Robes advanced north, establishing missions and reductions in the valleys of westward-flowing rivers. By 1636, they reached the Sonora River and, during the remainder of the century, slowly moved inland along the river and its tributaries into Arizona. In northern Sonora and in southern Arizona, a region that came to be called *Pimería Alta*, they established their most populous and prosperous reductions in North America under the leadership of Father Francisco Eusebio Kino, noted not only for his zeal and piety but for his extensive geographic explorations in northwestern Mexico.

The Jesuits did not have it all their own way for very long. As in the lands opened by the missionaries in the interior, the government built presidios near reductions to protect them from unpacified Indians. Stockmen soon appeared, attracted by pasturage on the slopes and in the upland basins of the Sonoran ranges. Small towns sprang up to serve the needs of soldiers and the civilian population.

In the late 1600s, the Jesuits established another missionary field on the peninsula of Baja California, whose coastal waters had been exploited intermittently by pearlers since the days of Cortés. In the middle decades of the seventeenth century, the crown granted several patents for its settlement, but its rugged terrain and extreme aridity discouraged Spanish efforts. Finally, in 1697, the king turned the peninsula over to the Black Robes. During the next decade, they managed to establish a handful of missions on its eastern coast, but only supplies coming from Sonora enabled them to survive into the eighteenth century.

New Mexico

While the occupation of the Mexican north was still under way, the Spanish made a 600-mile leap beyond their furthest outposts to occupy the lands that became known as Nuevo México (New Mexico). The enterprise showed a clear continuity with the Conquest tradition and was the last of the great *entradas*. Despite half a century of disappointment, the legend of the Seven Cities of Cíbola and Gran Quivira remained alive, and to the lure of these chimeras, hope and imagination added the Strait of Anian, linking the Atlantic and the Pacific far to the north. After Sir Francis Drake's voyage into the Pacific (1578–79) the crown became apprehensive that the English might find and seize the prize.

These several considerations induced the king to give Juan de Oñate, son of Cristóbal, one of the discoverers of the mines of Zacatecas, a patent to pacify and settle New Mexico. In 1593, the *adelantado* led a large expedition north from Durango and made extensive explorations beyond the Rio Grande. Although he failed to discover rich civilizations or the Strait of Anian, he managed to pacify the Pueblo Indians and distributed them in *encomiendas* to his men. In 1608 he founded Santa Fe as the capital of the new province. Franciscans who had accompanied him established missions among the pacified Pueblos. New Mexico was connected with settlements in Nueva Vizcaya and points farther south only by a long and hazardous trail, called rather pretentiously *El Camino Real de la Tierra Adentro* (The Royal Road from the Interior Lands).

By the end of the seventeenth century, the northern frontier of New Spain had reached an irregular and broken line running from the Jesuit missions in Lower California, through Pimería Alta and northern Chihuahua, to the mission and settlement of *Nuestra Señora de Guadalupe del Paso* (El Paso), where the *Camino Real* crossed the Rio Grande. From here the frontier turned southwest, roughly paralleling the Rio Grande, to the Spanish settlements in New Leon. Far to the north, New Mexico subsisted as "an islet of Christians." Far to the east, beyond unsettled Texas and Louisiana, lay another outpost of empire, St. Augustine and its satellite forts and missions.

Between the northern frontier and central Mexico, Spanish occupation consisted of thinly scattered mining and agricultural settlements, cattle haciendas, missions, and presidios, and a few incorporated towns that served as administrative centers. These population nuclei were connected only by rough tracks and trails. Father Domingo Lázaro de Arregui, who traversed much of northern Mexico in the seventeenth century relying solely on an astrolabe to determine his latitude, described the vastness and solitude of the land: "There is so much uninhabited space in these realms that I doubt whether Europe's entire population could fill them; not only do they have no boundaries, but all or nearly all is empty."[4]

Behind the frontier, also, pockets of native resistance remained, and pacified tribes frequently rebelled against Spanish rule and religion. Indian resistance climaxed toward the end of the seventeenth century. In 1680 the Pueblos rose and drove white settlers and missionaries from New Mexico, and, during the next decade, a series of revolts broke out along the northern frontier from Sonora to New Leon. Repacification of the rebels required extended and expensive campaigns. The Spanish were not able to reoccupy New Mexico until 1692.

Mining and Agricultural Frontiers in
Southern Mexico and Central America

Elsewhere in the Viceroyalty of New Spain, territorial expansion occurred on a smaller scale. In the late 1570s prospectors found rich silver veins in the mountains of central Honduras. The region soon became an important producer, although a distant third to Potosí and the mines of northern Mexico. Settlement followed the opening of the mines, beginning with the foundation of the Real de Minas de San Miguel de Tegucigalpa in 1578.

The expansion of grazing and agriculture also opened new territory. During the late sixteenth and the early seventeenth centuries, cattle herds spread throughout tropical and semitropical savannas, the main areas occupied being the Gulf Coast of Mexico from Tampico to Tabasco, northeastern Costa Rica, and southeastern Honduras. The last region became especially famous for the mules it bred and exported to Panama for use in transisthmian haulage.

The most dynamic center of agricultural expansion developed in Costa Rica. For more than a century after the Spanish established themselves in that province, the white population consisted of a few dozen families concentrated in the cool volcanic basin of Cartago. Then, for reasons by no means clear, the region came to life late in the seventeenth century, producing substantial amounts of wheat, which it exported to settlements on the Caribbean lowlands and even to Panama and Cartagena. By 1700 the basin had become so crowded that excess families spread out into other compartments in the central *meseta*, a move symbolized by the foundation of San José in 1736.

The Philippine Islands

The utmost territorial expansion originating in New Spain led far beyond the geographical scope of this work and is described only because of its economic effect on Spanish America. Despite the cession of the Moluccas to Portugal and several fruitless voyages across the Pacific from Mexico during the first half of the sixteenth century, the Spanish crown did not abandon hope of establishing a foothold in the Spice Islands. In 1559, King Philip ordered the viceroy of New Spain to send a force across the Pacific to occupy and pacify the archipelago that came to bear his name, the Philippines.

The expedition formed for this mission consisted of four ships carrying 400 men under the command of Miguel López de Legazpi. Leaving the Mexican Pacific port of Navidad in November 1564, the fleet reached the Philippine island of Cebu in February 1565. Legazpi sent three vessals back to New Spain, but, instead of trying to sail due west against wind and current, their commander, Andrés de Urdaneta, turned northward beyond the belt of trade winds and caught westerlies that carried him to the coast of California. From there he followed the coast south to home port. Although the voyage was long and hazardous, it pioneered a feasible return route free of Portuguese interference.

Meanwhile, Legazpi undertook the pacification of the archipelago, using peaceful means as he had been instructed to do by the king and relying heavily on the missionary efforts of a band of Augustinians who had accompanied him. By the early 1570s, Spanish dominion was firmly established on the islands of Cebu and Luzon, and, in 1571, the city of Manila was founded as their capital city. Settlement followed well-established methods. Legazpi, named royal governor of the Philippines, distributed natives in *encomiendas* to his followers. Franciscans, Jesuits, and Dominicans arrived to reinforce the Augustinians, and, by 1600, the several orders claimed some 600,000 Filipino converts. The economic reward of the Philippine enterprise came not from spices but from the opening of a profitable trans-Pacific trade involving the exchange of Oriental silks, porcelains, and other luxury items for American silver.

## Territorial Expansion in the Viceroyalty of Peru

The Agrarian Frontier in
the Rio de la Plata Region

In spatial terms, the greatest territorial expansion in Spanish South America occurred in the grasslands and savannas along the branches of the Rio de la Plata system. It began as an extension of the Conquest. The objectives, however, were no longer other Perus but the provision of *encomiendas* of Indians for settlers who had missed out in earlier distributions and the development of communications routes linking interior Argentina and Paraguay to Upper Peru and the Atlantic.

The cities of Tucumán and Asunción furnished the springboards. In 1573 the governor of Tucumán founded the city of Córdoba 300 miles to the south on the northern limit of the pampas. Settlement of northern Argentina proceeded slowly during the next hundred years, centering on new towns: Rioja (1591), San Luís (1596), and Catamarca (1680).

Settlers from Asunción first moved north and founded Santa Cruz de la Sierra (1561) in the western foothills of the Bolivian Andes as the first step in opening a land route to Upper Peru. Their main effort, however, followed the Paraguay and Paraná rivers to the Atlantic to fulfill a long-felt need to establish direct communications with Europe. In 1573, the *adelantado* Juan de Garay, armed with a patent from the governor of Asunción, founded Santa Fe some 600 miles downstream near the junction of the Paraná and Salado rivers. Seven years later, Garay, now elevated to the governorship of Paraguay, took another giant step, some 1000 miles, to the Rio de la Plata estuary, where he founded El Puerto de Santa María de Buenos Aires on the mudflats along the west bank, not far from the site where Pedro de Mendoza had placed the ill-fated first town of Buenos Aires. In 1588, Paraguayan colonists established the city of Corrientes midway between Asunción and Santa Fe, thus completing a chain of settlements linking the heart of the continent to the sea.

The towns founded in the late sixteenth century defined the limits of Spanish settlement in the Rio de la Plata region and created another great American frontier that ran roughly west to east from Mendoza and San Juan in the eastern foothills of the Andes through Córdoba and Santa Fe to Buenos Aires. To the south of this line lay the pampas, empty of human habitation except for bellicose Indians who, like the Chichimecas in northern Mexico, stubbornly resisted Spanish intrusions into their lands. North of the frontier ranches devoted to subsistence agriculture and cattle ranching partially filled the gaps between widely dispersed urban centers. Two thin and extended communications routes served the region. One followed the Paraná-Paraguay to Asunción and continued by land northwest through Santa Cruz de la Sierra to Upper Peru. The other branched inland from the river system at Santa Fe and led to Upper Peru via Córdoba, Santiago del Estero, Tucumán, and Salta.

Other Areas of Agrarian Expansion: Antioquia,
the Eastern Andes, and the *Llanos* of the Orinoco

A more concentrated and more dynamic area of agrarian expansion developed in the temperate valleys and basins of the central cordillera in New Granada, a region that came to be called Antioquia. Beginning in the late 1500s, settlers from the town of Santa Fe de Antioquia began to drift into the fertile and springlike valley of Aburra, where they engaged in small-scale cattle ranching and agriculture. During the seventeenth century the region's population grew steadily through natural increase and the arrival of settlers from other parts of New Granada and from metropolitan Spain. Many of its inhabitants lived rude, seminomadic lives, and in 1675 the crown authorized the founding of Nuestra Señora de Candelaria de Medellín in order to bring them together in Christian polity. The new town gradually replaced Santa Fe de Antioquia as the political and economic center of the district. Continued population growth produced an excess that, in the eighteenth century, began to spill over into neighboring valleys, a migration that continued into modern times.

Agrarian expansion occurred on a smaller scale in several parts of Spanish South America. Cattlemen and ranchers from highland Peru, Bolivia, and Ecuador slowly moved into temperate and semitropical lands along the eastern slopes of the Andes. Farther north, grazing spread out from the uplands of New Granada and the Venezuelan Andes into the *llanos* of the Orinoco. In the eighteenth century these plains became one of the three major cattle raising regions of Spanish America, the other two being northern Mexico and the Argentine pampas.

New Mining Districts: the
Central Andes and New Granada

The most important mines opened in South America after the Conquest were in the central Andes and in New Granada. The Spaniards made silver strikes at Oruro, some 150 miles northwest of Potosí, in 1606; at Pasco, in the high sierra northeast of Lima, in 1630; and at Laicacota, in southern Peru just west of Lake Titicaca, in 1657. All together their yields were much less than those of Potosí, but their discovery opened new regions for Spanish settlement and led to the foundation of new municipalities.

The advance of the mining frontier in New Granada followed new gold strikes made in the last decades of the seventeenth century in several regions: on the upper and middle stretches of the Cauca and Magdalena rivers; on the upper Nechí, one of the Magdalena's main tributaries; in the eastern cordillera near Pamplona; and in the Sierra Nevada de Santa Marta, which arose along the Caribbean coast.

The production of the new gold mines peaked in the early seventeenth century, and by 1650 many sites had been virtually abandoned. But mining left its mark on the land. A handful of camps became towns and villas and survived; Cáceres (f. 1576) and Zaragoza (f. 1581) are cases in point. In the eastern highlands, the Spaniards founded Bucaramanga as a deposit of Indian labor, and the town gradually supplanted Pamplona as the economic center of the region. Along the middle Cauca and the Nechí, mestizos and mulattoes settled around abandoned mines, where they eked out an existence panning tailings and growing subsistence crops.

Late in the seventeenth century, miners began to open new placers in the tropical lowlands of New Granada, especially in the Chocó, a district occupying the northern part of a structural depression lying between the western cordillera and the coastal Serranía de Baudó. Here tropical heat, dense and dripping rain forests, and unremitting Indian hostility slowed penetration. With the aid of missionaries, the Spaniards pacified the region toward the end of the century, and in the 1700s it became the main gold producer in the Spanish Indies. But it lacked agricultural and pastoral resources, and settlement remained limited to rude mining camps.

The Great Mission Arc in South America

Missionaries played a key part in territorial expansion along a rough arc that curved from the lower Paraná River to the Guianas, generally following the eastern and southern slopes of the Andes. The most populous and prosperous mission province lay in the south and was created by the Society of Jesus. Beginning in 1588 Jesuit fathers began to establish reductions among the Guaraní on the upper Paraná, a region that came to be known as Guairá. Unfortunately, it lay exposed to the raids of Brazilian slavers moving inland from São Paulo. Between 1629 and 1632 these raiders, called *mamelucos* after the ferocious Turkish mamelukes, virtually destroyed the reductions. The Black Robes, therefore, withdrew the survivors south into a region that later became the Argentine province of Misiones. The *mamelucos* followed, but the missionaries obtained permission from the Council of the Indies to arm their charges, and in 1641 an army of 4000 Guaraní under the command of the governor of Paraguay administered a resounding defeat to the invaders. Now secure, the Jesuit province of Paraguay entered its golden age. By the end of the seventeenth century, it had thirty prosperous reductions, each with a population of about 3500 Indians.

The other main sectors of the arc, tracing its curve from south to north, consisted of clusters of missions in the following regions: eastern Bolivia, established by the Jesuits in the 1560s; trans-Andean Ecuador (the Province of Maynas), formed by the Jesuits in the 1590s and shared with the Observant Franciscans after the 1630s; the *llanos* (savannas) of eastern Colombia, organized by the Jesuits in the early 1600s; the Venezuelan *llanos* south of Caracas, established by the Capuchin Franciscans in the last half of the seventeenth century; the Venezuelan interior south of Cumaná, established around 1650, also by the Capuchins; and the western Guianas, organized by the Jesuits in 1668 but reassigned to the Capuchins in 1681.

The trans-Andean, Venezuelan, and Guiana missions occupied precarious positions. They were remote from the centers of Spanish settlement; tropical pests and pestilences afflicted them; warlike Indian tribes harassed them; and

Brazilian slavers raided the Maynas province. The total reduction population, counting each province at its peak, came to only a fraction of that of the Paraguayan missions during their golden age. Yet, if the missionaries' presence was sometimes insecure and impermanent, they explored vast interior regions, gathered ethnological data, and pioneered communications routes, thus paving the way for future settlement. They also reinforced Spanish juridical claims to large territories in the interior of South America by at least symbolic occupation. As in North America, the crown of Spain used the mission system for geopolitical purposes: to signify its dominion, to create buffer zones against depredations of unreduced Indians and Portuguese expansion, and to resist the intrusions of northern Europeans in the Guianas.

Stalemate on the Chilean Frontier

On one important frontier, expansion remained stalled. In southern Chile campaigns of military pacification continued after the initial conquest but with scant success. In the 1590s massive Araucanian uprisings forced the abandonment of seven towns south of the Bío Bío River. At about this juncture, Jesuit Father Luis de Valdivia won royal support for a program of pacification through gentle preaching and teaching, and in 1612 the king ordered the suppression of personal services for Indians, a form of exploitation that had accounted for much of the Araucanians' hostility. He also fixed the limit of Spanish political jurisdiction at the Bío Bío but authorized missionaries to enter Arauca. At first the natives accepted the arrangement, but very soon they murdered three Jesuits and again rose in rebellion, thus ending the experiment. Thereafter the Spanish alternated campaigns of military and peaceful pacification but made little progress, and at the end of the century the territory beyond the Bío Bío remained a land of war.

## Territorial Expansion in Brazil

In Brazil, as in Spanish America, territorial expansion reflected diverse public and private interests and assumed various organizational forms. In geographical terms, it involved the extension of settlement in coastal regions and the penetration of the interior in several directions. An important governing circumstance was the union of the Hispanic crowns (1580–1640) under the Spanish Habsburgs. During this interlude, a political barrier to Brazilian expansion, the Line of Tordesillas, was weakened, and Habsburg imperial strategies influenced Luso-Brazilian affairs.

The Coasts: Sergipe,
Alagoas, and the Northeast

The establishment of new settlements along the coast began in the stretch between Pernambuco and Bahia. In the 1580s, Bahian cattlemen pushed north into a region that became known as Sergipe. In 1589 an official expedition from Bahia subdued its Indian inhabitants and in the same year founded the town of São Cristóvão de Rio Sergipe. Meanwhile, ranchers from Pernambuco drifted south into Alagoas, the two movements meeting at the mouth of the Rio São Francisco. In the newly occupied lands captains distributed *sesmarias* to settlers, who combined ranching with sugar planting.

The two other main areas of coastal expansion lay at the northern and southern extremes of Brazil. In both regions, imperial strategies provided the driving force. In the north and northeast, the primary goal was the expulsion of the French, who after their eviction from the central captaincies established posts at several points between the bulge of Brazil and the Amazon delta. These bases constituted a threat to Portuguese sovereignty in the region, and from them the French incited the Indians against settlers around Pernambuco. Furthermore, King Philip II of Spain (Philip I of Portugal) regarded France as his main enemy. The presence of its subjects on a broad front facing the Atlantic and flanking the Caribbean, constituted a threat to the Spanish Indies and to imperial communications.

The Luso-Brazilian offensive, on occasion supported by Spanish forces, consisted of a series of campaigns. The first three, undertaken between 1584 and 1615, drove the French from Rio Grande do Norte, Ceará, and Maranhão. The Portuguese secured their victories by founding the towns of Filipéia (after King Philip) in 1585, Natal in 1599, and São Luís de Maranhão in 1615.

A fourth campaign struck against the Amazon delta where the Dutch and English, as well as the French, had established trading posts and small plantations. It began with the founding of Belém on the Pará River in 1616. Using Belém as a base, the Portuguese during the next decade expelled the foreign intruders from the Delta region and pushed further to the north into a region called Amapá, which extended to the borders of French Guiana. When, in 1697, French forces from Guiana invaded Amapá, the Portuguese governor of Maranhão sent an expedition against them and drove them out. In the Treaty of Utrecht (1713), France recognized Portuguese claims to the disputed territory. Thus, the northwestern Boundary of modern Brazil was established.

## The South: Santa Catarina
## and Colônia do Sacramento

Brazilian expansion in the south began later than in the north and at first owed chiefly to private initiative. In the 1650s the discovery of modest deposits of gold at the southern extremes of the Captaincy of São Vicente led to the formation of several settlements at the mining sites. In the same decade emigrants from São Paulo started to drift southward into Santa Catarina, a region lying just south of the mines, and between 1653 and 1684 established three settlements on its coasts.

Official Portuguese interest extended much farther south — to the banks of the Rio de la Plata. Both Spain and Portugal claimed this region because of uncertainties about where the Line of Tordesillas intersected the South American continent. The treaty that had established the Line in 1494 had not specified the island in the Azores group from which 370 leagues were to be measured off westward to establish the division of the New World, nor had it defined the length of a league. In addition, contemporaries lacked the means of measuring longitude accurately. The Spanish consistently maintained that the line crossed the northeast coast of South America around Belém and the southeast coast just south of São Vicente. Portuguese writers contended that it lay far enough west to place the Plata estuary on their side, and some even claimed that it ran from the mouth of the Orinoco River in the north to Patagonia in the south.

These claims were largely academic during the union of the Hispanic crowns, but after Portugal finally gained its independence from the Spanish Habsburgs in 1665, they acquired practical strategic and economic importance. Portuguese officials now regarded control of the Rio de la Plata as vital to the security of Brazil and desirable for expanding an already flourishing clandestine trade with Upper Peru that involved bringing in African slaves and taking out silver. The Spanish felt that the presence of any foreign power on the estuary would pose a threat to the mines of Potosí and, of course, wished to halt the contraband that the Portuguese were so eager to foment.

At first officials in Lisbon and Brazil considered achieving their aims in one bold stroke by seizing Buenos Aires, but later settled for occupying the north bank of the Plata estuary, a region that came to be called the Banda Oriental (lying east of the Uruguay River). In 1680 Portuguese forces established the fortified post of Colônia do Sacramento just twenty-five miles across the upper estuary from Buenos Aires. This move provoked an armed struggle for the Banda Oriental that continued far beyond the temporal limits of this book. It is sufficient to say here that in that part of South America Spain enjoyed a strategic advantage, for the closest Portuguese base of support was Rio de Janeiro, several hundred miles to the north. In 1737 Portuguese forces attempted to close the gap by occupying the district of Rio Grande de São Pedro (Rio Grande do Sul) which extended south from Santa Catarina, but this move marked the southernmost limit of permanent Brazilian expansion. The Spanish eventually destroyed Colônia, and Spain sustained its claims to dominion in the Plata estuary.

The Interior:
The Paulistas and the *Sertão*

*Entradas* from coastal bases all the way from São Vicente to Pernambuco had begun to probe into the backlands in the 1560s, but deep and sustained penetration did not begin until later in the sixteenth century. The main base was the district of São Paulo. Its inhabitants, the Paulistas, were a hardy, enterprising, and independent people of mixed Portuguese and Indian blood, an apparent example of hybrid vigor. Since they could not raise sugar profitably owing to the costs of transportation to the coast, they looked into the interior for some source of wealth—preferably gold, silver, or precious gems.[5] But if treasure could not be found, Indian slaves would do, despite a series of royal orders prohibiting the enslavement of indigenes excepting those captured in a just war. The lay of the land favored their enterprises, for from their plateau homeland, rivers drained inland through open forest and grasslands.

The governor of São Paulo initiated the first Paulista *entradas* to punish hostile Indian tribes. These expeditions were organized as militia companies modeled on a metropolitan Portuguese army unit called a *companhia* or, because of the ensign under which it marched, a *bandeira* (banner). By extension, *entradas* in the south became known as *bandeiras*, and in the eighteenth century their members called *bandeirantes*. In the late 1500s the Paulistas began to organize *bandeiras* for their own purposes and in their own ways, and what began as an Old World military unit acquired New World organizational forms. *Bandeiras* varied in size from a few dozen members to as many as 3000, depending on the magnitude of their enterprises. Municipal officers of São Paulo with demonstrated prowess in Indian fighting and enjoying the headship of extended patriarchal families furnished the field masters. The expedition recruited its captains, lieutenants, and rank and file from free *vizinhos* and *moradores*, often tied to the leader by consanguinity or patron-client relationships. The total complement included wives and concubines, children down to babes in arms, servants, slaves both Indian and black, and native auxiliaries. As the American historian Richard Morse observed, they amounted to municipalities on the march.[6] Each *bandeirante* contributed to expenses and supplies according to his means and received in return a proportionate share of booty taken.

*Bandeiras* might be gone for many seasons — the longest of record spent eight years in the field — and they carried with them not only prepared rations, consisting mainly of manioc and dried corn and meat but seeds that they stopped to plant and await the harvest. They also drove livestock to be bred and slaughtered on the march. Although they generally followed rivers, they traveled on foot with native bearers providing transport for supplies. The *bandeirantes* were not only part Indian by birth but they adopted many indigenous usages and skills: on the march, techniques of pathfinding and the use of wild foods and medicaments; in tactics, the ambush and swift raid; in battle, the bow and arrow. They also favored a modified form of Indian apparel: short trousers and shirts of cotton and, perhaps, a leather jerkin or vest as an outer garment; for the head, a fur cap or broad-brimmed hat. Some wore leather boots, but most traveled barefoot. They slept on leather cots or in hammocks. For communication they employed the *lingua geral*, a form of the Tupí-Guaraní idiom that served as a lingua franca in the interior of southern South America.

By the end of the seventeenth century, the Paulistas had explored most of the territory forming the southern half of modern Brazil. They had penetrated south to the Uruguay River before being repulsed by the Guaraní militia, west to the eastern slopes of the Andes, and north to the upper Rio São Francisco and the tributaries of the Amazon. One of their *bandeiras* virtually "circumnavigated" Brazil. Led by Antônio Rapôso Tavares, it traveled west from São Paulo to Paraguay, north along the foothills of the Andes to the headwaters of the Madeira River, downstream to the Amazon, and then along the Great River to Belém. All in all, it traversed 8000 miles of wilderness, and its journey consumed most of the years 1648–51.

Although the Paulistas still served royal officials on occasion and took as many slaves as they could, in the last half of the seventeenth century they became increasingly interested in discovering precious metals. Their efforts eventually bore fruit. In the 1690s they found rich deposits of alluvial gold in the interior some 200 miles north of Rio de Janeiro. Their strike ended two centuries of Portuguese frustration and precipitated a rush of a magnitude not seen since the opening of Potosí and Zacatecas or again until the days of the California forty-niners. But the results of this bonanza fall beyond the time limits of this book.

The *bandeirantes* provided Brazil with its great colonial epic, and inevitably their exploits invite comparison with those of the Spanish conquistadors. Certainly the two types of adventurers possessed common attributes: physical hardihood, enterprise, audacity, and rapacity. They both ranged vast hinterlands, and, with their villainies filtered out by the mists of time, their deeds glow romantically. Like the expedition of conquest, the *bandeira* was an independent, freewheeling, quasi-military association, but it possessed a definable political, social, and economic organization. Some scholars, moreover, see structural and historical connections between the two types of enterprise. Many Spaniards joined the Paulista *entradas*, carrying with them the tradition of the Caribbean *compañía* and lending the vigorous spirit of the Spanish Conquest to the penetration of the *sertão*.[7] One authority views both the *compañía* and the *bandeira* as New World extensions of Reconquest *cabalgadas* and *algaras*.[8]

But the two types of New World *entradas* also had important differences. The conquerors were invading Europeans; they were medieval minded, subscribing to knightly virtues although not always practicing them; they rode horses when they could obtain them; many of them had an exalted sense of mission. And, although their flame burned high, it subsided quickly and in the end they became populators, the founders of towns. *Bandeirantes* were most emphatically of the New World by birth, identity, and loyalty; they slogged along faint tracks on foot for over a century; they were primarily pragmatic frontiersmen, and they left few permanent marks on the boundless backlands they roamed. In terms of historic role, they closely resembled the North American trapper and Indian fighter. They pointed the way.

Brazilian Cattle Frontiers

The epic of the *bandeirantes* tends to obscure the substantial achievements of other Brazilian frontiersmen. Bahian *entradas* continued well into the seventeenth century, exploring large stretches of territory in the drainage system of the Rio São Francisco and along the headwaters of the southern affluents of the Amazon. Meanwhile, cattlemen made important contributions to the opening of the interior. During the first stages of Portuguese colonization, stock raising developed as an adjunct to sugar planting, and plantations and ranches tended to be coterminous. Sugar, however, provided much better profits than livestock, and planting gradually squeezed herds out of valuable coastal lands, particularly after 1627, when the government imposed fencing laws to protect plantations. Thus, grazing began to creep into the interior along a broad front extending from São Paulo in the south to Ceará in the northeast.

The main avenue of advance led up the Rio São Francisco, beyond whose rather narrow valley stretched an upland country of grasslands and bush. During the 1600s, *vaqueiros* (cowmen) gradually moved up the river valley, reaching its middle course in the 1650s. At about this time Paulistas, called in to help put down Indian resistance, obtained lands on the upper stretches of the river, and toward the end of the century the two frontiers merged. In the early 1700s contemporaries reported that they could travel the 1500-mile length of the São Francisco, confident that they would find rest and rude hospitality at some ranch at the end of each day's journey.[9]

A second cattle frontier emerged somewhat farther to the north. In the early decades of the seventeenth century, ranchers from Paraíba and Ceará drifted inland to make the best of a land of eroded mesas and semiarid grasslands intermittently visited by drought. Advancing slowly to the south and west they eventually linked with the São Francisco frontier in the interior district called Piauí, thus creating a continuous cattle zone stretching from Ceará to the backlands of São Paulo. In the northeast, the Dutch occupation gave a substantial impetus to the movement forcing noncollaborating Brazilians back from the coast. In the eighteenth century another major ranching area developed in the Banda Oriental, but, as with the mining boom, its story lies beyond the scope of this book.

## Amazonia: The *Tropas*

Luso-Brazilians began to penetrate the Amazon basin shortly after the founding of Belém in 1616. Their *entradas* in that region were called *tropas*, and they fell into two functional categories. Public officials sent out *tropas de guerra* to conquer or punish hostile Indians. In some instances, missionaries accompanied them as vanguards of the faith and agents of pacification, serving in much the same way as Franciscans did on the northern frontier of New Spain. Private parties organized *tropas de resgate* to take slaves. The word *resgate* had a number of meanings. In this case it meant a rescue mission but in a euphemistic sense, that is, the "rescue" of "friendly" Indians taken captive by wild tribes. In terms of purpose, organization, range of operation, adaptation to native ways, intrepidity, and ruthlessness, the northern *tropas* resembled Paulista *bandeiras*. They differed, however, in their means of transport, for they traveled by canoe along interconnected interior waterways. The larger expeditions constituted veritable flotillas, bearing soldiers, families, native auxiliaries, and slaves, and were propelled along by Indian paddlers.

The most famous *tropa* had an overtly strategic mission. Its commander,

Captain Pedro Teixeira, had orders from the governor of Belém to assert Portuguese claims to Maynas, on the upper Amazon, where Spanish Franciscans had established reductions of Indians. Leaving Belém in October 1637, Teixeira voyaged up the main river and its tributaries into the foothills of the Ecuadorian Andes. There he left his flotilla and crossed the mountains to Quito, where he received a very stiff reception from Spanish officials. After returning to his fleet, he established a small station at a point roughly corresponding to the easternmost extension of modern Ecuador and then led his company back down the river to Belém, arriving in September 1639, after twenty-three months in the field.

During the next several decades the Portuguese consolidated their claims to the Amazon basin in several ways. The government placed forts at strategic points along the main river: in 1669, Fortaleza de São José da Barra do Rio Negro at the juncture of the Solimões and the Rio Negro; in 1697, Fortaleza de Santarém near the mouth of the Tapajoz; and in 1698, Forte d'Obidos where the Amazon narrows into a single channel only 1892 meters wide. Meanwhile Brazilian *tropas* probed the courses of the Amazon's main tributaries, and in the 1690s several *bandeiras* tried, unsuccessfully, to capture Santa Cruz de la Sierra. Then, in 1710, the governor of Belém forcibly expelled the Spanish missionaries from Maynas.

Scattered settlement followed in the wake of these penetrations. Small towns grew up around forts, inhabited by a few whites and rather more mixed bloods of diverse hues. At important river junctions, trading posts appeared to serve the needs of collectors of nuts, pepper, cloves, cinnamon, vanilla, indigo, pelts of animals, feathers of exotic birds, and other "harvests of the forests." At various points along the Great River and its tributaries, fishermen built tiny villages.

The Amazonian Missions

Missionaries played a part in the expansion of colonial Brazil, but it was more restricted than in the Spanish Indies. Their efforts lacked firm direction and the consistent support of the crown and its overseas officials. Also, their aim of converting and protecting the Indians conflicted with powerful local interests who wished to enslave the indigenes. In the south of Brazil, Jesuit protests against slaving so incensed the Paulistas that twice in the seventeenth century they expelled the Black Robes from São Paulo.

In the seventeenth century the main missionary frontier shifted north, supporting the advance of secular agencies into new territories. Jesuits aided in the pacification of the Indians along the northeast coast from Ceará to the island of Marajó, in the Amazon delta, and established missions in those regions. On the Amazon itself, Jesuits, Franciscans, and Carmelites served *tropas de guerra* as advance agents, interpreters, and negotiators. But they also tried to protect the Indians from enslavement. In the north, as in the south of Brazil, their humanitarian endeavors aroused the ire of slavers and local officials conniving in the slave trade.

During the latter half of the 1600s, the missionary effort became more determined, owing heavily to the conscience and enterprise of Antonio Vieira, S.J., who has sometimes been called the Las Casas of Brazil. In 1653 Vieira returned to Brazil from Lisbon, where he had gone to present a case for the evangelization and protection of the Indians. His arguments had been so persuasive that he brought back with him a royal order placing him in charge of missionary work in Brazil and enjoining royal officials, civil and religious corporations, and lay persons to assist and obey him.

Around 1660, Vieira drew up regulations for the organization and administration of *aldeias* that severely restricted civil access to Indian labor. Colonists in Maranhão responded to these measures just as they had in São Paulo. In 1661–62 and again in 1684, they rose against the missionaries and expelled them. These setbacks convinced the Jesuits and the crown that some compromise with settlers had to be made, and the outcome was the royal *Regimento das Missões do Estado do Maranhão e Grão-Pará* of 1686. This enactment provided that pacified Indians should be settled in *aldeias* under missionary management but that they could be drafted for service in households, on plantations, and as paddlers through *repartição* (allotment or partition) under regulated conditions, an arrangement closely resembling the Spanish American *repartimiento-mita*.

The role of the missionaries in frontier expansion increased substanially after the years 1693–95, when the king apportioned most of the Amazon Basin among the Jesuits, Franciscans, Carmelites, and Mercedarians. Their achievements, however, belong to the eighteenth century and are therefore beyond the scope of this book.

## Territorial Changes: A Summary Assessment

Territorial expansion and contraction in the seventeenth century pretty well defined the permanent external and internal boundaries of Hispanic America. Spain never regained the lands occupied by the northern European nations in North America and the Caribbean. In the eighteenth century it loosely occupied large regions north of Mexico, but it lacked the demographic resources to hold them. Ultimately, the northern limit of Spanish America fell back to approximately where it had been in 1700, along the "natural boundary" of the Rio Grande. Within Spanish America, the expansion of settlement helped to shape post-Independence political configurations. It extended or filled in the jurisdictions of audiencial districts and major provinces whose *uti possidetis* as of 1812 became the basis of the boundaries between the newly created nations.

In South America, Brazilian expansion bent the Line of Demarcation far to the west and eventually nullified it as a basis for territorial claims. Several circumstances contributed to this outcome.[10] Luso-Brazilians could use uncertainties about where the Line lay to justify advances far to the south and deep into the interior. The union of the Hispanic crowns between 1580 and 1640 favored Portuguese aspirations by loosening political boundaries between the Spanish and Portuguese empires in the New World. A case in point is the grant of two hereditary captaincies in the Amazon basin carelessly made by King Philip III of Spain (Philip II of Portugal) to two Portuguese nobles in 1637. According to Spanish interpretations the territory granted was far to the west of the boundary fixed at Tordesillas.

Logistical factors further favored the extension of Portuguese claims to the interior of South America. To reach it, Luso-Brazilians could move men and supplies up inland waterways; the Spaniards had first to cross infrequent and difficult Andean passes. Thus, after Teixeira's expedition, the viceroys of Peru warned the crown about Brazilian intentions in the upper Amazon and urged that defensive conquests be made in the region. Problems of moving an army across the cordillera, however, deterred such actions. A major exception to this generalization was the Rio de la Plata, where the Spaniards enjoyed a logistical advantage by virtue of their bases at Buenos Aires and Asunción.

Luso-Brazilians also had stronger motivations for pushing into the continental heartland. After sixteenth century *entradas* failed to discover other Perus, Spanish Americans tended to rest content with their mines and *repartimientos* in the sierras, and their kings, preoccupied with European affairs, had little interest in unmapped rain forests thinly inhabited by uncivilized indigenes. They left the defense of their claims to the missionary orders. In addition, some evidence suggests that Brazilian expansion expressed a deliberate geopolitical design, a conscious and powerful urge toward continental imperium. In the Amazon region, Teixeira ascended the Great River to establish Portuguese claims to its vast watershed; Jaime Cortesão, a leading historian of the *bandeirante* epic, believes that Rapôso Tavares "circumnavigated" Brazil for the same reason.[11] Luso-Brazilians drove the French from Maranhão and Amapá more to control the mouth of the river than for any intrinsic worth those regions possessed. As for the south, João Teixeira, a Portuguese royal cosmographer, declared in 1640 that the Rio de la Plata constituted the "natural boundary" of Brazil.[12] After Portugal regained its independence from Spain, and especially after the foundation of Colônia, its kings based their territorial claims in South America more on the principle of *uti possidetis de facto* than on *uti possidetis de jure*.

The extent to which geopolitical considerations guided Portuguese and Spanish expansion in South America is uncertain, but the efforts of both peoples produced important geopolitical consequences. By 1700 the effective boundaries between the Spanish and Portuguese empires in America generally conformed to the line where the furthest penetration of Brazilian *bandeiras* and *tropas* met the arc of Spanish trans-Andean, Venezuelan, and Paraguayan missions. In eighteenth-century treaties between the two Hispanic powers, Spain accepted the principle of *uti possidetis de facto*, and the limits just described became the basis of boundary settlements between Brazil and the Spanish American nations in the nineteenth century. The Banda Oriental constituted a special situation. It remained a bone of contention, first between Spain and Portugal, later between the Empire of Brazil and the Platine republics.

## American Roots of Hispanic Imperial Expansion

Some concluding remarks are in order about the kinds of people who added new territories to the Hispanic dominions in America. The Spanish and Portuguese crowns, united and separate, sometimes assigned directions and objectives for expansion and attempted to regulate procedures. But, for the most part, *hijos de la tierra* (sons of the land), Americans of all hues, followed their individual and collective urges and provided most of the energy and labor. The Brazilian *bandeirantes*, *tropas*, and *vaqueiros* were distinctively American types. In Mexico the generation of European conquerors opened the first northern mines and founded the first great haciendas, but their American-born sons, followed by mestizo and mulatto soldiers and cowboys, led subsequent expansion. In the Spanish Rio de la Plata the expedition that founded Santa Fe counted seventy-five mestizos in its full complement of eighty-four, and mixed bloods predominated in the company that refounded Buenos Aires. Rui Díaz, the mestizo grandson of Martín de Irala, recounted the colonizing exploits of his mixed-blood kin in *La Argentina*, published in 1612. In Chile many first-generation mestizos served Spain in the Araucanian wars. The governor of the kingdom informed the king in 1585 that, without them, all the land would be lost and exclaimed, "I should pray to God that there were as many good people among those sent to us from Spain as there are among these mestizos."[13]

# CHAPTER 16

# Post-Conquest Populations: Components, Numbers, Movements, Distribution

## Spanish America

Sources of Data

The kinds and spacing of data largely determine what can be said about the populations of Spanish America after the Conquest. In the seven decades or so that followed the preparation of López de Velasco's *Geografía y descripción universal de las Indias*,[1] a number of other "censuses" appeared. In 1577, the Council of the Indies sent out a questionnaire to provincial administrators eliciting detailed information on the political geography, topography, natural resources, defense, demography, and other features of their jurisdictions. During the next ten years returns slowly trickled in from Venezuela, New Granada, Quito, Peru, the Antilles, Central America, and New Spain, although many districts failed to comply, and subsequently a number of responses became lost. The surviving returns repose in Spanish archives, and a substantial part of them have been published.[2] Some decades later, in 1628, Antonio Vázquez de Espinosa wrote in his *Description of the Indies* (c. 1620), a province-by-province survey,[3] and in 1646 Juan Díaz de la Calle prepared another general description, *Memorial, y noticias sacras, y reales del imperio de las Indias occidentales*.[4]

Despite these compilations, systematically collected population data for the post-Conquest period tend to fall off in quality and quantity. Peter Boyd-Bowman's studies of European immigration end in 1600.[5] After 1610 or thereabouts, tribute lists and other fiscal documents that provide such a wealth of information about Indian demography become scattered in both time and space.

After 1640, it is much more difficult to determine slave imports. The Chaunu series stops in that year, and for a good reason.[6] During the union of the Hispanic crowns, the Portuguese had a monopoly on the slave trade to the Spanish Indies, and *asiento* records, if not entirely accurate, are reasonably complete and centralized for the period. Between 1640, when Portugal regained its independence, and 1651, the Spanish suspended the traffic, and, when Philip IV allowed it to resume, he gave contracts to companies of diverse nationalities so that data are scattered. Dutch and English traders, moreover, introduced a substantial number of Africans clandestinely via their islands in the Caribbean and through the Rio de la Plata. As for *mestizaje*, only one really systematic study of rates and qualitative and quantitative results exists, and it deals only with Mexico.[7] Substantial bodies of general and particular population data do not appear again until the 1740s.

It is tempting to speculate about the reasons for a hundred-year famine in demographic information. Does it simply mean that modern scholars have not gotten around to compiling information? Or does it reflect objective contemporary conditions: economic stagnation in many parts of the Indies in the seventeenth century, a withering of the vigor and efficiency of royal officials who were supposed to count people and things, the disappearance of curious and diligent cosmographers and geographers? In any event, the following sketch of demographic trends will have to rest on less substantial data than those used analyzing Conquest populations. This is especially true of observations made about the latter half of the seventeenth century.

The European Element:
Immigration and Natural Growth

The Swedish historian Magnus Mörner offers the most systematic estimates of post-Conquest Spanish emigration to the Indies. His figures are: for 1561–1600, 157,182; for 1601–25, 111,312; for 1626–50, 83,504. Yearly averages for each of the three periods are: for 1561–1600, 1587; for 1601–25, 4452; for 1626–50, 3340. Mörner's data did not permit him to extend his series beyond 1650 or to estimate the number of emigrants who eventually returned to Spain.[8]

The influences that governed the numbers and qualities of immigrants can only be inferred from contemporary conditions and sources. In Old Spain, the concentration of wealth and economic opportunity in the hands of the privileged classes continued in the late sixteenth century and on into the seventeenth. During the same years the Spanish kingdoms, especially Castile, fell on hard times owing to bad harvests and famines, plagues, excessive taxation, and monetary disorder. Some Spaniards, especially New Christians, found the religious climate intolerable. These circumstances unquestionably constituted push factors, encouraging or compelling emigration.

Pull factors also played a part. Although visions of conquest booty had largely vanished, the New World still appeared to offer brighter prospects to the disadvantaged and the improvident than did an impoverished homeland. The contemporary novelist Miguel de Cervantes described the Indies as "the refuge and haven of all poor devils of Spain, the sanctuary of the bankrupt, the safeguard of murderers, the way out for gamblers, the promised land for ladies of easy virtue, and a lure and disillusionment for the many, and an incomparable remedy for the few."[9] Spanish American viceroys, governors, and bishops fretted about the numbers of indigent, shiftless, and malicious Spaniards constantly arriving in their jurisdictions. The developing economies and expanding bureaucracies of the Indies also attracted more stable types: merchants, *letrados*, and clergy, although colonial officials complained about the mischief done by fee-hungry lawyers and licentious priests. Male immigrants still outnumbered female, but exact sex ratios have not been determined.

Most immigrants still came from southern and central Spain, but in the late 1600s an increasing proportion arrived from Galicia, the Asturias, Santander, and the Basque counties. Perhaps their emigration reflected overpopulation in the north and the need for the excess to seek their fortunes overseas. Immigrants continued to include a sprinkling of foreigners. Among them Portuguese still predominated owing to their traditional cultural affinities with Castilians and the loosening of restrictions occasioned by the union of the Hispanic crowns between 1580 and 1640. They appear to have been most numerous in the Rio de la Plata because of its proximity to Brazil. Significant Portuguese mercantile colonies also appeared in Potosí and on the West Indian islands. Italians, particularly Genoese, living in the principal commercial centers of the Indies made up the second largest identifiable foreign element. Despite the vigilance of the Holy Office, Jews and New Christians made their way to the Spanish New World in undetermined numbers, mainly from or via Portugal.

Most immigrants, perhaps a quarter of the total, went to the relatively stable, prosperous, and environmentally congenial Kingdom of New Spain. Peru, where colonization really did not get into full swing until the 1570s, attracted the second largest contingent. Numbers and proportions going to other parts of the Indies are uncertain, but probably the kingdoms of New Granada and Quito along with the recently occupied Rio de la Plata were the preferred destinations.

Spanish fecundity did not abate after the Conquest, and the disparate sex ratio narrowed, mainly through the increase of American-born women, including Europeanized *mestizas* as well as those of pure European stock. It was these circumstances, rather than 3000 to 4000 immigrants a year, that produced perhaps a threefold increase in the white population of the Indies between 1570 and the mid-seventeenth century.

What happened after that is uncertain, but some circumstantial evidence suggests that even before 1650 the rate of white population growth began to slow. A number of eminent scholars have proposed that the economy of the Indies contracted significantly beginning in the early decades of the seventeenth century.[10] The causes, extent, severity, and duration of the setback are still being debated and the issues will be examined in the following chapter. It may be observed here, however, that historically, long-term economic downturns are associated with demographic reversals, and this may have been the case in the Spanish Indies as it was in many parts of seventeenth-century Europe.

A more ponderable influence was disease. Epidemics struck American cities, where most of the European population lived, with destructive frequency in the seventeenth century. In some instances the attackers were smallpox and measles, which affected mainly indigenous inhabitants, but bubonic plague also appeared and it made no racial distinctions. Sometime before 1648 yellow fever, called *vómito negro* (the black vomit), arrived from Africa on the coasts of Cuba, Yucatán, and Veracruz. By the end of the seventeenth century it was endemic in most parts of tropical America, and, in contrast to measles and smallpox, it chose whites as its main victims. Earthquakes and volcanic eruptions also caused great destruction to population centers in a zone running through the American cordillera from Guatemala to southern Chile.[11]

The Indigenous Population:
Decline and Recovery

After the 1570s severe epidemics continued to afflict the American Indian, but scattered evidence, mainly from tributary counts, suggests that the demographic damage became progressively less catastrophic.

Trends appear to have varied from region to region. In central Mexico, the decline that began during the Conquest continued into the early seventeenth century, but data for selected towns in that region and for the Audiencia of New Galicia point to a slow increase in the latter half of the 1600s. Research on the native population of the province of Sonsonate in Central America shows a slight growth between the mid-sixteenth century and about 1680, and one scholar affirms that in Central America as a whole, an increase occurred in the seventeenth century.

In South America, studies of particular Indian districts of New Granada reveal a continued decline throughout most of the seventeenth century and possibly into the eighteenth. The most comprehensive figures for Peru show that the number of indigenes dropped by half between 1570 and 1630, from 1,290,680 to 601,645. In contrast, the *Relaciones geográficas* from the province of Quito in the late sixteenth century report that the Indians were increasing, and letters from the Audiencia of Quito to the king around 1700 assert that the indigenous population of the Ecuadorian sierra was growing. The compilers of the *Relaciones geográficas* offered an explanation of their findings. The Indians were much better treated under the Spaniards than they had been under the Incas. This opinion may have overstated the benignity of Spanish rule, but of all the major Indian areas in the New World Ecuador may have suffered the least from the Conquest and its aftermath.[12]

Translating these scattered estimates and impressions into gross trends and totals is very risky. In the first place, they are not necessarily representative or broadly indicative. In the second, figures based on head counts of tributaries mask a very important demographic variable, that is, internal migration, voluntary and involuntary. Throughout Spanish America Indians evaded the exactions of *encomenderos* and *corregidores* by fleeing their villages and hiding in the native *barrios* (wards) of European towns, by obtaining employment in mines and remote haciendas, and by finding refuge among unconquered tribes. Thus, in central Mexico many of the inhabitants in regions disturbed by exploitations and resettlement moved into the thinly occupied Bajío beginning in the last decades of the sixteenth century. The Spaniards also shifted large numbers of Indians around in connection with pacification and colonization. In New Spain, they brought Tlaxcalans and Tarascans north to settle the frontier. In the province of Tucumán, they shipped captives taken in wars wholesale to Catamarca, La Rioja, Santa Fe, and Buenos Aires. Because of these movements, reduced tributary counts in many regions may reflect displacement rather than demographic decline.

Finally, elusive and imponderable factors affected tallies of the native peoples. *Mestizaje* diminished the number of "pure" Indians without decreasing the indigenous gene pool. In some instances Indians, by changing residence or occupation, came to be counted as mestizos, thus accomplishing a cultural transference from one population group to another.

Although contemporary data on the indigenous population are deficient in quantity and quality, some general demographic trends may be postulated. By mid-seventeenth century, the decline had reached its nadir and recuperation had begun in some districts. Among the major Indian areas the tide turned first in Ecuador, next in central Mexico and perhaps Guatemala, and then in New Granada. In Upper and Lower Peru, the drop did not end until well into the eighteenth century. But even in the more fortunate regions recovery was slow and faltering. The indigenous peoples of Spanish America as a whole did not begin to approach pre-Conquest numbers until the middle of the twentieth century.

It is tempting to speculate about the causes of these trends. The general slowdown in population decline may be attributed to the development of resistance to European diseases among the Indians. Regional differences are harder to explain. Perhaps the contrasting experiences of New Spain and Peru stemmed from different working conditions in the two regions. The shift from forced to free wage labor in the seventeenth century proceeded more rapidly in Mexico and Central America than it did in New Granada and Peru. The case of Ecuador is an as yet unexplained anomaly.

The Black Population:
Numbers and Provenance

The black population of Spanish America grew significantly after the Conquest years. Professor Philip Curtin's calculations, based principally on *asiento* records, produce the most up-to-date and comprehensive estimates of the numbers arriving from Africa via the slave trade during the seventeenth century: for 1601–25, 75,000; for 1626–50, 52,500; for 1651–75, 62,500; for 1676–1700, 102,500.[13] Some apparent but undemonstrable correlations exist among this series, supply-demand situations, and organizational changes in the slave trade. During the second twenty-five-year period, imports fell off substantially from the first, reflecting perhaps the deflation of the great Indies boom after the 1620s as well as the suspension of the slave trade after 1640. During the third period, after the resumption of the traffic, volume picked up modestly, and during the fourth it almost doubled, possibly in response to economic recovery in the last decade of the seventeenth century. Professor Sánchez-Albornoz, however, believes that Curtin's figures for the latter half of the century are excessive in light of interruptions occasioned by inefficient organization of the trade as well as slack demand throughout most of the period.[14] The disagreement cannot be resolved at the present state of knowledge, especially in view of the lack of data on illicit importations.

In the seventeenth century the source of supply of slaves shifted heavily from the Sudanese on the Guinea coast to the Bantu peoples in Angola as a result of continued Portuguese-African and tribal wars in the latter region and possibly disruptions in the Guinea trade occasioned by Dutch and English intrusions. Unfortunately, no seventeenth-century series showing American destinations of African slaves are available. Curtin's do not begin until the eighteenth century. Neither can comprehensive sets of data be found on the demographic qualities of slave populations—family formation, fertility, sex ratios, birth and mortality rates—that affected natural growth. A sample of 6884 blacks sold in the Lima market between 1560 and 1650 shows 2726 (39.5 percent) to be women. Among *bozales* imported directly from Africa the percentage of females was 34.5.[15] This ratio would theoretically permit a natural increase, but the separation of the sexes, careful supervision of cohabitation by masters, and abortions inhibited fecundity, while the physical conditions of slavery produced a high mortality rate among both infants and adults. Free blacks did not suffer these disabilities, but they constituted a minority of the Afro-American population. It appears, therefore, that it could grow or even be maintained only by constant supplements from Africa.

## Asiatics

In the last quarter of the sixteenth century other ethnic elements appeared in the Indies, mainly as involuntary immigrants. They consisted of Filipino, Chinese, Japanese, and even a few East Indian slaves and servants whom the Spaniards brought from Manila to New Spain. From there some dispersed to other parts of the Indies, mainly to Peru, with which Mexican merchants had established a substantial trade. The Orientals imported, however, never numbered more than a few thousand and did not constitute a significant element in the American population mix.

## Mixed Bloods

Diverse influences affected the rate and forms of miscegenation in the late sixteenth and seventeenth centuries. Some were restrictive. The Spanish crown adopted a more rigorous policy of racial segregation, mainly to protect the Indians from exploitation and moral corruption. In 1578 it ordered blacks, mulattoes, and mestizos excluded from Indian villages, and in 1600 it extended the prohibition to Spaniards. It also tried to reinforce segregation in European towns and settlements. It required the permanent native population to live in clearly marked off wards, and, when *repartimientos* took villagers off to work in the mines and urban *obrajes*, they had to be kept in separate quarters. It is likely, also, that interracial marriages declined in the seventeenth century, at least proportionately. Spanish racial—or cultural—prejudices hardened perceptibly after the Conquest years; the crown took a stronger stand against such unions, and in any case, as the numbers of Spanish American women increased, seekers after brides had less occasion to turn to other racial groups.

But positive forces far outweighed legal and social inhibitions against miscegenation. Spanish males exhibited an unrestrained propensity for concubinage, and women of an "inferior" race tended to prefer liaison with a "superior" to marriage with men of their own kind. In addition, official segregation policies broke down everywhere. White and mixed-blood vagrants tarried in native communities long enough to leave their seed or settled permanently in them, procreating energetically. Conversely, village Indians seeking work or dodging tribute collectors drifted into European towns and mining camps and onto haciendas. In these places, it proved impossible to segregate them and, no one tried very hard to do so. Such migrations contributed not only to genetic but to cultural *mestizaje*, thus affecting population counts.

Territorial expansion in the seventeenth century also encouraged miscegenation. Spaniards and mestizo frontiersmen encountered new tribes of Indians and, as conquerors, had their way with native women. On a smaller scale, Spanish men and women captured in frontier wars mixed with unpacified tribes. Runaway black slaves established communities called *palenques* or *cumbes* in remote regions in Ecuador, Panama, Nicaragua, and New Granada, where they took Indian wives and sired a new generation of *zambos*. Meanwhile, in towns and countryside throughout the Indies, mixed bloods of all hues mated, generally without benefit of clergy, to produce a population whose genetic complexity increased to a point where fine distinctions became impossible.

The bulk of impressionistic evidence suggests a rapid increase in the mixed-blood population during the seventeenth century despite discriminatory legislation, plagues, natural disasters, and, possibly, economic depression. Cook and Borah's quantitative analysis of racial groups in Mexico supports this view. Their calculations yield 79,396 mestizos and *pardos* in 1646 amounting to 5.3 percent of the total population and 38.8 percent of the non-Indian component as compared with 24,973 mestizos and *pardos* in 1568–70, making up 0.9 percent of the total and 28.5 percent of the nonindigenous population.[16]

## The Population of Brazil

### The European Element

Brazilian population data are fuller for the seventeenth century than for the sixteenth, but only because more bits and pieces exist. Immigrants from Portugal contributed to the population of European origin at the rate of about 1000 a year during the first decades of the seventeenth century. The Dutch occupation of the north caused the volume to drop in the mid-1600s. When the intruders left, however, the flow resumed, and after about 1680 immigrants arrived at a rate of some 2000 annually.[17]

A contemporary Portuguese who knew Brazil well explained in 1645 why his compatriots left home for a new land: "Portugal has no other region more fertile, nor close at hand nor more frequented, nor have its vassals a better or safer refuge than Brazil. The Portuguese who is overtaken by any misfortunes at home emigrates thither."[18] What these misfortunes might have been can be inferred from what is known about seventeenth-century Portugal. The kingdom as a whole could not be said to have been overpopulated, but the province of Minho had a density of 800 per square mile, enough to create pressures, and both the Azores and the Madeiras had too many people for their resources. Other influences contributed to emigration. Portugal was a poor country in which commoners, both rural and urban, and many *fidalgos* lived at a bare subsistence level. Visitations of plagues and frequent famines made their lives even more precarious. The Azores, another source of immigrants, also suffered from plague and famine as well as earthquakes and storms.[19] Particular classes of people had their special misfortunes. During the union of the crowns, Spanish pressures brought Jews and New Christians under closer inquisitorial scrutiny and many sought refuge in Brazil. And, it must be said, some Portuguese created problems that induced them to seek refuge overseas: bankruptcy through improvidence, social ostracism because of dissolute behavior, and criminal acts of violence.

Studies of the regional origins of immigrants reveal the following patterns. Among those going to Pernambuco, northerners from Minho predominated, continuing a trend established by Duarte Coelho, who encouraged his compatriots from that province to immigrate to his captaincy. For São Vicente and São Paulo, a sample of wills and testaments of 113 persons shows that 42.5 percent came from the north (Galliza, Minho, Douro, Tras-os-Montes, and Beira) and 37 percent from the south (Alentejo, Estremadura, and the

Algarves).[20] Disagreement exists about the regional origins of Portuguese coming to Bahia. Carlos B. Ott, a leading Bahian art and cultural historian, finds that the northern province of Entre Douro e Minho provided nearly half of a sampling he made for the seventeenth century, and Estremadura, mainly Lisbon, a quarter. The southern provinces sent only about 2.5 percent.[21] The Brazilian social historian Thales de Azevedo, however, believes that most Bahian immigrants came from the "strongly arabized" southern provinces although they often sailed from northern ports, a practice that masked their actual origin.[22] Throughout the 1600s, the Azores and the Canaries contributed a significant number of immigrants, in some instances because of crown population policy. In the middle decades of the century some hundreds of islanders came to sparsely settled Maranhão and Pará under royal auspices.

The following assumptions are generally made about the social qualities of immigrants. Although records show entire families going to Brazil, especially from the Azores and the Canaries, most of those who left metropolitan Portugal continued to be single males, and the sex ratio among emigrants was probably more disproportionately male than among Spaniards going to America. The common element in Portuguese society predominated, but the mix within this class changed after about 1570. In the early years of colonization it contained a high proportion of *degredados*; in the seventeenth century most immigrants came voluntarily. Although peasants continued to be an important group, increasing numbers of urban dwellers—artisans, merchants, and professional people—arrived to swell the population of Brazilian towns. Jewish and New Christian immigration also increased in the 1600s, and by 1700 businessmen, planters, traders, masons, clergymen, teachers, and poets of Jewish origin constituted a significant proportion of the population. Many entered through the back door, so to speak. They had first fled to Holland and then came to Brazil during the Dutch occupation.

During the seventeenth century Brazil continued to accommodate an indeterminate number of foreigners including Flemish, Italian, German, and English residents, but Spain contributed most of the non-Portuguese element, a representation undoubtedly encouraged by the union of the Hispanic crowns. Inquisition records spanning the years 1591–93 for northern Brazil show that Spaniards constituted by far the largest component of the foreign population, some 37.8 to 55.0 percent. In the southern provinces of São Vicente and São Paulo, which abutted on the Spanish Rio de la Plata, their presence was even more noticeable.[23]

Just as in Spanish America, hardly anything is known about the rate of natural growth among whites in Brazil. In view of the rather meager flow of immigration, natural growth probably accounted for much of a rather substantial overall increase that occurred in the century as indicated in the following rough series: in 1570, 20,000; in 1583, 25,000; in 1600, 30,000; in 1624, 50,000; in 1650, 70,000; in 1700, 100,000.[24] It should be borne in mind, however, that the sums undoubtedly included a substantial number of assimilated mixed bloods. They had a cultural rather than a purely ethnic European identity.

Blacks, Indians, and Mixed Bloods

Estimates made by the Brazilian historian Mauricio Goulart show a rapid increase in the number of blacks in Portuguese America in the last decades of the 1500s and throughout most of the 1600s: 2000–3000 in 1570, 9000–10,000 in 1590, 12,000–15,000 in 1600, and 100,000 around 1670.[25] Slaves acccounted for most of these totals. Little is known about the demographic characteristics of the colonial Brazilian slave population, but it is generally assumed that natural increase within it was low or even negative because of high death rates and low birth rates. Its growth, therefore, must have owed to introductions from Africa. This conclusion is supported by Curtin's estimates of the volume of the slave trade to Brazil: for 1576-1600, 40,000; for 1601-25, 100,000; for 1626-50, 100,000; for 1651-75, 185,000; for 1676-1700, 175,000.[26] Thus, imports for the period 1576-1675 totaled 425,000, but, according to Goulart, around 1670 the black population was only 100,000.

Slaves introduced into Brazil in the 1600s came mainly from the Congo, Angola, and Benguela, although Guinea continued to supply significant numbers. During the Dutch occupation of Luanda, Angola, and of Benguela (1641-63), the Portuguese began tapping sources in Mozambique, and, in the latter half of the seventeenth century, Brazil received occasional shipments from that region.

Virtually no firm data exist for other racial groups in the Brazilian population, but contemporary observations and modern conjectures suggest that by mid-seventeenth century European diseases, slaving, and miscegenation had reduced the Indians to a minor component in that part of the colony effectively occupied by the Portuguese. The survivors lived chiefly in missions in São Vicente, around Bahia, and in Pará and Maranhão. Beyond the sketchily drawn frontiers of settlement, an uncounted number of unpacified natives maintained a seminomadic existence. As for mixed bloods, mestiçagem played an increasingly important part in population formation for familiar reasons: the shortage of European women, relaxed sexual attitudes among all classes of people, and the master-slave or master-servant relationships that prevailed between the Portuguese on the one hand and blacks, Indians, and early generations of mixed bloods on the other.

## The Population of Hispanic America at Mid-Seventeenth Century

Since the period covered by this book ends around 1700, it would be satisfying to present a numerical summary of the results of population formation in Hispanic America as of that date. Unfortunately, the absence of data for the last half of the seventeenth century would make such an exercise specious. Hence, figures for the mid-seventeenth century must serve. Again, as for the year 1570 (see table 1, p. 131), Angel Rosenblat's hemispheric compilation furnishes a point of departure if for no other reason than that it is the only one available. It is reproduced in table 6 with some changes and with totals for 1570 added for comparision.

The table gives a plausible ranking of the several regions of Hispanic America by the size of their populations. It also presents a verisimilar picture of the relative numerical strength of the several main groups—whites, blacks, Indians, and mixed bloods—in the total populations of both Spanish America and Brazil. Its absolute numbers, however, may be questioned on several grounds. Henry Dobyns believes that Rosenblat greatly overestimated the number of indigenous peoples in 1650 and that 4,000,000 for the entire hemisphere would be a generous figure.[27] Dobyns's skepticism is supported by several regional studies. Sherburne F. Cook and Woodrow Borah calculated that only 1,293,420 Indians survived in Mexico in 1646.[28] Noble David Cook, a leading North American authority on the indigenous population of Peru, concluded that it totaled no more than 598,026 in 1620.[29] Rosenblat's count of Indians raises another problem. It includes large numbers living outside of regions effectively occupied by Spain and Portugal and who, therefore, cannot be considered as part of the "effective population" of Hispanic America. This is especially true of Brazil, Chile, and the Rio de la Plata region.

With reference to non-Indian peoples, Sherburne F. Cook and Woodrow Borah calculated that 157,907 whites, blacks, mulattoes, and mestizos dwelt in Mexico in 1646, less than half of the total of these groups (400,000) in table 6.[30] The author of the present book believes that Rosenblat's estimates of whites in the Antilles and Argentina and of Antillean blacks are much too high.

Conflicting opinions of the sizes of Hispanic American populations around the mid-1600s lead to different interpretations of long-range trends. Assuming

Table 6

Estimated Population of Hispanic America in about 1650 (as Compared with 1570)

| Year | Region | Whites | Blacks | Mulattoes | Mestizos | Indians | Total |
|------|--------|--------|--------|-----------|----------|---------|-------|
| 1650 | Spanish North America | | | | | | |
| | Mexico | 200,000 | 30,000 | 20,000 | 150,000 | 3,400,000 | 3,800,000 |
| | Central America | 50,000 | 20,000 | 10,000 | 30,000 | 540,000 | 650,000 |
| | Antilles | 80,000 | 400,000 | 114,000 | 10,000 | 10,000 | 614,000 |
| | Subtotal | 330,000 | 450,000 | 144,000 | 190,000 | 3,950,000 | 5,064,000 |
| | Spanish South America | | | | | | |
| | Colombia | 50,000 | 60,000 | 20,000 | 20,000 | 600,000 | 750,000 |
| | Venezuela | 30,000 | 30,000 | 10,000 | 20,000 | 280,000 | 370,000 |
| | Ecuador | 40,000 | 60,000 | 10,000 | 20,000 | 450,000 | 580,000 |
| | Peru | 70,000 | 60,000 | 30,000 | 40,000 | 1,400,000 | 1,600,000 |
| | Bolivia | 50,000 | 30,000 | 5,000 | 15,000 | 750,000 | 850,000 |
| | Paraguay | 20,000 | 10,000 | 5,000 | 15,000 | 200,000 | 250,000 |
| | Uruguay | | | | | 5,000 | 5,000 |
| | Argentina | 50,000 | 10,000 | 10,000 | 20,000 | 250,000 | 340,000 |
| | Chile | 15,000 | 5,000 | 2,000 | 8,000 | 520,000 | 550,000 |
| | Subtotal | 325,000 | 265,000 | 92,000 | 158,000 | 4,455,000 | 5,295,000 |
| | Total Spanish America | 655,000 | 715,000 | 236,000 | 348,000 | 8,405,000 | 10,359,000 |
| | Percentage of total | 6.3 | 6.9 | 2.3 | 3.4 | 81.1 | 100.0 |
| 1570 | Total Spanish America | 118,000 | ← – – – – | – – – 230,000 | – – – → | 8,907,150 | 9,255,150 |
| | Percentage of total | 1.3 | | 2.5 | | 96.2 | 100.0 |
| 1650 | Brazil | 70,000 | 100,000 | 30,000 | 50,000 | 700,000 | 950,000 |
| | Percentage of total | 7.4 | 10.5 | 3.2 | 5.3 | 73.7 | 100.0 |
| 1570 | Brazil | 20,000 | ← – – – – | – – – 30,000 | – – – → | 800,000 | 850,000 |
| | Percentage of total | 2.4 | | 3.5 | | 94.1 | 100.0 |

Source: Adapted from table 3 in Angel Rosenblat, *La población indígena y el mestizaje en América, 1492–1950*, 2 vols. (Buenos Aires: Editorial Nova, 1954), I, 59.

that the totals in table 6 for 1570 are roughly verisimilar, Rosenblat's estimates show a small increase in the inhabitants of both Spanish America (from 9,255,150 to 10,359,000) and Brazil (from 850,000 to 950,000) between 1570 and 1650. This occurred because a growth in the number of Europeans, Africans, and mixed bloods more than offset indigenous losses. If more conservative estimates of the number of Indians surviving around the mid-seventeenth century are used, the populations of both regions would have declined significantly despite the increase in nonindigenous peoples. Furthermore, the proportion of Indians in the general population would have dropped significantly.

In the presence of these disagreements and in the absence of solid demographic information for many parts of the Hispanic New World, only conjectures can be offered about post-Conquest populations. The weight of existing evidence suggests that Rosenblat's totals for all main groups should be revised downward, and those for Indians substantially. It is likely, therefore, that total populations did actually decline between 1570 and 1650. But a steady growth in nonindigenous elements coupled with a slowdown in Indian losses portended a reversal of this trend that, in fact, happened in the eighteenth century and possibly earlier.

The formation of Hispanic American populations had important regional variations. In highland Middle America and in the central Andes, enough Indians survived to constitute a large majority. Whites and mixed bloods, especially mestizos, were a small but growing minority. In northern Mexico, central Chile, and the Rio de la Plata, where pre-Conquest inhabitants had been fewer, the disproportion between whites and Indians was smaller and the proportion of mestizos greater. In the Antilles, along the tropical coasts of the Caribbean and the Mexican Gulf, and in the coastal part of Brazil, the indigenous population had practically disappeared. It was replaced by a white minority and a black and mulatto majority. Thus, by the mid-seventeenth century three main ethnic and cultural areas had begun to emerge that some authorities have termed Indo-America, Mestizo-America, and Afro-America.

## The Territorial Organization of Spanish American Populations

### Spanish Urbanization

In the immediate post-Conquest decades, urbanization in the Spanish Indies continued unabated. The Spanish founded new towns in both newly occupied territories and previously conquered regions. In 1570, López de Velasco counted 225 Spanish municipalites; in 1628 Vázquez de Espinosa enumerated

331. In the same interval, the increase in the total number of *vecinos* was probably greater than these figures suggest because López gave population data for 189 of the 225 communities he listed whereas Vázquez did so for only 165 of his 331 towns and cities.

Two Argentine urban historians, Jorge Hardoy and Carmen Aranovich, have used the data compiled by López and Vázquez to calculate indices of growth. By dividing López's count of *vecinos* into that of Vázquez, they obtained an "absolute index" of 3.3 for Spanish America as a whole. By adjusting for the discrepancies between the numbers of vecinos and the number of municipalities counted by the two Spanish authorities, they arrived at an absolute index that is somewhat higher, 3.8.[31]

Hardoy and Aranovich also use regional data in López and Vázquez to calculate growth indices for the several audiencial districts in Spanish America between 1580 and 1630. As might be expected, the relative indices are above the general average in those districts possessing the richest and most diverse resources, the greatest stability, and the most salubrious natural environment: Quito (8.25), Mexico (5.82), Santa Fe de Bogotá (4.43), and Guadalajara (3.82). The depressed islands of the Audiencia of Santo Domingo also had an above average index (3.87), but this owed mainly to a twentyfold increase in the population of Havana. The indices for the Audiencias of Charcas (2.77) and Lima (2.67) fell below the average, despite the remarkable expansion of Potosí in Charcas and the substantial growth of the city of Lima, the viceregal capital. Possibly because of chronic problems in its cacao industry, the index for the Audiencia of Guatemala was only 1.32. That for Panama was only 1.32, owing mainly to a lack of indigenous labor. Among all the American audiencias, only Chile showed an index of decrease (0.95). Although its resources were bountiful and its natural environment hospitable, the Araucanian wars discouraged the growth of its towns and cities.[32]

Post-Conquest urbanization had still another aspect. Continuing a trend already well established by 1580, main centers — viceregal and audiencial capitals, the seats of bishoprics, and prosperous mining centers — grew most rapidly. In 1580, 40 percent of the total urban population lived in cities with more than 10,000 members of Spanish households, 60 percent in smaller places. Percentages for 1630 were 75 in the former category of municipalities and 25 in the latter.

Scattered evidence suggests that after about 1630 urban growth in the Indies may have slackened except, perhaps, in major administrative centers. This turn can be attributed tentatively to several circumstances. It may have meant that the sizes of towns had reached a limit imposed by the human and natural resources of their hinterlands. Perhaps it also reflected a slowdown in the rate of increase among Europeans and Europeanized mixed bloods, who constituted the officially enumerated residents of incorporated communities. This trend may have been accompanied by some migration from towns and cities to rural areas, a subject that will be examined later in this chapter.

Some communities experienced actual population losses owing to their particular economic circumstances. Thus, because of a sharp decline in silver production, the inhabitants of Potosí shrank from 160,000 souls in 1650 to perhaps 40,000 in 1705, and by the last part of the seventeenth century many mining communities in northern Mexico had lost half of the residents they had held in the early 1600s.[33]

Indian Urbanization in Spanish America:
Reductions, Civil Congregations, and *Resguardos*

Urbanization in the Spanish Indies also involved the indigenous population. In the last decades of the sixteenth century the royal government in Peru, New Granada, and Mexico undertook to concentrate or reconcentrate Indians in new corporate communities. The program resembled the congregation undertaken by the mendicant orders in Mexico and Guatemala immediately after the Conquest, but it differed in important respects. First, it had primarily civil objectives: to facilitate the collection of tribute and the distribution of labor; to integrate Indian administration more closely with royal government; to define and protect communal lands; and to separate the natives from contaminating contact with Europeans and mixed bloods. Civil officials planned and executed resettlement. Second, public convenience rather than traditional tribal and community associations governed the distribution and location of new settlements.

Officials in the three regions employed essentially the same procedures and organizational forms. They began with careful planning, which included population counts and land surveys. From the data collected they determined appropriate sites and the Indians to be moved to them. The physical layout of towns followed the most advanced tendencies in European urban planning. They had commodious central plazas faced by churches, often of outsized proportions and elaborate design, and municipal buildings. Streets were laid out at right angles from the ends of each side of the plaza and, intersecting with lateral thoroughfares, formed blocks. Each family received a residential lot, and some streets were set aside for shops. The crown granted newly founded communities rural lands in communal ownership and with inalienable tenure. One portion was reserved for subsistence crops, another for pastures and woodlands, and a third for commercial production. Cash flow from the last furnished capitalization for community needs such as tools, livestock, savings, and administration. Indian *cabildos* provided municipal government, although to convey legitimacy to such bodies royal officials allowed them to be dominated by local nobles, and *corregidores* and resident curates supervised local affairs closely.

The king's officials carried out Indian resettlement at different times and using different designations in the several regions affected. The program began first in Peru shortly after the arrival of Viceroy Toledo, perhaps because a more immediate need for it existed there. By the late 1560s the mines of Potosí and Huancavelica required massive and continuous drafts of labor but, despite the earlier efforts of mendicant friars to congregate the natives for religious purposes, most of them continued to dwell in isolated and dispersed hamlets close to ancient holy places. Consequently, *corregidores* found it difficult to mobilize them. In Peru the new settlements were called reductions, following religious usage.

In Mexico, officials did not undertake resettlement until somewhat later, between 1598 and 1606, perhaps because they perceived the need to be less urgent. Mexican mines did not depend as heavily on draft labor as those in Peru, and the mendicant friars had already made some progress in regrouping the native population. New Indian communities in Mexico were called *congregaciones civiles* (civil congregations). In New Granada congregation began in the 1580s and was closely associated with the creation of *resguardos de Indios* (lands reserved for the benefit of Indians), to be granted to newly formed indigenous communities.

The actual results of resettlement are hard to determine. Some quantative information is available for Mexico. The probable number of congregations created came to 187. Their size varied from a maximum of 850 tributaries to a minimum of 50, with most falling in the range 250–300. All told, congregation affected only about 80,000 tributaries or some 320,000 Indians, that is, no more than 16 percent of the indigenous population.[34] The explanation for this apparently modest result is uncertain. Congregation was certainly expensive and time-consuming and encountered opposition from *encomenderos*, landowners, and churchmen, who felt their vested interests threatened. Officials, therefore, may have limited their efforts to regions where they deemed the need to be greatest. Information on Peru is very summary, amounting to statements that the program was pan-Peruvian and completed during the early 1570s. In

New Granada, it appears that most of the Indians of the provinces of Tunja and Villa de Leiva (present-day Department of Boyacá) had been concentrated in reductions and provided with *resguardos* by 1642.

## Spanish American Ruralization

Urbanization was accompanied by an opposite movement, namely, ruralization, which is here taken to mean the settlement of individuals or the formation of permanent population nuclei outside of incorporated municipalities. Ruralization took a number of forms and had diverse causes. It began, or, at least, first became perceptible, in the late sixteenth century because of Indian population decline. When Spanish towns could no longer subsist on what could be obtained from the indigenes, Europeans turned directly to the commercial production of foodstuffs. To meet growing demands, they expanded their original land grants and obtained new ones from the crown, with the result that centers of agricultural production moved farther and farther from urban centers and often from sources of labor. Ranchers, therefore, built permanent installations on their haciendas and *estancias*, including residences for their permanent work forces and houses for themselves. They lived on their rural estates part of the year but retained their status as *vecinos* of the city or town of their primary residence. Some of the larger estates became rural population nuclei.

During the same period, along routes leading from towns to rural estates, crossroads settlements sprang up performing service functions for the inhabitants of the countryside and for travelers. They often had churches and resident priests. They were unincorporated and existed as administrative satellites of the chief town of the district. Their inhabitants were poor Spaniards and mixed bloods who could not find posts or livelihoods in urban centers. Indian depopulation also encouraged another kind of urban-rural migration. Town-dwelling *encomenderos*, unable to subsist on the tribute delivered to them through official channels, moved into the countryside to live directly from the production of the Indians. Spanish and mixed-blood indigents joined them. The magnitude of the various kinds of movements from towns to rural habitats is conjectural, but in some areas it was sufficient to concern public officials. The *alcalde* of Cartago in New Granada, for example, exhorted the inhabitants to *hacer vecinidad*, that is, to maintain a house and residence in the community, and reminded them that "the King was not a King over fields and pastures but over towns."[35]

In the vast territories occupied in post-Conquest expansion, ruralization proceeded on a larger scale than in older, more settled parts of the Indies. Towns were few and widely dispersed in frontier regions, so that owners of haciendas and *estancias* found it convenient to establish settlements on their estates and live in their rural residences for most of the year. Frontiers generated other forms of rural colonization. Poor Spaniards and mestizos established *ranchos* (family-sized ranches) in the large stretches of unused lands available. Retired soldiers and service personnel settled around forts and presidios, and small nuclei of permanent inhabitants formed along main communication routes to serve travelers and transport. Small camps developed to exploit minor mineral strikes or to mine the tailings of abandoned shafts and placers.

It has been proposed that economic contraction in the seventeenth century accelerated urban-rural migration. When hard times hit towns and cities, the owners of haciendas and *estancias* fled to their estates, where they could live self-sufficiently. Less fortunate urban dwellers found refuge in Indian or mestizo settlements or squatted on unused land. In some instances the desire to escape creditors and taxes provoked flight. A concurrent political and social development also contributed to the movement. By mid-seventeenth century the government of older municipalities had fallen into the hands of closed oligarchies that, to insure their preeminence, restricted *vecinidad*, that is, full citizenship, which conveyed important economic and civic rights. Many of those excluded departed to less urbane but more hospitable rural environments.[36]

In some regions, particular circumstances promoted ruralization. By the end of the sixteenth century virtually all of the good coastal lands in Santo Domingo, Cuba, and Puerto Rico belonged to the descendants of first settlers intermarried with wealthy merchants and royal officials. Poorer Spaniards and mixed bloods, therefore, moved into the interior, where they established *hatos* and *corrales*, that is, small ranches. In the Caribbean Islands, also, the threat of attack by corsairs, buccaneers, and Carib Indians induced the Spaniards to abandon unfortified coastal towns. In at least one instance the crown's mercantilist policies contributed to this kind of movement. In 1602 and 1603, the governor of Española ordered the destruction and abandonment of towns on the western half of the island, in part because of corsair attacks, but also to prevent the inhabitants from dealing with smugglers in nearby Tortuga. Retreat into the interior likewise occurred on the Caribbean coasts of Central America, where buccaneers and Mosquito Indians menaced settlements, and on the Pacific coast of New Spain, which was harassed by Dutch and English privateers during the last part of the sixteenth century and well into the seventeenth. Although some leading citizens of abandoned towns moved to safer incorporated municipalities, many of the inhabitants dispersed in the backlands to form *poblaciones campesinos* (peasant communities).

In addition to the formation of new population nuclei in the countryside, ruralization proceeded through what might be called the deurbanization of older established corporate municipalities, both Spanish and Indian. Many small and isolated European towns declined to the point that — although they retained their status as cities and *villas*, displayed rather tarnished coats of arms, and pointed proudly to royal cedulas declaring their nobility and loyalty — they amounted in fact to pueblos of Spaniards. Even their "Spanishness" faded through cultural and genetic *mestizaje*.

The civil congregations and reductions of Indians created in the late sixteenth and the seventeenth centuries were urban in form and constitution. But native resettlement helped to spread pestilence, which quickly reduced the population of the new communities. Their inhabitants, furthermore, tended to drift off to avoid tribute and personal service or were lured away by Spaniards seeking a permanent labor force. By the last part of the seventeenth century, many of the surviving congregations were urban only in name, and Spanish landowners had moved some of them to sites where the labor of their inhabitants could be exploited more conveniently. The outcome was the final breakdown of the old native structure of *cabecera* and satellite towns and the creation of undifferentiated *pueblos de Indios* (Indian pueblos) dispersed through the countryside.

No one knows what percentage of the Spanish America population was urban and what percentage rural in the late seventeenth century. It may be surmised, however, that most whites still lived permanently in towns and cities or at least maintained their primary residences in them. The European corporate municipality also remained the place where people dwelt in polity, the center of political authority and of social and economic intercourse for large hinterlands. But it had begun to be counterbalanced demographically and, in some measure, culturally by dispersed rural populations composed mainly of Indians and mixed bloods. Whereas urbanization was primarily a European phenomenon, ruralization was essentially American.

## Urbanization and Ruralization in Brazil

Brazil had comparable patterns of population movement and organization. In 1570, it boasted far fewer corporate municipalities than did Spanish America, and fewer were founded in ensuing decades. Yet for the most part Brazilian towns were vigorous civic entities and experienced healthy growth. Rates varied according to regional circumstances. Salvador (Bahia), the political capital and the economic center of the rich *recôncavo* (Bahian sugar-planting region), grew the fastest, having some 8000 white inhabitants in about 1600 and 21,601 *almas de confissão* (communicants, and a fair approximation of the "white" population) in 1709. In the Captaincy of Pernambuco, during the Dutch occupation, Recife replaced Olinda as the principal urban center. Between 1630 and 1639 it expanded from a village of 150 hearths to a sizable town of 2000 souls, and by 1709 it had at least 10,000 inhabitants, thus becoming the second largest town in Brazil. Beyond the plantation zone, urban growth also occurred. São Paulo had 600 white and *mameluco* inhabitants who could bear arms in 1646 and 3000 in 1676.[37]

The north American social historian James Lockhart offers a pungent observation on the vitality of Brazilian urbanization:

[There existed] a complex and flexible urban society in Brazil from an early time, a society amazingly like its Spanish American equivalent in organization, function, and tendency. Whatever its economic base, colonial Brazil was no mere rural or plantation society; the master-slave dichotomy is not an adequate analytical tool to comprehend it. What we see is a complete European-type, urban-oriented society in operation, with a strong tendency to grow because of entry of European immigrants into its middle levels and Africans into its lower levels.[38]

It may be ventured, furthermore, that towns in Brazil sustained their vigor longer into the seventeenth century than did those in the Spanish Indies because the Brazilian sugar boom, extending into the 1660s, outlasted the Peruvian and Mexican silver bonanzas by several decades.

Although Brazilian towns experienced a vigorous growth, ruralization also occurred on a large scale. Its original and most obvious form was the plantation as a rural population nucleus, and, as sugar zones expanded in the seventeenth century, new plantations became increasingly distant from urban centers. Meanwhile, ruralization proceeded in other ways. As Brazilians cleared their coasts of foreigners, small trading posts and fishing villages appeared in the gaps between older maritime towns. As *tropas* penetrated Amazonia, the same kinds of settlements sprang up on inland waterways, and people clustered around forts to seek security or serve the garrisons. In the *sertão*, dispersed cattle ranches and *fazendas* stretched from Ceará to the backlands of São Paulo, and crossroads settlements appeared along communication routes.

As in Spanish America, Brazilian population organization developed both a rural and an urban component: cities that were European in culture and orientation and smaller nuclei in plantation zones and in the backlands that were American in blood and culture. Geographically the distinction was more clearly defined in Brazil: coastal zones of urbanization and an overwhelmingly rural interior.

## Population and Territory: An Overview

Between about 1570 and the close of the seventeenth century, the enterprise of government officials, missionaries, miners, cattlemen, agriculturists, and enslavers of Indians tripled the American territories ruled nominally, at least, by the kings of Spain and Portugal. During the same period, the inhabitants of these territories probably declined in number or, at best, registered only a small increase. The result was a substantial decline in population density. In 1700 it could not have been greater than 3 per square mile. If regions as yet unsettled by Spain and Portugal be taken into account, the figure would be considerably less. At about the same date, overall density in Europe west of the Volga was 25 per square mile; in Italy, 102; in France, 95; and in the Iberian peninsula, about 40. Hispanic America was badly underpopulated.

Gross density figures do not present the whole picture of the relationship between people and territory. In 1700 most Hispanic Americans still dwelt in lands conquered and colonized in the sixteenth century, that is, where the Spaniards had found large concentrations of Indians and the Portuguese, good sugar lands. These regions had substantially higher population densities than did Hispanic America as a whole. Yet in 1700, as in 1570, their inhabitants were distributed in clusters centered on an urban core or nucleus. Between clusters stretched thinly peopled lands, or *despoblados*. There was little overlap between the territories served by the several centers, a condition that discouraged intercourse among them.

The clustered pattern of settlement had a close relationship with political and economic organization. In many parts of Spanish America, such as Chile, Paraguay, El Salvador, Ecuador, and Guatemala, one central cluster formed the core of major provinces and even audiencias. The boundaries of these administrative units ran through sparsely settled regions and were therefore only loosely defined. Their jurisdictions might be large, but their "effective" territories or ekumenes, that is, those parts that could be effectively governed from their centers and that contributed to their economies, were much smaller. When they became independent republics, they inherited these demographic defects. In regions such as Brazil, Mexico, and Colombia that held several major clusters, the distance between concentrations hindered the creation of truly national states.

Around 1800, as the colonial period drew toward its close, the Prussian scientist Alexander von Humboldt wrote a graphic description of the relationship between territory and people in Hispanic America: "In the Old World, nations and the distinctions of their civilizations form the principal point in the picture but in the New World, man and his production virtually disappear amidst the stupendous display of wild and gigantic nature."[39]

# CHAPTER 17

# Post-Conquest Economies

## Spanish America: General Trends

The territorial expansion that followed the Conquest greatly increased the natural resources available in the Indies, and mining and commerce generated new capital for their exploitation. The number of indigenes, however, continued to diminish, making labor the most critical factor of production. During the same period, the demands of a growing Spanish American population of European and mixed-blood origin and of a vigorous European economy stimulated the commerce of the Indies. Until the early 1600s this conjuncture of favorable production and market factors generated a steady expansion of the Spanish American economy. Then a contraction began, at least in mining and trans-Atlantic trade. Its causes, breadth, and duration are uncertain, and it is a major problem in the historiography of colonial Spanish America.

## The Factors of Production

### Land Tenure and Use

In the course of territorial expansion, the Spaniards found new deposits of precious metals and new sources of forest products such as hardwoods, medicinal plants, and food seasonings. Nevertheless, land continued to be the basic natural resource in the Indies, and, as frontiers advanced and the indigenous inhabitants declined in numbers, it became available to Spaniards and mixed bloods in large quantities. Much of the new territory occupied after the Conquest, however, was more suitable for grazing than for agriculture and lay so far from main population centers that it could not be exploited intensively.

Important changes occurred in the forms of land tenure and use. Beginning in the 1570s, most of the productive land in older conquered and newly pacified regions passed from the royal domain (*realengo*) into the possession of corporations and private parties. In connection with Indian resettlement in the sixteenth and early seventeenth centuries, the crown endowed indigenous towns with technically inalienable communal holdings. During the same period European appetites for land sharpened. With the expansion of commercial agriculture and grazing, it acquired a monetary value that increased in proportion to the demand for its fruits, and, in an expanding inflationary economy, it offered a secure and ultimately profitable store of wealth. In addition, land acquired a social value. After Spanish kings foiled attempts to transform *encomiendas* into *señorial* domains, settlers recalled their cultural heritage and found an alternative source of lordship in the landed estate with a dependent labor force. Although the crown made occasional half-hearted attempts to restrict concentration of ownership, it alienated its domain rather freely.

The Europeans acquired land in large, medium, and small quantities by various devices. They secured new municipal and royal grants. They bought property from original grantees legally and from indigenous communities illegally. They encroached on the royal domain, and Indian communal holdings or usurped them outright. In some instances, estates were created by the fusion of *encomiendas* and land grants, although this did not happen as commonly as once supposed.[1] Landed families enlarged their holdings through intermarriage. Following established Spanish practice, they sought to insure the indivisibility of their estates and to link them inalienably to the family name through entailment, which might also bring with it a noble title. The king, however, created *mayorazgos* (entailed estates) sparingly because of their historical association with *señorial* faculties and the unwillingness of applicants to pay for the privilege.

Informal usurpations and encroachments coupled with the loose metes and bounds defined in legal grants created enormous cadastral confusion. In 1591 the crown tried to impose order by declaring a general *composición*, an arrangement whereby those who held land legally or illegally could confirm or obtain proper title through paying a nominal fee to the royal treasury. In the course of territorial expansion, it allowed new *composiciones* in 1601, 1643, and 1674. *Composición* helped to extend and consolidate private ownership of land, but it never resolved problems of titles and limits completely. Old and new disputes constantly plagued the royal courts, and in many cases they were inherited by the independent Spanish American republics.

The church, especially the religious orders, also accumulated large holdings. Both the seculars and regulars believed that, if they were to perform their spiritual functions effectively, they could not depend entirely on royal subventions or private charties and would have to possess their own income-producing properties. A certain measure of worldly acquisitiveness undoubtedly complemented their religious considerations. In contrast to its position on private property, the crown tried to discourage ecclesiastical holdings, fearing that the affairs of Mammon would distract the clergy from their ministry and wishing to prevent accumulations held in mortmain. As early as 1538, Emperor Charles prohibited grants to churches and monasteries, but viceroys made exceptions in favor of needy convents, and pious settlers gave liberal donations and bequests to religious foundations. Informed contemporaries estimated in 1608–09 that ecclesiastical establishments owned one-third of the productive land of the Indies. As the principal lender on real estate, moreover, the church held mortgages on many private estates.[2]

Regional differences in original settlement patterns, in the availability of land, in population densities, and in access to markets created a bewildering variety of sizes and forms of holdings. Among them was the hacienda. Unfortunately, this institution has become identified primarily with the great cattle latifundia that dominated the rural landscape in many parts of nineteenth-century Spanish America and to which stereotypical characteristics have been assigned: low capitalization, backward technology, and a labor force of serflike peasants. In the seventeenth century the word had a much looser usage. Generically it meant an accumulation of any form of material wealth. Thus the crown's revenues constituted the royal hacienda, and a silver refining mill was a hacienda.

As applied to landholding in the seventeenth century, hacienda simply meant a landed estate, ranging in size from something larger than a family farm upward to a great latifundium. The closest approximations to the nineteenth-century hacienda were the great cattle ranches that spread over northern Mexico and throughout the central valley of Chile and its Andean flanks. But even in those regions the hacienda did not fit the stereotype. Owners adjusted capital investment and technology to market conditions, and, although they possessed a nuclear resident work force, they drew heavily on other sources of labor during peak seasons.

In the more densely populated and urbanized parts of the Indies, especially the temperate upland valleys and basins of the American cordillera from north central Mexico to Peru, smaller haciendas chiefly grew grain. But most of them also grazed some livestock for local consumption or for sale in regional markets. In tropical or subtropical regions there were haciendas specializing in the production of sugar, cacao, or indigo. They might be called plantations, but the term is anachronistic. Contemporary Spanish Americans did not use it, and their seventeenth-century "plantations" did not conform to the stereotype that developed from observations of British and French planting in the West Indies. They were rarely monocultural, they raised basic foodstuffs for local and regional markets, and, although they used black slaves, they also drew on Indian labor when it was available.

In the seventeenth-century Indies, haciendas did not everywhere preempt the countryside. Even in regions dominated by cattle latifundia, small ranches subsisted in the interstices between their loosely defined boundaries or within their confines. In other places, such as highland Costa Rica and Antioquia, small one-family properties devoted to farming or cattle ranching or combining the two predominated. In western Cuba the trend toward land concentration reversed during the seventeenth century as the owners of cattle latifundia formed a hundred years earlier subdivided their holdings in order to sort out boundaries and titles. Meanwhile, small ranchers and tobacco and ginger planters established themselves on larger estates by exercising squatters' rights. In regions with dense Indian populations, such as the Valley of Oaxaca and highland Bolivia, Indian communities managed to hold on to a good part of their lands.

Labor: Forms and Uses

The primary influence on the supply and forms of labor was the continuing decline in the indigenous population, as contemporaries were acutely aware. In 1594, the viceroy of Mexico, Luis de Velasco II, lamented: "The Spanish population grows daily, and public works and secular and religious buildings become more numerous; meanwhile, the Indians are becoming so scarce that it is extremely difficult to maintain such works with so little labor available."[3] And at the beginning of the seventeenth century, another Mexican viceroy, the Marquis of Montesclaros, lectured some of the descendants of the conquerors: "Far better it would be to discover an increase of Indians than mines of gold and silver."[4]

The Spaniards responded to the labor crisis in several ways. They tried to import more Africans, but the piecemeal licensing system introduced by Emperor Charles failed to meet colonial demands, and shortages along with speculation in licenses inflated slave prices severely. In 1595, therefore, Philip II turned to monopolistic contracts (*asientos*) with a series of Portuguese suppliers, now conveniently his own subjects. The conditions of the contracts, however, still imposed severe restrictions on the slave trade. The crown set prices, imposed duties, and fixed numbers to be delivered. At first it designated Cartagena as the only legal port of entry; later it allowed importations through Veracruz. At these two points, contractors or their representatives sold their human cargoes to merchants who marketed them throughout the colonies, except that regulations forbade sales in Tierra Firme and severely restricted them in Buenos Aires.

*Asientos* with Portuguese contractors continued until 1640, when their country broke with the Habsburg dynasty. The contracts brought a substantial increase in volume of the legal slave trade: from 36,300 Africans during the period 1551-95, to 132,600 during 1595-1640.[5] But royal regulations coupled with marketing factors effected an uneven distribution, favoring sales in regions close to legal ports of entry. The Antilles, Central America, and the west coast and interior of South America suffered shortages. Even in the most favored regions the prices of slaves remained so high that they could be used profitably for mass labor only in industries such as sugar production and gold mining, where high returns justified large capital outlays.

The Spaniards, officially and privately, sought a more comprehensive solution to their labor problems through reorganizing the use of the indigenous work force. The crown proposed to husband it more carefully and ration it more efficiently. To this end it ordered the resettlement of the Indians in civil congregations where they would be readily accessible to public and private employers and where their treatment could be closely supervised. This program was described in the preceding chapter. In addition, the viceroy of Mexico, Martín Enríquez (1568–80) and the viceroy of Peru, Francisco de Toledo (1569–81), issued detailed ordinances governing the kinds of tasks to which *repartimientos* and *mitas* could be assigned as well as wage scales and working conditions for these forms of labor. Nevertheless, employers of labor in conspiracy with *corregidores* soon found ways to avoid these inconveniences. In the early seventeenth century, therefore, the crown abolished the *repartimiento-mita* except in mining and other critical sectors of the economy.

Viceroys and governors in America interpreted critical needs as their consciences and local pressures dictated, but even with the most liberal and equitable distribution of Indians possible there were simply not enough to go around. For a permanent solution to their problems, settlers turned to what might be called loosely a free labor market, which had two main components. One was composed of *gañanes*, *yanaconas*, and other Indians not subject to the *repartimiento-mita*; the other, of free blacks and mixed bloods. To attract and retain workers, employers used various devices. In mining, where the demand for labor was greatest, they paid competitive wages and allowed employees to retain a share of the ore gathered. In agriculture and textile manufacturing, debt bondage came into fairly common use. To supplement nuclear resident work forces, particularly in agriculture with its seasonal demands, proprietors hired *repartimiento-mita* Indians between their turns of service.

The measures adopted by crown and colonists produced a general shift from forced drafts of labor to nominally free forms. The rate of change varied regionally. It was most rapid in areas where diversified economies created highly competitive demands for workers and that suffered a short supply either because of the absence of pre-Conquest Indian communities or drastic post-Conquest losses. In thinly populated northern Mexico, free labor predominated in mines and on haciendas from the beginning of settlement. In central Mexico, which suffered disastrously from epidemics, free workers outnumbered those drafted in all economic sectors by the 1630s. In Peru, the transition was slower. There mining dominated the economy more completely, and despite a long-term decline in the native population the *mita* provided a reliable source of labor for Potosí and Huancavelica until the mid-1600s. In the Kingdom of Quito, where Indians remained relatively abundant, the system furnished workers for haciendas and *obrajes* until the end of the seventeenth century.

Capital: Accumulation and Investment

After the Conquest, expanding economies in the Indies generated sizable amounts of capital, and decreasing dependence on European imports allowed more to remain at home. The government collected part of the surplus and spent it for administration, defense, and public works. Ecclesiastical government and construction absorbed another portion. Yet enough was left in the hands of individuals and corporations to make the Indies self-sufficient in investment capital and, indeed, to allow Spanish Americans to export it for their own rather than metropolitan purposes. As early as 1609, *peruleros* (agents of Lima merchants) began to appear in Seville in considerable numbers, bringing with them silver which they used to buy goods directly from Sevillian suppliers, and thereby bypassing the *consulado*'s monopoly.

The main source of private investment capital was wholesale commerce and silver banking conducted by the great mercantile houses of Mexico and Lima. In the early 1600s a contemporary observer reported, "There are merchants in Lima who have fortunes of a million pesos, many with 500,000 and very many with 100,000.''[6] Substantial capital formation also occurred in peripheral regions such as Venezuela where a merchant-planter aristocracy grew rich from exporting cacao to Mexico and came to be known as the *grandes cacaos*.

Yet it cannot be said that capital accumulated at rates or was employed in ways that would encourage stable, long-term economic growth. Spanish Americans certainly possessed acquisitive instincts and appreciated the value of money, but they regarded the pursuit of wealth not as a discrete and all-absorbing occupation but rather as a means to other ends and only part of a total way of life. Furthermore, social and political pressures and interests induced men of substance to divert their profits away from reinvestment into economically nonproductive channels: donations to the crown or to municipal causes, dowries for marriageable daughters, maintenance of a sumptuous life-style, bequests to the church, support for sons in the clergy and daughters in convents, and the purchase of landed estates which yielded meager returns.

Spanish Americans and Spaniards in the Indies also lagged in developing forms of business organization that would have encouraged continuing, large-scale capital accumulation. They did not wish to entrust their money to impersonal secular institutions such as banks and joint stock companies. In the seventeenth century, as in the sixteenth, they might form partnerships with *hombres de confianza* —intimate and trusted associates— but they much preferred to keep their enterprises in the family.

These organizational forms tended to make accumulations of capital vulnerable and ephemeral. Partnerships were generally formed for a particular enterprise and in any event were dissolved upon the death of one of the partners. As for family fortunes, Castilian family and property law, which governed in the Indies, provided that all capital accumulated during a marriage belonged equally to the two spouses. Thus, when one died, the survivor was entitled to only one-half of the estate. The other half, which had belonged to the deceased, was to be divided equally among his or her male and female children, generally numerous. When surviving partners died, the same disposition was to be made of their half of the estate. In addition, testators could bequeath a fifth of their estate to charities and other beneficiaries outside the family.

Ways did exist to limit the dispersion of family fortunes. Persons could separate a third of their estate from the rest and will it to a favorite child, commonly a son, but this device did not necessarily guarantee the continuity of family fortunes. As a Spanish Philippine historian of the times rephrased a venerable adage, "The father amasses a fortune, the son spends it, and the grandson is a pauper. The greatest amounts of capital are no more stable than the waves of the ocean across which they were amassed."[7] Another method available to merchants for perpetuating their fortunes was to withdraw from commerce, invest their money in land, and then entail their estate. But this method did not encourage capital accumulation, and in any event entailment was an expensive, prolonged process and not commonly used.

Finally, the will of kings and the whims of fortune constantly threatened the stability of capital accumulations. The flooding of mines, the exhaustion of veins of ore, or changes in the costs or availability of mercury could destroy a fortune made in the silver industry. A merchant could be ruined by the loss of a ship to storms or buccaneers, by mistaken estimates of demands and prices for imported merchandise, or by bad loans. All businesses were vulnerable to prolonged and costly litigation.

Another and more stable source of investment capital was religious corporations and foundations. Part of their revenues went for economically nonproductive activities, but enough remained to be put to work. They not only loaned substantial sums to private parties, secured by land mortgages, but also invested directly in entrepreneurial activities, especially commercial agriculture. Their accumulations of wealth were not vulnerable to dissolution through inheritance. By the late 1600s the Jesuit haciendas of Mexico and coastal Peru may well have been the most truly capitalistic enterprises in the Indies.

## Government Regulation and Taxation

In addition to changing market conditions and factors of production, government policies affected the organization and performance of the economy of the Indies, in the main adversely. Beginning in the reign of Philip II, the crown increased its direct and indirect intervention in all economic sectors. In the case of trans-Atlantic trade, in 1562–64 the crown required that two separate fleets go to the Indies and that all American shipping sail in one or the other. One of the convoys, which came to be called the *flota*, departed San Lucar, an outport of Seville, in the spring and followed well-established routes across the Atlantic and through the Caribbean to Veracruz. Toward the end of the century it became customary to detach from it two armed vessels to pick up silver in Honduras. The other fleet served South America, and, after the silver of Potosí became the main treasure of the Indies, it was called the *galeones* because of the six to eight galleons assigned as its escort. Regulations required it to leave San Lucar in August. After the Atlantic crossing it passed through the southern Caribbean and on to its isthmian destination, which, in 1597, was moved from the roadstead at Nombre de Dios westward to the deepwater harbor of Portobelo. It then proceeded to Cartagena. As the two fleets passed through the Caribbean, both released individually licensed vessels to serve ports in the Antilles and on Tierra Firme. After completing their main American unloadings and loadings, they rendezvoused in Havana, wintered there, and in early spring returned to Europe together, helped by the Gulf stream and Atlantic westerlies.

The crown took several other steps to tighten control of the *Carrera*. It designated Veracruz, Nombre de Dios (later Portobello), Cartagena, and Havana as the only legal American ports of entry for fleets. In 1573 it withdrew the rights of Spanish maritime cities other than Seville and Cadiz to trade with the Indies. In 1592 it chartered a *consulado* in Mexico and in 1613 another in Lima, thereby confirming the de facto monopoly of the overseas trade enjoyed by the mercantile houses of the two viceregal capitals. These several measures created an Atlantic mercantile system whose main features, with one major exception, remained unchanged for over a century. After the mid-1600s Cadiz replaced Seville as its main European terminal. The shift occurred primarily because of the silting of the Guadalquivir, which made river navigation hazardous for the larger vessels in the Indies trade.

Beginning during the reign of Philip II, the Spanish crown adopted new fiscal and regulatory measures affecting the domestic economy of the Indies. Faced by mounting costs of war and civil administration in its American dominions, it introduced a 2 percent *alcabala* (general sales tax) in Mexico in 1575, in Guatemala in the following year, and in Peru in 1591. In 1627 it imposed a special sales tax of 2 percent throughout its American dominions. Called the *derecho de unión de armas*, this levy was intended as America's contribution to the count duke of Olivares's Union of Arms and was to be used to support a fleet of galleons for the defense of the *Carrera*. In 1636 the original *alcabala* was doubled to 4 percent in New Spain to help pay for the defense of the Caribbean. Other important new sources of American revenues were royal monopolies established for the distribution of various commodities: mercury in 1559, playing cards in 1572, salt and pepper in 1631, and, in 1635, the stamped paper required for all legal documents. Beginning during the reign of Philip II also, Spanish kings imposed increasingly burdensome mercantilist controls on colonial production and commerce that will be noted in connection with the following descriptions of the several main sectors of the economy.

## Economic Sectors

### Agriculture and Grazing

Agricultural and pastoral expansion in older and newly settled regions yielded increasing supplies of foodstuffs. Little is known about the volume of production of indigenous crops such as maize, beans, potatoes, and manioc. It may have sufficed to provide the Indians with a minimum caloric intake. By the early 1600s the Indies enjoyed an overall self-sufficiency in wheat and other European grains. Extension of grazing along with omnipresent pigs and domestic fowl furnished an abundant supply of meat.

The expansion of agricultural and pastoral production did not mean that Europeans, mixed bloods, and Indians could obtain adequate supplies of meat and cereals at all times, in all places, and at prices they could afford. Growing demand, rising labor costs, and cheap silver inflated commodity prices. Transportation problems slowed or disrupted distribution. Unseasonable weather and pests brought intermittent crop failures, and pandemics and epidemics among the Indians disrupted planting and harvesting. Speculators and hoarders exploited agricultural crises to elevate prices exorbitantly, thereby inducing Mexican authorities to establish regulated markets and public granaries.

The vine and the olive flourished so well in the fluvial valleys of Peru and in central Chile that by the early 1600s these regions could produce potable vintages and acceptable oil at a fraction of the prices of Spanish imports and in quantities sufficient to permit export to other parts of South America and even to New Spain. The very success of the two products brought them trouble. Under pressure from Andalusian producers, the crown forbade the planting of new orchards and vineyards in the Indies and prohibited exports of wine and oil from Peru and Chile to regions that could conveniently be supplied from Spain. Colonial officials, however, enforced restrictions indifferently. The narrow range of soils and climates tolerated by the vine and the olive limited planting more than mercantilist regulations.[8]

Aside from basic foodstuffs, the chief products of field and range were sugar, dyes, hides, and cacao.[9] By the end of the sixteenth century the Indies had achieved self-sufficiency in sugar, and its production and sale generated substantial profits. Even earlier, beginning in the 1550s, Española and Puerto Rico enjoyed an export boom. It collapsed in the 1580s, however, and the Spanish American sugar industry in general failed to realize the potential of overseas markets for several reasons, all ultimately attributable to the bullionist concerns of crown, colonists, and metropolitan merchants. The production of silver diverted capital and Indian labor from less glittering enterprises. The fear that silver would escape into the hands of foreign suppliers induced Spanish kings to restrict imports of slaves needed on sugar plantations. The shipment of silver to Europe shaped the routes of fleets so that they bypassed the Antilles, which had the richest export potential. Finally, excessive reliance on bullion from the Indies weakened incentives to develop a good marketing system for sugar in Europe.[10]

American dyestuffs supplied the domestic textile industry but found their main market overseas. As exports they enjoyed certain advantages over sugar. Their production required less capital and labor, they catered to the greatest growth industry of Europe, and they had little competition from other sources. In the late sixteenth century Tlaxcala and Oaxaca increased their cochineal output, and highland Guatemala began to produce at a modest level. Quantities entering Seville illustrate the growth of the industry. In 1587 they amounted to around 5667 *arrobas* (about 142,000 pounds) annually and by 1600 averaged 10,000 to 12,000 *arrobas* (about 250,000 to 300,000 pounds) a year, worth upward of 600,000 pesos on the European market.[11] Indigo also experienced a boom beginning in the 1570s, when producers turned from gathering wild leaves to planting and built *obrajes* to process the harvest. The main centers of cultivation lay along the Pacific coast of Central America, with a secondary zone in Yucatán. Between 1590 and 1620 imports into Seville averaged 240,000 pounds annually.[12] Dyewood cutting continued in the Caribbean area, but in terms of value its production lagged well behind that of cochineal and indigo.

Hides, mainly cattle, had an expanding market in both the Indies and Europe. Their low bulk-to-value ratio, however, limited the export trade to regions having good access to water transport. Throughout the sixteenth and seventeenth centuries, Mexico was the main producer both for internal use and marketing abroad. In the Antilles, Española and Cuba gained an early lead in exports. Puerto Rico, Jamaica, and Trinidad followed. Around 1600 Venezuela entered the overseas market, and by 1620 hides accounted for 75 percent of its exports to Europe by value.[13] The herds of the Rio de la Plata provided a virtually unlimited supply, and access to the river system made exports feasible, but official restrictions on direct trade between Buenos Aires and Europe limited the expansion of the Platine hide industry.

The demand for cacao expanded because European-managed production lowered prices, and Central Americans discovered that brewing the pulverized product with vanilla, another indigenous American bean, yielded a potable hot chocolate. By 1580 or thereabout whites and mixed bloods throughout the Indies consumed the beverage in large quantities. Around the end of the sixteenth century the bean found a modest popularity in Spain, and in the 1600s its use spread to northern Europe, but the American market continued to absorb most of the output. Meanwhile the centers of production shifted. In the early 1600s planting began around Guayaquil, which supplied Peru, and in Venezuela, which sent substantial surpluses to Mexico. Competition from these sources completed the ruin of the Central American cacao industry.[14]

Other plantation-type products experienced varying fortunes. The growth of Mexican sericulture slowed after 1580 because of competition from Chinese silks imported from Manila and because of restrictions imposed by the crown in 1597 under pressure from merchants engaged in the Philippine trade. In contrast, the spread of smoking on both sides of the Atlantic encouraged tobacco planting in Mexico, the Antilles, and Venezuela. Since the weed could be grown in remote areas on small plots, it invited contraband trade, which the crown tried to prevent by intermittent restrictions on production. The expansion of the American textile industry stimulated cotton growing in subtropical regions from Yucatán to Paraguay, but a strong European market did not develop until the eighteenth century. In the Andean region, coca planting continued to flourish. In Brazil, the Rio de la Plata, Chile, and the central Andes, the white and mixed-blood population developed an enormous addiction to maté, the brewed leaves of a Paraguayan shrub. By the mid-1600s it was the principal cash crop of the Jesuit Guaraní missions.[15]

In addition to cultivated or herded products, Spanish America produced diverse "fruits of the forest": dyewood, seasonings such as vanilla and several kinds of spices, and a variety of medicinal plants. These items accounted for a significant part of exports to Europe in the late sixteenth and seventeenth centuries.

## Manufacturing

Food processing, pottery making, tanning, and other basic manufactures expanded to meet growing domestic demand, but, in the Indies as in Europe, shipbuilding, textiles, and mining were the principal growth industries. They are described here in ascending order of economic importance. Havana took the lead in maritime construction, beginning in the 1560s because of its key location on the *Carrera*. Cartagena, which also lay on the fleet route, followed. At first both ports built only small craft, up to frigate size, and repaired vessels engaged in trade with Europe, but, when Spanish shipbuilding declined in the early seventeenth century, they began to construct ships of up to 600 tons for the trans-Atlantic run. Maracaibo, which the *Carrera* bypassed, established its own yards to serve the cacao trade with Mexico. On the Pacific coast, Guayaquil, in Ecuador, and Realejo, in Nicaragua, were in that order the main centers. Both built galleons for the Manila trade and together created a sizable Pacific merchant marine. After the appearance of the Dutch in the South Sea in the early 1600s, naval contracts spurred their growth.[16]

American textile manufacturing grew in response to an expanding domestic market, the debility of the Spanish industry, and the high prices of European imports, both Spanish and foreign. By the opening of the seventeenth century several hundred licensed workshops and an uncounted number of illegal ones made cloth and textile products in nearly every part of the settled Indies.[17] In South America, Ecuador was the main center of production, the "sweatshop" of the continent, because of its abundant flocks and stable labor supply.[18] In New Spain, the industry centered in the valleys of Mexico, Puebla, and Tlaxcala. Kinds and organization of production followed patterns established during the Conquest period. Looms produced fabrics and manufactured items of wool, cotton, silk, linen, and hemp. Climates and the kinds of fibers available imposed some measure of regional specialization. Most workshops were privately owned, but in Mexico and Ecuador Indian communities held on to some, and in Ecuador a few belonged to the crown.

By the early 1600s the Indies enjoyed virtual self-sufficiency in cloth products of low and middling quality, but several circumstances prevented the American textile industry from developing its full potential. In the first place, it was heavily regulated. In 1565 the crown applied to its American dominions existing Spanish legislation governing production and marketing. Subsequently it issued orders dealing with workshops: their licensing, the kinds that could be built, the conditions of their sale and transfer, and production standards. It also closely controlled the use of Indian labor. The overall intent of these measures is uncertain, if, indeed, they had any common purpose.[19] In part they continued the medieval policy of regulating the prices and quality of industrial output in the public interest. Labor legislation in particular was intended to protect the Indians from exploitation. Some scholars believe that regulation was an indirect effort to reduce colonial competition with home industry, and this opinion is supported by occasional royal orders forbidding the manufacture of types of cloth competing directly with imports from Spain. Americans found innumerable ways to avoid restrictions, but state intervention undoubtedly limited growth.

Other restrictive influences included the nature of the domestic market, which consisted largely of Indians with minimal purchasing power; the length and hazards of transportation systems, which limited market ranges; and the diversion of capital into mining. Taken together, unfavorable conditions of production and distribution discouraged manufacturers from introducing more advanced European technologies.

Mining and Metallurgy

Mining and metallurgy in the Indies concentrated on the extraction and refining of precious metals. In terms of both volume and value, silver from the mines of Upper Peru and Mexico continued to account for most of the output. Honduras and the central Peruvian Andes added modest increments. Yields were unquestionably spectacular, but, owing to the scattered nature of production records, actual amounts must be inferred from other sources. For many years scholars used Hamilton's figures for registered Sevillian imports as a rough guide to volume and trends. More recently David Brading and Harry Cross devised a more direct approach based on two related assumptions: One is that the Spaniards refined most ores—some 70 to 87 percent, depending on time and place—by mercury amalgamation and the remainder by smelting. The other is that a direct relationship existed between silver output and quicksilver consumed, 100–125 marks of silver for each hundredweight of mercury.[20]

Using available statistics on mercury consumption and correcting for the percentage of silver yielded by smelting, the two authors arrived at a set of figures that they juxtaposed to Hamilton's (see table 7). As they, themselves, conceded, their results are still only estimates. But they are the best estimates available and they revise substantially traditional views on American silver production. A comparison of the first and third columns demonstrates, as might be expected, that mining yields exceeded registered Sevillian imports appreciably in most of the five-year periods from 1571 to 1660, raising more explicitly the question of what became of the difference. Comparison shows, moreover, that, whereas registered imports peaked in 1591–95 at 58.2 million pesos, actual production did not reach its highest level until 1636–40, when it stood at 64.8 million pesos.

The Brading and Cross study also finds important regional variations in silver production. In the last quarter of the sixteenth century, yields increased sharply in both Peru and New Spain including Honduras, with Peru leading because of the tremendous output of Potosí. After about 1603, however, Peruvian production began a slow decline owing to the depletion of Potosí's rich surface ores, tech-

Table 7
Estimated Minimum Spanish American
Bullion Production, 1571–1700
(in Millions of Pesos of 8 *Reales*)

| Year | Registered Bullion Imports into Seville* | Estimated Minimum Silver Production by Amalgamation | Adjusted Total Minimum Bullion Production |
|---|---|---|---|
| 1571–75 | 19.7 | 17.3 | 21.6 |
| 1576–80 | 28.5 | 35.5 | 44.4 |
| 1581–85 | 48.6 | 39.2 | 49.0 |
| 1586–90 | 39.4 | 49.2 | 61.5 |
| 1591–95 | 58.2 | 47.4 | 59.3 |
| 1596–1600 | 57.0 | 41.3 | 51.6 |
| 1601–05 | 44.9 | 31.6 | 39.5 |
| 1606–10 | 52.0 | 34.5 | 43.1 |
| 1611–15 | 40.6 | 49.3 | 61.6 |
| 1616–20 | 49.8 | 50.5 | 63.1 |
| 1621–25 | 44.7 | 62.3 | 77.9 |
| 1626–30 | 41.3 | 39.1 | 48.9 |
| 1631–35 | 28.3 | 46.3 | 57.9 |
| 1636–40 | 27.0 | 51.9 | 64.8 |
| 1641–45 | 22.8 | 49.2 | 61.4 |
| 1646–50 | 19.5 | 36.8 | 45.0 |
| 1651–55 | 12.1 | 49.7 | 62.1 |
| 1656–60 | 5.6 | 37.5 | 46.9 |
| 1661–65 | | 32.6 | 40.8 |
| 1666–70 | | 31.9 | 39.9 |
| 1671–75 | | 42.6 | 53.3 |
| 1676–80 | | 33.8 | 42.3 |
| 1681–85 | | 15.2 | 19.4 |
| 1686–90 | | 26.5 | 33.1 |
| 1691–95 | | 34.5 | 43.1 |
| 1696–1700 | | 31.9 | 39.9 |

*Source:* David A. Brading and Harry C. Cross, "Colonial Silver Mining: Mexico and Peru," *HAHR*, 52:579 (1972). Copyright © 1972 by Duke University Press (Durham, NC).

*Figures in this column are based on Hamilton's statistics, which end in the five-year period 1656–60.

nical problems at the Huancavelica mercury mine, and a gradual shrinkage in the supply of *mita* workers. These trends climaxed in a much sharper downturn in the 1680s and 1690s. In contrast, production in New Spain continued to increase until about 1635 because of the growth of free wage labor in Mexican mines and the continuing availability of high-grade ores. Then output dropped severely and remained low relative to peak years for the rest of the seventeenth century. The cause of the decline was simple: a severe mercury famine occasioned first by diversion of shipments from Almaden, in Spain, to Peru and then after 1645, when Mexico's supply had been restored, by a sharp drop in Almaden's production.[21]

The Spaniards continued to mine gold at scattered sites in Mexico, Central America, Colombia, Ecuador, Peru, and Chile, with the chief centers of production after about 1560 lying in the middle reaches of the Cauca Valley and in the province of Antioquia. The only clue to total American production is registered imports at Seville. These peaked just as the silver boom began, that is, in the decennium 1551–60, when they totaled 42,620,080 grams valued at 9,358,823 *pesos de oro*. Thereafter they fell off sharply to 8,885,940 grams (1,951,238 *pesos de oro*) in 1601–10 and continued to drop during the next fifty years.[22] The tribulations of gold mining arose in part from prohibitions on the use of indigenous labor in the industry and the high price of black slaves, but the main problem was technological. The Spaniards knew how to exploit economically only alluvial deposits and high-grade surface ores, both of which became exhausted quickly.

### Commerce: The Trans-Atlantic Sector

In the decades following the Conquest, the commerce of the Indies developed new patterns and directions. Thanks to the industry of Pierre and Huguette Chaunu, partial data are available on the kinds and value of American exports up to the middle of the seventeenth century. Precious metals, mainly silver, continued to furnish an overwhelming proportion, approximately 95 to 96 percent in the first decade of the seventeenth century.[23] For this reason, along with prevailing preoccupations with precious metals, contemporaries called the *galeones* and the *flotas*, "the fleets going to the Indies to bring back the gold and silver of his Majesty and private individuals."[24]

A regional breakdown of the Chaunu figures produces some significant contrasts. South American exports consisted almost exclusively of bullion. Small quantities of hides, tobacco, and medicinal plants made up the remainder. In the *flota* returning from New Spain, products other than precious metals constituted about 35 percent by value of cargoes. In approximate order of value, the most important were cochineal, mainly from Mexico; hides from Mexico, Central America, and the Antilles; indigo from Central America and Yucatán; sugar, mainly from Santo Domingo and Puerto Rico but including some from Cuba and Mexico; and medicinal plants gathered on the main islands and the periphery of the Caribbean.

Much less complete data indicate that until about 1570 the principal imports from Europe, by value, consisted of grain, oil, and wines but that thereafter, as the Indies produced more and more of these staples, the balance steadily shifted to mercury, fine foods and vintages, high-quality textiles, spices, books, paper, and other luxuries.

The Chaunus provide more complete serial data on the volume of trans-Atlantic traffic. As might be expected, its rate of flow corresponded closely to that of registered silver entering Seville. Between about 1550 and about 1610 both inbound and outbound sailings increased some threefold. Thereafter they begin to drop at an accelerating pace, until in 1650 they stood at around 50 percent of peak-year levels. Trends varied between Mexico and Peru, reflecting closely the shifting fortunes of the mining industry in the two viceroyalties. From 1581 to 1590 Peru accounted for somewhat over 40 percent of total volume, New Spain a little less than 40 percent, and the Antilles the remainder. Between 1596 and 1620, New Spain moved ahead by a few percentage points. Thereafter, the balance reversed sharply. In the quinquennium 1631–35, the Tierra Firme fleets carried 51.23 percent and the Mexican *flota* only 29.82 percent.

### Trans-Pacific Trade: The Manila Galleons

Beginning in the early 1570s the Spaniards opened a lucrative trade between Manila and Acapulco, which replaced Huatulco as the main Mexican west coast port. American exports consisted chiefly of silver; imports, of Chinese silks, porcelains, spices, and wax. As with the *Carrera*, the crown tried to supervise commerce with Manila closely, for it drained off bullion to the Orient. Regulations restricted sailings to two galleons annually and limited the quantities of oriental goods that could be sold in Mexico or reexported from Mexican ports. In 1579 direct trade between Peru and Manila received royal sanction, but, when Sevillian interests complained about competition of oriental goods with imports from Spain via Panama, the king revoked the privilege. Despite these restraints, Mexican-Philippine commerce prospered for several decades. Data compiled by Pierre Chaunu, however, demonstrate that its volume also dropped sharply in the mid-seventeenth century, a turn attributable to the declining fortunes of New Spain's silver industry.[25]

### Inter-American Commerce

Development of the domestic commerce of the Indies followed lines and patterns established during the period of conquest: the exchange of precious and non-precious products took place between more and less developed American kingdoms, between tropical and temperate zones, between mining and agricultural regions, and between textile centers and their market areas. In continental South America the main trading system served Potosí, whose mines supported a population of 160,000 souls in 1650.[26] To this center came textiles from as far away as Quito; grain from Arequipa; mining timbers from distant Cochabamba; wheat, fruits, and cotton from Tucumán and Santa Cruz de la Sierra; sugar from Peruvian coastal valleys; wines from vineyards around Lima and from Chile; cacao from Guayaquil; hides and tallow from Chile, Argentina, and northern Peru; and mules from Salta, in northwestern Argentina. Potosí paid for imports with its only product, silver. Secondary systems linked Lima with Cuzco and other parts of highland Peru, Quito with its port of Guayaquil, and Santa Fe de Bogotá with Cartagena.

In New Spain the main axis of commerce ran from Veracruz to Mexico City and thence along the *Camino Real* to the mining centers of Zacatecas, Durango, and Parral. From Veracruz came many kinds of European imports and coastal plantation products for distribution from the viceregal capital. As the route continued northwestward, it picked up manufactures from central Mexico and grain and cattle products for consumption in the mines. Offshoots from the *Camino Real* led west to Guadalajara and north to Saltillo and Monterrey. Return traffic from the north consisted principally of silver for coinage in the Mexico City mint and export to Seville and the Caribbean. In central Mexico hides and dyestuffs entered the flow of goods destined for shipment to Spain. Another important commercial route linked Mexico City to Acapulco. It brought in oriental products for internal consumption and reexport to Europe. It carried out Mexican silver bound for Manila and Mexican manufactures for export to the Pacific coasts of Central and South America. In addition to the import-export oriented commerce of New Spain, the major cities of the viceroyalty — Mexico City, Puebla, Oaxaca, Guadalajara, and Guatemala City — exchanged their manufactures for agricultural products from their hinterlands.

Two major maritime routes connected North and South America. The most important carried the Mexico-Peru trade, which grew with the internal development of the two viceroyalties and received a new stimulus from the opening of trans-Pacific commerce. After the termination of legal exchange between Peru and the Philippines, buyers from Lima appeared in Acapulco when the galleon from Manila arrived, bringing with them large quantities of silver with which they bought oriental imports. Such transactions, however, not only drained bullion from the Spanish mercantile system but circumvented the interests of Sevillian monopolists by absorbing much of the galleons' cargo and creating competition for oriental merchandise introduced into the Indies through Panama. The crown countered with measures of increasing severity. In 1585 it levied heavy duties on exports from Mexico to Peru; in 1587 and 1589 it limited trade between the viceroyalties to two vessels annually, which could carry only Mexican products; finally, in 1609, it forbade the traffic altogether. Another main route linked Veracruz with Venezuelan ports. It exchanged mainly Mexican silver and European reexports for Venezuelan cacao.[27]

Transportaton

Increases in the volume and range of commerce brought little improvement in transportation. On land the Europeans traced a track suitable for wheeled vehicles through the rolling lands between Buenos Aires and the Andean foothills, and they slowly extended their cart road north from Zacatecas to New Mexico. They also improved some sections of main trails, especially those from Potosí to Arica and from Veracruz to Mexico City. Along most routes, however, goods continued to move by mule train.

For oceanic transportation the Spaniards built larger and larger ships, but there is some evidence that a decline in the quality of construction partially offset increased carrying capacity. On the *Carrera*, furthermore, threats from privateers and bureaucratic aggravations often delayed or prevented annual fleet sailings. After 1580 convoys frequently skipped a year, and between 1600 and 1650 only twenty-nine departed Seville for Panama.

The enormous distances to be traversed on land and sea, coupled with obstacles raised by nature and humans, made transportation extremely slow. The following case illustrates the problems. In 1606 the *Casa de Contratación* reported that a shipment of silver took 15 days to get from Potosí to Arica; 8 from Arica to Callao; and 20 from Callao to Panama, counting stops made by the carriers at Paita and Trujillo to take on more silver. Adding the total, 43 days, to an average 6-day passage of the Isthmus of Panama and an average 91-day trans-Atlantic crossing, it required 140 days, better than a third of a year, to move the consignment from the mines to its first European destination.[28]

Illicit Commerce

The Spanish mercantile system was in many ways a remarkable human achievement. Its construction cost enormous amounts of labor, money, and blood. It carried unprecedented quantities of merchandise and treasure across continents and oceans. But it had one near fatal defect. Spain could not fulfill the contract implicit in mercantilist doctrine. The peninsula's industry lacked the ability to supply the Indies market with the merchandise it demanded, much less to do so at prices consumers were willing to pay. Nor could *asientos* meet American requirements for slaves. Conversely, the metropolis could not absorb colonial goods at prices producers and exporters found acceptable. The Spanish merchant marine lacked the capacity to handle the volume of trans-Atlantic shipping. Monopolistic organization and restrictive regulations further limited the system's capabilities.

These circumstances increasingly drove the commerce of the Indies into illegal channels dominated by foreigners who could draw directly on the manufactures of northern Europe and who had better access to African slaves than the Spaniards. The Portuguese, already well established in major Spanish American commerical centers, took advantage of the union of the crowns and of *asientos* to introduce contraband merchandise and slaves into the Spanish colonies. After their country regained its independence, they managed to maintain their trade networks. Northern European nations, especially the Netherlands and England, expanded their clandestine commerce after establishing entrepôts in their Antillean settlements in the mid-1600s. They stepped it up further during the last decades of the seventeenth century when they belatedly realized that smuggling yielded higher profits than privateering, buccaneering, and territorial seizures.

Smuggling flourished in all parts of the Indies but most vigorously in regions that the fleets bypassed, those to which foreigners had close access, and those that were farthest removed from the scrutiny of viceroys, audiencias, and principal treasury offices. The Caribbean most fully met these conditions. Within and around it a truly international trading community developed during the last decades of the seventeenth century. The English, Dutch, and French traded with each other, disregarding the mercantilist restrictions of their home governments and European wars pitting their nations against each other. All trafficked with the Spanish colonies, the main connections being between English Jamaica, and Spanish Cuba, Puerto Rico and Central America and between Dutch Curaçáo and Spanish Venezuela. The Rio de la Plata was another major theater of contraband. There the Portuguese, increasingly backed by the English in the late 1600s, made deep inroads into the Potosí trade. Everywhere local governors and treasury officials knew very well what was going on, but they lacked the means and the will to stop it. Indeed, many of them were personally involved, directly through buying or selling or indirectly through taking bribes.

Mercantile controls also broke down along legal trade routes. Foreign merchants established in Cadiz and Seville, most notably the French and the Genoese, colluded with Spanish firms and the House of Trade to supply goods for outbound fleets and to receive returning silver and merchandise. Foreign-owned ships made up a large part of the convoys. Spanish merchants in both European and American ports conspired with royal officials to falsify cargo manifests and evade duties. The Pacific was less vulnerable to foreign penetration, but there the Spaniards themselves engaged in large-scale fraud and contraband behind the legal facades of the Manila and Mexican-Peruvian trades.

It is impossible to calculate, even roughly, the volume and value of trade conducted outside the bounds of the Spanish mercantile regime. In the Indies, Spanish defrauders kept no public books of their transactions, and the records of foreign contrabandists are widely scattered in public and private archives. It may be guessed that by the mid-seventeenth century smuggling accounted for better than half of the commerce of the Spanish Caribbean. One source estimates that in the years 1600–21, 20 to 25 percent of Potosí's silver escaped through the Rio de la Plata.[29] Another affirms that in 1597 the value of bullion illegally sent to Manila exceeded that of the merchandise and silver carried by the Atlantic fleets.[30]

Two sets of figures suggest the scale of foreign penetration into the Indies trade at its European end toward the close of the seventeenth century. Of the 8,500,000 pesos brought to Spain by the 1670 Mexican fleet, the Genoese took 1,500,000, the French 1,300,000, the Dutch 700,000, the Germans 500,000, and the English 300,000.[31] And an often-cited memorial of French origin reports that in 1691 foreigners engrossed better than 90 percent of imports from America in the following order: French (25 percent), Genoese (21 percent), Dutch (19 percent), Flemings (11 percent), English (11 percent), and Hamburgers (7.6 percent).[32] These figures are not necessarily accurate, but if they are anywhere near the mark they demonstrate that the Spanish mercantile system had virtually collapsed by the end of the Habsburg era.

## The "Seventeenth-Century Depression": Theses and Countertheses

The most commonly used leading economic indicators for colonial Spanish America—registered silver entering Seville, the volume of trans-Atlantic commerce, and the size of the Indian work force—all point to a prolonged downturn beginning in the early 1600s. Several historians have interpreted the slump as a "seventeenth-century depression" in the Indies. Woodrow Borah made the seminal statement on the subject in 1951. The Mexican economy, he wrote, began to weaken in the 1590s and by 1650 had sunk into low-level stagnation. His case may be summarized as follows: The great *matlazahuatl* epidemic of 1576–79 dealt a near-mortal blow to the indigenous population and created an acute labor shortage. As a result, agricultural production dropped sharply, and commodity shortages and exorbitant prices brought severe hardships to cities and countrysides. For the same reason, mining production declined. It follows that miners could buy less from ranchers and merchants, and domestic commerce slackened. Furthermore, with less silver at their disposal, Mexicans could import fewer goods from Europe, so that the volume of the trans-Atlantic trade contracted.[33] François Chevalier takes much the same view in his study of the great Mexican hacienda, but, in contrast to Borah, he sees falling commodity prices as one of the causes of stagnation.[34] Pierre Chaunu also supports Borah's interpretation but interposes another variable to help explain the declining volume of overseas commerce, namely, the saturation of the Mexican import market.[35]

The depression thesis derived principally from observations of the behavior of the Mexican economy, but Borah further proposed that the same basic cause, an acute shortage of indigenous labor, brought prolonged hard times to other parts of the Indies. Murdo MacLeod's detailed socioeconomic history of colonial Central America supports this proposition.[36] Confirmative evidence also comes from studies of post-conquest Peru.[37] In the Antilles, the collapse of the sugar industry toward the end of the seventeenth century dealt a severe blow to island economies,[38] and a sharp drop in gold production in New Granada after 1620 visited hardship on that kingdom.[39] In the last two cases, however, the problem was not a shortage of Indian labor but market and technological factors. In sum, depression afflicted not only Mexico but all of Spanish America.

The depression thesis can be challenged on two grounds, one being the adequacy of the indicators on which it is based and the ways in which they have been interpreted. Peter Bakewell and others contend that the principal source of the Mexican mining industry's problems was interruptions in its mercury deliveries and tight credit rather than its labor supply, which, although not abundant, was sufficient for its needs.[40] As for American mining output, Brading and Cross assert that "Hamilton's import figures simply reflect official inefficiency and corruption; they bore little relation to the realities of silver production."[41] Their own calculations show that yields dropped later and much less sharply than Sevillian registrations indicate.

The Chaunu series on ship sailings also have shortcomings as general indicators. All they reveal is that legal Spanish trans-Atlantic and trans-Pacific trade declined during the first half of the seventeenth century. They say nothing about the volume of traffic after 1650, nor do they take into account the supportive and possibly stimulative effects of large-scale contraband trade on the Spanish American economy.

The other challenge to the depression thesis is evidence that directly contradicts it. As a number of scholars have observed, large parts of Spanish America subsisted on the margins of the monetary economy, consuming very few urban products.[42] Therefore, fluctuations in mineral production and trans-Atlantic trade affected them only marginally. Although it cannot be said that they prospered or expanded during the seventeenth century, and although different regions may have suffered short-term ups and downs in the level of their economic activity, they remained more or less stable over the long term.

It has been proposed further that even the monetary-based sectors of the Spanish American economy did not experience general or prolonged distress in the seventeenth century. On the contrary, the collapse of the *Carrera* along with the demands of a growing Europeanized and urbanized population for consumer goods produced internal growth. The English historian John Lynch first expounded this view explicitly: "The crisis in the *carrera de Indias* occurred not because the American economies were collapsing but because they were developing and disengaging themselves from their primitive dependence on the mother country. . . . Spain's recession was America's growth."[43]

Support for this proposition comes from data and observations on the major sectors of the economy of the Indies. Some branches of commercial agriculture appear to have flourished. The American historian Richard Boyer and the French historian François Chevalier estimate that Mexican sugar production increased substantially between 1620 and 1680.[44] Boyer also asserts that despite competition from cheaper and finer Chinese silk Mexican sericulture continued to produce large quantities of medium-grade fiber up to 1650 and probably thereafter.[45] The American historian Miles Wortman believes that Guatemalan indigo growers compensated for the loss of European markets by increasing exports to Mexico, northern South America, and, especially, to Quito and textile centers in Peru.[46]

In South America mining continued to dominate the economy of Peru, but the central and southern parts of the viceroyalty developed a more diversified economy based on artisan industry and on the production of wine, sugar, wheat, and olives along the Peruvian coast. Peruvian agriculture suffered a severe setback in 1687, when an earthquake devastated the coastal area, but one region's loss was another's gain: Chile found an expanding market for its grain in Lima and other Peruvian cities.[47] Farther north, both Guayaquil and Venezuela became important cacao producers in the seventeenth century. Trends in Venezuela's production are revealed by imports into Mexico, its principle market. In 1622 these amounted to only 60 *fanegas* (about 6960 pounds) annually, but during the period 1620–50 they averaged 1150 *fanegas* (about 133,400 pounds) a year and from 1651 through 1700, 6450 *fanegas* (about 748,200 pounds).[48]

The major industries of Spanish America experienced varied fortunes. The silver-mining boom unquestionably ended in the early 1600s, but Brading and Cross believe that thereafter production remained high enough to sustain a healthy level of economic activity.[49] John Lynch concurs and furthermore believes that in the seventeenth century a proportionately larger amount of silver stayed in the Indies than in the sixteenth. There it was used for civil and ecclesiastic expenditures, defense, and private investments and amounted to "a form of economic aid from the metropolis to its dependencies."[50] The Guatemalan historian Carmelo Sáenz de Santa María supports this view. In the 1600s, he reports, Guatemalans erected defensive works on their Caribbean coast, developed its harbors, and built roads into the interior. In their capital city they established a press and a university, raised many public works, and completely reconstructed the cathedral. The magnitude of these undertakings, he contends, does not square with economic stagnation.[51]

As for other major industries, the German historian Hans Pohl finds no evidence of a production crisis in Puebla's *obrajes*, nor does the American historian John Phelan detect one in Quito's.[52] These cities were the main textile centers in the Indies. Boyer estimates that Mexican manufacturing as a whole increased by 50 to 100 percent in the seventeenth century.[53] Spanish American shipbuilding probably expanded, especially in Guayaquil, whose yards increased the Peruvian merchant marine from thirty ships in 1590 to seventy a hundred years later and constructed naval vessels for its defense.[54]

Although the collapse of the *Carrera* initially depressed the commerce of the Indies, the development of internal trade helped to offset this effect. In some areas interregional exchange expanded in range and in volume. By overland routes and by sea, central Mexico imported cacao and dyestuffs from Central America, sending in return textiles and reexports from Europe.[55] The increase in Mexico's cacao trade with Venezuela and in Guatemala's commerce in indigo with South America have already been noted. In the Viceroyalty of

Peru silver, grain, oil, wine, tubers, lard, coca, maté, and textiles passed through a far-flung trading network.[56]

The most important boost to Spanish American commerce was an expansion of a trading system whose main marts were Mexico, the Philippines, and Lima. On paper Mexico's commerce with Manila was limited by the *permiso* (individual import-export license), and Chaunu's figures show a decline in the volume of trans-Pacific trade in the seventeenth century. According to the American historian Louisa Hoberman however, it increased substantially, owing to a growing Spanish American demand for Oriental products such as silks, porcelains, ivory, and exotic spices. A part of these goods was consumed in New Spain and another part was reexported to Europe, but a significant portion went to Peru along with Mexican wheat, cochineal, sugar, pottery, textiles, furniture, and European reexports. Peru returned wines, mercury, cacao from Guayaquil, and above all silver, which helped Mexicans pay for Oriental imports. The growth of the Mexico-Peru trade is indicated by the expansion of the Peruvian merchant marine on which it was carried. After the collapse of the *Carrera*, Hoberman suggests, Mexico City merchants simply shifted their assets from the Atlantic to the Pacific.[57]

Fiscal evidence collected and analyzed by John J. TePaske and Herbert S. Klein throw some flashes of light on seventeenth-century economic trends.[58] Their data are serial statistics on the inflow and outflow of revenues in the main treasuries of Mexico and in the treasury of Lima for the years 1580–1700. Their basic assumption is that changes in the volume of income provide a rough measure of the course of the economy, since revenues derived chiefly from taxes on production. Their conclusions may be summed up as follows. In New Spain economic trends were mixed. The amount of taxes collected from the mining industry reveals short- and intermediate-term fluctuations in silver production, but for the seventeenth century as a whole, yields increased modestly, a finding that confirms and extends the views of Bakewell, Brading, and Cross. The amount of taxes collected on agriculture and commerce also had cyclical ups and downs but over the long term, 1590–1700, changed very little. Because tax rates increased and many exemptions were eliminated in these sectors, the failure of these two economic sectors to generate larger revenues may be taken to mean that at best they stagnated.

TePaske and Klein's analysis of the outflow of revenues from Mexican treasuries confirms Lynch's thesis that in the course of the seventeenth century the proportion of Mexican silver remaining in Mexico increased since the amounts remitted to Castile and the Philippines dropped from slightly over one-half of total collections to about one quarter. Presumably more silver available meant that the government spent more and the private sector invested more, but the authors do not venture an opinion on whether these expenditures sustained or stimulated the economy.

What do the foregoing analyses reveal about the general state of the Mexican economy? The two authors are reluctant to commit themselves on the grounds that their data on sectors other than mining are not sufficiently complete. They simply venture this cautious statement: "If the data do indicate any trend, they suggest stagnation. . . . At the same time the sharp contrast between the public revenues generated in New Spain in the seventeenth century, and those produced in the eighteenth, may also support the view that the seventeenth century was a period of stability, recession, or even crisis."[59]

Although TePaske and Klein focus mainly on New Spain, they also analyze data from the Lima treasury and arrive at a more clear-cut conclusion. Up to 1600, the Peruvian economy had much the same characteristics as the Mexican. After that year, however, treasury revenues dropped sharply, probably because of declining silver production at Potosí and other mines in the viceroyalty. As a result, "Lima fell victim to a serious depression in the second half of the seventeenth century, a crisis lasting over a hundred years."[60]

What can be concluded from the foregoing muster of conflicting information and propositions? It cannot be affirmed with certainty that Spanish America suffered a severe and prolonged seventeenth-century depression marked by a general retreat to the self-sufficiency of rural estates. Although the Indian labor supply unquestionably declined sharply, the government and colonial employers devised ways to use remaining workers more efficiently. Although the silver boom ended, it did not end in a bust. And, although trans-Atlantic trade collapsed, the effect was at least partially offset by the growth of interregional and trans-Pacific commerce and by a sharp increase in contraband, especially in peripheral regions of the Indies where the king's regulations were only indifferently observed.

But neither can it be said that the seventeenth century was an epoch of sustained and vigorous prosperity. Instead, the picture that seems to be emerging from recent scholarship can be sketched out as follows. The economy of the Indies did become more diversified, less dependent on the metropolis, and overall more productive, except in precious metals. A greater amount of capital than previously remained in America to be invested in agriculture, manufacturing, and commerce. As a consequence of expanding regional and interregional trade, the circulation of money increased in areas that during the sixteenth century had primarily subsistence economies. Then, in the last two decades of the seventeenth century, a marked economic upswing began—before the advent of a reforming Bourbon dynasty. Within these general trends, different regions experienced short- and medium-term shifts in fortunes, owing to increases and decreases in mining production, changing market conditions, the fluctuating availability of labor, natural disasters such as droughts, earthquakes, and insect plagues, and the ravages of buccaneers. If any major region suffered a severe and prolonged depression, it was Peru after 1660.

## Structural Changes

In addition, seventeenth-century economic trends created two basic structural changes in the organization of Spanish colonial economies. One was their closer integration around primary and secondary centers. As the Spanish mercantile system decayed, Mexico City replaced Seville as the metropolis of the Indies because it held the largest accumulation of commercial capital in the New World and because it lay at the juncture of major trade routes, one running north-south by land from the northern mines into Central America and by sea into Peru and the other running east-west from Manila through Acapulco to Veracruz. At the same time Mexico City and regional capitals such as Guatemala City, Caracas, and Santiago de Chile extended their sway over their hinterlands.[61] These developments, however, did not alter the monopolistic character of Spanish American trade. It simply shifted monopolistic control from Spanish to American interests.

The other major structural change was the establishment of large-scale direct trade between Spanish America and the nations of northern Europe via contraband routes that bypassed Seville. The pattern of trans-Atlantic exchange, however, remained essentially the same: primary products of the Indies for European manufactures and luxury goods, with prices for both American exports and imports set in European markets.

## The Post-Conquest Brazilian Economy

Brazil had no mines of precious metals until the Paulistas discovered gold at the very end of the seventeenth century, nor did it have a good supply of cheap indigenous labor. Its small population generated only a small demand for goods, and its more or less uniform climate prevented diversified regional production of foods and fibers. As a result of these circumstances, domestic commerce was limited to local markets and manufacturing to local artisanry, domestic weaving, small-scale food processing, and the distillation of cheap spirits. The growth of the colonial economy depended heavily on the exploitation of agricultural, pastoral, and forest resources for export to Europe.

The Sugar Boom

The most important Brazilian export by far was sugar. Indeed the economic history of the colony after the Conquest is the history of a sugar cycle lasting more than a hundred years.[62] Several circumstances conjoined to fuel the boom phase that began in the 1570s and extended into the 1640s. The rise of sugar prices in Europe that began in the early sixteenth century continued into the 1600s, and in Brazil itself production factors generally favored the growth of the industry. An abundant supply of oxen for transport made it feasible to plant land up to two days' travel from the sea and to haul wood for fuel to plantations from a distance. Capital for expansion could be obtained from the swelling profits from the sale of sugar as well as from European investors.

At first glance it might appear that the supply of labor favored sugar production. Indigenous workers were inadequate in number and quality, but the Portuguese conquest of Angola in the 1570s opened a rich new source of African slaves, and Portugal controlled all African slaving stations until the Dutch seized El Mina and Luanda in the 1640s. All told some 500,000 Africans came to Brazil involuntarily in the seventeenth century.[63] But these data do not mean that slaves were cheap and plentiful. In 1575 the Portuguese government initiated a system of *contratos* or *asientos* (contracts), similar to the Spanish *asientos*, whereby contractors paid the royal treasury 22,000 to 80,000 *cruzados* annually for the right to introduce specified numbers of slaves at Brazilian ports. It was a monopolistic arrangement that artificially controlled supply and raised prices. Contractors and traders, moreover, preferred to divert shipments to Spanish America, where they brought even higher prices. The need for frequent replacement must also be taken into account in calculating labor costs. Field hands had an average working life of from seven to ten years only, and they generally failed to reproduce themselves. Although the supply of slaves was sufficient to support the growth of a planting, labor constituted the highest and most vulnerable fixed cost of the sugar industry.

The organization of sugar production remained essentially the same as in earlier years. The central unit was the mill, which processed cane grown by the owner or by independent small proprietors, lessees, and sharecroppers who could not afford their own equipment. Mills ranged in size from a few that had an annual capacity of 160 tons and employed upward of 100 slaves down to many more that could produce around 50 tons a year and that used some 20 slaves. The larger mills were water-powered (*engenhos d'agua*); many of the smaller ones (*trapiches* or *almajarras*) used oxen for power. Most mills of all sizes belonged to private parties, but colleges of the Society of Jesus owned some of the most profitable ones. Around the middle of the seventeenth century, white sugar accounted for from 65 to 70 percent of their total output by weight.[64]

The growth of the Brazilian sugar industry was reflected in both an increase in the number of mills and a rise in the average annual output per mill, as shown in table 8.

Table 8
Brazilian Sugar Production, 1576–1644
(Output in Short Tons [2000 pounds each])

| Year | Total Number of Mills | Average Output per Mill | Total Output* |
|---|---|---|---|
| 1576 | 57 | 44 | 2500 |
| 1584 | 120 | 46 | 5500 |
| 1610 | 230 | 61 | 14,000 |
| 1618 | . . . | . . . | 13,500 |
| 1623 | . . . | . . . | 18,700 |
| 1628 | 346 | 58 | 20,200 |
| 1637–44 (average) | 300 | 67 | 20,000 |

*Source:* David Denslow, "The First Brazilian Sugar Cycle, Growth and Maturity" an unpublished paper graciously lent to me by the author, p. 12.

*Celso Furtado, a leading Brazilian economic historian, puts annual production during the peak years of the cycle much higher, at about 32,500 tons (*Formação econômica do Brazil* [Rio de Janeiro: Editôra Fundo de Cultura, 1959], trans. Ricardo W. Aguiar and Eric C. Drysdale as *The Economic Growth of Brazil* [Berkeley: University of California Press, 1963], p. 45 of the English edition).

A report prepared in 1629 provides some information on sugar production by region. Of a total of 346 mills, Pernambuco had 150; Bahia, 80; and Rio de Janeiro, 60. The total output of each captaincy stood in the same order. Bahia, however, had the largest annual output per mill because it had more large *engenhos*. It was followed by Pernambuco and then by Rio de Janeiro, where the size of mills was below the general average for Brazil. The remaining mills, 56 in number, and the balance of production were distributed among the captaincies of São Vicente, Ilhéus, Pôrto Seguro, and Sergipe.[65]

The End of the Boom

The Brazilian sugar boom ended around the middle of the seventeenth century, not in a bust or in a depression but in a leveling off of production at

around 20,000 short tons annually. The slowdown resulted in part from changing market conditions. Prices dropped sharply in the last half of the seventeenth
century when production from the English and French West Indian islands began reaching Europe in large quantities. In the 1650s, sugar sold on the Amsterdam wholesale market at a high of 0.73 guilders a pound; in the 1670s it
brought only 0.27 to 0.28 guilders.[66] West Indian plantations also offered intense competition to the Brazilian industry because their soils were fresh, because they employed a more advanced technology introduced by the Dutch,
and because their location and nationality gave them quicker and more direct
access to northern European markets.

The continued expansion of the Brazilian industry was hindered further by
rising fixed production costs. These owed to the declining soil fertility in older
planting zones and the doubling of African slave prices between 1640 and
1680. The result of these circumstances was that between 1628 and 1710 the
total number of mills in Brazil increased from 346 to 528 but the average annual output per mill dropped from 58 to 40 short tons.

Still another adverse development was the Dutch occupation of Pernambuco
(1630–54), which was accompanied by the burning of fields and the slaughter
of oxen for food by both Hollanders and Brazilians. These depredations disrupted planting and milling for many years in what had been the colony's most
productive sugar captaincy. After the departure of the invaders, recovery came
slowly, principally because of time required to rebuild depleted oxen herds.

The difficulties of the Brazilian sugar industry climaxed in a sharp recession
in the 1680s, brought about by a succession of bad harvests and the appearance of yellow fever, which killed slaves, planters, technicians, and merchants
alike. Production recovered around the turn of the century and in the early
1700s reached about 21,000 short tons. Sugar continued to be an important
export commodity, but gold replaced it as the principal source of the colony's
wealth.[67]

## Brazilwood, Tobacco, Cotton, and Hides

Other products of fields, ranges, and forests made smaller and, in most
cases, cyclical contributions to Brazil's market economy.[68] Until the early seventeenth century, annual exports of dyewood fluctuated around 10,000 hundredweights (about 500 tons). By the mid-1600s they had fallen by half, because steady cutting had brought down prices and diminished accessible stands
of trees.[69] Bahia and Pernambuco produced tobacco on small plots worked
chiefly by *lavradores*. Some of the leaf was sent to Europe, but most went to

Africa to pay for slaves. Exports reached 1250 tons in 1610 and peaked some time after 1650.[70] Cotton planting made a good start in the northern captaincies during the last half of the sixteenth century, but exports dropped in the early 1700s owing to competition from Venetian-controlled sources of staple.

Brazilian cattle ranching invites particular mention because it developed in the interior, outside a predominantly plantation economy, and with its own organizational forms. By 1640 the spread of grazing in the interior ended dependence on leather imports from Portugal, the Cape Verdes, and the Rio de la Plata and permitted the export of hides, which in the 1670s reached a volume of 15,000 to 20,000 annually.[71] The emergence of an overseas market along with the emptiness of the backlands and the land hunger of cattle barons encouraged the concentration of grazing lands in great *fazendas*, similar in organization to and approaching in size the cattle haciendas of northern Mexico. But the great age of the Brazilian cattle industry did not open until the very end of the seventeenth century, when settlers began to move into the rich grasslands of the southernmost captaincies.

The Organization of
Brazilian Import-Export Commerce

The several products of Brazil fed into a triangular trading system whose corners lay in metropolitan Portugal, particularly Lisbon and Porto; in Luanda, in Angola; and in Brazil itself, especially Recife-Olinda, Bahia, and Rio. Exchange might be carried on in any direction along the three sides. Ships commonly left Portuguese ports for Luanda or Brazilian destinations carrying European manufactures, fine wines and foodstuffs, and Oriental reexports. Angolan exports consisted of some ivory to Europe but mainly of slaves to Brazil. Brazil sent sugar and other agricultural products to Europe to pay for imported goods, and tobacco and cheap spirits to Angola in return for slaves. Lusitanian Atlantic trade depended heavily on connections with northern European and Spanish commercial networks. Since Portugal manufactured very little, a large part of its own and its colonies' needs had to be obtained from other nations, among which England furnished a steadily growing share toward the end of the seventeenth century. Portugal's exports of wine, fruits, cork, and salt to northern Europe, however, did not suffice to pay for imports. Brazilian sugar along with Spanish silver obtained from the slave trade to the Caribbean, to the Rio de la Plata, and through Seville helped to redress the balance. Spanish American bullion also financed the remnants of commerce with the Orient and supplied the royal mints.[72]

The Portuguese mercantile regime had a much looser and more flexible organization than the Spanish. Until well into the 1600s the crown allowed all its subjects as well as friendly foreign nationals to traffic freely with Portuguese and Brazilian ports, subject only to the payment of import and export duties. The monopolistic slave and dyewood trades constituted important exceptions. The costs of the war for independence against Spain (1640–68), however, and the continued losses to Dutch privateers in the Atlantic induced the government to experiment with new revenue-producing and defense measures. Drawing on Spanish practice, in 1649 Portugal required shipping between Portugal and Bahia to sail in convoy, and, taking a lesson from the English and Dutch, it brought leading metropolitan merchants together in a joint stock venture called the Brazil Company. The company obtained a twenty-year monopoly of the wine, oil, flour, and cod trade with Portuguese America, to which the exploitation of brazilwood was later added. In return it had to provide armed escorts for trans-Atlantic fleets.

These organizational innovations had a short life span. The Brazil Company provoked the hostility of excluded merchants on both sides of the Atlantic, and Brazilians complained that fleets sailed so tardily and irregularly that warehoused sugar deteriorated while awaiting shipment. In 1658, therefore, the king disbanded the company, giving compensation to stockholders, and five years later organized in its stead the *Junta de Comercio* (Council of Trade) with powers to regulate the American trade. Under the council's auspices, convoyed fleets continued to sail until well into the eighteenth century, and intermittent efforts were made to regularize schedules, but the number of exempted vessels generally exceeded those going with the fleets.

By no means all of Brazil's commerce passed through legal channels. Colonials thought import, export, and reexport duties excessive, and their evasions of these imposts added up to a lively clandestine trade, especially in tobacco, which may help to account for the leveling off of officially recorded exports after 1650. Everyone who could participated: planters, merchants, meagerly paid royal officials, and officers and crews of outward bound vessels, including East Indiamen that came to call regularly at Bahia in the late 1600s. In addition to smuggling by Portuguese nationals, foreign vessels, especially English, openly picked up contraband at Bahia and Rio de Janeiro. As in Spanish America, no one knows the volume of clandestine traffic, but alarms sounded by the crown and its repeated warnings to colonial governors intimate that it was substantial.

## Structures of Dependency

A description of the economies of colonial Hispanic America would be incomplete without at least a nod to modern dependency theory. It has long been known, of course, that the Spanish and Portuguese possessions in the New World were economically dependent on Europe. According to classical economic theory, their dependent condition owed to a disadvantageous international division of labor imposed on them by superior European financial power supported by metropolitan mercantile policies. Under this arrangement they were required to produce primary goods for export at cheap prices and import finished goods at dear prices.

Beginning in the 1950s, efforts of Latin American social scientists to explain and remedy economic underdevelopment produced fresh theoretical formulations about the nature and consequences of dependency. In the 1960s a number of North American scholars, mostly from the New Left, joined their ranks. The new dependency theorists were often strident, dogmatic, and careless about their use of empirical data, but by the 1970s their writings had won a measure of respectability in academic circles.

Speaking very generally, modern dependency theory is based on the following set of propositions: (1) The development of an economically dominant region imposes dependency on other countries and regions that it dominates. (2) Dependency, however, cannot be attributed solely to external forces; it owes in part to internal infrastructural weakness. (3) Dependency creates underdevelopment, for it is not in the interests of dominant centers to encourage or even allow the development of subordinate regions. (4) Thus, underdevelopment is a chronic state that cannot be escaped through evolutionary stages of advancement; countries such as England were never dependent or *under*developed, they were simply once *un*developed. (5) Underdevelopment can only be remedied by the elimination of external and internal structures of dependency.[73]

Although sharing a consensus on the essential nature of dependency, modern theorists differ greatly in their methods of analysis, according to their ideological convictions, the relative weight they assign to external and internal forces, and the depth of their historical perspectives. Of particular relevance to the theme of this book are the writings of historically minded analysts, generally of Marxist or neo-Marxist persuasion, who find the origins of dependency and underdevelopment in the mercantile expansion of Europe in the sixteenth and seventeenth centuries. The most erudite and comprehensive exposition of

this view is the work of the American sociologist-historian Immanuel Wallerstein, *The Modern World-System*, vol. 1: *Capitalist Agriculture and the Origins
of the European World-Economy in the Sixteenth Century*, vol. 2: *Mercantilism
and the Consolidation of the European World-Economy, 1600–1750.*[74] With
more particular reference to colonial Hispanic America, the study best known
to historians is *The Colonial Heritage of Latin America: Essays on Historical
Dependency*, an essentially descriptive account by the American historians
Stanley and Barbara Stein.[75]

The most influential theoretical statement on colonial Hispanic American
dependency is, however, the essays of the Canadian social scientist Andre
Gunder Frank in his book *Capitalism and Underdevelopment in Latin America:
Historical Studies of Chile and Brazil.*[76] Frank's point of departure is an attack
on the conventional dualist conception of Latin American societies in which
one sector is identified as modern, capitalist, and linked to national and international markets while the other is viewed as agrarian, self-sufficient, and
"feudal," a part of the colonial heritage. The epitome of feudalism was the
great hacienda. Dualism was invented by nineteenth-century liberal elites who
thought that development could be achieved by modernizing the archaic sector. Marxists of the time accepted the idea of dualism, believing that the modernization of the feudal sector would complete the bourgeois revolution and
pave the way for the downfall of capitalism. In challenging the dualist position,
Frank argues that Hispanic America had a capitalist economy and was part of
an emerging world capitalist system from the sixteenth century onward, for
even its most remote and "feudal" areas were linked to regional and international markets.[77]

Frank conceputalized this relationship as a process of expropriation and appropriation of surpluses at various levels. Thus, the world capitalist "center"
or "metropolis" (Europe) expropriated the surpluses of peripheries or satellites
(the major regions of Latin America) and appropriated them for its development, leaving peripheries without resources for their own. The expropriation-
appropriation process continued downward to the economic relationships between colonial satellites such as Mexico City and Lima and subsatellites such
as Santiago de Chile, between subsatellites and mining areas and haciendas,
and, at the lowest level, between these units of production and the workers
who served them. In Frank's schema Spain and Portugal were briefly world
centers, but, as their economies lagged, they themselves became satellites of
the rising centers of northern Europe. Frank further proposes that, when the

centers of world capitalism experienced crises or hard times, as did much of Europe in the seventeenth century, the dependency of satellites loosened and they retained a larger proportion of their surpluses. But, when the centers recovered, they were invariably able to reimpose dependency.

In imposing this system, the forces of world capitalism were supported by the mercantile monopolists of Seville, the colonial merchant class in viceregal and provincial cities, and Spanish American landed interests, for, although each rendered its surplus to superordinate levels, each did very well by expropriating and appropriating from subordinate levels.

Frank concludes that colonial dependency structures have survived until the present day. They are so deeply rooted and so firmly fixed that they cannot be remedied by reforms within the capitalist system but can only be eliminated by destroying capitalism itself or escaping from its orbit.

The theories of Frank received a mixed reception. Doctrinaire Marxists accepted his expropriation-appropriation model but attacked his departure from orthodoxy; he described capitalism as simply a profit-driven market system rather than as a social mode of production, and he paid insufficient attention to the class struggle.[78] Non-Marxists found his work redundant, excessively dogmatic, and strident. The present author, a confessed non-Marxist, believes that both Frank and his Marxist critics disregard two important influences shaping colonial dependency. One was normative Hispanic social attitudes that discouraged efficient accumulation and uses of capital. The other was the social conservatism of colonial elites. Not only did they profit from their dependent status—as Frank pointed out—but they feared that modernization of production would loosen the bonds of servitude and subordination of the non-European population, which were the warp and woof of the social order.

Nevertheless, historical dependency theory has made significant contributions to colonial Hispanic American historiography. It has helped to dispose of artificial distinctions between feudal and capitalistic elements in colonial economies, and it has demonstrated, or at least confirmed, that production in the Indies was much more diversified and interregional trade wider in range than has commonly been assumed. Frank's expropriation-appropriation model itself is the most comprehensive conceptualization of the structures of Hispanic colonial economies that can be found. It defines the essential nature of economic exchange at and between local, regional, continental, and transoceanic levels; it accounts for the shift of economic dominance from Hispanic metropolises to northern European centers; and it accommodates the trends toward colonial diversification and self-sufficiency discussed earlier in this chapter.

It must be said, however, that dependency theory has inspired precious little empirical research—at least on sixteenth- and seventeenth-century Hispanic America—and that is the main utility of theory in the social as well as the natural sciences. Instead, dependency analysts have tended to expend their efforts on recasting known empirical data into their theoretical molds or on the elaboration of theory and increasingly sterile doctrinaire disputes.[79]

# CHAPTER 18

# American Societies and American Identities

Throughout the colonial era persons of European descent in the Indies still believed firmly that a properly formed republic should be constituted by a hierarchy of orders, each possessing distinct ascribed and juridical statuses. By the end of the Conquest, however, it had become clear that the traditional ordering—nobility, clergy, and commoners—could not be reproduced in America. They were already archaic in Europe, the crown opposed the presence of a powerful nobility in America, and, above all, the medieval concept of a republic could not accommodate the millions of non-Europeans who made up most of the American population.

For these reasons the social order in the seventeenth-century Indies was hierarchical, but its constituent elements were defined by the Spanish in ostensibly racial terms—a Republic of Spaniards, a Republic of Indians, and a "third order" of free blacks and mixed bloods who had not been assimilated into European or Indian society and who were presumed to have an African taint.[1] As in chapter 3 "race" is defined here not as a biologically distinct population but as a belief held by human groups that they are different from other groups by virtue of their innate and immutable physical characteristics, that these characteristics are intrinsically related to cultural attributes, and that such differences are a legitimate justification for invidious distinctions among peoples.

## The Republic of Spaniards and Its Ordering

The Spaniards made the rules and therefore constituted the superior order. Regardless of rank or provenance, they perceived themselves as descendants by legitimate lineage of a race of conquerors, as *gente de razón* (rational human beings capable of living in polity), and as Catholics of impeccable orthodoxy. They pretended to "purity of blood," which in the Indies meant freedom from African and pagan Indian contamination as well as from Jewish and Moorish taint. Their self-perception also had physical overtones. They saw themselves as vigorous, robust, and light complexioned, a hue that they ordinarily described as *bermejo* (ruddy or florid) rather than white (*blanco*). In law they possessed a wide range of behavioral and occupational freedoms and enjoyed exemptions from personal taxes.

The Aristocracy

The concept of functional orders continued to influence the internal con-stitution of the Republic of Spaniards, but important changes occurred in sources of status. The *encomendero* class, more or less conterminous with the sons of conquerors and first settlers, continued to be the most aristocratic group in colonial society, and the king declared its members to be *beneméritos de Indias* (the well-deserving in the Indies) by virtue of services rendered by their ancestors. It did not, however, complete its evolution into a true noble estate. Through its inability or unwillingness to fulfill its military obligations, the defense of the realm passed into the charge of municipal militias and royal companies and battalions. The king refrained from granting it the *fuero* of hidalgos on a wholesale basis, and, through the New Laws and subsequent anti-*encomienda* legislation, he deprived *encomenderos* of *señorial* rights and re-fused them perpetual tenure of their fiefs, an attribute essential to the existence of a nobility. Finally, the continuing decline in the indigenous population eroded the economic and territorial bases of their influence.

Meanwhile a new aristocracy emerged consisting of *moradores* and latter-day *adelantados* who created large haciendas. Although ownership of land even in great amounts, did not automatically convey honor and esteem, it furnished an economic and territorial base for social advancement that *hacendados* ex-ploited in various ways. They entailed their properties if they could afford to do so. They acquired resident work forces and, through the territorial union of their land and dependent labor, gained a form of de facto *señorío* much more durable than the *encomienda*. Like the old *encomendero* class, they main-tained imposing houses in towns of their provinces and obtained seats in *ca-bildos*. They reinforced their civil sources of status with officerships in local militias. Landowning families intermarried, thereby consolidating holdings and forming an ever-widening network of kinship influence.

A certain fusion between old and new aristocracies took place. Enterprising *encomenderos* created haciendas that they worked with their Indians. The crown gave vacant or escheated *encomiendas* to favored *hacendados*. The two groups intermarried to mutual advantage; *encomenderos* acquired haciendas or enlarged those they already had, and *hacendado* families joined their lineages to those of the *beneméritos*. But as *encomiendas* shrank in numbers and size and haciendas grew and multiplied, the landed estate became the most common source of aristocratic status in the Indies.

The landed aristocracy, like the *encomenderos*, gave some promise of evolving into a colonial nobility. Some of its members already possessed *nobleza* through descent from Spanish hidalgos or ennobled conquerors and first settlers. This was the most solid source, and the more ancient the lineage the better. But those who did not inherit nobility could win it in one of two ways. The more legitimate was through cedulas of *hidalguía* given by the king for distinguished services to the republic in military action, in civil government, or in the form of liberal donations to the royal treasury. If the contribution rendered was on a grand enough scale it might win a noble title. Such services might also be rewarded with knighthoods in the Spanish military orders that, although not inheritable, added luster to family names and amounted to a foot in the door of nobility.

Another route to nobility was through reputation. The essential requirement was well-known and undisputed purity of blood, but this attribute had to be complemented by behavioral qualities associated with nobility. These included honor, virtue, courage, charity, and generosity demonstrated by donations of money, land, and sons and daughters to the church and by liberal contributions to civic causes. They also included a noble life-style as evidenced by an elegant townhouse overflowing with hospitality, lordship over an extended household, and ostentatious expenditure. Through the display of these virtures, families "became known" as noble, and, if reputational status could be maintained for three generations on both the maternal and paternal sides, it could be formalized through a process of legal proof called *limpieza de nobleza*. Ennoblement by this method, however, did not have the same legitimacy as that conveyed by either lineage or royal grace.[2]

No one has counted the number of families who inherited or acquired formal, documented nobility. They probably amounted to only a small proportion of the Spanish American aristocracy. During the sixteenth and seventeenth centuries nearly 1000 Americans obtained titles in the Spanish military orders, but, again, the beneficiaries represented only a fraction of the families of quality.[3]

The king conceded a mere handful of titles of Castile for services in the Indies, and most of these went to royal officials who returned to Spain. Also, several titled families with roots in America, such as the marquises of the Valley of Oaxaca and the counts of Moctezuma, became expatriates. Reputational nobility, however, appears to have been common from Mexico to Chile.

### The Common Classes

Among the more common classes of Spaniards, the merchant community had the highest social rank. By the end of the Conquest it was firmly established in the major cities of the Indies, and during the mercantile and mining boom that began in the 1560s its numbers and wealth increased. The money it possessed went a long way toward compensating for the social stigma attached to buying and selling for gain. The rich importers and silver merchants of Mexico City and Lima constituted a mercantile elite. The chartering of *consulados* (merchant guilds) in these capitals (Mexico, 1594; Lima, 1613) enhanced their position by consolidating their monopoly of overseas trade, formalizing their corporate status, and providing them with a collective voice in their dealings with royal and municipal officials. The merchant guilds gained public favor by using their resources to build hospitals, charitable institutions, and roads and bridges.

Other common classes in the Republic of Spaniards grew in size: lawyers and notaries to document, argue, and judge a growing volume of civil and criminal suits; mine and mill owners; artisans, shopkeepers, itinerant traders, and small agriculturists to serve the material wants of an expanding population; and majordomos to manage the estates and households of the wealthy. The lowest stratum of Spanish society consisted of indigent laborers and vagabonds who lacked the ability or disposition to find respectable employment. Very little is known about the size or distribution of this class in the seventeenth century, but, if the reports of colonial officials are credited, it was large enough to create a serious social problem in many parts of the Indies.

### The Clergy and the Royal Bureaucracy

The status and influence of the church in the Indies increased greatly during the seventeenth century. The foundation of new towns, the growth of old ones, and the secularization of Indian congregations required the establishment of new parishes and swelled the lower ranks of the secular clergy. Territorial expansion and population growth led to the creation of new dioceses and more prelates, deans, and canons. Among the regulars, the populations of monasteries and nunneries multiplied, and the Society of Jesus dominated many frontiers. Land and capital accumulated by religious foundations and perpetuated through mortmain supported influence provided by function, numbers, and office. Despite restrictions imposed on the church by the *patronato real*, it enjoyed the generous support of the crown, and it attracted universal reverence, devotion, and generosity from its communicants. The ecclesiastical *fuero* gave it a secure corporate existence.

The king's officials in the Indies formed a growing component of the Republic of Spaniards. They were members of a "royal estate" performing a particular function and enjoying rank and privilege by virtue of royal grace. Their core consisted of *letrados*, staffing audiencias, lower magistracies, and treasury posts, who held university degrees in civil or canon law, an attribute that gave them a common professional identity.

## The Republic of Indians: Status and Ordering

In the last decades of the sixteenth century, the Spanish came to conceive of the indigenes not only as a conquered people, as *gente sin razón* (people incapable of rational behavior), and as *rústicas* (uncouth and untutored), but as irredeemably slothful, improvident, and defective in Christianity. Europeans also identified Indians by their physical traits. They were smaller and less robust than Europeans. Their hair was straight and coarse, and their beards grew sparsely.[4] Their color ran from medium to dark brown, a shade that the Spaniards described as *aindiado* (Indian colored).[5] It was not, however, so different from their own hue as to arouse strong antipathies.

As a complement to their social reputation, the Indians had a distinct juridical status, despite the fact that by the end of the sixteenth century Castilian substantive and procedural law, as adapted for use in America, had superseded native customs and usages in cases to which they were parties. They still had to pay tribute to their masters as a mark of their subjugation, and legal restrictions on their freedom of movement and behavior accumulated. But as perceptions of their rationality became more negative and the need for their protection grew more urgent, they gained compensatory advantages. First rhetorically and later (in the 1640s) juridically, they became identified as *miserables*, people recognized in the Old Testament and defined by Emperor Constantine's jurists as disadvantaged—widows, orphans, and the like—who deserved public compassion and protection.

The crown recognized the "miserable" condition of the Indians by various measures. It continued to appoint high-ranking civil and ecclesiastical officials as their "protectors"; it accorded them special testamentary rights; and it declared them immune from the direct jurisdiction of the Inquisition. Perhaps most important, it established general Indian courts (*juzgados de indios*) in Mexico in 1573 and in Lima in the early 1600s to take cognizance of suits between Indians and Spaniards and between Indian parties themselves.

The Republic of Indians had its own internal ordering. At its apex stood the decendants of the pre-Conquest nobility whose status had been confirmed by the crown through cedulas of *hidalguía* and grants of other privileges and immunities. In the seventeenth century, however, several circumstances combined to erode their preeminence. Indian resettlement disturbed the territorial and kinship bases of their power, and, as the royal bureaucracy expanded, the crown became less dependent on their political intermediation. In some instances commoners challenged their domination of indigenous municipal government. The growth of Spanish estates put pressure on their lands, and, as Indian populations declined or villagers migrated to towns and haciendas, nobles sometimes had to make up the tribute demanded by the royal treasury from their own pockets. Their fortunes varied from region to region, but as a class they tended to become proletarianized.

The commonality of Indians consisted of two classes. the largest was the *indios de pueblo*, that is, indigenes who were bound by law to live in fixed communities, pay tribute, and serve in *repartimientos* and *mitas*. It was principally this group that the Spaniards regarded as *sin razón*, *rústica*, and *miserable*. The second class, sometimes called *forasteros* (literally strangers), was formed by indigenes who escaped their villages and settled in *barrios* around Spanish towns or who became attached to Spanish landed estates. They had an ambiguous legal status and did not properly belong to the Repubic of Indians.

### The "Third Order" of Society: Mixed Bloods and Free Blacks

By the end of the 1600s, two centuries of widespread and indiscriminate miscegenation had produced in the Indies an increasingly homogenous mixed-blood population into which particular types of mixtures such as mestizos, mulattoes, and *zambos* tended to blend. Europeans assumed that it must be permeated by African blood owing to what today is called gene flow and linked it reputationally to the free black element. Thus, they came to define a third major grouping in the society of the Indies and attributed to its members a more or less common set of phenotypical and cultural characteristics that, according to the eminent seventeenth-century jurist Juan de Solórzano y

Pereyra, "are natural to them and are nurtured in their mother's milk."[6] On the average they were darker than were Europeans and Indians, of a color called *pardo* (brown). Because of the promiscuous conditions of their conception they were presumed to be illegitimate. The association of African heritage with slavery made them infamous in fact, if not in law. In European eyes they were addicted to idleness, vagabondage, licentiousness, insolence, unruliness, and irreverence. The Spaniards believed that these defects and vices made them a threat to religion and public order, and, as their numbers increased, so did their social visibility and the Spaniards' apprehensions.[7]

Because mixed bloods and free blacks reputedly lacked civic virtues and performed no useful social functions, they could not be constituted as a third republic. Nevertheless, they acquired a juridical status of sorts. The crown imposed legal disabilities upon them of much the same kind as those born by the Indians. They were required to pay tribute; their freedom of movement and assembly was severely restricted; and they were forbidden to bear arms, occupy public office, and enter universities. The church denied them admission to the clergy, and guilds excluded them. But unlike the indigenes they enjoyed no compensatory advantages. Although they were nominally free, their degraded reputational and legal status made them in effect a "third order" in Spanish colonial society.

As in the republics of Spaniards and Indians, social rankings existed in the third order. Pure mestizos, insofar as they could be identified, held a higher repute than blacks and mixtures stained by African blood. But a more general distinction emerged between a majority to whom ascribed defects continued to cling and a minority who managed to improve their reputation through sacramental marriage, by taking up an honest if not an honorable occupation, and by establishing a fixed residence.

## The Status of Slaves

Although Indian slavery survived surreptitiously after the Conquest, mostly on military frontiers, the vast majority of slaves in the seventeenth-century Indies were blacks and mulattoes. Unlike their free brethren, they were not properly part of the social order because of their most essential condition; they were human chattels subject to a substantial body of special law whose origins dated back to the Middle Ages and that defined the conditions under which people might be enslaved and the nature of their servitude. Yet status differences appeared even among slaves. Those who were Hispanicized and worked as domestics, especially in wealthy households, along with artisans and skilled laborers and those who were descendants of important African families formed an elite of sorts. *Bozales* and unskilled workers in mines and workshops and on plantations had a lower status both in the eyes of the Spaniards and within the slave population itself.

## Social Boundaries and Social Mobility

Differences in social rank and status were well fixed in Spanish opinion and law but were not immutable. Slaves could obtain freedom in one of several ways whose order of use was: first, purchase by the slave himself, by relatives, or by some other benefactor; second, voluntary action of a master; and, third, court award based on proof of illegal treatment by an owner. How many slaves were manumitted in colonial Spanish America is unknown, but the number was probably substantial. In any event, emancipation admitted the beneficiary into the lower ranks of the social order.

Since behavioral as well as physical characteristics influenced social status, Indians who escaped their villages, settled around Spanish towns, and learned European ways became cultural mestizos. Families of the third order who lived decently and who were not too dark blended culturally with lower-class Spaniards and occasionally intermarried with them. If the legitimate descendants of such families maintained socially acceptable forms of behavior, they might escape the legal disabilities imposed on mixed bloods and free blacks and become de facto Spaniards. Social mobility of this kind could be hastened if individuals moved from the towns of their birth to others where their family origins were unknown.

The practical needs of state and society contributed further to the erosion of boundaries between orders. In order to fill the poorly paid and relatively nonprestigious lower ranks of the guilds, the army, and even the clergy, prohibitions against the admission of mixed bloods and free blacks had to be overlooked or excused. This happened most openly and commonly in military service. In the seventeenth century, mixed bloods made up most of the strength of presidial companies in Chile and northern Mexico, and along the Caribbean coast of South America royal officials raised units of free mulattoes and blacks, some of which had colored officers.

One can only speculate about how general social mobility was among the lower orders in the seventeenth century. It was probably less common and less easy than during the disorderly Conquest era. After the Spaniards established their dominion firmly, their racial prejudices hardened and their anxieties about uprisings from below deepened. In addition, the lowest classes among them regarded the advancement of non-Spaniards as threats to their jobs and as encroachments on their privileged status. Furthermore, Spanish perceptions of race created differential opportunities for upward mobility and limited the level that could be achieved. As a general rule, the lighter the skin, the easier "passage" became, but the upper ranks of colonial society remained closed to persons of color.

The Republic of Spaniards itself lacked a well-defined hierarchy, for the identities of its several orders were only weakly developed and the functional lines between them loosely drawn. Like the old *encomendero* elite, the seventeenth-century aristocracy lacked the qualities of a true nobility. Since it was not a warrior class and did not occupy high posts in the royal service, it did not perform the traditional social functions of a noble order. Because it was of recent provenance and its *nobleza* largely reputational, its legitimacy was shaky. Although some of its members enjoyed the *fuero* of hidalgos, as a group it did not possess a corporate identity.

The aristocracy's widespread engagement in crass commerce further weakened its pretensions to nobility. Perhaps its preoccupation with buying and selling came from its inevitable absorption into an increasingly market-based economy, or perhaps it reflected an older relationship described by the sixteenth-century writer Juan Huarte de San Juan, in his *Examen de ingenios*: "To be well born and of famous lineage is a very highly esteemed jewel but it has one great fault, by itself it has little benefit . . . but linked to wealth there is no point of honor that can equal it."[8]

But beneath these particular sources of debility lay a more fundamental historical trend. By the seventeenth century, it was too late for a true nobility to develop in the Indies. Even in Europe noble status was no longer part of the natural order, sanctified by God and perpetuated by lineage, but a legal condition created by royal concession.

The American social environment also had dissolvent effects on the more firmly constituted upper "estates," the royal service, and the clergy. The crown forbade its servants to acquire local interests that compromised their official functions, but those born in America were already compromised at the time of their appointment, and those sent from Spain evaded such prohibitions or composed violations by money payments to the royal treasury. Clergymen, too, had or established secular connections that diverted them from their ministry. In the seventeenth century, the king's officials from viceroys to *corregidores* and churchmen from prelates to parish priests and friars commonly had family ties in the Indies and, like the nobility, engaged in commercial and real-estate ventures.

Spanish commoners also lacked a firmly defined identity. In Europe, their status rested on municipal *fueros* and representation in *cabildos* and cortes. But, even compared with the decaying municipalities of Castile, American towns and cities had few real liberties. Their *procuradores* could not gather in representative assemblies, and colonial aristocracies dominated municipal governments. The commonality, furthermore, did not regard itself as really common. All Spaniards in the Indies pretended to noble qualities and all enjoyed exemption from head taxes, a privilege reserved in Spain for proven hidalgos. The merchant class, which constituted the most vigorous element among commoners, showed a disposition to join the aristocracy through acquiring haciendas and marrying into landed families. In 1673 the viceroy of Mexico, the marquis of Mancera, wrote: "The merchants and traders who in the Indies comprise a good part of the Spanish nation, approach the nobility very much, affecting their carriage and style. . . . It can be generally reckoned that for the most part in these provinces the gentleman is a merchant and a merchant is a gentleman."[9]

Thus, the merchant class moving from one direction and the landed aristocracy from another tended to merge into an oligarchy characterized by pretensions to nobility and the possession of mercantile and landed wealth. The constitution of this group had contradictory features. On the one hand, its membership, individual and family, had a high rate of turnover, for landed estates as well as mercantile fortunes were vulnerable to dispersion under Spanish inheritance laws. Furthermore, they often had to be sold outside the family owing to unprofitable operation and an unpayable burden of debt. On the other hand, the oligarchy had a remarkable structural stability because as one landed or mercantile family sank from view it was replaced by another with the same sources of wealth and having or developing the same social pretensions.

The greatest hindrance to the proper ordering of the Republic of Spaniards was a fracture that ran through it from top to bottom, through all ranks and orders, separating those born in Spain from those born in America. European Spaniards called their American-born cousins *criollos* (creoles). Generically this word simply meant persons or animals indigenous or acclimated to a particular environment, but in the Indies it acquired a pejorative social meaning. American birth, Europeans believed, produced natural defects very likely worsened by African or Indian contamination, that manifested themselves in behavioral qualities: fecklessness, improvidence, and dilettantism.

Creoles sometimes called European Spaniards *peninsulares* (people from the peninsula), a neutral word. More commonly they used the terms *chapetón* (in

Peru) and *gachupín* (in Mexico), both of which had the pejorative meaning of rude or uncouth newcomer. They resented the arrogance and condecension of the recent arrivals and, even more, their successful attempts to obtain *encomiendas*, offices, and other spoils to which they believed they themselves held preemptive rights and to which the law gave them preferential entitlement. Nevertheless, American-born Spaniards tacitly acknowledged the social seniority of Europeans and knew that no matter what they achieved, one honor lay forever beyond their reach. They could not be born in Spain.

## Spanish American Identities

Creolism

The lines dividing colonial society by assigned rank and status defined another set of qualities, that is, the cultural and psychological identities felt or sought by peninsulars and creoles, by Indians and Africans, and by unassimilated mixed bloods.

Within the Republic of Spaniards, persons who came to the Indies from Spain at first had no doubts about who they were or where their hearts lay, but those who stayed on experienced a slow erosion of their Spanishness. The process began with the first generation of European arrivals, the men of the Conquest. Many of them may have dreamed of returning to the mother country, bathed in glory and laden with riches, there to become lords of land and vassals. But the tangible spoils of conquest proved to be ephemeral and quite insufficient to support their aspirations. Instead most of them remained in America to become *primeros pobladores* (first settlers), and as time passed they sank roots deeper and deeper into the land they had won. Its majesties and grandeurs gained a grip on their souls; its fruits sustained them; its *repartimientos* and offices ennobled them.

Even the conquerors who became repatriates never lost their attachment to the Indies. Hernán Cortés, the richest and most famous among them, would have preferred to remain in Mexico had Emperor Charles given him the deserts to which he felt entitled, and in his will he testified: "First of all, it is my wish that if I die in these Kingdoms of Spain my body be laid to rest in the Church . . . until it be time, and may seem so to my successor . . . to remove my bones to New Spain, which I hereby charge and order to be done within ten years, or earlier if possible."[10]

Among succeeding generations of *peninsulares*, some returned to the mother country after their terms of royal office expired or they had amassed fortunes or had been disappointed in their expectations. Others remained in the Indies as permanent settlers by original intention or because of circumstances. There they acquired mines, haciendas, and businesses, obtained local offices, and took American brides. They retained an emotional allegiance to the land of their birth, but more practical considerations bound them to the land of their adoption, and they adjusted to its social environment. They became, so to speak, "cultural creoles."

The true creole man, of course, had a more deeply rooted American identity whose essential qualities were much the same as those subsumed under the modern concept of *criollismo* (creolism). He was a *hijo de la tierra*, a native son who felt a deep sentimental and practical attachment to the land of his birth. To him its sights, sounds, and smells were dear and familiar things. His physical and social well-being depended on its mines, haciendas, and commerce. In it he would be laid to rest, but it would also sustain his lineage. The presence of black and brown people further diluted his Old World heritage. They filled his home with foreign voices, infiltrating Castilian with new words and softer cadences. Their women wet-nursed him with alien milk, prepared his meals with exotic ingredients, and introduced him to sex. Their herbalists soothed his agues and rashes with strange unguents and decoctions. Their craftsmen adorned his churches with carvings of American plants, animals, and, occasionally, human figures with an Indian or Negroid cast of feature.

Yet creolism had an ambivalent character. The native son was also an *español americano*, a Spaniard for whom fate had decreed an American birth. He felt a certain nostalgia for old Spain, a sense of inferiority because he could not claim it as his true *patria* (fatherland), and a resentment against those who could and who constantly reminded him of his defective birth.

Creolism permeated every aspect of the Spanish American social environment: institutions, art forms, life-styles, and popular culture. Its most direct expression appeared in literature. The sixteenth-century Mexican chronicler Juan Suárez de Peralta (born c. 1536) signed his works proudly as "a citizen and native of Mexico."[11] Far to the south, the Chilean poet Pedro de Oña (born c. 1570) wrote in his *Arauco domado* that the sole source of his literary inspiration was a desire "to render some service in the land (*tierra*) in which he was born."[12] Across the Andes, the Hispanicized mestizo historian Rui Díaz de Guzmán (1560–1629) spoke of Argentina as his *patria* (fatherland).[13]

In addition to expressing pride in their American birth, creole authors dwelt on American themes from grand to trivial and extolled the American scene, often in hyperbolic terms. They described the land as Columbus had seen it:

verdant and bountiful, its skies clear and limpid, its airs salutary and invigorating. They lauded the grandeurs (*grandezas*) of its great metropolises, their magnificent palaces and churches, their spacious avenues, their flowing aqueducts and canals, and the richness of their commerce.[14] They also extolled the personal virtues of their class: active and imaginative minds, discretion, liberality, courtesy, and unfailing honor. American culture, they contended, was in no way inferior to that of Old Spain. But these exuberant affirmations concealed a yearning to compensate for an irremediable defect of birth and a need to counter the calumnies of *peninsulares*. In some instances they have the appearance of deliberate attempts to arouse a spirit of creole self-consciousness and pride.[15]

Creole identity expressed itself most profoundly in religion. American-born Spaniards believed themselves to be the most devout, exemplary, and orthodox of all Catholics. Masses, baptisms, confirmations, confessions, prayers, and saints' days observances consumed a good part of their lives. They endowed chaplaincies and convents, made liberal bequests to religious foundations, and gave their daughters as brides of Christ. In the seventeenth century a multiplication of miraculous cures and apparitions gave rise to the conviction that God had chosen to reward especially the faithful of the Indies with a display of His wonders. Holy persons, both men and women, became reputational saints, and cults sprang up devoted to their veneration. In 1671, the church canonized Sister Rosa of Lima, giving Americans their first official saint. By the late 1600s hagiography had become one of the most popular genres of colonial literature.

Cultural and psychological identities had solid supports in wealth, power, and influence. Creoles owned mines of silver and gold as well as sugar, grain, and cattle haciendas. They controlled the labor of millions of Indians and tens of thousands of black slaves. Many were entrenched in trade and commerce, although in these activities *peninsulares* dominated, if not in numbers then in wealth. Spanish Americans lost the battle to feudalize the *encomienda* and they obtained only a minority of high public offices, but they gained political control of many towns and provinces as well as commissions in militias, garrisons of presidios, and frontier companies. In the ecclesiastical establishment, they held a minority of bishoprics, but they furnished not a few abbotts, numerous deans and canons, and a majority of the lower ranks of the secular and regular clergy.

## The Identity of the Indians

Being an Indian meant not just the possession of an ascribed and juridical status. It meant a way of life, a way of viewing the world, and a way of defining a place in it. By the nature of things, however, indigenes could not continue to be what they had been before the coming of the Europeans. They had to restructure their Indianism, blending what they could save from the past with what the Europeans offered them or imposed upon them.

The primary source of indigenous identity was the territorial community formed by the civil congregation, the reduction, and the *resguardo*. The community fixed Indians in place amid familiar surroundings. Its communal lands gave them roots in the soil, and the cultivation of those lands regulated their daily and seasonal rounds. Within its bounds they rebuilt old kinship structures and formed new ones, associations that shaped their interpersonal relations. The Christian institution of *compadrazgo* reinforced real and mythical consanguine ties. By the mid-seventeenth century a network of coparents (*compadres* and *comadres*) and cogodparents (*padrinos* and *madrinas*) contributed to community solidarity.

A syncretic religion furnished another source of Indian identity. By the mid-seventeenth century, virtually all indigenes under Spanish rule were Catholic communicants, but the forms and spirit of their devotions left much to be desired from the viewpoint of the clergy. In subtle and insidious ways saints took over the faculties of earth and fertility gods, and pagan practices infiltrated Christian rites. In religious pageantry performers acted out Spanish themes, such as Moors and Christians or the lives of saints, but they did so in strange combinations of European and native garb. Dancers stepped and shuffled in ancient rhythms to the accompaniment of *sonajes* (rattles) held in their hands. But, however heterodox Indian religion might have been, it was a real faith, providing spiritual sustenance to millions of *miserables*.

Religion linked intimately with community. Each town and village had its church. These churches loomed over civil edifices, and their construction and adornment strained communal resources to their limits. Each congregation had its pastor, resident or visiting, furnished mainly by the secular clergy to whom the regulars had grudgingly turned over the cure of souls. Every parish had its local madonna or patron saint who gave its needs special attention. Religion and civic life blended through another European introduction, the *cofradía* (religious confraternity). Its essential function was to serve the cult of the patron, but it also provided a measure of social security to its members and their families and helped to pay for the feasts, dances, processions, and fiestas that relieved the monotony of endless toil.

The indigene also found a post-Conquest identity in real or idealized pasts. Educated Indian and mestizo historians wrote annals of Aztec, Maya, and Inca dynasties.[16] These works, however, had European forms and, in part, European inspiration. In any event, ordinary Indians did not read them. The past had a more vital presence in covert loyalties to ancient ruling families, especially in Peru, and in folklore and mythology. In Guatemala, village elders told tales of Tecán Umán, a Quiché Indian hero in the Knight Roland/El Cid tradition who had done battle against the conquistador Pedro de Alvarado. Although he was finally slain, his bravery and honor shown brightly in defeat and was undiminished by the passage of time.[17]

Remembrances of things past found more forceful expression in "nativistic" or "revivalistic" movements that sprang up, generally a generation or more after European conquests and in regions such as northern Mexico and remote Andean valleys, where Spanish pacification was incomplete. They aimed at the elimination of alien persons, customs, and values, especially Christian influences, and the restoration of a golden age believed to have existed before the coming of the Europeans. Perhaps drawing on repudiated Christian teaching, they often expressed messianic or millennialist hopes. They took various forms of action. Some tribes simply abandoned routine activities and devoted themselves to ritual dancing, feasting, and drinking. Others set forth en masse to seek a mythical promised land. Still others, such as the Pueblos of New Mexico (1680-97) and the Tepehuanes of New Vizcaya (1616-22), rose in bloody rebellions and slew or expelled missionaries, officials, and settlers before being repacified.

## Afro-Americanism

Africans in Spanish America had a more severe identity problem than Indians. Enslavement had separated them physically and culturally from their homelands and distributed them individually and randomly in alien environments. Nevertheless, they displayed a remarkable capacity for survival that enabled them to restructure a group consciousness that was, if not truly African, at least Afro-American.

Generally speaking, Africans reformed their identity in much the same ways as Indians did. They began by reconstructing communities. Slaves from Africa remembered their languages, their folklore, and their gods. In places where they became concentrated they sought out their linguistic and cultural kin and met together whenever possible. These associations became more firmly established as favored slaves gained greater mobility and behavioral latitude through advancement from field hand to overseer and from domestic service to artisanry. Significant numbers of slaves won freedom and, in urban centers, settled in neighborhoods that provided loci for regular gatherings of blacks and mulattoes, both slave and free.

Religion contributed to community solidarity. Africans brought to the Indies became Christians, at least nominally. With the assent of the Spaniards they formed religious congregations and *cofradías* under the patronage of colored saints such as St. Benedict the Moor or Our Lady of the Rosary who especially looked after blacks. In cities with large black and mulatto populations, particular African nations formed their own sodalities, thus reconstituting Old World identities. Among all things remembered, however, old gods figured most prominently. Their worship not only crept into Christian observances but formed the basis of cults known variously as *vodun, condomblé*, and *macumba* that competed with Catholicism.

Africans sought to preserve or reconstitute identities through more direct action. Slave rebellions sometimes abetted by free blacks and mulattoes erupted frequently in the Indies. Overtly they were violent protests against exploitation and degradation, but many contained revitalization elements such as the restoration of a remembered way of life, the repudiation of Christian teachings and the restoration of old gods, the exhortations of cult leaders, and the election of kings.

Slaves also protested their servitude by flight, individually and in groups, to inaccessible mountains and forests, becoming known in contemporary Spanish terminology as *cimarrones*. Along the coasts of Veracruz, in Central America, and in New Granada escapees formed communities called *palenques* or *quilombos*. Free blacks and mulattoes joined them, and matings with the women of indigenous tribes further augmented their populations. *Cimarrón* settlements elected kings, drew up laws, raised military forces, built fortifications, established churches, and created a social order based on remembered African models. They constituted republics, but not of a sort that pleased the Spaniards, for they defied the rule of Castilian kings and harassed European settlements and communications. Despite the concerted efforts of viceroys and governors to destroy them, some remained independent for generations.

## Comparative Strengths of
## Creole, Indian, and African Identities

The strength of identities created or recreated by the principal social groups in the Indies varied. Creoles expressed their self-consciousness most positively for the simple reason that they possessed the social, political, and economic resources necessary to do so. Despite revivalist movements and occasional violent protests against particular abuses, Indian identity was mainly passive and unself-conscious. It did not develop a rationalized, assertive form until the appearance of Indian movements (*indigenismo*) in the twentieth century and then only under the leadership of white and mestizo intellectuals.

Africans asserted their identities more vigorously than Indians did, but against less favorable odds. In most parts of the Indies, their numbers lacked the mass and density that allowed the highland indigenes to retain and reconstruct their cultures. As individuals or dispersed groups, blacks and mulattoes had to adapt more completely to European ways, and meanwhile miscegenation continued to take toll of their physical and cultural qualities. Furthermore, as time passed free blacks and mulattoes sought to improve their status by escaping their African heritage. Isolated *palenques* had a greater capacity for resistance, but in these bastions inhabitants had to adopt European forms of political and military organization in order to survive, and they mixed their blood with Indian tribes. Afro-Americanism as a vigorous phenomenon in the Spanish New World did not appear until the very late eighteenth century, and then mainly in Cuba, where a developing plantation economy restored and swelled the black population.

### Mixed Bloods: Assimilation and Alienation

Mixed bloods had special difficulty finding a place in the sun, for they had multiple heritages, none of which was fully theirs. Assimilation into a primary parental group provided the only route to a firmly based group identity. The difficulty of passage varied according to the kind of ethnic mixture and the direction taken. Mulattoes found ready acceptance in African communities, and social and legal discrimination pushed them toward that destination. It was harder for mestizos to enter corporate Indian communities, and in any event they saw little advantage in doing so unless they could gain access to the cacique class. Through cultural adaptation, lighter-skinned mixed bloods could become reputational Spaniards, but, as their numbers swelled, mainly through illegitimate birth, and as presumption of African taint increasingly besmirched their reputation, they found assimilation into European society more and more difficult. Little is known about the rate and volume of movement in these several directions, but certainly large numbers of mixed bloods remained unassimilated. They could find identities only as individuals or at best as residents of unincorporated villages, rural estates, and urban neighborhoods.

## Social Cleavage and Social Cohesion in the Spanish Indies

Civil society in the Indies had an even more pronounced invertebrate character than in metropolitan Spain, and one may very well wonder what bound its mutually antipathetic orders and classes together.

As in the mother country, the king provided an instrument of organic cohesion. Ruling by God's grace and standing above the interests, he constituted a mystical and sacrosanct symbol of Catholic unity. As the custodian and giver of the law, he defined the constitution of the several orders and classes and prescribed the manner in which they were to serve each other in harmony and concord. But, although the mystique of the crown may have helped give unity to the Republic of Spaniards, it had less influence on the lower orders. The king appeared remote and foreign to the Indians and inspired little reverence among blacks and mixed bloods, who did not benefit much from his grace and mercy. As for the law, it was an effective instrument of social articulation only to the extent that the several orders accepted its spirit and chose to obey its rules.

Religion also provided a measure of unity. The modern Mexican writer Fernando Benítez describes its role: "The hallowed glow of the altar and the splendor of church ritual were shared by rich and poor, by white and Indians alike. Inequality ended at the church door, and it was not important whether the nobleman had a pew in the chancel or not. The disparate members of the congregation were united in the single desire for redemption."[18] Perhaps the passage exaggerates the social democracy of chapel and altar, but the fact remains that all elements of society shared their God, their saints, and a core of devotional forms.

The gradual Americanization of the Virgin contributed especially to the unifying influence of religion. Ever since the Conquest, the Holy Mother had manifested herself from time to time in various parts of the Indies, giving rise to many local madonnas, each with her own cult of Spaniards, Indians, or blacks. Some American virgins acquired a wider geographical and social following. The best known among them came to be Our Lady of Guadalupe. According to religoius tradition, she first appeared in 1531 to the Indian Juan Diego on the Hill of Tepeyac, which rises just outside of Mexico City and, in pre-Conquest times, was sacred to Tonantzín, the Aztec earth mother. The church accepted the authenticity of her appearance and erected a shrine to her on the site that became a center of worship for the Indians of central Mexico. Many years later, in 1649, its curate, Luis Lasso de la Vega, published a book about his patroness.[19] He wrote in Nahuatl in order to bring knowledge of her wonders to the Indians who used that tongue, but his message spread all over Mexico, not only among the indigenes but among creoles and mixed bloods, thus creating a "national" cult. Toward the end of the seventeenth century, builders completed a great basilica at Tepeyac that became the greatest center of religious pilgrimage in the New World, and, in 1737, the Virgin of Guadalupe was proclaimed *La Patrona de la Nación Mexicana* (The Patroness of the Mexican Nation).[20]

Resentment against Spanish exploitation as distinguished from the rule of the king constituted another kind of bond among the disparate elements of American society. For the most part it was latent, but on occasion it appeared openly. In 1624 and again in 1692 riots erupted in Mexico City. Ostensibly they were reactions to acute grain shortages, but they contained an undertone of protest against oppressive government. The rioters consisted mainly of the urban poor, but this class included persons of every ethnic group, and upper-class creoles gave Spanish officials little aid in suppressing the disorders.

The pervasiveness of anti-Spanish sentiment was also reflected in a plan for Mexican independence pronounced in 1642 by Don Guillén de Lampart, a minor member of the household of the viceroy, the marquis of Villena. Among other things it called for emancipation of slaves, abolition of tributes, confiscation of the enemies' (that is, the *gachupines'*) estates, and the assumption of government by a "royal council" of American notables. The conspiracy aborted, but the plan reveals a shrewd appreciation of the grievances and aspirations of the major groups in Mexican society.[21]

A tighter form of social articulation consisted of kinship and personal dependency structures that cut vertically through all the horizontal strata of colonial society. Extended families brought together in intimate association aristocratic creole paterfamilias, peninsular sons-in-law, close and distant blood kin of diverse ethnic origins, Spanish and mixed-blood dependents, Indian servants, and black slaves. In rural areas patron-client relationships linked *hacendados* not only to resident workers but to smaller landholders who depended on their more powerful neighbors for favor and protection and in return rendered respect and obedience. In the main urban centers merchant houses patronized a clientele extending downward through retailers to the most humble shopkeepers and outward to business agents and firms in satellite towns and ports. *Parentela* and *clientela* penetrated the church hierarchy and the royal bureaucracy. Through intermarriage among influential families, clans and clienteles interlocked, forming the warp and woof of the social fabric.[22]

Even added together, however, mystical, moral, and institutional forces lacked the strength to provide any significant measure of social cohesion. What held the social order together was simply the monopoly of economic resources, political influence, and powers of coercion held by the oligarchy. This group exploited its strengths to impose on the lower orders a graduated system of dependence and subordination that law and social theory simply rationalized. Although the dominant class included both American-born and European-born Spaniards, both elements had a common interest in maintaining their wealth and privileges and laid their differences aside when confronting the lower orders of society.

## Regional Diversities

The social groups and the identities described above had regional variations so numerous that they cannot be discussed individually, but broad patterns of diversification can be identified. The most elaborate social ordering and the most sharply defined social distinctions appeared in the upland basins and valleys of the great American cordillera. These regions were inhabited by a mass of Indians, a large mixed-blood population, and a dominant white minority, a well-defined division that lent itself to systematic classification. In these regions, also, a wide distributional range of wealth, offices, and honors encouraged hierarchal ranking. Finally, having been the first to be conquered and colonized, they had mature societies in which ruling elites had had time to sort out and fix statuses to their own satisfaction.

Colonial society had a much simpler ordering in other regions, where Indians did not exist as a republic but only as individuals and where populations consisted mainly of an increasingly homogeneous ethnic mixture. They were also the poorest and least-governed parts of the Indies, so that distinctions of wealth and office figured less prominently in social perceptions.

Geographic and demographic circumstances likewise affected the variety and forms of Spanish American identities. That of the Indians was most well formed and enduring in the highlands, where their numbers and density protected their culture from dissolution. The Americanism of the creole and the acculturated peninsular developed most strongly in the same regions, for there these groups had their deepest roots and held majority control of the factors of production. In the lowlands and especially in port provinces they tended to be more oriented toward Europe because of their dependence on overseas trade. These differences help to explain political and economic antagonisms that surfaced during the wars for independence and survived long after Spanish rule in the Indies had ended: between Mexico and Veracruz, between Cartagena and Bogotá, between Guayaquil and Quito.

## Colonial Brazilian Society:
## The Sugar Regions

Brazilian society in the seventeenth century had regional forms so distinct that they can best be described separately. The most highly developed social structures appeared in the coastal sugar zones stretching from Pernambuco in the north through Rio de Janeiro in the center. The Portuguese in these regions started out with much the same social values as the Spaniards, but several circumstances produced somewhat different configurations of rank and status. One was heavy dependence on black slavery, a condition that created a fundamental distinction between slaves and freemen and that in addition made persons of African descent the largest single component in the population. Another was the shrinkage of the coastal Indian population to the point where, by the latter half of the seventeenth century, it was no longer a significant social element. This trend meant also a decline in the growth rate of *mamelucos* and *caboclos* (white and Indian mixtures). A third factor was the relatively weak influence of the Portuguese crown in fixing rank and status.

### The Ruling Groups

By their own definition Portuguese of whatever rank and provenance constituted the superior class. They claimed purity of blood and Old Christian lineage, but many would have been hard put to sustain their pretensions. Although they had not conquered the land in the heroic sense of the word, they had occupied and settled it against considerable odds, an achievement that demonstrated to them their superiority. In addition, they were lighter in color than blacks, Indians, and mixed bloods.

Within the European element, the *senhores de engenho* formed an aristocracy roughly comparable to the Spanish American *hacendados*. Their status rested on much the same foundations: the economic and social value of land and the control of municipal offices and militias. Yet they differed from the *hacendados* in several respects. The sugar boom tied them more closely to the European mercantile economy. They enjoyed firmer bases of local power, because the Portuguese crown intervened in municipal government less generally and effectively than the Spanish kings. Finally, they possessed fewer of the attributes of nobility. Some were linked by lineage to Portuguese noble families and all considered themselves to be *fidalgos*, but few, if any, had their pretensions confirmed by royal concessions. None obtained noble titles for their services in Brazil. Why they ran to more common quality is uncertain. Perhaps it was because Brazil lacked the conquest tradition and *encomiendas*, circumstances that gave the *beneméritos* of the Spanish Indies a quasi-noble status. Perhaps the more capitalistic economy of Brazil diluted noble values. Or it may have been that Pernambuco, Bahia, and Rio de Janeiro did not have the elaborate civil and ecclesiastical hierarchies that created appetites for rank and title in the major administrative centers of the Spanish Indies.

Below the sugar aristocracy lay a middle sector of Portuguese American society. Its upper levels were occupied by import-export merchants resident in major ports who were overwhelmingly of European birth. Their status corresponded roughly to that of the merchants of Mexico and Lima, but with important differences. They were not as wealthy as their Spanish counterparts, for the Brazil trade amounted to only a fraction of that carried by Spanish fleets; they did not enjoy the advantages of corporate organization; and they were dominated socially by their planter neighbors.

The ecclesiastical estate in Brazil had essentially the same corporate organization, privileges, and immunities as in the Spanish Indies. But its presence did not loom so large, nor was its influence so great. Although no comparative counts are available, its members probably constituted a smaller proportion of the European population; it was not as well endowed with temporal wealth; and it had a less developed organization. In 1676 Portuguese America had only four sees: the Archdioceses of Bahia, and its suffragan dioceses of Rio de Janeiro and Olinda, and the Diocese of São Luís do Maranhão, suffragan to Lisbon. The distance between them virtually precluded episcopal intercourse and cohesion.

As for the regular clergy, monasteries and nunneries were few compared to their profusion in Spanish American cities. Believing that the few women in the white population should be encouraged to become wives and mothers, the crown did not authorize the establishment of a convent of nuns in the colony until 1665, and a second was not authorized until seventy years later. Brazil had no universities or major colleges to serve as centers of theological learning or to train clergymen. Excepting the Jesuits, the Brazilian clergy, secular and regular, had a reputation for ignorance and immorality that weakened its spiritual authority, although it would be difficult to demonstrate that its defects were more pronounced than those of its brothers in the king of Spain's dominions.

The "royal estate" was also weaker in Portuguese America than in the Spanish Indies. The king's officials in Brazil enjoyed ranks, titles, and privileges setting them off from other social groups, but they lacked the social density and visibility that characterized the bureaucracy in Spanish America. Nor did they enjoy the same preeminence in relation to local elites. Brazil did not have a court comparable in rank to the audiencia until one called a *relação* was created in Bahia in 1608. This tribunal, moreover, had an intermittent existence, being abolished in 1626 and not reestablished until 1652. After 1640 the Portuguese crown occasionally gave the governors-general in Bahia the title of viceroy but did not establish a viceregal system permanently until the middle of the eighteenth century. In any event, the presence of high-ranking officials in the colony's capital had little social influence on the residents of cities hundreds of miles away.

Status in Portuguese American society graded downward from landed, mercantile, ecclesiastical, and bureaucratic elements into urban shopkeepers, artisans, and accountants, and, in rural areas, to small sugar planters and plantation overseers and technicians. A high proportion of these classes were Portuguese immigrants, and they were constantly reinforced by new arrivals from the metropolis.

In Brazil as in the Spanish Indies, a clear social cleavage divided European- and American-born whites, called respectively *reinóis* and *mazambos*. The European Portuguese believed that American birth carried inherent defects including the presumptive taint of Indian or African blood. They regarded their Brazilian cousins as lazy, spendthrift, frivolous, and intellectually shallow. For their part, *mazambos* resented the *reinóis'* arrogance and condecension and the preferential treatment they received in the allocation of government posts. But they favored immigrants as husbands for their daughters, thus tacitly admitting the superiority of the Europeans.

## The Lower Classes

The two Hispanic peoples used much the same criteria in assigning statuses to non-Europeans. Both European and American-born Portuguese regarded persons of African or Indian blood as inferior species of humanity because of their savage and pagan origins and defects in their behavior and appearance. They expressed their prejudices in social discrimination, especially against interracial marriages, and by the imposition of legal restraints on the movement, behavior, and occupational freedom of the tainted classes.[23]

The Portuguese, like the Spaniards, made social and juridical distinctions among the several elements of non-European society. *Mamelucos* and *caboclos* suffered the least prejudice and discrimination, because they were free and most closely resembled Europeans in culture and behavior. Free blacks and mulattoes ranked lower on the reputational scale, because they bore the stigma of slave origin and African blood. For these reasons they were legally excluded from civil and ecclesiastical office and forbidden to wear European-style clothing. Black and mulatto slaves stood at the very bottom of the social hierarchy. Not only did they possess the worst possible combination of undesirable physical and cultural traits, they were legal chattels.

Social Mobility

Seventeenth-century Brazilian society offered much the same routes of upward mobility for disadvantaged elements as those available in Spanish America. Slaves might win freedom. Free blacks and mixed bloods could penetrate into the lower ranks of the white population through cultural adaptation, the performance of essential but nonprestigious services, and common law or sacramental intermarriage. However, formal recognition of de facto social advancement was not easy to come by. During the seventeenth and eighteenth centuries, the crown awarded *habitos* (robes—in effect, membership) in the several Portuguese military orders to a number of blacks who had distinguished themselves in wars, especially during the expulsion of the Dutch, but, before they could be inducted, the *Mesa da Consciência e Ordens* had to investigate their backgrounds for purity of blood and religion and to ensure that they had not soiled their hands with degrading work. In one investigation, the *Mesa* declared that "It does not seem right [that] the habit of São Bento de Avis [the Order of Avis] be seen on a person so despicable in the esteem of people as that of a Black." Dispensation from defects uncovered could be obtained only from the pope. He did in fact give dispensation in two cases, but there is no evidence that any black candidates actually entered one of the orders.

Mulattoes found the way somewhat easier. Of some thirty whose cases came before the *Mesa* between 1607 and 1723 most eventually received their robes. Only two of these, however, had had substantial military service in Brazil. The rest were natives of other parts of the empire.[24]

A fairly constant upward movement occurred within the white population. Newly arrived immigrants from Portugal, mainly of low birth, found employment as clerks, cashiers, and shop assistants in mercantile establishments. By dint of hard work some advanced into managerial positions and even partnerships.

In plantation regions, enterprising *lavradores* obtained titles to the lands they cultivated, bought slaves, and even acquired small mills, especially after the introduction of the economical Urrey *engenho* in the 1650s.

At the upper levels of Brazilian society, wealthy merchants managed to penetrate the planter aristocracy in various ways: by acquiring landed estates through purchase or government grant, by marrying the daughters of lords of mills, and by obtaining municipal offices, commissions in local militias, and membership in prestigious lay religious brotherhoods. Thus, they became a hybrid social type, the merchant-planter or the landed merchant, and divided their time between their two main enterprises. They also provided for a more definitive and permanent change in family status by establishing their sons as planters and directing their interests away from commerce.

## Backland Society

A quite different society formed in the Brazilian backlands stretching from Ceará and Piauí in the north to the highlands in back of São Paulo. These boundless expanses of desert, bush, and grassland constituted a melting pot that reduced Europeans, Africans, and Indians to a homogeneous mixed-blood population. Until the opening of the gold mines at the end of the seventeenth century, moreover, the products of the backlands brought in little ready cash. These circumstances made it difficult to assign social rank on the basis of either ethnic qualities or wealth.

Still another kind of society appeared in the Amazon region, composed of Portuguese and mixed-blood traders and gatherers of forest products, of missionaries and their charges, and of unreduced Indian tribes. Its elements were enormously dispersed and often transient. Its only stable centers were Indian reductions, military garrisons with small service sectors, trading posts, and fishing villages. These conditions were even less conducive to the creation of social ranks than those prevailing in the *sertão* to the south. Amazonian society could hardly be said to have a structure except at local levels.

## Brazilian Identities

### Portuguese Americans

The main groups in Brazilian society developed psychological and cultural identities comparable to those that appeared in Spanish America. American-born Portuguese regarded themselves as *filhos da terra* (sons of the land) and felt a deep affinity for it. They took pride in its paradisiacal vistas, its boundless expanses, and its rich and diverse fruits. It provided most of them with a livelihood and some with wealth. But they also cherished their Old World heritage, felt inferior to the haughty Portuguese immigrants who had the good fortune to have been born in the mother country, and resented their hauteur.

The Brazilian variety of creolism was not only an identity felt; the influence of an exotic environment gave it cultural and behavioral forms. The Portuguese language incorporated Indian and African words as well as new terms coined to describe the American scene. African cooks working with New World foodstuffs created a distinctively Brazilian cuisine for their masters. African influences gave religious festivities in the colony distinctive colors, sounds, and rhythms. More formal affirmations of creolism appeared in contemporary chronicles, histories, geographical descriptions, and poetry. Their authors repeated a constant theme, one that, in the eighteenth century, came to be called "the myth of *ufanismo*," that is, a lyrical exaltation of the beauty and bounty of the land.[25]

Brazilian creolism found a more forceful expression in resistance to European affronts to local interests. On more than one occasion municipal governments defied crown and church by expelling Jesuits whose concern for the Indians interfered with the native labor supply. A more violent reaction was the so-called War of the Mascates (1710–11), in which the Brazilian planters of Pernambuco led their militia and Paulista auxiliaries against the European-born merchants of the Port of Recife, who held them in debt. Although the Portuguese government subdued the uprising, the defeat and the reprisals that followed merely exacerbated planters' resentments.

Afro-Americanism

Persons of African origin created a stronger and more lasting identity in Brazil than they did in Spanish America, because they formed a relatively larger part of the population and lived in denser concentrations. These circumstances allowed closer and more constant associations among them, especially through the organization of powerful religious brotherhoods that, more than any other institution, preserved African culture in the New World.[26]

Another condition favoring the preservation of African culture in Brazil was the presence of limitless and empty backlands in which blacks and mulattoes who fled servitude could establish settlements (*quilombos*). Ten major slave communities are known to have existed for various lengths of time during the seventeenth and eighteenth centuries. The strongest and most enduring was the so-called Republic of Palmares, founded in the interior of Alagoas in the 1630s.

Its inhabitants surrounded it with palisades of palm trunks and within them built hundreds of homes, planted gardens, and created a lake well stocked with fish. They elected a king and lived in polity under their own laws. The refuge Palmares offered to plantation slaves and the depredations caused by the settement's army posed such a threat to the sugar lords of Pernambuco that in the last quarter of the seventeenth century the governors of that captaincy sent a series of powerful expeditions against it. The settlement did not fall, however, until 1694 and then did so only after a forty-two-day seige.

## Social Cohesion in Brazil

Several circumstances worked toward the formation of a more homogeneous society in seventeenth-century Brazil than existed in most parts of the contemporary Spanish Indies. Although the Portuguese colony had an enormous geographical extent and diverse terrains, climates, and vegetations, it was a single territorial entity, marked out by natural boundaries and undivided by seas and impassible cordilleras. Navigable rivers ran its length and breadth, connecting regions distant from each other. Brazilians were conscious of the unity of their land, for many of them had traveled it from one end to the other and had helped define its limits.

Brazil also had a relatively homogeneous population, owing principally to the absence of an unassimilated mass of Indians and to the rate and range of miscegenation between black and white, which created an ethnic continuum. The concepts of estate and corporation had scarcely any influence on social development, excepting the case of the corporate municipality. The debility of formal structures allowed the patriarchal family to assume an even more important integrative function than in the Spanish Indies. In sugar-growing regions it incorporated not only free kin and dependents but numerous household slaves and the illegitimate mulatto offspring of the paterfamilias and his sons. In this fashion it helped to ameliorate the infamy of slave origins. In the backlands its predominance was almost absolute. There neither civil nor ecclesiastical institutions existed that could challenge its authority.

Brazil had two particular seventeenth-century experiences that contributed to social solidarity. Settlers from every part of the colony and of every shade of color participated and intermingled in the penetration of the sertão. The same can be said about the war of liberation against the Dutch. Its national character was enhanced by the fact that little help came from metropolitan Portugal, which was too deeply involved in its own struggle for independence against Spain to risk outright war against the Netherlands.

## Race, Color, and Class

Chapter 3 of this book contains the observation that the Portuguese advance along the coast of sub-Saharan Africa opened a new and shameful chapter in the history of race relations; it led to the identification in the European mind of savagery, paganism, infamous slavery, and blackness as marks of human inferiority. In view of the observations made in this chapter about the ostensibly racial bases of social ordering and identification in Brazil and Spanish America, it seems appropriate to survey the problem of race relations in these regions after two centuries of close associations between white, black, and brown peoples.

It may well be, as a number of scholars have argued, that the prejudices of the Hispanic peoples were less pronounced than those of other Europeans, especially the English.[27] Nevertheless, the evidence is incontestable that at the end of the seventeenth century Spaniards and Portuguese in America regarded Africans, Indians, and mixed bloods as inferior species of humanity. This attitude was openly expressed by private persons, public officials, and learned jurists. It was manifested in various forms of legal and social discrimination. The question is which of the "defects" of the inferior orders were primary in shaping European perceptions of their inferiority and which were secondary or derivative?

Seventeenth-century Spaniards and Portuguese have left no clear-cut answers. Insofar as they tried to relate and order defective characteristics, they drew on Aristotelian precepts. Peoples who deviated markedly from European physical and cultural norms were "naturally" inferior and their inferiority became more pronounced in proportion to the magnitude of deviation. Natural defects provided a moral and legal justification for imposing servitude upon those who possessed them, thereby making them infamous in law and in fact. Then, in a circular, self-fulfilling fashion, the qualities justifying bondage became the marks of bondage and could not be entirely removed by manumission or emancipation. And by resisting servitude or other legal disabilities they suffered, inferior peoples disturbed the harmony of the republic, thus demonstrating and confirming their inferiority.

Modern scholars have attempted to sort out and order the sources of racial prejudices and disharmony and, generally speaking, have developed two different theories. One is social; that is, it holds that what appear to be "racial" attitudes actually derive from the structural relationships in a society. The other is racial; it holds that what appear to be racial attitudes are just that and that they help to shape the structures of multiracial societies. The following review will deal with these two theories in the order they were identified.

The social explanation takes several forms, depending on the particular structural features on which it is based. Among these forms, two are most widely known and debated. One derives from comparative studies of plantation slavery in the New World and holds that racial prejudice and ultimately virulent racism in that region sprang primarily from the conditions of slavery.[28] Masters, so the argument goes, subjected the slave to extremely harsh treatment in order to maximize their profits and to ensure slave docility. Slaves reacted defensively by adopting a posture of sloth, ignorance, and shuffling servility, or, as the North American historian Stanley Elkins put it, they became "infantilized." This behavior created in the minds of the master race a stereotypical image of slaves as "Sambo" or as the "lazy nigger" whose defects were ingrained in his nature. But lazy niggers could also be rebellious blacks, thus raising the specter of slave uprisings. Once these images and apprehensions became fixed in masters' minds, the physical appearance of blacks became the most convenient mark of their inferiority.

Manumission or emancipation did not change substantially the perceptions of black people held by whites, for freedmen and their descendants retained the behavioral patterns of their servile past: they could not shed their color and physiognamy, and the masters' fear of slave rebellion was replaced by white apprehensions of black encroachments on racial purity, especially through sexual aggression against white women.

A second and more universal social explanation is found in Marxist theory. It holds that what seem to be race relations are simply class relations in which physical and cultural differences between dominant and subordinate classes are only incidental. Vulgar Marxism attributes the racial projection of class interests to the desire of the European bourgeoisie to rationalize the exploitation of non-European peoples who happened to be colored and to divert to them the resentments of the domestic proletariat that otherwise might have led to revolution.

With particular reference to Hispanic America, the Argentine scholar Sergio Bagú maintained that, although the contrary might appear to be true, ethnic stratification was a consequence rather than the basis of differentiation into social classes.[29] In a similar vein, the Chilean, Alejandro Lipschütz observed that post-Conquest society in the Indies was ostensibly a "pigmentocracy" shaped by the "law of the spectrum of racial colors," but he contended that in fact the Spaniards simply used invidious color distinctions to justify and maintain their domination over subject and enslaved peoples.[30]

A number of Neo-Marxists who have analyzed multiracial societies offer a more sophisticated explanation of the relationship between class and race. The North American historian Eugene Genovese contends that slavery and other forms of unfree labor were simply archaic modes of production that the European bourgeoisie found it profitable to perpetuate in overseas colonies. Like more modern modes, servitude involved complex social and economic relations between dominant and subordinate classes including invidious class distinctions. American slaveholders displayed the same sort of contempt for their chattels as did medieval lords for peasants, and later, the bourgeoisie for the industrial proletariat. By no means all the "lazy niggers" in history have been black, as witnessed by the condition of the Russian serf.

Yet, Genovese continues, once capitalistically organized slavery was well and widely established in the Americas, the contempt of the dominant class turned rather rapidly into overt racial prejudice. And toward the end of his disquisition, he admits, "Yet slavery in the Americas had a racial basis and therefore must be understood not simply as a class question, but as a class question with a profound racial dimension." The Mexican sociologist Rodolfo Stavenhagen takes a similar view. Although the primary groups in social stratification are classes defined in terms of the social relations of production, race and ethnicity are "secondary or accessory factors" that are a part of these "social fixations." They may act to reinforce the system and "liberate" it from its economic base, thus maintaining it even when its economic base changes.[31]

The basic argument that racial prejudices are just what they seem to be is quite straightforward. They derive from a "primordial" ethnocentrism of peoples, reinforced and physically marked by differences in color between one another. Furthermore, the greater the differences in culture and color are, the deeper antipathies become. This kind of prejudice antedates others that might arise from conditions of servitude, colonialism, imperialism, or other types of exploitive relationships.[32] With particular reference to the connection between prejudice and color, the North American historian Winthrop Jordan found that Renaissance Europeans held strong antagonisms toward blacks owing to color symbolisms deeply embedded in Western Christianity. These associated whiteness with cleanliness, beauty, virtue, and the Dove of the Holy Spirit; blackness with ugliness, corruption, sin, and death. When Westerners came into large-scale association with Africans through the institution of slavery, their ingrained dislikes deepened into open prejudice and ultimately virulent racism.[33]

The Dutch sociologist Harry Hoetink added another dimension to the case for the cultural origins of racial attitudes, principally through his studies of the Caribbean area.[34] Patterns of race relations, he argues, have been shaped not by slavery or other forms of unfree labor but by the social values of the dominant race, which antedated servitude and survived its abolition. In multiracial societies these values create a racial hierarchy, but race relations actually develop at two levels of interaction. One consists of the nonintimate daily associations among groups that form "part of the social atmosphere."[35] At this level economic interdependence and transculturation of necessity soften the prejudices of the dominant group and over time permit some measure of upward social mobility for subordinate groups.

The other level involves more intimate associations among races, especially intermarriage. Here the critical factor is the "somatic norm image," that is, "the complex of physical (somatic) characteristics which are accepted by the group as its norm and ideal."[36] Persons seek mates most closely approaching their own group norm and shun others in proportion to their deviation from the norm. Somatic perceptions are not affected by the "social atmosphere" and remain fairly constant over generations. Furthermore, after prolonged subordination of one group to another, the "inferior" comes to regard the physical traits of the "superior" as more desirable.

None of the theories reviewed above have been proven or disproven. Perhaps they are not susceptible to empirical proof because of the imponderability of the variables in the equation of race relations and the emotion-laden nature of the problem. Perhaps, as the Swedish historian Magnus Mörner observed, the question of whether the attribution of human inferiority was racially or socially based in Hispanic America is sterile because what really counted was the precise correlation that existed between social and legal status on the one hand and skin color on the other.[37] Nevertheless, the search for an answer will continue, because the "racial" problems created by European expansion are very much a part of modern society.

Meanwhile, this author's own basic research and general reading incline him to believe that racial prejudices do spring from "primordial" antipathies toward differences in culture and physical appearance among peoples. The answer, however, is really not that simple, for the extent to which antipathies become open and generate racial disharmonies depends on the sharpness of differences among racial groups and the social and institutional forms interracial associations take. Furthermore, these forms change over time, making race relations a dynamic process rather than a static condition. Thus, the circular, self-fulfilling perceptions of racial inferiority held by seventeenth-century Spanish and Portuguese may have a genuine explanatory value.

Among the several modern theories of race relations reviewed above, Harry

Hoetink's seems to accommodate best what is known about race relations in colonial Hispanic America. By the end of the seventeenth century, Spanish and Portuguese societies were truly multiracial, and, although the dominant whites still ordered them according to racial characteristics, prolonged and widespread miscegenation among the several social groups made it impossible to maintain clear-cut boundaries between them. African slavery was an integral part of colonial society, but the majority of slaves labored individually as household servants, artisans, and skilled and unskilled workers rather than in harsher plantation environments. In addition, the Europeans depended on a large and growing population of free blacks and mixed bloods for nonprestigious but essential services. These conditions created the kind of "social atmosphere" that perforce suppressed the prejudices of the dominant group but did not eliminate them. They emerged when it came to the selection of marriage mates.

# CHAPTER 19

# Imperial Systems

Royal government in Spanish and Portuguese America expanded steadily after the era of the Conquest both territorially and in terms of its functions and powers. Newly occupied regions had to be provided with governors and magistrates, and in kingdoms and provinces settled earlier increasingly complex societies needed a larger governmental apparatus. The growth of royal absolutism in theory and fact led to the promulgation of more rigorous and detailed laws, and preoccupation with mercantilist doctrines produced a growing body of rules and regulations affecting production and commerce. The defense of trade and territory against mounting foreign threats required larger military and naval forces.

The expansion of government was accompanied by shifts in its meaning and ends. In law and in theory it was still the king's government, but in the last part of the sixteenth century the more impersonal concept of the "state," which encompassed the entire body politic, gained a certain currency among political thinkers. And, although law and theory still declared the primary purpose of government to be the provision of justice and the safeguarding of the common good—in America as well as in the metropolis—in practice it became more and more the exploitation of the colonies for the benefit of metropolitan interests.

## New Territorial Jurisdictions in Spanish America:
### Civil and Ecclesiastical

Territorial expansion in North America led to the creation of new superior provinces: the *gobernaciones* of New Vizcaya (1562), New Leon (1579), New

Mexico (1598), and Coahuila (1687). All of these came under the political and military command of the viceroy of New Spain. In matters of justice, New Vizcaya fell under the jurisdiction of the Audiencia of New Galicia; the other three provinces, under the Audiencia of Mexico. Far across the Pacific, the Spanish crown established the Captaincy-General of Manila in 1583 to govern and defend the pacified islands of the Philippine group and attached it to the Viceroyalty of New Spain.

In the Viceroyalty of Peru, the king suppressed the Audiencia of Chile in 1573 but then, in 1609, reestablished it with the status of a captaincy-general and relocated its seat in Santiago. Two thirds of a century later, in 1661, an audiencia was seated in Buenos Aires with jurisdiction over the province of the same name as well as over Paraguay and Tucumán. In matters of general government and defense it was dependent on Lima. The Platine provinces, however, were so poor and rustic that they could not support such a dignified tribunal in proper style. In 1671, therefore, it was disbanded, and its jurisdiction reverted to the Audiencia of Charcas.

The foundation of new audiencias in the Indies, including the Philippines, raised the total number of these jurisdictions to eleven by the end of the seventeenth century. Their identities, type, and official dates of establishment are listed in table 9; their territorial dimensions are shown on map 6.[1]

Within American audiencias, both old and newly established, the crown marked out additional *corregimientos*, *alcaldías mayores*, and minor *gobernaciones*. By 1700 there were some 200 such provinces within the territories of the Viceroyalty of New Spain alone.

New units of ecclesiastical administration were also created in the wake of pacification and settlement. In New Spain the diocese of Guadiana was established in 1623 with its seat in Durango and suffragan to the archbishopric of Mexico. In South America the list of new sees was longer: the archbishopric of Caracas (1638); the bishoprics of Trujillo (1577), Arequipa (1577), and Ayacucho (1609), all suffragan to Lima; and the bishoprics of Córdoba (1570), Santa Cruz de la Sierra (1605), La Paz (1608), and Buenos Aires (1620), all suffragan to the archbishopric of Sucre. The establishment of these sees raised the total in the Spanish Indies to five archdioceses and thirty-one dioceses, not counting the Philippines, which had one archbishopric and three suffragan bishoprics.

At lower levels of church government, parishes multiplied. Some were formed to serve new congregations of Spaniards and Indians, others by the secularization of the older indigenous congregations created by the missionary

Table 9
The Governmental Organization of Spanish America in About 1700

| Viceroyalty of New Spain | Audiencial Types |
|---|---|
| Mexico (1528, 1530) | Viceregal |
| Santo Domingo (1511) | Captaincy-General |
| Guatemala (1542) | Captaincy-General |
| Manila (1583) | Captaincy-General |
| New Galicia (1548) | *Presidencia* |
| Viceroyalty of Peru | |
| Lima (1542) | Viceregal |
| New Granada (1549) | Captaincy-General |
| Chile (1565, 1609) | Captaincy-General |
| Panama (1567) | *Presidencia* |
| Quito (1563) | *Presidencia* |
| Charcas (1559) | *Presidencia* |

orders. On the frontiers of empire, in northern New Spain, in Paraguay, and along the arc of the eastern Andes, the regular clergy established new missionary provinces and numerous Indian reductions. In addition, the structure of ecclesiastical administration and jurisdiction included ever-expanding numbers of cathedral chapters; convents of monks and nuns; universities and major and minor colleges; and hospitals, orphanages, and other ameliorative institutions.

## Expanding Functions and Powers of Royal Government in the Spanish Indies

The functions and powers of the king's government expanded in several areas. The crown intervened more openly in municipal affairs, beginning in Peru, where tensions and rivalries generated during the Conquest still disturbed the harmony of the republic. During the 1570s that fecund father of regulations Viceroy Francisco de Toledo issued ordinances for the governance of towns that spelled out in detail uniform procedures for the election of officials, their duties and responsibilities, and the kinds and qualities of the services they were to render.

Throughout the Indies royal and viceregal measures strengthened the powers of provincial governors to intervene in municipal elections, in the proceedings of *cabildos*, and in the management of municipal funds. Philip II and his successors extended two practices introduced by Emperor Charles. One was the appointment of *regidores* "at the king's will," or in perpetuity and heredity;

the other, the sale of offices, such as those of constable, collectors of fines, and inspectors of weights and measures, that had customarily been filled through appointment by town councils. Thus, municipal officials became increasingly beholden to royal favor. The several measures undertaken by the crown and its viceroys in effect made the *cabildo* an extension of royal government.

The crown likewise intruded more directly into the governance of the Indians, prompted by two inconsistent concerns: their protection and more efficient collection of revenues and services from them. Its measures included resettlement of indigenes in reductions, *resguardos*, and civil congregations; standardizing the bases and rates of tribute; and increasing the numbers and authority of *corregidores de indios*. Again Viceroy Toledo took the lead, issuing a spate of ordinances dealing with these matters. The erosion of the authority and prestige of *encomenderos* and Indian nobles helped to strengthen the powers of royal officials in indigenous affairs. Royal tribunals including the general Indian courts in Mexico City and Lima used simplified Castilian procedures rather than native customs and usages in judging cases to which indigenes were parties. In these several ways government by Europeans penetrated into all except the most remote native villages.

The evolution of Spanish mercantilist doctrines is described in chapter 17, but the principal measures adopted may be recapitulated: the regulation of the fleet system and limiting its ports of call; the restraints placed on trade between the Indies and Manila and between Mexico and Peru; the expansion of the functions of the House of Trade and the Merchant Guild of Seville; the chartering of merchant guilds in Mexico City and Lima; the limitations placed on the production of silk, olives, wine, and textiles in America; and the establishment of royal and private monopolies for the sale of essential commodities.

## Ecclesiastical Government: The Royal Patronage and the Royal Vicariate

In matters of ecclesiastical government, the crown reasserted and extended the royal patronage, especially during the reign of Philip II. The immediate occasion was the threat to the unity of the church posed by disputes between the regular and secular clergy in New Spain about episcopal jurisdiction over Indian congregations and about the indigenes' liability for payment of tithes. At first conflicting religious and political considerations restrained Philip from taking sides. On the one hand, the religious orders represented most clearly the missionary role of the state, the sole legal justification for Spain's presence in the Indies. They also provided a check on overweening secular prelates. On the other, the decisions of the Council of Trent had reaffirmed the exclusive jurisdiction of bishops in the temporal and spiritual governance of parishes. Perhaps most important, the king knew full well that the historic ties between the religious orders and the papacy imposed the only real obstacle to the crown's absolute dominion over the church in the Indies.

The obduracy of the regular clergy finally induced Philip to act decisively. In 1568 he convoked a *junta magna* (a supreme ad hoc council) to deliberate on the issues in dispute, and in 1574 it promulgated its decisions in a *Real Ordenanza del Patronazgo* (Royal Ordinance Governing the Patronage). The twenty-three chapters of the ordinance not only categorically reaffirmed established rights of patronage but made declarations on more recent points in contention. Henceforth, friars in charge of Indian congregations received their jurisdictions from bishops rather than directly from popes; regulars could not establish new religious foundations without royal and episcopal approval; and Indians had to pay tithes. These provisions opened the way for the ascendancy of the secular clergy in spiritual matters except in frontier missions and teaching and charitable activities, thereby permitting a much firmer exercise of the royal patronage.

The crown's rights of patronage were further strengthened by the theory of the Royal Vicariate, enunciated tentatively around the mid-sixteenth century by clerics of the mendicant orders and set forth in fuller form by the jurist Juan de Solórzano y Pereyra, in the early 1600s. It affirmed that the papal bulls of donation actually amounted to a jurisdictional delegation of apostolic authority in the newly discovered lands to the king of Spain, who thereby became "attorney general, patron and, as it were, legate in spiritual matters."[2] The papacy placed Solórzano's writings on the *Index*, but this did not prevent the theory from gaining currency among Spanish jurists and from evolving into an extreme regalist doctrine in the eighteenth century.

## The Holy Office of the Inquisition

The amplification of the patronage in the 1570s coincided with another measure that strengthened the king's hand in civil as well as ecclesiastical government. By royal order, tribunals of the Holy Office were installed in Lima in 1570 and in Mexico in 1571. These bodies took over the inquisitorial functions formerly exercised by bishops and occasional visitors from the Supreme and General Council of the Inquisition in Spain. The coincidence was not entirely fortuitous. The king was prompted mainly by growing threats to orthodoxy in the Indies posed by the appearance of Lutheran heretics, active *converso* communities, and an influx of heterodox literature. But the strife between seculars and regulars in New Spain also affected his decision. Efforts of bishop-inquisitors to impose their jurisdiction on the friars heightened tensions between the two parties and made it desirable to erect a tribunal independent of both.[3]

The Holy Offices in Lima and Mexico along with another installed in Cartagena in 1620 were each composed of two judge-inquisitors assisted by prosecutors, scriveners, and lay officers called *familiares* who served as informants, spies, and constables. Within their respective districts—Peru, New Spain, and New Granada—they exercised exclusive jurisdiction over all offenses against the purity of the faith except those involving Indians, who remained in the cognizance of bishops. They did in fact process a handful of Protestants, held to be relapsed Catholics, and rather more New Christians and crypto-Jews. They also exercised a careful although not entirely effective censorship of materials on the *Index*. Most of their prosecutions, however, dealt with more routine offenses against Catholic purity and morality: blasphemy and witchcraft, bigamy and adultery, and breaches of clerical discipline.

In addition to guarding purity of faith and morals, the Holy Office became an important political arm of the state in the Indies. The king had complete control over the Supreme Council and appointed American inquisitors. American tribunals were independent of all other civil and ecclesiastical authority. Their jurisdiction allowed them to keep an eye open for offenses against the royal patronage. They could also look into cases of treason and disloyalty, for these sins could hardly be distinguished from heresy and heterodoxy.

## The Defense of the Indies

### Indian Threats and Spanish Responses

The insults and depredations of Spain's enemies required a substantial expansion in the military functions of the government. Northern New Spain and southern Chile continued to be the major theaters of Indian wars. In the first region, unsubdued nations of great martial valor and skill resisted Spanish expansion and menaced frontier settlements and missions. In addition, pacified tribes rose against Spanish domination. Crown officials responded by building new presidios at strategic points, garrisoned by small permanent detachments of infantry and cavalry. In situations requiring offensive or counteroffensive action they raised companies and squadrons paid by the crown for the duration of the campaign.

In southern Chile, Araucanian raids continuously harassed an unstable frontier, and in 1599 the entire Indian nation took the offensive, scattering hastily organized Spanish field forces and destroying seven towns south of Concepción. It was this war that prompted the Jesuit father Luis de Valdivia to undertake a program of pacification by preaching and gentle persuasion. Crown officials, however, had little confidence in the outcome. In 1603, they raised a small permanent army, whose authorized strength varied from 1500 to 2500 men, to defend the marches. It was the first of its kind in the Indies.[4]

## The Foreign Threat: England, Holland, the Buccaneers, and Portugal

The growing foreign presence raised a more formidable threat to Spain's New World dominions and commerce. In the last quarter of the sixteenth century Elizabethan privateers appeared in force in the Caribbean, supplanting French corsairs as the chief enemy. In 1572 Francis Drake temporarily occupied Nombre de Dios, the American terminal of the Tierra Firme fleet, and in the following year crossed the isthmus to the outskirts of Panama. In 1586 he reappeared in American waters, seized and plundered Cartagena and Santo Domingo, and on his way home tarried to destroy St. Augustine. In 1598, George Clifford, earl of Cumberland, took San Juan de Puerto Rico and held it for six weeks.

The Treaty of London between England and Spain (1604) ended the great age of English privateering in the Indies, but the Spaniards still did not enjoy peace. In the late sixteenth century Dutch filibusters began to harass settlements and shipping in the Antilles and along the Main. In the 1620s fleets of the Dutch West India Company virtually dominated the Caribbean, capping their depredations in 1628 with the capture of the Mexican treasure fleet off Matanzas, Cuba.

A diversion of Dutch interests to India and Brazil gave the Spaniards a respite, but around midcentury English marauders reappeared. In 1655, after hostilities between Spain and England resumed, Oliver Cromwell sent out a fleet to take Santo Domingo, and, when repulsed, it rebounded and captured Jamaica. The following year another English squadron sacked Cartagena and Santa Marta on Tierra Firme. Meanwhile, American buccaneers gathered sufficient strength to take the offensive. In the 1660s and in the 1670s scarcely a town along the coasts of the Antilles, the Main, and Central America escaped their furious descents, and they even raided into the interior of Nicaragua and Costa Rica. The establishment of foreign settlements in the Caribbean facilitated their operations, for British and French governors gave them secure haven and on occasion employed them against the Spanish.

Foreign interlopers also appeared in the Pacific in much the same sequence. Francis Drake rounded Cape Horn in 1577, harassed coastal towns in Chile and Peru, and sailed north to California seeking the Strait of Anian before continuing his circumnavigation of the globe. In 1615 Admiral Joris von Spillbergen, commanding a Dutch East India fleet, entered the South Sea through the Strait of Magellan en route to reinforce the Moluccas. He decided to see first what the west coast of America had to offer and began with an attack on Valparaiso. He then sailed north, defeated a Spanish fleet off Callao, and continued to Acapulco, where he exchanged Peruvian prisoners for provisons to sustain his trans-Pacific voyage. Nine years later a large Dutch armada made an unsuccessful attack on Callao but managed to ravage Guayaquil and harassed the coast as far north as Mexico. The prospect that the intruders might ally themselves with the Araucanians or disaffected Peruvian Indians heightened Spanish alarm.[5]

The Dutch menace proved to be short-lived, but in the second half of the seventeenth century buccaneers arrived in the Pacific in strength via Cape Horn or overland across Central America. Their most famous, or infamous, exploit was Henry Morgan's sack of Panama in 1671. Their intrusions climaxed in two great maritime raids, coming respectively in 1680 and 1684, that took Spanish ships and ravaged coastal settlements from Peru to Mexico.

The Portuguese expansion in Brazil created still another threat to Spanish America, especially after Portugal regained its independence in 1640. By the late 1600s Brazilian frontiersmen had pushed inland to the eastern slopes of the Andes, challenging Spain's claim to more than half of South America. The foundation of Colônia do Sacramento in 1680 created a more immediate problem for Spain. The settlement not only provided the Portuguese with a center for smuggling silver from Peru, but from it they and their English allies could conceivably mount an attack on Potosí itself.

## Defensive Strategies and Measures:
## Atlantic and Caribbean Sea Routes

The defense of the Indies was based on one fundamental consideration. The vast extent of theaters of hostilities and the initiative enjoyed by foreign intruders made it impossible to defend every bit of territory and every ship at sea. The Spaniards therefore concentrated on defending that which metropolitan Spain deemed most important and which at the same time was most vulnerable, namely, the sea routes that carried American treasure to Seville and the ports that served them.

The means to this end were set forth systematically in a plan prepared by the Spanish *adelantado* and naval captain Pedro Menéndez de Aviles in the early 1560s. They were: (1) the provision of strong naval escorts for the trans-Atlantic fleets; (2) the creation of cruiser squadrons based permanently in the Caribbean to seek out and destroy corsairs and smugglers; and (3) the strengthening of the fortifications of the ports serving the *Carrera* and the provision to them of strong permanent garrisons.[6] Philip II approved Menéndez's proposals and they guided Spanish defensive strategy for the remainder of the Habsburg era. The construction and maintenance of warships and fortifications, however, cost enormous sums of money, always in desperately short supply, and colonial officials were more than a little dilatory. Consequently, the implementation of plans proceeded slowly and fitfully, accelerating when threats mounted, slowing down when they slackened.

The fundamental features of the defense of the treasure fleets took form during the last four decades of the sixteenth century. In 1565 the crown decreed that the *capitanas* (flagships of the commander) of both the Tierra Firme and Mexican fleets must be large galleons carrying at least twelve large cannon and twenty-four smaller artillery pieces. In the following year it extended this requirement to *almirantes* (flagships of the second-in-command). A *capitana* and an *almirante* were generally the only warships accompanying the Mexican *flota*. The Tierra Firme fleet, however, passed through more dangerous waters and carried a more valuable cargo of precious metals. In the later years of Philip II's reign, therefore, it became customary to reinforce its two flagships from the *Armada de la Guardia de la Carrera de Indias*, which had been formed to protect the Atlantic approaches to Seville. The *Armada* normally contributed eight galleons, but the number varied according to the magnitude of foreign naval threats and the availability of seaworthy ships. In 1595, when Drake and Hawkins were ravaging the Caribbean, it furnished twenty warships; in 1655, only four. The Armada's contingent generally carried a regiment (*tercio*) of infantry. Two infantry companies sailed on the *flota*'s flag vessels.

Plans for a permanent naval force in American waters lagged until the 1640s, when the crown formed the *Armada de las Islas de Barlovento y Seno Mexicano* (Windward Squadron) to patrol the seas between the Windward Islands and the Gulf of Mexico. It had a strength of from six to eight frigates and a home station in San Juan de Puerto Rico. During the middle decades of the seventeenth century, however, it was frequently diverted to convoy duty or service in Europe and did not settle down to its original mission until 1672.

## Fortifications in the Caribbean and the Gulf of Mexico

For two decades after the approval of Menéndez's plan, military construction consisted mostly of strengthening the works begun during the French corsair threat in the first half of the sixteenth century. The English privateering offensive and especially Drake and Hawkins's sack of Santo Domingo and Cartagena imparted urgency to the program. In 1586, King Philip II commissioned the military engineers, Juan de Tejada and Juan Bautista Antonelli, to prepare an overall plan for the fortification of Caribbean ports. On the basis of their site selections and plans, new works began to rise. After the English threat abated in the early seventeenth century, construction lagged, but it accelerated again in the mid-1600s when the buccaneers took the offensive. At this time, too, the Spaniards began to fortify the coasts of the Gulf of Mexico and Central America, which earlier corsairs and privateers had left largely unmolested.

Despite the intermittent pace of construction, by the end of the seventeenth century a far-flung system of fortifications guarded the Atlantic prospects of the Indies. Its linchpins were the great stone curtains, bastions, redoubts, and terrepleins that defended Havana, Veracruz, Cartagena, Santo Domingo, and San Juan de Puerto Rico. Less impressive but respectable masonry forts and presidios protected places of secondary importance: Campeche in Yucatán; the entrance to the Gulf of Honduras; the mouth of the Chagres River and Portobelo on the Isthmus of Panama; the Island of Margarita; Santa Marta, and Rio de la Hacha on Tierra Firme; and St. Augustine in Florida. Most fortifications had permanent garrisons whose strength ranged from small detachments to several hundred men.

## The Defense of the Pacific

The appearance of first Drake and then Spillbergen in the Pacific induced the Spanish to strengthen the defenses of those waters, especially the sea lane from Arica to Panama that carried the silver from Potosí. In the late sixteenth century the crown formed the *Armada de la Mar del Sur* (the South Sea Squadron) with a normal strength of five galleons and a home station in Callao. For operational purposes it was divided into two squadrons of two galleons each, one guarding Chilean and Peruvian coasts, the other ranging as far north as Mexico. The fifth vessel remained in reserve at Callao. The South Sea Squadron performed continuous service in the seventeenth century, but its galleons often required beaching for repairs, and in 1692 it had to be completely rebuilt. In the course of the seventeenth century, the Spaniards also fortified or refortified important sites on the Pacific coast: Acapulco, Panama, Guayaquil, Callao, Valparaiso, Valdivia, and the island of Chiloé off southern Chile.

## The Ground Forces of the Indies: Regulars and Militias

The garrisons of coastal fortifications together with presidial troops and scattered field units on Indian frontiers constituted what might loosely be called the regular or standing army of the Indies. Even at prescribed strengths, its several units could not have exceeded a total of several thousand men, but all were chronically undermanned and for the most part they were short of armament, poorly uniformed, undisciplined, and indifferently led.

Several kinds of auxiliary forces stood behind regular troops. In some regions, such as the Kingdom of Quito, *encomenderos* still rallied to the king's standard when summoned, but not without voluble protestations about the expenses and inconveniences that military services caused them. In northern Mexico *hacendados* raised small private armies to defend their properties against Indian incursions. In addition, the crown renewed its efforts to create colonial militias; in 1570 Philip II ordered viceroys and governors to see to it that able-bodied *vecinos* of American port towns had at hand horses and arms according to their means and that they muster every four months for review and inspection.[7] Toward the end of the seventeenth century, urban militia units were formed in some interior provinces, more to preserve domestic tranquillity than to repel foreign invaders. Such was the case in Mexico City, where in 1683 the guild of silversmiths raised a company of grenadiers and, following the riots of 1693, the *consulado* sponsored a "Regiment of Commerce."

Little is known about the history of the militia in the seventeenth-century Indies, very likely because it had none of consequence. Some units apparently had a more or less continuous existence, a more or less fixed organization, and some semblance of training. Such was the case with the so-called *compañías de número* raised in Chile and Peru at the end of the sixteenth century, several companies recruited around Cartagena in the early 1600s, the militia of the coasts of Veracruz organized in the 1680s, and the urban units of Mexico City. For the most part, however, the colonial militia existed only on paper or, at best, rarely mustered in proper order and with serviceable equipment. Although the descendants of conquerors coveted military titles, they had no taste for the inconveniences of military service, and crown officials showed scant organizational zeal.

When measured against the size of Spain's American dominions and the many military fronts they presented, their armed forces appear pitiably inadequate in numbers and quality. Habsburg kings, however, never saw fit to create large colonial armies. As they well knew from their treasurers' doleful reports, regiments of infantry and squadrons of cavalry devoured royal revenues. Also, hints exist that they were reluctant to place concentrations of arms in the hands of Spanish Americans, especially since the aristocracy scorned military service, and the enlisted strength of units had to be recruited from the turbulent lower orders of society.[8]

## The Size and the Costs of Government

The growth of royal government in the Indies swelled the number of officials serving its several branches and offices. Only a handful of scriveners had assisted the early viceroys, Antonio de Mendoza and Francisco de Toledo. By the beginning of the eighteenth century, the viceroys of Mexico and Peru had secretariats whose members performed various specialized functions. The original Audiencia of Mexico consisted of four *oidores* and a president. By the late seventeenth century it had expanded to twelve judges divided into a civil chamber of eight *oidores* and a criminal chamber of four *alcaldes del crimen*. Its personnel also included a host of subordinate functionaries: a chancellor, a high constable, and a chaplain and crown attorneys, reporters, notaries, and clerks. The viceregal audiencia in Lima had much the same organization. The principal treasury offices in the Indies were filled by corps of treasurers, accountants, auditors, and administrative and clerical assistants. Staffs of officers and legal advisors served the commanders of major military installations.

The territorial and functional expansion of the state greatly increased the costs of its governance, and the crown held to the policy that these had to be paid by colonial exchequers. The only extended series of data on their expenditures is from the records of the central office in Mexico. These show approximate annual outlays rising from 1,190,577 silver pesos of eight *reales* in 1577–78 to amounts ranging around 2,500,000 in the first half of the 1600s, and between 3,000,000 and 5,000,000 in the last twenty-five years of the seventeenth century. Direct and indirect costs of defense accounted for the single largest outlay, followed by civil and ecclesiastical salaries.[9]

Since many provinces did not generate enough revenues to cover the expenses of their own government, the crown required the central treasury offices in Mexico and Lima to give them annual subsidies called *situados*, a large part of which went for the construction of fortifications and war vessels, and the support of ships' crews and garrisons. Under this arrangment Lima provided for Chile, Panama, and Cumaná; Mexico, for Venezuela, the Antilles, Florida, and the Philippines. In many years the sums sent to Manila constituted the largest itemized entry in the accounts of the Mexican office.[10]

## The Legal and Theoretical Foundations
### of the State in the Indies

The state in the Indies rested on massive legal foundations. Its expansion was accompanied by an outpouring of royal orders, declarations, cedulas, and pragmatics dealing with particular matters and of ordinances and regulations with broader application. By the end of the Conquest these enactments filled some 200 registry books in the files of the Council of the Indies.

Governors and magistrates found the accumulated legislation very difficult to use, because, aside from its volume, enactments were recorded in chronological order without any subject classification. King Philip II, therefore, determined to codify them and in 1570 placed the task in the charge of Juan de Ovando, a distinguished jurist who had just completed a visitation to the Council of the Indies. Ovando, however, was soon promoted to the presidency of the Council, and the assignment passed from hand to hand for several decades until it fell to Antonio León Pinelo, an attorney of the Council who worked under the supervision of Councilor Juan de Solórzano y Pereyra. León and Solórzano had served respectively as crown attorney and *oidor* of the Audiencia of Lima, and their experience with peculiarly American jurisprudence unquestionably influenced the form and content of their work.

By 1635 León had completed his task, but the compilation was not published, owing mainly to the penury to which the royal treasury had been reduced. Revision and updating followed, however, and in 1681, over eighty years after Philip II had been laid to rest, the code finally emerged from the press bearing the title *Recopilación de leyes de los reinos de las Indias* (Compilation of the Laws of the Kingdoms of the Indies).

The *Recopilación* contained some 6400 separate laws, ordered in nine subject books (*libros*) subdivided into 218 titles (*títulos*). Many laws dealt with matters that today seem trivial. The House of Trade should have a clock; the doorkeeper of its Chamber of Government should receive appropriate gratuities; gunpowder should not be wasted on salutes; the judges of the Audiencia of Manila should not accept chickens as gifts or purchase them at lower than going market prices. Many laws were inconsistent with each other and some were obsolete at the time of publication. Taken together they lacked the consistency of a modern code.

These defects do not prevent the *Recopilación* from being a document of immense historical value and a monument of jurisprudence. It records the construction of an imperial system in the Indies and defines its structures and functions. It reveals a patrimonial philosophy of government combining high idealism with pragmatic political considerations. If its laws were frequently disobeyed, evaded, or deliberately misinterpreted, it still guided the formation of American societies by establishing the limits of what could and could not be done. And it had great durability, for it strongly influenced the legal codes of the independent Spanish American republics.

A growing corpus of political theory rationalized the structures and functions of the state. Its main current of development ran toward the amplification of royal authority, thus reflecting the triumph of the Roman civil law in Spanish universities as well as the absolutist pretensions of Habsburg monarchs, under whose patronage jurists and theologians wrote. When Philip II succeeded to the throne of Spain in 1556, the most widely accepted explanation of the origins and attributes of sovereignty still rested on principles set forth in the *Siete Partidas*, as reformulated by neo-Thomist schoolmen at the University of Salamanca. Sovereign power reposed in God. From Him it passed to the people, who in turn delegated it to the prince through a "pact of submission." By virtue of the transfer, the prince became superior to the people but remained bound by the end to which he was the means, that is, the common good, and by the laws, although without being subject to legal coercion.

During the seventeenth century, jurists and theologians still had no doubt about the divine origins of sovereignty, but they came to hold that in the process of transmission to earthly agencies the people were a passive rather than an active instrument. The king was God's legate and therefore possessed absolute and extraordinary power. The laws shaping the common welfare became the untrammeled expression of his will. The obverse of absolute power was a diminution of the popular right of resistance to the point of negation. Jurists still affirmed that the king could not be a tyrant, and the Jesuit Juan de Mariana condoned tyrannicide in certain circumstances.[11] His position, however, was not widely accepted, on the grounds that punishment was an exclusive prerogative of sovereignty. The only real restraint on the power of kings was their consciences. If the people believed themselves to be misgoverned, all they could do was supplicate and pray for better times following the counsel of the Old

Testament. Absolutist theory applied separately and equally to all the Spanish kingdoms, but it had special force in the realms of the Indies. The crown had created them de novo. The concept of a pact of submission had no validity in them; no question existed about the route of transmission of sovereignty over them.

Two subjects of political inquiry related more particularly to the Indies. The most controversial was the papal donations as a source of juridical title. In Spain, the issue developed through increasingly explicit definitions of the apostolic character of the monarchy's role in America, the first being the doctrine of the Royal Vicariate adumbrated by the missionary orders. Subsequently a line of regalist jurists extending from Juan de Ovando to Solórzano y Pereyra refined this concept for a practical political purpose, the aggrandizement of the royal patronage.[12] Although their arguments were convoluted and often inconsistent, they had a central thesis. God had miraculously revealed the New World to the Catholic Kings and commanded the pope to entrust its governance to them and their successors so that the barbarous nations that might be found there would be converted to the True Religion. By accepting the task and discharging it faithfully and well, the kings of Castile acquired temporal dominion directly through God's will. The papal grants were merely instruments.

But the nature of the papal bulls was more than a matter between the king of Spain and the Holy See. The counterclaims of foreign kings supported by Dutch and French jurists and, ironically, by a Spaniard, Francisco de Vitoria, changed the dimensions of the problem. It passed from the domain of the laws of Christendom, of which the pope was the supreme adjudicator, into the realm of the law of nations, which derived from natural law and in which secular authorities claimed competence. Most Spanish thinkers refused to recognize this shift and still contended that their kings exercised legitimate sovereignty in the Indies by virtue of their preeminent services to Christendom, first in the New World, later as defenders of the faith against heretics and infidels. As Spanish influence waned, however, and as Spain grudgingly accepted the principal of uti possidetis de facto, the issue of the papal donations lost its relevance in international affairs. It remained alive in Spain only as it affected the royal patronage.

Another line of political inquiry concerned the constitutional status of the Indies in relation to other dominions of the Spanish crown. Solórzano delivered the most incisive opinion on the subject. The king's realms, he declared, fell into two classes. The first consisted of those united to Castile "with equal principality." They were governed as though the "King who ruled them all together was King of each one separately." Each had its own estates and cortes and subsisted under its own laws. Within each, native subjects had preferential claims to public office. The king governed each through a supreme council. Into this class fell Aragon, Navarre, Flanders, the Italian kingdoms, and Portugal while ruled by the Spanish Habsburgs. The second class consisted of "appendages" that were subject to the laws of Castile, had no representative assemblies, and were administered by whomsoever the ruler wished to appoint. The realms of the Indies constituted appendages even though they were governed by a supreme council.[13]

## The Spanish State in the Indies toward the End of the Habsburg Era

In the century following the Conquest, the state in the Indies grew into a monumental structure of theories, laws, offices, agencies, and institutions. Yet its power was not commensurate with its size and weight. This disproportion owed in part to the inability of Spain in decline to impose strong rule on its American possessions, a condition of which colonials were well aware. In addition, the way in which the state grew enhanced its inherent structural weaknesses. Territorial expansion lengthened already overextended imperial communications, leaving outlying provinces increasingly remote from metropolitan and even American centers of authority. Everywhere in the Indies, the growth in the number, size, and duties of governmental agencies—unaccompanied by clearer-cut divisions of power among them—generated more and more jurisdictional disputes and encouraged bureaucratic sluggishness. Meanwhile, legal and illegal methods of evading the king's writ and the intrusion of private interests into the performance of public duties became deeply entrenched in the political culture of Spanish America.

The overall quality of the royal service in the Indies also declined in the post-Conquest era. Although precedent and law established some rough norms governing the conditions of employment, especially in the judiciary and the military, the bureaucracy remained essentially patrimonial, for the crown could change the rules at its pleasure. As the seventeenth century advanced, the defects inherent in this system were enhanced by two developments. One was the passage of patrimonial rights from Philip II to the less conscientious and strong-minded Philip III and Philip IV and, by default of their leadership, to their favorite ministers, the duke of Lerma and the count duke of Olivares. These functionaries, in turn, dispensed public offices to their own favorites or to persons to whom they were beholden, without too much concern about the competence or rectitude of their appointees.

The other abuse of patrimonialism was the widespread sale of royal offices. This practice was rationalized on the grounds that the purchase price constitued a nonrefundable bond for correct performance, but it was used in fact as a source of revenue. The early Spanish Habsburgs limited sales to minor nonsalaried positions such as that of notary, whose emoluments came from fees charged for services, but, as the needs of the treasury became desperate, seventeenth-century monarchs openly sold posts, first in the exchequer and then in the judiciary, to the highest or most influential bidder. Positions could also be obtained less directly by appropriate "donations" to the royal treasury or by "gifts" to royal favorites.

## Royal Government in Post-Conquest Brazil

### Territorial Expansion

Immediately following the occupation of the north and northeastern parts of Brazil, the crown created six new captaincies in those regions: Sergipe (detached from the Captaincy of Bahia), Paraiba, and Rio Grande do Norte, all in the late sixteenth century; and Ceará, Maranhão, and Pará, all in the early 1600s. Although private initiative had played an important part in their conquest, they were all constituted as royal captaincies. Furthermore, in the first half of the seventeenth century, the king repossessed three of the original private captaincies: São Tomé by cession in 1619, and Pernambuco and Itamaracá by confiscation in 1654, ostensibly because of the defection of their donatarial heir to Spain during Portugal's struggle for independence against Habsburg rule. Both newly created and regained royal captaincies were placed under the civil and military governship of officials called *capitães mores*. Thus, the most important parts of Brazil came under direct royal rule.

### Territorial Decentralization

Territorial decentralization of royal government accompanied territorial expansion. This development reflected several influences. One was the reluctance of the king to entrust too much power to a governor-general residing in distant Bahia. Another was the desire of the governors of the several captaincies to exercise as much authority as they could obtain. Still another, and probably the most powerful was the population geography of Brazil. By the end of the sixteenth century, three widely separated concentrations of population and economic activity had developed in the colony: around Pernambuco, Bahia, and Rio de Janeiro. Some 500 miles of coast separated Bahia from Pernambuco;

nearly 1000 stretched between Bahia and Rio. Land communications among the centers were undeveloped, and wind patterns in the South Atlantic hindered communication by sea. The occupation of the northeast coast added another remote region to the colony. In terms of elapsed sailing times, its captaincies were closer to Lisbon than to Bahia. Portuguese kings recognized the extreme difficulty of governing the dispersed captaincies of Brazil from any one capital.

The Portuguese crown laid the legal foundations of territorial decentralization through acts of omission in the several *regimentos* (standing instructions) that it gave to governors-general and that together formed the basic constitution of Brazil.[14] In both the *regimento* issued to Tomé de Sousa in 1548 and that to Roque da Costa Barreto in 1677 — over 125 years later — it conferred upon them supreme military and political command in all of the colony, but it neglected to spell out the powers reserved or denied to subordinate governors, thereby encouraging them to resist inconvenient orders from Bahia. The king never resolved this ambiguity, perhaps by design, perhaps because of irresolution, but in any event its continued existence stunted the growth of the governorship-general.

The crown also furthered decentralization through acts of commission. In 1614 it forbade the governors-general to travel outside the captaincy of Bahia without its express permission, thereby limiting the range of their actual authority. Earlier, in 1572, it detached the southern captaincies of Pôrto Seguro, Espírito Santo, and São Vicente from the military and political command of Bahia and placed them under that of the governor of Rio de Janeiro, who, at the same time, was promoted to captain-general, a rank hitherto held only by the governor-general. This arrangement had a checkered history. In 1578 the three provinces were returned to Bahia, in 1608 were reassigned to Rio, and in 1612 again reverted to Bahia. Rio de Janeiro, however, retained a large measure of de facto authority in the governance of southern Brazil.

The crown made a firmer and more lasting division in northern Brazil. In 1621 it created the *Estado do Maranhão* (State of Maranhão), which included the newly established captaincies of Maranhão, Pará, and Ceará and which had its capital fixed in São Luís de Maranhão. The new "state" was completely independent of Bahia and its governor responsible directly to Lisbon. Thereafter, all the rest of Brazil became known as the *Estado do Brasil* (the State of Brazil). Its capital remained in Bahia.

Both de facto and de jure decentralization continued throughout the rest of the seventeenth century and on into the eighteenth. The struggle against the Dutch further weakened the power of governors-general. Being fully engrossed with defending Bahia and instigating revolts in Dutch-occupied territory, they had neither the time nor the resources to assert their authority outside of their immediate command. Consequently, subordinate captains became accustomed to a considerable measure of independence, which they did not wish to relinquish after the invaders had been expelled. This was especially true of the powerful governors of Pernambuco and Rio de Janeiro. Not only did they consolidate their semiautonomous status, but they extended their sway over the captaincies adjacent to them.

Around the turn of the seventeenth century, the regional subdivision of Brazil became even more firmly established. In 1697, the king again named the governor of Rio de Janeiro captain-general, and in the early 1700s the governor of Pernambuco assumed the same rank. By the end of the seventeenth century, furthermore, the captaincies grouped around Rio, Pernambuco, and Bahia came to be known as *capitanías subalternas* (subordinate captaincies), and were governed by *capitães mores*. Supreme political and military command in the State of Brazil still pertained to the governor-general in Bahia, but except for the coordination of defense his actual authority was limited to his own captaincy and adjacent subordinate captaincies. The territorial organization of Brazil resulting from these developments is shown in table 10.

Table 10
The Governmental Organization of
Portuguese America in About 1700

| |
| --- |
| State of Maranhão |
|     Captaincy of Maranhão (royal) |
|     Captaincy of Pará (royal) |
|     Captaincy of Ceará (royal) |
| State of Brazil |
|     Governorship-General and Captaincy-General of Bahia |
|         Captaincy of Bahia (royal) |
|         Captaincy of Sergipe (royal) |
|         Captaincy of Ilhéus (hereditary) |
|         Captaincy of Pôrto Seguro (hereditary) |
|     Captaincy-General of Pernambuco |
|         Captaincy of Pernambuco (royal) |
|         Captaincy of Rio Grande do Norte (royal) |
|         Captaincy of Paraíba (royal) |
|         Captaincy of Itamaracá (royal) |
|     Captaincy-General of Rio de Janeiro |
|         Captaincy of Rio de Janeiro (royal) |
|         Captaincy of Espírito Santo (hereditary) |
|         Captaincy of São Vicente (hereditary), which had |
|             incorporated the Captaincy of São Tomé in 1619 |

## Territorial Organization of the Church in Brazil

Church governance developed along much the same regional lines as civil administration, although somewhat more slowly. In 1676, more than a century after its founding in 1551, the see of Bahia was elevated to an archbishopric, and the bishoprics of Rio de Janeiro and Olinda were created suffragan to it. In 1677 a fourth diocese was established with jurisdiction over the State of Maranhão and suffragan to Lisbon rather than to Bahia.

## The Growth of the Powers of the State in Brazil

### Defense

The Portuguese recognized the same primary functions of government as did the Spanish: the provision of justice, the making and execution of the laws, treasury management, and military command. Although territorial decentralization distributed their exercise among regional centers, each function expanded after the Conquest era in response to demographic and economic growth and to the imperatives of defense.

From the very beginning of Portuguese colonization in Brazil, security took precedence over all other concerns. Indian tribes constantly harassed the first settlements, and the advance to the northeast and into the backlands created new Indian frontiers. Meanwhile, northern European nations offered an ever-present threat to the colony. Throughout the sixteenth century the French attempted to establish footholds on the coast, first in the southeast and then in the northeast. The English attacked Santos in 1582 and 1591, Bahia in 1587, and Recife in 1595. In 1604 the Dutch made an unsuccessful assault on Bahia but in 1624 and again in 1627 managed to occupy the city temporarily. In the 1630s they began their conquest of Pernambuco and its neighboring captaincies. Portuguese expansion to the Rio de la Plata in the 1680s brought a military confrontation with Spain. At the end of the seventeenth century Brazil remained very vulnerable to foreign attack, for in contrast to the Spanish Indies its main centers of wealth and population still lay on its coasts.

Despite these dangers, for over a century following the settlement of Brazil the crown did not maintain a permanent defense establishment in the colony. Instead Indian wars were fought by settlers who took up arms for the occasion. Colonial governors expelled the French with troops raised for particular campaigns. Brazilian irregulars reconquered the northeast from the Dutch, and, although some units engaged in the struggle acquired a regimented organization, they were disbanded after victory had been won. In the later 1600s, however, when rivalries with Spain over the Platine area intensified, the crown placed permanent garrisons of regular troops in Bahia and Pernambuco and raised militia units in Brazilian towns. In addition, it strengthened the fortifications of major ports, but even those guarding Bahia were modest compared to the bastions of the Spanish Caribbean.

The imperatives of defense reflected most strongly in the structure of colonial government and the kinds of men who occupied its principal offices. All the governors of Bahia held the prestigious rank of captain-general, and, in contrast with Spanish American viceroys, most were professional soldiers with previous field experience in Europe, Asia, or Africa. As observed in the preceding section of this chapter, when the crown separated Rio de Janeiro, Pernambuco, and Maranhão from the command of Bahia, it promoted their governors to captains-general, whereas governors of subordinate royal captaincies held the military rank of *capitão mór*.

From captains-general and *capitães mores*, the military command structure extended downward to *sargentos mores*, who were directly responsible for the organization and administration of troops and the maintenance of fortifications in the several captaincies, to the commanders of permanent garrisons, and to the colonels of militia units. Many of the last-named officers were also landed magnates and held posts in municipal councils. By combining military rank with economic and civic influence, they dominated their districts. They were the prototypes of the colonels (*coroneis*) who played such an important part in the affairs of Brazil after it gained its independence.

## Civil Government

Although the government of Brazil was preoccupied with defense, its civil functions also expanded in response to the demographic and economic growth of the colony and, to some extent, the propensities of Portugal's Habsburg rulers for bureaucratization. In the department of general administration, the governors of the State of Brazil and the governor of the State of Maranhão were obliged to execute a swelling body of royal laws and regulations and to make decisions on a widening range of public matters. They also were heads of the treasury offices located in their capitals, and, in this capacity, they had to oversee the management of an increasing volume of royal revenues. To assist them in these tasks, they required the services of more and more clerks, notaries, and scribes.

The royal judiciary developed a three-tiered structure. The lowest level consisted of *juizes ordinários* (municipal magistrates) who throughout most of the sixteenth and seventeenth centuries enjoyed a considerable measure of independence in adjudicating local cases. In the 1690s, the crown appointed *juizes de fora* (royal judges) to take their places in the more important towns, such as Olinda, Salvador, and Rio de Janeiro. The second level was composed of *ouvidorias* (circuit courts). The first of these had been established in the royal captaincy of Bahia when it was founded in 1549. A second was seated in Rio de Janeiro in 1572 when the southern captaincies were separated from the command of Bahia, and it continued to function after the separation was abandoned. A third was established in 1611 in the newly created State of Maranhão, and a fourth in Pernambuco after the crown confiscated that captaincy from its donatary. Judges of these courts traveled throughout the districts governed from their headquarters to hear appeals from lower courts.

The superior tribunal in Brazil was a *relação* (high court of appeals), established in Bahia in 1608 in connection with metropolitan judical reforms undertaken by the Habsburg kings of Portugal. It was composed of several senior magistrates (*desembargadores*) presided over ex officio by the governor-general, and its jurisdiction extended throughout Brazil, excepting the state of Maranhão. Appeals from its decisions went to the king's courts in Lisbon. In addition to hearing appeals from lower courts, it reviewed the conduct of royal officials at the end of their terms of office and conducted special investigations upon the orders of the crown or the governor-general. Its organization and jurisdiction resembled that of the Spanish American audiencia.

In 1624 the *Relação* was abolished, the immediate reason being that the government needed the money it cost to pay for the garrison established in Bahia in the same year. Perhaps a more fundamental consideration, however, was the opposition it drew from the powerful donatary of Pernambuco, who feared its intrusion into his private jurisdiction. In 1652 it was reestablished in response to complaints from various captaincies about the high costs of appeal directly to Lisbon. By that time, also, the unpatriotic conduct of the donatary family of Pernambuco had cost it its influence at court.[15]

## Metropolitan Agencies of Colonial Government

The growth of Brazil together with Spanish Habsburg influence induced Portugal to centralize the metropolitan governance of the colony, which, until the early seventeenth century, had been distributed among various offices and agencies in Lisbon. In 1614 it organized a *Concelho da India e Conquistas Ultramarinas* (Council of India and Overseas Conquests) on the model of the Spanish Council of the Indies. The council had jurisdiction over Brazil as well as Portuguese overseas possessions in the Old World. However, the agencies into whose customary competences it intruded opposed it, and furthermore it was suspected of being a Castilian device for gaining access to Portuguese colonial revenues. It was therefore abolished after only ten years of existence. In 1642 the new Braganza dynasty created another superior council for overseas government, the *Concelho Ultramarino* (Overseas Council), which managed to survive, but it never enjoyed the same power and prestige as the Council of the Indies.

## The Governance of Brazil toward the End of the Seventeenth Century

The Portuguese state in Brazil rested on the same fundamental principle as the Spanish state in the Indies. It was part of the patrimony of the Portuguese crown and was governed at the king's will by a patrimonial bureaucracy whose various agencies possessed coordinate and overlapping functions. The declared purpose of the state was to provide justice and good government to the king's American subjects, but in practice its aim was to exploit the colony in his interests and those of the metropolitan mercantile community. In Brazil, as in Spanish America, the royal writ was weakened by bureaucratic squabbling, favoritism in appointment to public offices, and conflicts between public and private interests to which royal officers were susceptible.

Yet the governmental apparatus in Spanish and Portuguese America were dissimilar in important respects. The Brazilian bureaucracy was much smaller and less complex, and the balance between its several functional departments was different. In contrast to the power and prestige enjoyed by the courts and, especially, the audiencias in the king of Spain's dominions, the Brazilian judiciary was underdeveloped. The government of the colony was essentially a military command structure dominated by governors as captains-general and their subordinate *capitães mores*.[16]

Furthermore, whereas Spain created a large legal code, the *Laws of the Indies*, specifically for its American possessions, Brazil remained subject to metropolitan compilations, first the *Ordenações Manuelinas* and then the *Ordenações Filipinas*, prepared under the auspices of Philip I (Philip II of Spain) and promulgated in 1603. Portuguese jurists gave relatively little thought to the theoretical underpinnings of the state in Brazil, nor did they give it a particular status within the empire such as that possessed by Spanish American "kingdoms." Early in the seventeenth century, the Council of India advised the crown that its overseas possessions were in no way distinct from metropolitan Portugal nor were they joined to it. Rather they were all parts of the same kingdom.

The reasons for these divergences are not hard to find. The governance of Brazil did not require a large and complex bureaucracy or an elaborate code of colonial law. It was smaller and less diverse than the Spanish Indies; it had a much smaller population; it had far fewer Indians who required special governance; and its economy was less rich and diversified and therefore required less regulation. Neither could the colony's revenues support viceregal courts, august magistracies, and large numbers of civil and ecclesiastical functionaries. It is worth remarking, however, that, after its rich gold mines came into production in the eighteenth century, the crown gave the chiefs of state in Brazil the title of viceroy along with viceregal status and powers, enlarged both the judiciary and the royal treasury, and attempted to regulate the economy of the colony more closely. Finally, the emphasis placed on military defense in Brazil at the expense of other functions of government simply reflected the continued vulnerability of its principal settlements to invasion.

## Hispanic American Empires: Imperial Control and Imperial Survival

The post-Conquest history of Hispanic America raises a number of questions, all related to the decline of Spain and Portugal as European and imperial powers. One is: How did the two nations manage to expand their empires in America under these conditions? The answer lies in a shift in the source of expansive energy. The conquest and colonization of America were accomplished by the export of men and goals and enterprise from Spain and Portugal in their prime. But by the end of the sixteenth century the Hispanic New World possessions had generated their own expansive forces and had bred the men to direct them: miners, ranchers, *bandeirantes, tropas,* captains and soldiers, and creolized friars and padres.

Another question is: How did Spain and Portugal in decline manage to preserve the territorial integrity of their American empires against the attacks of northern European enemies whose maritime power was waxing? The answer lies not so much in formal Hispanic defense measures as in fortuitous circumstances. Throughout most of the seventeenth century, northern Europeans had only a peripheral interest in America. Although stimulated by American silver, their economies were based primarily on Old World production and commerce, and Old World concerns prevented them from giving full and continuous attention to exploiting Spanish and Portuguese weaknesses. England was diverted by the Puritan Revolution and problems associated with the restoration of the Stuarts; France, by dissensions among its great noble houses; Holland, by its efforts to extend its carrying trade in Europe, Africa, and Asia. In addition, the enemies of Spain and Portugal were preoccupied with European wars: the Thirty Years' War (1618–48) and the three Dutch-English naval wars (fought between 1652 and 1678), which pitted the two powers most capable of attacking Hispanic America against each other.

The other and most fundamental safeguard of the Spanish and Portuguese American colonies was their geographical layout and their climates. The northern European powers demonstrated their capability to seize temporarily Spanish Caribbean and Brazilian ports, but, to hold and expand their lodgments, they would have had to mount prolonged and costly campaigns in inhospitable and thinly populated hinterlands, perfectly suited for guerrilla resistance from inhabitants who regarded all foreigners as heretics. Meanwhile their enclaves were vulnerable to attack from unconquered settlements and their garrisons to tropical diseases, especially after yellow fever appeared in America. Nothing illustrates better the way in which geography assisted the defense of Brazil than the failure of the Dutch conquest. The Hollanders were able to seize a large part of the northeastern coast, but resistance generated in the backlands and threats from unconquered Bahia on their southern flank ultimately made their occupation untenable.

The geography of settlement gave the Spanish Indies a special advantage. Their main centers of wealth and population lay in interior uplands, guarded by pestilential maritime frontiers and towering ranges or steep escarpments and approachable only by poorly developed roads. None of Spain's enemies had the logistical capabilities to conquer these regions. Indeed, no major inland city in Spanish America fell to a foreign power until United States armies took Mexico City in 1847, and, although the gringos had the advantage of adjacent territorial bases of operations, they had to fight a bitter war to achieve their objective.

The Spaniards understood and exploited the advantages that geography gave them. They withdrew from regions such as the Lesser Antilles and the North American mainland beyond Florida whose defense did not justify heavy and, probably, fruitless expenses. In the Greater Antilles and on the Pacific coast of Mexico, authorities allowed and in some instances ordered the depopulation of threatened maritime provinces. In contrast they encouraged missionaries to occupy the open frontiers of their empire, such as northern Mexico, Guairá in Paraguay, and the eastern slopes of the Andes, in order to create buffer zones guarding its heartland. Colonial governments refrained from improving roads, hoping to discourage the passage of enemies, as in the cases of the trail across the Isthmus of Panama and routes from coastal Ecuador to the interior. As one

Spanish official put it, "The major security of these provinces [Quito] consists of the inaccessibility of the roads."[17]

The largely unproductive forays of privateers and buccaneers, the inglorious Cromwellian invasion of Española, and the failure of the Dutch in Brazil gave northern Europeans an appreciation of the strategic advantages enjoyed by Spain and Portugal in those parts of America they had occupied effectively. In the latter half of the seventeenth century, therefore, the enemies of the Hispanic powers turned more and more to less bloody and more profitable forms of intrusion: planting in regions left unoccupied by the Hispanic nations and contraband trade, which they exploited with increasing success. Thus, it might be said that, although Spain and Portugal maintained the territorial integrity of their American possessions, they lost a good part of the profits of empire.

A third question is how enfeebled Spain and Portugal were able to impose an increasingly burdensome government on American colonies that were growing more and more populous, wealthier, less economically dependent on their mother countries, and increasingly aware of their own identities and interests. The political aspects of this relationship have been pointed out by two distinguished modern historians. Speaking of New Spain, Lesley Byrd Simpson wrote, "By 1700 [the kingdom] was firmly in the hands of a vast interlocking system of [creole] family interests, which the able servants of the latter Bourbons conspicuously failed to break up."[18] As for Brazil, Pedro Calmon observed, "[It] was governed in fact not by the king in Lisbon, nor by the Governor General in Bahia, but by the municipal *câmaras* in the cities and towns, by the *capitães mores* where they existed and by the heads of families in their sparsely settled and vast zones of influence."[19] To put the question another way: Why did Spanish Americans and Brazilians wait until the nineteenth century to renounce imperial systems that they knew were designed to exploit them?

The answer cannot be found in the coercive instruments at the disposal of the Hispanic states. In both Spanish America and Brazil, the permanent armed forces were too small and scattered and the militia and the constabulary too poorly trained and armed to be able to cope with general or even regional rebellions. In any event, most of the personnel of military and police units were American born, and their loyalties to the government could not be relied upon. Neither could colonial officials count on ready help from the mother country. During long periods in the seventeenth century, Spain's military resources were fully committed to safeguarding imperial interests in northern Europe and to suppressing revolts in Catalonia and Portugal. As for Portugal, it was deeply involved in preserving its eastern empire and in defending its independence from Habsburg rule.

The durability of Hispanic imperial systems derived rather from their territorial and social organization. The several regions of both the Spanish Indies and Brazil had separate identities born of geographical separation, administrative decentralization, varying population mixtures, and different natural resources. In addition, they often had competing economic interests that the crown could manipulate by the bestowal or withdrawal of favors. These circumstances tended to limit overt resistance against metropolitan rule to local protests against specific grievances.

The hierarchical organization of colonial societies had a comparable effect. The social separation of the several orders and classes precluded broadly based resistance to metropolitan rule. The Spanish government understood this, as evidenced by the following excerpt from a *consulta* (formal opinion) delivered by the Council of the Indies as late as 1806:

If it is undeniable that the existence of various hierarchies and classes is of the greatest importance to the existence and stability of a monarchical state, since a graduated system of dependence and subordination sustains and insures the obedience and respect of the last vassal to the authority of the sovereign, with much more reason such a system is necessary in America, not only because of its greater distance from the throne, but also because of the number of that class of people who, because of their vicious origin and nature, are not comparable to the commoners of Spain and constitute a very inferior species.[20]

The key to the system described by the Council was an alliance between the crown and colonial elites that was characteristic of Spanish Habsburg rule in metropolitan Spain, in Italy, and in Flanders as well as in the Indies and that also existed in Brazil.[21] The rich, the powerful, and the wellborn in Hispanic America had a profoundly traditional mentality. They could not conceive of a republic without a prince who ruled by legitimate dynastic succession, his majesty sanctified by God and time. The clergy, secular and regular, high and low, reminded them from the pulpit and in the confessional that they owed allegiance to their monarch. A large measure of self-interest reinforced their loyalty. They knew that the king was the ultimate source of *legitimate* ranks, offices, titles, perquisites, property rights, and mercantile privileges, in short, all of those benefits from which their elevated status derived. Although they might protest or evade particular royal policies or laws, they never questioned the right of their monarch to rule. Moreover, they lived in fear of risings from below and hoped for the assistance of the king in keeping the lower orders in subjugation.

For their part, Spanish and Portuguese kings counted on colonial elites to set standards of loyalty and respect for royal authority and to use their power and influence to keep the servile population in its place. In return, Hispanic monarchs recognized their superior status, granted them honors and material benefits, accepted their influence in local government, and allowed them considerable latitude in observing the law, balking only at lese majesty and misdeeds so blatant that they could not be overlooked.

The patrimonial bureaucracy in America provided the essential instrument of this compact. Its members were bound to serve their kings, but most of them had or soon acquired local kinship and economic interests and, being in America, understood and often sympathized with American sentiments. Thus, through their dual status, they "brokered" relations between their distant masters and American elites. They interpreted and applied royal orders in terms of colonial needs and political feasibility. They spoke to their princes for colonial interests and tried to restrain them from ill-considered actions.[22]

The efficacy of these alliances was demonstrated by what happened when monarchs forgot or disregarded them. The abridgment of ancient *fueros* and privileges or the fear of such an affront caused Castilians to rebel against Charles I in 1520, the Flemings against Philip II in the 1560s, and the Catalans against Philip IV in the 1640s. In each instance many nobles at first joined the revolt or stood aloof. But, when revolutions took a popular turn, they resumed their allegiance to the crown.[23]

The test of the compact in America came later. The attempts of the Spanish Bourbons in the late eighteenth century to reassert metropolitan domination in the Indies undermined the loyalty of the privileged classes and ultimately contributed to colonial rebellions. In most regions, however, revolution took on popular overtones, and aristocracies did not support them until conservative forces gained control of their direction. Even after independence, colonial elites retained an allegiance to monarchical principles.

Events took a comparable turn in Brazil. In the third quarter of the eighteenth century, the marquis of Pombal, Portugal's dictatorial chief minister, introduced reforms in the colony intended to strengthen royal government. Powerful landed and mercantile elements, however, felt that his measures threatened their entrenched privileges. Later, in 1808, the Portuguese court fled from Lisbon to escape Napoleon's troops and settled down in Rio de Janeiro. Its presence raised the specter of closer scrutiny of Brazilian affairs, more taxes to support the immigrant government, and the intrusion of arrogant *reinóis* courtiers into public offices. And, when in 1822 the colonial aristocracy finally renounced its allegiance to the king of Portugal, it acted not only to gain independence but also to forestall a more popular revolution. It also opted for a monarchy rather than a republic and chose a prince of the royal house to reign.

# CHAPTER 20

# Epilogue: European Reactions to Hispanic Expansion in America

The impact of Hispanic expansion on America was direct, massive, and permanent. It involved the rapid conquest of large parts of two continents, the sudden destruction of great Indian civilizations, and the decimation of indigenous populations. In the wake of conquest the Spaniards and Portuguese created new American societies with the unwilling help of the conquered peoples and slaves brought from Africa.

As they existed at the end of the seventeenth century, these societies give the appearance of archaic structures when compared with those of northern Europe, but less so if their mother countries are used as the standard of measurement. Except for a few favored locations, they had low population densities and poorly developed urban networks; they were economically backward and dependent; they possessed hierarchically ordered social structures in which status ostensibly was based on racial qualities and various degrees of servitude; and their governments were inefficient and corrupt. They were insulated from the currents of change flowing in early modern Europe by distance, metropolitan policies, the vigilance of the church, and the conservatism of their elites. The sharp cleavages among their social classes, moreover, make them appear fragile and vulnerable to eruptions from within and subversion from without. Nonetheless, they proved to have a remarkable durability, and, even after they became independent, they stood as clearly visible marks of the work of Spain and Portugal in America.

The impact on Europe of Hispanic expansion in America is much more difficult to assess. Indeed, except for the shock of the Discovery and the arrival of large quantities of American treasure, the effects could hardly be called an impact. They amounted, rather, to the slow infiltration of material things and intangible influences. Furthermore, it is hard to isolate American influences from changes already under way in Europe at the time of the Discovery, and historians of Europe have implicitly assumed that what Europe gave was more important than what it received in return.

For these reasons the effects of the opening of the New World on the Old have been less thoroughly studied than the creation of Hispanic empires in America, and what has been written on the former subject has not been fully synthesized. Nonetheless, the theme of this series, "Europe and the World in the Age of Expansion," demands at least a survey of what scholars think Europe received in the "Columbian Exchange."[1]

## Information about the New World: Accumulation, Dissemination, and Assimilation

Information about the New World accumulated steadily in Europe beginning with Columbus's first voyage. At first it came chiefly from Spanish sources and fell into several categories: (1) the charts and notes of navigators, which were mainly of cartographical interest; (2) the reports to the crown of discoverers, conquerors, and colonial officials, which were full of miscellaneous information but often unbalanced by a desire to please or impress; (3) the chronicles of conquest, which varied widely in quality according to the education and perception of their authors;[2] (4) the writings of the first generation of missionaries, especially in Mexico, which contained a wealth of ethnographic data;[3] and (5) the histories, "general," "natural," and "moral," written by men on the scene, which described the New World's physical features, its climates, its minerals, its flora and fauna, and, above all, its indigenous peoples.[4]

After the middle of the sixteenth century, Spanish sources were supplemented by Portuguese chronicles and histories of the conquest and colonization of Brazil and by the writings of foreigners who penetrated Hispanic America. The last-named category included the descriptions of Brazil by Frenchmen who participated in Huguenot efforts to settle in Brazil, and Sir Walter Raleigh's *The Discovery of the Large, Rich, and Beautiful Empire of Guiana*.[5] Although numerous works on the Hispanic New World were written in the seventeenth century, the great age of information gathering was the sixteenth, and by its end these regions had been very well described.

The dissemination of information about America occurred more slowly than its gathering. Most of the official accounts reposed in Seville, Madrid, and

Lisbon, far distant from the most important centers of learning in Europe, and Spanish and Portuguese kings restricted their use because they did not wish to draw foreign attention to their American dominions. As for private chronicles and histories, many were not published in full, in part, or at all until the nineteenth century. Furthermore, the works that did appear in print during the era of the Conquest were in Latin, Spanish, or Portuguese, and their translation into other European languages was often long delayed.

The assimilation of information about the New World proceeded even more slowly than dissemination for several reasons. One was that discoveries in those regions had to compete for attention with developments closer to home. Humanist scholars were making their own "discoveries" about the classical world, which was just as new to them as America. Among more practical-minded men, the Portuguese voyages to India excited greater interest than the Enterprise of the Indies; the former produced rich and immediate profits through rerouting a familiar trade, whereas the latter was an economic disappointment until after the mid-sixteenth century, when Spanish American mines and Brazilian sugar plantations began to pour out their riches. European monarchs had immediate and pressing Old World problems: the advance of the Turks in the Mediterranean and in southeastern Europe, the Habsburg-Valois wars, the revolt of the Netherlands, and the religious schism in Germany.

A psychological problem further delayed European appreciations of America. How were the newly found lands to be accommodated to the classical and scriptural knowledge that formed the basis of existing views of the nature of the world? The things that the Europeans found could not be fitted into the fixed and static Aristotelian system of classification. Ptolemy's geography accounted for only three continents; Pliny's *Natural History* made no mention of the llama or the tapir; Hippocrates, Galen, and Avicenna said nothing about American dysenteries, fevers, and eruptive diseases. Even more troublesome was the realization by Old World savants that the distinctive biota of America could not be accounted for in the Old Testament relation of the single creation of species and their survival through the Great Flood. As a result of these dilemmas, various kinds of information about America entered European awareness in ways and at rates governed by their practical utility and the ease with which they could be assimilated with deeply rooted cosmological and religious preconceptions.

## The Intellectual Influence of the New World

### Imaginative Literature and Utopias

The discovery of new continents and seas unquestionably stimulated imaginative thought and writing in Europe. Not only were these regions excitingly novel, but they were distant, vast, and empty of civilization as Europeans knew it. In them, therefore, almost anything might be found or be placed by the imagination. Thus, Spanish discoverers, stimulated by medieval legends and chronicles, believed that somewhere in their depths lay El Dorado, Gran Quivira, the Seven Cities of Cíbola, and the formidable Nation of the Amazons.

The advance of discovery finally forced the Spaniards to abandon these chimeras and filled in vacant spaces with detail, but European writers could still regard America as empty for literary purposes. Thus, it became the "Faery Land" of Edmund Spenser's unfinished masterpiece, *The Faerie Queen*, of which the first six books were published in 1596, and the vague locus of William Shakespeare's *The Tempest* (first published in 1623). These works were more than simple fantasies; they had a moral content. In a New World, unencumbered by Old World restraints, men could fulfill their potential for true civility. Thomas More dealt more explicitly with this theme in a much earlier work, *Utopia* (first published in 1516). To More, America was politically free space, and in it he placed an ideal republic formed and guided by reason. There men lived in civil and religious freedom without the inequities created by private property. *Utopia* was a very subversive book and quite dangerous to read in Tudor England.

It cannot be said, however, that the opening of the New World greatly enriched the imaginative literature of early modern Europe. Works using it as a theme or locus were few and scattered. Their historical importance lay in the new vistas they opened and the new hopes they created. They formed part of the root system of the modern concept of a free society and, perhaps, helped to form the perception of America as a land of opportunity.

### Science: Geography, Cartography, and Navigation

America made its first and greatest impact on early modern European science in the field of geography, then subsumed under the more general science of cosmography. In 1512, the German humanist Cochleus haughtily asserted that, whether the reports of the Discovery were true or not, "it has nothing . . . to do with Cosmography and the knowledge of History. For the peoples and places of that continent are unknown and unnamed to us and sailings are only made there with the greatest dangers. Therefore it is of no interest to geographers at all."[6] A French description of the world that went through five editions between 1539 and 1560 fails to mention America and adheres to the classic concept of a tripartite world comprising Asia, Europe, and Africa, and their surrounding oceans.[7]

By around 1560, however, the course of discovery had discredited the recalcitrants and greatly changed European perceptions of the world on which they dwelt. Long before Columbus, educated people had believed that it was spherical, but the circumnavigation of the Magellan expedition, other voyages that together spanned the Atlantic, Pacific, and Indian oceans, and a widening range of celestial observations made cosmographers more keenly aware of sphericity. The discovery that the Ocean Sea was not one but two bodies of water, each thousands of miles wide, and that great land masses separated them, demonstrated that the earthly sphere had a much greater circumference than the ancients had allowed.

Changing concepts of the size of the earth coupled with the practical needs of navigators led to significant changes in methods of measuring distance and direction on the earth's surface. For centuries navigators had used mainly portalan charts that simply showed compass bearings and distances between points. Toward the end of the 1500s these were increasingly replaced by charts based on a grid of latitude and longitude. At first two difficulties limited their accuracy. One was how to project a spherical surface onto a geometrical plane. It was solved in 1569 by the Flemish cartographer Gerardus Mercator, using the grotesque but verisimilar projection that bears his name. The other problem was the lack of seaworthy chronometers that could help determine accurate longitudinal distances. Such instruments did not appear until the eighteenth century, but by the beginning of the seventeenth voyagers were already cut loose from local systems of navigation and could range freely over the entire globe.

By the 1560s, too, European perceptions of the configuration of the earth's surface had changed markedly. Cartographers had defined roughly the dimensions of the New World, although they were still uncertain about the shape and limits of its northern and southern projections. They had traced the contours of its coastline in the Atlantic from Labrador to the Strait of Magellan and in the Pacific from southern Chile to the northern part of Lower California. They had mapped the main Caribbean islands quite accurately and had fixed them in the correct spatial relationship with each other.

Sixteenth-century maritime discoveries gave empirical support to the notion and the hope that the world's oceans linked its continents rather than constituting obstacles to global communications. The presence of the American continents, however, posed a problem: How to get through or around them except by the long and hazardous routes through the Strait of Magellan or later around Cape Horn. This difficulty coupled with uncertainties about the northern extent of North America generated two efforts that extended into modern times. One was the search for a strait through the American Isthmus and, in its absence, the construction of an interoceanic water route in that region. The other was the search for a northwest passage.

Information about the interior of the American continents accumulated and spread more slowly than knowledge of their position and shape. Nonetheless, by 1560, European cartographers were able to sketch in roughly the course of the Marañon (Amazon) River, the Platine River system, and the delta of the Orinoco. The location and general configuration of the great American cordillera from the tip of South America to northern Mexico was known, although its exploration had scarely begun. Much the same can be said of South American rain forests, deserts, and savannahs, and the arid region of northern Mexico. There was nothing strikingly new about these features. Counterparts existed in the Old World. Their impact rather came through enhancing European perceptions of the scale of things. According to the "Anonymous Chronicler" of the Conquest of Mexico, "The land of New Spain is similar to [Old Spain] . . . except that the mountains are more terrible and rugged."[8] The towering Andes were even more awesome; they dwarfed the Alps and the Pyrenees. Of American volcanoes, the Jesuit historian José de Acosta wrote: "Although in other regions *bocas de fuego* [mouths of fire] are found, those of the Indies are much more numerous and notable."[9] As for American rivers, Father Acosta declared, "Among all the rivers not only in the Indies but of the entire world, the first is the Rio Marañon or the Amazon."[10] So vast were its waters that the Portuguese called it *O Rio Mar*, The River Sea.

## Natural History and Medicine

The effect of the opening of the New World on the biological sciences, then subsumed under natural history and medicine, is uncertain. Botany and zoology in early modern Europe were mainly descriptive, and work in these fields consisted of preparing herbals and bestiaries, that is, illustrated descriptions of plants, especially those deemed useful for medical purposes, and of animals. The animal world attracted less interest than the vegetable because it included fewer useful species. In both types of works, varieties were generally listed alphabetically by their Latin or vernacular names, following the practice of classical writers. In some instances, species were grouped into rough categories on the basis of impressionistic similarities and differences.

The early histories and descriptions of the New World written in the first half of the sixteenth century introduced Europeans to many species of plants and animals previously unknown to them. Later in the century, these were notably complemented by drawings and descriptions of some 1200 plants brought back from Mexico to Spain in 1577 by the Spanish doctor Francisco Hernández and by Father Acosta's *Natural and Moral History of the Indies*. It might be expected that this inflow of information would have stimulated the development of natural history in Europe, and perhaps it did. The British historian G. B. Masefield observed that the arrival of so many unknown species "preceded, and perhaps partly inspired, the golden age of the great herbalists."[11]

But inspiration came slowly. Otto Brunfel's herbal, published between 1530 and 1536, made no reference to American plants, and that of Leonard Fuchs, which appeared in 1542, illustrated only three American species, maize and two varieties of squash.[12] As the century advanced, interest in New World biota slowly increased, a landmark being the work of the Spaniard Nicolás Monardes, first published in 1569 but best known in its English translation, *Joyfull Newes Out of the Newefound World* (London, 1577). This work described many useful plants, herbs, and barks as well as a number of exotic animals such as the armadillo. Yet the work of sorting and description proceeded slowly, hampered by attempts to identify American species with those listed in classical references or those known in Europe and by the outlandish names they bore. The task, indeed, was so great that it may have delayed the development of systematic taxonomy and of evolutionary and migrational theory.[13]

Natural history was linked to medicine through interest in curative or stimulative plants, barks, and herbs. Apothecaries and doctors prescribed the sweet potato as an aphrodisiac, a highly regarded property. The kidney bean was an obvious specific for ailments of the organ that gave it its name. Tobacco taken as snuff or in liquid decoctions was regarded as a panacea for many infirmities, including "diseases of the chest and wasting of the lungs." Jesuit bark (chinchona) was helpful in treating malaria. One modern scholar, however, contends that, while American medicinal plants may have enriched the apothecaries and merchants who traded in them, their influence on medical science was minimal, owing to ignorance of their proper use, professional conservatism, and suspicions of their value aroused by the exaggerated claims of quacks.[14]

In summary, the scattered evidence available suggests that the New World did not begin to make significant contributions to the advancement of the biological sciences in Europe until the latter half of the seventeenth century. By that time, accumulated scientific data on Spanish America and Brazil had become widely disseminated; northern Europeans had begun to gather information from their own colonies; and the Scientific Revolution had created an intellectual environment in which these data could be assimilated.

## European Perceptions of Race:
## Noble and Ignoble Savages

Among all things in the New World, its indigenous peoples created the most interest and, at the same time, the greatest intellectual predicament for sixteenth- and seventeenth-century European scholars, already concerned about the varieties of mankind. The existence of the Indians involved several interrelated problems. Were they actually human, or did they belong to some inferior species? Pope Paul III provided an official answer in the bull *Sublimus Deus* of 1536, which declared them to be truly men, but the bull was denied the *pase regio* (royal license for publication) in the Indies, and it never circulated widely there. Furthermore, Spanish settlers, officials, and even some missionaries—persons who had to contend with the recalcitrance and uncivil behavior of the American natives—had serious reservations about their rational qualities.

But, if the Indians were indeed men, whence had they come? The Book of Genesis did not specifically account for their existence, let alone their presence in America. Some heterodox thinkers sought a historico-environmental answer, first proposed by classical philosophers and reaffirmed by the French scholar Jean Bodin in the mid-sixteenth century.[15] That is, men were created by several divine acts, at different moments in time, and in different places. Thus, they may originally have had different cultural and physical qualities, or dissimilar natural environments may have caused them to evolve along different paths.

This view, however, was not widely held or vigorously propounded in the religious climate prevailing in early modern Europe. A more orthodox and widely held explanation of American Indian origins derived from a reinterpretation of scriptural accounts. After the Lord created a babel of tongues and scattered men over the face of the earth, some nations eventually found their way to the New World after a long migration across Asia and a Bering land-mass. Indeed, a number of early Spanish missionaries believed that the American indigenes were descendants of the ten lost tribes of Israel.

Still another question was: If the American Indians were in fact of the lineage of Adam and Noah, what manner of men were they? The several European peoples approached the question from somewhat different points of view. From the moment of the Discovery onward, the Spanish and the Portuguese had accepted the responsibility for evangelizing the people they had conquered, and their inquiries into the nature of indigenes related mainly to their capacity for conversion. Northern Europeans took a more secular and scientific approach: Where could Indians be placed in the family of mankind? In addition, they had little extended contact with them until the seventeenth century, and then only in cultures much less advanced than the Mayas, Mexicans, and Incas.

Despite their differing points of observation, European savants tended to view American Indians in much the same ways. Clearly, they belonged in the category of "savages," people who lived without law, civility, and true religion. But savagery had different meanings. To some it was a "primitive" condition, a state of innocence unspoiled by the accumulated vices of civilization and existing in rustic and idyllic surroundings. Savagery, moreover, was redeemable through patient precept and example. One of the earliest and certainly most vocal exponents of this view was the Spanish Dominican friar Bartolomé de Las Casas (1474-1566).[16] This image lingered on through the sixteenth and seventeenth centuries and in the eighteenth resurfaced as the fetish of the "noble savage," used by the French *philosophes* to attack inherited privilege and power in Europe.

Other observers took an "antiprimitivistic" view. Savages were naturally and irredeemably corrupt, shiftless, treacherous, and addicted to bestial vices. The earliest and most influential exponent of this position was the Spanish historian and colonial official Gonzalo Fernández de Oviedo (1478-1557).[17] His attitudes were echoed by others, persisted in the writings of northern Europeans, and were epitomized in the often quoted dictum of the English philosopher Thomas Hobbes (1588-1679): The life of the supposedly noble savage was "solitary, poore, nasty, brutish, and short."[18]

Still other observers took an intermediate, or what might be called today a "relativistic," position. Some of the first generation of Spanish missionaries such as the Franciscan friar Bernadino de Sahagún (c. 1500-90) found much that was deplorable in Indian culture: dress (or state of undress), polygamy, and, worst of all, cannibalism. But some advanced nations such as the Aztecs were superior to Europeans in many respects such as their family organization and their care of children.[19] Jean de Léry, who participated in the abortive French attempt to settle on Rio de Janeiro Bay (1555-65), regarded the Brazilian Indians' lack of religion as brutish, but they were happy folk; their nudity deserved reproach, but it was no more offensive than the brazen coquetry of European women.[20] Writing later in the sixteenth century, the French savant Michel de Montaigne developed more systematically the theme of the infinite variety of customs and beliefs among the nations of mankind, including the American Indian, and declared that differences were all relative, being based on the perceptions and prejudices of the observer.[21]

Speculations and theories about the origin and nature of Indians made positive contributions to the development of such modern anthropological concepts as environmentalism, evolutionism, and cultural relativism and diffusion. But, on the negative side, their image as ignoble savages gained ascendancy. They were indeed men, but marginal ones, deficient in rationality and incapable of civility. This perception owed to several circumstances: unshakable European prejudices against deviations from their own cultural norms; the need to rationalize the despoilation of the American indigenes; and, quite possibly, the destruction of their most rational and civil qualities by exploitation, mistreatment, and prolonged exposure to European vices. Contemporary thinkers explained their defects in terms of arrested development in the progress toward civilization, which was assumed to be the natural course of human evolution, or, alternatively, as a result of degeneration or declension believed to occur when an ancestral culture was diffused through migration.

The expansion of Spain and Portugal not only brought a new people to the attention of Europeans but placed black Africans in a new and less favorable perspective. Their existence had been known, of course, since ancient times, but, owing to their remote habitats and to lack of extended European contacts with them, Europeans had given relatively little thought to their biological and cultural characteristics. Their appearance in the Americas in the hundreds of thousands brought them under closer scrutiny and generated more intensive speculation about their qualities, not only by their Spanish and Portuguese masters but by other Europeans engaged in the slave trade. The results were greatly to their disadvantage. Europeans came to doubt their essential humanity because of their cultural deviancy, their dark hue, and their physiognomy, which Europeans regarded as apelike. If they were indeed men, they were unquestionably savages but, unlike Indians were never noble. The Spaniards and the Portuguese did not make concerted efforts to teach them to live in Christian polity, nor did northern Europeans when they began to establish New World plantations. Europeans in general regarded them as irredeemably uncivilized and depraved. Most, moreover, knew them as slaves, a status for which their perceived natural defects suited them.

In summary, Hispanic expansion greatly increased European awareness of the varieties of mankind, but it also helped to fix ideas about the qualitative differences among them. American Indians and African blacks came to be regarded as inferior races, or marginal men whose defects were very likely uncorrectable. These perceptions departed from the long-established theological dogma of the homogeneity of mankind, deriving from a common Adamic heritage, and ushered in the modern era of race relations.[22]

## The Economic Impact of the Hispanic New World on Europe

### The Indies Trade

During the early modern period the economies of the several nations of western Europe had widely differing structures, and each had its particular short-term and intermediate-term ups and downs. Nevertheless, economic historians generally agree on long-term trends in the region as a whole. In the last half of the fifteenth century a cycle of vigorous growth began, first in the Mediterranean, then spreading west and north. The upward swing halted in the 1620s and a period of decline or, at best, stagnation ensued. Recovery began in the last two decades of the seventeenth century, but strong growth did not resume until the middle of the eighteenth. Only the Dutch Republic and, to a lesser extent, England managed to escape the crisis. When it ended, the economic center of gravity of Europe had shifted from the Mediterranean to those two states and to the Atlantic ports of France.

The growth phase of this cycle is commonly attributed to several complementary influences. The most fundamental was the doubling of Europe's population between 1460 and 1620. Also contributing to the upturn was the expansion of established trading systems, especially commerce with the Baltic, which brought to the western nations wheat from eastern Europe to feed a growing population and forest products from Scandinavia in return for exports of textiles, dyestuffs, wine, vegetable oils, and fruits. Other stimulating factors were the progressive economic unification of national states that broke down internal barriers to commerce and the development of more efficient financial and commercial practices, especially in international transactions.

Several explanations are also offered for the decline or stagnation that followed. One is Malthusian. By the early seventeenth century, the argument goes, the amount of land that could be brought under cultivation practically and profitably had reached a limit, thereby placing a ceiling on further population growth. In addition, adverse climatic changes produced many years of bad harvests. Another explanation is the frequency and duration of international and civil wars that not only devastated large areas but diverted capital to economically unproductive ends. Still another was the survival of archaic political institutions and social structures, which discouraged further economic expansion.

But developments external to Europe also affected its economic trajectory. In the sixteenth century, explorers, conquerors, and merchant adventurers opened up lucrative new trading areas in other parts of the world. In an often-quoted passage from *Das Kapital*, Karl Marx assessed the consequences of this expansion: "The discovery of gold and silver in America, the extirpation, enslavement and entombment in mines of the aboriginal population, the beginning of the conquest and looting of the East Indies, the turning of Africa into a warren for the commercial hunting of black-skins, signalised the rosy dawn of the era of capitalist production."[23]

The wording of Marx's statement is a bit purplish, but the thesis propounded is worthy of consideration. This chapter, however, lacks space to probe the complex problems of the nature and origin of the capitalist system whether it be defined in Marxist or non-Marxist terms. Nor is it within the scope of this book to assess the economic effect of the opening of Africa and the Orient on Europe. Rather, the question to be addressed here is: What were the empirical effects of the colonization and exploitation of the Hispanic New World on Europe's economic fortunes in the sixteenth and seventeenth centuries?

Only a partial and inconclusive answer can be given. Relevant firm data are mainly statistics compiled by Pierre and Huguette Chaunu on the Spanish Indies trade and, earlier, by Earl J. Hamilton on imports of American precious metals in Seville.[24] These show that in the 1540s the cargoes of fleets outbound to the Indies averaged about 10,000 tons a year. By 1570 this volume had tripled and by 1608, the peak year of the trade, had quadrupled. European exports consisted principally of textiles and other manufactured goods, fine wines and foods, and other luxury items. The returning fleets brought dye-stuffs, hides, and other nonprecious commodities, but their richest cargo by far was gold and silver. In 1609 this treasure constituted 84 percent by value of imports from the Indies, and by that time the total value of silver imports greatly exceeded those of gold.[25] Thus, it was silver that paid for most American imports, and between 1540 and 1608 the amount of this metal arriving in Seville increased sevenfold. Between the last date and 1620, however, the volume and value of the trans-Atlantic trade, including shipments of precious metals, leveled off and thereafter it fell into a deep and prolonged slump.

During this cycle the trade of the Indies increasingly fell into the hands first of the Italians and then of northern Europeans. Spanish industry could not meet the demands of its colonies, and foreign manufacturers and merchants gladly made up the deficiency, acting through commerical agents in Seville. Of the silver imported, some remained in Spain to serve fiscal and commercial needs or to be fashioned into jewelry and ornaments for churches, chapels, and shrines. The rest of it, and probably the most, escaped to Italy and the north to redress unfavorable trade balances, pay Spanish troops in the field, and retire or service imperial debts.

How is this information to be interpreted? Little can be said about the importance of European trade with Hispanic America in nonprecious commodities because relevant monographic studies are lacking. It was probably marginal.[26] The most striking commercial development of the sixteenth century was not the opening of America but the phenomenal expansion of the Baltic trade, whose volume in the late sixteenth century exceeded that carried by the Indies fleets.[27] Furthermore, it has been estimated that in 1666 three-quarters of the capital active in the Amsterdam bourse was engaged in Baltic commerce.[28] The experiences of the Dutch West India Company provide additional corroborative evidence. One of the reasons it decided to abandon its conquests in Brazil is that the Dutch believed the Portuguese salt trade to be more lucrative than the Brazilian sugar trade. Furthermore, although the company occasionally paid large dividends from its operations in the Hispanic New World, in most years it declared none at all and in 1674 it went into bankruptcy.[29]

The importance of American silver is another matter. Pierre Chaunu argues that the rate and volume of its arrival in Seville played a major part in shaping economic trends in western Europe. In the first half of the sixteenth century, he proposes, that region suffered a chronic shortage of circulating money that hindered further economic growth. The several European states responded with currency debasements, but this solution was only temporary and, in the end, self-defeating. By the end of the 1570s, however, the outpouring of the mines of Mexico and Peru had relieved the scarcity, thereby encouraging production, lubricating the flow of commerce, and stimulating the growth phase of the cycle. As Pierre Chaunu expressed it, the arrival of the annual fleets in Seville set the pulse of financial markets in Italy, southern Germany, and the Low Countries. In addition, the influx of silver encouraged European states to stabilize their currency by ending debasements.

The sequel is that the end of the American bonanza produced a sharp financial and commercial crisis in Europe in 1619–22, and thereafter an economy that had come to depend on annual infusions of precious metals suffered a prolonged slump. Furthermore, lacking adequate supplies of silver, European states again turned to debasements and devaluations of their currencies, thus creating monetary disorder.[30]

As it applies to the growth phase of the European economy, the Chaunu thesis is convincing. The correlation between the volume of incoming silver registered in Seville and increased levels of economic activity in Europe is incontestable, and it is plausible to assume that a rapidly increasing money supply had the stimulative effects postulated. Data on the movement of interest rates, prices, and wages lend some support to Chaunu's arguments. Between 1540 and 1570, interest rates hovered around 5.5 percent, but between 1570, when the inflow of silver reached bonanza proportions, and 1620 they dropped to an average of 2.0 percent.[31] According to modern monetary theory, an increase in money supply would have contributed to lower interest rates, and this would have encouraged trade and manufacturing.

The general level of prices unquestionably rose from the mid-sixteenth century into the early seventeenth. Hamilton's calculations show that in Spain the increase was over threefold and in England and France more than twofold.[32] By today's standards inflation of this magnitude does not seem inordinate, but compared with the price stability that existed before and afterward it amounted to what had been termed a "Price Revolution." The contribution of American treasure to this movement was observed as early as 1556 by Martín Azpilcueta de Navarro, a canon lawyer and economist of the Spanish "Salamanca School." Everything in Spain, he observed, cost less before the flood of gold and silver began to arrive from the Indies. "The reason for this," he concluded, "is that money is worth more where and when it is scarce than where and when it is plentiful."[33]

Over 350 years later Hamilton gave statistical confirmation to Azpilcueta's theory. After analyzing data from various Spanish archives, he concluded: "The extremely close correlation between the increase in the volume of treasure imports [registered at Seville] and the advance of commodity prices throughout the sixteenth century, particularly from 1535 on, demonstrates beyond question that the 'abundant mines of America' were the principal cause of the Price Revolution in Spain."[34] Later, Hamilton and other scholars following his lead developed the thesis that, beginning in the 1550s, the flow of Spanish silver into other parts of Europe produced similar results. Further, the return to relative price stability in the first part of the seventeenth century coincided with the drop in the volume of precious metals reaching Seville.

Data for wages are scarcer than for prices, but scattered studies suggest that wages lagged behind prices, especially those for basic commodities. If this is true, a general decline in living standards may be postulated. But the differential may have produced a more salutary economic effect, that is, accumulations of growth stimulating investment capital through the inflation of trading profits.[35]

There are, however, reasons to be skeptical about the Chaunu thesis and the supporting arguments outlined above. Economic growth had been under way for some time before silver from the New World began to arrive in Europe in amounts sufficient to increase the money supply substantially. In addition, not enough is known about the disposition of this metal after its arrival to assess its impact accurately. How rapidly did it reach Italy and northern Europe, and in what quantities? How much of it remained in circulation and at what velocity? How much of it was accumulated as capital for investment? How much of it was hoarded or sunk into landed estates for security or for social purposes? How much of it escaped to the East, never to return?

Furthermore, the argument that American treasure was primarily responsible for the Price Revolution has been criticized on several grounds. One is its failure to give sufficient weight to monetary factors other than the volume of silver in circulation. These include the rate of circulation of money; the debasement of currencies to which European kings still resorted despite the increased amount of precious metals available to them; an inflation in monies of account such as the English pound sterling, the French *livre tournais*, and the Spanish *maravedí*; and, finally, an inflation in credit reflected in the great mass of bills of exchange in circulation.

Empirical regional studies further challenge the Hamiltonian thesis by demonstrating that price movements did not always synchronize with the flow of silver. In Spain the average annual rise in general price levels between 1501 and 1562 was about 2.8 percent, but between 1562 and 1600 the rate dropped to 1.3 percent. Thus, the greatest increase occurred *before* the full flood of American treasure began to reach Spain.[36] In Italy the sharpest increase, about 2.0 percent annually, came during the first half of the sixteenth century, when the peninsula did not receive unusual quantities of silver. After the revolt of the Spanish Netherlands in the 1560s more treasure passed through Italian hands, especially those of Genoese bankers, on its way to the Low Countries via the Spanish Road. But, beginning in the 1570s, Italian prices began to fall.[37]

The sharpest criticism of the Hamiltonian thesis comes from scholars who attribute the Price Revolution primarily to a real cause, that is, the sharp increase of the European population between 1460 and the early 1620s without a corresponding increase in agricultural production. This explanation can be traced back to statements of Alderman Box in 1576 and began to gather modern support in M. J. Elsas, "Price Data from Munich in 1500-1700."[38] It rests on the statistical observation that prices of agricultural commodities, especially grain, rose sooner and faster than those of other items and on the proposition that the bidding up of agricultural prices eventually caused a general increase in price levels.

As for the downward turn in the European economy, again a clear correlation exists between the end of the silver bonanza and the economic crisis of 1619-22. Beyond that, however, the evidence becomes rather shaky and contradictory. In the first place, the arguments of Chaunu and Hamilton are based on the belief that the American mining industry collapsed after the 1620s and on calculations of the amount of silver entering Seville legally. Recent research, however, shows that silver production in the Indies did not drop as soon or as drastically as once supposed and that throughout the seventeenth century enough of this metal reached Europe through Seville and a growing clandestine trade with Spanish America to support a healthy level of economic activity.[39] In addition, the increased use of bills of exchange and other circulating credit instruments may have compensated for any contraction in the supply of real money. The case for an adequate supply of money is supported by evidence that interest rates remained stable and in some regions actually dropped.

It is even more difficult to discern an important connection between the economic recovery that began in the late 1600s and European trade with Hispanic America. Revival came rather from the construction of a new Atlantic economy, begun by the Dutch but later taken over by England. This structure included the Hispanic possessions in America. By that time they offered a much larger market than they had a century earlier, owing to a substantial increase in European and Europeanized inhabitants as well as the incorporation of much of the Indian population into the market system. By that time also, European demand for Hispanic American sugar, tobacco, cotton, and cacao had increased. These circumstances, along with the collapse of Hispanic mercantile systems, induced northern Europeans to step up their illicit trade with both the Spanish Indies and Brazil.

But, in addition, the Atlantic economy now incorporated the growing English North American colonies and the English and French Caribbean Islands. These regions also provided an overseas market as well as plantation products for export, and with mercantilist controls European metropolises could exploit trade with them more efficiently than they could traffic illegally with the Hispanic New World possessions.

The most dynamic force in the new Atlantic economy, however, was the expansion of the internal European market, in part for exotic imports but mainly for European-produced goods. This phenomenon was the product of two complementary forces. One was slowly developing structural changes in European society that turned a larger proportion of the population into market-oriented consumers. The other was organizational changes in agriculture and manufacturing that lowered production and transaction costs, thereby making more goods available to consumers at home and overseas. England took the lead in the new order because it experienced these changes sooner and more fully than its neighbors and because of its more effective mercantilist policies.[40]

The problems raised in the foregoing review cannot be resolved without extended and painstaking research. Meanwhile, existing evidence suggests that internal forces were primarily responsible for shaping long-range economic trends in early modern Europe. The Hispanic American trade in both precious and nonprecious commodities had a marginal influence, with one major exception. Although it cannot be said that imports of American silver generated the era of growth, a plausible case can still be made that they provided a strong stimulus for expansion and perhaps extended its duration.

## The Transference of American Plants to Europe

In addition to treasure and raw materials, Hispanic America sent back to Europe many plants whose adaptation and dispersion in their new environment had important nutritional consequences as well as economic effects. This process, however, was much slower than the transference of Old World species to the New. In contrast with the immediate requirements of the Spaniards in America for accustomed foods and fibers, Europeans could not perceive an urgent need for new crops. Tastes for them had to be cultivated; prejudices against strange flavors, smells, and textures overcome; and suitable habitats located for those ultimately found to be useful.

American plants caught on as food sources first in home gardens and later as field crops. Maize cultivation began in southern Spain and Portugal in the middle of the sixteenth century, but it required irrigation in those regions and agriculturists felt that water could be put to better use. Toward the end of the century, its planting spread to the northern part of the peninsula, where more rain fell. There maize displaced rye and millet and revolutionized diet. Elsewhere, Italians began planting maize in the Po delta by 1554 and shortly thereafter in Lombardy and the Piedmont. In eastern Europe, its adoption came slower. It did not become a major crop in Rumania, eventually one of Europe's largest producers, until about 1700.

The sweet potato became popular as a garden crop in Spain and Portugal by mid-sixteenth century. It did not do well farther north, but the Spaniards exported small quantities to England, where they fetched luxury prices. Europeans at first shied away from the "Irish" potato, perhaps because of its kinship to the deadly nightshade, but eventually they discovered its virtues. By 1573 the Spaniards cultivated it in a small way, and in the next decade the Italians planted it as a garden vegetable. It found its true foster home, however, in northern Europe, especially in Ireland, where the peasantry subsisted off tiny plots of land and found that potatoes gave a higher nutritional yield per acre than cereals then in use. It also better survived the tramplings of marauding soldiers. By the end of the seventeenth century, the potato constituted the chief article of diet for the poorer classes of that troubled land and, from there, found its way back to its native America via emigrants to the English colonies. On the continent, Germany became an important producer as a result of the famine conditions of the Seven Years' War. Throughout Europe potatoes were at first consumed mainly by peasants, but, when King Louis XVI and Marie Antoinette began serving them at the royal table, they entered haute cuisine.

Among American fruits, the tomato became the most popular. It was well established in southern Europe in the sixteenth century, although it aroused little interest in the north until the eighteenth. The only species of American spices that grew well in Europe were red peppers. Their cultivation became common in Spain in the second half of the 1500s and began in England toward the end of the century. Although tomatoes and peppers had low caloric values, they were rich in vitamins and added savor and color to the rather drab cuisine of the common folk.

The only domesticated American livestock to find favor in Europe was the turkey. The Spanish introduced the bird very early, and its breeding spread rapidly. It reached England in the 1530s, and turkeys graced festive Yule boards there by the 1570s.

The transference of American plants to the Old World also had important nutritional results in Africa. In the 1500s the Portuguese brought maize, cassava, and the sweet potato to tropical Africa, which, at the time, had the most limited selection of indigenous food crops of any cultivated region on the globe. In high-rainfall areas there, maize gave a greater nutritional yield than native cereals. Cassava and sweet potatoes increased the number of available crops that locusts left alone. Cassava also kept well in the ground for long periods and thereby provided reserves against famine. By the eighteenth century these three crops were well integrated into tropical African agricultural systems and very probably saved large numbers of Africans from starvation.

G. B. Masefield offers a trenchant judgment on the significance of the migration of flora and fauna initiated by the opening of the New World: "It was the unforseen discovery of America which changed the agricultural map of the world. . . . Thus at one stroke the potential vegetable resources of the known world had been doubled. The dispersal of crops and livestock which followed was the most important in human history, and perhaps had the most far-reaching effects of any result of the Discoveries."[41]

## Malevolent Transfers: The Case of Syphilis

Early in the sixteenth century, Ulrich von Hutten, one of Erasmus's correspondents, reported: "In the year of Chryst 1493 or there aboute, this most foul and most grevous disease beganne to sprede amonge the people."[42] Its symptoms included disfiguring rashes, ulcers that commonly extended into the throat and mouth, violent fevers, and painful bone aches. It was not only a loathsome but a virulent affliction; it did irreparable damage to the internal organs and frequently caused quick death.

Contemporary observers reported that it appeared first in Spain, that in 1494 or 1495 it reached epidemic proportions in Italy, and that by 1500 it had spread throughout Europe. Its dispersion coincided with the departure of Spanish troops from Barcelona to Italy and the return of French soldiers to northern Europe from Italian wars. Physicians, surgeons, and laymen believed that it was a new disease, that it was transmitted by venereal contact, and that Columbus's men had brought it back from Española. By the 1520s, some Europeans called it syphilis, but this name did not come into general use until the nineteenth century. Meanwhile, the French called it the disease of Naples; the Italians, the French disease; and the English, the French or Spanish disease or, simply, the pox.

The coincidence of the malady's appearance with the Columbian voyages, along with medical analyses of contemporary literature and paleopathological evidence from America, led a number of modern scholars to hypothesize an American origin of syphilis. Others, however, did not find the case convincing and instead found evidence that the disease had existed in the Old World long before 1493. Europeans simply did not diagnose it properly until the end of the fifteenth century. But the disagreement may now be outdated. More recent research indicates that venereal syphilis, like yaws, *pinta*, and endemic syphilis, is but one syndrome of treponematosis, an infection that in one form or another had been present in Europe, Asia, Africa, and America since ancient times. Its sudden and virulent appearance in Europe can be explained by postulating that Columbus's men brought back an American treponema organism that, in European bodies, quickly evolved into a deadly venereal disease. Perhaps, after all, American Indians gained a measure of revenge against their European despoilers.[43]

## Hispanic America and European Political Systems

### The National State

During the early years of the sixteenth century, the development of national states and national monarchies in Europe was well under way, owing to the breakdown of the feudal order, the weakening of the supranational powers of the papacy, the dissolution of the Holy Roman Empire, and the rise of Protestant nations. It may reasonably be assumed that the opening of the New World hastened this process in at least two ways. American silver and profits from the Indies trade encouraged the expansion of a money economy in Europe, thereby contributing to the breakdown of feudal and manorial relations and weakening the power of nobilities vis-à-vis national monarchs. In addition, American wealth flowing into royal coffers helped to pay for the growth of bureaucracies and armies, the principal instruments of the national state. With reference to armies, one modern author summed up the effect neatly: "Salvation for paymasters came from the Andes; for recruiting officers from the Alps."[44]

### International Relations and
### International Law

The opening of the New World influenced the relations among European nations by creating new sources of contentions and extending the range of international rivalries to America. Northern European governments never accepted the Papal Donation as a legitimate source of territorial and commercial monopoly and rather freely raided, traded, and colonized in territories claimed by Spain and Portugal. These incursions, however, more often than not represented private commerical enterprises, and kings authorized, overlooked, or discouraged them depending on how they affected national interests in Europe. The rule of "No peace beyond the line," accepted by both the Hispanic powers and their rivals, further insured that American affairs remained separate from European diplomacy and wars. It was not until the very end of the seventeenth century that widening European commercial rivalries and the greater effectiveness of navies began to make America the focus rather than the occasional locus of international wars.

Although the establishment of Hispanic colonies in the Indies extended the range of European hostilities, the Spanish experience also contributed to the development of laws that to some extent mitigated and regulated trade rivalries and the conduct of war. The Spanish Conquest unfolded at a time when the international order badly needed redefinition, for the emergence of national states, some adhering to the Lutheran heresy, undermined the concept of a Christian ekumene ruled spiritually by the pope and temporally by the Holy Roman Emperor. The establishment of Spanish dominion over numerous American peoples added a new ingredient to the ferment.

The immediate question raised was how to justify the conquest of the Indies. At first this was primarily a Spanish problem, addressed by Spanish jurists and theologians. Among their writings and teachings, those of Francisco de Vitoria (c. 1480–1546), head professor of theology at the University of Salamanca, had the widest influence. His ideas were sometimes contradictory or ambivalent because he was in a position where he had to reconcile legal and moral principles with pragmatic Spanish actions and policies. Nevertheless, a set of propositions emerged from his work that may be summarized as follows.

First, the community of mankind, including non-Christians as well as Christians, was composed of essentially rational individuals who together constituted a "republic of the world" governed by divine and natural law. Should one nation violate the law, another could intervene to restore the rightful order if no other redress was available. Second, the members of the several nations of the republic had a right, without hindrance of their lords, to communicate with each other, including travel, sojourn, immigration, and the establishment of domicile abroad. Third, the pope's spiritual competence was limited to Christian peoples, and his temporal jurisdiction extended only as far as was required to exercise his spiritual functions. Other sixteenth-century Spanish theologians reaffirmed and refined Vitoria's propositions. Thus, the Jesuit Francisco Suárez declared that the republic of the world was a community of nations whose relations with each other were regulated by the *jus gentium*, and the Franciscan Alfonso Castro argued around 1550 that the seas should not be the exclusive preserve of any particular state.[45]

The doctrines of Spanish jurists had an applicability much wider than the legal bases of Spain's presence in the Indies. They redefined on a universal scale the nature of sovereignty, developed the existing laws of war on practicable yet charitable bases, and declared for the principle of freedom of the seas. They slowly filtered into the mainstream of European thought and eventually were amplified and reformulated by the Dutch jurist Hugo Grotius (1583–1645) and incorporated into his legal and theoretical structure of international law. It is ironic that Spanish jurists played such an important part in breaking down Spain's claims to territorial and commercial monopoly in the Indies.

## Hispanic American Colonies and Their Mother Countries

### The Indies and Spain

As might be expected, the impact of the New World was greatest on the Hispanic nations who first discovered, conquered, and colonized it. This was especially true of Spain, which took the leading role in these enterprises. Yet the effect was not immediate or general, for, like other Europeans, Spaniards had more immediate concerns at home. Most men of letters expressed more interest in what was going on in Italy and Africa than in the *hechos de los Castellanos* (the great deeds of Castilians) in America. The Emperor Charles did not see fit to mention the Indies in his published memoirs, although in fairness to him it must be said that he was writing mainly about his personal travels and campaigns, which did not take him across the Atlantic. Columbus himself was not well known in Spain, and, when he died in Valladolid in 1506, the city chronicler did not think the event important enough to record. Indeed discoverers and conquerors received but meager acclaim or even appreciation from the public, a slight that rankled them throughout their lifetimes.

Nevertheless, the opening of the New World made important contributions to Spanish intellectual life in the six decades following the discovery, among which two were particularly notable. One was a genre of literature comprising the chronicles and histories of discovery and conquest. Although the styles of these works were noninnovative and often unpolished, their content was instructive, vivid, and vital. How widely they were read is uncertain, but it can reasonably be assumed that many educated persons were familiar with them and that the events they recounted and the things they described became known by oral transmission to common folk. The other contribution was the juridical and theological literature generated by the Conquest.

The duration of these contributions, however, was relatively short-lived. Although Spaniards continued to write histories and descriptions of the Indies, such works lost their vitality and epic quality after the Conquest ended. By the 1570s, also, the status and nature of the Indians had been fixed in fact and law, and the source of Spain's just title settled for all practical purposes. Thereafter, jurists and theologians produced little that was new but rather turned to the exegesis and interpretation of earlier texts. Furthermore, the concerted efforts of King Philip II to impose strict Counter-Reformation orthodoxy on his Spanish and American subjects stifled intellectual inquiry about what was already known or about what might be discovered. It cannot be said, therefore, that the opening of the New World had a lasting and profound impact on the intellectual life of Spain, perhaps because Spain denied it the opportunity.

In practical matters, the American influence was more pronounced and lasting. The Enterprise of the Indies dramatically changed the position of Spain in the geopolitical configuration of Europe. The Spanish humanist Hernán Pérez de Oliva recognized the shift as early as 1524. "Formerly we were at the end of the world," he exclaimed, "and now we are in the middle of it with an unprecedented change in our fortunes."[46]

In more specific terms, the conquest of America was a Castilian enterprise. Its achievement increased the predominance of Castile among the Spanish kingdoms and enhanced the status of the monarchy in various ways. In the language of the times, the new kingdoms overseas added luster and honor to the crown. In addition it extended and strengthened the royal patronage over the church and created numerous offices to be filled through civil patronage. Together with the Habsburg alliance, it gave the king a more powerful voice in European affairs.

The wealth that the colonies produced was even more important than the reputational status and the patronage they conveyed. In the first six decades of the sixteenth century, at least, the Indies trade contributed to a boom in the Spanish textile and shipbuilding industries and in Andalusian agriculture. Duties on commerce with America and, more important, American silver, decreased the dependence of the king on taxes and subsidies voted by the cortes. Revenues from the New World could be used to pay bureaucracies as well as the armies sent to fight in Italy, the Low Countries, and Germany. In sum, the Indies made a major contribution to the rise of Spain as a European and imperial power.

But what about decline? It has been argued that the creation of an empire in the Indies overextended the power of Spain and created a severe drain on its resources. In purely fiscal terms, this position cannot be sustained. Almost from their start, conquest and colonization paid their own way, and, after the rich mines of Peru and Mexico had been opened, the colonies not only financed their own government and defense but remitted surpluses to the Castilian treasury.

But strain and drain took other forms, according to Spanish political economists of the times, the so-called *arbitristas* (those who propose *arbitrios* [remedies]). Some among them thought that emigration to the Indies was a major cause of the depopulation of Castile, which deprived the kingdom of workers and its army of soldiers. Writing in 1626, one author estimated emigrants at 40,000 persons a year.[47] Modern demographic research tends to depreciate this opinion. There is some question as to whether the Castilian population declined during the seventeenth century or simply ceased to grow, and it is possible that the *arbitristas* mistook rural-urban migrations and the emptying of the countryside for a general decline. In addition, the volume of emigration to America was much smaller than they thought; it probably averaged no more than 3000 to 4000 persons annually between 1561 and 1650.[48] Perhaps, however, even such a modest number of departures did some cumulative demographic damage in southern and central Castile, whence came most of the emigrants, since those who left were young people at the peak of their reproductive capacity. Also, emigration per se tends to drain off the most vigorous and enterprising elements of a nation's people.

The riches of the Indies, contemporaries claimed, was another source of harm to the mother country. American treasure and the profits to be had from American trade distracted the attention of the government and private parties from development of the domestic agriculture, manufacturing, and commerce that constituted the true sources of a nation's wealth. In the same vein, they argued that hopes for quick and easy profits from the New World corrupted the industry of entrepreneurial classes. Some *arbitristas* offered a variation on these themes. It was not American wealth per se that caused the injury but rather its diversion into economically unproductive channels such as foreign wars, religious foundations, and the creation of *señorial* domains. The proponents of these views were intelligent and thoughtful men, but their vision was myopic. They interpreted a temporal coincidence between the decadence they saw around them and the influx of American wealth as a clear-cut cause-and-effect relationship. Their analyses failed to take into account that inattention to balanced economic development, uneconomic uses of capital, and the depreciation of bourgeois virtues antedated the Enterprise of the Indies. The *arbitristas*, however, may not have been entirely off the mark. It is a plausible proposition that riches from the New World strengthened values hostile to the productive use of capital already well rooted in Spanish culture.

Modern historians have also blamed American silver for some of Spain's economic woes. The Hamilton Price Revolution theory maintains that, since silver arrived and circulated first in Spain, prices there rose sooner and faster than in other parts of Europe. In addition, wages kept better pace with rising prices than elsewhere. These circumstances placed Spanish industry, especially textile manufacturing, at a competitive disadvantage with cheaper foreign imports and hindered the accumulation of investment capital, thus causing industrial decay and restraining economic growth. This view, however, must be accepted with caution. As observed above, Hamilton and his followers provide a plausible explanation for a century-long rise in general price levels in Europe, but their theory does not accommodate particular regional and temporal price changes. In this author's judgment, the most destructive effect of American treasure on Spain was the deceptive encouragement it gave to imperial adventures in Europe. It was these rather than the Enterprise of the Indies that drained Spain's strength.

## Brazil and Portugal

Expansion in America had less far-reaching effects on Portugal than on Spain. The conquest of the Brazilian Indians did not stir as much intellectual ferment as the Spanish Conquest did, for the natives conquered were far fewer and had not created advanced civilizations. Nor did the Portuguese find precious metals in Brazil until the very end of the 1600s. In his great epic of Portuguese expansion in the sixteenth century, *Os Lusíadas*, Luís de Camões mentioned Brazil only three times, and then only in passing.[49] The great deeds recounted were done in Portugal's Old World Empire.

Much the same can be said about the effects of American possessions on the Portuguese state and the Portuguese economy. Insofar as the loot and profits of empire strengthened the monarchy in the sixteenth century, they came from the east, not the west. Like the Spanish *arbitristas*, Portuguese political economists blamed their country's woes on overseas empire. In 1608 the historian Luís Mendez Vasconcellos wrote that imperial expansion brought great wealth to Lisbon, but "it gave us no fields in which to sow or to pasture cattle, or labourers to cultivate fields. On the contrary, it took away those who might have served us in this. . . . For a state cannot be great without an abundance in itself."[50]

But Vasconcellos and others who shared his views laid the blame on the *Estado da India*, not on Brazil. It was wealth from the Orient and not Brazilian sugar that diverted attention from the development of the nation's internal economy. Furthermore, they believed that most immigrants went east and, to make matters worse, were replaced by an influx of blacks from Africa. Portuguese going to Brazil were relatively few and, moreover, included a large proportion of *degredados*, a type that the country was well rid of.[51]

Indeed, a case can be made that in the long-term Brazil had a sustaining effect on Portugal. The colony came to the rescue of the mother country in times of great need. In 1648 an expedition manned largely by Brazilians, financed from Brazilian resources, and launched from Bahia drove the Dutch from Angola. In the 1640s Brazilian irregulars began a counteroffensive in the northeastern captaincies that culminated in 1654 with the withdrawal of the Hollanders from the colony. In contrast with the decline of Spain's commerce with the Indies, the Brazilian sugar trade held up well during most of the seventeenth century, compensating for commercial losses in the Orient.

Notes

and

Bibliographical Essay

# Abbreviations

## Periodicals and Series

| | |
|---|---|
| *AHR* | *American Historical Review* (Washington, D.C.) |
| *TA* | *Americas, The* (Washington, D.C.) |
| *AESC* | *Annales: Économies, Sociétés, Civilisations* (Paris) |
| *AEA* | *Anuario de Estudios Americanos* (Seville) |
| *AHDE* | *Anuario de Historia del Derecho Español* (Madrid) |
| *HAHR* | *Hispanic American Historical Review* (Durham, N.C.) |
| *HM* | *Historia Mexicana* (Mexico City) |
| *JGSW* | *Jahrbuch für Geschichte von Staat, Wirtschaft und Gesellschaft Lateinamerikas* (Cologne) |
| *JIAS* | *Journal of Inter-American Studies* (Miami, Fla.) |
| *LARR* | *Latin American Research Review* (Albuquerque, N.M.) |
| *PICA* | *Proceedings of the International Congress of Americanists* |
| *PEEHA* | *Publicaciones de la Escuela de Estudios Hispano-Americanos* (Seville, Spain) |
| *RHA* | *Revista de Historia de América* (Mexico City) |
| *RI* | *Revista de Indias* (Madrid) |

## Publishers

| | |
|---|---|
| *C.S.I.C.* | *Consejo Superior de Investigaciones Científicas* (Madrid) |
| *E.E.H.A.* | *Escuela de Estudios Hispano-Americanos* (Seville) |
| *U.N.A.M.* | *Universidad Nacional Autónoma de México* (Mexico City) |

# Notes

## CHAPTER 1: THE MATRIX OF HISPANIC SOCIETIES: RECONQUISTA AND REPOBLACIÓN

1. *Aproximación a la historia de España* (2nd ed.; Barcelona: Editorial Teide, 1960), trans. Joan Connelly Ullman as *Approaches to the History of Spain* (Berkeley: University of California Press, 1967), p. 39. The quotation is from the English translation.

2. The extent to which the Reconquest experience shaped Spanish culture and character and in what ways provoked a lively debate among a generation of distinguished Hispanic scholars, including philosopher José Ortega y Gasset, philosopher and philologist Américo Castro, and historians Claudio Sánchez-Albornoz and Jaime Vicens Vives. The polemics are fascinating but too prolix to review here. Joseph F. O'Callaghan, *A History of Medieval Spain* (Ithaca, N.Y.: Cornell University Press, 1975), pp. 17-21, and John Ramsey, *Spain: The Rise of the First World Power* (Tuscaloosa, Ala.: University of Alabama Press, 1973), pp. 49-51, summarize the issues and arguments.

3. As quoted in Alfred F. Havinghurst, ed., *The Pirenne Thesis* (rev. ed.; Lexington, Mass.: D. C. Heath, 1969), p. viii. For a fuller treatment of Christian-Muslim relations in the Mediterranean see Archibald R. Lewis, *Naval Power and Trade in the Mediterranean, A.D. 500-1100* (Princeton, N.J.: Princeton University Press, 1951), especially pp. 152-163.

4. George M. Foster, *Culture and Conquest: America's Spanish Heritage* (Chicago: Quadrangle Books, 1960), pp. 28, 29.

5. Perhaps the most eloquent of many statements on this point is Claudio Sánchez-Albornoz, "La Edad Media y la empresa de América," in his *España y el Islam* (Buenos Aires: Editorial Sudamericana, 1943), pp. 181-189.

6. *Primera parte de la historia general de las Indias*, in *Historiadores primitivos de Indias*, gen. ed. Don Enrique de Vedia, Biblioteca de Autores Españoles, vols. 22, 26 (Madrid: Ediciones Atlas, 1946-47), vol. 22, p. 156.

## CHAPTER 2: RECONQUEST HISPANIA

1. Spanish and Portuguese interpretations, especially the latter, are summarized in Jaime Cortesão, "The Portuguese Imprint on Brazil," in Harold B. Johnson, ed., *From Reconquest*

*to Empire: The Iberian Background to Latin American History* (New York: Alfred A. Knopf, Borzoi Books, 1970), pp. 209-224. For further observations on cultural and ethnic factors in the shaping of Portuguese identity see H. V. Livermore, *A New History of Portugal* (Cambridge: Cambridge University Press, 1966), pp. 9-32; and Antonio H. de Oliveira Marques, *History of Portugal*, 2 vols. (New York: Columbia University Press, 1972), I, chap. 1. For the importance of maritime influences see Bailey W. Diffie, *Prelude to Empire: Portugal Overseas Before Henry the Navigator* (Lincoln: University of Nebraska Press, Bison Books 108, 1960), pp. 20-28, 67.

2. *The Individuality of Portugal: A Study in Historical Political Geography* (Austin: University of Texas Press, 1959), especially pp. 204-217.

3. *Ibid.*, p. 213.

4. French historians of the "Annales" school have been instrumental in working out long-term demographic and economic trends. For insights into their contributions see Peter Burke, "Introduction," and Fernand Braudel, "History and the Social Sciences," in *Economy and Society in Early Modern Europe: Essays from Annales*, ed. Peter Burke (New York: Harper and Row, Harper Torchbooks, 1972), pp. 1-10 and 11-42. See particularly François Simiand, *Les fluctuations économiques à longue période et la crise mondiale* (Paris: F. Alcan, 1932). Simiand's general thesis is that long-term upswings (A-Phases) are associated with economic and demographic expansion, and downswings (B-Phases) with economic and demographic contraction. It is not certain which factor, demographic or economic, is the chicken and which the egg. Climatic and epidemiological variables, moreover, enter the picture. For a critique of their influence see Immanuel Wallerstein, *The Modern World-System, Vol. I: Capitalist Agriculture and the Origins of the European World-Economy in the Sixteenth Century* (New York: Academic Press, 1974), pp. 33-38.

5. Jaime Vicens Vives, with the collaboration of Jorge Nadal Oller, *Manual de historia económica de España* (4th ed.; Barcelona: Editorial Vicens Vives, 1965), trans. Frances M. López-Morillas as *An Economic History of Spain* (Princeton, N.J.: Princeton University Press, 1969), pp. 250-251.

6. Julian J. Bishko, "The Peninsular Background of Latin American Cattle Ranching," *HAHR*, 32:491-515 (1952).

7. *L'Espagne de Charles Quint*, 2 vols. (Paris: Société d'Edition d'Enseignement Supérieur, 1973), I, chap. 2.

8. The text along with critical annotations may be found in *Los códigos españoles concordados y anotados*, 12 vols. (Madrid, 1872-73), II-IV.

9. The French historian Roland Mousnier has made the fullest study of the "society of orders." He presents a summary of his work in *Les hiérarchies sociales de 1450 à nos jours* (Paris: Presses Universitaires de France, 1969), trans. Peter Evans as *Social Hierarchies, 1450 to the Present*, ed. Margaret Clarke (New York: Schocken Books, 1973), chap. 1 in the English edition.

10. The difference between feudal and *señorial* organization in Reconquest Hispanic societies and the degree to which feudal elements were present in Hispanic American societies are still debatable issues. A detailed study of Spanish and, especially, Castilian feudalism is Claudio Sánchez-Albornoz, *En torno a los orígenes del feudalismo*, 3 vols. (Mendoza, Arg.: Universidad Nacional de Cuyo, 1942). A more recent and more critical analysis is Luis García de Valdeavellano, "Prólogo y apéndice sobre las instituciones feudales en España," in F. L. Ganshof, *El feudalismo* (Barcelona: Ariel, 1963), a Spanish translation of Ganshof's classic *'Qu'est-ce que la féodalité?'* The best explanation of feudalism in Portugal is Marques, *History of Portugal*, I, chap. 2.

11. The classical statement on these points is Miguel de Unamuno, "Spanish Individualism," in his *Essays and Solioquies* (New York: Alfred A. Knopf, 1925), pp. 38-51.

12. For example, see Américo Castro, *The Meaning of Spanish History* (Princeton, N.J.: n.p., 1941). A more recent expression of this view may be found in Luis García Valdeavellano, *Orígenes de la burguesía en la España* (Madrid: Espasa-Calpe, 1969); and Richard M. Morse, "Trends and Issues in Latin American Urban Research, 1965-1970," part 1, *LARR*, 6(no. 1):3-52 (Spring 1961).

13. Gabriel Jackson, *The Making of Medieval Spain* (New York: Harcourt Brace Jovanovich, 1972), p. 88; and Diffie, *Prelude to Empire*, pp. 30, 34, 41, 61.

14. Fernand Braudel, *La Méditerranée et le Monde Méditerranéen à l'époque de Philippe II* (Paris: Librairie Armand Colin, 1966), trans. Siân Reynolds as *The Mediterranean and the Mediterranean World in the Age of Philip II*, 2 vols. (New York: Harper and Row, 1972), II, 725-734.

15. On this point see Robert S. Chamberlain, "The Concept of the *Señor Natural* as Revealed by Castilian Law and Administrative Documents," *HAHR*, 19:130-137 (1939).

16. *España invertebrada: Bosquejo de algunos pensamientos históricos* (4th ed.; Madrid: Revista de Occidente, 1934), trans. Mildred Adams as *Invertebrate Spain* (New York: W. W. Norton, 1937).

## CHAPTER 3: HISPANIC EXPANSION IN THE OLD WORLD

1. A concise interpretation of Europe's setback is Robert E. Lerner, *The Age of Adversity: The Fourteenth Century* (Ithaca, N.Y.: Cornell University Press, 1968). See also the stimulating article by Archibald Lewis, "The Closing of the Medieval Frontier," *Speculum*, 33:475-483 (1958).

2. The long-term significance of the Revolution of 1385 is still a contentious subject in Portuguese historiography. I have listed several works in the bibliographical essay for this chapter that sample the several interpretations.

3. Louis Ruchames, "The Sources of Racial Thought in Colonial America," *The Journal of Negro History*, 52:255-256 (1967); Real Academia Española, *Diccionario de Autoridades*, vol. III (Madrid: Editorial Gredos, 1963), p. 501.

4. Pierre L. van den Berghe, *Race and Racism* (New York: John Wiley and Sons, 1967), pp. 9, 11.

5. For an exposition of the last point see Winthrop D. Jordan, *White over Black: American Attitudes toward the Negro, 1550-1812* (Chapel Hill, N.C.: University of North Carolina Press, 1968; reprinted, Baltimore: Pelican Books, 1969), pp. 5-7, 17-19, 28-31. Citations are from the reprinted edition.

6. As quoted in Carter G. Woodson, "Attitudes of the Iberian Peninsula," *Journal of Negro History*, 20:202 (1935).

7. As quoted in Margaret T. Hogden, *Early Anthropology in the Sixteenth and Seventeenth Centuries* (Philadelphia: University of Pennsylvania Press, 1964), p. 362.

8. Stephen H. Haliczer, "The Castilian Urban Patriciate and the Jewish Expulsions," *AHR*, 78:35-58 (1973), offers new insights into the politics of the Jewish expulsions.

9. An especially important article on this subject is Paul Stewart, "The Soldier, the Bureaucrat, and Fiscal Records in the Army of Ferdinand and Isabella," *HAHR*, 49:281-292 (1969). It examines the development of administrative procedures for the new army.

10. On the role of the Italians see Charles Verlinden, "Italian Influence on Spanish Economy and Colonization During the Reign of Ferdinand the Catholic," in his *The Beginnings of Modern Colonization*, trans. Yvonne Freccero (Ithaca, N.Y.: Cornell University Press, 1970).

11. A concise interpretation of the turn of the tide is Jarah Johnson and William A. Percy, *The Age of Recovery: The Fifteenth Century* (Ithaca, N.Y.: Cornell University Press, 1977).

12. Julio Caro Baroja, *Los moriscos del reino de Granada, ensayo de historia social* (Madrid: Instituto de Estudios Políticos, 1957), is an outstanding study of *morisco* society and the problems it created for Christian Spain. Albert A. Sicroff, *Les controverses des statuts de "pureté de sang" en Espagne du xv$^e$ au xvii$^e$ siècle* (Paris: Didier, 1960), is a careful investigation into the religious and social origins of the concept of "pure blood" and its popular and statutory expressions.

13. As quoted in Silvio Zavala, "La conquista de Canarias y América," in his *Estudios indianos* (Mexico: El Colegio Nacional, 1948), p. 13.

14. Charles Verlinden, "The Italians in the Economy of the Canary Islands at the Beginning of Spanish Colonization," in his *The Beginnings of Modern Colonization*, pp. 132-157.

## CHAPTER 4. THE CONDITIONS OF CONQUEST AND COLONIZATION: GEOGRAPHY AND PEOPLES

1. The observations attributed to Columbus are from the *Journal of Christopher Columbus*, trans. Cecil Jane (London: Anthony Blond, 1968), *passim*.

2. The quotations are from *Inter caetera divinae* as translated in W. Eugene Shiels, S.J., *King and Church: The Rise and Fall of the Patronato Real* (Chicago: Loyola University Press, 1961), p. 80.

3. Charles E. Nowell, "The Discovery of Brazil: Accidental or Intentional?" *HAHR*, 16:311-338 (1936), makes a strong argument for this case. More recent scholarship, however, tends to be skeptical. See, for example, Manuel Nunes Dias, "Descobrimento do Brasil: Tratados biláterais e partilha do Mar Oceano," *Studia* (Lisbon), 25:7-29 (1968).

4. Nowell, "The Discovery of Brazil."

5. "The Letter of Pero Vaz de Caminha," May 1, 1500, in *A Documentary History of Brazil*, ed. E. Bradford Burns (New York: Alfred A. Knopf, 1966), p. 28.

6. Juan Pérez de Tudela, "La quiebra de la factoría y el nuevo poblamiento de la Española," *RI*, 15:197-252 (1955).

7. The concept of "verticality" as it applied among the Indians of Andean America is developed in John V. Murra, *Formaciones económicas y políticas del mundo andino* (Lima: Instituto de Estudios Peruanos, 1975).

8. Howard Cline, "Hernando Cortés and the Aztec Indians in Spain," *Quarterly Journal of the Library of Congress*, 26:70-90 (1969), gives a delightful description of the Aztecs whom Cortés brought to Spain in 1528-29 and the reaction of the Spaniards to them.

9. As quoted in Shiels, *King and Church*, p. 80.

10. As quoted in James Lockhart, *Spanish Peru, 1532-1560: A Colonial Society* (Madison: University of Wisconsin Press, 1968), p. 34.

11. As quoted in Carl O. Sauer, *The Early Spanish Main* (Berkeley: University of California Press, 1966), p. 229.

12. Francisco López de Gómara, *Cortés: The Life of the Conqueror by His Secretary*, trans. and ed. Lesley Byrd Simpson (Berkeley: University of California Press, 1964), p. 58.

13. *Visión de los vencidos*, ed. and intro. Miguel León-Portilla (Mexico: U.N.A.M., 1959), trans. Lysander Kemp as *The Broken Spears: The Aztec Account of the Conquest of Mexico* (Boston: Beacon Press, 1962), p. 51. The quotation is from the English edition.

14. "A Letter written by Don Christopher Columbus, Viceroy and Admiral of the Indies, to the most Christian and mighty Sovereigns, the King and Queen of Spain . . ." Jamaica, July 7, 1503, in *Christopher Columbus, Four Voyages to the New World: Letters and Selected Documents*, trans. and ed. R. H. Major (New York: Corinth Books, 1961), p. 196.

15. *Historia verdadera de la conquista de la Nueva España*, ed. Genaro García, 2 vols. (Mexico: Oficina Tipográfica de la Secretaría de Fomento, 1904–5), trans. Alfred P. Maudslay as *The True History of the Conquest of New Spain*, Works issued by the Hakluyt Society, series II, vols. XXIII-XXV, XXX, XL (London, 1908–16), XXIII, 10.

16. Summaries and evaluations of early Spanish estimates may be found in Woodrow Borah, "¿América como modelo? El impacto demográfico de la expansión europea sobre el mundo no europeo," *Cuadernos Americanos*, 21:176-185 (1962); and in Sauer, *The Early Spanish Main*, pp. 65-69.

17. The *Brevissima relación* in F. A. MacNutt, *Bartholomew de las Casas, His Life, His Apostolate, and His Writings* (New York: G. P. Putnam's Sons, 1909), p. 317.

18. These first modern estimates are reviewed briefly in Borah, "¿América como modelo?" p. 177, and Henry F. Dobyns "Estimating Aboriginal American Population. An Appraisal of Techniques with a New Hemispheric Estimate," *Current Anthropology*, 7:396 and *passim* (1966).

19. "El desarrollo de la población indígena de América" (three parts), *Tierra Firme* (Madrid), no. 1:115-133, no. 2:117-148, no. 3:109-141 (1935). Rosenblat still held to approximately the same figure nearly twenty years later in *La población indígena y el mestizaje en América*, 2 vols. (Buenos Aires: Editorial Nova, 1954), I, 102.

20. *Cultural and Natural Areas of Native North America*, University of California Publications in American Ethnology, 38 (Berkeley: University of California Press, 1939).

21. Sherburne F. Cook and Woodrow Borah, *The Aboriginal Population of Central Mexico on the Eve of the Spanish Conquest*, Ibero-Americana: 45 (Berkeley: University of California Press, 1963), pp. 88, 157. A more recent report on the methods and findings of the "Berkeley School" is Cook and Borah, *Essays in Population History*, 3 vols. (Berkeley: University of California Press, 1971–79). The assumptions and methods employed by the "Berkeley School" and the results it has obtained have been challenged by a number of scholars. See for example Rudolph A. Zambardino, "Mexico's Population in the Sixteenth Century: Demographic Anomoly or Mathematical Illusion?" *The Journal of Interdisciplinary History*, 11:1-27 (1980–81). Zambardino estimates the Indian population of Central Mexico in 1518 to have been only between 5,000,000 and 10,000,000.

22. "¿América como modelo?" p. 179.

23. "Estimating Aboriginal American Population," p. 415.

24. William M. Denevan, ed., *The Native Population of the Americas in 1492* (Madison: University of Wisconsin Press, 1976), contains the most recent statements of Borah, Rosenblat, and other authorities and constitutes a survey of the state of the controversy.

25. *Ibid.*, "Epilogue," p. 291.

26. Sherburne F. Cook, "Human Sacrifice and Warfare as Factors in the Demography of Pre-Colonial Mexico," *Human Biology*, 18:81-102 (1946). The quotation is from Woodrow Borah, "New Demographic Research on the Sixteenth Century in Mexico," in *Latin American History: Essays on Its Study and Teaching, 1898-1965*, comp. and ed. Howard F. Cline, 2 vols. (Austin: University of Texas Press, 1967), II, 720.

27. A good general treatment of the health of the pre-Conquest American Indian is Alfred W. Crosby, Jr., *The Columbian Exchange: Biological and Cultural Consequences*

*of 1492* (Westport, Conn.: Greenwood Press, 1972), pp. 31, 37, and chap. 4. For a more recent and more specialized research report see Marvin J. Allison, "Paleopathology in Peru," *Natural History*, 88(no. 2):74-82 (February 1979).

28. *Historia del Nuevo Mundo*, Biblioteca de Autores Españoles, vols. 91, 92 (Madrid: Ediciones Atlas, 1964), vol. 92, p. 15 (*lib*. xi, *cap*. 4).

29. Contemporary historian Gonzalo Fernández de Oviedo y Valdés sensed the Indian's perception of the ecological unity of the human, natural, and supernatural environment (*Sumario de la natural historia de las Indias* [Mexico and Buenos Aires: Fondo de Cultura Económica, 1950], pp. 115-142 [*cap*. x]). For modern interpretations of the Indian ethos see Miguel León-Portilla, *Aztec Thought and Culture: A Study of the Ancient Nahuatl Mind*, trans. Jack E. Davis (Norman: University of Oklahoma Press, 1963); and Terence Grieder, *Ecología pre-colombina*, Institute of Latin American Studies, University of Texas, Offprint Series, no. 99 (Austin: University of Texas, 1971).

## CHAPTER 5. MUNDUS NOVUS: DISCOVERY AND CONQUEST

1. Almost contemporary definitions of these terms may be found in Sebastián de Horozco Covarrubias, *Tesoro de la lengua castellana o española según la impresión de 1611*, ed. Martín de Riquer (Barcelona: S. A. Horta, 1943). On discovery alone see Wilcomb E. Washburn, "The Meaning of 'Discovery' in the Fifteenth and Sixteenth Centuries," *AHA*, 68:1-21 (1962). Irving A. Leonard, *Books of the Brave; Being an Account of Books and Men in the Spanish Conquest and Settlement of the Sixteenth Century New World* (Cambridge, Mass.: Harvard University Press, 1949), examines the effect of romances of chivalry on the minds of discoverers and conquerors.

2. Manuel Fernández Alvarez, *Charles V: Elected Emperor and Hereditary Ruler* (London: Thames and Hudson, 1975), pp. 188-190.

3. As quoted in Lewis Hanke, *The Spanish Struggle for Justice in the Conquest of America* (Boston: Little, Brown, 1965), p. 33.

4. As quoted in *ibid.*, pp. 33-34.

5. *De Orbe Novo, the Eight Decades of Peter Martyr d'Anghera*, trans. and ed. F. A. MacNutt, 2 vols. (New York: G. P. Putnam's Sons, 1912), I, 83.

6. Charles Gibson, *Spain in America* (New York: Harper and Row, 1966), p. 12.

7. Carl O. Sauer, *The Early Spanish Main* (Berkeley: University of California Press, 1966), pp. 1-4.

8. Francisco Morales Padrón, "Descubrimiento y toma de la posesión," *AEA*, 12:321-380 (1955).

9. As quoted in Burr Brundage, *A Rain of Darts: The Mexican Aztecs* (Austin: University of Texas Press, 1972), p. xvi.

10. On the differing organizations of the Inca and Aztec states and their influence on Spanish conquest and pacification see Charles Gibson, *The Inca Concept of Sovereignty and Spanish Administration in Peru* (Austin: University of Texas Press, 1948); George Kubler, "The Neo-Inca State, 1537–1572," *HAHR*, 27:189-203 (1947); and R. C. Padden, *The Hummingbird and the Hawk: Conquest and Sovereignty in the Valley of Mexico* (Columbus: Ohio State University Press, 1967).

## CHAPTER 6. COLONIZATION: THE POPULATORS OF THE INDIES

1. T. Lynn Smith, "Studies of Colonization and Settlement," *LARR*, 4(no.1):93-96 (Spring 1969), discusses the meaning of colonization and settlement in the Hispanic context.

2. *Bases y puntos de partida para la organización política de la República Argentina* (Buenos Aires: La Cultura Argentina, 1915), p. 219.

3. Richard Konetzke, ed., *Colección de documentos para la historia de la formación social de Hispanoamérica, 1493–1810*, 3 vols. in 5 (Madrid: C.S.I.C., 1953–62), I, 5-6.

4. *Ibid.*, p. 9.

5. As quoted in Lewis Hanke, *The Spanish Struggle for Justice in the Conquest of America* (Boston: Little, Brown, 1965), p. 57.

6. Ed. Cristóbal Bermúdez Plata, 3 vols. (Madrid: C.S.I.C., 1940–46).

7. Boyd-Bowman summarizes and analyzes this data in "Patterns of Spanish Emigration to the New World (1493–1580)," Council on International Studies, State University of New York at Buffalo, Special Studies, mimeo (Buffalo, 1973); and in "Patterns of Spanish Emigration to the Indies until 1600," *HAHR*, 56:580-604 (1976). Data given for the period 1493–1580 are basically the same in both items, but the figures cited in the following pages are taken from the first named, since it is more detailed and its summaries correspond more closely to the end of the time span covered in this chapter.

8. *Culture and Conquest: America's Spanish Heritage* (Chicago: Quadrangle Books, 1960), chap. 2, and pp. 33, 227-234.

9. Boyd-Bowman, "Patterns of Spanish Emigration to the New World," pp. 9-10.

10. James Lockhart, *Spanish Peru, 1532-1560: A Colonial Society* (Madison: University of Wisconsin Press, 1968), pp. 224-255; and his "The Social History of Colonial Spanish America," *LARR*, 7(no. 1):18 (Spring 1972).

11. *Geografía y descripción universal de las Indias*, ed. Don Marcos Jiménez de Espada, Biblioteca de Autores Españoles, vol. 248 (Madrid: Ediciones Atlas, 1971), p. 283.

12. *La población indígena y el mestizaje en América, 1492-1950*, 2 vols. (Buenos Aires: Editorial Nova, 1954), I, 88.

13. *Geografía y descripción universal*, p. 1.

14. *New Spain's Century of Depression*, Ibero-Americana: 35 (Berkeley: University of California Press, 1951), pp. 7-11.

15. *The Population of Latin America: A History*, trans. W. A. R. Richardson (Berkeley: University of California Press, 1974), p. 69.

16. Las Casas's views are contained in his *Historia apologética de las Indias* (Madrid, 1867), completed around 1550. Motolinía's observations are from his *History of the Indians of New Spain*, trans. and ed. Francis B. Steck (Washington, D.C.: Academy of American Franciscan History, 1951), pp. 87-94.

17. Peter Gerhard, *A Guide to the Historical Geography of New Spain*, Cambridge Latin American Studies, 14 (Cambridge: Cambridge University Press, 1972), p. 23, contains a tabulation of epidemics in New Spain.

18. *La población indígena*, I, 83-95.

19. For example, Cook and Borah arrived at a factor of 2.8 for central Mexico in the later sixteenth century (*The Indian Population of Central Mexico, 1531-1610*, Ibero-Americana: 44 [Berkeley: University of California Press, 1960], p. 3).

20. *The Aboriginal Population of Central Mexico on the Eve of the Spanish Conquest*, Ibero-Americana: 45 (Berkeley: University of California Press, 1963), p. 4. It should be noted that other scholars have criticized Cook and Borah's methods and results and have calculated a much lower rate of decline. Thus Rudolph Zambardino estimates that the Indian population of Central Mexico in 1568 was between 2.6 ± 0.4 million, that is, approximately the same as the Cook and Borah figure. His estimate for 1518, however, is 5-10 million, considerably less than Cook and Borah's ("Mexico's Population in the

Sixteenth Century: Demographic Anomoly or Mathematical Illusion?" *The Journal of Interdisciplinary History*, 11:1-27 [1980-81]).

21. The "Aboriginal Population of Hispaniola," in their *Essays in Population History*, 3 vols. (Berkeley: University of California Press, 1971-79), I, chap. 6, and "The Population of Yucatán, 1517-1960," in *ibid.*, II, chap. 1.

22. *Spanish Central America: A Socioeconomic History, 1520-1720* (Berkeley: University of California Press, 1973), pp. 98-100, 131, 204-205.

23. Juan Friede, "Algunas consideraciones sobre la evolución demográfica de la provincia de Tunja," *Anuario Colombiano de Historia Social y de la Cultura*, 2(no. 3):5-19 (1965).

24. *Demographic Collapse: Indian Peru, 1520-1620* (Cambridge: Cambridge University Press, 1981), table 18, p. 94.

25. The organization of the slave trade is discussed in more detail in chapters 11 and 17 of this book.

26. The problems of estimating the volume of the African slave trade to the Indies are summarized in Philip D. Curtin, *The Atlantic Slave Trade: A Census* (Madison: University of Wisconsin Press, 1969), pp. 15-23.

27. Huguette Chaunu and Pierre Chaunu *Séville et l'Atlantique (1504-1650)*, 8 vols. in 11 parts (Paris: Librairie Armand Colin, 1955-59), VI, part 1, pp. 41-42, and tables 185-188, pp. 396-403.

28. Curtin, *Atlantic Slave Trade*, pp. 23-24.

29. *Ibid.*, pp. 95-101, 109-111.

30. *Geografía y descripción universal*, p. 1.

31. *La crónica del Perú* (Buenos Aires: Espase-Calpe, 1945), p. 145, quoted in Magnus Mörner, *Race Mixture in the History of Latin America* (Boston: Little, Brown, 1967), p. 24.

32. *Historia general y natural de las Indias, lib.* xxvi, *cap.* x, quoted in Rosenblat, *La población indígena*, II, 22.

33. Carl O. Sauer, *The Early Spanish Main* (Berkeley: University of California Press, 1966), p. 199.

34. *Historia apologética, cap.* 14, as cited in Lesley Byrd Simpson, *The Encomienda in New Spain: The Beginning of Spanish Mexico* (Berkeley: University of California Press, 1966), p. 177, n. 3.

35. Raimundo Rivas, *Los fundadores de Bogotá (diccionario-biográfico)* (Bogotá: Imprenta Nacional, 1923), cited in Rosenblat, *La población indígena*, II, 71.

36. As quoted in Rosenblat, *La población indígena*, II, 110.

37. As quoted in Harris G. Warren, *Paraguay: An Informal History* (Norman: University of Oklahoma Press, 1949), pp. 79-80.

38. *Geografía y descripción universal*, pp. 22-23.

39. "Racial Groups in the Mexican Population," in their *Essays in Population History*, II, table 2.1, p. 197.

## CHAPTER 7. INSTRUMENTS OF COLONIZATION: THE CASTILIAN MUNICIPIO

1. As quoted in Richard M. Morse, "Some Characteristics of Latin American Urban History," *AHA*, 67:319 (1962).

2. Quotations are from William L. Schurz, *This New World: The Civilization of Latin America* (New York: E. P. Dutton, 1954; reprinted, New York: E. P. Dutton [Paperback D 137], 1964). The quotations are from the latter edition, p. 343.

3. *Repartimientos* and *encomiendas* of Indians will be treated more fully in chapter 8 following.

4. On the Spanish American fortress-church see Leopoldo Castedo, *A History of Latin American Art and Architecture from Pre-Columbian Times to the Present*, trans. and ed. Phyllis Freeman (New York: Praeger, 1969), p. 105.

5. The count is based on Juan López de Velasco, *Geografía y descripción universal de las Indias*, ed. Don Marcos Jiménez de Espada, Biblioteca de Autores Españoles, vol. 248 (Madrid: Ediciones Atlas, 1971), *passim*.

6. The forms of classification employed in the following pages are my own, although I have borrowed heavily from various authorities on Spanish American urbanization, particularly Jorge Hardoy, J. M. Houston, and Richard M. Morris, whose works are listed in the bibliographical essay for this chapter. The data on numbers of *vecinos* and *encomenderos* are taken from López de Velasco, *Geografía y descripción universal, passim*.

7. López de Velasco, p. 283.

8. López de Velasco gives status rankings of Spanish American municipalities around 1570.

9. The problem of the origins of the gridiron layout has generated a lively polemic among students of Spanish American urban and architectural history. The following items are good introductions to the issues and to the various points of view: Morse, "Some Characteristics"; and George M. Foster, *Culture and Conquest: America's Spanish Heritage* (Chicago: Quadrangle Books, 1960), chap. 4.

10. For the following analysis I have relied heavily on Morse, "Some Characteristics"; J. M. Houston, "The Founding of Colonial Towns in Hispanic America," in *Urbanization and Its Problems: Essays in Honor of E. W. Gilbert*, ed. R. P. Beckinsdale and J. M. Houston (Oxford: Basil Blackwell, 1968), pp. 352-390; Nicolás Sánchez-Albornoz, *The Population of Latin America: A History*, trans. W. A. R. Richardson (Berkeley: University of California Press, 1974), pp. 76-85; and Walter D. Harris in collaboration with Humberto L. Rodríguez-Camilloni, *The Growth of Latin American Cities* (Athens, Ohio: Ohio University Press, 1971), pp. 1-38.

## CHAPTER 8. COLONIZATION: EFFORTS TO INCORPORATE THE INDIANS

1. *Historia general y natural de las Indias, primera parte, lib.* I, *cap.* 6; *lib.* IV, *cap.* 2; *lib.* V, *prohemio* and *caps.* 2-3; *lib.* VI, *cap.* 9, as quoted in Lewis Hanke, *The Spanish Struggle for Justice in the Conquest of America* (Boston: Little, Brown, 1965), p. 11.

2. As cited in Hanke, *The Spanish Struggle for Justice*, pp. 11-12.

3. As quoted in *ibid.*, p. 11.

4. As quoted in *ibid.*, p. 73.

5. Richard Konetzke, ed. *Colección de documentos para la historia de la formación social de Hispanoamérica, 1493-1810*, 3 vols. in 5 (Madrid: C.S.I.C., 1953-62), I, 9-13.

6. *Ibid.*, I, 6, 16-17.

7. The text of the Laws of Burgos may be found in *The Laws of Burgos of 1512-1513: Royal Ordinances for the Good Government and Treatment of the Indians*, trans. and ed. Lesley B. Simpson (San Francisco: John Howell, 1960).

8. As quoted in Magnus Mörner, *La Corona Española y los foráneos en los pueblos de indios de América* (Stockholm: Almqvist and Wiksell, 1970), p. 27.

9. As quoted in Florentino Pérez-Embid and Francisco Morales Padrón, *Acción de España en América* (Barcelona: Editiorial AHR, 1958), p. 217.

10. Diego de Encinas, comp., *Cedulario indiano*, 4 vols. (Madrid, 1596), III, 7, as trans. by Lesley B. Simpson in *The Encomienda in New Spain: The Beginning of Spanish Mexico* (Berkeley: University of California Press, 1966), p. 85.

11. As quoted in François Chevalier, *Land and Society in Colonial Mexico: The Great Hacienda* (Berkeley: University of California Press, 1963), p. 36.

12. The text of the New Laws may be found in J. F. Pacheco, F. de Cardenas, and L. Torres de Mendoza, eds., *Colección de documentos inéditos relativos al descubrimiento, conquista y organización de las antiguas posesiones españoles* . . . , 42 vols. (Madrid, 1864–89), XVI, 376-408. For an English translation see H. Stevens and F. W. Lucas, trans. and eds., *The New Laws of the Indies for the Good Treatment and Preservation of the Indians* (London, 1892).

13. *Geografía y descripción universal de las Indias*, ed. Don Marcos Jiménez de Espada, Biblioteca de Autores Españoles, vol. 248 (Madrid: Ediciones Atlas, 1971), p. 1.

14. *The Encomienda in New Spain*, p. 145.

15. Historiographic articles analyzing problems and issues are listed in the bibliographical essay for this chapter.

16. "Castilian Backgrounds of the *Repartimiento-Encomienda*," in Carnegie Institution of Washington, Contributions to American Anthropology and History, 5(no. 25):19-66 (1939).

17. As quoted in Simpson, *The Encomienda in New Spain*, p. xvi.

18. *Hernando Cortés: Five Letters, 1519–1526*, trans. and ed. J. Bayard Morris (New York: W. W. Norton, The Norton Library [N 180], 1962), p. 240 (Third Letter), p. 280 (Fourth Letter).

19. As quoted in Charles S. Braden, *Religious Aspects of the Conquest of Mexico* (Durham, N.C.: Duke University Press, 1930), p. 133.

20. As cited in Pedro Borges, O.F.M., *Métodos misionales en la cristianización de América* (Madrid: C.S.I.C., 1960), p. 460.

21. As quoted in *ibid.*, p. 204.

22. As quoted in Robert Ricard, *The Spiritual Conquest of Mexico: An Essay on the Apostolate and the Evangelizing Methods of the Mendicant Orders in New Spain, 1523–1572* (Berkeley: University of California Press, 1966), p. 143.

23. Fray Pedro Juárez de Escobar, as quoted in Ricard, *The Spiritual Conquest of Mexico*, p. 150.

24. Konetzke, *Colección de documentos*, I, 186-187.

25. *Recopilación de leyes de los reynos de las Indias*, 4 vols. (Madrid: 1681), II, 198 (*lib*. VI, *tít*. iii, *ley* 1).

26. *Geografía y descripción universal*, pp. 48, 169.

27. Carmelo Sáenz de Santa María, "La 'reducción a poblados' en el siglo xvi en Guatemala," *AEA*, 29:200-201 (1972).

28. *Geografía y descripción universal*, p. 169.

29. Contemporary citations and quotations are as given in Borges, *Métodos misionales*, pp. 471, 473-474, 482-483.

30. Contemporary citations and quotations are from *ibid.*, pp. 464, 475, 486, 489.

31. Anita Brenner, *Idols behind Altars* (New York: Payson and Clark, 1929).

32. Quoted in Silvio Zavala, *Ensayos sobre la colonización española en América* (Buenos Aires: Emecé Editores, 1944), p. 126.

33. *Gobierno del Perú* (1567), ed. and intro. Guillermo Lohmann Villena (Paris and Lima: L'Institut Français d'Études Andines, 1967), p. 84.

34. *Geografía y descripción universal*, p. 22.

## CHAPTER 9. THE ROYAL SEÑORÍO IN THE INDIES

1. Disagreements exist about the origins of the American viceregal system. Jaime Vicens Vives, "Precedentes mediterráneos del virreinato colombino," *AEA*, 5:571-614 (1948), forcefully defends Aragonese precedents. Ciriaco Pérez Bustamente, "Sobre los precedentes del virreinato colombino," *RI*, 12:241-248 (1952), analyzes the title of viceroy given to Columbus and, while admitting Aragonese influences, affirms that it had primarily Castilian origins and implies the same for later American viceroyalties. Sigfrido Augusto Radaelli, *La institución virreinal en las Indias: Antecedentes históricos* (Buenos Aires: Editorial Perrot, 1957), finds no Aragonese precedent for Columbus's title and concludes that the viceregal system instituted in 1535 had neither Aragonese nor Columbian antecedents.

2. As far as I have been able to determine, this typology was first developed in Enrique Ruiz Guinazú, *La magistratura indiana* (Buenos Aires: Universidad de Buenos Aires, 1916).

3. *Recopilación de leyes de los reynos de las Indias*, 4 vols. (Madrid: 1681), II, 94 (*lib.* IV, *tít.* viii, *ley* 2).

4. C. H. Haring, *The Spanish Empire in America* (New York: Oxford University Press, 1947), p. 180.

5. *Church and State in Latin America: A History of Politico-Ecclesiastical Relations* (rev. ed.; Chapel Hill: University of North Carolina Press, 1966), p. 36.

6. As quoted in Philip W. Powell, *Soldiers, Indians and Silver: The Northward Advance of New Spain, 1550-1600* (Berkeley: University of California Press, 1952), p. 47.

7. The distinguished Spanish historian Guillermo Céspedes contends that the crown reposed extraordinary confidence in its appointed officials in contrast to those who obtained their positions by patent (*Latin America: The Early Years* [New York: Alfred A. Knopf, 1974], p. 96).

8. Max Weber, *The Theory of Social and Economic Organization*, trans. A. M. Henderson and Talcott Parsons (New York: Free Press of Glencoe, 1947), pp. 329-358.

9. Pierre Chaunu, *Conquête et exploitation des nouveaux mondes (xvi$^e$ siècle)*, Nouvelle Clio, L'histoire et ses problèmes, 26 *bis* (Paris: Presses Universitaires de France, 1969), pp. 277-290, discusses time-distance factors in trans-Atlantic communication.

10. *Descripción breve de todo la tierra del Perú, Tucumán, Rio de la Plata y Chile* (Lima: 1908), p. 525.

11. I am indebted for this information to two unpublished papers prepared in my seminar at the University of Florida in August 1972: Daniel Jares, "Colonial Land Transportation Systems: Spanish Colonies in South America, and Lisandro O. Pérez, "Colonial Transportation Systems in Mexico: A Time-Distance Analysis."

## CHAPTER 10. THE FRUITS OF THE LAND

1. *Sumario de la natural historia de las Indias*, ed. José Miranda (Mexico and Buenos Aires: Fondo de Cultura Económica, 1950), p. 254 (*cap.* lxxxii).

2. *Gobierno del Perú*, ed. Guillermo Lohmann Villena (Paris and Lima: Institut Français d'Études Andines, 1967), p. 25 (*primera parte, cap.* 8).

3. Bailey W. Diffie, *Latin-American Civilization: Colonial Period* (Harrisburg, Pa.: Stackpole Sons, 1945), p. 107.

4. *Historia de las Indias*, ed. Agustín Millares Carlo, and intro. Lewis Hanke, 3 vols. (Mexico and Buenos Aires: Fondo de Cultura Económica, 1951), II, 225 (*lib.* ii, *cap.* 6).

5. *Historia del Nuevo Mundo*, in *Obras del P. Bernabé Cobo*, ed. P. Francisco Mateos, 2 vols. Biblioteca de Autores Españoles, vols. 91, 92 (Madrid: Ediciones Atlas, 1964), vol. 91, p. 154 (*lib.* iv, *cap.* 1).

6. Raymond L. Lee, "Cochineal Production and Trade in New Spain to 1600," *TA*, 4:451 (1947-48).

7. *Relation of the Discovery and Conquest of the Kingdoms of Peru*, trans. Philip A. Means, 2 vols., Documents and Narratives concerning the Discovery and Conquest of Latin America, no. 4 (New York: The Cortes Society, 1921), II, 363.

8. *Gobierno del Perú*, p. 163 (*primera parte, cap.* 44).

9. Earl J. Hamilton, *American Treasure and the Price Revolution in Spain, 1501-1650* (Cambridge, Mass.: Harvard University Press, 1934), table 3, p. 42. I have divided weights in grams given in the table by 4.219, the weight of the *peso de oro de minas*, to arrive at values.

10. The series referred to were constructed by Hamilton and are presented in tabular and graphic forms in his *American Treasure and the Price Revolution*, pp. 34, 35, 40, 41, 42, and 43.

11. *Ibid.*, table 3, p. 42. I have divided weights in grams as given in the table by 25.56, the weight of the silver *peso fuerte*, to arrive at values.

12. Calculations are based on *ibid.*, table 2, p. 40, and table 3, p. 42.

13. *Ibid.*, table 4, p. 71.

## CHAPTER 11. THE COMMERCE OF THE INDIES

1. *Hernando Cortés: Five Letters, 1519-1526*, trans. and ed. J. Bayard Morris (New York: W. W. Norton, The Norton Library [N 180], 1962), pp. 271, 273.

2. Woodrow Borah, *Early Colonial Trade and Navigation between Mexico and Peru*, Ibero-Americana: 38 (Berkeley: University of California Press, 1954), p. 13.

3. *The Atlantic Slave Trade: A Census* (Madison, University of Wisconsin Press, 1969), table 5, p. 25. The figure 16,200 is based on Curtin's annual average of 810 for the period 1551-95.

4. *Historia natural y moral de las Indias*, ed. Edmundo O'Gorman (2nd ed.; Mexico-Buenos Aires: Fondo de Cultura Económica, 1962), p. 108 (*lib.* iii, *cap.* 10).

5. An excellent survey of monetary systems in the Indies is Manuel Luengo Muñoz, "Sumario noción de las monedas de Castilla e Indias en el siglo xvi," *AEA*, 7:325-366 (1950). The tables of equivalencies included are especially useful.

6. On the use and rates of credit in the Indies trade consult Ruth Pike, *Enterprise and Adventure: The Genoese in Seville and the Opening of the New World* (Ithaca, N.Y.: Cornell University Press, 1966), especially chaps. 2 and 4.

7. *Summa de tratos y contratos* (Seville, 1587), pp. 45, 47.

8. Woodrow Borah and Sherburne F. Cook, *Price Trends of Some Basic Commodities in Central Mexico, 1531-1570*, Ibero-Americana: 40 (Berkeley: University of California Press, 1958), *passim*.

9. *Ibid.*, p. 49.

10. Earl J. Hamilton, *American Treasure and the Price Revolution in Spain, 1501-1650* (Cambridge, Mass.: Harvard University Press, 1934), table 1, p. 34; Huguette Chaunu and Pierre Chaunu, *Séville et l'Atlantique (1504-1650)*, 8 vols. in 11 parts (Paris: Librairie Armand Colin, 1955-59), VI, part 2, pp. 980, 1004, 1012. The values are for quantities arriving legally in Seville.

## CHAPTER 12. THE CONQUEST OF BRAZIL

1. Joseph François Lafitau, *Histoire des découvertes et conquestes des Portugais dans le Nouveau Monde*, 2 vols. (Paris, 1733), I, xv, as quoted in Richard M. Morse, ed., *The Bandeirantes: The Historical Role of the Brazilian Pathfinders* (New York: Alfred A. Knopf, Borzoi Books, 1965), p. 9.

2. Antonio H. de Oliveira Marques, *History of Portugal*, 2 vols. (New York: Columbia University Press, 1972), I, 261-262.

3. James Lang, *Portuguese Brazil: The King's Plantation* (New York: Academic Press, 1979), p. 18.

4. *Decadas da Asia* (Lisbon, 1777-78), as quoted in Charles R. Boxer, *Four Centuries of Portuguese Expansion 1415-1825: A Succinct Survey* (Berkeley: University of California Press, 1969), p. 64.

5. As quoted in Antonio da Silva Rêgo, *Portuguese Colonization in the Sixteenth Century: A Study of Royal Ordinances (Regimentos)* (Johannesburg: Witwatersrand University Press, 1957), pp. 35-36.

6. As quoted in *ibid.*, p. 38.

7. *História econômica do Brasil (1500/1820)* (4th ed.; São Paulo: Companhia Editora Nacional, 1962), p. 61.

8. Marques, *History of Portugal*, I, 253.

9. *História da colonização portuguesa do Brasil: Edição monumental comemorativa do primeiro centenário de independência do Brasil*, gen. ed. Carlos Malheiro Dias, 3 vols. (Oporto: Litografia Nacional, 1921-26), III, 309, as quoted in E. Bradford Burns, ed., *A Documentary History of Brazil* (New York: Alfred A. Knopf, Borzoi Books, 1966), p. 34.

10. The text of the royal letter declaring the king's intentions may be found in Pero Lopes de Sousa, *Diario da navegação [de 1530 a 1532] de Pero Lopes de Sousa*, ed. Eugenio de Castro, 2 vols. (6th ed.; Rio de Janeiro, Typographia Leuzinger, 1927), I, 433-435.

11. The best analysis of these documents and their Old World origins is Harold B. Johnson, "The Donatary Captaincy in Historical Perspective: Portuguese Backgrounds to the Settlement of Brazil," *HAHR*, 52:203-214 (1972).

12. Luis de Góes to D. João III, May 12, 1548, *História da colonização portuguesa do Brasil*, III, 259, as quoted in Alexander Marchant, *From Barter to Slavery: The Economic Relations of Portuguese and Indians in the Settlement of Brazil, 1500-1580* (Baltimore: Johns Hopkins University Press, 1942), p. 80.

13. The text of the *regimento* may be found in *História da colonização portuguesa do Brasil*, III, 345-350.

14. Rêgo, *Portuguese Colonization*, pp. 101-102.

15. *Ibid.*, pp. 105-112.

16. *Cartas de Duarte Coelho a el Rei*, ed. José A. Gonsalves de Mello and Cleonir X. de Albuquerque, *Documentos para la história do nordeste*, vol. II (Recife-Pernambuco: Imprensa Universitaria, 1967), *passim*. The quotation is from p. 28.

17. *História da Prouincia de Sãncta Cruz a que vulgarmente chamamos Brasil* (Lisbon, 1576), trans. John B. Stetson, Jr., as *The Histories of Brazil*, 2 vols. in 1, Documents and Narratives concerning the Discovery and Conquest of America, Old Series, no. 5 (New York: The Cortes Society, 1922). The citation is from the translation, II, 32-38.

18. As quoted in Burns, *A Documentary History of Brazil*, p. 39.

19. Johnson, "The Donatary Captaincy," *passim.*

20. Francisco Adolpho de Varnhagen, *História geral do Brasil antes da sua separação e independência de Portugal,* annotated by João Capistrano de Abreu and Rodolfo Garcia, 6 vols. in 3 (7th ed.; São Paulo: Edições Melhoramentos, 1962), I, 73-74.

21. I know of no systematic comparative analyses of Spanish American patents and instructions for conquest and Brazilian charters and *forais.* The above observations are based on my own reading of a few samples of the several types of documents. They are therefore impressionistic and quite open to challenge.

## CHAPTER 13. THE COLONIZATION OF BRAZIL TO ABOUT 1570

1. Richard M. Morse, "A Prolegomenon to Latin American Urban History," *HAHR,* 52:387 (1972).

2. *Geografía y descripción universal de las Indias,* ed. Don Marcos Jiménez de Espada, Biblioteca de Autores Españoles, vol. 248 (Madrid: Ediciones Atlas, 1971), p. 287.

3. Frei Vicente do Salvador, *História do Brasil, 1500-1627,* ed. Capistrano de Abreu, Rodolfo Garcia, and Venancio Willeke, O.F.M. (5th ed.; São Paulo: Edições Melhoramentos, 1965), p. 61 (*liv.* 1, *cap.* 3).

4. Antonio H. de Oliveira Marques asserts, "For more than two centuries the history of Brazil was above all the history of a desperate effort to find gold." (*History of Portugal,* 2 vols. [New York: Columbia University Press, 1972], I, 355.) On the "Edenic Vision" see Sergio Buarque de Holanda, *Visão do paraiso: Os motivos edênicos no descobrimento e colonização do Brasil* (2nd ed. rev.; São Paulo: Companhia Nacional Editora da Universidade de São Paulo, 1969). See also the contemporary Pedro de Magalhães de Gandavo, *História da Prouincia de Sãncta Cruz a que vulgarmente chamamos Brasil* (Lisbon, 1576), trans. John B. Stetson, Jr., as *The Histories of Brazil,* 2 vols. in 1, Documents and Narratives concerning the Discovery and Conquest of America, Old Series, no. 5 (New York: The Cortes Society, 1922). In vol. II, 117-121, of the English edition, Magalhães voices contemporary convictions "About the Great Riches which They Expect in the Region of the Sertão" and speaks of the nameless persons who were lost in the pursuit.

5. Stuart B. Schwartz, "Cities of Empire: Mexico and Bahia in the Sixteenth Century," *JIAS,* 11:632, n.64 (1969).

6. Alexander Marchant, *From Barter to Slavery: The Economic Relations of Portuguese and Indians in the Settlement of Brazil, 1500-1580* (Baltimore: Johns Hopkins University Press, 1942), pp. 116-117.

7. Stetson, *Histories of Brazil,* II, 165.

8. On this point Robert Ricard, "Comparison of Evangelization in Portuguese and Spanish America," *TA,* 14:444-453 (1958), is well worth reading.

9. The word *reduções* derives from the Latin *reduco,* meaning to lead or conduct back. The missionaries used it to describe their congregations because many of them believed that the Indians had once known Christ but had been seduced and perverted by Satan. Thus, they were bringing them back to the True Faith.

10. Roberto Simonsen, *História econômica do Brasil 1500/1820* (4th ed.; São Paulo: Companhia Editora Nacional, 1962), table following p. 382, and pp. 61-64.

11. Stetson, *Histories of Brazil,* II, 77.

12. *The Atlantic Slave Trade: A Census* (Madison: University of Wisconsin Press, 1969), table 33, p. 116.

13. Frédéric Mauro, *Le Portugal et l'Atlantique au xvii$^e$ siècle (1570-1670): Étude économique* (Paris: S.E.V.P.E.N., 1960), pp. 194-195.

14. Simonsen, *História econômica do Brasil*, p. 102.

15. *Ibid.*, table following p. 381.

16. Respectively, Stetson, *Histories of Brazil*, II, 131-148; and *Geografía y descripción universal*, pp. 287-289.

17. Marchant, *From Barter to Slavery*, p. 125.

18. I am greatly obliged to Michael D. Worth, a former doctoral candidate at the University of Florida, for pulling together for me scattered data on Portuguese immigration in an unpublished paper, "Brazil: Demographic Characteristics, 1534-1700."

19. *La población indígena y el mestizaje en América, 1492-1950*, 2 vols. (Buenos Aires: Editorial Nova, 1954), I, tables on pp. 88 and 102.

20. Marchant, *From Barter to Slavery*, p. 108.

21. *La población indígena*, I, table on p. 88.

22. As quoted in Magnus Mörner, *Race Mixture in the History of Latin America* (Boston: Little, Brown, 1967), p. 49.

23. I am indebted for the following analysis of the growth of royal government to two unpublished master's theses prepared under the direction of Professor Neill Macaulay and submitted in 1971 at the University of Florida: William S. Devine III, "Royal Government in Colonial Brazil: The Governors-General"; James B. Sivells, "The Hereditary Captaincies of the State of Brazil: Structure, Jurisdiction and Reversion to the Crown."

24. As quoted in Devine, "Royal Government," p. 29.

25. Schwartz, "Cities of Empire," p. 634; Sidney M. Greenfield, "Slavery and the Plantation in the New World: The Development and Diffusion of a Social Form," *JIAS*, 11:51 (1969).

26. This is one of the main themes in James Lang's fine synthesis of the colony's economic history, *Portuguese Brazil: The King's Plantation* (New York: Academic Press, 1979).

27. As quoted in J. B. Trend, *Portugal* (New York: Praeger, 1957), p. 145.

## CHAPTER 14. THE IMPERIAL CONTEXT: THE HISPANIC WORLD IN THE AGE OF THE HABSBURG KINGS

1. As quoted in Charles R. Boxer, *Four Centuries of Portuguese Expansion, 1415-1825: A Succinct Survey* (Berkeley: University of California Press, 1969), p. 45.

2. *Description of the Indies (c. 1620)*, trans. Charles Upson Clark (Washington, D.C.: Smithsonian Institution Press, 1968), p. 4.

3. As quoted in John H. Elliott, *Imperial Spain, 1469-1716* (New York: The New American Library, Mentor Books, 1966), p. 245.

4. For a summary of Spanish population trends in the seventeenth century, see Jaime Vicens Vives with the collaboration of Jorge Nadal Oller, *Manual de historia económica de España* (3rd ed.; Barcelona: Editorial Vicens Vives, 1964), trans. Frances M. López-Morillas as *An Economic History of Spain* (Princeton, N.J.: Princeton University Press, 1969), pp. 411-416 in the English edition.

5. *History of the Reign of Philip III* (London: 1783), p. 309, as quoted in John H. Elliott, "The Decline of Spain," in *Crisis in Europe, 1560-1660*, ed. Trevor Aston (New York: Basic Books, 1965), p. 193.

6. A good summary of the price history of pepper may be found in Fernand Braudel, *La Méditerranée et le Monde Méditerranéen à l'époque de Philippe II* (Paris: Librairie Armand Colin, 1966), trans. Siân Reynolds as *The Mediterranean and the Mediterranean World in the Age of Philip II*, 2 vols. (New York: Harper and Row, 1972), I, 543-560 in the English edition.

7. Stanley G. Payne, *A History of Spain and Portugal*, 2 vols. (Madison: University of Wisconsin Press, 1973), II, 400.

## CHAPTER 15. TERRITORIAL CHANGES IN THE HISPANIC NEW WORLD: CONTRACTIONS, EXPANSIONS, ADJUSTMENTS

1. In crediting the Dutch with opening the way for northern European colonization, I am following Engel Sluiter, "Dutch Maritime Power and the Colonial Status Quo, 1585-1647," *Pacific Historical Review*, 11:29-41 (1942).

2. The full Spanish titles and texts of the 1563 and 1573 ordinances may be found in *Colección de documentos inéditos relativos al descubrimiento, conquista y organización de las antiguas posesiones españoles de América y Oceanía*, 42 vols. (Madrid, 1864-84), VIII, 484-537, and XVI, 142-187, respectively.

3. As quoted in Enrique Florescano, "Colonización, ocupación del suelo y 'frontera' en el norte de Nueva España, 1521-1750," in Alvaro Jara and others, *Tierras nuevas: Expansión territorial y ocupación del suelo en América (siglos xvi-xix)* (Mexico: El Colegio de México, 1969), p. 56.

4. *Descripción de Nueva Galicia*, PEEHA, 24 (Seville, 1946), as quoted in François Chevalier, *La formation des grands domaines au Mexique: Terre et société aux xvi^e-xvii^e siècles* (Paris: Université de Paris, 1952), trans. Alvin Eustis as *Land and Society in Colonial Mexico: The Great Hacienda* (Berkeley: University of California Press, 1963), p. 8. The quotation is from the English edition.

5. The lure of the fabulous in the Portuguese penetration of the *sertão* is described in Sérgio Buarque de Holanda, *Visão do paraiso: Os motivos edênicos no descobrimento e colonização do Brasil* (2nd ed. rev.; São Paulo: Companhia Editora Nacional, 1969).

6. *The Bandeirantes: The Historical Role of the Brazilian Pathfinders*, ed. Richard M. Morse (New York: Alfred A. Knopf, Borzoi Books, 1965), p. 331.

7. Cassiano Ricardo, *La marcha para oeste*, 2 vols. (2nd ed.; Rio de Janeiro: José Olympio, 1942), I, 19-33, *passim*.

8. Mário Góngora, *Los grupos de conquistadores en Tierra Firme, 1509-1530: Fisonomía histórico-social de un tipo de conquista* (Santiago: Universidad de Chile, 1962), chap. 4.

9. André João Antonil, *Cultura e opulencia do Brasil* (Bahia: Livraría Progresso Editora, 1950), pp. 291-294.

10. For the following observations on the geopolitics of Brazilian expansion, I am especially indebted to Lewis A. Tambs, "Geopolitics of the Amazon," in *Man in the Amazon*, ed. Charles Wagley (Gainesville: The University Presses of Florida, 1974), pp. 45-87; and Arlene Kelly, "An Attempt at the Historiography of Boundary Settings and Disputes during the Colonial Period in Brazil," unpublished seminar paper, University of Florida, 1976.

11. *Rapôso Tavares e a formação territorial do Brasil* (Rio de Janeiro: Ministério da Educação e Cultura, 1958).

12. E. Bradford Burns, *A History of Brazil* (New York: Oxford University Press, 1970), p. 49.

13. As quoted in *Colección de documentos inéditos para la historia de Chile*, 2nd series, ed. José Toribio Medina, 6 vols. (Santiago: Fondo Histórico y Bibliográfico J. T. Medina, 1956-63), III, 268-269.

## CHAPTER 16. POST-CONQUEST POPULATIONS: COMPONENTS, NUMBERS, MOVEMENTS, DISTRIBUTION

1. First published in Madrid, 1574.

2. Howard F. Cline, "The *Relaciones Geográficas* of the Spanish Indies," *HAHR*, 44:341-374 (1964), provides a guide to surviving returns. The major published collection is Marcos Jiménez de la Espada, ed., *Relaciones geográficas de Indias* (Madrid: Tip. de M. G. Hernández, 1881-97), whose contents are mainly from the Viceroyalty of Peru.

3. Washington, D.C.: Smithsonian Institution, 1942.

4. Mexico: Bibliófilos Mexicanos, 1932.

5. "Patterns of Spanish Emigration to the Indies until 1600," *HAHR*, 56:580-604 (1976).

6. Huguette Chaunu and Pierre Chaunu, *Séville et l'Atlantique (1504-1650)*, 8 vols. in 11 parts (Paris: Librairie Armand Colin, 1955-59), VI, part 1.

7. Sherburne F. Cook and Woodrow Borah, "Racial Groups in the Mexican Population since 1519," in the same authors' *Essays in Population History*, 3 vols. (Berkeley: University of California Press, 1971-79), II, 180-269.

8. Magnus Mörner, "Spanish Migration to the New World Prior to 1800: A Report on the State of Research," in *First Images of America: The Impact of the New World on the Old*, ed. Fredi Chiappelli, co-eds. Michael J. B. Allen and Robert L. Benson, 2 vols. (Berkeley: University of California Press, 1976), II, especially pp. 766-767.

9. From the opening lines of *El Celoso Extremeño* [1613], one of the *Novelas ejemplares*, as quoted in Irving A. Leonard's review of Valentín de Pedro, *América en las letras españolas del siglo de oro* (Buenos Aires: Editorial Sudamericana, 1954), in *HAHR*, 35:514 (1955).

10. The seminal statement on this subject is Woodrow Borah, *New Spain's Century of Depression*, Ibero-Americana: 35 (Berkeley: University of California Press, 1951).

11. Nicolás Sánchez-Albornoz, *The Population of Latin America*, trans. W. A. R. Richardson (Berkeley: University of California Press, 1974), pp. 100-103.

12. The information cited is drawn mainly from *ibid.*, pp. 88-94. However, the figures for Peru are from Noble D. Cook, *Demographic Collapse: Indian Peru, 1520-1620* (Cambridge: Cambridge University Press, 1981), table 18, p. 94, and the statement on the general increase of the indigenous population in Central America from Miles Wortman, "Elites and Habsburg Administration: Adaptations to Economic Fluctuations in Seventeenth-Century Central America," paper presented at the Annual Meeting of the American Historical Association, 1980, p. 7. I am much obliged to the author for providing me with a copy.

13. *The Atlantic Slave Trade: A Census* (Madison: University of Wisconsin Press, 1969), table 34, p. 119.

14. *Population of Latin America*, p. 98.

15. Frederick P. Bowser, "The African in Colonial Spanish America: Reflections on Research Achievements and Priorities," *LARR*, 7(no. 1):91, n.40 (Spring 1972).

16. "Racial Groups in the Mexican Population since 1519," table 2.1B, pp. 197-198.

17. Charles R. Boxer, *Four Centuries of Portuguese Expansion, 1415-1825: A Succinct Survey* (Berkeley: University of California Press, 1969), p. 70.

18. As quoted in *ibid.*, pp. 69-70.

19. Frédéric Mauro, *Le Portugal et l'Atlantique au xvii^e siècle (1570-1670): Étude économique* (Paris: S.E.V.P.E.N., 1960), pp. 308-309, 331-348.

20. Alfredo Ellis Júnior, *Os primeiros troncos paulistas e o cruzamento euro-americano* (São Paulo: Companhia Editora Nacional, 1955), pp. 122-126.

21. *Formação e evolução étnica da Cidade do Salvador*, 2 vols. (Salvador: Prefeitura Municipal do Salvador, 1955-57), I, tables 2-7, pp. 77-89.

22. *Povoamento da Cidade do Salvador* (2nd ed. rev.; São Paulo: Companhia Editora Nacional, 1955), pp. 236-239.

23. As cited in Stuart B. Schwartz, "Luso-Spanish Relations in Hapsburg Brazil, 1580-1640," *TA*, 25:35 (1968).

24. These figures are my own estimates based on a collation of various sources. They have no statistical validity.

25. Maurício Goulart, *A escravidão africana no Brasil (das origines à extinção do tráfico)* (São Paulo: Livraría Martins, 1950), p. 106.

26. *The Atlantic Slave Trade*, table 33, p. 116; table 34, p. 119.

27. Professor Dobyns offered this opinion in a critique that he generously made of this chapter.

28. "Racial Groups in the Mexican Population since 1519," table 2.1B, pp. 197-198.

29. *Demographic Collapse*, table 18, p. 94.

30. "Racial Groups in the Mexican Population since 1519," table 2.1B, pp. 197-198.

31. "Urban Scales and Functions in Spanish America Toward the Year 1600: First Conclusions," *LARR*, 5(no. 3):66 (Fall 1970).

32. *Ibid.*, pp. 67-74. The authors' calculations of regional indices are not always accurate. In cases of error, I have recalculated them.

33. Nicolás Sánchez-Albornoz and José Luis Moreno, *La población de América Latina: Bosquejo histórico* (Buenos Aires: Editorial Paidos, 1968), p. 75.

34. Howard F. Cline, "Civil Congregations of the Indians in New Spain," *HAHR*, 29:336, table 3 (1949).

35. As quoted in Peter Marzahl, "Creoles and Government: The Cabildo of Popayán," *HAHR*, 54:639 (1974).

36. Borah, *New Spain's Century of Depression*, pp. 30-44; Murdo MacLeod, *Spanish Central America: A Socioeconomic History, 1520-1720* (Berkeley: University of California Press, 1973), chap. 16.

37. I have taken these figures from an unpublished collation and analysis of various sources prepared for me by Mr. Michael Worth, a former doctoral candidate at the University of Florida, entitled "Brazil: Demographic Characteristics, 1534-1700."

38. "The Social History of Colonial Spanish America: Evolution and Potential," *LARR*, 7(no. 1):20-21 (Spring 1972).

39. *Voyage aux regions equinoxiales du Nouveau Continent*, vol. IV (Paris: 1817), p. 64, as quoted in William L. Schurz, *This New World: The Civilization of Latin America* (New York: E. P. Dutton, 1964), pp. 7-8.

## CHAPTER 17. POST-CONQUEST ECONOMIES

1. The connection between *encomienda* and hacienda is still a disputed subject. Various aspects of the problem are examined in James Lockhart, "Encomienda and Hacienda: The Evolution of the Great Estates in the Spanish Indies," *HAHR*, 49:411-429 (1969); Robert G. Keith, "Encomienda, Hacienda and Corregimiento in Spanish America: A Structural Analysis," *HAHR*, 51:431-446 (1971); and Magnus Mörner, "The Spanish American Hacienda: A Survey of Recent Research and Debate," *HAHR*, 53:183-216 (1973).

2. Ralph Davis, *The Rise of the Atlantic Economies* (Ithaca, N.Y.: Cornell University Press, 1973), p. 165.

3. As quoted in Nicolás Sánchez-Albornoz, *The Population of Latin America*, trans. W. A. R. Richardson (Berkeley: University of California Press, 1974), p. 64.

4. As quoted in Angel Rosenblat, *La población indígena y el mestizaje en América, 1492-1950*, 2 vols. (Buenos Aires: Editorial Nova, 1954), I, 93.

5. Philip D. Curtin, *The Atlantic Slave Trade: A Census* (Madison: University of Wisconsin Press, 1969), table 5, p. 25.

6. *Descripción del Virreinato del Perú: Crónica inédita de comienzos del siglo xvii*, ed. Boleslao Lewin (Rosario, Arg.: Universidad Nacional del Litoral, 1958), p. 59, as quoted in John Lynch, *Spain under the Hapsburgs*, 2 vols. (New York: Oxford University Press, 1964-69), II, 214.

7. As quoted in Fernando Benítez, *Los primeros Mexicanos: La vida criolla en el siglo xvi* (Mexico: Ediciones ERA, 1962), trans. Joan MacLean as *The Century after Cortés* (Chicago: University of Chicago Press, 1965), p. 58. The quotation is from the English edition.

8. I have found no useful data on the volume and value of wine and olive production in the Indies.

9. The most comprehensive set of indicators of the volume and value of these products is the export series in Huguette Chaunu and Pierre Chaunu, *Séville et l'Atlantique*, 8 vols. in 11 parts (Paris: Librairie Armand Colin, 1955-59), VI, part 2, pp. 981-1035.

10. Some clues to the volume and value of Antillean sugar production can be found in the export figures given in Frank Moya Pons, *Historia colonial de Santo Domingo* (Santiago: Dom. Rep.: Universidad Católica Madre y Maestra, 1974), chap. 4; and Julio Le Riverend Brusone, *Historia económica de Cuba* (2nd ed.; Havana: Editorial Nacional de Cuba, 1965), pp. 75-76, 110-111. Ward Barrett, *The Sugar Hacienda of the Marqueses del Valle* (Minneapolis: University of Minnesota Press, 1970), *passim*, and especially pp. 127 ff., has some good local production figures for Mexico.

11. The figures are from Raymond L. Lee, "Cochineal Production and Trade in New Spain to 1600," *TA*, 4:462 (1947-48), and the same author's "American Cochineal in European Commerce, 1526-1625," *The Journal of Modern History*, 23:206 (1951).

12. Chaunu and Chaunu, *Séville et l'Atlantique*, VI, part 2, p. 980.

13. For Venezuela see the export data for the years 1620-1700, in Eduardo Arcila Farías, *Economía colonial de Venezuela* (Mexico: Fondo de Cultura Económica, 1946), pp. 99-101.

14. Partial data on Central American cacao production can be found in Murdo J. MacLeod, *Spanish Central America: A Socioeconomic History, 1520-1720* (Berkeley: University of California Press, 1973), chaps. 5, 12, and 18. On Venezuela see the export figures for the period 1620-1700 in Arcila Farías, *Economía colonial*, pp. 95-98. Dora León Borja and Adam Szaszdi Nagy, "El comercio de cacao de Guayaquil," *RHA*, nos. 57-58:1-50 (1964), has some information on Ecuadorian production.

15. Very few data on the volume and value of silk, cotton, coca and maté production in the Indies exist except for particular places and periods. On Venezuelan tobacco see export figures for 1620-1700 in Arcila Farías, *Economía colonial*, pp. 99-101. Woodrow Borah, *Silk Raising in Colonial Mexico*, Ibero-Americana: 20 (Berkeley: University of California Press, 1943), contains some estimates of Mexican silk production toward the end of the sixteenth century.

16. Very few statistical data are available on American shipbuilding.

17. Little is known about the volume and value of American textile production.

18. So termed by John L. Phelan, *The Kingdom of Quito in the Seventeenth Century: Bureaucratic Politics in the Spanish Empire* (Madison: University of Wisconsin Press, 1967), p. 67.

19. On this point see Richard E. Greenleaf, "The Obraje in the Late Mexican Colony," *TA*, 23:228-232 (1967).

20. David A. Brading and Harry C. Cross, "Colonial Silver Mining: Mexico and Peru," *HAHR*, 52:570 (1972).

21. *Ibid.*, pp. 567-570.

22. Calculated from Earl J. Hamilton, *American Treasure and the Price Revolution in Spain, 1501-1650* (Cambridge, Mass.: Harvard University Press, 1934), table 3, p. 42. Statistical data on gold production in New Granada are presented in Germán Colmenares, *Historia económica y social de Colombia, 1537-1719* (2nd ed.; Medellín, Col.: Editorial La Carreta), pp. 306-330.

23. Chaunu and Chaunu, *Séville et l'Atlantique*, VI, part 2, pp. 981-1035, and VIII, part 3. A convenient synthesis of the Chaunu data may be found in John Lynch, *Spain under the Habsburgs*, II, 184-193.

24. As quoted in Hamilton, *American Treasure*, p. 34.

25. The fullest collection of statistical data on Spanish trans-Pacific commerce is Pierre Chaunu, *Les Philippines et le Pacifique des Ibériques (xvi$^e$, xvii$^e$, xviii$^e$ siècles)* (Paris: S.E.V.P.E.N., 1960).

26. Lewis Hanke, *The Imperial City of Potosí: An Unwritten Chapter in the History of Spanish America* (The Hague: Nijhoff, 1956), pp. 1, 3.

27. Meaningful statistics for the Mexican-Peruvian trade are lacking. Data on the Mexican-Venezuelan trade are contained in Eduardo Arcila Farías, *Comercio entre Venezuela y México en los siglos xvi y xvii* (Mexico: El Colegio de México, 1950).

28. Joseph de Veitia Linage, *Norte de la Contratación de las Indias Occidentales* (Seville, 1672). The quote is from the edition published in Buenos Aires (Talleres Gráficos Bartolomé U. Chiesino, 1945), pp. 514-515 (*lib.* II, *cap.* iv, *núm.* 9).

29. Lynch, *Spain under the Habsburgs*, II, 179.

30. Guillermo Céspedes, *Latin America: The Early Years* (New York: Alfred A. Knopf, 1974), p. 106.

31. Lynch, *Spain under the Habsburgs*, II, 192.

32. Jaime Vicens Vives in collaboration with Jorge Nadal Oller, *An Economic History of Spain*, trans. Frances M. López-Morillas (Princeton, N.J.: Princeton University Press, 1969), p. 433.

33. Woodrow Borah, *New Spain's Century of Depression*, Ibero-Americana: 35 (Berkeley: University of California Press, 1951).

34. *Land and Society in Colonial Mexico: The Great Hacienda*, trans. Alvin Eustis (Berkeley: University of California Press, 1963), *passim*, and especially pp. 39, 41, 178-180, 291-292, 310.

35. *Séville et l'Atlantique*, VIII, part 3, pp. 1531ff.

36. *Spanish Central America*, part 3.

37. Lynch, *Spain under the Habsburgs*, II, 219-224; Brading and Cross. "Colonial Silver Mining," pp. 574-575.

38. Moya Pons, *Historia colonial de Santo Domingo*, chaps. 4, 10.

39. Colmenares, *Historia económica y social de Colombia*, chap. 6.

40. *Silver Mining and Society in Colonial Mexico: Zacatecas, 1546-1700* (Cambridge: Cambridge University Press, 1971), pp. 225, 234-235. On the problem of mercury supply see also M. F. Lang, "New Spain's Mining Depression and the Supply of Quicksilver from Peru," *HAHR*, 48:632-641 (1968).

41. "Colonial Silver Mining," p. 574.

42. Recent statements on this subject are Richard Boyer, "Mexico in the Seventeenth Century: Transition of a Colonial Society," *HAHR*, 57:461 (1977), and Miles Wortman, "Elites and Habsburg Administration: Adaptations to Economic Fluctuations in Seventeenth-Century Central America," paper presented at the Annual Meeting of the American Historical Association, 1980, pp. 4, 7-8. I am much obliged to Professor Wortman for giving me a copy of his paper.

43. *Spain under the Habsburgs*, II, 193, 195. This thesis is also expounded in Bakewell, *Silver Mining and Society*, chap. 9.

44. Boyer, "Mexico in the Seventeenth Century," p. 476; Chevalier, *Land and Society*, p. 79.

45. "Mexico in the Seventeenth Century," p. 474.

46. "Elites and Habsburg Administration," p. 3.

47. Kenneth J. Andrien, "Bureaucratic Responses to the Fiscal Crisis of Seventeenth Century Peru," paper presented at the Annual Meeting of the American Historical Association, 1980, p. 3. I am very grateful to the author for sending me a copy of his paper.

48. Arcila Farías, *Comercio entre México y Venezuela*, pp. 106, 134-135.

49. "Colonial Silver Mining," p. 576.

50. *Spain under the Habsburgs*, II, 200.

51. "El siglo xvii en el reino de Guatemala a través de su cronista Don Francisco Antonio Fuentes y Guzmán," *AEA*, 28:163 (1971).

52. Pohl, "Algunas consideraciones sobre el desarrollo de la industria hispanoamericana — especialmente la textil — durante el siglo xvii," *AEA*, 28:472 (1971); Phelan, *The Kingdom of Quito*, chap. 4, passim.

53. "Mexico in the Seventeenth Century," p. 473.

54. Lawrence Clayton, "Trade and Navigation in the Seventeenth-Century Viceroyalty of Peru," *Journal of Latin American Studies*, 7:17 (1975).

55. Boyer, "Mexico in the Seventeenth Century," pp. 455-456; Wortman, "Elites and Habsburg Administration," pp. 3-5; and William B. Taylor, "Landed Society in New Spain: A View from the South," *HAHR*, 54:394 (1974).

56. Carlos Sempat Assadourian, "Sobre un elemento de la economía colonial: Producción y circulación de mercancías en el interior de un conjunto regional," *Revista Latinoamericana de Estudios Urbano Regionales* (*EURE*), 3(no. 8):135-181 (December 1973).

57. "Merchants in Seventeenth-Century Mexico City: A Preliminary Portrait," *HAHR*, 57:490-492 (1977). Clayton, "Trade and Navigation," pp. 1-21, describes the structure of the Mexico-Peru trade.

58. "The Seventeenth-Century Crisis in New Spain: Myth or Reality?" *Past and Present*, no. 90:116-135 (February 1981).

59. *Ibid.*, p. 134.

60. *Ibid.*, pp. 120, 123.

61. The following works touch upon regional economic integration: Hoberman, "Merchants in Seventeenth-Century Mexico City"; Marcelo Carmagnani, *Les mécanismes de la vie économique dans une société coloniale: Le Chile, 1680-1830* (Paris: École Pratique des Hautes Études, 1973); Analola Borges, "La estructura socioeconómica de la gobernación de Venezuela (1690–1700), *AEA*, 28:101-120 (1971); and John V. Lombardi, "The Rise of Caracas as a Primate City," in *Social Fabric and Spatial Structure in Colonial Latin America*, ed. David J. Robinson (Ann Arbor, Mich.: University Microfilms, 1979), pp. 433-443.

62. I know of no full and thorough study of the Brazilian sugar industry in the sixteenth and seventeenth centuries. Observations and data on its organization and output

502 NOTES TO PP. 382-88

are scattered through various published sources and are conflicting. The best attempt at synthesis and reconciliation I have found is David Denslow, "The First Brazilian Sugar Cycle: Growth and Maturity" an unpublished paper written at the University of Florida, which the author graciously permitted me to use. Kit Sims Taylor, "The Economics of Sugar and Slavery in Northeastern Brazil," *Agricultural History*, 44:267-280 (1970) is also useful, especially for information on the organization of production.

63. This is a very rough estimate based on figures in Maurício Goulart, *A escravidão africana no Brasil: Das origens à extinção do tráfico* (3rd ed. rev.; São Paulo: Editôra Alfa-Omega, 1975), Goulart's figures are on the conservative side.

64. Denslow, "The First Brazilian Sugar Cycle," *passim*; and Taylor, "The Economics of Sugar and Slavery," *passim*.

65. "Descripción de la Provincia del Brasil," in Frédéric Mauro, *Le Brésil au xvii<sup>e</sup> siècle: Documents inédits relatifs a l'Atlantique Portugais* (Coimbra, Portugal: n.p., 1961), pp. 170-182, cited in Denslow, "The First Brazilian Sugar Cycle," p. 10.

66. Nicolaas W. Posthumus, *Inquiry into the History of Prices in Holland* (Leiden: E. J. Brill, 1946), pp. 122-123.

67. The decline of the Brazilian industry is analyzed in Denslow, "The First Brazilian Sugar Cycle"; Mathew Edel, "The Brazilian Sugar Cycle of the 17th Century and the Rise of West Indian Competition," *Caribbean Studies*, 9:24-44 (1969); and Alice P. Canabrava, "A fôrça motriz: Um problema da técnica da industria do açucar colonial (a solução antilhana e a brasileira)," in *Annais do Primero Congresso de História da Bahía*, vol. IV (Salvador, 1950), pp. 351-387.

68. I have found no statistically reliable data on agricultural and pastoral production other than for sugar. Some partial figures can be found in Roberto C. Simonsen, *História económica do Brasil (1500/1820)* (4th ed.; São Paulo: Companhia Editôra Nacional, 1962). A good overview of Brazil's agrarian economy right after the turn of the seventeenth century can be found in André João Antonil (pseudo. João Antonio Andreoni), *Cultura y opulência do Brasil por sus drogas y minas* (Lisbon, 1711).

69. Antonio H. de Oliveira Marques, *History of Portugal*, 2 vols (New York: Columbia University Press, 1972), I, 362-363.

70. Céspedes, *Latin America*, p. 34; Vitorino Magalhães Godinho, "Portugal and Her Empire," in *The Ascendancy of France, 1648-88*, ed. F. L. Carsten, vol. 5 of *The New Cambridge Modern History* (Cambridge: Cambridge University Press, 1961), p. 385.

71. Magalhães Godinho, "Portugal and Her Empire," p. 385.

72. The best available data on Brazil's Atlantic trade are in Frédéric Mauro, *Le Portugal et l'Atlantique aux xvii<sup>e</sup> siècle (1570-1670). Étude économique* (Paris: S.E.V.P.E.N., 1960).

73. Two good surveys of dependency theory are C. Richard Bath and Dilmus D. James, "Dependency Analysis of Latin America," *LARR*, 11(no. 3):3-54 (1976); and Ronald H. Chilcote and Joel C. Edelstein, eds., *Latin America: The Struggle with Dependency and Beyond* (Cambridge, Mass.: Schenkman, 1974), pp. 1-87.

74. New York: Academic Press, 1974, 1980.

75. New York: Oxford University Press, 1970.

76. Rev. ed.; New York: Modern Reader Paperbacks, 1969, especially "Capitalist Development of Underdevelopment in Chile," pp. 1-120. This work was first published in 1967 (New York: Monthly Review Press).

77. Frank's criticism of the concept of colonial "feudalism" is aimed in part at the influential work of the Chilean historian Anibal Pinto Santa Cruz, *Chile: Un caso de desarrollo frustrado* (Santiago: Editorial Universitaria, 1962), which maintained that Chile had a closed subsistence economy until the nineteenth century.

78. Examples of such criticisms are Carlos Sempat Assadourian and others, "Modos de producción en América Latina," *Cuadernos de Pasado y Presente* (Córdoba, Arg.), no. 40:1-242 (1967); and Ernesto Laclau, *Politics and Ideology in Marxist Theory: Capitalism-Facism-Populism* (London: Verso Editions, 1979), especially chap. 1, "Feudalism and Capitalism in Latin America."

79. Among the rare exceptions to this criticism are Bernard Slicher van Bath, "Economic Diversification in Spanish America Around 1600: Centres Intermediate Zones and Peripheries," *JGSW*, 16:53-95 (1979), an empirical demonstration of the hierarchical order of economic power posited by dependency theorists; and Carlos Sempat Assadourian, "Sobre un elemento de la economía colonial: Producción y circulación de mercancías en el interior de un conjunto regional," *Revista Latinoamericana de Estudios Urbano Regionales (EURE)*, 3(no. 8):135-181 (December 1973), which is a fine analysis of the structure of the economy of the Viceroyalty of Peru in the seventeenth century.

## CHAPTER 18. AMERICAN SOCIETIES AND AMERICAN IDENTITIES

1. In the eighteenth century, the Spaniards commonly called the major racial groupings *castas* (castes), and the social order they formed has been described as a society or *régimen* of *castas*. (The *régimen* of *castas* is described in Nicolás León, *Las castas del México colonial o Nueva España, noticias etno-antropológicas* [Mexico: Talleres Gráficos del Museo Nacional de Arqueología, Historia y Etnografía, 1924], and more recently in Magnus Mörner, *Race Mixture in the History of Latin America* [Boston: Little, Brown, 1967], chap. 5). Casta in both Spanish and Portuguese originally meant simply a population of people or animals possessing common inherited traits. The Portuguese subsequently used the term to describe the social groups of Hindu India, and apparently the Spaniards in America adopted this usage. As will be shown later in this chapter, however, the *casta* in the Indies did not fit even the minimum modern definition of the word caste, that is, a hierarchally ordered endogamous social group into which people are born and from which they cannot escape. The characteristics of a caste society are analyzed in Roland Mousnier, *Les hiérarchies sociales de 1450 à nos jours* (Paris: Presses Universitaires de France, 1969), trans. Peter Evans as *Social Hierarchies, 1450 to the Present*, ed. Margaret Clarke (New York: Schocken Books, 1973), pp. 29-33.

2. This paragraph is based on Juan A. Villarmarín, "The Concept of Nobility in the Social Stratification of Santa Fe de Bogotá," an unpublished paper graciously given to me by the author. It is an exceptionally good piece of social analysis.

3. Guillermo Lohmann Villena, *Los americanos en las órdenes nobiliarias (1529-1900)*, 2 vols. (Madrid: C.S.I.C., 1947).

4. For contemporary Spanish perceptions of the Indians' physical traits consult Bernabé Cobo de Peralta, *Historia del Nuevo Mundo*, Biblioteca de Autores Españoles, vol. 91 (Madrid: Ediciones Atlas, 1964), pp. 16-20 (*cap.* iv). (Written between 1642 and 1653.)

5. Gonzalo Aguirre Beltrán, *La población negra de México, 1519-1810: Estudio etnohistórico* (Mexico: Ediciones Fuentes Cultural, 1946), p. 266.

6. *Política indiana*, Biblioteca de Autores Españoles, vols. 252-256, 5 vols. (Madrid: Ediciones Atlas, 1972), vol. 252, pp. 445-446 (*lib.* II, *cap.* 30, *núm.* 21).

7. Spanish perceptions of the somatic qualities of blacks and mixed bloods are described in Aguirre Beltrán, *La población negra de México*, especially chaps. 9, 14.

8. As quoted in Juan Beneyto Pérez, *Historia social de España y de Hispanoamérica* (Madrid: Aguilar, 1961), p. 215.

9. As quoted in David A. Brading, *Miners and Merchants in Bourbon Mexico, 1763–1810* (Cambridge: Cambridge University Press, 1971), p. 21.

10. As quoted in Fernando Benítez, *Los primeros Mexicanos: La vida criolla en el siglo xvi* (Mexico: Ediciones ERA, 1962), trans. Joan MacLean as *The Century after Cortés* (Chicago: University of Chicago Press, 1965). The quotation is from the English edition, p. 155.

11. As quoted in *ibid.*, p. 243.

12. Lima, 1596. The citation is from the edition published in Santiago (Imprenta Universitaria, 1917), pp. 26-27.

13. *Historia argentina del descubrimiento, población y conquista de las provincias del Rio de la Plata: Escrita en el año de 1612* (Buenos Aires: Espasa-Calpe, 1945), p. 21.

14. See, for example, Bernardo de Balbuena, *Grandeza mexicana* (Mexico, 1604), and the rare Diego Ojeda Gallinato, *Grandezas de Lima* (Lima, n.d.).

15. This theme is apparent in Francisco Antonio de Fuentes y Guzmán (1643 – c. 1699), *Recordación florida: Discurso historial y demonstración natural, material, militar y política del reyno de Guatemala*, 3 vols. (Guatemala: Sociedad de Geografía e Historia de Guatemala, 1932–33).

16. Their works are identified and discussed in Francisco Esteve Barba, *Historiografía indiana* (Madrid: Editorial Gredos, 1964), pp. 211-237, 282-288, 470-481. For Mesoamerica alone see the more analytical articles by Charles Gibson in *Handbook of Middle American Indians*, XV, 311-400.

17. John T. Reid, "Folkloric Symbols of Nationhood in Guatemala," *Southern Folklore Quarterly*, 28:135-137 (1974).

18. Benítez, *The Century after Cortés*, p. 90.

19. *Hvei Tlamahviçoltica Omonexiti in ilhvicac tlatoca Cihvapilli Santa Maria Totloconantzin Gvadalvpe in nican hvei altepe-nahvac Mexico itocayocan Tepeyayac (Gran viñeta de N.S. de Guadalupe)* (Mexico, 1649).

20. The theme of the Mexicanization of the Virgin is developed most fully in Jacques la Faye, *Quetzalcóatl et Guadalupe: La formation de la conscience nationale au Mexique, 1531–1813* (Paris: Editions Gallimard, 1974), trans. Benjamin Keen as *Quetzalcóatl and Guadalupe: The Formation of Mexican National Consciousness, 1531–1813* (Chicago: University of Chicago Press, 1976).

21. This episode is described in Luis González Obregón, *D. Guillén de Lampart, La Inquisición y la independencia en el siglo xvii* (Paris: Librería de la V^da de C. Bouret, 1908).

22. The only systematic study of clientage in the colonial Spanish Indies I know of is Stephanie Blank, "Patrons, Clients, and Kin in Seventeenth-Century Caracas: A Methodological Essay in Colonial Spanish American Social History," *HAHR*, 54:260-283 (1974).

23. On this matter I concur with the skepticism about Luso-Brazilian racial tolerance expressed in Charles R. Boxer, *Race Relations in the Portuguese Colonial Empire, 1415–1825* (Oxford: Oxford University Press, 1963). His views are supported by a wealth of documentation.

24. Francis A. Dutra, "Blacks and the Search for Rewards and Status in Seventeenth-Century Brazil," in *Revolution in the Americas, Proceedings of the Pacific Coast Council on Latin American Studies*, vol. VI (1977-79), pp. 25-35. The quotation is from p. 29.

25. Examples are Ambrósio Fernandes Brandão, *Diálagos das grandezas do Brasil* (Dialogues on the Grand Resources of Brazil), written in 1618 but not published until the nineteenth century; and Frei André João Antonil (pseudo. for João Antonio Andreoni [1650-1716?]), *Cultura e Opulência do Brasil* (Culture and Opulence of Brazil) (Lisbon, 1711).

26. The importance of African confraternities is discussed in A. J. R. Russell-Wood, "Black and Mulatto Brotherhoods in Colonial Brazil: A Study in Collective Behavior," *HAHR*, 54:567-602 (1974); and Roger Bastide, *Les amériques noires: Les civilisations africaines dans le Nouveau Monde* (Paris: Payot, 1967), trans. Peter Green as *African Civilizations in the New World* (New York: Harper and Row, 1971), *passim*.

27. The case for relative Hispanic tolerance is based on two principal arguments. One is that, in contrast to northern Europeans, the Hispanic peoples had become accustomed to both nonintimate and intimate associations with a darker-skinned people—the Moors—long before their overseas expansion began. This proposition is plausible but has not been demonstrated empirically. The other argument is that black slavery was less harsh and degrading and manumission much easier and more common in the Hispanic colonies than in those of the northern European peoples, especially the English. The difference owed to the relatively humane provisions and precepts of Hispanic law and the Roman Catholic religion. As a result, slaves in Spanish and Portuguese America were not regarded with the same contempt as they were in other parts of the New World and after manumission found readier acceptance in the general society. A number of studies of comparative slavery in the Americas cast serious doubt on this proposition. However, disputes over this issue seem to have abated, and in any event are peripheral to the theme of this book. Those who wish to inquire into them may begin by consulting John V. Lombardi, "Comparative Slave Systems in the Americas: A Critical Review," in *New Approaches to Latin American History*, ed. Richard Graham and Peter H. Smith (Austin: University of Texas Press, 1974), pp. 156-174.

28. The argument that racism was a direct product of slavery is developed in Eric Williams, *Capitalism and Slavery* (Chapel Hill: University of North Carolina Press, 1944); Stanley Elkins, *Slavery: A Problem in American Institutional and Intellectual Life* (Chicago: University of Chicago Press, 1959); and Marvin Harris, *Patterns of Race in the Americas* (New York: Walker and Company, 1964).

29. *Estructura social de la colonia: Ensayo de historia comparada de América Latina* (Buenos Aires: Librería "El Ateneo" Editorial, 1952), pp. 53-54.

30. *El problema racial en la conquista de América y el mestizaje* (Santiago: Editora Austral, 1963).

31. Eugene Genovese, *The World the Slaveholders Made: Two Essays in Interpretation* (New York: Pantheon Books, 1969), pp. ix, 3-21, 105, 113; Stavenhagen, *Las clases sociales en las sociedades agrarias* (Mexico: Siglo Vientiuno Editores, 1969), trans. Judy Adler Hellman as *Social Classes in Agrarian Societies* (Garden City, N.Y.: Anchor/Doubleday, Anchor Books, 1975), p. 33. See also pp. 115-116.

32. This view is examined in Franklin Knight, *The African Dimension in Latin American Societies* (New York: Macmillan, 1974), pp. 52-55; David B. Davis, *The Problem of Slavery in Western Cultures* (Ithaca, N.Y.: Cornell University Press, 1966), pp. 281-282; and Edward Shils, "Color, the Universal Intellectual Community, and the Afro-Asian Intellectual," in *Color and Race*, ed. John Hope Franklin (Boston: Houghton Mifflin, 1968), especially pp. 3-4.

33. Winthrop Jordan, *White over Black: American Attitudes toward the Negro, 1550-1812* (Chapel Hill: University of North Carolina Press, 1969), pp. 5-7, 17-19.

34. *Caribbean Race Relations: A Study in Two Variants* (Oxford: Oxford University Press, 1967). Hoetink's theories are developed further in his *Slavery and Race Relations in the Americas: Comparative Notes on Their Nature and Nexus* (New York: Harper and Row, 1973).

35. Hoetink, *Caribbean Race Relations*, p. 21-23.

36. *Ibid.*, p. 120.

37. "The History of Race Relations in Latin America: Some Comments on the State of Research," *LARR*, 1(no. 3):25 (Summer 1966).

## CHAPTER 19. IMPERIAL SYSTEMS

1. The several types of audiencias are discussed in chapter 9, pp. 190-91.

2. Solórzano expounds his ideas in *Política indiana*, Biblioteca de Autores Españoles, vols. 252-256 (Madrid: Ediciones Atlas, 1972), vol. 252, pp. 107-116 (*lib.* I, *cap.* xi).

3. The influence of strife between seculars and regulars on the establishment of the tribunal in Mexico is brought out in Richard E. Greenleaf, *The Mexican Inquisition of the Sixteenth Century* (Albuquerque: University of New Mexico Press, 1970), p. 152.

4. Roberto Oñat and Carlos Roa, *Régimen legal del ejército en el Reino de Chile: Notas para su estudio* (Santiago: Universidad Católica de Chile, 1953), pp. 158-163.

5. Pierre Duviols makes an interesting comparative observation about Spanish apprehensions. The failure of the *moriscos* of Spain to convert to Christianity and their treacherous associations with the North African Moors induced the crown to expel them in 1609-13. In Peru, the persistence of paganism among the Indians and the fear that they might ally themselves with foreign Protestants created a comparable situation. But, because it was patently impossible to expel the indigenes, civil and ecclesiastical officials launched in 1609-10 a massive campaign to extirpate idolatry among them. ("La represión del paganismo andino y la expulsión de los moriscos," *AEA*, 28:201-207 [1971].)

6. The best study of the evolution of Spanish policy for the defense of the Indies in the sixteenth century is Paul E. Hoffman, *The Spanish Crown and the Defense of the Caribbean, 1535-1585* (Baton Rouge: Louisiana State University Press, 1980).

7. *Recopilación de leyes de los reynos de las Indias*, 4 vols. (Madrid: 1681), II, 26 (*lib.* III, *tít.* iv, *ley* 19).

8. Such a reservation is suggested in "Consulta del Consejo de las Indias sobre la milicia que el virrey ha introducido en la ciudad de Lima," Madrid, September 29, 1591, in Richard Konetzke, ed., *Colección de documentos para la historia de la formación social de Hispanoamérica, 1493-1810*, 3 vols. in 5 (Madrid: C.S.I.C., 1953-58), I, 612-614.

9. John TePaske in collaboration with José and Mari Luz Hernández Paloma, *La Real Hacienda de Nueva España: La Real Caja de México (1576-1816)* (Mexico: Instituto Nacional de Antropología e Historia, 1976), *passim*.

10. *Ibid.*

11. *De rege et regis institutione* (Toledo, 1599), *lib.* I, *cap.* vi.

12. Juan de Ovando, "Libro de gobernación espiritual" (1571), in Victor M. Maurtúa, *Antecedentes de la Recopilación de Indias* (Madrid: Imprenta de B. Rodríguez, 1906), 21-181; Solórzano, *Política indiana*, I, 87-129 (*lib.* I, *caps.* ix-xii).

13. *Política indiana*, I, 393-394 (*lib.* III, *cap.* 32, *núm.* 23); II, 299-301 (*lib.* IV, *cap.* xix, *núms.* 31, 37); III, 260 (*lib.* V, *cap.* xvi, *núm.* 12). Solóranzo's reflections on these points are ably summarized and analyzed in Mario Góngora, *Studies in the Colonial History of Spanish America* (Cambridge: Cambridge University Press, 1975), pp. 79-82.

14. The number of *regimentos* issued by the crown is uncertain. There were definitely three: those given to Tomé de Sousa (1548), Manuel Teles Barreto (1583), and Roque da Costa Barreto (1677). Another was prepared for Francisco Geraldes (1588), but it did not go into effect, because the appointee never took office. It is possible that still another was given to Duarte da Costa (1553), but the evidence is not conclusive. In addition three documents called *regimentos* were issued in 1621, 1638, and 1642, but these may have been intended as ad hoc rather than as standing instructions. The historiography of the

problem is discussed in William S. Devine, "Royal Government in Colonial Brazil: The Governors General" (M.A. thesis, University of Florida, 1971), pp. 66-69.

15. I am obliged to Professor Stuart B. Schwartz for these explanations.

16. I offer this as a proposition based on strong impressions gained from contemporary and modern sources. Demonstration will require more research.

17. As quoted in Agustín Zapata Gollán, *Caminos de América* (Santa Fe, Arg.: Ministerio de Instrucción Pública y Fomento, 1940), pp. 72-73.

18. Lesley Byrd Simpson, "Mexico's Forgotten Century," *Pacific Historical Review*, 22:117 (1953).

19. Pedro Calmon, *História social do Brasil*, 3 vols. (2nd ed.; São Paulo: Companhia Editôra Nacional, 1937-39), I, 240.

20. As quoted in Richard Konetzke, "Estado y sociedad en la Indias," *EA* 3(no. 8):58 (January 1951).

21. The alliance as it existed in the Spanish Italian possessions is described in H. G. Koenigsburger, *The Practice of Empire* (Ithaca, N.Y.: Cornell University Press, 1951), pp. 50-51.

22. The best-developed exposition of the "brokerage" function is Stuart B. Schwartz, *Sovereignty and Society in Colonial Brazil: The High Court of Bahia and Its Judges, 1609-1751* (Berkeley: University of California Press, 1973).

23. The attitude of the nobility in these instances is discussed in Joseph Pérez, *La révolution des "Comunidades" de Castille, 1520-21* (Bordeaux: Institut d'Études Ibériques et Ibéro-américaines de l'Université de Bordeaux, 1970); Gordon Griffiths, "The Revolutionary Character of the Revolt of the Netherlands," *Comparative Studes in Society and History*, 2:452-472 (1960); and John H. Elliott, *The Revolt of the Catalans: A Study in the Decline of Spain (1598-1640)* (New York: Cambridge University Press, 1963).

## CHAPTER 20. EPILOGUE: EUROPEAN REACTIONS TO HISPANIC EXPANSION IN AMERICA

1. The term is borrowed from Alfred W. Crosby, Jr., *The Columbian Exchange: Biological and Cultural Consequences of 1492* (Westport, Conn.: Greenwood Press, 1972).

2. Probably the best of this class is Pedro Cieza de León, *Parte primera de la crónica del Perú* (Seville, 1553).

3. The most systematic works in this class are Bernardino de Sahagún, *Historia general de las cosas de Nueva España* (Mexico; 1829-30, 1840); and Diego Durán *Historia de las Indias de Nueva España y islas de Tierra Firme* (Mexico, 1867 80).

4. The first of this category was Gonzalo Fernández de Oviedo y Valdés, *Historia general y natural de las Indias*, of which the first nineteen books were published in Seville in 1535 and the twentieth in Valladolid in 1557. The best is José de Acosta, *Historia natural y moral de las Indias* (Seville, 1590).

5. London, 1596. Probably the best of the early histories of Brazil is Gabriel Soares de Souza, *Tratado descriptivo do Brasil en 1587* (Rio de Janeiro, 1851). The chief French accounts of Brazil are André Thevet, *Les singvlaritez de la France Antarctiqve avtrement nommée Amerique* (Paris, 1557); and the more reliable Jean de Léry, *Histoire d'un voyage fait en la terre du Bresil autrement dite Amerique* (La Rochelle, 1578).

6. As quoted in John S. Elliott, "Renaissance Europe and America: A Blunted Impact?" in *First Images of America: The Impact of the New World on the Old*, ed. Fredi Chiappelli, coed. Michael J. B. Allen and Robert L. Benson, 2 vols. (Berkeley: University of California Press, 1976), I, 14.

7. Hildegard B. Johnson, "New Geographical Horizons: Concepts," in *First Images of America*, II, 616.

8. *Narrative of Some Things of New Spain and of the Great City of Temistitán*, (New York, 1917), p. 15.

9. *Historia general y moral de las Indias* (Mexico City and Buenos Aires: Fondo de Cultura Económica, 1962), p. 133 (*lib*. III, *cap*. 24).

10. *Ibid*., p. 122 (*lib*. III, *cap*. 18).

11. "Crops and Livestock," in *The Economy of Expanding Europe in the 16th and 17th Centuries*, vol. IV of *The Cambridge Economic History of Europe*, ed. E. E. Rich and C. H. Wilson (Cambridge: Cambridge University Press, 1967), p. 287.

12. Joseph Ewan, "The Columbian Discoveries and the Growth of Botanical Ideas with Special Reference to the Sixteenth Century," in *First Images of America*, II, 807-808.

13. This opinion is expressed in Jonathan D. Sauer, "Changing Perception and Exploitation of New World Plants in Europe, 1492–1800," in *First Images of America*, II, 823.

14. This opinion is offered in Charles H. Talbot, "America and the European Drug Trade," in *First Images of America*, II, 841.

15. Bodin's theories are discussed in Margaret T. Hodgen, *Early Anthropology in the Sixteenth and Seventeenth Centuries* (Philadelphia: University of Pennsylvania Press, 1964), p. 209, and *passim*.

16. Las Casas's opinions on the matter run through his writings and especially his *Historia apologética de las Indias* (Madrid, 1867).

17. Oviedo's opinions about the Indians are scattered through his *Historial general y natural de las Indias*.

18. *The English Works of Thomas Hobbes of Malmsbury, now first Collected and ed. by Sir William Molesworth*, 11 vols. (London: J. Bohn, 1839–45), III, 112-113.

19. *Historia general de las cosas de Nueva España*, *passim*.

20. As interpreted in Gilbert Chinard, *L'exotisme américain dans la litérature française au xvi^e siècle* (Paris: Hachette, 1911), pp. 125-148.

21. *Des cannibales* as analyzed in Aldo Scaglione "A Note on Montaigne's *Des cannibales* and the Humanistic Tradition," in *First Images of America*, II, 63-70. See also Hodgen, *Early Anthropology*, pp. 191-194, and *passim*.

22. The opinions expressed above about the effect of Hispanic expansion on race relations are my own.

23. As quoted in Immanuel Wallerstein, *The Moden World-System, Vol. I: Capitalist Agriculture and the Origins of the European World-Economy in the Sixteenth Century* (New York: Academic Press, 1974), p. xv.

24. Huguette Chaunu and Pierre Chaunu, *Séville et l'Atlantique (1504–1650)*, 8 vols. in 11 parts (Paris: Librairie Armand Colin, 1955–59); Earl J. Hamilton, *American Treasure and the Price Revolution in Spain, 1501–1650* (Cambridge, Mass.: Harvard University Press, 1934).

25. Hamilton, *American Treasure*, p. 34.

26. This opinion is expressed categorically in Celso Furtado, *Economic Development of Latin America* (Cambridge: Cambridge University Press, 1970), p. 11.

27. Astrid Friis, "An Inquiry into the Relations between Economic and Financial Factors in the Sixteenth and Seventeenth Centuries," *Scandinavian Economic History Review*, 1:193, 209-213 (1953), as cited in Wallerstein, *The Modern World-System*, p. 198.

28. Violet Barbour, *Capitalism in Amsterdam in the Seventeenth Century* (Ann Arbor: University of Michigan Press, Ann Arbor Paperbacks, 1963), p. 27.

29. Jan de Vries, *The Economy of Europe in an Age of Crisis, 1600-1750* (Cambridge: Cambridge University Press, 1976), pp. 138, 141.

30. Chaunu and Chaunu, *Séville et l'Atlantique*, VIII, part 2, chaps. 6-10.

31. Carlo M. Cipolla, "Nota sulla storica del saggio d'interesse . . . ," *Economia Internazionale* 5:266 (2, magg. 1952), as cited in Wallerstein, *The Modern World-System*, pp. 76-77.

32. *American Treasure, passim*, and especially pp. 206-208.

33. As quoted in Marjorie Grice-Hutchinson, *The School of Salamanca: Readings in Spanish Monetary Theory* (Oxford: The Clarendon Press, 1952), p. 95.

34. *American Treasure*, p. 301.

35. F. C. Spooner, "The Economy of Europe 1559-1609," in *The Counter-Reformation and Price Revolution 1559-1610*, ed. R. B. Wernham, vol. III of *The New Cambridge Modern History* (Cambridge: Cambridge University Press, 1968), pp. 20-21.

36. Jorge Nadal Oller, "La revolución de los precios españoles en el siglo xiv: Estado de la cuestión," *Hispania*, 19:503-529 (1959).

37. Carlo M. Cipolla, "The So-Called 'Price Revolution': Reflections on the Italian Situation," in *Economy and Society in Early Modern Europe: Essays from Annales*, ed. Peter Burke (New York: Harper and Row, Harper Torchbooks, 1972), pp. 43-46.

38. *Economic History* (supplement to the *Economic Journal*), 3(no. 10):63-68 (February 1935). The development of the demographic school is described briefly in Dennis O. Flynn, "A New Perspective on the Spanish Price Revolution: The Monetary Approach to the Balance of Payments," *Explorations in Economic History*, 15:388-406 (1978).

39. Peter Bakewell, *Silver Mining and Society in Colonial Mexico: Zacatecas, 1546-1700* (Cambridge: Cambridge University Press, 1971), pp. 230-232; and David A. Brading and Harry C. Cross, "Colonial Silver Mining: Mexico and Peru," *HAHR*, 52:576 (1972).

40. This interpretation draws heavily on De Vries, *The Economy of Europe in an Age of Crisis*.

41. "Crops and Livestock," pp. 275-276.

42. *Of the Wood Called Guaiacum*, trans. Thomas Payne (London, 1540), p. 1, as quoted in Crosby, *Columbian Exchange*, p. 123.

43. The controversy over the origins of syphilis is discussed briefly in layman's language in Crosby, *Columbian Exchange*, pp. 122-164; and Francisco Guerra, "The Problem of Syphilis," in *First Images of America*, II, 845-851.

44. V. G. Kiernan, "Foreign Mercenaries and Absolute Monarchy," in *Crisis in Europe*, ed. Trevor Aston (New York: Basic Books, 1965), p. 123.

45. The contributions of Vitoria and Suárez to international law are examined in Bernice Hamilton, *Political Thought in Sixteenth-Century Spain: A Study of the Political Ideas of Vitoria, DeSoto, Suárez and Molina* (Oxford: The Clarendon Press, 1963). The writings of Castro are discussed briefly in John S. Elliott, *The Old World and the New, 1492-1650* (Cambridge: Cambridge University Press, 1970), p. 102; and Lewis Hanke, "The Theological Significance of the Discovery of America," in *First Images of America*, I, 369-370.

46. *Las obras* (Córdoba, Spain, 1586), fs. 129v-139v, as quoted in Elliott, *The Old World and the New*, p. 73.

47. The writings of the *arbitristas* are surveyed and evaluated in Magnus Mörner, "Spanish Migration to the New World Prior to 1800: A Report on the State of Research," in *First Images of America*, II, 758-764; and Woodrow Borah, "The Mixing of Populations," in *ibid.*, II, 712-713.

48. Mörner, "Spanish Migration," p. 767.

49. In Canto VII, stanza 14, and Canto X, stanzas 63, 140 (English edition, ed. Frank Pierce [Oxford: The Clarendon Press, 1933] ).

50. *Diálogos do sitio de Lisboa*, as quoted in J. B. Trend, *Portugal* (New York: Frederick A. Praeger, 1957), p. 146.

51. The opinions of Portuguese writers of the times on the effects of overseas emigration on their country are summarized in Borah, "Mixing of Populations," p. 713.

# Bibliographical Essay

This essay is organized as follows: It begins with a section on general works dealing with Hispanic expansion in America. Thereafter, entries are grouped by chapters in the text and, as far as possible, by sections and subjects within chapters. The first time an item is listed, full bibliographical information is provided. If it is repeated in the same chapter essay, only the author's name and a short title are given. If repeated in a later chapter essay, the author's name and the short title are listed followed by the number of the chapter essay, printed in italics and enclosed in brackets, in which the work was first cited.

In view of the many thousands of books, monographs, and articles that have been written about the various aspects of Hispanic expansion in the New World, I have had to select items to be included very rigorously. As a general rule, I have chosen works of modern scholarship that I regard as the best or, at least, representative in their categories. Exceptions are made in the following classes of writings: (1) the publications of earlier generations of scholars that have an abiding value; (2) unpublished manuscripts on important subjects not covered by works in print, and (3) contemporary sources that have a very special relevance to the subject under discussion.

## GENERAL WORKS

General works dealing with Hispanic expansion in the New World fall into three main categories. The first places Spanish and Portuguese enterprises within the broad context of European expansion. I have found John H. Parry, *The Age of Reconnaissance* (New York: Mentor Books, 1964), to be the best balanced and most readable book of this class. The French "*Annales* School" has produced two noteworthy items of a more analytical nature: Pierre Chaunu, *Conquête et exploitation des nouveaux mondes (xvi$^e$ siècle)*, Nouvelle Clio, L'histoire et ses problèmes, 26 *bis* (Paris: Presses Universitaires de France, 1969); and Frédéric Mauro *L'expansion européene (1600–1870)*, Nouvelle Clio, 27 (Paris: Presses Universitaires de France, 1967). The "History of the Americas School" has also made significant contributions, including Silvio Zavala, *El mundo americano en la época*

511

*colonial,* 2 vols. (Mexico: Editorial Porrúa, 1967); and *Historia de América y de los pueblos americanos,* gen. ed. Antonio Ballesteros y Beretta, 27 vols. (Barcelona: Editorial Salvat, 1936–56), relevant volumes of which will be mentioned separately.

Some scholars may not agree with its schema or ideological slant, but Emmanuel Wallerstein, *The Modern World-System,* vol. I: *Capitalist Agriculture and the Origins of the European World-Economy in the Sixteenth Century,* vol. II: *Mercantilism and the Consolidation of the European World-Economy, 1600–1750* (New York: Academic Press, 1974–1980), are erudite analyses of the economic dimensions of European expansion.

A second category deals with Hispanic expansion in the New World as chapters in the imperial history of Spain and Portugal. For Portugal, Charles R. Boxer, *The Portuguese Seaborne Empire, 1415–1825* (New York: Alfred A. Knopf, 1969), is the best synthesis. The standard monumental work, António Baião, gen. ed., *História da expansão portuguesa no mundo,* 3 vols. (Lisbon: Editorial Atica, 1937–40), contains contributions ranging from excellent to indifferent. On Spain and its empire, Roger B. Merriman, *The Rise of the Spanish Empire in the Old World and in the New,* 4 vols. (New York: Macmillan, 1918–34), remains a classic institutional history. The more recent Jaime Vicens Vives, ed., *Historia de España y América,* 5 vols. (Barcelona: Editorial Vicens Vives, 1961), gives more attention to social and economic themes. John H. Lynch, *Spain under the Habsburgs,* 2 vols. (Oxford: Oxford University Press, 1964–69), is a fine treatment of imperial rise and decline.

A third class of works is concerned more specifically with the formation and internal organization of Hispanic empires in the New World. Three dealing with both Spanish America and Brazil may be singled out: Bailey W. Diffie, *Latin American Civilization: Colonial Period* (Harrisburg, Pa.: Stackpole Sons, 1945), is outdated but contains a valuable compendium of information and some original insights; Richard Konetzke, *Die Indianerkulturen Altamerikas und die Spanisch-Portugiesische Kolonialheerschaft* (Frankfort: Fischer Bucharei, 1965), is a masterly synthesis. Stanley J. Stein and Barbara H. Stein, *The Colonial Heritage of Latin America: Essays on Economic Dependence in Perspective* (Oxford: Oxford University Press, 1970), is particularly useful for its treatment of American economies, but its interpretations are somewhat bound by dependency theory.

A number of good synthetic studies of the Spanish American colonies alone are available. Clarence H. Haring, *The Spanish Empire in America* (Oxford: Oxford University Press, 1947), employs a legal and institutional approach. John H. Parry, *The Spanish Seaborne Empire* (New York: Alfred A. Knopf, 1966), emphasizes maritime aspects. Charles C. Gibson, *Spain in America* (New York: Harper and Row, 1966), is a shorter but well-balanced treatment. Salvador de Madariaga, *The Rise of the Spanish American Empire* (New York: Macmillan, 1947), is rich in subjective perceptions. Finally, I particularly like the mature topical essays in Mario Góngora, *Studies in the Colonial History of Spanish America* (Cambridge: Cambridge University Press, 1975).

Although it is heavily weighted toward economic organization, the best synthesis of the history of colonial Brazil is James Lang, *Portuguese Brazil: The King's Plantation* (New York: Academic Press, 1979). Good, straight traditional surveys are Francisco Adolpho de Varnhagen, *História geral do Brasil antes da sua separação e independencia de Portugal,* 6 vols. in 3 (7th ed.; São Paulo: Edições Melhoramentos, 1962), and the shorter Jaime Cortesão and Pedro Calmon, *Brasil,* vol. 26 of *Historia de América y de los pueblos americanos* (Barcelona: Editorial Salvat, 1956).

Interpretive works of merit include: Caio Prado, Jr., *Formação do Brasil contemporâneo, colônia* (7th ed.; São Paulo: Editora Brasiliense, 1963), trans. Suzette Macedo as *The Colonial Background of Modern Brazil* (Berkeley: University of California Press,

1969); and Dauril Alden, ed., *Colonial Roots of Modern Brazil* (Berkeley: University of California Press, 1973). Both, however, emphasize the eighteenth century rather than the formative years. Charles R. Boxer, *The Golden Age of Brazil, 1695-1750* (Berkeley: University of California Press, 1964), also deals mainly with the eighteenth century but offers some valuable backlooks.

Any listing of general works must begin or end with two basic reference items: *Diccionario de la historia de España*, gen. ed. Germán Bleiberg, 3 vols. (2nd ed.; Madrid: Ediciones de la Revista de Occidente, 1968-69); and *Dicionário de história de Portugal*, ed. Joel Serrão, 4 vols. (Lisbon: Iniciativas Editoriais, 1963-70). Both contain alphabetically arranged short articles on people, places, and things written by specialists. Although some contributions are indifferent, the overall quality ranges from good to high.

For those who wish to pursue the literature of Hispanic expansion in America beyond this selective essay, the needs of most will be served by *Latin America: A Guide to the Historical Literature*, ed. Charles C. Griffin, asst. ed. J. Benedict Warren (Austin: University of Texas Press, 1971); and *The Handbook of Latin American Studies*, vols. 1-13 (Cambridge, Mass.: Harvard University Press, 1935-51); vols. 14-40 (Gainesville, Fla.: University of Florida Press, 1951-78); vols. 41- (Austin: University of Texas Press, 1979- ), an annual survey of books and articles about Latin America published in all parts of the world.

## CHAPTER 1. THE MATRIX OF HISPANIC SOCIETIES
## CHAPTER 2. RECONQUEST HISPANIA

Since these parts of the book are closely related and deal essentially with "background" materials, I have combined the bibliographical references for both into a single essay, avoided for the most part the listing of monographs and specialized articles and, instead, included only general histories and interpretations.

The best-balanced synthesis of the history of medieval, or Reconquest, Spain is Angus MacKay, *Spain in the Middle Ages: From Frontier to Empire, 1000-1500* (London: Macmillan, 1977). The accompanying bibliographical essays are an excellent guide to more specialized works on the period. Other good surveys are José A. García de Cortazar, *La época medieval* (Madrid: Alianza Editorial, 1973); and Joseph F. O'Callaghan, *A History of Medieval Spain* (Ithaca, N.Y.: Cornell University Press, 1975). A more controversial work stressing acculturation and the Muslim influence is Thomas F. Glick, *Islamic and Christian Spain in the Early Middle Ages: Comparative Perspectives on Social and Cultural Formation* (Princeton, N.J.: Princeton University Press, 1979). An older history that has aged very well is Merriman, *The Rise of the Spanish Empire* [General Works], vol. I.

The classic work on Muslim Spain is still Evaristé Lévi-Provençal, *Histoire de l'Espagne musulmane*, 3 vols. (new ed., rev. and enl.; Paris: G. P. Maisonneuve, 1950-53). A more recent synthesis is W. Montgomery Watt and Pierre Cachia, *A History of Islamic Spain* (Edinburgh: Edinburgh University Press, 1965).

The only work I have found dealing primarily and specifically with the process of reconquest is Derek W. Lomax, *The Reconquest of Spain* (New York: Longman, 1978). The classic study of frontier resettlement in Castile-León is Claudio Sánchez-Albornoz, *Despoblación y repoblación del Valle del Duero* (Buenos Aires: Instituto de Historia de España, 1966). The repopulation of other regions in Spain is treated in *La reconquista y la repoblación del país*, ed. J. M. Lacarra (Zaragoza: Instituto de Estudios Pirenáicos, 1947); Julio González, *La repoblación de Castilla la Nueva*, 2 vols. (Madrid: C.S.I.C., 1975-76); and the same author's *Repartimiento de Sevilla*, 2 vols. (Madrid: C.S.I.C., 1951).

An excellent study of the development of political and legal institutions in medieval Spain is Luis García de Valdeavellano, *Curso de historia de las instituciones españolas, de los orígenes al final de la Edad Media* (2nd ed., rev. and enl.; Madrid: Ediciones de la Revista de Occidente, 1970). Medieval social organization and economies are surveyed unevenly but, on balance, well in Vicens Vives, *Historia de España y América* [*General Works*], vols. I and II. However, the best purely economic survey of the period is unquestionably Jaime Vicens Vives with the collaboration of Jorge Nadal Oller, *Manual de historia económica de España* (3rd ed.; Barcelona: Editorial Vicens Vives, 1964), trans. Frances M. López-Morillas as *An Economic History of Spain* (Princeton, N.J.: Princeton University Press, 1969), parts 2 and 3. There is no satisfactory history of the Spanish church in the Middle Ages, but an indispensable reference work is *Diccionario de historia eclesiástica de España*, ed. Quintín Alda Vaquero, Tomás Marín Martínez, and José Vives Gatell, 3 vols. (Madrid: C.S.I.C., 1972).

Among interpretations of the medieval Spanish experience, the best known are the polemical Américo Castro, *The Spaniards: An Introduction to Their History*, trans. Willard F. King and Selma Margaretten (Berkeley: University of California Press, 1971); and the equally polemical Claudio Sánchez-Albornoz, *España, un enigma histórico*, 2 vols. (2nd ed.; Buenos Aires: Editorial Sudamericana, 1962). Castro contends that the most distinctive features of Spanish society and character resulted from the prolonged and intimate interaction among Christians, Moors, and Jews and were permanently fixed by the end of the Reconquest. Sánchez-Albornoz argues that the principal formative force was Christian and European and, further, that the process of formation continued into modern times. A more concise and better balanced view can be found in Jaime Vicens Vives, *Aproximación a la historia de España* (2nd ed.; Barcelona: Universidad de Barcelona, 1960), trans. and ed. Jean Connelly Ullman as *Approaches to the History of Spain* (Berkeley: University of California Press, 1967), chaps. 5-12.

Compared with that of the Spanish kingdoms, the historiography of medieval Portugal is relatively thin. The best syntheses are Antonio H. de Oliveira Marques, *History of Portugal*, vol. I: *From Lusitania to Empire* (New York: Columbia University Press, 1972), chaps. 1-2; and the seminal Vitorino de Magalhães Godinho, *Estrutura de antiga sociedade portuguesa* (2nd ed., rev. and enl.; Lisbon: Arcádia, 1975). A solid factual chronicle is Harold V. Livermore, *A New History of Portugal* (2nd ed.; New York: Cambridge University Press, 1966). Somewhat dated but still valuable monumental histories are Alexandre Herculano, *História de Portugal*, 4 vols. (Lisbon, 1846–53), and Damião Peres, *História de Portugal: Edição monumental*, 8 vols. (Barcelos: Portucalense Editora, 1928–38). Political and administrative history is the focus of Henrique da Gama Barros, *História da administração pública em Portugal nos séculos xii-xv*, 11 vols. (2nd ed.; Lisbon: Livraria Sá da Costa, 1945–54). Its topical scope, however, is much broader than its title indicates. For economic history, the patient scholar will find a wealth of detail in the ambitious Armando Castro, *A evolução económica de Portugal dos séculos xii a xv*, 9 vols. to date (Lisbon: Portugália Editôra, 1964–   ).

The ecclesiastical history of Portugal in the Middle Ages is recounted uncritically in Fortunato de Almeida, *História da igreja em Portugal*, 4 vols. in 8 parts (Coimbra: Imprensa Académica, 1910–22). José António Saravia, *Para la história da cultura em Portugal*, 2 vols. (2nd ed; Lisbon: Publicações Europa-América, 1961), provides insights into medieval social values. An especially good analysis of the emergence of Portugal as a state and a nation is Dan Stanislawsky, *The Individuality of Portugal: A Study in Historical Political Geography* (Austin: University of Texas Press, 1959).

On the controversial question of the extent to which feudalism existed in Hispanic medieval societies, the classic exposition is Claudio Sánchez-Albornoz, *En torno a los orígenes del feudalismo*, 3 vols. (Mendoza, Arg.: Universidad Nacional de Cuyo, 1942). A more critical analysis is Luis García de Valdeavellano, "Prólogo y apéndice sobre las instituciones feudales en España," in F. L. Ganshof, *El feudalismo* (Barcelona: Ariel, 1963), a Spanish translation of Ganshof's classic *Qu'est-ce que la féodalité?*

Feudalism and *señorialism* are, of course, neologisms used by scholars from the eighteenth century onward to describe "systems" they perceive to have existed in medieval times. I have analyzed these systems in traditional terms, that is, as contractual political and economic relationships among the members of the warrior class, because technically that was what they were. The works cited in the previous paragraph employ this definition—with some variations. A number of scholars, however, prefer to use the broader concept of "feudal society," which encompassed all social classes. The most influential work in this category is, of course, Marc Bloch, *La société féodal*, 2 vols. (Paris: A. Michele, 1939–40), trans. L. A. Manyon as *Feudal Society* (Chicago: University of Chicago Press, 1961). Marxist historians employ the same approach, but within their own frame of reference. That is, feudalism was a mode of production characterized by the extraction of the surplus production of peasants and serfs by the lords of the land. A sampling of their analyses may be found in the essays by several authors in *Sur le féodalisme* (Paris: Editions Sociales, 1972). An excellent critical review of recent Marxist and non-Marxist works on feudalism and the transition to capitalism is William Letwin, "The Contradictions of Serfdom," *Times Literary Supplement*, March 25, 1977, pp. 373-375.

With particular reference to the influence of the medieval experience on Hispanic expansion in America, a good but now dated survey of the pertinent literature is Charles J. Bishko, "The Iberian Background of Latin American History," *HAHR*, 36:50-80 (1956). A classic but somewhat impassioned statement on the subject is Claudio Sánchez-Albornoz, "La Edad Media y la empresa de América," in his *España y el Islam* (Buenos Aires: Editorial Sudamericana, 1943), pp. 181-199. Also useful is the collection of readings in *From Reconquest to Empire: The Iberian Background of Latin American History*, ed. H. B. Johnson, Jr. (New York: Alfred A. Knopf, Borzoi Books 1970).

## CHAPTER 3. HISPANIC EXPANSION IN THE OLD WORLD

Recommendable works on early Castilian and Catalan interests in Africa and its offshore islands are Charles-Emmanuel Dufourcq, *L'Espagne catalane et le Maghrib aux xiii^e et xiv^e siècles* (Paris: Presses Universitaires de France, 1966); and Antonio Rumeu de Armas, *España en el Africa Atlántico*, 2 vols. (Madrid: C.S.I.C., 1956–57), I. The political and diplomatic aspects of Aragonese aggrandizements in Sicily are introduced in J. Lee Schneidman, *The Rise of the Aragonese-Catalan Empire, 1200-1350*, 2 vols. (New York: New York University Press, 1970), I, part 3.

The best summary of what is known about medieval Atlantic exploration is Carl O. Sauer, *The Northern Mists* (Berkeley: University of California Press, 1968). Bailey W. Diffie, *Prelude to Empire: Portugal Overseas before Henry the Navigator* (Lincoln: University of Nebraska Press, 1960), deals more particularly with early Portuguese Atlantic voyages.

Good introductions to Europe's misfortunes in the fourteenth century and the slackening of overseas expansion are Robert E. Lerner, *The Age of Adversity: The Fourteenth Century* (Ithaca, N.Y.: Cornell University Press, 1969); and Harry A. Misimkin, *The Economy of Early Renaissance Europe, 1300-1460* (Englewood Cliffs, N.J.: Prentice-Hall, Spectrum Books, 1969). Spanish adversities after the end of the High Reconquest are surveyed in J. N. Hillgarth, *The Spanish Kingdoms 1250–1516*, 2 vols. (Oxford: Oxford University Press, 1976–78); Luis Suárez Fernández, *Nobleza y monarquía: Puntos de vista sobre la historia castellana del siglo xv* (Valladolid, Spain: Universidad de Valladolid, Facultad de Filosofía y Letras, 1959), and William D. Phillips, *Enrique IV and the Crisis of Fifteenth-Century Castile* (Cambridge, Mass.: Medieval Academy of America, 1978). The best general work on the Jewish and *converso* problem is Yitzak F. Baer, *History of the Jews in Christian Spain*, 2 vols. (Philadelphia: The Jewish Publication Society of America, 1961–66).

Fourteenth-century Portuguese problems, the climactic succession crisis of 1383, and the foundation of the House of Avis are analyzed in Salvador Dias Arnaut, *A crise nacional dos fins do século xiv*, vol. I: *A sucessão de D. Fernando* (Coimbra: Faculdade de Letras, 1960); and António Borges Coelho, *A revolução de 1383* (Lisbon: Portugália Editôra, (1965).

A fine essay on the incoming demographic and economic tides that helped to regenerate European expansion is Jarah Johnson and William H. Percy, Jr., *The Age of Recovery: The Fifteenth Century* (Ithaca, N.Y.: Cornell University Press, 1970). The most up-to-date and best-balanced treatment of the pioneer role played by Portugal in the great age of expansion is Bailey W. Diffie and George Winius, *Foundations of the Portuguese Empire, 1450–1580*, vol. I of *Europe and the World in the Age of Expansion*, ed. Boyd Shafer, (Minneapolis: University of Minnesota Press, 1977). A number of more specialized studies, however, merit mention. On economic aspects see the detailed but somewhat disjointed Vitorino de Magalhães Godinho, *L'economie de l'Empire Portugais aux xv^e et xvi^e siècles* (Paris: S.E.V.P.E.N., 1969). Also worthy of mention is E. W. Bovill, *The Golden Trade of the Moors* (2nd ed., rev.; Oxford: Oxford University Press, 1968). The crusading element is covered in Robert Ricard, *Études sur l'histoire des Portugais au Maroc* (Coimbra: Universidade de Coimbra, 1955); and Francis M. Rogers, *The Quest for Eastern Christendom: Travels and Rumors in the Age of Discovery* (Minneapolis: University of Minnesota Press, 1962). The standard work on cartography is Armando Cortesão, *Cartografia e cartógrafos portugueses dos séculos xv e xvi* (Lisbon: Seara Novo, 1935).

I have found the most useful analyses of the institutional forms employed in the colonization of the African offshore islands to be Charles Verlinden, "Feudal and Demesnial Forms of Portuguese Colonization in the Atlantic Zone in the Fourteenth and Fifteenth Centuries, Especially under Prince Henry the Navigator," in his *The Beginnings of Modern Colonization*, trans. Yvonne Freccero (Ithaca, N.Y.: Cornell University Press, 1970), pp. 203–240; and Harold B. Johnson, "The Donatary Captaincy in Perspective: Portuguese Backgrounds to the Settlement of Brazil," *HAHR*, 52:203-214 (1972). An excellent introduction to sugar planting on the Madeiras is Sidney Greenfield, "Madeira and the Beginnings of New World Sugar Cane Cultivation and Plantation Slavery: A Study in Institution Building," in *Comparative Perspectives on Slavery in New World Plantation Societies*, ed. Vera Rubin and Arthur Tuden, Annals of the New York Academy of Sciences, vol. 292 (New York: A.N.Y.A.S., 1977), pp. 536-552.

The juridical problems raised by Hispanic overseas expansion are examined in Frederick H. Russell, *The Just War of the Middle Ages* (Cambridge: Cambridge University Press, 1975); and Silvio Zavala, "La conquista de Canarias y América," in his *Estudios indianos* (Mexico: El Colegio Nacional, 1948), pp. 7-94. On the subject of race relations see Charles R. Boxer, *Race Relations in the Portuguese Colonial Empire, 1415-1825* (Oxford: Oxford University Press, 1963); and A. J. R. Russell-Wood, "Iberian Expansion and the Issue of Black Slavery," *AHR* 83:16-42 (1978).

The classic history of the reign of Ferdinand and Isabella is still Jean H. Mariejol,

*L'Espagne sous Ferdinand et Isabelle* (Paris, 1892), trans. and ed. Benjamin Keen as *The Spain of Ferdinand and Isabella* (New Brunswick, N.J.: Rutgers University Press, 1961). The editorial comments of Keen help to bring this work up-to-date. A good modern survey emphasizing political developments is Hilgarth, *The Spanish Kingdoms*, vol. II. The best analysis of the Spanish economy under the dual monarchy is Vicens Vives, *An Economic History of Spain* [*Chaps. 1* and 2], part 4. The organization of the royal treasury is ably described in Miguel A. Ladero Quesada, *La Hacienda Real de Castilla en el siglo xvi* (La Laguna [Santa Cruz de Tenerife]: Universidad de Tenerife, 1973). The religious policies of the Catholic Kings are studied in Henry Kamen, *The Spanish Inquisition* (London: Weidenfeld and Nicolson, 1965). The military organization and tactics of the last campaigns against the Spanish Moors are analyzed in Miguel A. Ladero Quesada, *Castilla y la conquista del Reino de Granada* (Valladolid: Universidad de Valladolid, Secretario de Publicaciones, 1967).

A standard narrative and institutional history of the Spanish conquest and colonization of the Canaries is Merriman, *The Rise of the Spanish Empire* [*General Works*], vol. II, chap. 16. Zavala, "La conquista de Canarias," emphasizes moral and juridical aspects, while bringing out precedents established for Spanish enterprises in the New World. There is no good economic history of the islands but two works may be cited that cast some light on the subject. Charles Verlinden, "The Italians in the Economy of the Canary Islands at the Beginning of Spanish Colonization," in his *The Beginnings of Modern Colonization*, trans. Yvonne Freccero (Ithaca, N.Y.: Cornell University Press, 1970), pp. 132-57; and Vitorino de Magalhães Godinho, *A economia das Canárias nos séculos xiv e xv* (São Paulo: n.p., 1952). Florentino Pérez-Embid, *Los descubrimientos en el Atlántic y la rivalidad castellano-portuguesa hasta el Tratado de Tordesillas*, PEEHA, 19 (Seville, 1948), examines Castilian-Portuguese contentions in the Atlantic as precedents for later negotiations about titles to the New World.

The circumstances bringing Columbus to the court of the Catholic Kings and the negotiations leading up to his patent are examined in his standard biography, Samuel E. Morison, *Admiral of the Ocean Sea: A Life of Christopher Columbus*, 2 vols. (Boston: Little, Brown, 1942), I. Antonio Muró Orejón, *El original de la capitulación de 1492 y sus copias contemporáneas*, PEEHA, 25 (Seville, 1951), analyzes the contents of the patent of Santa Fé.

## CHAPTER 4. THE CONDITIONS OF CONQUEST AND COLONIZATION: GEOGRAPHY AND PEOPLES

An excellent account of Columbus's discovery is contained in his standard biography, Morison, *Admiral of the Ocean Sea* [*Chap. 3*]. Works on Columbus as a person, a discoverer, and a colonizer and on his place in history are evaluated in Charles E. Nowell, "The Columbus Question: A Survey of Recent Literature and Present Opinion," *AHR*, 44:802-822 (1939); and Martin Torodash, "Columbian Historiography since 1939," *HAHR*, 41:409-428 (1966).

The jurisdictional issues between Spain and Portugal raised by Columbus's discovery are fully treated in Alfonso García Gallo, "Las bulas de Alejandro VI y el ordenamiento jurídico de la expansión portuguesa y castellana en Africa e Indias," *AHDE*, 27-28:461-829 (1957-58); and Coloquio Luso-Español de Historia Ultramarina, 1st, Valladolid, Spain, 1972, *El Tratado de Tordesillas y su proyección*, Presentación de Luis Suárez Fernández, 2 vols. (Valladolid: Seminario de Historia de América, 1973).

On the Portuguese "discovery" of Brazil and its historiography, see Diffie and Winius,

*Foundations of the Portuguese Empire* [*Chap. 3*], chap. 10. A balanced Portuguese interpretation of the discovery and of negotiations with Spain about the division of the New World is Manuel Nunes Dias, "Descobrimento do Brasil: Tratados biláterais e partilha do Mar Oceano," *Studia* (Lisbon), 25:7-29 (1968).

The single best treatment I have found of the geographical factors affecting the course of Hispanic discovery, conquest, and colonization in America is Oscar Schmieder, *Die Neue Welt*, 2 vols. (Heidelberg: Keysersche Verlagsbuchhandlung, 1962–63). An excellent shorter analysis may be found in Kempton E. Webb, *Geography of Latin America: A Regional Analysis* (Englewood Cliffs, N.J.: Prentice-Hall, 1972). A larger and more specialized work on Mesoamerica is Robert C. West and John P. Augelli, *Middle America: Its Lands and Peoples* (Englewood Cliffs, N.J.: Prentice-Hall, 1960). Unfortunately, no comparable study of South America exists.

A most perceptive analysis of the interests of the Spanish crown and private parties in the Enterprise of the Indies is Góngora, *Studies* [*General Works*], chaps. 1-3. A good specialized study of evolving royal policy is Manuel Giménez Fernández, *Política inicial de Carlos I en Indias* (Zaragoza: Hesperia, 1960). On private and *señorial* interests see Silvio Zavala, *Los intereses particulares en la conquista de América* (Mexico: U.N.A.M., 1964), and Alfonso María Guilarte, *El régimen señorial en el siglo xvi* (Madrid: Instituto de Estudios Políticos, 1962). Good studies of the social backgrounds of conquistadors are Mario Góngora, *Los grupos de conquistadores en Tierra Firme, 1509-1530: Fisonomía histórico-social de un tipo de conquista* (Santiago: Universidad de Chile, 1962); and James Lockhart, *The Men of Cajamarca* (Austin: University of Texas Press, 1972).

It is difficult to find good up-to-date syntheses of pre-Conquest Indian history because of the rapid advance of archaeological research and sharp differences of opinion among specialists about the results of findings, both old and new. For the nonspecialist, the best survey of the histories of the "high civilizations"—Inca, Maya, and Aztec—I have found is Friedrich Katz, *Vorkolumbische Kulturen: Die grossen Reiche des alten Amerika* (Munich: Kindler Verlag, 1969), trans. K. M. Lois Simpson as *The Ancient American Civilizations* (New York: Praeger, 1972). The reader, however, must be alert for occasional factual errors. Although it is directed more toward archaeologists than historians, a good culture history of pre-Columbian Mesoamerica is Muriel P. Weaver, *The Aztecs, Maya, and Their Predecessors* (2nd ed.; New York: Academic Press, 1981). For the general reader, the best history of the Incas is Alfred Métraux, *Les Incas* (Paris: Éditions du Seuil, 1963), trans. George Ordish as *The History of the Incas* (New York: Pantheon Books, 1969). On the Chibcha culture of the northern Andes see Sylvia M. Broadbent, *Los Chibchas: Organización socio-política* (Bogotá: Universidad Nacional de Colombia, 1964). An excellent synthetic article on the indigenous peoples of the Antilles is Irving Rouse, "Prehistory of the West Indies," *Science*, 144:499-513 (1964).

The following items provide introductions to the controversial subject of pre-Conquest Indian populations: Henry F. Dobyns, "Estimating Aboriginal American Population: An Appraisal of Techniques with a New Hemisphere Estimate," *Current Anthropology*, 7:395-416, 425-435 (1966); and the more recent collection of essays in William M. Denevan, ed., *The Native Population of the Americas in 1492* (Madison: University of Wisconsin Press, 1976).

Two good works on the "African background" are Robert W. July, *Precolonial Africa: An Economic and Social History* (New York: Charles Scribner's Sons, 1975); and *History of West Africa*, ed. J. F. A. Ajayi and Michael Crowder, vol. I-   (London: Longman, 1971-   ), I.

## CHAPTER 5. MUNDUS NOVUS: *DISCOVERY AND CONQUEST*

Among the many works on the juridical aspects of conquest, the following provide good analyses of the sources of Spain's just title to the Indies and of the requirements for a just war in those regions: Góngora, *Studies [General Works]*, chap. 2; and Lewis Hanke, *The Spanish Struggle for Justice in the Conquest of America* (Boston: Little, Brown, 1965). On the legal instruments of discovery and conquest see Bernardo García Martínez, "Ojeada a las capitulaciones para la conquista de América," *RHA*, no. 69:1-40 (1970), which analyses the content of seventy-four patents given out by the Spanish crown between 1492 and 1570.

The fullest accounts of the spread of maritime discovery in the New World after Columbus's first voyage are Samuel E. Morison, *The European Discovery of America: The Southern Voyages, A.D. 1492-1616* (Oxford: Oxford University Press, 1974); and the same author's, *The European Discovery of America: The Northern Voyages, A.D. 500-1600* (Oxford: Oxford University Press, 1971). A good introduction to the controversial voyages of Amerigo Vespucci and the naming of America is Frederick J. Pohl, *Amerigo Vespucci: Pilot Major* (New York: Columbia University Press, 1944). Attempts to find ways around or through the "American Nuisance" to the Pacific are surveyed in María L. Díaz Trechuelo Spinola, "La conexión entre el Atlántico y el Pacífico hasta Fray Andrés de Urdaneta," *AEA*, 25:469-494 (1968).

The most thorough study of the Spanish occupation of the Greater Antilles and the first mainland penetrations in northern South America is Carl O. Sauer, *The Early Spanish Main* (Berkeley: University of California Press, 1966). I think that for the general reader the best narrative account of the great mainland conquests is F. A. Kirkpatrick, *The Spanish Conquistadores* (London: A. & C. Black, 1946). Shorter interpretive syntheses of the process of conquest may be found in Huguette Chaunu and Pierre Chaunu, *Séville et l'Atlantique (1504-1650)*, 8 vols. in 11 parts (Paris: Librairie Armand Colin, 1955-59), VIII, part 1, pp. 114-155; and in Francisco Morales Padrón *La fisonomía de la conquista* (Seville: E.E.H.A., 1955).

Accounts of the conquest of particular regions abound, and the following listing is highly selective. William H. Prescott, *History of the Conquest of Mexico*, 2 vols. (New York, 1843), is outdated in some of its details and, by modern standards, overromanticizes events. However, it is still the best narrative of the conquest of central Mexico. For northwestern Mexico see José López-Portilla y Weber, *La conquista de la Nueva Galicia* (Mexico: Talleres Gráficos de la Nación, 1935); and for the Mexican southeast see the meticulous Peter Gerhard, *The Southeast Frontier of New Spain* (Princeton, N.J.: Princeton University Press, 1979). A good introduction to Spanish land explorations north of Mexico and in Florida is Herbert E. Bolton, *The Spanish Borderlands: A Chronicle of Old Florida and the South-West* (New Haven, Conn.: Yale University Press, 1921). On Pacific explorations north of Mexico see Henry R. Wagner, *Spanish Voyages to the Northwest Coast of America in the Sixteenth Century* (San Francisco: California Historical Society, 1929). Early trans-Pacific exploration from Mexico is ably reported and analyzed in O. H. K. Spate, *The Pacific since Magellan*, vol. I: *The Spanish Lake* (Minneapolis: University of Minnesota Press, 1979). Also valuable for the way in which it places Spanish voyages in the broader context of European expansion is Pierre Chaunu, *Les Philippines et le Pacifique des Ibériques (xvi$^e$, xvii$^e$, xviii$^e$ siècles)*, 2 vols. (Paris: S.E.V.P.E.N., 1960), I.

Substantial works on the conquest of Central America are Robert S. Chamberlain, *The Conquest and Colonization of Yucatan, 1517-1550* (Washington: Carnegie Institution,

1948); the same author's *The Conquest and Colonization of Honduras, 1502–1550* (Washington: Carnegie Institution, 1953); and Victoria Urbano, *Juan Vásquez de Coronado y su ética en la conquista de Costa Rica* (Madrid: Ediciones Cultura Hispánica, 1968). The best-balanced and most readable account of Spanish discoveries and conquests in South America is J. H. Parry, *The Discovery of South America* (New York: Taplinger, 1979).

Following are basic works on the conquests of major South American regions: for the Northern Region; Juan Friede, *Descubrimiento del Nuevo Reino de Granada y fundación de Bogotá, 1536–1539* (Bogotá: Banco de la República, 1960); for Peru, John Hemming, *The Conquest of the Incas* (New York: Harcourt Brace Jovanovich, 1970), a particularly noteworthy book; for Chile, Francisco Esteve Barba, *Descubrimiento y conquista de Chile*, vol. XI of *Historia de América y de los pueblos americanos* [*General Works*]; for the Rio de la Plata, Julián M. Rubio, *Exploración y conquista del Rio de la Plata: Siglos xvi y xvii*, vol. VIII of *Historia de América y de los pueblos americanos* [*General Works*].

The following items deal with particular aspects of conquest: on the influence of myth and legend see Irving A. Leonard, *Books of the Brave* (Cambridge, Mass.: Harvard University Press, 1949); on arms and equipment see Alberto M. Salas, *Las armas de la conquista* (Buenos Aires: Emece Editores, 1950); on pathogenic factors see Alfred A. Crosby, Jr., *The Columbian Exchange: Biological and Cultural Consequences of 1492* (Westport, Conn.: Greenwood Press, 1972), chap. 2; on social and economic organization of expeditions see Demetrio Ramos, "Funcionamiento socio-económico de una hueste de conquista: La de Pedro de Heredia en Cartagena de Indias," in *Homenaje a Don Ciriaco Pérez Bustamante* (Madrid: C.S.I.C., 1969), pp. 393-526.

Attempts to explain the Indian view of the Conquest include Miguel León-Portilla, ed., *Visión de los vencidos* (Mexico: U.N.A.M., 1959), trans. Lysander Kemp as *The Broken Spears: The Aztec Account of the Conquest of Mexico* (Boston: Beacon Press, 1962); and Nathan Wechtel, *La vision des vaincus: Les Indiens du Pérou devant la conquête espagnole, 1530–1570* (Paris: Éditions Gaillimard, 1971), trans. Ben and Siân Renolds as *The Vision of the Vanquished: The Spanish Conquest of Peru through Indian Eyes, 1530–1570* (New York: Barnes and Noble, 1977).

## CHAPTER 6. COLONIZATION: THE POPULATORS OF THE INDIES

The quick shift of Spanish policy from simple commercial exploitation to deliberate colonization is analyzed in Juan Pérez de Tudela, "La quiebra de la factoría y el nuevo poblamiento de la Española," *RI*, 15:197-252 (1955); and in the same author's "Política de poblamiento y política de contratación de las Indias, 1502–1505," *RI*, 15:371-420.

The best general survey of the population history of Latin America is Nicolás Sánchez-Albornoz, *The Population of Latin America*, trans. W. A. R. Richardson (Berkeley: University of California Press, 1974). Chap. 4 deals with the Conquest period. A more ambitious study, organized century by century, is Angel Rosenblat, *La población indígena y el mestizaje en América*, 2 vols. (Buenos Aires: Editorial Nova, 1954). Despite its title, it includes information on white and black as well as Indian and mixed-blood population components. It is rich in descriptive material, but the validity of its quantitative data is debatable.

Magnus Mörner summarizes what is known about European emigration to the Indies in "Spanish Migration to the New World prior to 1810: A Report on the State of Research," in *First Images of America: The Impact of the New World on the Old*, ed. Fredi Chiappelli, co-ed. Michael J. B. Allen and Robert L. Benson, 2 vols. (Berkeley: University of California

Press, 1976), II, 737-782. Jorge Nadal Oller, *La población española (siglo xvi-xx)* (Barcelona: Ediciones Ariel, 1966), provides information on the demographic background of population movements to the Indies, and Woodrow Borah, "The Mixing of Populations," in *First Images of America*, II, 707-722, is a thoughtful essay on the social conditions in Spain that influenced emigration. Crown emigration policy is discussed in Richard Konetzke, "Legislación sobre inmigración de extranjeros en América durante la época colonial," *Revista Internacional de Sociología* (Madrid), 3(nos. 11-12):269-299 (July-December, 1945).

The most thorough study of the numbers, regional origins, social qualities, and American destinations of European emigrants during the Conquest period is Peter Boyd-Bowman, "Patterns of Spanish Emigration to the New World (1493-1580)," Special Studies, Council on International Studies, State University of New York at Buffalo (Buffalo, 1973, mimeo). The author has abridged and revised this work in "Patterns of Spanish Emigration to the Indies until 1600," *HAHR*, 56:580-604 (1976).

Boyd-Bowman's work includes data on particular classes of immigrants but the following items have supplementary descriptive value: on Canary Islanders, Francisco Morales Padrón, "Colonos canarios en Indias," *AEA*, 8:399-441 (1951); on foreigners in general, William L. Schurz, *This New World: The Civilization of Latin America* (New York: E. P. Dutton, 1964), chap. 6; on Portuguese, Henry H. Keith, "New World Interlopers: The Portuguese in the Spanish West Indies from the Discovery to 1640," *TA*, 25:360-371 (1968-69); and Lewis Hanke, "The Portuguese in Spanish America with Special Reference to the Villa Imperial de Potosí," *RHA*, no. 51:1-48 (June 1960); on Italians, Ruth Pike, *Enterprise and Adventure: The Genoese in Seville and the Opening of the New World* (Ithaca: N.Y.: Cornell University Press, 1966); on women, Analola Borges, "La mujer pobladora en los orígenes americanos," *AEA*, 29:389-444 (1972); on Jews, Martin Cohen, *The Martyr: The Story of a Secret Jew and the Mexican Inquisition in the Sixteenth Century* (Philadelphia: The Jewish Publication Society of America, 1973).

Rosenblat, *La población indígena*, I, is the most comprehensive account of demographic trends among the post-Discovery Indian population of the American hemisphere. As remarked earlier, however, the author's methods and findings are controversial. A shorter synthetic study is Alejandro Lipschütz, "La despoblación de las Indias después de la conquista," *América Indígena*, 26:229-247 (1966).

An indispensable introduction to population trends among North American Indians are the titles and commentary in Henry F. Dobyns, *Native American Historical Demography: A Critical Bibliography* (Bloomington: Indiana University Press, 1976). Among substantive works, Sherburne F. Cook and Woodrow Borah, *Essays in Population History*, 3 vols. (Berkeley: University of California Press, 1971-79), stands out. It brings together almost three decades of the "Berkeley School's" work on Mexico, and, although the methods used and the results obtained by the School's members have been sharply criticized, the work is a monument of pioneer scholarship on the population history of the American Indian. Murdo J. MacLeod, *Spanish Central America: A Socioeconomic History, 1520-1720* (Berkeley: University of California Press, 1973), examines the decline of the Indian population in Central America.

The fullest and most up-to-date study of the historical demography of Peru during and after the conquest is Noble D. Cook, *Demographic Collapse: Indian Peru, 1520-1620* (Cambridge: Cambridge University Press, 1981). Population trends in two provinces of New Granada are analyzed in Juan Friede, "Algunas consideraciones sobre la evolución demográfica de la provincia de Tunja," *Anuario Colombiano de Historia Social y de la Cultura*, 2(no. 3):5-19 (1965); and Germán Colmenares, *Encomienda y población en la Provincia de Pamplona (1549-1650)* (Bogotá: Universidad de los Andes, 1969).

A fine general view of European diseases introduced into the New World and their effects on the indigenous population is William H. McNeill, *Plagues and People* (Garden City, N.Y.: Anchor Press-Doubleday, 1976), especially chap. 5. The population history of blacks in the Indies is thin, especially in quantitative data. Most of what is known derives from studies of the slave trade. The standard general work on the volume and destinations of slave imports is Philip D. Curtin, *The Atlantic Slave Trade: A Census* (Madison: University of Wisconsin Press, 1969). Studies of black slavery and other aspects of the black presence in America contain scattered information on numbers and distribution of Africans and on the conditions that affected demographic trends among them. Literature in this category is ably surveyed in Frederick P. Bowser, "The African in Colonial Spanish America: Reflections on Research Achievements and Priorities," *LARR*, 7(no. 1):77-94 (Spring 1972). General works meriting mention are Roger Bastide, *Les Amériques Noires: Les civilisations africaines dans le Nouveau Monde* (Paris: Payot, 1967), trans. Peter Green as *African Civilizations in the New World* (New York: Harper and Row, 1971); Franklin W. Knight, *The African Dimension of Latin American Societies* (New York: Macmillan, 1974); and Lesley B. Rout, Jr., *The African Experience in Spanish America* (Cambridge: Cambridge University Press, 1976). An older but useful study of the geographical distribution of black populations is Wilbur Zelinsky, "The Historical Geography of the Negro Population in America," *Journal of Negro History*, 34:153-219 (1949).

Important regional works include Gonzalo Aguirre Beltrán, *La población negra de México, 1519-1810: Estudio etnohistórico* (Mexico: Ediciones Fuentes Cultural, 1946); Frederick P. Bowser, *The African Slave in Colonial Peru, 1524-1560* (Stanford, Calif.: Stanford University Press, 1973); and Rolando Mellafe, *La introducción de la esclavitud negra en Chile: Tráfico y rutas* (Santiago: Universidad de Chile, 1959).

The best introduction to a rather substantial corpus of literature on miscegenation and mixed bloods in Spanish America is Magnus Mörner, *Race Mixture in the History of Latin America* (Boston: Little, Brown, 1967). Fuller descriptions are Rosenblat, *La población indígena*, II; and Alejandro Lipschütz, *El problema racial en la conquista de América y el mestizaje* (Santiago: Editora Austral, 1963). Papers dealing with diverse aspects of *mestizaje* including regional forms are contained in two published symposia: "Estudio sobre el mestizaje en América, Contribución al XXXVI Congreso Internacional de Americanistas," *RI*, 24:1-354 (1964); and *El mestizaje en la historia de Ibero-América* (Mexico: PIGH, 1961).

An excellent regional study of miscegenation is Elman R. Service, *Spanish-Guaraní Relations in Early Colonial Paraguay* (Westport, Conn.: Greenwood Press, 1971), first published in 1954 by the University of Michigan Museum of Anthropology. Sherburne F. Cook and Woodrow Borah, "Racial Groups in the Mexican Population," in their *Essays in Population History*, II, 180-269, deserves special mention because of its attempts to quantify systematically rates and kinds of race mixture.

## CHAPTER 7. INSTRUMENTS OF COLONIZATION: THE CASTILIAN MUNICIPIO

The literature on the function of towns in Spanish American colonization can be grouped into five categories. One consists of theoretical or analytical articles and includes Richard M. Morse, "Some Characteristics of Latin American Urban History," *AHR*, 67:317-338 (1962); the same author's "A Prolegomenon to Latin American Urban History," *HAHR*, 52:359-394 (1972); Robert Smith, "Colonial Towns in Spanish and Portuguese America,"

*Journal of the Society of Architectural Historians*, 14(no. 4):3-72 (December 1955); and Jean Tricart, "Quelques caractéristiques generales de villes latinamericaines," *AESC*, 15:15-30 (1965).

A second category deals with the process and progress of town founding. Although it contains some factual errors, I think the best general survey in this class is J. M. Houston, "The Founding of Colonial Towns in Hispanic America," in *Urbanization and Its Problems: Essays in Honor of E. W. Gilbert*, ed. R. P. Beckinsdale and J. M. Houston (Oxford: Basil Blackwell, 1968), pp. 352-390. The importance of parishes in town founding is examined in Gary W. Graff, "Spanish Parishes in Colonial New Granada: Their Role in Town Building on the Spanish American Frontier," *TA*, 33:336-351 (1976-77).

The following are good regional studies of early urbanization: on central Mexico, George Kubler, "Mexican Urbanism in the Sixteenth Century," *Art Bulletin*, 24:161-171 (1942); on northern South America, Carlos Martínez, *Apuntes sobre el urbanismo en el Nuevo Reino de Granada* (Bogotá: Ediciones Banco de la República, 1967); Graziano Gasparini, "Formación de ciudades coloniales en Venezuela, siglo xvi," in *PICA*, 38th, Munich, 1968, vol. IV (Munich: Kommissionsverlag Klaus Renner, 1962), pp. 225-238; on Lower and Upper Peru, Ralph A. Gackenheimer, "The Peruvian City of the Sixteenth Century," in *The Urban Explosion in Latin America: A Continent in the Process of Modernization*, ed. Glenn H. Beyer (Ithaca, N.Y.: Cornell University Press, 1967), pp. 35-56, and the same author's "The Early Colonial Mining Town: Some Special Opportunities for the Study of Urban Structure," in *PICA*, 39th, Lima, 1970, vol. II (Lima: Instituto de Estudios Peruanos, 1972), pp. 359-372, which deals mainly with Potosí; on western Argentina, Jorge Comadrán Ruiz, "Nacimiento y desarrollo de los nucleos urbanos y el poblamiento de la campaña del país de Cuyo durante la época hispana," *AEA*, 19:145-246 (1962); on Chile, Gabriel Guarda, *Historia urbana del Reino de Chile* (Santiago: Editorial Andrés Bello, 1978).

A third category of works deals with municipal organization and function. It includes the following: Constantino Bayle, *Los cabildos seculares en la América española* (Madrid: Sapienta, 1952); essays by various authorities in Rafael Altamira and others, *Contribuciones a la historia municipal de América*, (Mexico: PIGH, 1951); and John P. Moore, *The Cabildo in Peru under the Habsburgs* (Durham, N.C.: Duke University Press, 1954). An excellent case study is Hildegard Krüger "Función y estructura social del cabildo colonial [sic] de Asunción," *JGSW*, 18:31-51 (1981).

Fourth, a number of maps and plans of colonial towns have been published, the most comprehensive collection being Instituto de Estudios de Administración Local, Seminario de Urbanismo (Spain), 1951, *Planos de ciudades iberoamericanas y filipinas existentes en el Archivo de Indias*, 2 vols. (Madrid: Casa de Silverio Aguirre, 1951).

## CHAPTER 8. COLONIZATION: EFFORTS TO INCORPORATE THE INDIANS

Standard works on Spanish Indian policy during the Conquest period are: Hanke, *The Spanish Struggle for Justice in the Conquest of America* [*Chap*. 5]; Magnus Mörner, *La Corona Española y los foráneos en los pueblos de Indios de América* (Stockholm: Almqvist and Wiksell, 1970); and Silvio Zavala, *New Viewpoints on the Spanish Colonization of America* (Philadelphia: University of Pennsylvania Press, 1943). A recent supplement to these works is *Estudios sobre política indigenista española en América*, vol. II: *Evangelización, régimen de vida y ecología, servicios personales, encomienda y tributos*, Seminario de Historia de América (Valladolid, Spain: Universidad de Valladolid, 1976).

Spanish perceptions of the Indian are examined by various authorities in "Symposium: El concepto del indio americano en la España de los siglos xvi y xvii," *PICA*, 36th Barcelona, Madrid, Seville, 1964, vol. IV (Seville: Editorial Católica Española, 1966), pp. 69-178. The role played by Las Casas in Indian affairs is evaluated in Juan Friede and Benjamin Keen, eds., *Bartolomé de Las Casas in History: Toward an Understanding of the Man and His Work* (DeKalb: Northern Illinois University Press, 1971).

The following articles are useful introductions to the Spanish American *encomienda* and, especially, its controversial features: Robert S. Chamberlain, "Castilian Backgrounds of the *Repartimiento-Encomienda*," in Carnegie Institution of Washington, *Contributions to American Anthropology and History*, 5(no. 25):19-66 (1939); the same author's "Simpson's *The Encomienda in New Spain* and Recent Encomienda Studies," *HAHR*, 34:238-250 (1954); F. A. Kirkpatrick, "Repartimiento-encomienda," *HAHR*, 19:372-379 (1939); the same author's "The Landless Encomienda," *HAHR*, 22:765-774 (1942); James Lockhart, "Encomienda and Hacienda: The Evolution of the Great Estate in the Spanish Indies," *HAHR*, 49:411-429 (1969); and Robert G. Keith, "Encomienda, Hacienda and Corregimiento in Spanish America," *HAHR*, 51:431-466 (1971).

A pioneer substantive study of the *encomienda* with emphasis on its juridical features is Silvio Zavala, *La encomienda indiana* (Madrid: Centro de Estudios Históricos, 1935). Standard regional works include Lesley B. Simpson, *The Encomienda in New Spain: The Beginnings of Spanish Mexico* (rev. and enl., ed.; Berkeley: University of California Press, 1966); William L. Sherman, *Forced Native Labor in Sixteenth-Century Central America* (Lincoln: University of Nebraska Press, 1979); Eduardo Arcila Farías, *El régimen de la encomienda en Venezuela*, PEEHA, 106 (Seville, 1957); Colmenares, *Encomienda y población en la provincia de Pamplona, 1549-1650* [*Chap. 6*]; M. Darío Fajardo, *El régimen de la encomienda en la Provincia de Vélez (Población indígena y economía)* (Bogotá: Universidad de los Andes, 1969); Manuel Belaúnde Guinassi, *La encomienda en el Perú* (Lima: Biblioteca Mercurio Peruano, 1945); Néstor Meza Villalobos, *Política indiana en los orígenes de la sociedad chilena* (Santiago: Universidad de Chile, 1951); and Elman R. Service, "The Encomienda in Paraguay," *HAHR*, 31:230-252 (1951).

On the Indian *corregimiento* see Guillermo Lohmann Villena, *El Corregidor de Indios en el Perú bajo los Austrias* (Madrid: Ediciones Cultura Hispánica, 1957); on Indian tributes see José Miranda, *El tributo indígena en la Nueva España durante el siglo xvi* (Mexico: El Colegio de México, 1952).

The religious climate that generated and formed the missionary enterprise in the Indies is treated in Marcel Bataillon, *Érasme et l'Espagne: Recherches sur l'histoire spirituelle du xv^e siècle* (Paris: E. Droz, 1937); and in José García Oro, *Cisneros y la reforma del clero español en tiempo de los Reyes Católicos* (Madrid: C.S.I.C., 1971).

Good general surveys of the early missionary effort in the Indies are Pedro Borges, *Métodos misionales en la cristianización de América, siglo xvi* (Madrid: C.S.I.C., 1960); and Lino Gómez Canedo, *Evangelización y conquista: Experiencia franciscana en Hispanoamérica* (Mexico: Editorial Porrúa, 1977). See also Constantino Bayle, *El clero secular y la evangelización de América* (Madrid: C.S.I.C., 1950), which emphasizes the contribution of the secular clergy.

In the genre of regional works, the classic study of the evangelization of Mexico is Robert Ricard, *Conquête spirituelle du Mexique*, Travaux et mémoires de l'Institut d'Ethnologie, vol. XX (Paris: University of Paris, 1933), trans. Lesley B. Simpson as *The Spiritual Conquest of Mexico* (Berkeley: University of California Press, 1966). For Guatemala, especially the creation of *congregaciones*, see Carmelo Sáenz de Santa María, "La 'reducción a poblados' en el siglo xvi en Guatemala," *AEA*, 29:187-228 (1972). Perhaps the best account of the missionary effort in Peru is Pierre Duviols, *La lutte contre les religions au- tochtones dans le Pérou colonial: "Extirpation de l'idolâtrie" entre 1532 et 1660* (Lima: Institut Français d'Études Andines, 1971). Also useful are Fernando de Armas Medina, *Cristianización del Perú, 1532-1660*, PEEHA, 75 (Seville, 1953); and Antonine Tibesar, O.F.M., *Franciscan Beginnings in Peru* (Washington, D.C.: Academy of American Francis- can History, 1953).

The literature on the adaptation of the Indian to Spanish culture and institutions is surveyed in Karen Spalding, "The Colonial Indian: Past and Future Research Perspectives," *LARR*, 7(no. 1):47-76 (Spring 1972). Among particular works on the subject, Charles Gibson, *The Aztecs under Spanish Rule: A History of the Indians of the Valley of Mex- ico, 1519-1810* (Stanford, Calif.: Stanford University Press, 1964), stands out. A short but perceptive analysis of Mayan reactions is Inga Clendinnen, "Landscape and World View: The Survival of Yucatec Maya Culture under Spanish Conquest," *Comparative Studies in Society and History*, 22:374-393 (1980). For Peru see Wechtel, *The Vision of the Vanquished [Chap. 5]*; and the older but still respectable George Kubler, "The Quechua in the Colonial World," in *Handbook of South American Indians* ed. Julian H. Steward, vol. II: *The Andean Civilizations* (Washington, D.C.: U.S. Government Printing Office, 1946), pp. 331-410.

The particular problem of the Indian's acceptance of Christianity is discussed and de- bated in Ursula Lamb, "Religious Conflicts in the Conquest of Mexico," *Journal of the History of Ideas*, 17:526-539 (1956); Nicolau D'Olwer, "Comments on the Evangeliza- tion of New Spain," *TA*, 14:399-410 (1957-58); Wigberto Jiménez Moreno, "The In- dians of America and Christianity," *TA*, 14:411-431; and Duviols, *La lutte contre les religions autochtones*, already cited in this chapter essay.

An excellent introduction to the study of colonial Spanish American societies is James Lockhart, "The Social History of Colonial Spanish America: Evolution and Potential," *LARR*, 7(no. 1):6-45 (Spring 1972). The author, however, raises a definitional problem. He makes a distinction between the "informal, the unarticulated, the daily and ordinary manifestations of human existence," which he regards as the substance of true social his- tory, and the more formal structuring of society into classes and ranks, a theme that might better be termed "the history of societies." He also makes the point that social history — or the history of societies — is general history. It cannot be separated from the economic, political, and demographic forces that help to shape it.

In the text of this chapter and in chapter 18, "American Societies and American Iden- tities," I have used a structural treatment if for no other reason than that it lends itself more readily to synthesis than does an infinite range of informal and unarticulated social phenomena. The titles listed in the corresponding bibliographical essays reflect this ap- proach. Also, I have selected only items that deal explicitly or primarily with social orga- nization but remind the reader that many of the works listed in other chapter essays con- tain relevant materials.

In my estimation, the best general survey of the social order in the Spanish Indies is Guillermo Céspedes del Castillo, "La sociedad colonial americana en los siglos xvi y xvii," in Jaime Vicens Vives, ed., *Historia de España y América [General Works]*, III, 388-578. Also useful is Sergio Bagú, *Estructura social de la colonia: Ensayo de historia comparada de América Latina* (Buenos Aires: El Ateneo, 1952), which gives an economic interpreta- tion of social structures in both Spanish America and Brazil. A short but important spe- cialized essay is Richard Konetzke, "Estado y sociedad en las Indias," *Estudios Amer- icanos*, 3(no. 8):33-58 (1951), which deals with the role of the state in the formation of colonial society.

Studies of colonial societies in various regions of the Indies include: Lyle N. McAlister, "Social Structure and Social Change in New Spain," *HAHR*, 43:349-370 (1963), which the author now admits oversimplifies; John K. Chance, *Race and Class in Colonial Oaxaca* (Stanford, Calif.: Stanford University Press, 1978); MacLeod, *Spanish Central America* [*Chap. 6*]; Frank Moya Pons, *Historia colonial de Santo Domingo* (Santiago, D.R.: Universidad Católica Madre y Maestra, 1974); and Germán Colmenares, *Historia económica y social de Colombia, 1537-1719* (2nd ed.; Medellín, Col.: Editorial La Carretera, 1975). Recommendable works dealing particularly with the societies of the Conquest period are Peggy K. Liss, *Mexico under Spain, 1521-1556: Society and the Origins of Nationality* (Chicago: University of Chicago Press, 1975); Manuel Tejarda Fernández, *Aspecto de la vida social en Cartagena de Indias durante el seiscientos*, *PEEHA*, 87 (Seville, 1954); James Lockhart, *Spanish Peru, 1532-1560: A Colonial Society* (Madison: University of Wisconsin Press, 1968); and Josep M. Barnadas, *Charcas, 1535-1565: Orígenes históricos de una sociedad colonial* (La Paz: Centro de Investigación y Promoción del Campesinado, 1973). Tomás Thayer Ojeda, *Formación de la sociedad chilena y censo de la población de Chile en los años de 1540 a 1565*, 3 vols. (Santiago: Universidad de Chile, 1939-41), is a rich mine of information but deficient in classification and analysis.

## CHAPTER 9. THE ROYAL SEÑORÍO IN THE INDIES

Historians have devoted more pages to the government of the Indies than any other aspect of Spain's presence in the New World. Most of their output has run to descriptions of laws and institutions and legalistic interpretations. The best general survey in this category is still Haring, *The Spanish Empire in America* [*General Works*]. Eulália María Lahmayer Lôbo, *Processo administrativo ibero-americano* (São Paulo: Biblioteca do Exército-Editôra, 1962), is also valuable, especially because of its comparative treatment of colonial Brazilian and Spanish American administrative organization and practice. Although rather narrow in scope and concept, the standard work on Spanish colonial law is José María Ots Capdequí, *Historia del derecho español en América y del derecho indiano* (Madrid: Aguilar, 1969). The thinking of leading political theorists of the times about the nature of the incipient Spanish state in the Indies is reviewed and analyzed in Bernice Hamilton, *Political Thought in Sixteenth-Century Spain: A Study of the Political Ideas of Vitoria, De Soto, Suárez, and Molina* (Oxford: The Clarendon Press, 1963).

Unquestionably the most perceptive interpretation of the formative years of Spanish colonial government is Mario Góngora, *El estado en el derecho indiano* (Santiago: Universidad de Chile, 1951). Some of its content appears in English in the author's *Studies* [*General Works*].

"Private" government as represented by the *adelantado* is described in a general way in Roscoe R. Hill, "The Office of *Adelantado*," *Political Science Quarterly*, 28:646-668 (1913). A meticulous case study of this office is Eugene Lyon, *The Enterprise of Florida: Pedro Menéndez de Avilés and the Spanish Conquest of 1565-68* (Gainesville: The University Presses of Florida, 1976). Works dealing with conflicts between royal government and the *señorial* aspirations of conquerors and first settlers include Troy S. Floyd, *The Columbus Dynasty in the Caribbean, 1492-1526* (Albuquerque: University of New Mexico Press, 1973); Bernardo García Martínez, *El Marquesado del Valle: Tres siglos de régimen señorial en Nueva España* (Mexico: El Colegio de México, 1969); Luís González Obregón, *Los precursores de la independencia mexicana en el siglo xvi* (Paris: Viuda de C. Bouret, 1906), which describes the conspiracy of the Avila brothers; and Marcel Bataillon,

"Les colons du Pérou contra Charles Quint: Analyse du mouvement pizarriste," *AESC*, 3:479-494 (1967), a study of the Gonzalo Pizarro revolt in Peru. On the political rise and decline of Spanish American towns see Frederick R. Pike, "The Municipality and the System of Checks and Balances in Spanish American Colonial Administration," *TA*, 15:139-158 (1958-59); and Woodrow Borah, "Representative Institutions in the Spanish Empire in the Sixteenth Century: The New World," *TA*, 12:246-256 (1955-56).

Following are respectable works dealing with superior agencies of royal government in the Indies: on the Council of the Indies, Ernst Schäfer, *El Consejo Real y Supremo de las Indias: Su historia, organización y labor administrativo hasta la terminación de la Casa de Austria*, 2 vols. (Seville: Centro de Historia de América and E.E.H.A., 1935-47); and Demetrio Ramos and others, *El Consejo de las Indias en el siglo xvi* (Valladolid, Spain: Universidad de Valladolid, 1970); on the viceregal system, Lillian E. Fisher, *Viceregal Administration in the Spanish Colonies* (Berkeley: University of California Press, 1926); and the citations in note 2 for this chapter, which debate the origins of the system; on the *audiencia*, Charles C. Cunningham, *The Audiencia in the Spanish Colonies* (Berkeley: University of California Press, 1919); and John H. Parry, *The Audiencia of New Galicia in the Sixteenth Century* (Cambridge: Cambridge University Press, 1948).

The organization and operation of the royal treasury in the Indies is described in Ismael Sánchez-Bella, *La organización financiera de las Indias (siglo xvi)*, *PEEHA*, 179 (Seville, 1968).

Studies of lower levels of royal government include Alfonso García Gallo, "Alcaldes mayores y corregidores en Indias," in Congreso Venezolano de Historia, 1st, Caracas, 1971, *Memoria*, 2 vols. (Caracas: Academia Nacional de las Historia, 1972), I, 301-347; and Carlos Castañeda, "The *corregidor* in Spanish Colonial Administration," *HAHR*, 9:446-461 (1929). On specialized institutions for the governance of the Indians see Lohmann Villena, *El Corregidor de Indios [Chap. 8]*. The works of Bayle, Altamira, and Moore listed in the essay for chapter 7 describe municipal government and its connections with royal administration.

The function of inspection is treated in Guillermo Céspedes del Castillo, "La visita como institución indiana," *AEA*, 3:984-1025 (1946); Charles H. Cunningham, "The *residencia* in the Spanish Colonies," *Southwestern Historical Quarterly*, 21:253-278 (1917-18); and José María Mariluz Urquijo, *Ensayo sobre los juicios de residencia indianos*, *PEEHA*, 70 (Seville, 1952).

The best introduction to ecclesiastical organization and government in the Indies is the article "Latin America, Church in," in *New Catholic Encyclopedia*, vol. VIII (New York: McGraw-Hill, 1967), pp. 448-469. Although it overemphasizes Jesuit contributions, a satisfactory comprehensive history of these subjects is León Lopétegui, Félix Zubillaga, and Antonio de Egaña, *Historia de las iglesia en la América española desde el descubrimiento hasta comienzos del siglo xix*, 2 vols. (Madrid: Editorial Católica, 1965-66). Two important regional studies are Mariano Cuevas, *Historia de la Iglesia en México*, 5 vols. (5th ed.; Mexico: Editorial Patria, 1946-47), I, II; and Rubén Vargas Ugarte, *Historia de la Iglesia en el Perú*, 3 vols. (Lima: Imprenta Santa María, 1953-61), I. A brief but well-documented study of the *real patronato* is Manuel Gutiérrez de Arce, "Regio patronato indiano: Ensayo de valorización histórico-canónica," *AEA*, 11:107-168 (1954). A satisfactory account in English is William E. Shiels, S.J., *King and Church: The Rise and Fall of the Patronato Real* (Chicago: Loyola University Press, 1961).

Compared with work done on civil and ecclesiastical government, studies of the defense of the Indies are few. The juridical bases of Spain's defense policy and the issues that brought northern European intruders into Spanish American waters are examined in Paul E. Hoffmann, "Diplomacy and the Papal Donation, 1493-1585," *TA*, 30:151-183 (1973-74). The best survey of the activities of these interlopers is Kenneth R. Andrews, *The Spanish Caribbean: Trade and Plunder, 1530-1630* (New Haven, Conn.: Yale University Press, 1978). The best work on the evolution of Spanish defensive measures and, especially, their fiscal aspects is Paul E. Hoffmann, *The Spanish Crown and the Defense of the Caribbean, 1535-1585: Precedent, Patrimonialism and Royal Parsimony* (Baton Rouge: Louisiana State University Press, 1980). The classic Cesáreo Fernández Duro, *Armada española desde la unión de los reinos de Castilla y León*, 9 vols. (Madrid: Est. Tipográfico "Sucesores de Rivadeneyra," 1895-1903), especially vol. II, contains a wealth of detail on naval operations. A more concise account of the defense of maritime trade routes is Clarence H. Haring, *Trade and Navigation between Spain and the Indies in the Time of the Habsburgs* (Cambridge, Mass.: Harvard University Press, 1918).

Good short accounts of the defense of Indian frontiers are Philip W. Powell, *Soldiers, Indians and Silver: The Northward Advance of the Frontier of New Spain, 1550-1600* (Berkeley: University of California Press, 1952), chaps. 1-5; and Alvaro Jara, *Guerre et société au Chile* (Paris: Université de Paris, 1961), chaps. 1-4.

The best survey of imperial communications is Ernst Schäfer, "Comunicaciones marítimas y terrestres de las Indias españolas," *AEA*, 3:969-983 (1946). A much more detailed analysis of Atlantic maritime routes, distances, and elapsed times may be found in Chaunu and Chaunu, *Séville et l'Atlantique* [*Chap. 5*], VIII, part 1. On the royal mails see Cayetano Alcázar Molina, *Historia del correo en América (notas y documentos para su estudio)* (Madrid: Sucesores de Rivadeneyra, 1920).

Works on the men and classes of men who governed the Indies during the Conquest are considerably scarcer than institutional studies. Among them are Ursula Lamb, *Frey Nicolás de Ovando, gobernador de las Indias, 1501-1509* (Madrid: C.S.I.C., 1956); Arthur S. Aiton, *Antonio de Mendoza, First Viceroy of New Spain* (Durham, N.C.: Duke University Press, 1927); María Justina Sarabia Viejo, *Don Luis de Velasco: Virrey de Nueva España* (Seville: E.E.H.A., 1978); and Javier Malagón-Barcelo, "The Role of the Letrado in the Colonization of America," *TA*, 18:1-17 (1961-62).

## CHAPTER 10. THE FRUITS OF THE LAND

The economic historiography of the Spanish Indies is still an underdeveloped field. It has tended to emphasize externally oriented forms of activity, especially mining, trans-Atlantic commerce, and the slave trade, and has neglected internal production and trade. Most of the literature in the field is descriptive of the organization and regulation of economic activities. With some exceptions that will be noted later, it is deficient in serial statistical data on the factors of production and the quantities and prices of goods produced and exchanged. This is particularly true of the earlier years, that is through the 1560s, with which this chapter is concerned.

These deficiencies have induced a new generation of economic historians, mostly Latin American and French scholars trained in or influenced by the "Annales School" to examine the state of their field in terms of what needs to be done and methodologies to be employed. The most comprehensive summary of their conclusions and proposals is *La historia económica en América Latina*, 2 vols. (Mexico: Sep/Setentas, 1972). See also Alvaro Jara, *Problemas y métodos de la historia económica hispanoamericana* (Caracas: Universidad Central de Venezuela, 1969); and Frédéric Mauro, *Des produits et des hommes: Essais historiques latino-américains, xvi-xx siècles* (The Hague: Mouton, 1972).

Until the "new economic history" is written we must do with what we have. To begin with, a solid general economic history of the colonial era cannot be found, nor will one be written until great lacunae in quantitative data are filled. However, some partial treatments and broadly constructed overviews are available. Chaunu and Chaunu, *Séville et l'Atlantique* [*Chap.* 5] is concerned mainly with trans-Atlantic trade, but vol. VIII, part 1, contains valuable information on internal production and trade along with wide-ranging and stimulating interpretations and propositions. Sergio Bagú, *Economía de la sociedad colonial: Ensayo de historia comparada de América Latina* (Buenos Aires: El Ateneo, 1949), is a provocative attempt to compare the economies of the Spanish Indies, Brazil, and the English, French, and Dutch New World colonies within what I take to be a neo-Marxist framework. Vicens Vives, *An Economic History of Spain* [*Chaps.* 1 and 2], has some good textbook-level chapters on Spanish America and has the additional merit of relating developments in Spain and the Indies. Hans Pohl, *Studien zur Wirtschafts-geschichte Lateinamerikas* (Wiesbaden: Franz Steiner Verlag, 1976), is a wide-ranging and thoughtful collection of essays on the Spanish colonial economy, although it is relatively thin on the sixteenth century. Laura Randall, *A Comparative Economic History of Latin America, 1500-1914*, 4 vols. (Ann Arbor, Mich.: University Microfilms International, 1977), is an ambitious attempt to compare the economies of Mexico, Argentina, Brazil, and Peru over four centuries, but its treatment is conventional and the formative sixteenth century is given scant attention.

The writing of regional economic histories has also been handicapped by a lack of basic data, especially for the earlier years. The following, however, are commendable efforts and devote considerable attention to the sixteenth century: Alejandra Moreno Toscano, *Geografía económica de México, siglo xvi* (Mexico: El Colegio de México, 1968); Moya Pons, *Historia colonial de Santo Domingo* [*Chap.* 8], especially part 1; Leví Marrero y Artiles, *Cuba: Economía y sociedad*, 8 vols. (vol. I, Rio Piedras, P.R.: Editorial San Juan, 1972; vols. II-VIII, Madrid: Editorial Playor, 1974–80), especially vol. II; MacLeod, *Spanish Central America* [*Chap.* 6]; Eduardo Arcila Farías, *Economía colonial de Venezuela* (Mexico: Fondo de Cultura Económica, 1946); Colmenares, *Historia económica y social de Colombia* [*Chap.* 8]; José M. Vargas, *La economía política de Ecuador durante la colonia* (Quito: Editorial Universitaria, 1957); Emilio Romero, *Historia económica del Perú* (Buenos Aires: Editorial Sudamericana, 1949), especially part 2; Ceferina Garcón Maceda, *Economía de Tucumán: Economía natural y economía monetaria* (Córdoba, Arg.: Editorial Sudamericana, 1968); and Alfredo Castillero Calvo, *Estructuras sociales y económicas de Veragua desde sus orígenes históricos, siglos xvi y xvii* (Panama: Editora Panamá, 1967).

A special category of general and regional views of the colonial Spanish American economy is the works of dependency theorists. These are discussed in the notes and bibliographical essay for chapter 17.

The factors of production in Conquest economies are rather unevenly covered in existing literature. A good general introduction to forms of land distribution, appropriation, and tenure is Juan Friede, "Proceso de formación territorial en la América intertropical," *JGSW*, 2:75-87 (1965). Important regional studies are Lesley B. Simpson, *Exploitation of Land in Central Mexico in the Sixteenth Century*, Ibero-Americana: 36 (Berkeley: University of California Press, 1952); François Chevalier, *La formation des grands domaines au Mexique: Terre et société aux xvie-xviie siècles* (Paris: Institut d'Ethnologie, 1952), trans. Alvin Eustis as *Land and Society in Colonial Mexico: The Great Hacienda* (Berkeley: University of California Press, 1963), chaps. 2-4; G. Michael Riley *Fernando Cortés and* the Marquesado in Morelos, 1522-1547: A Case Study in the Socioeconomic Development of Sixteenth-Century Mexico (Albuquerque: University of New Mexico Press, 1973); Hanns J. Prem, Milpa y hacienda: Tenencia de la tierra indígena y española en la Cuenca del Atoyac, Puebla, México, 1520-1650 (Wiesbaden: Franz Steiner Verlag, 1978); José M. Ots Capdequí, España en América: El régimen de tierras en la época colonial (Mexico: Fondo de Cultura Económica, 1959), which deals mainly with New Granada; and Jean Borde and Mario Góngora, Evolución de la propiedad rural en el Valle del Puangue, 2 vols. (Santiago: Universidad de Chile, 1956), I, chaps. 1-3.

Works on Indian labor are relatively abundant. The most comprehensive and up-to-date survey of the various forms employed is Juan A. Villamarín and Judith E. Villamarín, Indian Labor in Mainland Colonial Spanish America, University of Delaware, Latin American Studies Program, Occasional Papers and Monographs, no. 1 (Newark, 1975). Some of its definitions and interpretations, however, may be questioned. An important documentary study of the several forms is Silvio Zavala, El servicio personal de Indios en el Perú, vol. I: Extractos del siglo xvi (Mexico: El Colegio de México, 1978).

Following are more specialized studies: on Indian slavery see Jean-Pierre Berthe, "Aspects de l'esclavage des Indiens en Nouvelle-Espagne pendant la première moitié du xvi^e siècle," Journal de la Société des Americanistes (Paris), 54:189-209 (1965); and Silvio Zavala, "Los esclavos indios en Guatemala," HM, 19:459-465 (1969-70); on the encomienda see the works listed in the essay for chapter 8; on the repartimiento-mita see Lesley B. Simpson, Studies in the Administration of the Indians in New Spain, vol. III; The Repartimiento System of Forced Native Labor in New Spain and Guatemala, Ibero-Americana: 13 (Berkeley: University of California Press, 1938); Alberto Crespo Rodas, "La 'mita' de Potosí," Revista Histórica (Lima), 22:169-182 (1955-56); and Aquíles R. Pérez Tamayo, Las mitas en la Real Audiencia de Quito (Quito: Impresa del Ministerio del Tesorero, 1947).

Studies on the use of black slave labor as distinct from the institutional and social features of African slavery are relatively scarce compared to works on Indian labor. The best survey of the subject is Rolando Mellafe, Breve historia de la esclavitud negra en América Latina (Mexico: Secretaría de Educación Pública, 1973), trans. J. W. S. Judge as Negro Slavery in Latin America (Berkeley: University of California Press, 1975). Important regional studies are Bowser, The African Slave in Colonial Peru [Chap. 6]; and Mellafe, La introducción de la esclavitud negra en Chile [Chap. 6]. Information on the use of black slaves may also be found scattered throughout the general works on the African presence in the Indies listed in the essay for chapter 6, in the general and regional surveys of the colonial economy cited earlier in this chapter essay, and in the studies of particular economic sectors discussed immediately following.

I know of no monographic works on capital formation and investment during the Conquest period. Clues to the process, however, may be found in studies of the business activities of particular individuals and groups such as the following: Pike, Enterprise and Adventure [Chap. 6]; Enrique Otte, "Mercaderes burgaleses en los inicios del comercio con México," HM, 18:258-285 (1968-69); Guillermo Lohmann Villena, Les Espinosa: Une famille d'hommes d'affaires en Espagne et aux Indies à l'époque de la colonisation (Paris: S.E.V.P.E.N., 1968); and José Miranda, La función económica del encomendero en los orígenes del régimen colonial (2nd ed.; Mexico: U.N.A.M., 1965).

The most substantial work on the agricultural sector in the Indies is Victor M. Patiño, Historia de la actividad agropecuaria en América equinoccial (Cali, Col.: Imprenta Departamental, 1965). It is not properly a history, however, but rather a catalog of indigenous products and European introductions, conditions and methods of cultivation, forms of labor employed, and agrarian legislation. The following items are much briefer surveys of the state of the agricultural historiography of the Indies and problems needing attention: Demetrio Ramos, "Notas sobre historia de la economía agrícola de Hispanoamérica," *RI*, 26:79-96 (1966); and Rolando Mellafe, "Agricultura e historia colonial Hispanoamericana," in A. Jara and others, *Temas de historia económica hispanoamericana* (The Hague: Mouton, 1965), pp. 23-32.

The following items deal with the production of particular crops: on wheat, Chevalier, *Land and Society*, especially pp. 59-71; on sugar, Mervyn Ratekin, "The Early Sugar Industry in Española," *HAHR*, 34:1-19 (1954); and Fernando B. Sandoval, *La industria de azúcar en Nueva España* (Mexico: Editorial Jus, 1951); on dyestuffs, Jacques Heers, "La busqueda de colorantes," *HM*, 11:1-27 (1961-62); Raymond L. Lee, "Cochineal Production and Trade in New Spain to 1600," *TA*, 4:449-473 (1947-48); and Jean-Pierre Berthe, "El cultivo del 'pastel' en Nueva España," *HM*, 9:340-367 (1959-60); on cacao, J. Eric Thompson, "Notes on the Use of Cacao in Middle America," *Notes on Middle American Archeology and Ethnology*, no. 128:95-116 (1956); on silk, Woodrow Borah, *Silk Raising in Colonial Mexico*, Ibero-Americana: 20 (Berkeley: University of California Press, 1943). Many of the more general studies of colonial economies listed earlier in this chapter essay contain important information on agricultural production. See especially the materials on cacao in MacLeod, *Spanish Central America*, chaps. 4-5 [*Chap. 6*].

Early stockraising and grazing in the Indies awaits substantial monographic treatment. The following items, however, help to fill the gap: John J. Johnson, "The Introduction of the Horse into the Western Hemisphere," *HAHR*, 23:587-610 (1942); José Matesanz, "Introducción a la ganadería en Nueva España," *HM*, 14:533-566 (1964-65); Chevalier, *Land and Society*, chap. 3; William H. Dusenberry, *The Mexican Mesta* (Urbana: University of Illinois Press, 1963).

The most general survey of what is known about textile manufacturing in the Indies is Hans Pohl, "Algunas consideraciones sobre el desarrollo de la industria hispanoamericana—especialmente la textil—durante el siglo xvii," *AEA*, 28:459-477 (1951). Although concentrating on the seventeenth century, it contains useful information on sixteenth-century beginnings. Works on the industry in Mexico include Manuel Carrera Stampa, "El obraje novohispano," *Memorias de la Academia Mexicana de Historia*, 20:148-171 (1961); and William H. Dusenberry, "Woolen Manufacture in Sixteenth Century New Spain," *TA*, 4:223-234 (1947-48). For Peru see Fernando Silva Santisteban, *Los obrajes en el virreinato del Perú* (Lima: Museo Nacional de Historia, 1964).

Basic works on colonial guilds are Manuel Carrera Stampa, *Los gremios mexicanos: La organización gremial de Nueva España, 1521-1861* (Mexico: Edición y Distribución Ibero-Americano de Publicaciones, 1954); Héctor H. Samayoa Guevara, *Los gremios de artesanos en la Ciudad de Guatemala* (Guatemala: Editorial Universitaria, 1962); and Emilio Harth-Terre and Alberto Márquez Abanto, *Perspectiva social y económica del artesano virreinal en Lima* (Lima: Librería e Imprenta Gil, 1963).

The state of the historiography of the colonial mining industry is explored in Alvaro Jara, *Tres ensayos sobre la economía minera hispanoamericana* (Santiago: Universidad de Chile, 1966). For the general reader a satisfactory substantive survey is the semipopular Carlos Prieto, *La minería en el Nuevo Mundo* (Madrid: Ediciones de la Revista del Occidente, 1968), trans. as *Mining in the New World* (New York: McGraw-Hill, 1973). A more technical but rather poorly organized study is Modesto Bargallo, *La minería y la metalurgía en América española durante la época colonial* (Mexico: Fondo de Cultura Económica, 1955). Those who wish to pursue the subject further will find a great compendium of substantive, bibliographical, and historiographical information in *La minería hispana e iberoamericana: Contribución a su investigación histórica*, Proceedings of the Congreso Internacional de Minería Hispano e Hispano-Americano, 6th Madrid, 1970, 7 vols. (León: Cátedra de San Isidro, 1970- ).

Among works dealing with silver mining alone, a concise review of the factors and conditions of production is David A. Brading and Harry C. Cross, "Colonial Silver Mining: Mexico and Peru," *HAHR*, 52:545-579 (1972). A fine study of Mexico's most productive mining district in the sixteenth and seventeenth centuries is Peter J. Bakewell, *Silver Mining and Society in Colonial Mexico: Zacatecas, 1546-1700* (Cambridge: Cambridge University Press, 1972). On Peruvian mercury mining see Guillermo Lohmann Villena, *Las minas de Huancavelica en los siglos xvi y xvii, PEEHA*, 50 (Seville, 1949). The most substantial work on gold mining in the Indies is Robert C. West, *Colonial Placer Mining in Colombia* (Baton Rouge: Louisiana State University Press, 1952).

Earl J. Hamilton, *American Treasure and the Price Revolution in Spain, 1501-1650* (Cambridge, Mass.: Harvard University Press, 1934), is still the standard work on the volume and value of precious metals produced in the Indies. The serial data it contains, however, are on legally registered imports at Seville and, therefore, are not an accurate measure of total production.

## CHAPTER 11. THE COMMERCE OF THE INDIES

The general and regional economic histories and studies of the particular sectors of production listed in the preceding chapter essay contain useful materials on trade. I will relist here only those that have a special relevance to the subject under discussion.

The literature on pre-Conquest and post-Conquest markets is surveyed in R. J. Bromley and Richard Symanski, "Marketplace Trade in Latin America," *LARR*, 9(no. 3):3-39 (Fall 1974). The works by Manuel Carrera Stampa and Emilio Harth-Terre and Alberto Márquez Abanto cited in the previous chapter essay contain materials on the function of the guilds in local commerce. The following items deal with the marketing of basic food items: Enrique Florescano, "El abasto y la legislación de granos en el siglo xvi," *HM*, 14:567-630 (1964-65); and William H. Dusenberry, "The Regulation of Meat Supply in Sixteenth-Century Mexico," *HAHR*, 28:38-52 (1948).

Interregional and interprovincial trade in the Indies is surveyed in Demetrio Ramos, *Minería y comercio interprovincial en hispanoamérica (siglos xvi, xvii y xviii)* (Valladolid, Spain: Universidad de Valladolid, 1970), especially part 2. Its main theme is the role of mining in fomenting commerce. It is, however, short on detail and statistical data. More specialized studies are Woodrow Borah, *Early Trade and Navigation between Mexico and Peru*, Ibero-Americana: 38 (Berkeley: University of California Press, 1954); and Eduardo Arcila Farías, *Comercio entre Venezuela y México en los siglos xvi y xvii* (Mexico: El Colegio de México, 1950).

Any listing of works on trans-Atlantic trade must begin with the Chaunus's *Séville et l'Atlantique [Chap. 5]*, a monumental collection of serialized statistics on the owners, masters, kinds, cargoes, tonnage, and routes of ships sailing to and from the Indies during the period 1504-1650. Vol. VIII, bound in three parts, synthesizes much of the statistical material in the rest of the work and contains invaluable interpretations. A condensation of the materials in the master work may be found in Pierre Chaunu, *Conquête et exploitation des nouveaux mondes [General Works]*. Haring, *Trade and Navigation [Chap. 9]*, is still a useful descriptive treatment of the organization of the *Carrera*. A concise survey of forms of shipping is A. P. Usher, "Spanish Ships and Shipping in the Sixteenth and

Seventeenth Centuries," in *Facts and Factors in Economic History* (Cambridge, Mass.: Harvard University Press, 1932), pp. 189-211.

The most up-to-date compilation of data on traffic in African slaves is Curtin, *The Atlantic Slave Trade* [*Chap. 6*], chaps. 2, 4. For a detailed treatment of the organizational forms and legal aspects of the trade see the classic Georges Scelle, *La traite négrière aux Indes de Castille: Contrats et traités d'assiento*, 2 vols. (Paris, 1906); and for a shorter description, Mellafe, *Negro Slavery* [*Chap. 10*], chaps. 2, 3.

The marketing of slaves in the Indies is described in Robert L. Brady, "The Domestic Slave Trade in Sixteenth-Century Mexico," *TA*, 24:281-289 (1967-68), Bowser, *The African Slave in Colonial Peru* [*Chap. 6*], chaps. 3-4; and Mellafe, *La introducción de la esclavitud negra en Chile* [*Chap. 6*]. The standard monograph on the Canaries trade with the Indies is Francisco Morales Padrón, *El comercio canario-americano (siglos xvi, xvii y xviii)*, *PEEHA*, 89 (Seville, 1955). We know little about clandestine commerce in the sixteenth century except for the general circumstances that created it.

Shäfer, "Comunicaciones marítimas y terrestres de las Indias españolas" [*Chap. 9*], is a succinct description of sea and land routes carrying the commerce of the Indies. Pierre Chaunu's analyses of trans-Atlantic routes are summarized in his "Les routes espagnoles de l'Atlantique," *AEA*, 25:95-128 (1968). Following are more specialized works on land transportation routes in the Indies: West and Augelli, *Middle America* [*Chap. 4*], pp. 299-302; Ronald D. Hussey, "Spanish Colonial Trails in Panama," *RHA*, no. 6:47-74 (1939); María T. Menchen Barrios, "Los caminos del Perú en el siglo xvi," in *PICA*, 36th Barcelona, Madrid, Seville, 1964, vol. III (Seville: Editorial Católica Española, 1966), pp. 253-263; Gwendolin B. Cobb, "Supply and Transportation for the Potosí Mines, 1545-1640," *HAHR*, 29:24-45 (1949); and Humberto Vázquez-Machicado, "Los caminos de Santa Cruz de la Sierra en el siglo xvi," *RHA*, no. 40:487-551 (1955). On forms of carriage see David R. Ringrose, "Carting in the Hispanic World: An Example of Divergent Development," *HAHR*, 50:30-51 (1970).

Very few works exist dealing specifically with water transport in the internal commerce of the Indies. However, the studies of Arcila Farías and Borah listed earlier in this chapter essay include substantial information on maritime routes. The following items deal with inland waterways: Lyle N. McAlister, "The Discovery and Exploration of the Nicaraguan Transisthmian Route, 1519-1545," *TA*, 10:259-276 (1953-54); and Raúl A. Molina, "Las primeras navegaciones del Rio de la Plata después de la fundación de Juan de Garay," *RHA*, no. 45:49-92 (1958).

Two excellent introductions to the kinds and values of money used in the Indies are Manuel Luengo Muñoz, "Sumario noción de las monedas de Castilla e Indias en el siglo xvi," *AEA*, 7:325-366 (1950); and Manuel Moreyra y Paz-Soldán, "La técnica de la moneda colonial: Unidades, pesos, medidas y relaciones," *RHA*, no. 20:347-369 (1945). Both contain tables relating kinds, weights, and values of monies of exchange and account. On American mints see Robert I. Nesmith, *The Coinage of the First Mint of the Americas at Mexico City, 1536-1572* (New York: American Numismatic Society, 1955); Humberto F. Burzio, *La ceca de Lima, 1565-1824* (Madrid: Fábrica Nacional de Moneda y Timbre, 1958); the same author's *La ceca de la Villa Imperial de Potosí y la moneda colonial* (Buenos Aires: Imprenta J. Peuser, 1945); and Martin L. Seeger, "Media of Exchange in 16th Century New Spain and the Spanish Response," *TA*, 35:168-184 (1978-79), which discusses unofficial media of exchange as well as mintage.

I know of no monographic study on the use of credit in the overseas or internal trade of the Indies. Scattered information on the subject may be found in the items listed in the preceding chapter essays that deal with capital, especially, Pike, *Enterprise and Adventure* [*Chap. 6*]. Perhaps the best source of information is a contemporary account, Fray Tomás de Mercado, *Summa de tratos y contratos* (Seville, 1587).

On metrology in the Indies see Manuel Carrera Stampa, "The Evolution of Weights and Measures in New Spain," *HAHR*, 29:2-23 (1949). J. Villasana Haggard, *Handbook for Translators of Spanish Documents* (Ann Arbor, Mich.: University Microfilms, 1941), is a useful reference for translating Spanish colonial units into modern units.

With reference to regulation of trade, the standard work on Spanish mercantilism is José López Larraz, *La época del mercantilismo en Castilla, 1500-1700* (2nd ed.; Madrid: Ediciones Atlas, 1943). Haring, *Trade and Navigation* [*Chap. 9*], is useful on regulatory measures and mechanisms. The function of *consulados* is examined in Robert S. Smith, *The Spanish Guild Merchant: A History of the Consulado, 1250-1700* (Durham, N.C.: Duke University Press, 1940), chap. 6 of which deals with the Seville merchant guild.

Taxes bearing on commerce are discussed in Sánchez-Bella, *La organización financiera de las Indias* [*Chap. 9*], and Ramón Carande, *Carlos V y sus banqueros*, vol. II: *La hacienda real de Castilla* (Madrid: Sociedad de Estudios y Publicaciones, 1949). The standard monograph on the *avería* is Guillermo Céspedes del Castillo, *La avería en el comercio de Indias*, *PEEHA*, 15 (Seville, 1945).

The following items discuss intrusion of foreigners into the Spanish monopoly: Pike, *Enterprise and Adventure* [*Chap. 6*]; Pauline Croft, *The Spanish Company*, London Record Society, Publications, vol. IX (London: The Record Society, 1973); and Albert Girard, *Le commerce français à Séville et à Cadix au temps des Habsbourgs: Contribution a l'étude du commerce étranger en Espagne aux xvi^e et xvii^e siècles* (Paris: E. de Boucard, 1932).

Problems of prices and price history are considered in Enrique Florescano, "La historia de los precios en la época colonial de Hispanoamérica: Tendencias, métodos de trabajo y objetivos," *Latino América: Anuario/Centro de Estudios Latinoamericanos*, U.N.A.M., 1:111-130 (1968); and Ruggiero Romano, "Historia colonial hispanoamericana e historia de los precios," in *Temas de historia económica hispanoamericana* [*Chap. 10*], pp. 11-21. Both articles make the point that scarcity of data and the pervasiveness of nonmonetary economies prevent systematic work on price history in the Spanish Indies before about 1700. Some efforts in this direction have, however, been made, including Woodrow Borah and Sherburne F. Cook, *Price Trends of Some Basic Commodities in Central Mexico, 1531-1570*, Ibero-Americana: 40 (Berkeley: University of California Press, 1958); and Manuel Luengo Muñoz, "Sumaria noción del poder adquisitivo de la moneda en Indias durante el siglo xvi," *AEA*, 8:35-57 (1951). The latter work contains scattered samplings of prices of domestic and imported commodities and of incomes of various classes of persons from sailors to viceroys.

## CHAPTER 12. THE CONQUEST OF BRAZIL

Compared with the enormous volume of literature on the Spanish Conquest, the historiography of the conquest of Brazil is thin, and for obvious reasons. Much less happened on the Portuguese side of the Line of Demarcation.

Unquestionably the best-balanced account of the Brazilian conquest in the sixteenth century is John Hemming, *Red Gold: The Conquest of the Brazilian Indians, 1500-1760* (Cambridge, Mass.: Harvard University Press, 1978), chaps. 1-7. As a shorter synthesis, the older William B. Greenlee, "The First Half-Century of Brazilian History," *Mid-America*, 25:91-120 (1943), is still useful. Mention must also be made of the series of specialized papers by various authorities on discovery and conquest contained in *História da coloni-zação portuguesa do Brasil: Edição monumental comemorativa do primeiro centenário da independência do Brasil*, gen. ed. Carlos Malheiro Dias, 3 vols. (Oporto: Litografia Nacional, 1921-26). The essays themselves reflect the nationalistic spirit of the occasion that inspired them and have a rather restricted point of view. They are greatly enriched, however, by their heavy documentation. When individually cited hereinafter, the *História* will be abbreviated as *HCPB*.

Regarding the so-called period of neglect, the brazilwood trade is described in António Baião, "O comércio do pau Brasil," in *HCPB*, II, 317-347; and John L. Vogt, "Fernão de Loronha and the Rental of Brazil in 1502, a New Chronology," *TA*, 24:153-159 (1967-68). What little is known about the first Franciscans is summarized in Dagoberto Romag, "História dos Franciscanos no Brasil desde os princípios até a criação da província franciscana de Santo Antônio (1500-1659)," *Vita Franciscana* (Curitiba, Brazil), 16:179-187, 233-239 (1939). On *degredados* see Emília Viotti da Costa, "Primeiros povoadores do Brasil: O problema dos degredados," *Revista de História* (São Paulo) 13(no. 27):3-23 (July-September 1956).

The French presence in Brazil and Portuguese reactions are introduced in Charles Nowell, "The French in Sixteenth Century Brazil," *TA*, 5:62-67 (1967-68). The voyage of Martim Afonso de Sousa and its significance are the subjects of Jordão de Freitas, "A expedição de Martim Afonso de Sousa," in *HCPB*, III, 97-164.

The best analysis of the donatary or captaincy system is Johnson, "The Donatary Captaincy in Historical Perspective: Portuguese Backgrounds to Colonial Brazil" [*Chap. 3*]. On the first donataries see Elaine Sanceau, *Capitães do Brasil*, trans. António Álvaro Doria (Oporto: Livraria Civilização-Editora, 1956); and Pedro Azevedo, "Os primeiros donatários," in *HCPB*, III, 191-216. The life and works of Duarte Coelho, the most famous among the captains-donatary, are surveyed in Francis A. Dutra, "Duarte Coelho Pereira, First Lord-Proprietor of Pernambuco; The Beginnings of a Dynasty," *TA*, 29:415-441 (1972-73).

For a succinct account of the foundation of Salvador (Bahia) and the establishment of the governorship-general see Ruth L. Butler, "Thomé de Sousa, First Governor-General of Brazil, 1549-1553," *Mid-America*, 24:229-251 (1944). See also Thales de Azevedo, *Povoamento da Cidade do Salvador* (2nd ed., rev.; São Paulo: Companhia Editôra Nacional, 1955); and Pedro Azevedo, "a instituição do govêrno geral," *HCPB*, III, 327-383. Ruth L. Butler, "Mem de Sá, Third Governor-General of Brazil, 1557-1572," *Mid-America*, 24:111-137 (1942), covers the founding of Rio de Janeiro and the administration of its founder.

## CHAPTER 13. THE COLONIZATION OF BRAZIL TO ABOUT 1570

The theory and practice of town founding and early patterns of urbanization in Brazil are discussed in Paulo F. Santos, "Formação de cidades no Brasil colonial," in *Colóquio Internacional de Estudos Luso-Brasileiros*, 5th, Coimbra, Portugal, 1963, *Actas* (Coimbra: Gráfica de Coimbra, 1968), pp. 7-116; Aroldo de Azevedo, *Vilas e cidades do Brasil colonial: Ensaio de geografia urbana retrospectiva* (São Paulo: Universidade de São Paulo, 1956); Edmundo Zenha, *O município no Brasil* (São Paulo: Instituto Progresso Editorial, 1948); and Pierre Deffontains, "The Origin and Growth of the Brazilian Network of Towns," *Geographical Review*, 28:379-399 (1938).

The following works are concerned especially with municipal organization and government: Charles R. Boxer, *Portuguese Society in the Tropics: The Municipal Councils of*

*Goa, Macao, Bahia, and Luanda, 1510-1800* (Madison: University of Wisconsin Press, 1965), especially chap. 3; Affonso Ruy de Sousa, *A história da câmara municipal da cidade do Salvador* (Salvador, Brazil: Câmara Municipal, 1953); and Maria da Concepção Martins Ribeiro, "Os oficiais da câmara de São Paulo no século xvi," in Congresso de História Nacional, 4th, Rio de Janeiro, 1951, *Anais*, vol. IX (Rio de Janeiro, 1951), pp. 461-500.

Odulfo Van der Vat, *Princípios da Igreja no Brasil* (Rio de Janeiro: Editôra Vozes, 1952), describes the first parishes in Brazil. Manoel S. Cardozo, "The Lay Brotherhoods of Colonial Bahia," *Catholic Historical Review*, 33:12-30 (1947), is a good introduction to the *irmandade*. A. J. R. Russell-Wood, *Fidalgos and Philanthropists: The Santa Casa de Misericórdia of Bahia, 1550-1775* (Berkeley: University of California Press, 1968), is a fuller study of Brazil's most prestigious sodality. Both Cardozo's and Russell-Wood's work, however, is mainly concerned with the institution in full bloom in the seventeenth and eighteenth centuries.

Comparative analyses of Brazilian and Spanish American towns and patterns of urbanization may be found in Morse, "Some Characteristics of Latin American Urban History" [*Chap.* 7]; the same author's "Recent Research on Latin American Urbanization: A Selective Survey with Commentary," *LARR*, 1(no. 1):35-74 (Fall 1965); Frédéric Mauro, "Prééminence et réseau urbain dans l'Amérique coloniale," in *PICA*, 39th [*Chap.* 7], II, 115-132; Stuart B. Schwartz, "Cities of Empire: Mexico and Bahia in the Sixteenth Century," *JIAS*, 11:616-637 (1969); and Smith, "Colonial Towns of Spanish and Portuguese America" [*Chap.* 7]. For a comparison of European backgrounds of Spanish American and Brazilian towns see Robert Ricard, "Recherches sur la toponymie urbaine du Portugal et de l'Espagne," *Bulletin Hispanique* (Bordeaux), 66:133-166 (1954).

The most complete description of Portuguese Indian policy and the role of the Indian in the early colonization of Brazil is Georg Thomas, *Die portugiesische indianerpolitik in Brasilien, 1500-1640* (Berlin: Ibero-Amerikanisches Institut, 1968). Alexander Marchant, *From Barter to Slavery: The Economic Relations of Portuguese and Indians in the Settlement of Brazil, 1500-1580* (Baltimore: Johns Hopkins University Press, 1942), contains some important although controversial sections on this subject. An interpretative overview of the problem of a "Just War" against the Indians and of doctrines and methods for their conversion may be found in Thales de Azevedo, *Igreja e estado em tensão a crise: A conquista espiritual e o Padroado na Bahia* (São Paulo: Editora Atica, 1978).

On the Jesuits in Brazil see Serafim Leite, *Suma histórica da Companhia de Jesús no Brasil: Assistência de Portugal, 1549-1760* (Lisbon: Junta de Investigações do Ultramar, 1965), an abridgement of the author's multivolume and heavily documented study of the society and its works. Its labors may also be appreciated through the following biographical treatments of two of its leaders: Helen G. Dominian, *Apostle of Brazil: The Biography of Padre José de Anchieta, S.J., 1534-1597* (New York: Exposition Press, 1958), a rather adulatory work; and the briefer Jerome V. Jacobsen, "Nóbrega of Brazil," *Mid-America*, 24:151-187 (1942). A thoughtful comparative essay is Robert Ricard, "Comparison of Evangelization in Portuguese and Spanish America," *TA*, 14:444-453 (1957-58). A succinct account of the struggle between Jesuits and labor-hungry settlers is Dauril Alden, "Black Robes versus White Settlers: The Struggle for the 'Freedom of the Indians' in Colonial Brazil," in *Attitudes of the Colonial Powers towards the Americans*, ed. Howard Peckham and Charles Gibson (Salt Lake City: University of Utah Press, 1969), pp. 19-45.

Among the several economic histories of Brazil, Roberto Simonsen, *História econômica do Brazil* (4th ed.; São Paulo: Companhia Editôra Nacional, 1962), is the best source of data on the early colonial period. Caio Prado, *História econômica do Brasil* (São Paulo:

Editora Brasiliense, 1949), followed by numerous new editions, is a clear and concise interpretation of the major economic cycles in the history of Brazil by one of the country's leading Marxist historians. However, it is a bit thin on the early colonial period. Luiz Amaral, *História geral da agricultura brasileira*, 3 vols. (São Paulo: Companhia Editora Nacional, 1939–40), II, is a general history of the agricultural products that provided the bases of Brazil's economy in the sixteenth and seventeenth centuries. The best work on colonial land grants is José da Costa Pôrto, *Estudo sobre o sistema sesmarial* (Recife, Brazil: Imprensa Universitária, 1965).

A substantial corpus of writing exists about the Brazilian sugar industry, although most of it deals with the seventeenth century, when production and profits peaked. Perhaps the best and most succinct introduction to its organization is Kit Sims Taylor, "The Economics of Sugar and Slavery in Northeastern Brazil," *Agricultural History*, 44:267-280 (1970). A longer account of the early history of the industry is Basílio de Magalhães, *O açúcar nos primórdios do Brasil colonial* (Rio de Janeiro: Instituto do Açúcar e do Alcool, 1953). Carl Laga, "O engenho de Erasmos em São Vicente," *Estudos Históricos* (Marília, Brazil), 1:113-143 (1963), sheds some light on the contribution of Flemish capital to the construction of one of Brazil's first *engenhos*.

The best general work on the slave trade that furnished the labor for the sugar industry is Mauricio Goulart, *A escravidão africana no Brasil: Das origens à extinção do tráfico* (3rd ed., rev.; São Paulo: Editora Alfa-Omega, 1975). Goulart's figures on the volume of imports are controversial. Curtin, *The Atlantic Slave Trade* [*Chap. 6*], p. 47, deals sketchily with the early trade, admittedly because little information is available.

On the importance of the *engenho* in the formation of Brazilian population and society see Simonsen, *História econômica do Brasil*, p. 98; Taylor, "The Economics of Sugar," *passim*; Boxer, *Portuguese Society in the Tropics*, chap. 3; and Sidney M. Greenfield, "Slavery and the Plantation in the New World: The Development and Diffusion of a Social Form," *JIAS*, 11:51 (1969).

Very few monographic studies of other Brazilian products exist. Some information on brazilwood production may be found in Simonsen, *História econômica do Brasil*, *passim*; and Marchant, *From Barter to Slavery*. Rollie Poppino, "The Cattle Industry in Colonial Brazil," *Mid-America*, 31:219-247 (1948), touches briefly on early grazing, and Myriam Ellis Austrégesilo, *Aspectos da pesca da baleia no Brasil colonial* (São Paulo: Universidade de São Paulo, 1958), on whaling enterprises.

The standard work on Brazilian trade with Europe and Africa is Frédéric Mauro, *Le Portugal et l'Atlantique au xviie siècle (1570-1670): Étude économique* (Paris: S.E.V.P.E.N., 1960). Charles R. Boxer, *The Portuguese Seaborne Empire* [*General Works*], pp. 220-221, examines briefly the question of why the Portuguese did not see fit to develop convoyed fleets in the sixteenth century.

What little is known about early Brazilian population history is summarized in Sánchez-Albornoz, *The Population of Latin America* [*Chap. 6*], pp. 60-85, and *passim*. Scattered information on Portuguese immigration may be found in Sérgio Buarque de Holanda, *História geral da civilização brasileira*, 5 vols. to date (São Paulo: Difusão Européia do Livro, 1960-  ), I. Regional studies throwing some light on the subject are Thales de Azevedo, *Povoamento da Cidade do Salvador* [*Chap. 12*]; and Carlos B. Ott, *Formação e evolução étnica da cidade do Salvador*, 2 vols. (Salvador: Prefeitura Municipal do Salvador, Tipografia Manú, 1955-57). On Jewish immigration in particular see Arnold Wiznitzer, *Jews in Colonial Brazil* (New York: Columbia University Press, 1960); and José Gonçalves Salvador, "Os Cristãos-Novos nas capitanias do sul (séculos xvi e xvii)," *Revista de História* (São Paulo), 25:49-86 (1962).

In regard to the Indian element, Rosenblat, *La población indígena* [*Chap. 6*], I, tables on pp. 88 and 102, and pp. 256-257, offers some conjectural figures for pre-Conquest populations and subsequent trends. Some information on the effects of European diseases on the indigenes may be found in Marchant, *From Barter to Slavery*; and Florestan Fernandes, *Organização social dos Tupinambás* (2nd ed.; São Paulo: Instituto Progresso Editorial, 1963). The main source of information on the volume of black slave imports is Goulart, *A escravidão africana*, and Curtin, *The Atlantic Slave Trade* [*Chap. 6*]. Ott, *Formação e evolução do Salvador*, is a good case study of the formation of a black population in early Brazil.

General treatments of miscegenation in Brazil may be found in Rosenblat, *La población indígena* [*Chap. 6*], II, 98-109; Mörner, *Race Mixture in the History of Latin America* [*Chap. 6*], pp. 49-51, 73; Boxer, *Race Relations in the Portuguese Empire* [*Chap. 3*], especially pp. 86-87, and the note on p. 116; and Gilberto Freyre, *Casa-Grande & Senzala* (4th ed.; Rio de Janeiro: José Olympio, 1943), trans. Samuel Putnam as *The Masters and the Slaves* (New York: Alfred A. Knopf, 1946), especially chap. 1. Important regional studies are Azevedo, *Povoamento do Salvador*; Ott, *Formação e evolução do Salvador*; and Alfredo Ellis Júnior, *Os primeiros troncos paulistas e o cruzamento euro-americano* (São Paulo: Companhia Editôra Nacional, 1936). The items cited are mainly descriptive of the conditions affecting miscegenation and the qualitative results.

Works on the captaincy system listed in the essay for chapter 12 describe the first phases of the development of colonial Brazilian government. Among more general studies, I think Lahmayer Lôbo, *Processo administrativo ibero-americano* [*Chap. 9*], is the best balanced and has the additional merit of comparing Brazilian and Spanish American organization and practice. See also Rodolfo Garcia, *Ensaio sôbre a história política e administrativa do Brazil, 1500-1810* (Rio de Janeiro: José Olympia, 1956), chaps. 2-5; and the older but still useful Max Fleiuss, *História administrativa do Brasil* (2nd ed.; São Paulo: Companhia Melhoramentos de São Paulo, 1925). The preponderance of the crown's commercial interests in shaping the apparatus of royal government in Brazil is stressed in Lang, *Portuguese Brazil: The King's Plantation* [*General Works*].

Standard works on ecclesiastical organization and administration are Van der Vat, *Princípios da Igreja no Brasil*; and Paulo F. da Silveira Camargo, *História eclesiástica do Brasil* (Petropolis, Brazil: Editôra Vozes, 1955). A brief but stimulating interpretation of church-state relations is contained in Azevedo, *Igreja e estado*.

The organization of conquest societies in Brazil receives partial treatment in works listed earlier in this chapter essay, especially Boxer, *Race Relations in the Portuguese Empire*; Azevedo, *Povoamento do Salvador*; Ott, *Formação e evolução do Salvador*; and Ellis Júnior, *Os primeiros troncos paulistas*.

## CHAPTER 14. THE IMPERIAL CONTEXT: THE HISPANIC WORLD IN THE AGE OF THE HABSBURG KINGS

A good traditional biography of the second Spanish Habsburg is Peter Pierson, *Philip II of Spain* (London: Thames and Hudson, 1975). The older Roger Bigelow Merriman, *The Rise of the Spanish Empire in the Old World and the New*, vol. IV: *Philip the Prudent* [*General Works*], is still useful for its descriptions of events and institutions. Broader based and more interpretive recent works are Fernand Braudel, *La Méditerranée et le Monde Méditerranéen à l'Époque de Philippe II* (Paris: Librairie Armand Colin, 1966), trans. Siân Reynolds as *The Mediterranean and the Mediterranean World in the Age of Philip II*, 2 vols. (New York: Harper and Row, 1972-1973); and John Lynch, *Spain under the Habsburgs*, vol. I: *Empire and Absolutism, 1516-1598* [*General Works*].

The reign of Dom Sebastian and events leading up to the union of the Hispanic crowns are treated in the following works: José M. de Queiróz Velloso, *D. Sebastião* (3rd ed., rev.; Lisbon: Empresa Nacional de Publicidade, 1945); the same author's *O reinado do Cardinal D. Henrique* (Lisbon: Empresa Nacional de Publicidade, 1946); E. W. Bovill, *The Battle of Alcazar* (London: Batchworth Press, 1952); and Alfonso Danvila y Buguero, *Felipe II y la sucesión de Portugal* (Madrid: Espasa-Calpe, 1956).

Good general interpretations of the decline of Spain are John H. Elliott, *Imperial Spain, 1479–1716* (New York: New American Library, Mentor Books, 1966), especially chaps. 8-10; the same author's contribution, "The Decline of Spain," in *Crisis in Europe, 1560–1660*, ed. Trevor Aston (New York: Basic Books, 1965), pp. 167-193; and Antonio Domínguez Ortiz, *Crisis y decadencia en la España de los Austrias* (2nd ed.; Barcelona: Ariel, 1971). Henry Kamen, *Spain in the Late Seventeenth Century, 1665-1700* (London: Longman, 1980), offers a tentative revisionist interpretation of the reign of Charles II and suggests that Spanish recovery actually began before the reforming Bourbons came to the throne. Also worth noting is *Historia económica y social de España*, ed. V. Vázquez de Prado, vol. III: *Los siglos xvi y xvii* (Madrid: Confederación Española de Cajas de Ahorros, 1978), which emphasizes the primary role of the state in shaping economic and social life.

On demographic aspects of Spain's decline see the standard Nadal Oller, *La población española* [*Chap. 6*]. The most straightforward account of economic trends in late sixteenth- and seventeenth-century Spain is Vicens Vives, *An Economic History of Spain* [*Chaps. 1 and 2*], especially chaps. 29-31. A provocative economic interpretation of decline is José Gentil da Silva, *En Espagne: Développement économique, subsistance, déclin* (The Hague: Mouton, 1965). A substantial work on seventeenth-century Spanish society is Antonio Domínguez Ortiz, *La sociedad española en el siglo xvii*, 2 vols. (Madrid: C.S.I.C., 1963, 1970). Thoughtful insights into the mentality of Spanish elites in the age of decline are offered in Antonio J. Maravall, *Poder, honor y élites en el siglo xvii (Historia)* (Madrid: Siglo Veintiuno Editores, 1979). John H. Elliott, *The Revolt of the Catalans: A Study in the Decline of Spain (1593-1640)* (New York: Cambridge University Press, 1963), is the standard work on this subject.

Spanish imperial diplomacy and wars are treated in Manuel Fernández Alvarez, *Política mundial de Carlos V y Felipe II* (Madrid: C.S.I.C., 1966); H. G. Koenigsburger, *The Habsburgs and Europe, 1516-1660* (Ithaca, N.Y.: Cornell University Press, 1971); and Bohdan Chudoba, *Spain and the Empire, 1519-1643* (Chicago: University of Chicago Press, 1952).

Sound studies of Habsburg monetary and fiscal policies are Carande, *Carlos V y sus banqueros*, vol. II: *La hacienda real de Castilla* [*Chap. 11*]; Modesto Ulloa, *La hacienda real de Castilla en el reinado de Felipe II* (2nd ed.; Madrid: Fundación Universitaria Española, 1977); and Antonio Domíguez Ortiz, *Política y hacienda de Felipe IV* (Madrid: Editorial de Derecho Financiero, 1960). The pernicious effects of the decentralization of military and naval recruitment and procurement are analyzed convincingly in I. A. A. Thompson, *War and Government in Habsburg Spain, 1560-1620* (London: Athlone Press, 1976).

The best general account of Portuguese vicissitudes in the late sixteenth and the seventeenth centuries are Marques, *History of Portugal* [*Chaps. 1 and 2*], vol. I, chap. 6; Boxer, *The Portuguese Seaborne Empire* [*General Works*], especially part 1; and Vitorino de Magalhães Godinho, "Portugal and Her Empire," in *The New Cambridge Modern History*, vol. V: *The Ascendancy of France*, ed. F. L. Carsten (Cambridge: Cambridge University Press, 1961), pp. 384-397.

Good monographic works on seventeenth-century Portugal are scarce. A fine study of the nation's Atlantic trade is Mauro, *Le Portugal et l'Atlantique au xvii$^e$ siècle (1570–1670)* [*Chap. 13*]. The classic account of the restoration of Portuguese independence is still the near-contemporary Conde de Ericeira, *Portugal restaurado*, 2 vols. (Lisbon, 1679–1698). On the Brazilian contribution to the recovery of Portugal's Atlantic empire see Charles R. Boxer, *Salvador de Sá and the Struggle for Brazil and Angola, 1602–1686* (London: Athlone Press, 1952); and the same author's *The Golden Age of Brazil* [*General Works*]. The beginnings of close mercantile relations between England and Portugal are discussed in Harold E. S. Fisher, *The Portugal Trade: A Study of Anglo-Portuguese Commerce, 1700–1770* (London: Methuen, 1971). Carl A. Hanson, *Economy and Society in Baroque Portugal, 1668–1703* (Minneapolis: University of Minnesota Press, 1981) is a scholarly account of the reign of Pedro II.

## CHAPTER 15. TERRITORIAL CHANGES IN THE HISPANIC NEW WORLD: CONTRACTIONS, EXPANSIONS, ADJUSTMENTS

The best general narrative account of northern European territorial intrusions into lands claimed by Spain is Arthur P. Newton, *The European Nations in the West Indies, 1493–1688* (London, A. & C. Black, 1933). More recent and more analytical treatments of the subject are K. G. Davies, *The North Atlantic World in the Seventeenth Century*, vol. IV of *Europe and the World in the Age of Expansion*, ed. Boyd C. Shafer (Minneapolis: University of Minnesota Press, 1974); and Mauro, *L'expansion européenne (1600–1870)* [*General Works*].

A survey of Dutch activities in the New World may be found in Charles R. Boxer, *The Dutch Seaborne Empire, 1600–1800* (New York: Alfred A. Knopf, 1965). Their actions in the Spanish Indies are narrated in more detail in Cornelis Ch. Goslinga, *The Dutch in the Caribbean and on the Wild Coast, 1580–1680* (Assen, The Netherlands: Van Gorcum, 1971). The best-balanced account of Dutch conquests in Brazil is Charles R. Boxer, *The Dutch in Brazil, 1624–1654* (Oxford: The Clarendon Press, 1957). It can well be supplemented by a Brazilian interpretation, José A. de Gonçalves de Mello Neto, *Tempo dos Flamengos: Influência da ocupação holandesa na vida e na cultura do norte do Brasil* (Rio de Janeiro: José Olympio, 1947).

Among the many works on the English in the Spanish Indies, I prefer the perceptive and well-written Carl Bridenbaugh and Roberta Bridenbaugh, *No Peace Beyond the Line: The English in the Caribbean, 1624–1690* (Oxford: Oxford University Press, 1972). Nothing comparable in quality is available for French enterprises, but a satisfactory narrative account is the older Nellis M. Crouse, *French Pioneers in the West Indies, 1624–1664* (New York: Columbia University Press, 1940). Territorial settlements among the several colonizing nations are surveyed concisely in Gordon C. Ireland, *Boundaries, Possessions and Conflicts in Central and North America and in the Caribbean* (Cambridge, Mass.: Harvard University Press, 1941).

The following short articles give an overview of territorial expansion in the Viceroyalty of New Spain: Florentino Pérez Embid, "La expansión geográfica de la Nueva España en el siglo xvii," *RI*, 11:501–531 (1951); and Peter Gerhard, "El avance español en México y Centroamérica," *HM*, 9:143–152 (1959–60), which is enriched by maps illustrating the several stages of advance.

An introduction to the advance of frontiers in the northern part of the viceroyalty is Enrique Florescano, "Colonización, ocupación del suelo y 'frontera' en el norte de Nueva España, 1521–1750," in Alvaro Jara and others, *Tierras nuevas: Expansión territorial y ocupación del suelo en América (siglos xvi-xix)* (Mexico: El Colegio de Mexico, 1969), pp. 43-76. A seminal article on the work of missionaries in those regions is Herbert E. Bolton, "The Mission as a Frontier Institutuion in the Spanish Colonies," *AHR* 23:42-61 (1917).

A large volume of more specialized literature deals with territorial expansion in the several regions of northern New Spain, and listings must be highly selective. The most thorough study of the Spanish conquest of Florida is Lyon, *The Enterprise of Florida: Pedro Menéndez de Avilés and the Spanish Conquest of 1565-1568* [*Chap. 9*]. The precarious history of the colony during the remainder of the sixteenth century is recounted briefly in Charles W. Arnade, *Florida on Trial, 1593-1602* (Coral Gables, Fla.: University of Miami Press, 1959). The best published survey of missionary enterprise in Florida during the sixteenth and seventeenth centuries is Michael V. Gannon, *The Cross in the Sand: The Early Catholic Church in Florida, 1513-1870* (Gainesville: University of Florida Press, 1965), chaps. 1-5.

The life and times of one of the great *adelantados* who won and settled New Vizcaya is the subject of J. Lloyd Mecham, *Francisco de Ibarra and Nueva Vizcaya* (Durham, N.C.: Duke University Press, 1927). The contribution of less eminent folk, in this instance an American mestizo, is Philip W. Powell, *Mexico's Miguel Caldera: The Taming of America's First Frontier, 1548-1597* (Tucson: University of Arizona Press, 1977). The military aspects of frontier expansion in this region to about 1600 are discussed in more detail in Powell, *Soldiers, Indians and Silver* [*Chap. 9*]. The part played by mining and by the great hacienda are treated respectively in Bakewell, *Silver Mining and Society* [*Chap. 10*], chaps. 1 and 2; and Chevalier, *Land and Society* [*Chap. 10*]. Missionary contributions are synthesized in Kieran R. McCarty, "Los Franciscanos en la frontera chichimeca," *HM*, 11:321-360 (1961-62).

A compact analysis of the Spanish occupation of northeastern Mexico is José Miranda, "Fisonomía del noroeste de México en la época colonial," *Cuadernos americanos*, 21:135-150 (1962). A much more detailed narrative can be found in Vito Alessio Robles, *Coahuila y Téxas en la época colonial* (Mexico: n.p., 1938). Foreign stimuluses to colonization along the Gulf Coast are discussed in William E. Dunn, *Spanish and French Rivalry in the Gulf Region of the United States: The Beginnnings of Texas and Pensacola, 1678-1702* (Austin: University of Texas Studies in History, 1917).

The most complete account of the occupation of the Mexican northwest is Luis García Navarro, *Sonora y Sinaloa en el siglo xvii* (Seville: E.E.H.A., 1967). The key role played by the Jesuits in this region is emphasized in John F. Bannon, *The Mission Frontier in Sonora, 1620-1687* (New York: United States Catholic Historical Society, 1955). Very much worth reading is Herbert E. Bolton, *Rim of Christendom: A Biography of Eusebio Francisco Kino, Pacific Coast Pioneer* (New York: Macmillan, 1936).

The Spanish conquest of New Mexico is examined in the heavily documented and annotated George P. Hammond and Agapito Rey, eds. and trans., *Don Juan de Oñate, Colonizer of New Mexico, 1595-1628*, 2 vols. (Albuquerque: University of New Mexico Press, 1953). The following two articles deal with important themes in the subsequent history of that province: France V. Scholes, "Civil Government and Society in New Mexico in the Seventeenth Century," *New Mexico Historical Review*, 10:71-111 (1935); and Manuel J. Espinosa, "The Recapture of Santa Fe, New Mexico, by the Spaniards — December 29-30, 1693," *HAHR*, 19:443-463 (1939).

To conclude this listing of works on territorial expansion in the Mexican north, Oakah I. Jones, Jr., *Los Paisanos: Spanish Settlers on the Northern Frontier of New Spain* (Norman: University of Oklahoma Press, 1979), deserves mention because it deals not with soldiers, missionaries, miners, or territorial barons but with the common settlers and the society they created.

Territorial expansion in the central and southern parts of the Viceroyalty of Spain was on a much smaller scale and lacked the epic character of the northward advance. Therefore, it has been studied in less detail. The fullest account available is Gerhard, *The Southeast Frontier of New Spain* [*Chap. 5*]. Brief accounts of advances in particular regions may be found scattered through chaps. 8 and 9 of West and Augelli, *Middle America* [*Chap. 4*]. Developments in Central America, in particular, are touched upon in MacLeod, *Spanish Central America* [*Chap. 6*], especially part 3.

A good short introduction to the motives for the Spanish conquest and colonization of the Philippines and to the methods employed is Luis González, "Expansión de Nueva España en el Lejano Oriente," *HM*, 14:206-226 (1964–65). Standard longer accounts are John L. Phelan, *The Hispanization of the Philippines: Spanish Aims and Filipino Responses (1576-1700)* (Madison: University of Wisconsin Press, 1959); and H. de la Costa, *The Jesuits in the Philippines, 1581-1768* (Cambridge, Mass.: Harvard University Press, 1967).

A solid history of Spanish expansion in the Rio de la Plata region is Rubio, *Exploración y conquista del Rio de la Plata* [*Chap. 5*]. The most substantial work on agrarian frontiers in other parts of the Viceroyalty of Peru is James J. Parsons, *Antioqueño Colonization in Western Colombia* (rev. ed.; Berkeley: University of California Press, 1968). Alvaro Jara, "Fontera agraria: El caso del virreinato peruano en el siglo xvi," in Jara and others, *Tierras nuevas*, pp. 11-42, contains some useful information on the Peruvian agricultural frontier in the late 1500s.

The part played by mining in opening new territory in South America is treated in the following works: in Peru, Alberto Crespo Rodas, "Fundación de la Villa de San Felipe de Austria y Asiento de Minas de Oruro," *Revista Histórica* (Lima), 29:3-25 (1967); and Cobb, "Supply and Transportation for the Potosí Mines" [*Chap. 11*]; in New Granada, West, *Colonial Placer Mining in Colombia* [*Chap. 10*], particularly pp. 9-34, and William F. Sharp, *Slavery on the Spanish Frontier: The Colombian Chocó, 1680-1810* (Norman: University of Oklahoma Press, 1976).

An overview of the mission as a frontier institution in South America is presented in Constantino Bayle, "Las misiones, defensa de las fronteras: Mainas," *Missionalia Hispánica*, 8:417-503 (1951). Among the numerous writings on the Jesuit missions in Paraguay, Guillermo Furlong Cardiff, *Misiones y sus pueblos de Guaraníes, 1610-1813* (Buenos Aires: Ediciones Teoría, 1962), is the best rounded. Magnus Mörner, *The Political and Economic Activities of the Jesuits in the Rio de la Plata: The Habsburg Era* (Stockholm: Library and Institute of Ibero-American Studies, 1953), gives a more specialized treatment of the Guaraní missions. The semipopular J. Fred Rippy and Jean T. Nelson, *Crusaders of the Jungle* (Chapel Hill: University of North Carolina Press, 1936), is the best general account of the Spanish trans-Andean and Venezuelan missions, and its ample bibliography lists works dealing with particular missionary provinces.

The special case of the southern frontier of Chile is described in Jara, *Guerre et société au Chile* [*Chap. 9*]; and in Eugene Korth, *Spanish Policy in Colonial Chile: The Struggle for Social Justice, 1535-1700* (Stanford, Calif.: Stanford University Press, 1968).

The best general account of territorial expansion in colonial Brazil is Basílio de Magalhães, *Expansão geográfica do Brasil colonial* (3rd ed.; Rio de Janeiro: Espasa, 1944). Also recommendable is the more recent Amadeu Cunha, *Sertões e fronteiras do Brasil: Noticia de época colonial* (Lisbon: Agência Geral das Colônias, 1945).

The occupation of northern and northeastern Brazil is emphasized in João Capistrano de Abreu, *Caminhos antigos e o povoamento do Brasil* (Rio de Janeiro: Livraria Briquiet, 1930). More specialized works on expansion in those regions are João F. de Almeida Prado, *Pernambuco e as capitanias do norte do Brasil, 1530-1630*, 4 vols. (São Paulo: Companhia

Editôra Nacional, 1939-42); the same author's *A conquista da Paraiba (séculos xvi a xviii)* (São Paulo: Companhia Editôra Nacional, 1964), especially pp. 145-196; Ernesto Cruz, *História do Belém*, 2 vols. (Pará: Universidade Federal do Pará, 1973), especially I, 111-170; and Francis A. Dutra, "Matias de Albuquerque and the Defense of Northeastern Brazil, 1620-1626," *Studia: Revista Semestral* (Lisbon), 36:117-166 (1973).

A short but important account of expansion in the far south of Brazil is José Honório Rodrigues, *O continente do Rio Grande* (Rio de Janeiro: Edições S. José, 1954). A more detailed work leading up to the founding of the principal Portuguese settlement in that region is Moacyr Domingues, *A Colônia do Sacramento e o sul do Brasil* (Porto Alegre, Brazil: Secretaria de Educação e Cultura, 1973).

The best introduction to the *bandeirantes* is the translated selections from Portuguese works and the accompanying commentary in Richard M. Morse, ed., *The Bandeirantes: The Historical Role of the Brazilian Pathfinders* (New York: Alfred A. Knopf, Borzoi Books on Latin America, 1965). The fullest study of this subject is the richly documented but rambling Affonso de Escragnolle Taunay, *História geral das bandeiras paulistas*, 11 vols. (São Paulo: Typografia Ideal, H. L. Canton, 1924-50). Also useful are Jaime Cortesão, *Rapóso Tavares e a formação territorial do Brasil* (Rio de Janeiro: Ministério da Eduçacão e Cultura, 1958), which recounts the achievements of one of the most famous *bandeirantes*; and Cassiano Ricardo, *A marcha para oeste: A influência da "bandeira" na formação social e política do Brasil*, 2 vols. (2nd ed.; Rio de Janeiro: José Olympio, 1942), which makes some provocative comparisons between the *bandeirantes* and Spanish conquistadors.

Literature on Brazil's pastoral frontier is sparse. The best introduction to the subject is Poppino, "The Cattle Industry in Colonial Brazil" [*Chap. 13*]. Pedro Calmon, *História da Casa de Tôrre uma dinastia de pioneiros* (2nd ed.; Rio de Janeiro: José Olympio, 1958), deals with a famous ranching family that built a vast rural empire along the Rio São Francisco.

Arthur C. Ferreira Reis, *A expansão portuguêsa na Amazônia nos séculos xvii e xviii* (Rio de Janeiro: Superintendencia do Plano de Valorização Economia de Amazonia, 1959), offers a compact account of Brazilian penetration into the Amazon basin. The work of the *tropas* is discussed more particularly in José Alipio Goulart, *Tropas y tropeiros na formação do Brasil* (Rio de Janeiro: Conquista, 1961). Although devoted mainly to the eighteenth century, Boxer, *The Golden Age of Brazil* [*General Works*], pp. 271-292, introduces the work of the religious orders in the Amazon. Mathias C. Kieman, *The Indian Policy of Portugal in the Amazon, 1614-1693* (Washington: Catholic University of America, 1954), describes the interplay of crown policy, missionary enterprise, and private interests in the Amazon.

Geopolitical and diplomatic aspects of Brazilian expansion are emphasized in the following works: Lewis A. Tambs, "Geopolitics of the Amazon," in *Man in the Amazon*, ed. Charles Wagley (Gainesville: The University Presses of Florida, 1974), pp. 45-87; Stuart Schwartz, "Luso-Brazilian Relations in Colonial Brazil," *TA*, 25:33-48 (1968-69), which discusses the effects of the union of the Hispanic crowns; and Luis Ferrand de Almeida, *A diplomacia portuguesa e os limites meridionais do Brasil*, vol. I: *1493-1700* (Coimbra: Faculdade de Letras da Universidade de Coimbra, 1957).

## CHAPTER 16. POST-CONQUEST POPULATIONS: COMPONENTS, NUMBERS, MOVEMENTS, DISTRIBUTION

General treatments of colonial Hispanic American populations and of major components thereof—Europeans, Indians, Africans, and mixed bloods—are listed in the bibliographical essays for chapter 6 (Spanish America) and chapter 13 (Brazil). The following essay introduces more specialized studies of areas and groups after the Conquest and repeats selectively works listed in earlier essays whose coverage extends into the post-Conquest era.

The following works cover European emigration to the Indies after the Conquest: Boyd-Bowman, "Patterns of Spanish Emigration to the Indies until 1600" [*Chap. 6*]; and Mörner, "Spanish Migration to the New World prior to 1810" [*Chap. 6*]. Studies of particular groups in the European population in the Indies include J. I. Israel, "The Portuguese in Seventeenth Century Mexico," *JGSW*, 11:12-32 (1974); Hanke, "The Portuguese in Spanish America" [*Chap. 6*]; Keith, "New World Interlopers" [*Chap. 6*]; Lucía García de Proodian, *Los Judios en América: Sus actividades en los virreinatos de Nueva Castilla y Nueva Granada, s. xvii* (Madrid: C.S.I.C., 1966); and Seymour Liebman, *The Jews in New Spain* (Coral Gables, Fla.: University of Miami Press, 1970).

The most comprehensive coverage of post-Conquest Indian populations is Cook and Borah, *Essays in Population History* [*Chap. 6*], which contains essays on Mexico, Yucatán, the Antilles, and Colombia. The best general study of indigenous population trends in Peru is Cook, *Demographic Collapse* [*Chap. 6*]. Other good regional studies are José Miranda, "La población indígena de México en el siglo xvii," *HM*, 12:182-189 (1962-63); Francisco de Solano y Pérez-Lila, "La población indígena de Yucatán durante la primera mitad del siglo xvii," *AEA*, 28:165-200 (1971); and Juan Friede, "Demographic Changes in the Mining Community of Muzo after the Plague of 1629," *HAHR*, 47:338-359 (1967).

For the post-Conquest period, the following supplement the works on the black population listed in the essay for chapter 6: Colin A. Palmer, *Slaves of the White God: Blacks in Mexico, 1570-1650* (Cambridge, Mass.: Harvard University Press, 1976); and David L. Chandler, "Health Conditions in the Slave Trade in New Granada," in *Slavery and Race Relations in Latin America*, ed. Robert B. Toplin (Westport, Conn.: Greenwood Press, 1974), pp. 57-88, which discusses survival and reproduction rates of slaves. The most systematic treatment of miscegenation yet published is Sherburne F. Cook and Woodrow Borah, "Racial Groups in the Mexican Population since 1519," in their *Essays in Population History* [*Chap. 6*], II, 180-269.

Most of the works on the population of Brazil listed in the essay for chapter 13 carry forward to the late sixteenth century or into the seventeenth. In addition, the following studies are worth consulting: Tarcizio do Rêgo Quirino, *Os habitantes do Brasil no fim do século xvi* (Recife: Imprensa Universitária, 1966), which analyzes population structure by region, social origins, sex, age and marital status toward the end of the 1600s; Pierre Verger, *Flux et reflux de la traité des nègres entre le Golfe de Bénin et Bahia de Todos os Santos, du xvii^e au xix^e siècle* (The Hague: Mouton, 1968), which supplements the work of Mauricio Goulart on the volume of the slave trade; Anita Novinsky, *Cristãos novos na Bahia* (São Paulo: Editora Perspectiva, 1972), which throws additional light on Brazil's New Christians; and Odair Franco, *História da febre amarela* (Rio de Janeiro: Ministério de Saúde, 1969), which describes the appearance of yellow fever in Brazil, an important demographic factor in the late seventeenth century.

The works on urbanization listed in the essay for chapter 7 may be supplemented by Jorge Hardoy and Carmen Aranovich, "Urban Scales and Functions in Spanish America toward the year 1600: First Conclusions," *LARR*, 5(no. 3):57-91 (Fall 1970), a systematic study of urban growth rates in the post-Conquest decades.

Two important works on civil congregations of Indians in Mexico are Lesley B. Simpson, *Studies in the Administration of the Indians in New Spain: The Civil Congregation*, Ibero-Americana: 7 (Berkeley: University of California Press, 1934); and Howard F. Cline,

"Civil Congregations of the Indians in New Spain," *HAHR*, 29:349-369 (1949). Good studies of Indian resettlement in New Granada are Orlando Fals-Borda, "Indian Congregations in the New Kingdom of Granada: Land Tenure Aspects," *TA*, 13:331-351 (1956-57); and Margarita González, *El resguardo en el Nuevo Reino de Granada* (Bogotá: Universidad Nacional de Colombia, 1970). I have found no articles or monographs dealing systematically with Viceroy Toledo's program of congregation in Peru. The following works provide evidence on how the Indians reacted to Spanish efforts to gather them into European-style nucleated villages: Woodrow Borah and Sherburne F. Cooke, "A Case History of the Transition from Precolonial to the Colonial Period in Mexico: Santiago Tejupan," in *Social Fabric and Spatial Structure in Colonial Latin America*, ed. David J. Johnson (Ann Arbor, Mich.: University Microfilms International, 1979), pp. 409-432; and Juan A. Villamarín and Julia Villamarín, "Chibcha Settlement under Spanish Rule: 1537-1810," in *Social Fabric and Spatial Structure in Colonial Latin America*, pp. 25-84.

The only explicit treatment of ruralization in the Spanish Indies I know of is a short passage in Góngora, *Studies [General Works]*, pp. 149-158. The decline of towns and migration to the countryside in several regions of the Indies are described incidentally in Peter Marzahl, "Creoles and Government: The Cabildo of Popayán," *HAHR*, 54:636-656 (1974); Leví Marrero, *Historia económica de Cuba: Guía de estudio y documentación* (Havana: Universidad de la Habana, 1956; and Enriqueta Vila Vilar, "Condicionamientos y limitaciones en Puerto Rico durante el siglo vii," *AEA*, 28:219-244 (1971).

The effect of economic contraction on urban-rural migration is examined in Woodrow Borah, *New Spain's Century of Depression*, Ibero-Americana: 35 (Berkeley: University of California Press, 1951); and in other studies dealing with the "Seventeenth-Century Depression" mentioned in the following chapter essay. The depopulation of coastal towns because of the intrusions of privateers and smugglers is described in Peter Gerhard, *Pirates on the West Coast of New Spain, 1565-1742* (Glendale, Calif.: A. H. Clark, 1960); and Concepción Hernández Tapia, "Despoblaciones de la Isla de Santo Domingo en el siglo xvii," *AEA*, 27:281-320 (1970).

The ruralization of Indian communities in Mexico is described in Charles Gibson, "The Transformation of the Indian Community of New Spain, 1500-1800," *Cahiers d'Histoire Mondiale* 2:581-607 (1954-55), and more fully in the same author's *The Aztecs under Spanish Rule [Chap. 8]*. The same process in Peru is discussed in Kubler, "The Quechua in the Colonial World" [*Chap. 8*]; and Spalding, "The Colonial Indian" [*Chap. 8*].

Several works on the growth of towns in Brazil are mentioned in the bibliographical essay for chapter 13. Others dealing more especially with the post-Conquest period include Sérgio Buarque de Holanda, "Movimentos da população em São Paulo no século xviii" [*sic*], *Revista do Instituto de Estudos Brasileiros*, 1:55-111 (1966), which actually deals with the seventeenth century; and J. da Costa Rêgo Monteiro, *A Colônia do Sacramento, 1680-1777*, 2 vols. (Porto Alegre: Oficinas Gráficas de Livraria do Globo, 1937), I.

Ruralization in Brazil was practically the same as expansion into the backlands, and relevant books and articles are listed in the essay for chapter 15, immediately preceding. To these may be added Lycurgo de C. Santos Filho, *Uma comunidade rural do Brasil antigo* (São Paulo: Companhia Editôria Nacional, 1956), a detailed account of the cattle *fazenda* of Brejo do Campo Seco. Although concerned mainly with the eighteenth and nineteenth centuries, its observations are pertinent for the late 1600s.

I know of no works containing firm data on overall population distribution and density in seventeenth-century Hispanic America or of any that analyze the political significance of the population geography of that period. Two works describing more recent patterns, however, may legitimately be extrapolated backward in time. These are Schmieder,

*Die Neue Welt* [*Chap. 4*], *passim*; and Preston James, "The Distribution of People in South America," in *Geographic Aspects of International Relations*, ed. Charles C. Colby (Chicago: University of Chicago Press, 1938), pp. 217-240.

## CHAPTER 17. POST-CONQUEST ECONOMIES

The literature dealing with colonial Hispanic American economies is discussed at some length in the bibliographical essays for chapters 10 and 11 (Spanish America) and for chapter 13 (Brazil). This essay will introduce or repeat studies of particular relevance to developments after the Conquest period.

The main development in land tenure and land use in post-Conquest Spanish America was the growth of the Spanish landed estate, generally at the expense of Indian holdings. Yet until recently research on this institution lagged. In the early 1950s, two pioneer works were published: Chevalier, *Land and Society* [*Chap. 10*]; and Borde and Góngora, *Evolución de la propiedad rural en el Valle del Puangue* [Chile] [*Chap. 10*]. It was not until the 1970s, however, that hacienda studies began to appear in substantial numbers.

Recent works on the colonial landed estate fall into two categories. One consists of articles and books attempting to define, describe, classify, and determine the origins of Spanish landholdings. It includes: Magnus Mörner, "The Spanish American Hacienda: A Survey of Recent Research and Debate," *HAHR*, 53:183-216 (1973); Keith, "Encomienda, Hacienda and Corregimiento" [*Chap. 8*]; Lockhart, "Encomienda and Hacienda" [*Chap. 8*]; and *Haciendas and Plantations in Latin American History*, ed. Robert G. Keith (New York: Holmes and Meier Publishers, 1977).

The second category comprises empirical studies of the formation and organization of haciendas in particular regions or of particular haciendas, especially those of the Jesuits. Solid works in this class are William B. Taylor, *Landlord and Peasant in Colonial Oaxaca* (Stanford, Calif.: Stanford University Press, 1972); Herman W. Konrad, *A Jesuit Hacienda in Colonial México: Santa Lucía, 1576-1767* (Stanford, Calif.: Stanford University Press, 1980); Ursula Ewald, *Estudios sobre la hacienda colonial en México: Las propiedades rurales del Colegio Espíritu Santo en Puebla*, trans. Luis R. Cerna (Weisbaden, Franz Steiner Verlag, 1976); Prem, *Milpa y hacienda* [*Chap. 10*]; Robert G. Keith, *Conquest and Agrarian Change: The Emergence of the Hacienda System on the Peruvian Coast* (Cambridge, Mass.: Harvard University Press, 1976); Nicolas P. Cushner, *Lords of the Land: Sugar, Wine, and Jesuit Estates of Coastal Peru, 1600-1767* (Albany: State University of New York Press, 1980); and Segundo E. Moreno Yáñez, "Traspaso de la propriedad agrícola indígena a la hacienda colonial: El caso de Saquisilí" [Ecuador], *JGSW*, 17:79-119 (1980).

The processes of entailment and of *composición* are given special attention respectively in G. S. Fernández de Recas, *Mayorazgos de la Nueva España* (Mexico: Instituto Bibliográfico Mexicano, 1965); and Christiana Borchart de Moreno, "Composiciones de tierras en la Audiencia de Quito: El Valle de Tumbaco a finales del siglo xvii," *JGSW*, 17:121-155 (1980).

Most of the works dealing with black slave labor listed in the bibliographical essay for chapter 10 extend their coverage into the post-Conquest period. To these may be added Palmer, *Slaves of the White God* [*Chap. 16*]. A listing of *repartimiento-mita* studies appears in the essay for chapter 10. It may be supplemented by Julián B. Ruíz Rivero, *Encomienda y mita en Nueva Granada*, PEEHA, 228 (Seville, 1975); and the documentary study Silvio Zavala, *El servicio personal de Indios en el Perú*, vol. II: *Extractos del siglo xvii* (Mexico: El Colegio de México, 1979). Also meriting mention is Robert J. Ferry, "Encomienda, African Slavery and Agriculture in Seventeenth-Century Caracas," *HAHR*, 61:609-636 (1981).

Monographs and articles dealing with the various forms of free and nominally free labor used in the Indies include Silvio Zavala, "Orígenes coloniales del peonaje en México," *El Trimestre Económico* (Mexico), 10:711-748 (1944); Mario Góngora, *Origen de los "inquilinos" de Chile Central* (Santiago: Universidad de Chile, 1960); and Alvaro Jara, *Los asientos de trabajo y la provisión de mano de obra para los no-encomenderos en la ciudad de Santiago, 1586-1600* (Santiago: Universidad de Chile, 1959). Studies dealing specifically with the formation and use of capital in the post-Conquest Indies are rare. The following items, however, cast some light on the subject: Louisa S. Hoberman, "Merchants in Seventeenth-Century Mexico City: A Preliminary Portrait," *HAHR*, 57:479-503 (1977); John C. Super, "Partnership and Profit in the Early Andean Trade: The Experience of Quito Merchants, 1580-1610," *Journal of Latin American Studies*, 11:265-282 (1979); Bryan R. Hamnett, "Church Wealth in Peru: Estates and Loans in the Archdiocese of Lima in the Seventeenth Century," *JGSW*, 10:113-132 (1973); and Marcello Carmagnani, "Formación de un mercado cumpulsivo y el papel de los mercaderes: La región de Santiago de Chile (1559-1600)," *JGSW*, 12:104-133 (1975). A perceptive explanation of how noneconomic considerations hampered capital formation and investment in colonial society may be found in Juan A. Villamarín, "The Concept of Nobility in the Social Stratification of Colonial Santa Fé de Bogotá," a paper prepared for the 41st International Congress of Americanists, 1974.

The following works are useful additions to materials on government regulation and taxation of the colonial Spanish American economy listed in the bibliographical essay for chapter 11: Sergio Florescano, "La política mercantilista española y sus implicaciones en la Nueva España, *HM*, 17:455-468 (1967-68), a regional study of the theory and practice of Spanish mercantilism; Allyn C. Loosely, "The Puerto Bello Fairs," *HAHR*, 13:314-335 (1933), which deals with the organization of commercial exchange in Panama when the fleets arrived from Spain; Robert S. Smith, "The Institution of the Consulado in New Spain," *HAHR*, 24:61-83 (1944); María E. Rodríguez Vicente, *El Tribunal del Consulado de Lima en la primera mitad del siglo xvii* (Madrid: Ediciones Cultura Hispánica, 1960); Robert S. Smith, "Sales Taxes in New Spain, 1575-1770," *HAHR*, 28:2-37 (1948); and Fred Bronner, "La Unión de Armas en Perú: Aspectos político-legales," *AEA*, 24:1133-1176 (1967), which discusses the imposition of special defense taxes in Peru. The organization and operation of the most important royal monopoly in the Indies is described in M. F. Lang, *El monopolio estatal del mercurio en el México colonial, 1550-1710*, trans. Roberto Gómez Ciriza (Mexico: Fondo de Cultura Económica, 1977).

For post-Conquest developments in the agricultural sectors of the colonial economy, the following works supplement materials listed in the essay for chapter 10: on grain production, Raymond L. Lee, "Grain Legislation in Colonial Mexico, 1575-1585," *HAHR*, 27:647-660 (1947); and the exceptionally able Demetrio Ramos, "Trigo chileno, navieros del Callao y hacendados limeños entre la crisis agrícola del siglo xvii y la comercial de la primera mitad del xviii, *RI*, 26:209-324 (1966); on dyestuffs, Robert S. Smith, "Indigo Production and Trade in Colonial Guatemala," *HAHR*, 39:181-211 (1959); and Raymond L. Lee, "American Cochineal in European Commerce, 1526-1625," *The Journal of Modern History* 23:205-224 (1951); on cacao, Michael T. Hamerly, "El comercio de cacao de Guayaquil durante el período colonial: Un estudio cuantavivo," *Historia Marítima del Ecuador*, 4(no. 4):1-75 (August 1976); and Dora León Borja and Adam Szaszdi Nagy, "El comercio del cacao de Guayaquil," *RHA*, nos. 57-58:1-50 (1964).

Studies of manufacturing in the Indies are rather scarce. For shipbuilding see David R. Raddell and James J. Parsons, "Realejo—A Forgotten Colonial Port and Shipbuilding Center in Nicaragua," *HAHR*, 51:295-312 (1971); and Lawrence A. Clayton, *Caulkers and Carpenters in a New World: The Shipyards of Colonial Guayaquil* (Athens, Ohio: Center for International Studies, Ohio University, 1980). Materials on shipbuilding in seventeenth-century Havana are included in Irene A. Wright, *Historia documentada de San Cristóbal de la Habana en el siglo xvii* (Havana: Imprenta "El Siglo XX," 1930), chap. 9. Useful supplements to studies of the colonial textile industry listed in the essay for chapter 10 are Richard E. Greenleaf, "The Obraje in the Late Mexican Colony," *TA*, 23:227-250 (1966-67); John C. Super, "Querétaro Obrajes," *HAHR*, 56:197-216 (1976); and John L. Phelan, *The Kingdom of Quito in the Seventeenth Century* (Madison: University of Wisconsin Press, 1967), chap. 4. A solid case study of colonial artisanry is Armando de Ramón, "Producción artesanal y servicios en Santiago de Chile (1650-1700)," *JGSW*, 12:134-166 (1975).

Major works on colonial mining are listed in the essay for chapter 10, but two bear repeating because of the overall view they give of the industry in the late sixteenth century and in the seventeenth. They are: Brading and Cross, "Colonial Silver Mining," and West, *Colonial Placer Mining in Colombia*. On gold mining in Colombia see also Sharp, *Slavery on the Spanish Frontier* [*Chap. 15*].

The most complete analysis of Spain's trans-Atlantic trade is, of course, the Chaunus' *Séville et l'Atlantique* [*Chap. 5*]. Its serial data are mostly for ship sailings, but vol. VI, part 2, pp. 981-1034, contains statistics on the quantities and value of commodity exports. The flow of trade in one of the principal ports of the *Carrera* is examined in Pierre Chaunu, "Veracruz en la segunda mitad del siglo xvi y primera mitad del xvii," *HM*, 9:521-557 (1959-60). A good indicator of the prices of American goods in the European market is the Amsterdam price series in Nicolaas W. Posthumus, *Inquiry into the History of Prices in Holland* (Leiden: E. J. Brill, 1946).

The materials on the remission of American precious metals to Spain contained in Hamilton, *American Treasure* [*Chap. 10*], are supplemented by Carmen Bancora Cañero, "Las remesas de metales preciosos desde el Callao a España en la primera mitad del siglo xvii," *RI*, 19:35-88 (1959); and María E. Rodríguez Vicente, "Los caudales remitidos desde el Perú a España por cuenta de la Real Hacienda: Serie estadística (1651-1739)," *AEA*, 21:1-24 (1964).

An excellent addition to materials on the African slave trade to the Indies listed in the essays for chapters 6 and 11 is the compact quantitative article Enriqueta Vilavilan, "The Large Scale Introduction of Africans into Veracruz and Cartagena," in *Comparative Perspectives on Slavery in New World Plantation Societies* [*Chap. 3*], pp. 267-280.

The counterpart of *Séville et l'Atlantique* for Spain's Pacific trade is Pierre Chaunu, *Les Philippines et le Pacifique des Ibériques* [*Chap. 5*]. A more readable descriptive account is William L. Schurz, *The Manila Galleon* (New York: E. P. Dutton, 1939).

Materials on Inter-American trade listed in the essay for chapter 11 are supplemented by Lawrence A. Clayton, "Trade and Navigation in the Seventeenth-Century Viceroyalty of Peru," *Journal of Latin American Studies*, 7:1-21 (1975); Marie Helmer, "Le Callao (1615-1618)," *JGSW*, 2:145-195 (1965), which provides an intimate view of commercial life in Spanish America's busiest Pacific port; and Carlos Sempat Assadourian, "Sobre un elemento de la economía colonial: Producción y circulación de mercancias en el interior de un conjunto regional," *EURE*, 3(no. 8):135-181 (December 1973), a fine description of patterns of commerce within the Viceroyalty of Peru. Ricardo Zorraquín Becú, "Orígenes del comercio rioplatense, 1580-1620," *Anuario de Historia Argentina*, 5:71-105 (1943-45), explores the beginning of commerce in the Rio de la Plata area.

Works on contraband trade in the Indies are descriptive rather than analytical for obvious reasons. A good compact overview is Dolores Bonet de Sotillo, *El tráfico ilegal en las colonias españolas* (Caracas: Universidad Central de la Cultura, 1955). See also G. Earl Sanders, "Counter-Contraband in Spanish America, Handicaps of the Governors of the Indies," *TA*, 34:59-80 (1977-78).

Following is a sampling of regional descriptions of contraband trade: Irene A. Wright, "Rescates with Special Reference to Cuba, 1599-1610," *HAHR* 3:333-361 (1920); Adam Szaszdi Nagy, "El comercio ilícito en la provincia de Honduras," *RI*, 17:271-283 (1967); and Marie Helmer, "Comercio y contrabando entre Bahia e Potosí no século xvi," *Revista de História*, vol. IV (São Paulo: Universidade de São Paulo, 1953). The operations of foreign merchants in Spanish America are examined in Hermann Kellebenz, "Mercaderes extranjeros en América del sur a comienzos del siglo xvii," *AEA*, 28:377-403 (1971).

The penetration of foreign merchants into the Indies trade at its European end is described in the following books: for the English, Croft, *The Spanish Company* [*Chap. 11*]; and Jean O. McLachlan, *Trade and Peace with Old Spain, 1667-1750* (Cambridge: Cambridge University Press, 1940); for the French, Girard, *Le commerce français à Séville et à Cadix au temps des Habsbourgs* [*Chap. 11*]; for the Flemish, John E. Everaert, "Le commerce colonial de la 'Nación Flamande' à Cadix sous Charles II, ca. 1670-1700," *AEA*, 28:139-151 (1971); and Eddy Stohls, *De Spaanse Brabanders of de Handelsbetrekkingen der Zuidelijke Nederlanden met de Iberische Wereld, 1598-1648*, 2 vols. (Brussels: Paleis der Academiën, 1971).

Works dealing with the controversial "depression" and structural changes in the economy of the seventeenth-century Indies are listed and discussed in the text and notes of chapter 17.

General economic histories of Brazil and histories of the colony's sugar industry are listed in the bibliographical essay for chapter 13. More specialized treatments of sugar production are José W. de Araújo Pinho, *História de um engenho do Reconcavo: Moatim, Caboto, Freguezia* (Salvador: Editôra Beneditina, 1968), one of the few case studies of an *engenho* in print; Stuart B. Schwartz, "Free Labor in a Slave Economy: the *Lavradores de Cana* of Colonial Brazil," in *Colonial Roots of Modern Brazil* [*General Works*], pp. 147-198; Mathew Edel, "The Brazilian Sugar Cycle of the 17th Century and the Rise of West Indian Competition," *Caribbean Studies*, 9:24-44 (1969); and Alice P. Canabrava, "A fôrça motriz: Um problema da técnica da industria do açucar colonial (a solução antilhana e a brasileira)," in *Anais do Primeiro Congresso de História da Bahía*, vol. IV (Salvador, 1950), pp. 351-387. The articles by Edel and Canabrava offer somewhat different interpretations of the causes and effects of West Indian competition.

Monographic works on other sectors of the economy in post-Conquest Brazil are very scarce. The essay for chapter 13 lists a few titles dealing with brazilwood cutting and cattle ranching. I know of no solid published studies of tobacco or cotton planting. The whaling industry is described in Austregésilo, *Aspectos da Baleia no Brasil colonial* [*Chap. 13*], and the colonial salt monopoly in the same author's *O monopólio do sal no estado do Brasil (1631-1801)* (São Paulo: Universidade de São Paulo, 1955). A good description of colonial land transportation is Richard P. Momsen, *Routes over the Serra do Mar: The Evolution of Transportation in the Highlands of Rio de Janeiro and São Paulo* (Rio de Janeiro: n.p., 1964).

Brazil's Atlantic trade in the seventeenth century is surveyed in Lang, *Portuguese Brazil* [*General Works*], chap. 3; and Pierre Chaunu, "Bresil et l'Atlantique au xvii$^e$ siècle," *AESC*, 6:1176-1207 (1961). A more detailed analysis is Mauro's *Le Portugal et l'Atlantique* [*Chap. 13*]. A standard book on Portuguese mercantile doctrine is José Calvet de Magalhães, *História do pensamiento econômica em Portugal* (Coimbra: n.p., 1967). The history of the Brazil Company is recounted in Gustavo de Freitas, *A Companhia Geral do Comércio do Brasil (1649-1720): Subsídios para a história económica de Portugal e do Brasil* (São Paulo: n.p., 1951).

More specialized works on Brazil's commerce include Verger, *Flux et reflux de la traité des nègres* [*Chap. 16*]; David D. Smith, "Old Christian Merchants and the Foundation of the Brazil Company, 1649," *HAHR*, 54:233-259 (1974); and Jerônimo de Viveiros, *História do comércio do Maranhão, 1612-1895*, 2 vols. (San Luis: Associação Comercial Maranhão, 1954).

Several important works link or compare Brazilian and Spanish American economies in the seventeenth century. Frédéric Mauro, "México y Brasil: Dos economías coloniales comparadas," *HM*, 10:571-587 (1960-61), makes some broad, high-level comparative observations. The effects of the union of the Spanish and Portuguese crowns on Hispanic American colonial economic relations are discussed in Schwartz, "Luso-Spanish Relations in Hapsburg Brazil, 1580-1640" [*Chap. 15*]. The importance the Portuguese attached to their Spanish American slave trade is brought out in Walter Rodney, "Portuguese Attempts at Monopoly on the Upper Guinea Coast," *Journal of African History*, 6:307-322 (1965). Eulália M. Lahmayer Lôbo, *Aspectos da influência dos homens de negócios na política comercial ibero-americana* (Rio de Janeiro: Universidade do Guanabara, 1963), advances the thesis that, since Portugal's mercantile policy was much more realistic than Spain's, Portuguese trade survived seventeenth-century vicissitudes much better.

A number of key works on dependency theory are identified and discussed in the last section of the text of chapter 17 and in the accompanying notes. The literature on the subject and associated controversies are analyzed more fully in Richard C. Bath and Dilmus D. James, "Dependency Analysis of Latin America," *LARR*, 11(no. 3):3-54 (1976); Ronald H. Chilcote and Joel C. Edelstein, "Introduction," in *Latin America: The Struggle with Dependency and Beyond*, ed. Ronald H. Chilcote and Joel C. Edelstein (New York: John Wiley and Sons, 1974), pp. 1-87; Steven Jackson and others, "An Assessment of Empirical Research on *Dependencia*," *LARR*, 14(no. 3):7-28 (1979); and Tulio Halperin-Donghi, "Dependency Theory and Latin American Historiography," *LARR*, 7(no. 1):115-130 (1982).

## CHAPTER 18. AMERICAN SOCIETIES AND AMERICAN IDENTITIES

General works on the social history of Spanish America are surveyed in the bibliographical essay for chapter 8. The following essay discusses those that have a special relevance for post-Conquest developments.

Changing Spanish perceptions of the Indian are examined in Mörner, *La corona española y los foráneos* [*Chap. 8*]; and Paulino Delgado Castañeda, "La condición miserable del Indio y sus privilegios," *AEA*, 28:245-335 (1971). The emergence of the concept of the "two republics" is described in Góngora, *Studies* [*General Works*], pp. 116-119.

A fine essay on the internal constitution of the republic of Spaniards may be found in Góngora's *Studies* [*General Works*], chap. 3. Good descriptions of the aristocracy are Chevalier, *Land and Society* [*Chap. 10*], chap. 4, which deals with the *hacendados* of northern Mexico; Fred Bronner, "Peruvian Encomenderos in 1630: Elite Circulation and Consolidation," *HAHR*, 57:633-659 (1977); Mario Góngora, *Encomenderos y estancieros: Estudios acerca de la constitución social aristocrática de Chile después de la Conquista, 1580-1660* (Santiago: Universidad de Chile, 1970); and Peter Marzahl, *Town in the Empire: Government, Politics, and Society in Seventeenth-Century Popayán*, Latin American

Monographs, 45 (Austin: Institute of Latin American Studies, University of Texas, 1978), whose main theme is the consolidation of a local aristocracy in this Colombian municipality.

The concept of *nobleza* (nobility) in the Indies is examined in Richard Konetzke, "La formación de la nobleza en Indias," *Estudios Americanos*, 3(no. 10):329-360 (1951); and Juan E. Villamarín, "The Concept of Nobility in the Social Stratification of Colonial Santa Fe de Bogotá," [*Chap. 17*]. American membership in the Spanish military orders is the subject of Guillermo Lohmann Villena, *Los americanos en las órdenes nobiliarias (1529-1900)*, 2 vols. (Madrid: C.S.I.C., 1947). The titled nobility of Mexico in the sixteenth and seventeenth centuries is discussed in Doris M. Ladd, *The Mexican Nobility at Independence, 1780-1826*, Latin American Monographs, 40 (Austin: Institute of Latin American Studies, University of Texas, 1976), chap. 1.

I know of no studies dealing explicitly with the clergy as an estate or a social class. However, information on the subject can be found in the books and articles on missionary activities and the institutional church listed in the essays for chapters 8 and 9 and for chapter 19. Also useful are the following: on the secular clergy, José Restrepo Posada, *Arquidiócesis de Bogotá: Datos biográficos de sus prelados*, 3 vols. (Bogotá: Editorial Lumen Christi, 1961-66); and Fernando Armas Medina, "La jerarquía eclesiástica peruana en la primera mitad del siglo xvii," *AEA*, 22:673-703 (1965); on the regular clergy, Francisco Morales, *Ethnic and Social Backgrounds of the Franciscan Friars in Seventeenth Century Mexico*, Monograph Series, 10 (Washington, D.C.: Academy of American Franciscan History, 1973).

Analytical studies of the "royal estate" are also scarce. Approaches to the subject are explored in two excellent historiographical articles: Stuart B. Schwartz, "State and Society in Colonial Spanish America: An Opportunity for Prosopography," in *New Approaches to Latin American History*, ed. Richard Graham and Peter H. Smith (Austin: University of Texas Press, 1974), pp. 3-35; and Margaret C. Crahan, "Spanish and American Counterpoint: Problems and Possibilities in Spanish Colonial Administrative History," pp. 36-70 in the same volume. The interpenetration of the magistracy and the colonial aristocracy is explored in Pedro Rodríguez Crespo, "Sobre parentescos de los oidores con los grupos superiores de la sociedad limeña (a comienzos del siglo xvii)," *Mercurio Peruano*, nos. 447-450:3-15 (1965).

Colonial historiography is likewise poor in monographic studies of the more common elements in the republic of Spaniards. A good regional introduction to the subject is Mario Góngora, "Urban Social Stratification in Colonial Chile," *HAHR*, 55:421-448 (1975). The following works contain information on particular groups: on merchants, Hoberman, "Merchants in Seventeenth-Century Mexico City" [*Chap. 17*]; and Rocío Caracuel Moyano, "Los mercaderes del Perú y la financiación de los gastos de la monarquía, 1650-1700," in *PICA*, 36th [*Chap. 8*], IV, 333-343; on miners, Bakewell, *Silver Mining and Society*, especially chap. 5 [*Chap. 10*]; and D. A. Brading, *Miners and Merchants in Bourbon Mexico, 1763-1810* (Cambridge: Cambridge University Press, 1971), especially the "Introduction"; on textile manufacturers, Super, "Querétaro Obrajes" [*Chap. 17*]; on lawyers, Héctor García Chuecas, *Abogados en la colonia* (Caracas: Imprenta Nacional, 1958); on guildsmen, see the works on guilds listed in the essays for chapters 10 and 17.

One of the few close looks at women in colonial society is Asunción Lavrin and Edith Couturier, "Dowries and Wills: A View of Women's Socioeconomic Role in Colonial Guadalajara and Puebla, 1640-1790," *HAHR*, 59:280-304 (1979).

The theme of creole-peninsular rivalry runs through much of the social history of colonial Spanish America. It is developed most colorfully in Thomas Gage, *The English-American, His Travail by Sea and Land* (London, 1648), subsequently published in many editions and with varying titles, the most common being *A New Survey of the West Indies*. Specialized modern studies are Antonine Tibesar, "The Alternativa: A Study of Spanish-Creole Relations in Seventeenth Century Peru," *TA*, 11:229-283 (1954-55); and Morales, *Ethnic Backgrounds of the Franciscan Friars in Seventeenth Century Mexico*, listed early in this chapter essay.

Information on the constitution of the republic of Indians may be found scattered through works on the American Indian listed in previous chapter essays, especially in those for chapter 16 and for chapters 6 and 8. The most comprehensive among them are Gibson, *The Aztecs under Spanish Rule* [*Chap. 8*]; and Mörner, *La corona española y los foráneos*. The social history of the Indians of Upper Peru from the 1570s onward is the principal theme of Nicolás Sánchez-Albornoz, *Indios y tributos en el Alto Perú* (Lima: Instituto de Estudios Peruanos, 1978).

More specialized studies dealing with or touching closely on this subject include François Chevalier, "Les muncipalités indiennes en Nouvelle Espagne, 1520–1620," *AHDE*, 15:352-368 (1944); Charles Gibson, "The Aztec Aristocracy in Colonial Mexico," *Comparative Studies in Society and History*, 2:169-196 (1959-60); Guillermo S. Fernández de Recas, *Cacicazgos y nobilario indígena de la Nueva España* (Mexico: Instituto Bibliográfico Mexicano, 1961); and Waldemar Espinoza Soriano, "El alcalde mayor indígena en el virreinato del Perú," *AEA*, 17:183-300 (1960).

Ethnic qualities, circumstances of birth, and condition of servitude fixed the status of blacks and mixed bloods in the colonial order. General and specialized works dealing with these several attributes are listed in the essay for chapter 4 and in the essays dealing with colonial populations (chapters 6 and 16) and with slavery (chapters 10 and 17). Additional studies of the status of the African component of colonial society are Palmer, *Slaves of the White God* [*Chap. 16*]; Gonzalo Vial Correa, *El Africano en el Reino de Chile: Ensayo histórico-jurídico* (Santiago: Universidad Católica de Chile, 1957); and Edgar Love, "Marriage Patterns of Persons of African Blood in a Colonial Mexico City Parish," *HAHR*, 51:79-91 (1971), a pioneer work. The handiest general survey of miscegenation and its social consequences is Mörner, *Race Mixture in Latin America* [*Chap. 6*]. A useful supplement to this work is Colin M. MacLachlan and Jaime O. Rodríguez, *The Forging of the Cosmic Race: A Reinterpretation of Colonial Mexico* (Berkeley: University of California Press, 1980), in which a major theme is the formation and status of the *castas*. Praiseworthy specialized studies of social mobility and assimilation, especially at the lower levels of society, are Luz María Martínez Montiel, "Integration Patterns and the Assimilation of Negro Slaves in Mexico," in *Comparative Perspectives on Slavery in New World Plantation Societies* [*Chap. 3*], pp. 446-454. Karen Spalding, "Changing Patterns of Mobility Among the Indians of Colonial Peru," *HAHR*, 50:645-664 (1970); and Emilio Harth-Terré, *Cauces de españolización en la sociedad indoperuano de Lima virreinal* (Lima: Editorial Tierra y Arte, 1964), which deals with the rate of acceptance of mixed-blood children by their Spanish fathers.

The best general treatments of creolism in colonial society are Leopoldo Zea, *América como conciencia* (Mexico: n.p., 1953); and José J. Arrom, *Certidumbre de América, estudios de letras, folklore y cultura* (Havana: Anuario Bibliográfico Cubano, 1959). Important regional studies are Liss, *Mexico under Spain, 1521-1556* [*Chap. 8*], especially chapter 6; Irving A. Leonard, *Baroque Times in Old Mexico: Seventeenth-Century Persons, Places and Practices* (Ann Arbor: University of Michigan Press, 1959); Severo Martínez Peláez, *La patria del criollo: Ensayo de la realidad colonial guatemalteca* (Guatemala:

Ediciones Universitaria, 1970); and André Saint-Lu, *Condition coloniale et conscience créole au Guatemala (1524-1821)* (Paris: Presses Universitaires de France, 1970). The economic bases of creole self-consciousness are examined in John Lynch, *Spain under the Habsburgs* [*General Works*], II, chaps. 7-8, *passim*. The influence of creoles in local political affairs is analyzed in Peter Marzahl, "Creoles and Government: The Cabildo of Popayán," *HAHR*, 54:636-656 (1974). The long-term implications of creole political aspirations are discussed in Gonzáles Obregón, *Los precursores de la independencia mexicana en el siglo xvi* [*Chap. 9*].

The theme of Indian identity as such has not been well developed by historians and anthropologists. It is, however, closely related to the process of acculturation, transculturation, syncretism, and the like, about which a large body of books and articles have been published. Some of these are listed in the essay for chapter 8. Good general syntheses are Eric Wolf, *Sons of the Shaking Earth* (Chicago: University of Chicago Press, 1959), especially chaps. 8-10, which deals with Mexico and Central America; and Henry F. Dobyns and Paul L. Doughty, *Peru: A Cultural History* (Oxford: Oxford University Press, 1976), chaps. 3-4.

For particular expressions of Indian identity in Mesoamerica, John T. Reid, "Folkloric Symbols of Nationhood in Guatemala," *Southern Folklore Quarterly*, 28:136-153 (1974), is very much worth reading. A catalog, description, and set of explanations of thirty important Indian revolts may be found in *Rebeliones indígenas de la época colonial*, comp. María Teresa Huerta and Patricia Palacios (Mexico: Sep/Inah, 1976). A typology of revivalist and nativist movements is presented in Anthony F. C. Wallace, "Revitalization Movements," *American Anthropologist*, 58:264-281 (1956). Good brief descriptive studies are William B. Griffen, "A North Mexican Nativistic Movement, 1684," *Ethnohistory*, 17:95-116 (1970); and Alicia M. Barabas, "Profetismo, milenarismo y mesianismo en las insurrecciones mayas de Yucatán," in *PICA*, 41st, Mexico, 1974, vol. II (Mexico: Instituto Nacional de Antropología e Historia, 1976), pp. 609-622.

The most systematic treatment of survival or re-creation of indigneous identities in the Andean region is Wechtel, *The Vision of the Vanquished* [*Chap. 5*], organized around the themes of structuration, destructuration, and restructuration and stressing folkloric influences and revolutionary movements. A specialized study of Andean Indian political consciousness is George Kubler, "The Neo-Inca State, 1537-1572," *HAHR*, 27:189-203 (1947).

Among the various works on blacks and mulattoes listed in earlier chapter essays, the most sophisticated and imaginative study of the formation of Afro-American identities in the Indies is Bastide, *African Civilizations in the New World* [*Chap. 4*]. It is especially good on the role of religion. On this point the short but pithy paper Monserrat Palau Martí, "Africa en América a través de sus dioses," in *PICA*, 36th [*Chap. 11*], III, 627-632, is also worth reading. Palmer, *Slaves of the White God* [*Chap. 16*], investigates the problems experienced by the blacks of colonial Mexico in forming an identity. The role of kinship in Afro-American society and its historiography are the subjects of the comparative article, A. J. R. Russell-Wood, "The Black Family in the Americas," *JGSW*, 16:267-309 (1979).

The more violent expressions of Afro-American identities are discussed in Edgar S. Love, "Negro Resistance to Spanish Rule in Colonial Mexico," *Journal of Negro History*, 52:89-103 (1967); David M. Davidson, "Negro Slave Control and Resistance in Colonial Mexico, 1519-1650," *HAHR*, 46:235-253 (1966); and the concise Angelina Pollak-Eltz, "Slave Revolts in Venezuela," in *Comparative Perspectives on Slavery in New World Plantation Societies* [*Chap. 3*], pp. 439-445.

Essays on marronage in Spanish America in general and in Cuba, Venezuela, and Mexico in particular are included in *Maroon Societies: Rebel Slave Communities in the Americas*, ed. Richard Price (Garden City, N.J.: Anchor Press/Doubleday [Anchor A954], 1973), part 1. María del Carmen Borrega Plá, *Palenques de Negros en Cartagena de Indias a finés del siglo xvii, PEEHA, 216* (Seville, 1973), deals with *cimarron* communities in the hinterlands of the port of Cartagena.

Monographic studies of mestizo identity deal almost exclusively with the nineteenth and twentieth centuries, and for a good reason: it was only an incipient phenomenon in the colonial world. The most perceptive treatment of it as such is Wolf, *Sons of the Shaking Earth*, chap. 11, mentioned earlier in this chapter essay.

An imaginative investigation of the unifying role of religion in colonial society is Jacques La Faye, *Quetzalcóatl et Guadalupe: La formation de la conscience nationale au Mexique, 1531–1813* (Paris: Editions Gallimard, 1974), trans. Benjamin Keen as *Quetzalcóatl and Guadalupe: The Formation of Mexican National Consciousness, 1531–1813* (Chicago: University of Chicago Press, 1976).

Monographs on informal social "microstructures" and their cohesive functions are poorly represented in colonial historiography, although they were powerful and pervasive. The importance of the family is surveyed in Elda R. González and Rolando Mellafe, "La función de la familia en la historia social de Hispanoamérica colonial," in *América colonial: Población y economía* (Rosario, Arg.: Instituto de Investigaciones Históricas, Universidad Nacional del Litoral, 1965), pp. 57-71. Although not primarily concerned with colonial forms of fictive and ritual kinship relationships, the following articles throw some light on the continuous historical importance of these phenomena in Hispanic societies: George Foster, "Cofradía and Compadrazgo in Spain and Spanish America," *Southwestern Journal of Anthropology*, 9:1-28 (1953); and Sidney W. Mintz and Eric H. Wolf, "An Analysis of Ritual Co-Parenthood (*compadrazgo*)," *Southwestern Journal of Anthropology*, 6:341-68 (1950).

The only systematic study of clientage in sixteenth- and seventeenth-century Spanish America I have come across is Stephanie Blank, "Patrons, Clients and Kin in Seventeenth-Century Caracas: A Methodological Essay in Colonial Spanish American Social History," *HAHR*, 54:260-283 (1974). Although it deals mainly with more recent periods, some retrospective illumination of the problem in colonial times comes from Arnold Strickon and Sidney M. Greenfield, *Structure and Process in Latin America: Patronage, Clientage, and Power Systems* (Albuquerque: University of New Mexico Press, 1972).

The standard social history of Brazil is Pedro Calmon, *História social do Brasil*, 3 vols. (2nd ed.; São Paulo: Companhia Editôra Nacional, 1937–39). More widely known is Freyre, *The Masters and the Slaves* [*Chap. 13*]. It has been criticized on the grounds that it is unsystematic and impressionistic and generalizes on the basis of Pernambucan society. But these defects are counterbalanced by deep erudition and rich intuitive insights. Another sociological contribution of general interest is Emilio Willems, "Social Differentiation in Colonial Brazil," *Comparative Studies in Society and History*, 12:31-49 (1970).

Important regional social histories are José W. de Araújo Pinho, *História social da cidade do Salvador*, vol. I: *Aspectos da história social da cidade, 1549-1650* (Salvador: Editôra Beneditina, 1968); and Nelson Omegna (pseudo. for Luís Jardim), *A cidade colonial* (Rio de Janeiro: Livraria J. Olympia, 1961).

There are a few monographic studies of major groups in Brazilian white society. I know of no comprehensive work on the sugar aristocracy that measures up to the standards of modern scholarship, although much can be learned about the constitution of the Bahian elite from Russell-Wood, *Fidalgos and Philanthropists* [*Chap. 13*]; and Ray Flory and David Smith, "Bahian Merchants and Planters in the Seventeenth and Early Eighteenth

Centuries," *HAHR*, 58:571-594 (1978). On upper-class women see Susan A. Soeiro, "The Social and Economic Role of the Convent: Women and Nuns in Colonial Bahia, 1677-1800," *HAHR*, 54:209-232 (1974).

The only thorough work on the royal bureaucracy is Stuart B. Schwartz, *Sovereignty and Society in Colonial Brazil: The High Court of Bahia and Its Judges* (Berkeley: University of California Press, 1973), which also helps to illuminate the constitution of Bahian elites. Brief information on the upper clergy is contained in Francis A. Dutra, "The Brazilian Hierarchy in the Seventeenth Century," *Records of the American Catholic Historical Society*, 83:171-186 (1972). The influential Jewish community in Brazil is described in Wiznitzer, *Jews in Colonial Brazil* [*Chap. 13*]; and Anita Novinsky, *Cristãos novos na Bahia* [*Chap. 16*].

The best general treatment of the status of Africans in colonial Brazilian society is Bastide, *African Civilizations in the New World*, mentioned earlier in this chapter essay. Other useful general works are Emília Viotti da Costa, *Da senzala à colônia* (São Paulo: Difusão Européia do Livro, 1966); the older Arthur Ramos, *The Negro in Brazil* (Washington, D.C.: The Associated Publishers, 1939); and Donald Pierson, *Negroes in Brazil: A Study of Race Contact in Bahia* (Chicago: University of Chicago Press, 1942). See also Russell-Wood, "The Black Family in the Americas." The religious element in the formation of Afro-Brazilian identities is examined in René Ribeiro, "Relations of the Negro with Christianity in Portuguese America," *TA*, 14:454-484 (1957-58); and A. J. R. Russell-Wood, "Black and Mulatto Brotherhoods in Colonial Brazil: A Study in Collective Behavior," *HAHR*, 54:567-602 (1974). Brazilian *quilombos* are surveyed in a series of essays by R. K. Kent, Roger Bastide, and Stuart B. Schwartz in Price, ed., *Maroon Societies*, mentioned earlier in this chapter essay, pp. 169-226. A fuller treatment of the "Republic" of Palmares is Edison Carneiro, *O quilombo dos Palmares* (2nd ed.; São Paulo: Companhia Editôria Nacional, 1958).

Among works on the *bandeirantes* listed in the essay for chapter 15, Leite, *Marcha para Oeste*, bears repeating because of its rich social content. See also José de Alcântara Machado, *Vida e morte do bandeirante* (São Paulo: Martins, 1953). Among the few studies on cattle-ranching societies, the following merit mention: Calmon, *História da Casa de Tórre, uma dinastia de pioneiros* [*Chap. 15*]; and Santos Filho, *Uma comunidade rural do Brasil antigo* [*Chap. 16*], a detailed description of a cattle *fazenda*.

The text and accompanying notes of the last section of chapter 18 identify and discuss some of the important studies of race relations in the Hispanic colonies and, from a comparative point of view, in the New World in general.

## CHAPTER 19. IMPERIAL SYSTEMS

General works on Spanish colonial government and its principal institutions are surveyed in the bibliographical essay for chapter 9. The following essay discusses books and articles that are especially relevant to the growth of the state after the Conquest.

The best survey of the territorial expansion of government is Haring, *The Spanish Empire in America* [*General Works*], chaps. 4, 5. Specialized studies of major new jurisdictions and commands are Cunningham, *The Audiencia in the Spanish Colonies as Illustrated by the Audiencia of Manila* [*Chap. 9*]; Ricardo Zorraquín Becú, *La organización judicial argentina en el período hispánico* (Buenos Aires: Librería de Plata, 1952); and the same author's *La organización política argentina en el período hispánico* (3rd ed.; Buenos Aires: Emecé Editores, 1967). On expanding episcopal government see A. C. van Oss, "Comparing Colonial Bishoprics in Spanish South America," *Boletín de Estudios Latinoamericanos y del Caribe* (Amsterdam), no. 24:27-65 (June 1978).

The functional expansion of the state may be traced in works dealing with its several departments or divisions. The development of the office of viceroy is examined and copiously documented in Ignacio Rubio Mañé, *Introducción al estudio de los virreyes de Nueva España, 1535-1746*, 4 vols. (Mexico: U.N.A.M., 1955-61), especially vols. I, IV. A more specialized work illustrating the rapid growth of viceregal government during the reign of Philip II is Roberto Levillier, *Don Francisco de Toledo, supremo organizador del Perú: Su vida, su obra (1515-1582)*, 2 vols. (Buenos Aires: Biblioteca del Congreso Argentino, 1935-42). A shorter account of Toledo's viceregency is Arthur F. Zimmerman, *Francisco de Toledo, Fifth Viceroy of Peru* (Caldwell, Idaho: The Caxton Printers, 1938). The function of *jurisdicción* (justice) is surveyed concisely in Louis G. Kahle, "The Spanish Colonial Judiciary," *Southwestern Social Science Quarterly*, 32:26-37 (1951). A fuller treatment is Enrique Ruiz-Guiñazú, *La magistratura indiana* (Buenos Aires: Universidad de Buenos Aires, 1916). A fine study of the functioning of an individual *audiencia* is Phelan, *The Kingdom of Quito* [*Chap. 17*].

Information on the organization and operations of the royal exchequer after the conquest period is provided by Fabián de Fonseca and Carlos Urrutia, *Historia general de real hacienda*, 6 vols. (Mexico: 1845-53), which deals with New Spain; John J. TePaske in collaboration with José and Mari Luz Hernández Palomo, *La Real Hacienda de Nueva España: La Real Caja de México (1576-1816)* (Mexico: Instituto Nacional de Antropolgía e Historia, 1976), an enormously valuable series of data on the income and expenditures of the main treasury office in Mexico City; and Amy Bushnell, *The King's Coffer: Proprietors of the Spanish Florida Treasury, 1565-1702* (Gainesville: University Presses of Florida, 1981), which provides a close look at a provincial treasury office and the men who staffed it.

Useful supplements to works on the royal patronage discussed in the essay for chapter 9 are Robert C. Padden, "The Ordenanza del Patronazgo, 1574," *TA*, 12:333-354 (1955-56), which examines the extension of the royal patronage under Philip II; and Reynerio Lebroc, "Proyección tridentina en América," *Missionalia Hispánica*, 26:129-207 (1969), which deals with the influence of the proceedings of the Council of Trent on ecclesiastical government in the Indies. Antonio de Egaña, *La teoría del regio vicariato español en Indias* (Rome: Apud Aedes Universitatis Gregorianae, 1958), is a solid monograph on the various theories advanced about the royal vicariate. The most systematic analysis of the management of ecclesiastical tithes is Woodrow Borah, "Tithe Collection in the Bishopric of Oaxaca, 1601-1867," *HAHR*, 29:498-517 (1949).

The classic work on the Spanish American Inquisition is a series of studies by the prolific Chilean scholar and bibliographer José Toribio Medina totaling ten volumes and published in Santiago de Chile between 1887 and 1914. They deal individually with the introduction of the inquisitorial function in the Indies and with the Holy Office in Lima, Chile, Cartagena, the Philippines, the Rio de la Plata, and Mexico. A shorter and disapproving general synthesis is Henry C. Lea, *The Inquisition in the Spanish Dependencies: Sicily, Naples, Sardinia, Milan, the Canaries, Mexico, Peru, New Granada* (New York: Macmillan, 1908). An excellent example of modern scholarship on the subject is Richard E. Greenleaf, *The Mexican Inquisition of the Sixteenth Century* (Albuquerque: University of New Mexico Press, 1970).

Compared with the volume of published scholarship on civil and ecclesiastical government, works on the military function in the Indies are few. I have not found any satisfactory general work on the subject. Good specialized studies of the defense of the northern frontier of New Spain are Max L. Moorhead, *The Presidio: Bastion of the Spanish Borderlands* (Norman: University of Oklahoma Press, 1975), which is concerned chiefly with the eighteenth century but which has an introductory chapter on "Historical Evolution," and Woodrow Borah, "La defensa fronteriza durante la gran rebelión tepehuana," *HM*, 16:15-29 (1966-67), a compact case study of the recruitment, organization, and armament of companies formed in San Luis Potosí to put down an Indian rebellion in 1616-18. The role of the missions in defending the northern frontier is developed in Herbert E. Bolton, "The Mission as a Frontier Institution in the Spanish Colonies" [*Chap. 15*]. Robert A. Matter, "Missions in the Defense of Spanish Florida," *Florida Historical Quarterly*, 54:18-38 (1975), expresses doubts about their effectiveness in this capacity.

The defense of the Indian frontier in Chile is described in Agustín Toro Dávila, *Síntesis histórico militar de Chile* (Santiago: Fondo Editorial Educación Moderna, 1969), I, 8-56; Jara, *Guerre et société au Chile* [*Chap. 9*]; and Fernando Márquez de la Plata, *Arqueología del antiguo reino de Chile* (Santiago: Imprenta Artes y Letras, 1953), which is especially useful for its information on fortifications and weapons. On frontier defense in the Platine region see Alfred J. Tapson, "Indian Warfare on the Pampa during the Colonial Period," *HAHR*, 42:1-28 (1962).

Works on northern European intrusions into the Indies are discussed in the bibliographical essay for chapter 15. The fullest description of Spanish naval responses in both the Caribbean and the Pacific is Fernández Duro, *Armada española* [*Chap. 9*], especially vols. III-V. The work, however, is weak on strategic analysis and naval organization.

The beginnings of a systematic defense policy in the Caribbean, especially its financing, are discussed in Hoffman, *The Spanish Crown and the Defense of the Caribbean* [*Chap. 9*]. Further developments are traced in Roland D. Hussey, "Spanish Reaction to Foreign Aggression in the Caribbean to About 1680," *HAHR*, 9:286-302 (1929). A basic description of the military and naval organization of the Atlantic fleets is contained in Haring, *Trade and Navigation* [*Chap. 9*], chaps. 9, 10, and 11. Aspects of the organization and operation of the "Windward Squadron are discussed in Bibiano Torres Ramírez, "Los primeros intentos de formación de la Armada de Barlovento," *JGSW*, 11:33-51 (1974); and María del Carmen Velázquez, "Una misión de la Armada de Barlovento," *HM*, 8:400-406 (1958-59).

The closest approach to a general survey of fortification in the Caribbean and the Gulf of Mexico is Diego Angulo Iñiguez and Enrique Marco Dorta, *Historia del Arte Hispanoamericano*, 3 vols. (Barcelona and Buenos Aires: Salvat Editores, 1945-56), I, chaps. 10, 13. The planning of fortifications and the first stages of their construction are examined in Diego Angulo Iñiguez, *Bautista Antonelli: Las fortificaciones americanas en el siglo xvi* (Madrid: Hauser y Menet, 1942). Studies of individual major fortifications are Irene A. Wright, *Historia documentada de San Cristóbal de la Havana en el siglo xvii* (Havana: Imprenta El Siglo XX, 1930); José A. Calderón Quijano, *Fortificaciones en Nueva España*, PEEHA, 60 (Seville, 1953); Enrique Marco Dorta, *Cartagena de Indias: Puerto y plaza fuerte* (Cartagena: A. Amado, 1960); and Guillermo Céspedes del Castillo, "La defensa militar del Istmo de Panamá a finés del siglo xvii y comienzos del xviii," *AEA*, 9:235-275 (1952).

A concise description of Spanish defenses in the Pacific is Peter T. Bradley, "Maritime Defense of the Viceroyalty of Peru (1600-1700)," *TA*, 36:155-174 (1979-80). Information on the subject may also be found in Lawrence A. Clayton, "Local Initiative and Finance in Defense of the Viceroyalty of Peru," *HAHR*, 54:284-304 (1974). The fortifications of principal Pacific ports are treated in Engel Sluiter, "The Fortification of Acapulco, 1615-1616," *HAHR*, 29:69-80 (1949); and Guillermo Lohman Villena, *Las defensas militares de Lima y Callao hasta 1746*, PEEHA, 154 (Seville, 1964).

The patrimonial and bureaucratic features of the Spanish State in the Indies are examined at a theoretical level in Magali Sarfatti, *Spanish Bureaucratic-Patrimonialism in*

*America* (Berkeley: Institute of International Studies, University of California, 1966). Tentative explorations into the structure of the royal bureaucracy are included in Schwartz, "State and Society in Colonial Spanish America" [*Chap. 18*]; and Crahan, "Spanish and American Counterpoint" [*Chap. 18*]. John L. Phelan theorizes about the functioning of the bureaucracy in "Authority and Flexibility in the Spanish Imperial Bureaucracy," *Administrative Science Quarterly*, 5:47-65 (1960). Phelan's *Kingdom of Quito* [*Chap. 17*], is the closest approach available to a substantive work on the royal bureaucracy in the Indies. An important study of royal patrimonialism is John H. Parry, *The Sale of Public Office in the Spanish Indies under the Habsburgs*, Ibero-Americana: 37 (Berkeley: University of California Press, 1953).

The historical development of the legal foundations of the state in the Indies along with the relevant literature is surveyed in Alfonso García Gallo, "El desarrollo de la historiografía jurídica indiana," *Revista de Estudios Políticos*, 48:163-185 (1953). The standard history of the Laws of the Indies is Juan Manzano Manzano, *Historia de las Recopilaciones de Indias*, 2 vols. (Madrid: Ediciones Cultura Hispánica, 1950–56).

The best introduction to the theoretical foundations of the state is Góngora, *Studies* [*General Works*], chaps. 2, 3. A fuller monographic treatment of the subject is José A. Maravall, *La teoría española del estado en el siglo xvii* (Madrid: Instituto de Estudios Políticos, 1944). As for more specialized studies, the evolution of the doctrine of "Just Title" is traced in Alfonso García Gallo, "Las Indias en el reinado de Felipe II: La solución del problema de los justos títulos," *Anuario de la Asociación Francisco de Vitoria*, 13:93-136 (1960–61); and the constitutional relationship between Castile and the American kingdoms is explained in Antonio Muro Orejón, "El problema de los 'Reinos Indianos'," *AEA*, 28:45-56 (1971).

I think the most thoughtful and best-balanced survey of the Portuguese state in Brazil after about 1580 is Lahmayer Lôbo, *Processo administrativo ibero-americano* [*Chap. 9*], chap. 3. The territorial expansion of royal government is traced in Varnhagen, *História geral do Brasil* [*General Works*], II, 29-185. On the state of Maranhão see Carlos Studart Filho, *O antigo Estado do Maranhão e suas capitanias feudais* (Fortaleza: Universidade do Ceará, 1960).

Very few scholarly studies of particular institutions and features of government in colonial Brazil have been published. Among them, the best treatment of the governorship general is Dauril Alden, *Royal Government in Colonial Brazil* (Berkeley: University of California Press, 1968). Although it concentrates on the eighteenth century, pp. 29-45, and *passim*, contain valuable information on the development of the office in earlier times. A fine monograph on the judiciary and, indeed, a major contribution to the administrative and social history of colonial Brazil, is Schwartz, *Sovereignty and Society in Colonial Brazil* [*Chap. 18*]. A good case study of the conflict between royal and private government is Francis A. Dutra, "Centralization vs. Donatarial Privilege: Pernambuco, 1602-1630," in Alden, ed., *Colonial Roots of Modern Brazil* [*General Works*]. Some aspects of ecclesiastical government and church-state relationships are examined in Francis A. Dutra, "The Brazilian Hierarchy in the Seventeenth Century" [*Chap. 18*].

Regarding the military functions of government, works on foreign threats to Brazil are surveyed briefly in the bibliographical essay for chapter 15. The Dutch conquest of the northeast was, of course, the chief danger, and Portuguese responses are recounted in Charles R. Boxer, *Salvador de Sá and the Struggle for Brazil and Angola, 1602-1686* (London: Athlone Press, 1952). A more detailed examination of Brazilian military organization and operations during the Dutch occupation can be found in José A. Gonsalves de Mello, *Antônio Dias Cardoso, Sargento-Môr do Têrço de Infantaria de Pernambuco* (Recife:

Universidade de Recife, 1954), one of several biographical studies of leaders of Brazilian liberation by the same author.

Other good studies of defense include Francis A. Dutra, "Matías de Albuquerque and the Defense of Northeastern Brazil, 1620–1626" [*Chap. 15*], which covers the crucial period immediately before the appearance of the Dutch in force; Gilberto Ferrez, *O Rio de Janeiro e a defesa do seu porto, 1555–1800* (Rio de Janeiro: Serviço de Documentação Geral da Marina, 1972), which deals with the defense of one of colonial Brazil's major cities; and Domingues, *A Colônia do Sacramento e o sul do Brasil* [*Chap. 15*], which describes conflicts with Spain in the far south of Brazil and the founding of the chief Portuguese outpost in that region.

Metropolitan agencies of colonial government are described in Francisco P. Mendes da Luz, *O Conselho da India, contributo a o estudo da história da administração e do comércio do ultramar português nos princípios do século xvii* (Lisbon: Divisão de Publicações e Biblioteca, Agência Geral do Ultramar, 1952); and Mathias C. Kieman, "The Conselho Ultramarino's First Legislative Attempt to Solve the Indian Question in America," *TA*, 14:259-271 (1957–58).

## CHAPTER 20. EPILOGUE: EUROPEAN REACTIONS TO HISPANIC EXPANSION IN AMERICA

I know of no comprehensive synthesis of the effects of the opening of the Hispanic New World on Europe. The most ambitious attempt to handle the subject is Walter P. Webb, *The Great Frontier* (Boston: Houghton Mifflin, 1952), which interprets America as a great frontier that shaped and transformed Western civilization. A number of scholars, however, regard Webb's thesis as overdrawn. A shorter and carefully thought-out synthesis is John S. Elliott, *The Old World and the New, 1492–1650* (Cambridge: Cambridge University Press, 1970). A comprehensive topical treatment is the wide-ranging collection of papers in *First Images of America* [*Chap. 6*]. An imaginative overview by an erudite nonprofessional historian is Germán Arciniegas, *América en Europa* (Buenos Aires: Sudamérica, 1975).

The impact of information about the natural history of America on Europe has not yet been thoroughly studied. A preliminary attempt to evaluate early European reactions to New World explorations, flora and fauna, and Indians is Antonello Gerbi, *La naturaleza de las Indias nuevas: De Cristóbal Colón a González Fernández de Oviedo*, trans. Antonio Alatorre (Mexico: Fondo de Cultura Económica, 1978). The best bio-bibliographical studies of early Spanish chroniclers and historians who described these phenomena are Francisco Esteve Barba, *Historiografía indiana* (Madrid: Editorial Gredos, 1964); and *Handbook of Middle American Indians*, gen. ed. Robert Wauchope, vol. XIII, part 2: *Guide to Ethnohistorical Sources*, ed. Howard C. Cline (Austin: University of Texas Press, 1973). A work that was very influential in shaping northern European perceptions of America is the richly illustrated Theodor de Bry, *Americae sive peregrinationum in indiam occidentalem*, which was published in installments in Frankfurt between 1590 and 1634 and which has since appeared in many editions in many languages. The intellectual problems Europeans encountered in assimilating and appreciating the New World are discussed in Elliott, *The Old World and the New*; and Edmundo O'Gorman, *The Invention of America: An Inquiry into the Historical Nature of the New World and the Meaning of History* (Bloomington: Indiana University Press, 1961).

The effects of the opening of the New World on European literature are discussed in a series of essays making up part 2, "Angles of Perception: Myth and Literature," of *First*

*Images of America* (vol. I, 27-135). General histories of science in early modern Europe treat American influences rather cursorily. Some useful observations may be found in Marie Boas, *The Scientific Renaissance, 1450-1630*, vol. II of *The Rise of Modern Science*, gen. ed. A. Rupert Hall (New York: Harper and Row, 1962); and *La science moderne*, ed. René Taton (Paris: Presses Universitaires de France, 1958), trans. A. J. Pomerans, as *History of Science: The Beginnings of Modern Science from 1450 to 1800* (London: Thames and Hudson, 1964).

In particular fields of science, the mapping of America may be traced in Raleigh A. Skelton, *Explorer's Maps: Chapters in the Cartographic Record of Geographical Study* (London: Routledge and Kegan Paul, 1958); and the popular Ernst Lehner and Johanna Lehner, *How They Saw the New World*, ed. Gerard L. Alexander (New York: Tudor Publishing, 1966). The influence of American discoveries on geographical concepts and the science of navigation is examined in the papers making up part 8, "The New Geography," of *First Images of America* (vol. II, pp. 615-704). The development of awareness that all the world's seas were connected is skillfully traced and analyzed in John H. Parry, *The Discovery of the Sea* (Berkeley: University of California Press, 1980).

Works dealing specifically with the effects of the opening of the New World on the biological sciences in Europe are few in number. Some short interpretive treatments of the subject may be found in part 10, "Science and Trade," of *First Images of America* (vol. II, pp. 807-884). Also useful is Enrique Alvarez López, "Las plantas de América en la botánica europea del siglo xvi," *RI*, 6:221-288 (1945).

Literature on developing European perceptions of the mental and moral qualities of the American Indian is somewhat more plentiful. Spanish views are summarized in Hanke, *The Spanish Struggle for Justice* [*Chap. 5*], those of the Portuguese in Hemming, *Red Gold* [*Chap. 12*], especially chap. 1. The roots of the concept of the noble savage are discussed in Gilbert Chinard, *L'exotisme américain dans la littérature française au xvi^e siècle* (Paris: Hachette, 1911). On this subject see also Hayden White, "The Noble Savage Theme as Fetish," in *First Images of America*, I, 121-137. An important specialized monograph is Benjamin Keen, *The Aztec Image in Western Thought* (New Brunswick, N.J.: Rutgers University Press, 1971). European views of the Indian are placed in a broad scientific context in Margaret T. Hodgen, *Early Anthropology in the Sixteenth and Seventeenth Centuries* (Philadelphia: University of Pennsylvania Press, 1964).

A seminal but now controversial study of the effect of the opening of the New World on the European economy is Chaunu and Chaunu, *Séville et l'Atlantique* [*Chap. 5*], vol. VIII, parts 1, 2, 3 ("Partie Interprétive"). More recent works containing useful information and views are *The Counterreformation and the Price Revolution, 1559-1610*, ed. R. B. Wernham, vol. III of *The New Cambridge Modern History* (Cambridge: Cambridge University Press, 1968), pp. 14-43; Ralph E. Davis, *The Rise of the Atlantic Economies* (Ithaca, N.Y.: Cornell University Press, 1973), chaps. 1-7; and Jan de Vries, *The Economy of Europe in an Age of Crisis, 1600-1750* (New York: Cambridge University Press, 1976). The subject is treated within the context of the growth of European capitalism in Immanuel Wallerstein, *The Modern World-System* [*General Works*].

Works dealing more specifically with the effects of American precious metals on European prices are Earl J. Hamilton, "The History of Prices before 1750," in 11th Congrès International des Sciences Historiques, Stockholm, 1960, *Rapports* (Göteborg, Sweden: Almqvist and Wiksell, 1960), I, 144-164; Fernand Braudel, "Prices in Europe from 1470 to 1750," in *The Economy of Expanding Europe in the 16th and 17th Centuries*, ed. J. P. Cooper, vol. IV of the *Cambridge Economic History of Europe* (Cambridge: Cambridge University Press, 1967), pp. 378-486; and the papers by various authorities in *Economy and Society in Early Modern Europe: Essays from Annales*, ed. Peter Burke (London: Routledge and Kegan Paul, 1972).

Good introductions to the transference of American plants to Europe and their economic and nutritional effects in their new habitat are G. B. Masefield, "Crops and Livestock," in *The Economy of Expanding Europe in the 16th and 17th Centuries*, pp. 276-301; Crosby, *The Columbian Exchange* [*Chap. 5*], chap. 5; and Jonathan D. Sauer, "Changing Perception and Exploitation of New World Plants in Europe, 1492–1800," in *First Images of America*, II, 813-832. The question of the origin of syphilis is examined in Crosby, *The Columbian Exchange* [*Chap. 5*], chap. 4; and Francisco Guerra, "The Problem of Syphilis," in *First Images of America*, II, 845-851.

I have found no monographs dealing explicitly with the effect of the New World on the development of national states in Europe. Its influence on international relations and international law are examined in Charles H. Carter, "The New World as a Factor in International Relations, 1492–1739," in *First Images of America*, I, 231-264; three essays by John T. Lanning in *Colonial Hispanic America*, ed. A. Curtis Wilgus (Washington, D.C.: The George Washington University Press, 1936), chaps. 12-14; James B. Scott, *The Spanish Origins of International Law: Francisco Suárez and His Law of Nations* (Oxford: The Clarendon Press, 1934); and Hamilton, *Political Thought in Sixteenth Century Spain* [*Chap. 9*].

The best general treatment of the effects of the possession of an American empire on Spain is Lynch, *Spain under the Habsburgs* [*General Works*], especially vol. II, chaps. 7-10. Economic influences are surveyed in Vicens Vives, *An Economic History of Spain*, especially part 4: "The Mercantile Economy" [*Chaps 1 and 2*]. The seminal work relating American treasure to Spanish prices and wages is Hamilton, *American Treasure* [*Chap. 10*]. Hamilton's conclusions are questioned in Jorge Nadal Oller, "La revolución de los precios españoles: Estado de la cuestión," *Hispania* 19:503-559 (1959). A more recent interpretation is Denis O. Flynn, "A New Perspective on the Spanish Price Revolution: The Monetary Approach to the Balance of Payments," *Explorations in Economic History*, 15:388-406 (1978). The effects of the opening of the Indies on the power of the Spanish state are surveyed in Elliott, *The Old World and the New*, chap. 4.

The best survey of the influence of Brazil on Portugal is Lang, *Portuguese Brazil* [*General Works*]. A good short synthesis covering the period 1550–1658 is Vitorino de Magalhães Godinho, "Portugal and Her Empire," [*Chap. 13*], pp. 384-397. The importance of the Brazil trade in particular is assessed in Mauro, *Portugal et l'Atlantique au xvii siècle* [*Chap. 13*].

# Index

# Index

Aburra, Valley of, 318
Acapulco, 371, 372, 381, 430, 433
Acosta, Father Joseph (José) de, 239, 458
Adelantados, 35, 36, 63-64, 65, 91-92, 96, 97-99, 135, 137, 184, 186, 188, 191, 209, 267, 309-10, 312, 313, 392
Afonso I, Henriques (king of Portugal), 14, 15, 18, 34
Afonso V (king of Portugal), 66, 252
Africa: Hispanic expansion in, 153, 251, 300; slave trade of, 235-36; American plants in, 470. See also Blacks, Slave Trade
Africans: early Portuguese contact with, 49-50, 54-55. See also Blacks, Slave Trade
Afro-Americanism: in Spanish America, 405-7; in Brazil, 416-17
Agadir, 47
Agriculture: in medieval Spain and Portugal, 19, 23, 61; of pre-Columbian American Indians, 86; transfer of plants from Europe, 214-18; production of in Spanish America, 218-24, 312, 316, 364-66; in Brazil, 275-78, 382-85; transfer of American plants to Europe and Africa, 468-70. See also Labor, Land
Aguardiente, 220, 233
Alagoas, 322, 416-17

Albuquerque, Afonso de, 255, 257
Alcabala, 244, 363
Alcáçovas, Treaty of, 63
Alcaides, 35, 203
Alcalá, 25
Alcalde, 162, 171, 349
Alcaldes del crimen, 434
Alcaldes mayores, 187
Alcaldes ordinarios, 135, 192
Alcaldías mayores, 187, 424
Alcántara, Military Order of, 7, 157, 164
Aldeias, 274, 282, 329
Alentejo, 15, 23, 340
Alexander VI, Pope, 59-60, 78, 90, 182
Alfares, 271
Alférez real, 135
Alfonso I (king of Castile), 21
Alfonso I (king of Asturias), 128
Alfonso II (king of Aragon), 16-17
Alfonso VI (king of Leon and Castile), 14
Alfonso VII (king of Leon and Castile), 14
Alfonso IX (king of Leon), 17
Alfonso X, "the Wise," (king of Castile), 25, 242
Alfonso XI (king of Castile), 25, 57
Alfoz, 8
Algaras, 4, 326
Algarve, 8, 9, 15, 21-22, 43, 48, 112. 341
Algeçiras, 8
Algeria, 42

*Alguacil mayor*, 135, 190
*Alguaciles*, 171
Aljubarrota, Battle of, 66
All Saints, Bay of, 271
Almadén, 228, 370
Almagrists, 192
Almagro, Diego de, 98, 106-7
Almohad sect, 7
*Almojarifazgo*, 186, 243
Almoravid sect, 7
Alto Peru, 102. *See also* Bolivia
Alvarado, Pedro de, 405
Amazon River, 76, 85, 94, 283, 306, 322, 325, 326, 327, 328, 329, 330, 340, 415, 457. *See also* Rio Maranhão, Rio Solimões
Amazons, 89, 455
America: geography of and influence on Spanish and Portuguese conquest and colonization, 76-77, 251, 329-30; origins of name, 92-93
Amapá, 322, 330
Amsterdam, 384, 464
Anchieta, Father José de, 281, 282
Andalusia: 6-9, 15, 17; trade of, 21-22; cattle in, 22, 44, 219; farmland in, 22; Reconquest in, effect on economy of, 23-24; pogroms in, 44; sheep in, 44; *cabalgadas* and slave trade in, 55; citrus and wine of, 61, 215; emigration from, 111, 220; resettlement of, 112; immigration, 114; French raids on ports of, 200, 235; sugar in, 220; agriculture and the New World, 364, 474
Andes, 77, 83, 84, 86, 102, 141, 142, 143, 215, 319-20, 325, 328, 330-31, 357, 366, 368, 373, 425-27, 430, 457
Angola: slave trade of, 88, 338, 342; Portuguese in, 267, 382; Dutch in, 301, 342, 477; trade with Brazil, 385
Anian, Strait of, 101, 314, 430
Antilles: factories in, 95; as base for exploration, 102; epidemic in, 105; colonization of, 109; language of, 114; disease in, 118; population of, 119, 202, 343, 345; free blacks in, 122; urbanization of, 138; *encomienda* in, 157-59; audiencias in, 188; incorporated into the Viceroyalty of New Spain, 189; French raids on, 200, 235; products of, 212, 216, 221, 222, 224, 366, 370, 376; trade of, 233, 234, 236, 363, 365; water routes of, 238; economy of, 248; slave shortage in, 359. *See also* Greater Antilles; Lesser Antilles
Antioquia, 142, 227, 318-19, 358, 370
Aragon, 13, 15-17, 21, 42, 43, 45, 61, 111, 291, 294, 437-38
Arauca, 107, 143, 165, 198, 207, 321, 331, 346, 429, 430
Araucanian Indians, 85, 143, 198, 321
*Arauco domado*, 402
Arawak Indians, 73, 85, 94, 138
*Arbitristas*, 297, 475-76
Archivo General de Indias, 110
Arequipa, 226, 230, 233, 372, 424
Argentina, 102, 142-43, 214, 317-19, 372
Arguim, 49
Arica, 237, 373
*Armada de la Guardia de la Carrera de Indias*, 201, 431
*Armada de la Mar del Sur*, 432
*Armada de las Islas de Barlovento y Seno Mexicano*, 431
Arrabida, Order of, 258
*Arrieros*, 237
Artisans, 30, 62, 79, 100, 115, 178-79, 278, 281, 341, 413. *See also* Guilds
*Asientos*, 123, 298, 333, 337, 359, 374, 382
Asturians, 6, 10
Asturias, 13, 334
Asunción, 102, 116, 127, 143, 145, 220, 224, 317, 318, 330
Atacama Desert, 143
Atahualpa, 212-13, 230
Atlantic Ocean: wind systems in, 9, 76, 201; pre-Columbian explorations in, 43, 47-49; Portuguese and Spanish claims in, 63, 74, 253, 302; Portuguese and Spanish trade across, 233-36, 279-80, 370-71, 375, 385
Audiencias: in Castile, 57; in Canary Islands, 65; organization and functions of in Spanish America, 188-91, 204, 423-25, 434
Augustinians, 167, 168, 171, 174, 196, 274, 317

*Avería*, 244-45
Avila Brothers Conspiracy, 310
Avilés, 234
Avis, House of, 46-47, 304
*Ayuntamiento*, 135
Azpilcueta de Navarro, Martín, 465
Azores, 43, 50-51, 74, 200, 245, 251, 254, 281, 323, 340, 341
Aztec Indians, 84-87, 100, 104, 118, 139, 404-5
Azurara (or Zurara), Gomes Eanes de, 55

Bahia: settlers in, 264, 273; Captaincy of, 264-65, 283, 439, 444; Jesuits in, 274-75; whaling in, 276; sugar mills in, 277, 278, 383; population of, 282; role in Brazilian government, 285; Dutch in, 306; Portuguese immigration to, 341; tobacco production in, 384; Brazilian trade center in, 385; Portuguese trade with, 386; governor-general of, 439; isolation of, 439-40; capital of *Estado do Brasil*, 440; archbishopric of, 442
Bajío, 140, 230, 336
Balboa, Vasco Núñez de, 80, 93, 98
Balearic Islands, 43
Baltic Sea, 288, 462, 464
Banda Oriental, 323, 327, 331
*Bandeiras*, 324-28, 331
Barcelona, 11, 13, 16-17
*Barcos*, 239
Barreto, Roque da Costa, 440
*Barrios*, 176, 396
Basques, 6, 10, 13, 61, 293, 334
Bayonne, 234
Belalcázar, Sebastián de, 141-42
Belém, 322, 323, 325, 327, 328
Benedictines, 26
*Beneméritos de Indias*, 392, 393, 412
Benguela, 301, 342
Betanzos, Domingo de, 154, 177
Béthancourt, Jean de, 55
Bío Bío River, 143, 198, 321
Biscay, Bay of, 21, 112
Blacks: European prejudices against, 53-55, 461-62; role in the Spanish conquest, 88, 121-22; population of in Spanish America, 121-24, 130-32, 337-38, 344; social status of in Spanish

America, 180-81, 287, 396-98; as freedmen, 180, 396-97, 398, 405-6, 419; in Brazil, 282-83, 304, 342-43, 344; social status of in Brazil, 287, 413-14. *See also* Africans, Miscegenation, Race
Bodin, Jean, 459
Bogotá, 126, 142, 145, 149, 189, 195, 207, 238, 331, 336, 346, 411
Bolivia, 86, 102, 142, 319, 320, 358
Borah, Woodrow: on American Indian populations, 84, 121, 343; on economic trends in seventeenth-century Spanish America, 375-76
Bourbon Dynasty, 381, 450
Boyd-Bowman, Peter, on European emigration to Spanish America, 111-15
*Bozales*, 122, 180, 338, 398
Brading, David, on Spanish American silver production, 368-70, 376
Bragança Dynasty, 304
Brazilwood, 257-59, 260, 262, 386
British East India Company, 300
Bucaramanga, 319
Buccaneers, 307, 429-30
Buenos Aires, 102, 143, 318, 323, 331, 336, 359, 365, 373, 424
Bulls, papal, 52, 65, 74, 167, 172-73, 199, 437, 459
Burgos, Laws of, 158, 183
*Burgueses*, 31

*Cabalgadas*, 4, 47, 55, 326
*Caballerías*, 8, 137, 185, 209, 218
*Caballeros*, 27, 62, 68-69, 79, 97, 144-45, 177
*Cabeceras*, 169, 351
*Cabildos*, 65, 135-37, 144-45, 161, 171, 178, 185-87, 192, 209, 270-71, 285, 348, 392, 400, 425, 426
*Caboclos*, 283, 411, 414
Cabot, John, 259, 260
Cabral, Pedro Alvares, 75-76
Cacao, 221-22, 233, 241, 248, 265-66, 364, 379, 467
Caciques, 125, 129, 161, 162, 165, 170, 180, 193, 407
Cadiz, 21, 43, 201, 233, 363
*Cafusos*, 282

Cajamarca, 225
Calatrava, Order of, 7
Cali, 145
Calicut, 251
California, Lower (Baja), 101, 310, 314, 456
Callao, 146, 237, 373, 430, 432, 433
*Calpixquis*, 162
*Calpulli*, 86
*Câmaras*, 254, 276, 279, 285, 448
Caminha, Pero Vaz de, 75
*Camino Real de la Tierra Adentro, El*, 315, 372
Camões, Luís de, 300, 476
Campeche, 221, 234, 432
*Cañadas*, 19, 21, 22
Cananéa, Island of, 260
Canary Islands, 43, 55, 63-65, 125, 155, 164, 200, 201, 215, 220, 236, 341; conquest and colonization of, 50, 89-90, 91, 99, 182, 268
*Cancillerías*, 57, 188
Cape Bojador, 63
Cape Horn, 430, 457
Cape Verde Islands, 48, 50, 74
*Capitães mores*, 441-48
Capital: sources of in Old World Portuguese and Spanish expansion, 48, 51, 59, 63; in American conquests, 98, 263; accumulation and investment of in the Spanish colonial economy, 212-13, 360-62; in Brazil, 277, 382. *See also* Monies
Capitalism: of *encomenderos*, 164; on Jesuit haciendas, 362; and Dependency Theory, 389; in Brazil, 412; effects of Hispanic expansion on development of in Europe, 462. *See also* Capital
*Capitanía general*, as a function and branch of government, 182, 190-91, 197
*Capitanías subalternas*, 441
*Capitão mór da costa*, 284
*Capitulaciones*, 96, 137, 184, 267
*Capitulaciones de Sante Fe*, 69
Captaincies, in Brazil, 260-66, 283-85, 439-41
Caracas, 141, 320, 381, 424
Caramurú, 265
Caribbean, 76, 77, 118, 140, 202-3, 238-40, 248, 374, 457; slaves imported

to, 124, 333, 385; Northern European colonization of, 306-8; fortifications of, 431-32
Carib Indians, 85, 94, 138, 350
*Carreira da India*, 251, 259, 266, 300
*Carrera de Indias*, 201-2, 206, 224, 233-42, 362-63, 366-67, 377-79, 431
*Carretera*, 237
*Carro*, 238
*Carta de doação*, 50, 261-62
Cartagena, New Granada, 141, 142, 146, 147, 149, 175, 178, 187, 206, 234, 316, 359, 363, 366-67, 372, 428, 429, 432, 433
Cartagena, Spain, 234
Cartago, New Granada, 140, 316, 349
*Casa da India*, 252, 253, 280
*Casa de Contratación* (Spanish House of Trade), 95, 110, 122, 236, 244, 245, 373, 426, 435
*Casa de Guiné e India*, 95
*Casa de Guiné e Mina*, 49
Castile, 13-14, 20-21, 25, 42, 44; status of in Hispania, 15-19, 474; products of, 21, 22, 23, 35, 61, 226, 300; succession crisis of, 45-46; claim to Canary Islands, 50, 63, 65; reign of Ferdinand and Isabella, 56-63; in Indies, 78, 95, 212; and New World, 95, 177, 185, 402; economic problems of, 293, 333-34
*Castizos*, 128-29
Catalonia, 13, 15, 17, 42, 295, 448
Catamarca, 317, 336
Cateau-Cambrésis, Treaty of, 201, 235
*Catequil*, 211
"Catholic Kings," 59-61, 65, 68, 268, 309; and Christopher Columbus, 69, 73; rights of in New World, 74, 78, 194, 437; and emigration, 110, 112. *See also* Ferdinand and Isabella
Cauca River Valley, 142, 222, 319, 370
*Causas de patronato*, 195
*Cavaleiros*, 27
Ceará, 263, 307, 322, 326, 327, 328, 415, 439
Cebu, 316, 317
Ceuta, 47, 49
Ceylon, 251, 256
Chagres River, 239, 432

*Chapetón*, 400-401
Charcas: Audiencia of, 190, 312, 346, 424, 425; mines of, 312
Charles V (Holy Roman Emperor), 42, 96, 101, 103, 172, 179, 192, 233-34, 236, 239; and emigration, 110, 113; and the *encomienda*, 159, 160; and evangelization, 166-67; and *corregimientos*, 161-63; and New World, 134, 183-84, 224, 240, 357; and Hernán Cortés, 191-92, 231, 401; and slave trade, 235, 358; and taxes, 297-98; abdication of, 298; memoirs of, 473
Charles I (king of Castile), 45. *See also* Charles V (Holy Roman Emperor)
Charles II (king of England), 302
Charles II (king of Spain), 295
Charles VIII (king of France), 59
Chaunu, Pierre and Huguette: on African slave trade, 123; on Spanish trans-Atlantic commerce, 370-71, 377, 463, 464, 465, 466, 467
Chevalier, François, 376-77
Chiapas, 101, 173-74
Chibcha Indians, 85, 102, 103, 107, 126, 142
Chichimeca Indians, 101, 139-40, 198, 207, 311, 318
Chihuahua, 313, 315
Chile, 398, 428-30, 433, 435, 456; Araucanians of, 85, 198, 331, 428, 429; conquest of, 97, 98, 107, 127; disease in, 118; colonization of, 143, 145, 146-47, 199; Audiencia of, 190, 224; Indian resistance in, 198; products of, 208, 214, 215, 216, 219, 227, 357, 370, 372; trade of, 233, 378; economy of, 248, population of, 343, 345
Chiloé, Island of, 433
Chivalry, romances of, 89, 96
Chocó, 319-20
Christ, Order of, 46, 50, 253, 262
Christianity. *See* Church, Roman Catholic; Religion, Roman Catholicism
Church, Roman Catholic: relations with Spanish and Portuguese crowns, 18, 34, 56, 65, 194-97, 285, 426-28; position of on conquest and sovereignty, 51-52, 63, 74-75, 77-78, 90, 182-83, 267, 436-37, 471-73; on racial differences, 53, 125; on nature of the American Indian, 154-179; territorial organization of in Spanish America, 194-95, 285, 424-25; in Brazil, 285, 442; as landowner, 357, 362. *See also* Clergy, Evangelization, Religion
Cíbola, Seven Cities of, 102, 255, 314
Cid, the, 31, 405
Cieza de León, Pedro de, 125, 215
*Cimarrones*, 406
Cinnabar, 228
Cipango, 69
Cisneros, Cardinal Jiménez de, 167
Cistercians, 6, 26
*Ciudad*, 148
*Ciudadanos*, 99
Clergy: as a social "order," 26-27, 178, 394-95, 412; divisions of, 26, 167, 172-73; role in government, 35, 57, 156, 194; sources of recruitment of, 274, 403. *See also* Church, Evangelization, Religion
*Clientela*, 39-40, 409
Clifford, George (earl of Cumberland), 429
Cobo, Father Bernabé, 87, 217
Coca, 222-23, 366
Cochabama, 372
Cochin, 251, 254
Cochineal, 221, 233, 234, 247, 365, 370, 379
*Cocolitzli*, 118
Coelho, Duarte, 258-59, 263, 267, 277, 281, 340
*Cofradías*, 136, 173, 179, 404, 406
Coimbra, 6
*Colégios*, 128, 144, 256, 265, 274, 275
Colombia, 102, 103, 141, 190, 320, 353. *See also* New Granada
Colónia do Sacramento, 323, 324, 331, 430
Colonization: on the medieval Spanish frontier, 5-9; in Portuguese Africa and Asia, 49-50, 254-57; of Portugal in the Azores, Madeira, and Cape Verde Islands, 50-51; of Castile in the Canary Islands, 63-65; aims and methods of in Spanish America, 108-9, 133; in Brazil, 260-64, 270-72, 278-79

Columbus, Christopher, 69, 76, 91, 124-25, 191, 215-17, 402, 453; discovery of New World by, 73, 250; second voyage of, 79-80; search for gold by, 80-81; geographical beliefs of, 92-93, 456; introduced sugar into New World, 220, 224; and syphilis, 470-71; death of, 473
Commerce: in Reconquest Hispania, 20-22, 23, 42-43; of Portugal with Africa and Asia, 47-49, 252; overseas and internal of Spanish America, 231-36, 242-45, 363, 370-77; of Brazil, 279-80, 385-86. See also Fleets, Merchants, Slave Trade, Transportation
Commoners, 18, 177, 261, 265, 340, 394; function of, 30-32; status of, 30, 68-69, 100, 400
Communications: in the Spanish American empire, 206-7, 286, 315, 444-48; in the Portuguese empire, 251, 264, 286, 330, 439-40
Compadrazgo, 39, 404
Composición, 204, 356
Compostela, Mexico, 190, 227
Comuneros, Revolt of in Castile, 82, 156, 185, 188-89
Concelho da India e Conquistas Ultramarinas, 444-45
Concelhos, 7, 47, 254
Concepción, 143, 190, 206, 429
Conchos Indians, 313
Condomblé, 406
Congo, 88, 123, 251, 256, 282, 342
Congo River, 66
Congregaciones civiles, 348
Congregaciones, of Indians, 170-73, 195-96
Conquest, rationale and legal bases of, 51-52, 63-64, 74-75, 89-90, 103, 154-55, 182-83, 253, 309-10
Conquistadors: regional and social origins of, 79, 111-12; motives and interests of, 79-82; as first settlers, 136, 177
Consejos, 7, 78, 186
Consulados: of Burgos, 58-59; of Seville, 245, 360, 426; of Mexico and Lima, 363, 394, 426, 533
Consulate of the Sea, Catalan, 58-59
Contador, 186
Contadores mayores, 183

Conversos, 56, 112, 115; converted Jews, 44-45; economic impact of attacks on, 61, 62; communities of in New World, 427-28
Cook, Sherburne, on American Indian populations, 84, 121, 343
Coquimbo, 206
Córdoba, Spain, 6; Argentina, 230, 317, 424
Coro, 141, 146
Coromandel coast, 251, 256
Coroneis, 443
Corpus juris civilis, 25
Corrales, 350
Corregedores, 253, 262
Corregidores, 36, 57, 172-73, 187, 197, 336, 348, 399
Corregidores de españoles, 187
Corregidores de indios, 197, 426
Corregimiento, 161-63, 176, 187, 225, 303, 424
Correia, Jorge Figueiredo, 261
Corrientes, 318
Corsairs, 147, 200, 201, 202, 203, 234, 237-39, 244, 247, 350, 429, 431, 432
Cortes, 35, 203
Cortés, Hernán, 96, 98, 107, 115, 139, 146, 177, 188, 230-32; conquests in North America, 100-105; and encomiendas, 159, 160; evangelism of, 166-67; royal rewards to, 177, 191-92; and sugar industry, 220, 224; capital of, 212-13
Cortés, Martín, 193
Coruna, 234
Costa Rica, 101, 141, 206, 316, 358, 429
Cotton, 222, 225, 246, 276, 366, 367, 372, 385, 467
Council of the Indies, 170, 183, 188, 190, 191, 195, 202, 204, 206, 244, 309, 320, 332, 435-38, 445
Couto, Diogo do, 253
Covadonga, Battle of, 3
Creoles, 401-3, 406-7, 409, 410
Creolism, 401-3, 406, 407
Crespy, Treaty of, 200
Cross, Harry, on Spanish American silver production, 368-70, 376
Cuba, 74, 83, 94, 138, 156, 185, 208, 335, 350, 358, 365, 370, 374, 407; gold in, 94, 226, 227; trade routes to, 201, 238

Cuenca, 125
Cuernavaca, 224
Culiacán, 206
Cumaná, 141, 320, 435
Curaçāo, 307, 308, 374
Curtin, Philip: on African slave trade, 123, 237, 238
Cuyo, 102
Cuzco, 101-2, 106, 142, 145, 149, 207, 225, 230, 233, 237, 372

Da Gama, Vasco, 251, 252
d'Ango, Jean, of Dieppe, 200
Darién, 83, 93, 94, 101
Dávila, Governor Pedrarias (Pedro Arias de Avile), 133-34, 140
Defense: as a function of royal government, 34, 182; of Spanish America, 197-203, 308, 310, 313, 330, 428-34, 447-48; of Brazil, 260, 262, 263, 265, 266, 307, 308, 322, 323-24, 442-43, 447-48
Degredados, 75, 258, 260, 265, 341, 477
Denevan, William, 119-20
Dependency, nature and theory of, 387-90
Depression, in seventeenth-century Spanish America, 375-81
Derecho: as unwritten law or custom, 25
Derecho de unión de armas, 363. See also Union of Arms
Derecho propiamente indiano, 184
Desembargadores, 444
Despoblados, 6, 139, 353
Dias, Bartolomeu, 66
Dias de Novais, Paulo, 267
Díaz de Fonseca, Juan, 183
Díaz de Guzmán, Rui, 331, 402
Díaz de la Calle, Juan, 332
Díaz del Castillo, Bernal, 81-82
Diezmo, 186. See also Tithes
Dinis, "the Farmer," (king of Portugal), 23
Doctrina, 170-73
Dominicans, 64, 156, 158-59, 167, 168, 173, 174, 175, 177, 222, 317
Doña Marina ("La Malinche"), 97-98
Donatary (Captain-donatary), in the Azores and Madeiras, 50. See also Captaincies
Douro, Portuguese province of, 340

Downs, Battle of the, 294, 307
Drake, Sir Francis: in Caribbean, 429, 431, 432; in Pacific, 314, 430, 432
Duarte, son of John of Avis, 46, 47
Duero (Douro) River, 6, 7, 13, 14-15, 19, 20, 133
Durango, 312, 313, 315, 372, 424
Dutch, 300, 301, 307, 308, 350, 352, 367, 374, 375, 384, 386, 437; in Brazil, 295, 307, 327, 340, 341, 414, 417, 440-42, 447, 448, 477; in Americas, 306, 429; slave trade of, 333, 338; occupation of African areas by, 342, 382
Dutch East India Company, 300, 306
Dutch East India Fleet, 430
Dutch-English wars, 307, 447
Dutch West India Company, 294, 301, 306, 307, 429, 464
Dyewood, 258, 275-76, 279, 365, 366, 384, 386

Ebro River, 13
Ebro, Valley of, 7
Ecuador, 141, 238, 248, 319, 320, 339, 353, 447; products of, 208, 222, 367; Indian population of, 336, 337; industry in, 367, 370. See also Quito
Ejido, 136
El Dorado, 213, 455
El Ksar-el-Kebir, Battle of, 292, 300
El Salvador, 139, 140, 353
Elizabeth I (queen of England), 200
Emigration: to Spanish America, 78-80, 109-16, 333-34, 475; to Brazil, 280-82, 340-41, 476-77
Encomenderos, 145-47, 158-59, 172-73, 176-77, 180, 184-86, 192, 193, 195, 198-99, 204-5, 213, 222, 286, 336, 348, 349, 392-93, 399, 433
Encomienda, 157-66, 173, 176, 185, 189, 210-11, 225, 248, 266, 286, 309, 313, 315, 317, 356, 392, 393, 401, 403, 412
Engenho, 277-79, 312, 382
England, 21, 22, 31, 44, 108, 113, 199, 200, 294, 300, 302, 305, 311, 429, 442, 446, 469, 470; and Portugal, 302, 385; and New World, 308, 322, 333, 338, 341, 374, 384

Enriques, Martín (viceroy of New Spain), 359
Entradas, 96-100, 102, 103, 142-43, 160-61, 260, 272, 314, 324, 327, 330
Entre Douro e Minho, 341
Epidemics, 83, 105, 139, 171-72, 211, 217, 302, 360, 364, 376
Escrivão, 270
Española (also Hispaniola), 74, 76, 94, 108, 113, 115-16, 122, 156, 157, 164, 177, 183, 185, 201, 308, 470; population of, 83, 116; products of, 208, 212, 213, 224, 226, 227, 364, 365; and English, 307, 448
Espírito Santo, Captaincy of, 264, 440
Estado da India, 251-57, 288, 300, 302, 477
Estado do Brasil, 440
Estado do Maranhão, 440. See Maranhão
Estancias, 219, 349, 350
Estremadura, Portugal, 15, 23, 340, 341
Evangelization: of Indians in Spanish America, 75, 108-9, 155, 166-75, 311, 313-15, 320-21; in Portuguese Asia, 256-57; of Indians in Brazil, 274, 328-29. See also Church, Clergy, Missionaries
Extremadura, Spain, 15, 22; emigration from, 111, 114; livestock in, 219

Factor, 186
Fazendas, 352, 385
Feitorias, 254
Ferdinand I (king of Aragon), 91, 110, 158, 160, 242; reign of, 56-58; and Christopher Columbus, 69, 74. See also Catholic Kings; Isabella
Ferdinand I (king of Portugal), 46
Ferdinand III, "the Saint" (king of Castile and Leon), 17, 36-37, 42, 58
Fernández de Oviedo, Gonzalo, 90, 125, 153-54, 460
Fernando, son of John of Avis, 46
Fernando Po, Island of, 48
Feudalism, 28-30, 38-39, 164, 388, 389, 471
Fiel ejecutor, 135
Fidalgos, 112, 261, 262, 265, 286, 340, 412

Filhos da terra, 415
Filipéia, 322
Fiscal (crown attorney), 190
Flanders, 21, 22, 31, 67, 212, 252, 281, 341, 375, 437-38, 449, 450
Fleets: Spanish trans-Atlantic, 201-2, 233-34, 362-63, 370-71, 430-31; Portuguese Asian, 251-52; Brazilian, 386
Fleury, Jean, 200, 201
Florentines, 21, 48, 63, 257
Florida, 94, 98, 139, 146, 156, 189, 310-11, 435, 447
Forais, 49, 67, 267
Foral, 262
Foresteros, 396
Fort Caroline, 310, 311
Fort Orange, 306
Fortaleza de Santarém, 328
Fortaleza de São José da Barra do Rio Negro, 328
Forte d'Obidos, 328
Forum Iudiciorum, 25
France, 31, 44, 105, 113, 288, 308, 353, 374, 384, 437, 462; and war with Spain, 45, 58, 101, 234, 294; and Corsair raids, 138, 141, 187, 259; in Indies, 200-201, 375; in Brazil, 264, 322, 330, 442; in New World, 268, 305-8, 313, 358
Francis I (king of France), 199
Franciscans, 64, 167, 169, 171, 173, 174-75, 256, 258, 311, 312, 313, 315, 317, 328, 329
Frank, Andre Gunder, on colonial dependency, 388-89
Frontiers: in Reconquest Spain and Portugal, 4-5; in Spanish America, 310-21; in Brazil, 321-29
Fuero, 7, 25, 27, 30, 32-34, 37, 61, 65, 82, 178, 180, 184-85, 195, 203, 296, 392, 399, 400
Fuero Juzgo, 25
Funchal, Diocese of, 254

Gachupín, 401, 409
Galicia, 6, 9, 10, 13, 20, 281, 334, 424
Galleon, 202, 239, 362, 363, 367, 371
Galliza, 340
Gambia, 123

*Gañanes*, 359
Garcia, Aleixo, 259
García Bravo, Alonso, 149-50
Genoa, 21-22, 41-43, 48, 59, 63, 69, 113, 241-42, 257, 334, 375
*Gente de razón*, 392
*Gente sin razón*, 395, 396
Germany, 67, 80, 105, 212, 375; and trade with Portugal, 67, 252; religious schism in, 82, 454; and New World, 221, 227-28
Gibraltar, Strait of, 8, 42
Ginés de Sepulveda, Juan, 169
Goa, 251, 253, 254, 256, 257, 300
*Gobernaciones*, 187, 423-24
*Gobierno* (as governmental function), 182
Goes, Damião de, 288
Gold: from Africa, 42, 48, 252; as an incentive for exploration and conquest in America, 73, 74, 76, 80-81, 263, 324; zones of production of in Spanish America, 94, 95, 124, 138, 140, 142, 208, 212, 226, 248, 319-20, 370; exports of to Europe, 227, 234; discovery of in Brazil, 381, 384, 415. *See also* Mining, Monies
Gold Coast, 48, 66
González de Avila, Alonso, 193
González de Avila, Gil, 193
Goulart, Mauricio, 342
Gracias a Dios, Cape, 140-41
Grain, 61, 223, 233, 357, 371, 372, 379
Gran Chichimec, 101, 198
Gran Quivira, 102, 314, 455
Granada, 9, 42, 44, 65, 99, 155; as Muslim stronghold, 8, 45, 149; conquest of, by Ferdinand and Isabella, 56, 59, 69; armies of, 61-62
*Grandes cacaos*, 361
Grazing: in medieval Spain and Portugal, 19-20, 22, 23, 59, 61; transfer of animals to America, 215-16; in Spanish America, 219-20, 312-13, 316, 318, 319, 355-58, 364-65; in Brazil, 326-27
Greater Antilles, 76, 83, 85, 94, 100, 124, 151, 202, 447. *See also* Antilles
Grotius, Hugo, 473
Guadalajara, Mexico, 139, 140, 145, 222, 346, 372

Guadalquiver River, 206, 239, 363
Guadalupe, Our Lady of, 408, 409
Guadarrama Mountains, 15
Guadiana, Diocese of, 424
Guairá, 320, 447
Guanabara Bay, 266
Guanahaní, 124-25
Guanajuato, 149, 228, 230
Guanches, 43, 64-65
Guaraní Indians, 85, 102, 107, 259, 320, 325, 366
Guatemala: conquest and colonization of, 101, 139; population of, 121, 337, 346; City of, 145, 150, 335, 372, 378; evangelization of, 173-74; Audiencia of, 189, 191, 425
Guayaquil, 142, 226, 366, 367, 372, 378, 379, 430, 433
Guiana, 120, 306, 307, 320, 321, 322, 453
Guilds, 23, 58-59, 296, 397, 398; formation of, 178, 179; in Mexico City, 226, 394, 426
Guillén de Lampart, Don, 409
Guinea, 76, 88, 123, 253, 282, 338, 342
Guinea, Gulf of, 48-49, 66, 80, 123, 253
Guzmán, Nuño de, 188

Habsburg kings (Spanish), 185, 200, 431, 436, 439, 443, 444; war with Valois, 200, 201, 202, 235, 454; silver in dominions of, 228; and Spain, 285, 296, 321, 375, 449, 474; and Portugal, 323, 359, 438, 439
*Hacendados*, 312, 392, 393, 409, 411, 433
Hacienda: as a function and branch of Spanish government, 82; as a landed estate, 312-13, 357-58, 388, 392-93. *See also* Treasury
*Haciendas de minas*, 228
Hamilton, Earl J., on imports of precious metals at Seville and effects on the European economy, 229-30, 376, 463, 465, 466-67
Hardoy, Jorge, on Spanish American urbanization, 148, 346-47
*Hatos*, 350
Havana, 138, 139, 147, 150, 201, 202, 247, 346, 363, 366-67, 432
Hawkins, John, 200, 431, 432

Henry, Prince (son of John of Avis), 46, 47, 49, 50, 51
Henry II (king of Aragon), 45
Henry III, "the Sufferer" (king of Castile), 55
Henry IV (king of Castile), 56, 60
Hernández, Father Bartolomé, 170, 175
Hernández, Francisco, 458
Heyn, Admiral Piet, 306, 307
Hidalgos, 27, 58, 68-69, 79, 89, 100, 112, 115, 177, 392, 399, 400
Hidalgos de solar conocido, 309-10
Hidalguía, 393, 396
Hijos de la tierra, 331, 402
Hoetink, Harry, on race relations, 420-22
Hohenstaufen, House of, 43
Holy Roman Empire, 471, 472
Holy See, 34, 194-95
Hombres de confianza, 361
Homens bons, 270
Honduras, 101, 174, 202, 308; gold in, 140, 208, 227; other products of, 208, 221, 234, 316, 362, 368
Honduras, Gulf of, 432
Horses, 98, 103-4, 198, 215-18, 326
Hostiensis (Henry of Sousa, Cardinal), 52, 90
Huancavelica, 228, 348, 360, 369
Huascar, 104
Huatulco, Mexico, 238, 371
Hudson River, 306
Huguenots, French, 266, 310, 453
Humbolt, Alexander von, 354

Iguaraçú, 263
Ilhéus, 264, 273, 274, 284, 383
Incas, 83, 85-86, 87, 101-4, 106, 142, 227, 237 336, 404-5
Index (of forbidden books), 427, 428
India, 66, 75, 429; route to, 74, 252; Portugal in, 300, 454
Indian Ocean, 251, 300
Indianism, 403-5, 407
Indians, in America: population history of, 83-85, 118-21, 130, 282, 320, 335-37, 342, 343, 344, 349, 358, 413; cultural characteristics of, 85-86, 104, 410, 460-61; physical attributes of, 86-87; as native labor
supply, 87-88, 137-38, 140, 154-55, 164, 185, 210-12, 226, 229, 237, 246, 247, 272-74, 358, 365, 367, 370, 380, 393, 416; hostilities of, 102, 311, 313, 327, 428-29; social structure of, 104, 177-81; rebellions of, 139-40, 313, 315, 321, 405, 433; Spanish view of and policy on, 153-54, 172, 174-77, 179, 197, 426, 427; evangelization of, 155, 168-69, 170, 174, 175, 313, 320, 328, 329, 409; land possession of, 160, 219; tributes paid by, 163, 186, 213; Doctrina, 170-73; congregaciones of, 170-73, 359, 394, 404; clothing of, 176, 246; status of, 179-80, 287; and blacks, 180, 338; resistance to Spanish, 197-98, 207, 315, 318; products of, 220-25; enslavement of by Portuguese donataries, 262, 265, 273, 320, 324, 325, 329, 397; resistance to Portuguese, 262, 263, 264, 274, 442; in Brazil, 265, 272-75; epidemics among, 273; pacification of, 312, 315, 328-29; urbanization of, 347-49; resettlement of, 348, 356, 359; municipal government of, 348, 396; identity of, 403-5, 407; Christianity and, 404
Indies, Spanish, origins and use of name, 73-74, 76, 93
Indigo, 221, 365, 378
Indios de pueblo, 396
Ingenios, 65, 223, 224, 278
Inquisition, 56, 65, 112, 115-16, 396, 427-28
Inter Caetera, Bull of, 199
Irala, Martín de, 128, 331
Irmandades, 254, 271
Isabella I (queen of Castile), 95, 110, 126, 158, 170; reign of, 56-58; death of, 62, 82, 110; and Canary Islands, 63, 64; and Christopher Columbus, 69, 74; and expansion into Indies under, 76, 183; and New World colonization, 108-9, 153-54, 156, 179, 182, 186, 210. See also Catholic Kings; Ferdinand I
Isidore of Seville, Saint, 24

Islam, 6-9, 11, 21, 59, 62, 292
Italy: and Hispanic commerce and expansion, 21-22, 59, 68-69, 464; and infantry of Ferdinand and Isabella, 59-60, 61-62; and emigration, 113, 334; settlers in Brazil, 281, 341; in Indies trade, 212, 464
Itamaracá, 264, 267, 307, 439

Jalapa, 221
Jalisco, 101
Jamaica, 94, 191, 220, 224, 308, 365, 374, 429
James I (king of Aragon), 15, 36-37
Jeronymites, 158-59
Jesuits, 175, 256, 282, 328, 329, 366, 395; in Brazil, 265, 273-75, 412, 416; in North America, 311, 313, 314, 315; in Chile, 320, 321
Jews, 115-16; merchants and bankers, 20, 22; place in Hispania, 32, 45, 56, 58; social mobility of, 33; and anti-Semitism, 44, 53, 54, 61; conversion of, 44-45, 169; in Portugal, 68, 252; emigration of, 110, 112; as immigrants to Brazil, 281, 340, 341
Jiménez de Quesada, Gonzalo, 97
John I (king of Castile), 46
John I (king of Portugal), 46, 47
John II (king of Portugal), 66-67, 68
John III (king of Portugal), 251, 258-59, 260, 261-65, 267, 273
John IV (king of Portugal), 302
Juana, "la Loca" (daughter of Ferdinand and Isabella), 60, 82
Juderías, 68
Juezes de visita, 187
Juezes pesquisadores, 187
Juiz dos orfãos, 271
Juizes de fora, 36, 67, 444
Juizes ordinarios, 67, 270, 443-44
Junta de Comercio (Portuguese Council of Trade), 386
Jurisdicción, as governmental function, 182
Juros, 46, 298
Juzgados de indios, 396

Kino, Father Francisco Eusebio, 314

Labor, free wage, 359-60. See also Encomienda, Mita, Repartimiento, Slavery
La Rioja, 336
Ladinos, 122
Lagos, 49
Laicacota, 319
Land: forms of use and tenure during Reconquest, 5, 6, 7, 8, 9, 19-20, 22-23, 28-30; in Spanish America, 136-37, 165, 209, 312-13, 313-14, 318, 349-51, 355-58, 392-93; in Brazil, 262, 265, 271, 276, 277-78, 326-27, 352, 385, 411, 414-15, See also Agriculture, Engenho, Hacienda, Plantation
La Paz, Bishopric of, 424
La Plata (Chuquisaca), 190
Laredo, 234
Las Casas, Father Bartolomé de, 83-84, 90, 109, 118, 126, 154, 156, 158-59, 169, 214, 460
Las Navas de Tolosa, Battle of, 8, 31
Latifundium, 357, 358
Lautaro, 143
Lavradores, 277, 384, 415
Laws of Burgos, 358
Leon, Kingdom of, 8, 13, 14, 15, 17, 20, 22, 35, 137, 155
León Pinelo, Antonio, 435
Lepanto, Battle of, 291, 292
Lerma, Duke of, 438
Léry, Jean de, 461
Lesser Antilles, 120, 138, 307, 447. See also Antilles
Letrados, 62, 178, 334, 395
Lex Visigothorum, 25
Lima, Audiencia of, 151, 189, 346, 424, 434
Lima, City of, 142, 143-45, 199; merchants of, 242, 245, 287, 360, 394, 412; as a commercial center, 247, 372, 378, 379; treasury of, 397, 380
Limpieza de nobleza, 393
Limpieza de sangre, 62, 68
Line of Demarcation, 74-75, 78, 101, 260, 264, 267, 279, 330. See also Tordesillas
Lingua geral, 325

Lisbon, 7, 69, 75, 252, 257, 260, 271, 277, 283, 285, 288, 442, 444, 450, 453-54, 476; merchants of, 46-48; and Brazil, 323, 385, 440; immigrants from, 341
*Llanos*, 319, 320
*Loco tenentes*, 263
London, Treaty of, 429
López de Gómara, Francisco, 12
López de Legazpi, Miguel, 316-17
López de Velasco, Juan, 116-17, 120, 124, 129, 130, 163, 173, 174, 180-81, 271, 280-81, 332, 345, 346
Louis XVI (king of France), 469
Luanda, 342, 382, 385
Lucayan Indians, 73-74
Luna, Alvaro de, 128
Lynch, John, on seventeenth-century economic trends in Spanish America, 377, 378

Macao, 251, 254, 300
MacLeod, Murdo, 121, 376
*Macumba*, 406
Madeira Islands, 43, 48, 50, 51, 55, 251, 254, 268, 281, 288, 340
Madeira River, 325
Madrid, 206, 260, 291, 308, 453
Magalhães de Gondavo, Pedro, 267, 273-74, 280-81
Magdalena Valley, 142
Magellan, Ferdinand, 93, 456
Magellan, Strait of, 77, 94, 430, 456, 457
Maize: in America, 218, 312, 323, 364; in European herbals, 458; transferred to Europe, 469, 470
Majordomos, 394
Malabar, 251
Malacca, 251, 254
Málaga, 234
Malagueta pepper, 252
Malaria, 86, 119, 458
Mallorca, 43
*Mamelucos*, 282, 283, 320, 352, 411, 414
Mancera, marquis of (viceroy of New Spain), 400
Manila, 317, 366, 367, 371, 372, 381, 424, 426, 435
Manila Galleons, 371
Manioc, 214, 218, 276, 325, 364

Manuel I (king of Portugal), 67, 68, 75-76
Manufacturing: in pre-Columbian Spain and Portugal, 22-23; in Spanish America, 223-26, 366-67; in Habsburg Spain, 293-94. *See also* Textile industry
Maracaibo, 367
Marajó, Island of, 328-29
Maranhão: Region of, 264, 322, 330, 341; State of, 329, 440, 441, 442, 443, 444; Captaincy of, 439, 441. *See also* Rio Maranhão
Margarita, Island of, 432
Mariana, Juan de, 436
*Marranos*, 44-45
Marroquín, Bishop Francisco, 173-74
Martyr, Peter, 92
Marxism: contributions of to dependency theory, 387-89; on the nature of feudalism, 388; on racial attitudes, 419-20; on European expansion and the rise of capitalism, 463
Mascates, War of, 416
Masefield, G. B., on New World herbs, 458, 470
*Massapé*, 276
Matanzas, 429
Maté, 241, 366, 379
Matienzo, Juan de, 180, 223
*Matlazáhuatl*, 118, 376
Maya Indians, 83, 85-86, 87, 104, 139, 404-5, 460
Maynas, 320, 321, 328
*Mayorazgos*, 29-30, 310, 356
*Mazambos*, 413
Medina, Bartolomé de, 228
Medina del Campo, Fair of, 61
Medina del Rio Seco, Fair of, 61
*Medio general*, 298
*Meirinhos-mores*, 35, 268
Mendoza, Antonio de (viceroy of New Spain), 165, 188-89, 205, 214, 216, 222, 434
Mendoza, Argentina (colonial Chile), 102, 143
Mendoza, Pedro de, 318
Menéndez de Avilés, Pedro, 310-11, 431, 432
Mercado, Fray Tomás, 245

Mercantilism: Spanish, 59, 242-45, 362-63, 367, 373-75; Portuguese, 280, 386; European, 467-68
Mercator, Gerardus, 456
Mercedarians, 173, 174, 329
Merchants, 334, 394; Jewish, 20; French, 20, 31, 201; Italian, 20, 41, 42, 43, 48, 51, 95, 288; English, 31; Flemish, 31, 288; Spanish, 21, 42, 235, 394; Portuguese, 42, 67, 112; charter of, 46-47; in New World, 178, 323, 412; in Indies, 213; in Brazil, 281, 286-87, 412; German, 288
Mercury, 228-30, 243, 247, 363, 368, 369, 370, 371, 376, 379. See also Silver
Merino sheep, 21, 216
Merino, office of, 36
Mesa de Conciência e Ordens, 273, 414
Meseta, 6, 15, 19, 316
Mestas, 19-20, 21, 22, 23, 31, 85, 219-20
Mestiços, 282
Mestizos, 124-25, 127, 130, 180-81, 319, 331, 336, 339, 343, 344, 345, 396-407
Mexico, 77, 102, 104, 105; population of, 83, 84, 120, 130, 151, 335, 343, 345, 358; Conquest of, 106-7, 118, 126, 232; slaves in, 122, 123, 232-33; mining in, 124, 146, 208, 227, 228, 234, 368, 370, 371, 379, 464; towns in, 139-40, 199; evangelization of, 168-73, 178; Audiencia of, 188, 424, 434; Cortes' holdings in, 191; Indian rebellions in, 193, 198; cattle in, 215, 219, 316, 319; trade of, 233, 371, 378, 379; economy of, 248, 376, 380; Jesuits in, 311, 362. See also New Spain
Mexico City, 143-45, 149-50, 151, 198, 206; founded on Tenochtitlán, 100, 136, 139; mercantile houses in, 245, 287, 394, 426; economy of, 247; trade of, 372, 379, 381
Mexico, Gulf of, 76, 77, 431, 432
Minho, Province of, 281, 340
Minho River, 14
Mining, in Spanish America: regulation and taxation of, 186, 226-27, 228-29, 376; as a major industry, 226-30, 368-70; volume and value of production of, 227, 229, 368-71, 376, 378;

importance in stimulating settlement, 230, 311-12, 319-20. See also Capital, Gold, Labor, Mercury, Silver
Minorca, 43
Mints, in Spanish America, 241
Miscegenation: in Portuguese Africa and Asia, 49, 255; in the Canary Islands, 64; in Spanish America, 124-30, 180-81, 331, 336, 338-39, 351, 396-97; in Brazil, 282-83, 287, 342-43, 413-14. See also Population, Race
Miserables, 395-96, 404
Misiones, Province of, 320
Missionaries: conflicts of with other Spanish and Portuguese interests, 172-73, 328-29; achievements of among Indians, 174-76, 214, 274-75; in the advance of Spanish American frontiers, 311, 312-13, 320-21, 447. See also Evangelization
Mita, 211, 229, 247, 287, 303, 329, 359, 360, 369, 396
Mixton War, 139-40
Moctezuma, 105, 180, 212-13, 394
Moluccas, 101, 251, 316, 430
Monarchy, as an institution: status and powers of in Spain and Portugal, 28-29, 33-34, 36-38, 39, 45, 46, 56-58, 60, 66-67, 292, 474; in Spanish America, 78-79, 81-82, 162-63, 182, 192-94, 196, 303, 425, 426-27, 436-38, 448-51; in Brazil, 262, 283-86, 304, 443-46, 448-51
Monies: Spanish, 59, 240-42; Portuguese, 66
Monopolies: royal, 243, 252, 257, 363; commercial, 245, 363, 386
Monterrey, 313, 372
Montesclaros, marquis of (viceroy of New Spain), 358
Monzón, Ordinances of, 303
Moors, 7, 20, 36, 43, 51, 52, 99, 155, 198, 292, 404; wars against, 15, 33; place in Hispanic community, 32, 58; prejudice against, 53, 54, 392; under Ferdinand and Isabella, 62, 65, 78
Morador, 178, 181, 262, 271, 324, 392
Môrdomos, 262
Moriscos, 56, 61, 62, 110, 175, 294

Morocco, 47, 55, 65, 67, 69, 76, 267, 300
Mörner, Magnus, 333, 421
Mosquito Indians, 350
Motolinia, Toribio, 118
Mozambique, 251, 300, 342
Mozarabes, 10
Mudéjares, 32
Muladíes, 10
Mulattoes: status of, 127, 180, 396-98, 414; defined, 282, 331; in Brazil, 304, 414, 416; settlements of, 319; assimilation of, 338, 406, 407; population of, 343, 344, 345
Mundus Novus, 89-107
Municipalities: function and government of in Reconquest Spain and Portugal, 7-8, 17-18, 30-31; in Hispanic Old World expansion, 49, 50, 65; in Spanish America, 91, 106, 133, 152, 170-72, 192, 345-49, 404, 425-26; in Brazil, 270-72, 285, 331-53. See also Cabildo, Urbanization
Münster, Treaty of, 308
Murcia, Kingdom of, 15

Naborías, 210
Nahuatl, 409
Não, 239
Narváez, Pánfilo de, 122
Nassau, Maurice of, 307
Natal, 322
Navarre, Kingdom of, 13, 16, 111, 437-38
Navidad, 316
Nechi River, 142, 319
New Cadiz, 141
New Castile, 15, 22
New Galicia: conquest and settlement of, 101, 139, 145, 168; Audiencia of, 190, 424, 425; silver mines of, 227; population of, 335, 346
New Granada, 118, 248, 348, 428; emigration to, 114, 334; products of, 124, 222, 225, 319-20, 376; founding of, 140, 141, 142, 143, 145; Audiencia of, 190, 191; population of, 336, 337; runaway black slaves in, 339, 406; Indian urbanization in, 347-49
New Laws of the Indies, 162-63, 189
New Leon, 140, 313, 315, 423

New Mexico, 122, 314-15, 405, 423-24
New Spain, 183, 193, 306, 316, 338, 350, 363, 379, 428, 448; jurisdiction of, 136, 424; evangelization of, 173, 175; viceroyalty of, 188, 191, 313; agriculture in, 216, 222, 230; products of, 225, 367, 368, 371; trade of, 232, 243, 364, 370-71, 372; settlers to, 234, 334; expansion of, 310-17. See also Mexico
New Vizcaya, 311-13, 315, 405, 423, 424
Nicaragua, 101, 140, 162, 193, 227, 233, 238, 239, 310, 323, 339, 367, 429
Nicoya, Gulf of, 221
Nobility, 27-30, 45, 392-94
Nobleza, 27-30, 393, 399
Nóbrega, Father Manuel da, 265, 283
Nombre de Dios, 140, 201, 234, 363, 429

Oaxaca, 146, 168, 177, 222, 224, 225, 358, 365, 394
Obrajes, 225, 230, 233, 255, 339, 360, 365, 378
Oficiais da câmara, 270
Oficiales reales de hacienda, 186
Olinda, 263, 271, 352, 412, 442, 444
Olivares, count duke of, 294, 297, 363, 438
Olmos, Father Andrés de, 169
Oña, Pedro de, 402
Oñate, Juan de, 315
Ordenações Afonsinas, 252
Ordenações Filipinas, 445
Ordenações Manuelinas, 252, 271, 445
Ordenanza del Patronazgo, 303, 427
Orellana, Francisco de, 103
Orinoco River, 103, 238, 319, 457, 323
Ormuz, 251, 300
Oruro, 319
Os Lusíadas, 476
Otomí Indians, 104
Ouvidores geral, 253, 284
Ouvidorias, 444
Ovando, Juan de, 435, 437
Ovando, Nicolás de, governor of Española, 108, 126, 149, 153, 157

Pacheco, Duarte, 55
Pachuca, 228
Pacific Ocean: discovery and early exploration of, 9, 93, 94, 101, 316-17; Spanish

trade in, 232-33, 317, 371, 379; defense of, 432-33
Padrinos, 404
Padroado real, 253, 285
Padrões, 48, 260
Padrões de juro, 68
Paita, 373
Palacios Rubios, Juan de, 90
Palenques, 339, 406
Palmares, Republic of, 416-17
Palos, 74
Pampas, 85
Pamplona, New Granada, 319
Panama: Isthmus of, 83, 140, 146, 151, 237; Region of, 86, 101, 118, 193, 202, 227, 237, 316, 339; City of, 94, 133-34, 146, 178, 206, 247, 371, 373, 429, 430; Audiencia of, 190, 424
Papacy, 14, 34, 427
Papal donations, 182, 194-95, 306, 427, 437, 472
Pará, 263, 341, 342, 439-40
Pará River, 322
Paraguay, 85, 107, 126-27, 143, 165, 190, 216, 248, 317-20, 366, 424, 425, 447
Paraíba, 327, 439
Paraná River, 143, 260, 317-18
Pardos, 130, 283, 339, 397
Parentela, 39, 409
Parral, 312, 372
Pasco, 319
Pase regio, 459
Patagonia, 323
Patrimonialism, in royal government, 34, 78, 183, 203, 205-6, 438-39, 445
Patrimonio real, 34
Patronato real, 34, 56, 65
Patronato real de Indias, 194-95, 303, 395, 426-27
Pau-brasil, 76
Paul III, pope, 1, 459
Paulistas, 324-26, 327, 328, 381, 416
Pechos, 27
Pedidos, 36
Pelayo, 3, 13
Peninsulares, 400, 401, 403, 410-11
Peões, 262
Peonías, 8, 137, 185, 209, 218

Pernambuco, 263, 439-41, 444; and Bahia, 264, 443; Jesuits in, 274; products of, 276, 277, 278, 383, 384; settlers in, 281, 322, 340; government of, 284-85; captaincy of, 352, 439; Dutch occupation of, 384, 442-43
Persian Gulf, 251, 300
Peru: Conquest of, 79, 98, 106-7; Incan dominion over, 86, 104; exploration of, 101; epidemics in, 105, 118; emigration to, 113, 114; slaves in, 123, 124, 232; mining in, 124, 146, 208, 227, 228, 319, 368, 370, 464; urbanization in, 142-43, 145; evangelization in, 174, 175; viceroyalty of, 189-90, 424-26; products of, 214, 215, 216, 222-23, 224, 225, 364, 366; trade of, 233, 243, 323, 363, 371, 372, 379, 381; settlers in, 234; economy of, 248, 380, 381; expansion of, 317-21; population of, 336, 337, 343; orientals in, 338; Indians in, 347-48; merchant marine of, 378, 379
Peruleros, 360
Pesquisa, 57, 191
Peter III (king of Aragon), 43
Peter IV (king of Aragon), 43
Peter I, "the Cruel," (king of Castile), 45
Phelan, John, 378
Philip, Archduke (House of Habsburg), 60
Philip I (king of Portugal). See Philip II of Spain
Philip II (king of Portugal). See Philip III of Spain
Philip II (king of Spain), 193, 200, 291-92, 295, 426, 432-33, 435-36, 445, 450, 474; and evangelization, 170, 175; and trade regulation, 236, 358, 362-63; and taxes, 297-98; Spanish America under, 302-3; and Brazil, 303-4, 332; and principles of expansion, 309-10, 316; and Indies, 425, 431; rights of patronage and patrimony, 427, 438
Philip III (king of Spain and Philip II of Portugal), 296-97, 330, 438
Philip IV (king of Spain), 296-97, 333, 438, 450
Philippa of Lancaster (wife of John of Avis), 46

Philippines, 101, 316-17, 366, 317-72, 379, 435
Piauí, 327, 415
Pieza de Indias, 123
Pimería Alta, 314
Pinta, 73, 86, 471
Piratininga, 260, 275
Pizarro, Francisco, 103-4, 128, 160, 177, 260; and conquest of Peru, 97, 98, 220; and civil war, 106-7
Pizarro, Gonzalo, 103, 192-93, 227
Pizarro, Pedro, 222-23
Plague, 44, 105, 223; in Spain, 60, 294; bubonic, in the New World, 118, 335; of insects, 141, 381
Plantations, 277-78, 288, 358, 366, 384
Platine provinces, 331, 424
Plaza mayor, 136
Población, 108, 109, 172, 174, 208
Poblaciones campesinos, 351
Polo de Ondegardo, Juan, 175
Ponce de León, Juan, 98, 156
Popayán, 136
Population: of pre-Columbian America, 83-85; summary of size and components of in Spanish America and Brazil, 130-32, 280, 343-45. See also Blacks, Emigration, Indians, Miscegenation
Port Royal, 310
Porto, 14, 272, 288, 385
Pôrto Seguro, 274, 284, 383, 440
Portobelo, 363, 432
Potato: as an indigenous American crop, 218; introduction into Europe, 469
Potosí, 146, 149, 247, 334; mines of, 113, 143, 190, 228, 229, 248, 312, 316; silver in, 142, 222, 228, 229, 235, 368, 380; population of, 346, 347; labor for, 348, 360; trade of, 362, 372, 374
Povoamento, 254
Presidios, 146, 313, 314, 428
"Price Revolution," in Europe, 465-67, 476
Prices: of commodities in Spanish America, 246, 376; of pepper, 300; of American cochineal, 365; of Brazilian sugar, 382-84; trends of in sixteenth- and seventeenth-century Europe, 465-67
Primeros pobladores, 136, 177, 401

Principales, 170
Principe, Island of, 48, 251, 288
Privateers, 294, 386, 429
Procurador general, 135
Procuradores, 185, 400
Provedores môr, 253, 284
Puebla, 149, 225, 226, 233, 367, 378
Pueblo Indians, 85, 315, 405
Pueblos de españoles, 117
Pueblos de Indios, 351
Pueblos de visita, 170
Pueblos sujetos, 169, 170
Puerto Rico, 94, 201, 208, 220, 224, 226, 227, 248, 350, 365, 370, 374
Puertoviejo, 142
Pyrenees, 13, 20, 457

Quetzalcoatl, 105
Quiché Indians, 405
Quilombos, 406, 416
Quinto (royal fifth), 4, 49, 98, 186, 209, 213, 229, 247, 262
Quiroga, Rodrigo de (governor of Chile), 97
Quiroga, Vasco de, 159
Quito: conquest of, 102-3, 107; City of, 141, 411; population of, 151, 334, 336; Audiencia of, 190, 425; economy of, 225, 230, 233, 372, 377, 378

Race: definitions of, 52-53; fifteenth-century European attitudes toward, 53-55, 459-62; relations in Portuguese Africa and Asia, 54-55, 255-56; in Spanish and Portuguese America, 418-22. See also Blacks, Indians, Miscegenation
Raleigh, Sir Walter, 306, 453
Ramalho, João, 260
Ranches, 218-19, 313, 322, 349, 352, 376
Realejo, 226, 367
Realengos, 137
Receptor de penas, 135
Recife, 307, 352, 385, 416, 442
Recôncavo, 352
Recopilación de leyes de lost reinos de las Indias, 435
Recuas, 237
Reducciones, of Indians, 172, 314, 320-21

Reduções, of Indians, 274
Regalías, 34, 203, 209, 242
Regidores, 171, 425
Regimentos, 135, 252, 264-65, 268, 271, 283, 284, 440
Regimento das Missões do Estado do Maranhão e Grão-Pará, 329
Reinóis, 413, 451
Relação, 413, 444
Relaciones geográficas, 336
Religion, Roman Catholic: importance of in unifying Hispanic societies, 16, 18, 39, 58, 408; as a force behind Hispanic overseas expansion, 63-64, 78-79, 108-9, 256; Indian adaptations to, 175, 404; African adaptations to, 405-6, 416. See also Church, Clergy, Evangelizaton
Repartição, 329
Repartimientos: of land, 65, 136-37, 219; of Indians, 81, 126-27, 137, 146, 151, 163-65, 172, 184; as institutionalized form of Indian labor, 210-11, 229, 247, 339, 360, 396
Requerimiento, 64, 90, 94, 103, 106
Rescate, 91
Resguardos de Indios, 348, 350, 404, 426
Residencia, 65, 187, 191, 205
Ricos hombres, 29, 36, 44, 45, 112, 186
Rio de Janeiro, 271, 274, 277-78, 324-25, 383, 411-12, 439-44, 450; Captaincy of, 263, 266, 283
Rio de la Hacha, 432
Rio de la Plata, 76, 102, 143, 214-15, 238, 260-61, 304, 317-18, 323, 330-34, 343-45, 365-66, 374, 385, 442-43
Rio Grande River, 120, 314, 315, 330
Rio Grande de São Pedro, region of, 324
Rio Grande do Norte, region of, 322, 439
Rio Maranhão, 260, 261, 263. See also Amazon River
Rio Marañon, 457. See also Amazon River
Rio Negro, 328
Rio São Francisco, 307, 322, 325, 326, 327
Rio Solimões, 328. See also Amazon River
Rioja, 317
Rocroi, Battle of, 294
Rodríguez, Isabel, 97

Rosenblat, Angel: on size and composition of American populatíons, 84, 117, 119, 130-31, 343, 344
Royal Vicariate, 427
Ruralization: in Spanish America, 349-51; in Brazil, 351-52
Ryswyk, Treaty of, 308

Sá, Mem de, 266
Sáenz de Santa María, Carmelo, 378
Sahagún, Bernadino de, 460
Sahara Desert, 74, 254
St. Augustine, Florida, 146, 311, 315, 429, 432
St. Domingue, 308
St. Eustatius, Island of, 307
St. Johns River, 310
St. Martins, Island of, 307
Salamanca, University of, 25, 436, 456
Salta, 372
Saltillo, 313, 372
Salvador, Bahia, 101, 265, 271, 272, 352
San Francisco, Father Jacinto de, 174-75
San José, 316
San Juan, Argentina, 143
San Juan de Puerto Rico, 201, 206, 431, 432
San Juan River, 107, 238
San Lucar, 362
San Luis, Argentina, 317
San Luis Potosí, Mexico, 312
San Marcos, Univeristy of, 144
San Salvador, 73, 75, 150
San Sebastián, 234
Sancho VII (king of Navarre), 31
Sant' Ana, Captaincy of, 263
Santa Catarina, 323
Santa Cruz de la Sierra, 317, 328, 372, 424
Santa Elena, Florida, 146
Santa Hermandad, 69
Santa Fe de Antioquia, 318
Santa María, 74
Santa Marta, 141, 142, 429, 432
Santander, 334
Sante Fe, New Mexico, 315
Sante Fe, Spain, 69, 194

Santiago (Saint James the Greater), 11, 18
Santiago, Chile, 102, 127, 143, 145, 381, 388, 424
Santiago, Order of, 7, 46
Santiago Atitlán, Pueblo of, 121
Santiago de Compostela, 11, 18, 20, 22
Santiago de Cuba, 201
Santiago de los Caballeros, Española, 148
Santiago del Estero, 318
Santo Amaro, 263
Santo Domingo: Island of, 94, 126, 224, 248, 350, 370; City of, 100, 139, 150, 201, 234, 238, 429, 432; Audiencia of, 151, 188, 189, 191, 346; Archdiocese of, 195
Santos, 263, 442
São Cristóvão de Rio Sergipe, 322
São Jorge da Mina (El Mina), 66, 251, 301, 382
São Luís de Maranhão, 322, 412, 440
São Paulo, 275, 320, 323, 324, 325, 326, 328, 341, 352, 415
São Tomé, 48, 251, 262, 264, 288, 439
São Vicente, 260, 263, 264, 271, 274, 275, 276, 277, 278, 281, 284-85, 300, 303, 323, 324, 340, 341, 342, 440
Sargentos mores, 443
Sebastian I (king of Portugal), 66, 267, 273, 292
Senado da câmara, 270
Senegal, 42, 123
Senegambia, 49
Senhores de engenho, 278, 279, 286, 411
Senhorio, 258
Señorío: rights of, 28-29; and king, 34, 106, 184-86, 193, 194, 195-96, 296, 309; in Canary Islands, 55, 64-65; conceded to Columbus, 69; in New World, 78, 81, 89-90, 92, 392; in Indies, 182-207
Sergipe, 322, 383, 439
Serranía de Baudó, 320
Sertão, 271, 272, 274, 326, 352, 415
Servicios, 36
Sesmarias, 262, 271, 276
Sesmos, 8
Seven Bishops, Island of the, 43
Seven Years' War, 469

Seville, 21, 150, 206, 239, 241-42, 243, 244, 288; as maritime center, 22, 381; gold in, 227, 368, 369, 370; silver in, 229, 299, 368, 369, 370, 371, 376, 467; trade of, 233, 256, 362, 363, 365, 371, 372, 373, 389, 426, 463, 464, 465, 466
Shipbuilding: in Spain and Portugal, 21, 23, 48, 61, 293; in Spanish America, 226, 366-67, 373, 378
Sicily, 11, 43
Sierra Leone, 251
Sierra Madre Mountains, 311-12, 313, 314
Sierra Morena Mountains, 215
Sierra Nevada de Santa Marta Mountains, 319
Sierra Nevada Mountains, 8
Siete Partidas (Law of Seven Parts), 25, 33, 37, 252
Silk, 209, 222, 225, 366, 367, 371, 377, 379, 426
Silver: zones of production of in Mexico, 140, 208, 227-28, 312 368; in Peru, 142, 208, 227-28, 229, 319, 368; exports to Europe, 201, 229-30, 235, 239, 303, 370, 373; in Honduras, 208, 316, 362, 368; technology of production of, 227-29, 368; total American production of, 368-70; use in inter-American commerce, 371-73; in the Manila trade, 371, 379; in the Portuguese Asian trade, 385; impact of on the European economy, 464-67, 471; on the Spanish economy, 474-76. See also Mercury, Mining, Monies
Sinaloa, 101, 314
Síndico, 135
Sitios, 219
Situados, 435
Slave Coast, 48
Slave Trade: beginnings in Africa, 48; to Spanish America, 121-23, 312, 323, 337-38; to Brazil, 282, 342, 358-59, 382. See also Blacks, Slavery
Slavery: legal status of, 54, 180, 287, 397-98; of Indians in Spanish America, 140, 154-55, 162, 210-11, 232; of blacks in Spanish America, 212, 358, 365; in Brazil, 273, 320, 324, 325, 327; of

blacks in Brazil, 277, 282, 382, 384.
  See also Slave Trade
Smallpox, 105, 118-19, 122, 273, 335
Smuggling, 236-37, 374, 380, 431, 448
Sofala, 251
Solórzano y Pereyra, Juan de, 396-97,
  427, 435, 437
Sonora, 314, 315
Sonsonate, 221, 335
Soto, Hernando de, 98, 102
Sousa, Pero Lopes de, 261, 267
Sousa, Martim Afonso de, 260, 263, 277,
  281
Sousa, Tomé de, 264, 266, 274-75, 277,
  284, 440
Spanish Main, 93, 95, 200, 201
Spice Islands, 66, 101, 300, 301, 316
Spices, 42, 67, 76, 252, 262, 371
Spillbergen, Admiral Joris von, 430, 432
Suárez, Father Francisco, 473
Suárez, Inés, mistress of Pedro de
  Valdivia, 97
Suárez de Peralta, Juan, 402
Sublimus Deus, Bull of, 459
Sucre, Archbishopric of, 424
Sudan, 66, 80, 338
Sugar: cultivation and production of in
  the Madeira Islands, 51, 66; in the
  Canary Islands, 65; in Spanish
  America, 212, 220, 223-24, 247, 248,
  364-65, 377; in Brazil, 264, 276-79,
  288, 300, 322, 326, 352, 382-84, 385,
  386, 411, 454, 464
Sultepec, 277
Syphilis, 86, 223, 470-71

Tagus (Tejo) River, 6, 7, 8, 281
Taina Indians, 74
Talavera, Hernando de, 155
Tamazula, 277
Tamemes, 237
Tampico, 168, 222, 316
Tapajoz River, 328
Tarahumara Indians, 313
Tarasco Indians, 85-86, 336
Tarifa, 8
Tavares, Antônio Rapôso, 325
Tegucigalpa, 195
Tehuantepec, Isthmus of, 101, 175, 221, 239

Teixeira, Captain Pedro, 328, 330
Teixeira, João (cosmographer), 331
Tejada, Juan de, 432
Tello de Sandoval, Gonzalo, 193
Tenerife, 55, 63
Tenochtitlán, 96, 100, 103, 106, 139,
  150, 178
Tepehuane Indians, 405
Tepeyac, 408, 409
Tercios, 63, 431
Término, 8, 136, 137
Termo, 271
Tesorero, 186
Tesoureiro das rendas, 284
Tetuán, 55
Texas, 313, 315
Textile industry: in Spain, 22, 23, 60-61,
  293, 474; in Spanish America, 224-26,
  360, 365, 367, 372, 378, 426
Thirty Years' War, 297, 447
Three Kings, Battle of the, 292
Tierras baldías, 219
Tierras de realengo, 137
Tierra Firme, 94, 100, 102, 153-54, 188,
  202, 221, 232, 235, 248, 359, 363,
  371, 431
Tin, 208, 241
Tithes, 186, 194, 195, 427
Titicaca, Lake, 319
Títulos de Castilla, 45
Tlaxcala, 173, 336, 365, 367
Tobacco: planting in Spanish America,
  222, 358, 366, 370; in Brazil, 276,
  384-85, 386; use of in Europe, 458, 467
Todos os Santos, Bay of, 264
Toledo, 6, 7, 16, 18, 20
Toledo, Francisco de, (viceroy of Peru),
  303, 348, 359, 425, 426
Toral, Francisco de, 169
Tordesillas: Treaty of, 75; Line of, 199,
  261, 293, 304, 321, 323
Toro, Laws of, 183-84
Tortuga, 308
Tourinho, Pero Campo do, 261
Tours, Battle of, 3
Transportation: systems and forms of in
  the Spanish American Empire, 201-2,
  237-40, 373; in Brazil, 280, 386
Trapiches, 223, 278, 383

Tras-os-Montes, 340
Traza, 149
Treasury: of Spanish kings, 34, 61-62, 78, 97, 182, 186-87, 189, 204, 297-99, 363-64, 379, 434, 439; of Portuguese kings, 252-53, 270, 443, 446. See also Hacienda, Monies
Trent, Council of, 294, 427
Treponematosis, 86, 471
Tribute: in Reconquest Hispania, 8-9, 36; of American Indians, 79, 81, 90, 157, 160, 161, 163, 164, 179, 186, 197, 210, 211, 218, 303, 395, 426; of free blacks and mixed bloods, 397
Trinidad, 365
Tripoli, 42
Tropas, 327, 329, 331, 352
Trujillo, Honduras, 140-41, 142, 373, 424
Tucumán, 225, 230, 317, 318, 336, 372, 424
Tunis, 42
Tupí-Guaraní Indians, 274, 325
Tupinambá Indians, 85
Turkey, 48, 82, 291, 454, 469-70
Tuxtla, 224
Typhus, 118

Ufanismo, myth of, 416
"Union of Arms," 294, 297, 363
Universities, in Mexico and Peru, 178
Urbanization: in Spanish America, 149-52, 345, 349-50; in Brazil, 271, 351-53. See also Municipalities
Urdaneta, Andrés de, 317
Uruguay, 261, 323, 325
Uti possidetis de facto, 306, 308, 330, 331, 437
Uti possidetis de jure, 306, 308, 331
Utrecht, Treaty of, 322

Valdivia, Chile, 143, 433
Valdivia, Father Luis de, 321, 429
Valdivia, Pedro de, 97, 98
Valencia, Kingdom of, 15
Valencia, Martín de, 169
Valladolid, Mexico, 145, 473
Valois, House of, 113, 200-202, 235, 454
Valparaiso, 430, 433
Vaqueiros, 327, 331
Vaqueros, 313, 327

Vázquez de Coronado, Francisco, 102
Vázquez de Espinosa, Antonio, 332
Vecinidad, 160-61, 350
Vecinos, 7-8, 17-18, 30, 99, 116-17, 126-27, 129, 135, 136, 139, 141, 144-48, 150, 171, 185, 199, 203, 204, 346, 349, 433
Vecinos moradores, 178
Velasco, Luis de (viceroy of New Spain), 193
Velasco II, Luis de (viceroy of New Spain), 358
Vellon, 59, 299
Venezuela, 102, 141, 156, 189, 208, 226, 307, 319, 320, 361, 365-66, 373-74, 378, 435
Venice, 41, 300, 385
Vera Paz, Guatemala, 126
Veracruz, 136, 146, 147, 178, 187, 206, 224, 234, 237, 247, 335, 359, 362, 363, 373, 381, 406, 432, 433
Veracruz, Ilha da, 257
Veragua, Dukedom of, 191
Vereadores, 270
Vespucci, Amerigo, 92-93
Viceroy: in Spanish America, 188, 192-93, 195, 204, 303, 425, 426, 433, 434; status and functions of office in Portuguese Asia, 253
Viceroyalties: territorial extent and organization of, 189, 424, 425. See also New Spain, Peru, Viceroys
Vieira, S. J., Antonio, 329
Viejo cristianidad, 62
Vilcabamba, 106
Villa, 148, 149, 187, 351
Villa de la Navidad, 74
Villegaignon, Vice Admiral Nicolas Durand de, 266
Viruelas, 105
Visigoths, 3, 6, 10, 16, 25, 64
Visitas, 191, 197, 205
Vitoria, Francisco de, 437, 472-73
Vitruvius, 149
Vizinhos, 7-8, 271, 280-81
Vodun, 406

Waldseemüller, Martin, 93
Wallerstein, Immanuel, 388

Weber, Max, 205
West Indies: *See* Antilles
Wheat, 51, 140, 214, 219, 246, 279, 288, 312, 316, 323, 364, 372, 377, 379
Wine, 223, 279, 364, 371, 377, 379, 385, 386, 426, 462
Woad, 51, 221
Women: role of in New World, 97-98, 335; immigration of, 115, 117; Indian, 119, 125; of Castile and Cuenca, 125; American-born Spanish, 126; black, 127, 338; mixed bloods, 131; Portuguese in Brazil, 281, 282, 412; shortage of European, 282, 342-43
Wool, 21-23, 59, 61, 220, 225, 367

Xavier, Father Francis, 256

*Yanaconas*, 210, 359
Yaws, 86, 471
Yellow fever, 335, 384, 447
Yucatán, 96, 104, 139, 174, 189, 221, 222, 238, 335, 365, 366, 370, 432

Zacatecas, 187, 206, 230, 237, 247, 311, 312, 313, 372-73; silver mining at, 140, 228, 229, 235, 315
*Zambaigos*, 181
*Zambos*, 125, 129, 302, 339, 396
Zaragoza, Spain, 319
Zaruma, 227
Zumpango, 227

Lyle N. McAlister earned his doctorate in history at the University of California, Berkeley, in 1950, and has taught for many years at the University of Florida, where he is is now Distinguished Service Professor of History. He was director of the Center for Latin American Studies at Florida in the mid-1960s, and in 1972 chaired the Conference on Latin American History. McAlister is the author of *The Fuero Militar in New Spain, 1764–1800*, and editor and principal author of *The Military in Latin American Sociopolitical Evolution*.